Communication Technology Update and Fundamentals

12th Edition

Communication Technology Update and Fundamentals

12th Edition

Editors
August E. Grant
Jennifer H. Meadows

In association with Technology Futures, Inc.

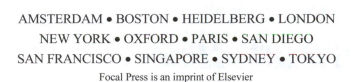

AMSTERDAM • BOSTON • HEIDELBERG • LONDON
NEW YORK • OXFORD • PARIS • SAN DIEGO
SAN FRANCISCO • SINGAPORE • SYDNEY • TOKYO
Focal Press is an imprint of Elsevier

Editors:

August E. Grant
Jennifer H. Meadows

Technology Futures, Inc.:

Production & Art Editor: Helen Mary V. Marek
Production Associates: Carrie Vanston & Henry Elliott

Focal Press is an imprint of Elsevier
30 Corporate Drive, Suite 400, Burlington, MA 01803, USA
The Boulevard, Langford Lane, Kidlington, Oxford, OX5 1GB, UK

Notices
Knowledge and best practice in this field are constantly changing. As new research and experience
broaden our understanding, changes in research methods, professional practices, or medical
treatment may become necessary.

Practitioners and researchers must always rely on their own experience and knowledge in evaluating
and using any information, methods, compounds, or experiments described herein. In using such
information or methods they should be mindful of their own safety and the safety of others, including
parties for whom they have a professional responsibility.

To the fullest extent of the law, neither the Publisher nor the authors, contributors, or editors, assume
any liability for any injury and/or damage to persons or property as a matter of products liability,
negligence or otherwise, or from any use or operation of any methods, products, instructions, or
ideas contained in the material herein.

Library of Congress Cataloging-in-Publication Data
Application submitted

British Library Cataloguing-in-Publication Data
A catalogue record for this book is available from the British Library.

ISBN: 978-0-240-81475-9

For information on all Focal Press publications visit our website at www.elsevierdirect.com

Companion Web site for Recent Developments: http://www.tfi.com/ctu

10 11 12 13 5 4 3 2 1

Printed in the United States of America

Working together to grow
libraries in developing countries

www.elsevier.com | www.bookaid.org | www.sabre.org

ELSEVIER   BOOK AID International   Sabre Foundation

Table of Contents

Glossary and Updates can be found on the
Communication Technology Update and Fundamentals Home Page
http://www.tfi.com/ctu/

Preface

We are excited about the new edition of *Communication Technology Update and Fundamentals*. This edition has three new chapters covering new technologies that, although they have been covered in the past, have now earned their own chapters. Cinema Technologies (Chapter 12) reviews changes in cinema production, post production, distribution and exhibition. Digital Signage (Chapter 11) reviews everyday technologies that range from those electronic billboards by the side of the road, to the digital menu at the corner coffee shop. The last new chapter (Chapter 20) covers a technology that has become a daily distraction for many: social networking.

While communication technologies have become a more important part of daily living over the years, their impact on the environment has been ignored for most of those years. That situation has changed as sustainability and green technology have become increasingly important to reduce waste, toxic materials, and energy consumption. In this edition each chapter has a sustainability sidebar that discusses sustainability issues related to that technology.

We are grateful to our authors for sharing their passion for communication technology. In order to keep this book as current as possible we ask the authors to work under extremely tight deadlines. Authors begin working in January 2010 and most chapters were submitted in April 2010 with the final details added in May 2010. Individually, the chapters provide snapshots of the state of the field for individual technologies, but together they present a broad overview of the role that communication technologies play in our everyday lives. The efforts of these authors have produced a remarkable compilation, and we thank them for all for their hard work in preparing this volume.

The impetus to include the sustainability sidebars came from a series of conversations with Focal Press' Elinor Actipis. Focal Press' Michelle Cronin, provided encouragement and feedback to help guide the new edition. TFI's Helen Mary Marek played the pivotal role in production, moving all 23 chapters from draft to camera-ready. Previously this difficult job was handled by Debra Robison, who worked on editions 1 through 11, We miss you Deb and hope you are back on your feet soon. Helen Mary also provided on-demand graphics production, adding visual elements to help make the content more understandable. Finally, we could not generate and edit so much text in so short a time without the support of our spouses, Diane Grant and Floyd Meadows. More than anyone else, your encouragement and patience have helped us keep doing what we do.

The companion Web site for the *Communication Technology Update and Fundamentals* is www.tfi.com/ctu. The complete Glossary for the book is on the site, where it will be much easier to find individual entries than in the paper version of the book. We have also moved the vast quantity of statistical data on each of the communication technologies that were formerly printed in Chapter 2. Our long-term goal is to continue to add content and value to the Web site, allowing you to stay better informed about these technologies. As always, we will periodically update the Web site to supplement the text with new information and links to a wide variety of information available over the Internet.

As a reader of this book, you are also part of the *Communication Technology Update* community. Each edition of this book has been improved over previous editions with the help and input from readers like you. You are also invited to send us updates for the Web site, ideas for new topics, and other contributions that will inform all members of the community. You are invited to communicate directly with us via e-mail, snail mail, or voice.

Thank you for being part of the CTU community!

Augie Grant and Jennifer Meadows
May 12, 2010

Augie Grant
College of Mass Communications & Information Studies
University of South Carolina
Columbia, SC 29208
Phone: 803.777.4464
augie@sc.edu

Jennifer H. Meadows
Department of Communication Design
California State University, Chico
Chico, CA 95929-0504
Phone: 530.898.4775
jmeadows@csuchico.edu

Introduction to Communication Technologies

August E. Grant, Ph.D.[*]

Communication technologies are the nervous system of contemporary society, transmitting and distributing sensory and control information and interconnecting a myriad of interdependent units. These technologies are critical to commerce, essential to entertainment, and intertwined in our interpersonal relationships. Because these technologies are so vitally important, any change in communication technologies has the potential to impact virtually every area of society.

One of the hallmarks of the industrial revolution was the introduction of new communication technologies as mechanisms of control that played an important role in almost every area of the production and distribution of manufactured goods (Beniger, 1986). These communication technologies have evolved throughout the past two centuries at an increasingly rapid rate. This evolution shows no signs of slowing, so an understanding of this evolution is vital for any individual wishing to attain or retain a position in business, government, or education.

The economic and political challenges faced by the United States and other countries since the beginning of the new millennium clearly illustrate the central role these communication systems play in our society. Just as the prosperity of the 1990s was credited to advances in technology, the economic challenges that followed were linked as well to a major downturn in the technology sector. Today, communication technology is seen by many as a tool for making more efficient use of energy sources.

Communication technologies play as big a part in our private lives as they do in commerce and control in society. Geographic distances are no longer barriers to relationships thanks to the bridging power of communication technologies. We can also be entertained and informed in ways that were unimaginable a century ago thanks to these technologies—and they continue to evolve and change before our eyes.

This text provides a snapshot of the state of technologies in our society. The individual chapter authors have compiled facts and figures from hundreds of sources to provide the latest information on more than two dozen communication technologies. Each discussion explains the roots and evolution, recent developments, and current status of the technology as of mid-2010. In discussing each technology, we will address these technologies from a systematic perspective, looking at a range of factors beyond hardware.

---

[*] Professor, College of Mass Communications and Information Studies, University of South Carolina (Columbia, South Carolina).

The goal is to help you analyze technologies and be better able to predict which ones will succeed and which ones will fail. That task is harder to achieve than it sounds. Let's look at Google for an example of how unpredictable technology is.

The Google Tale

As this book goes to press in mid-2010, Google is the most valuable media company in the world in terms of market capitalization (the total value of all shares of stock held in the company). To understand how Google attained that lofty position, we have to go back to the late 1990s, when commercial applications of the Internet were taking off. There was no question in the minds of engineers and futurists that the Internet was going to revolutionize the delivery of information, entertainment, and commerce. The big question was how it was going to happen.

Those who saw the Internet as a medium for information distribution knew that advertiser support would be critical to its long-term financial success. They knew that they could always find a small group willing to pay for content, but the majority of people preferred free content. To become a mass medium similar to television, newspapers, and magazines, an Internet advertising industry was needed.

At that time, most Internet advertising was banner ads, horizontal display ads that stretched across most of the screen to attract attention, but took up very little space on the screen. The problem was that most people at that time accessed the Internet using slow dial-up connections, so advertisers were limited in what they could include in these banners to about a dozen words of text and simple graphics. The dream among advertisers was to be able to use rich media, including full-motion video, audio, animation, and every other trick that makes television advertising so successful.

When broadband Internet access started to spread, advertisers were quick to add rich media to their banners, as well as create other types of ads using graphics, video, and sound. These ads were a little more effective, but many Internet users did not like the intrusive nature of rich media messages.

At about the same time, two Stanford students, Sergey Brin and Larry Page, had developed a new type of search engine, Google, that ranked results on the basis of how often content was referred to or linked from other sites, allowing their computer algorithms to create more robust and relevant search results (in most cases) than having a staff of people indexing Web content. What they needed was a way to pay for the costs of the servers and other technology.

According to Vise & Malseed (2006), their budget did not allow Google to create and distribute rich media ads. They could do text ads, but they decided to do them differently from other Internet advertising, using computer algorithms to place these small text ads on the search results that were most likely to give the advertisers results. With a credit card, anyone could use this "AdWords" service, specifying the search terms they thought should display their ads, writing the brief ads (less than 100 characters total—just over a dozen words), and even specifying how much they were willing to pay every time someone clicked on their ad. Even more revolutionary, the Google founders decided that no one should have to pay for an ad unless a user clicked on it.

For advertisers, it was as close to a no-lose proposition as they could find. Advertisers did not have to pay unless a person was interested enough to click on the ad. They could set a budget that Google computers could follow, and Google provided a control panel for advertisers that gave a set of measures that was a dream for anyone trying to make a campaign more effective. These measures indicated not only overall effectiveness of the ad, but also the effectiveness of each message, each keyword, and every part of every campaign.

The result was remarkable. Google's share of the search market was not that much greater than the companies that had held the number one position earlier, but Google was making money—lots of money—from these little text ads. Wall Street investors noticed, and, once Google went public, investors bid up the stock price, spurred by increases in revenues and a very large profit margin. Today, Google is involved in a number of other ventures designed to aggregate and deliver content ranging from text to full-motion video, but its little text ads are still the primary revenue generator.

In retrospect, it was easy to see why Google was such a success. Their little text ads were effective because of context—they always appeared where they would be the most effective. They were not intrusive, so people did not mind the ads on Google pages, and later on other pages that Google served ads to through its "content network." And advertisers had a degree of control, feedback, and accountability that no advertising medium had ever offered before (Grant & Wilkinson, 2007).

So what lessons should we learn from the Google story? Advertisers have their own set of lessons, but there are a separate set of lessons for those wishing to understand new media. First, no matter how insightful, no one is ever able to predict whether a technology will succeed or fail. Second, success can be due as much to luck as to careful, deliberate planning and investment. Third, simplicity matters—there are few advertising messages as simple as the little text ads you see when doing a Google search.

The Google tale provides an example of the utility of studying individual companies and industries, so the focus throughout this book is on individual technologies. These individual snapshots, however, comprise a larger mosaic representing the communication networks that bind individuals together and enable them to function as a society. No single technology can be understood without understanding the competing and complementary technologies and the larger social environment within which these technologies exist. As discussed in the following section, all of these factors (and others) have been considered in preparing each chapter through application of the "umbrella perspective." Following this discussion, an overview of the remainder of the book is presented.

The "Umbrella Perspective" on Communication Technology

The most obvious aspect of communication technology is the hardware—the physical equipment related to the technology. The hardware is the most tangible part of a technology system, and new technologies typically spring from developments in hardware. However, understanding communication technology requires more than just studying the hardware. It is just as important to understand the messages communicated through the technology system. These messages will be referred to in this text as the "software." Note that this definition of "software" is much broader than the definition used in computer programming. For example, our definition of computer software would include information manipulated by the computer (such as this text, a spreadsheet, or any other stream of data manipulated or stored by the computer), as well as the instructions used by the computer to manipulate the data.

The hardware and software must also be studied within a larger context. Rogers' (1986) definition of "communication technology" includes some of these contextual factors, defining it as "the hardware equipment, organizational structures, and social values by which individuals collect, process, and exchange information with other individuals" (p. 2). An even broader range of factors is suggested by Ball-Rokeach (1985) in her media system dependency theory, which suggests that communication media can be understood by analyzing dependency relations within and across levels of analysis, including the individual, organizational, and system levels. Within the system level, Ball-Rokeach (1985) identifies three systems for analysis: the media system, the political system, and the economic system.

These two approaches have been synthesized into the "Umbrella Perspective on Communication Technology" illustrated in Figure 1.1. The bottom level of the umbrella consists of the hardware and software of the technology (as previously defined). The next level is the organizational infrastructure: the group of organizations involved in the production and distribution of the technology. The top level is the system level, including the political, economic, and media systems, as well as other groups of individuals or organizations serving a common set of functions in society. Finally, the "handle" for the umbrella is the individual user, implying that the relationship between the user and a technology must be examined in order to get a "handle" on the technology. The basic premise of the umbrella perspective is that all five areas of the umbrella must be examined in order to understand a technology.

(The use of an "umbrella" to illustrate these five factors is the result of the manner in which they were drawn on a chalkboard during a lecture in 1988. The arrangement of the five attributes resembled an umbrella, and the name stuck. Although other diagrams have since been used to illustrate these five factors, the umbrella remains the most memorable of the lot.)

Adding another layer of complexity to each of the five areas of the umbrella is also helpful. In order to identify the impact that each individual characteristic of a technology has, the factors within each level of the umbrella may be identified as "enabling," "limiting," "motivating," and "inhibiting," depending upon the role they play in the technology's diffusion.

Enabling factors are those that make an application possible. For example, the fact that the coaxial cable used to deliver traditional cable television can carry dozens of channels is an enabling factor at the hardware level. Similarly, the decision of policy makers to allocate a portion of the spectrum for cellular telephony is an enabling factor at the system level (political system). One starting point to use in examining any technology is to make a list of the underlying factors from each area of the umbrella that make the technology possible in the first place.

Limiting factors are the opposite of enabling factors; they are those factors that create barriers to the adoption or impacts of a technology. A great example is related to the cable television example above. Although coaxial cable increased the number of television programs that could be delivered to a home, most analog coaxial networks cannot transmit more than 100 channels of programming. To the viewer, 100 channels may seem to be more than is needed, but to the programmer of a new cable television channel unable to get space on a filled-up cable system, this hardware factor represents a definite limitation. Similarly, the fact that the policy makers discussed above initially permitted only two companies to offer cellular telephone service in each market was a system-level limitation on that technology. Again, applying the umbrella perspective to create a list of factors that limit the adoption, use, or impacts of any specific communication technology is useful.

Figure 1.1
The Umbrella Perspective on Communication Technology

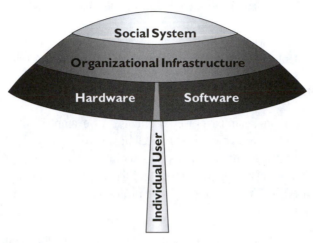

Source: A. E. Grant

Motivating factors are a little more complicated. They are those factors that provide a reason for the adoption of a technology. Technologies are not adopted just because they exist. Rather, individuals, organizations, and social systems must have a reason to take advantage of a technology. The desire of local telephone companies for increased profits, combined with the fact that growth in providing local telephone service is limited, is an organizational factor motivating the telcos to enter the markets for new communication technologies. Individual users desiring information more quickly can be motivated to adopt electronic information technologies. If a technology does not have sufficient motivating factors for its use, it cannot be a success.

Inhibiting factors are the opposite of motivating ones, providing a disincentive for adoption or use of a communication technology. An example of an inhibiting factor at the software level might be a new electronic information technology that has the capability to update information more quickly than existing technologies, but provides only "old" content that consumers have already received from other sources. One of the most important inhibiting factors for most new technologies is the cost to individual users. Each potential user must decide whether the cost is worth the service, considering his or her budget and the number of competing technologies. Competition from other technologies is one of the biggest barriers any new (or existing) technology faces. Any factor that works against the success of a technology can be considered an inhibiting factor. As you might guess, there are usually more inhibiting factors for most technologies than motivating ones. And if the motivating factors are more numerous and stronger than the inhibiting factors, it is an easy bet that a technology will be a success.

All four factors—enabling, limiting, motivating, and inhibiting—can be identified at the system, organizational, software, and individual user levels. However, hardware can only be enabling or limiting; by itself, hardware does not provide any motivating factors. The motivating factors must always come from the messages transmitted (software) or one of the other levels of the umbrella.

The final dimension of the umbrella perspective relates to the environment within which communication technologies are introduced and operate. These factors can be termed "external" factors, while ones relating to the technology itself are "internal" factors. In order to understand a communication technology or be able to predict the manner in which a technology will diffuse, both internal and external factors must be studied and compared.

Each communication technology discussed in this book has been analyzed using the umbrella perspective to ensure that all relevant factors have been included in the discussions. As you will see, in most cases, organizational and system-level factors (especially political factors) are more important in the development and adoption of communication technologies than the hardware itself. For example, political forces have, to date, prevented the establishment of a single world standard for high-definition television (HDTV) production and transmission. As individual standards are selected in countries and regions, the standard selected is as likely to be the product of political and economic factors as of technical attributes of the system.

Organizational factors can have similar powerful effects. For example, as discussed in Chapter 4, the entry of a single company, IBM, into the personal computer business in the early 1980s resulted in fundamental changes in the entire industry, dictating standards and anointing an operating system (MS-DOS) as a market leader. Finally, the individuals who adopt (or choose not to adopt) a technology, along with their motivations and the manner in which they use the technology, have profound impacts on the development and success of a technology following its initial introduction.

Perhaps the best indication of the relative importance of organizational and system-level factors is the number of changes individual authors made to the chapters in this book between the time of the initial chapter submission in March 2010 and production of the final, camera-ready text in May 2010. Very little new information was added regarding hardware, but numerous changes were made due to developments at the organizational and system levels.

To facilitate your understanding of all of the elements related to the technologies explored, each chapter in this book has been written from the umbrella perspective. The individual writers have endeavored to update developments in each area to the extent possible in the brief summaries provided. Obviously, not every technology experienced developments in each of the five areas, so each report is limited to areas in which relatively recent developments have taken place.

So Why Study New Technologies?

One constant in the study of media is that new technologies seem to get more attention than traditional, established technologies. There are many reasons for the attention. New technologies are more dynamic and evolve more quickly, with greater potential to cause change in other parts of the media system. Perhaps the reason for our attention is the natural attraction that humans have to motion, a characteristic inherited from our most distant ancestors.

There are a number of other reasons for studying new technologies. Perhaps you want to make a lot of money off a new technology—and there is a lot of money to be made (and lost!) on new technologies. If you are planning a career in the media, you may simply be interested in knowing how the media are changing and evolving, and how those changes will affect your career.

Or you might want to learn lessons from the failure of new communication technologies so you can avoid failure in your own career, investments, etc. Simply put, the majority of new technologies introduced do not succeed in the market. Some fail because the technology itself was not attractive to consumers (such as the 1980's attempt to provide AM stereo radio). Some fail because they were far ahead of the market, such as

Qube, the first interactive cable television system, introduced in the 1970s. Others failed because of bad timing or aggressive marketing from competitors that succeeded despite inferior technology.

The final reason we offer for studying new communication technologies is to identify patterns of adoption, effects, economic opportunity, and competition so that we can be prepared to understand, use, and/or compete with the next generation of new media. Virtually every new technology discussed in this book is going to be one of those "traditional, established technologies" in just a few short years, but there will always be another generation of new media to challenge the status quo.

Overview of Book

The key to getting the most out of this book is therefore to pay as much attention to the reasons that some technologies succeed and others fail. To that end, this book provides you with a number of tools you can apply to virtually any new technology that comes along. These tools are explored in the first five chapters, which we refer to as the *Communication Technology Fundamentals*. You might be tempted to skip over these to get to the "fun facts" about the individual technologies that are making an impact today, but you will be much better equipped to learn lessons from these technologies if you are armed with these tools.

The first of these is the "umbrella perspective" discussed before that broadens attention from the technology itself to the users, organizations, and system surrounding that technology. To that end, each of the technologies explored in this book provides details about all of the elements of the umbrella.

Of course, studying the history of each technology can help you find patterns and apply them to different technologies, times, and places. In addition to including a brief history of each technology, the following chapter, Historical Perspectives on Communication Technologies, provides a broad overview of most of the technologies discussed later in the book, allowing a comparison along a number of dimensions: the year each was first introduced, growth rate, number of current users, etc. This chapter anchors the book to highlight commonalties in the evolution of individual technologies, as well as present the "big picture" before we delve into the details. By focusing on the number of users over time, this chapter also provides the most useful basis of comparison across technologies.

Another useful tool in identifying patterns across technologies is the application of theories related to new communication technologies. By definition, theories are general statements that identify the underlying mechanisms for adoption and effects of these new technologies. Chapter 3 provides an overview of a wide range of these theories and provides a set of analytic perspectives that you can apply to both the technologies in this book and to any new technology that follow.

The structure of communication industries is then addressed in Chapter 4. The complexity of organizational relationships, along with the need to differentiate between the companies that make the technologies and those that sell the technologies, are explored in this chapter. The most important force at the highest level of the umbrella, regulation, is then introduced in Chapter 5.

These introductory chapters provide a structure and a set of analytic tools that define the study of communication technologies in all forms. Following this introduction, the book then addresses the individual technologies.

The technologies discussed in this book are organized into three sections: electronic mass media, computers and consumer electronics, and networking technologies. These three are not necessarily exclusive; for example, Internet video technologies could be classified as either an electronic mass medium or a computer technology. The ultimate decision regarding where to put each technology was made by determining which set of current technologies most closely resembled the technology from the user's perspective. Thus, Internet video was classified with electronic mass media. This process also locates the discussion of a cable television technology—cable modems—in the Broadband and Home Networks chapter in the Networking Technology section.

Each chapter is followed by a brief bibliography. These reference lists represent a broad overview of literally thousands of books and articles that provide details about these technologies. It is hoped that the reader will not only use these references, but will examine the list of source material to determine the best places to find newer information since the publication of this *Update*.

For the first time, each chapter in this book includes a sidebar discussing sustainability issues that relate to the technologies discussed in that chapter. These chapters explore a range of sustainability factors ranging from energy consumption and savings to the environmental impact from manufacturing and disposing of these technologies. These sidebars provide you with insight that can help you understand the impact of communication technologies on the environment, as well as helping you discover ways of minimizing your own environmental impact.

Most of the technologies discussed in this book are continually evolving. As this book was completed, many technological developments were announced but not released, corporate mergers were under discussion, and regulations had been proposed but not passed. Our goal is for the chapters in this book to establish a basic understanding of the structure, functions, and background for each technology, and for the supplementary Internet home page to provide brief synopses of the latest developments for each technology. (The address for the home page is http://www.tfi.com/ctu.)

The final chapter returns to the "big picture" presented in this book, attempting to place these discussions in a larger context, noting commonalties among the technologies and trends over time. Any text such as this one can never be fully comprehensive, but ideally this text will provide you with a broad overview of the current developments in communication technology.

Bibliography

Ball-Rokeach, S. J. (1985). The origins of media system dependency: A sociological perspective. *Communication Research, 12* (4), 485-510.

Beniger, J. (1986). *The control revolution.* Cambridge, MA: Harvard University Press.

Grant, A. E. & Wilkinson, J. S. (2007, February). *Lessons for communication technologies from Web advertising.* Paper presented to the Mid-Winter Conference of the Association of Educators in Journalism and Mass Communication, Reno.

Rogers, E. M. (1986). *Communication technology: The new media in society.* New York: Free Press.

Vise, D. & Malseed, M. (2006). *The Google story: Inside the hottest business, media, and technology success of our time.* New York: Delta.

2

Historical Perspectives on Communication Technology

Dan Brown, Ph.D.*

The history of communication technologies can be examined from many perspectives: telling stories about the creators, discussing the impacts of the technologies, or analyzing competition among these technologies. Each chapter in this book provides a brief history of the technology discussed in that chapter, but it is also important to provide a "big picture" discussion that allows you to compare technologies.

For that type of comparison, the most useful perspective is one that allows comparisons among technologies across time: numerical statistics of adoption and use of these technologies. To that end, this chapter follows patterns adopted in previous summaries of trends in U.S. communications media (Brown & Bryant, 1989; Brown, 1996, 1998, 2000, 2002, 2004, 2006, 2008). To aid in understanding rates of adoption and use, the premise for this chapter is that non-monetary measures such as the number of users or percentage of adoption are a more consistent evaluation of a technology's impact than the dollar value of sales. More meaningful media consumption trends emerge from examining changes in non-monetary media units and penetration (i.e., percentage of marketplace use, such as households) rather than on dollar expenditures, although frequent mentions of dollar expenditures are offered. Box office receipts from motion pictures offer a notable exception; here, the dollar figure has emerged as the de facto standard of measuring movie acceptance in the market.

Another premise of this chapter is that government sources should provide as much of the data as possible. Researching the growth or sales figures of various media over time quickly reveals conflict in both dollar figures and units shipped or consumed. Government sources sometimes display the same variability seen in private sources, as the changes in the types of data used for reporting annual publishing of book titles will show. Government sources, although frequently based on private data, provide some consistency to the reports. However, many government reports in recent years offered inconsistent units of measurement and, as a result, annual market updates were discontinued. Readers should use caution in interpreting data for individual years and instead emphasize the trends over several years. One limitation of this government data is the lag time before statistics are reported, with the most recent data being a year or more old. To compensate for the delay, the companion Web site for this book (www.tfi.com/ctu) reports more up-to-date statistics than could be printed in this chapter.

---

* Associate Dean of Arts & Sciences, East Tennessee State University (Johnson City, Tennessee).

Both of these assumptions have been challenged by such trends as declining coverage over the years of non-monetary units in census reports and lack of issuing of other governmental sources, such as Federal Communications Commission annual reports. Therefore, units other than monetary ones appear when they were available, often from commercial sources.

Figure 2.1 illustrates relative startups of various media types and the increase in the pace of introduction of new media technologies. This rapid increase in development is the logical consequence of the relative degree of permeation of technology in recent years versus the lack of technological sophistication of earlier eras. This figure and this chapter exclude several media that the marketplace abandoned, such as quadraphonic sound, CB radios, 8-track audiotapes, and 8mm film cameras. Other media that receive mention may yet suffer this fate. For example, long-playing vinyl audio recordings, audiocassettes, and compact discs seem doomed in the face of rapid adoption of newer forms of digital audio recordings. This chapter traces trends that reveal clues about what has happened and what may happen in the use of respective media forms.

To help illustrate the growth rates and specific statistics regarding each technology, a large set of tables and figures have been placed on the companion Web site for this book at www.tfi.com/ctu. Your understanding of each technology will be aided by referring to the Web site as you read each section. To help, each discussion makes specific reference to the tables and figures on the Web site.

Figure 2.1
Communication Technology Timeline

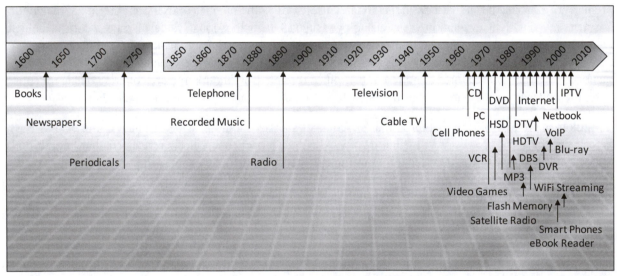

Source: Technology Futures, Inc.   *Image:* ©Jupiterimages Corporation

Print Media

The U.S. printing industry in recent year was characterized as the largest such industry among the printing countries of the world (U.S. Department of Commerce/International Trade Association, 2000). The U.S. Bureau of the Census (2010) counted nearly 142,000 publishing industry establishments involved in print media. These include publishers of newspapers, periodicals, books, databases, directories, greeting cards, and other print media.

Newspapers

Publick Occurrences, Both Foreign and Domestick was the first newspaper produced in North America, appearing in 1690 (Lee, 1917). As illustrated in Table 2.1 and Figure 2.2 from the companion Web site for this book (www.tfi.com/ctu), U.S. newspaper firms and newspaper circulation had extremely slow growth until the 1800s. Early growth suffered from relatively low literacy rates and the lack of discretionary cash among the bulk of the population. The progress of the industrial revolution brought money for workers and improved mechanized printing processes. Lower newspaper prices and the practice of deriving revenue from advertisers encouraged significant growth beginning in the 1830s. Newspapers made the transition from the realm of the educated and wealthy elite to a mass medium serving a wider range of people from this period through the Civil War era (Huntzicker, 1999).

The Spanish American and Civil Wars stimulated public demand for news by the middle 1800s, and modern journalism practices, such as assigning reporters to cover specific stories and topics, began to emerge. Circulation wars among big city newspapers in the 1880s featured sensational writing about outrageous stories. Both the number of newspaper firms and newspaper circulation began to soar. Although the number of firms would level off in the 20th century, circulation continued to rise.

The number of morning newspapers more than doubled after 1950, despite a 16% drop in the number of daily newspapers over that period. Overall newspaper circulation remained higher at the start of the new millennium than in 1950, although it inched downward throughout the 1990s. Although circulation actually increased in many developing nations, both U.S. newspaper circulation and the number of U.S. newspaper firms remain lower than the respective figures posted in the early 1990s. The decline in 2003 reversed a string of five consecutive years of small increases in the number of American newspaper firms that began in 1998. After increasing again in 2004, the figure declined every year through 2008, the last year for which the Bureau of the Census reported the data.

Newspaper operations in the United States are largely concentrated to a few companies. Among the more than 1,400 American daily newspapers operating in 2007, 24% of the total circulation was generated by top 20 newspapers. The largest 10 newspaper owners held more than 260 newspapers and accounted for about 44% of the industry circulation (Peters, 2009).

As with the downward trend in the number of newspaper firms, the same trend occurred with newspaper circulation. In fact, the last increase in annual circulation occurred in 1987. The average hours spent with daily newspapers per person per year declined annually from 201 hours in 2000 to 171 hours in 2007 (U.S. Bureau of the Census, 2008, 2010).

In the six-month period ending in March 2008, the daily circulation of all the newspapers audited by the Audit Bureau of Circulation fell by 3.6% from the 2007 figure (Peters, 2009). This decline represented an accelerated shrinking of circulation that fell by 2.1% the six-month period ending in March 2007, as compared with from that of the same period in 2006 (Peters & Donald, 2007). Circulation of Sunday newspapers declined in the six-month period ending in March 2008 by 4.6%, and only two (*Wall Street Journal*, up 0.35%; *USA Today*, up 0.27%) of the top 10 American newspapers experienced an increase in circulation (Peters, 2009).

Although 74.5% of adults older than 18 years reported reading newspapers within the previous week during 2008 (U.S. Bureau of the Census, 2010), the *Newspaper Association of America* (as cited in Peters, 2009) reported that the proportion of regular daily newspaper readers aged 18 and older in the 50 largest American cities declined from 52.8% in 2004 to 48.4% in 2007. The proportion declined annually in that period, as did the proportion of such readers of Sunday newspapers in the same period, dropping from 61.2% to 55.4%. In 2007, people over age 55 years made up the age group that most regularly read daily newspapers (63.7%). The age group that least regularly read daily newspapers in 2007 included people 25-35 years (33.7%). Factors that produced declining newspaper circulation included an increasing variety of attractions for consumer attention and an increased presence of advertising-supported free-circulation newspapers (Peters, 2009).

Newspaper advertising revenues have been declining for about 50 years, going back to the growth of broadcast television, cable, and more recently the Internet. In the 10-year interval that ended in 2006, media advertising increased by 4.9%. During that period, newspaper advertising grew annually by an average of 3.3%, while national cable television advertising increased by 11.3% and Internet advertising grew by 45% (Peters & Donald, 2007). In 2007, the share of the American advertising pie held by newspapers declined to 17.6% from 18.8% in 2006 and 20.4% in 2004. Global trends, however, revealed a 3.4% increase to $57.9 million in 2007 from the previous year. (Peters, 2009). The world-wide increasing trend was expected to increase through 2010, but the proportion of total advertising devoted to newspapers was projected to decline over that period (Zenith Optimedia, as cited in Peters, 2009).

Periodicals

"The first colonial magazines appeared in Philadelphia in 1741, about 50 years after the first newspapers" (Campbell, 2002, p. 310). Few Americans could read in that era, and periodicals were costly to produce and circulate. Magazines were often subsidized and distributed by special interest groups, such as churches (Huntzicker, 1999). *The Saturday Evening Post*, the longest running magazine in U.S. history, began in 1821 and became the first magazine to both target women as an audience and distribute to a national audience. By 1850, nearly 600 magazines were operating.

By early in the 20th century, national magazines became popular with advertisers who wanted to reach wide audiences. No other medium offered such opportunity. However, by the middle of the century, many successful national magazines began dying in face of advertiser preferences for the new medium of television and the increasing costs of periodical distribution. Magazines turned to smaller niche audiences that were more effective at reaching these audiences. Table 2.2 and Figure 2.3 on the companion Web site for this book (www.tfi.com/ctu) show the number of American periodical titles by year, revealing that the number of new periodical titles nearly doubled from 1958 to 1960.

In the 10 years beginning in 1990, the average annual gain in the number of periodical titles was by only 20, despite the average of 788 new titles published annually in the 1990s. The difference occurred from the high mortality rate, as evidenced by a loss in total titles in six of the 10 years in the decade. The rebound in 2000 and 2001 did not continue in 2002. "Approximately two-thirds of all new titles fail to survive beyond four or five years" (U.S. Department of Commerce/International Trade Association, 2000, p. 25-9).

By 2004, the U.S. periodicals industry included 7,602 firms that employed just more than 1.5 million people. The number of firms grew by 1,350, or 13.6%, since 2000, and the number of employees increased by 13.9%. In 2000, however, Americans averaged 135 hours per person per year reading consumer magazines and spent $47.58 per person per year buying them. By 2004, time spent with periodicals decreased by 8.1% to 124 hours per person per year, and spending remained about level (U.S. Bureau of the Census, 2008).

Periodicals earn revenue through advertising and purchase prices for their circulated issues. Most magazine circulation, however, is generated by annual subscriptions, which have steadily increased by about 2% annually from the late 1980s (Peters & Donald, 2007). However, single-copy magazine sales fell by 3.1% over the 10-year period ending in 2006. That rate slowed in 2007 to 0.6% as compared with the previous year (Peters, 2009). "Factors include rising cover prices, declining numbers of retail outlets that carry magazines, consolidation among wholesale distributors, and competition from other media" (p. 15).

The MPA (as cited by Peters & Donald, 2007) reported that 18,267 consumer and business publications appeared in 2005, including 6,325 consumer magazines. In 2007, 19,532 consumer and business publications (including 6809 consumer titles) were published, and the 10 largest ones accounted for only 20.7% of the revenues recorded among the top 300 magazines (*Advertising Age*, as cited by Peters, 2009).

Subscriptions increased by 0.7% annually in the 10-year period ending in 2007 to 322.4 million units. In 2007, single-copy sales accounted for 13% of all magazines sold and 32% of revenues from magazine sales. Subscriptions accounted for 87% of sales and 68% of revenues. The Audit Bureau of Circulation, which audits nearly 500 periodicals annually, reported (as cited by Clifford, 2010) that magazine circulation, including subscriptions, declined in the last half of 2008 by 0.86%. During the two six-month periods of 2009, total magazine subscriptions fell respectively by 1.19% and 2.23%.

Although subscription sales held steady for several years before 2008, single-copy sales figures are more vulnerable to economic downturns because they represent more of an impulse purchase than subscription sales. Publishing professionals are not yet certain what the recent drops in single-copy sales mean to long term health of the magazine industry (Clifford, 2010).

Online distribution of periodicals is in its infancy. This media form offers many advantages over the traditional printed copies, such as interaction with magazine writers and staffers, electronic bulletin boards, chat features, audio and video, and the ability to cut and paste content into other materials. The increasing availability of personal digital assistants (PDA) and other handheld devices, including e-readers and tablet computers, promotes magazine products and perhaps places them in the hands of people who might otherwise not see them (Peters, 2009).

Books

Books obviously enjoy a history spanning many centuries. Stephen Daye printed the first book in colonial America, *The Bay Psalm Book*, in 1640 (Campbell, 2002). Books remained relatively expensive and rare until after the printing process benefited from the industrial revolution. Linotype machines developed in the 1880s allowed for mechanical typesetting. After World War II, the popularity of paperback books helped the industry expand. The current U.S. book publishing industry includes 87,000 publishers, most of which are small businesses. Many of these literally operate as "mom-and-pop desktop operations" (Peters & Donald, 2007, p. 11).

Table 2.3 and Figures 2.4 and 2.5 from the companion Web site (www.tfi.com/ctu) shows new book titles published by year from the late 1800s through 2008. These data show a remarkable, but potentially deceptive, increase in the number of new book titles published annually, beginning in 1997. The U.S. Bureau of the

Census reports that provided the data were based on material from R. R. Bowker, which changed its reporting methods beginning with the 1998 report. Ink and Grabois (2000) explained the increase as resulting from the change in the method of counting titles "that results in a more accurate portrayal of the current state of American book publishing" (p. 508). Data for previous years came from databases compiled, in part by hand, by the R. R. Bowker Company. The older counting process included only books included by the Library of Congress Cataloging in Publication program. This program included publishing by the largest American publishing companies, but omitted such books as "inexpensive editions, annuals, and much of the output of small presses and self publishers" (Ink & Grabois, 2000, p. 509). Ink and Grabois observed that the U.S. ISBN (International Standard Book Number) Agency assigned more than 10,000 new ISBN publisher prefixes annually.

After a drop in annual book title production in 2004 from the output of the previous year, the number of book titles increased for three consecutive years before dropping again (Barr & Harbison, 2009). The drop was most likely due to the general malaise in the economy.

Book publishers shipped nearly 3.1 billion books in 2006 (U.S. Bureau of the Census, 2008). The figure for 2007 reached 3.126 billion (U.S. Bureau of the Census, 2010). Pfanner (2009) cited European trade organization data showing that book sales in early 2009 increased slightly in European countries such as France and Germany. He cited Nielsen BookScan reports showing that sales in the United States and Great Britain were down by less than one percent during 2008 and down by about one percent in early 2009. Nielsen BookScan reported that 750 million books were sold in the United States during 2009 (752 million in 2010).

In 1999, more than 40% of U.S. adults (79,218,000) reported reading books at least once as a leisure activity during the previous 12 months, and more than 20% (43,919,000) reported such participation at least twice each week (U.S. Bureau of the Census, 2003). From 1999 to 2004, the number who reported reading books fell by 2.2% to 77,472,000. The number of adults who reported reading books at least twice weekly dropped from 1999 to 2004 by 2.4% to 42,861,000 (U.S. Bureau of the Census, 2006).

In 2007, Americans spent more money buying books than they devoted to any other mass medium except cable television (Book Industry Study Group, as cited in Peters, 2009). Annual expenditures for consumer books per American consumer in 1999 averaged $87.34 (U.S. Bureau of the Census, 2005). The figure increased to $94.60 per person in 2004 and grew slightly each year to reach $103.60 in 2007 (U.S. Bureau of the Census, 2008, 2010).

The same trend occurred in consumer time spent with books, with the number of hours per person per year growing by only one hour from 2000 through 2004 to 110 hours before slipping by an hour per year in 2005 and fluctuating by one hour in 2006 and 2007. The average for 2007 fell to 109 hours per year (U.S. Bureau of the Census, 2008, 2010). Fears that Americans might stop reading books appear to have been exaggerated.

Amazon's Kindle and the Nook from Barnes & Noble, both selling in early 2010 for $259, were popular readers for electronic books (Rich, 2010). Other competition came from Apple's iPod Touch and iPhones, and Apple introduced the larger iPad in 2010. Electronic books had been available for several years before achieving much notice in the market, but pricing at $9.99 for e-books seemed to stimulate sales of both readers and books (Grossman, 2010). Amazon accepted losses on most new and popular e-books in hopes of stimulating Kindle sales (Rich & Stone, 2010). On Christmas Day 2009, Amazon for the first time received more orders for e-books than paper versions (Grossman, 2010).

The introduction of the Apple iPad in early 2010 accompanied reports of negotiations involving Apple and several of the largest publishing houses that suggested e-book prices of $12.99–$14.99, higher than the Amazon model but considerably below the $26 average price for a hardcover book (Rich, 2010). Rich and Stone (2010) soon reported that book publishers had been unhappy for more than a year with the Amazon pricing scheme but had been unable to control it because of Amazon's market dominance. The Kindle accounted for 70% of e-book readers and 80% of e-book sales by the end of 2009 (Stone & Rich, 2010). Amazon responded to the news of Apple's pricing deals by agreeing to higher prices with at least one major publisher (Rich & Stone, 2010).

Rich (2010) cited the *Bureau of Labor Statistics* reports of the *Consumer Price Index* as showing price decreases of 3% on recorded music during the period from 2000–2009, compared with a 6% increase for recreational books during the period. At first glance, the reduction in book prices offered via e-books might suggest the potential for increasing demand by lowering book pricing, but publishers argue that many of their costs (e.g., author royalties, editors, type-setting, overhead, and marketing) apply no matter what the mode of publication. The book publishers operate within a system that assumes that only 30% of book titles published will earn profits. The share of e-books accounted for only 3-5% of the overall market by the end of 2009, and the impact of reduced pricing of e-books on publisher profits and retail sales remains unknown (Rich, 2010).

TelepHONE

Alexander Graham Bell became the first to transmit speech electronically, that is, to use the telephone, in 1876. By June 30, 1877, 230 telephones were in use, and the number rose to 1,300 by the end of August, mostly to avoid the need for a skilled interpreter of telegraph messages. The first exchange connected three company offices in Boston beginning on May 17, 1877, reflecting a focus on business rather than residential use during the telephone's early decades. Hotels became early adopters of telephones as they sought to reduce the costs of employing human messengers, and New York's 100 largest hotels had 21,000 telephones by 1909. After 1894, non-business telephone use became ordinary, in part, because business use lowered the cost of telephone service. By 1902, 2,315,000 telephones were in service in the United States (Aronson, 1977). Table 2.4 and Figure 2.6 on the companion Web site (www.tfi.com/ctu) document the growth to near ubiquity of telephones in U.S. households and the expanding presence of wireless telephones.

Wireless telephones

Guglielmo Marconi sent the first wireless data messages in 1895. The growing popularity of telephony led many to experiment with Marconi's radio technology as another means for interpersonal communication. By the 1920s, Detroit police cars had mobile radiophones for voice communication (ITU, 1999). The Bell system offered radio telephone service in 1946 in St. Louis, the first of 25 cities to receive the service. Bell engineers divided reception areas into cells in 1947, but cellular telephones that switched effectively among cells as callers moved did not arrive until the 1970s. The first call on a portable, handheld cell phone occurred in 1973. However, by 1981, only 24 people in New York City could use their mobile phones at the same time, and only 700 customers could have active contracts. The Federal Communications Commission (FCC) began offering cellular telephone system licenses by lottery in June 1982 (Murray, 2001). Other countries, such as Japan in 1979 and Saudi Arabia in 1982, operated cellular systems earlier than the United States (ITU, 1999).

The U.S. Congress promoted a group of mobile communication services in 1993 by creating a classification of commercial mobile services that became known as Commercial Mobile Radio Service. This classification allowed for consistent regulatory oversight of these technologies and encouraged commercial competition among providers (FCC, 2005). By the end of 1996, about 44 million Americans subscribed to wireless telephone services (U.S. Bureau of the Census, 2008). Ten years later, the number of wireless subscribers exceeded 230 million in the United States. Subscriber growth rose by 11% between the end of 2005 and early 2007 (U.S. Bureau of the Census, 2008).

By the end of 2008, 25 million mobile wireless subscribers owned mobile devices with high-speed Internet access plans including laptop computers and smartphones (FCC, 2010b). Another 86 million subscribers used devices that transmitted at speeds above 200 kbps. This group included subscribers to voice service plans, data service plans customized for mobile content (e.g., text, multimedia messaging, downloading capability with ringtones and games). The latter group also included 25 million subscribers with data plans for full Internet access. Changes in reporting practices precluded comparing these numbers with previous estimates of the number of subscribers to high-speed wireless services. Earlier predictions (Stellin, 2002) that the wireless telephone phenomenon was reaching the saturation point proved incorrect.

The sale of wireless handsets is the "world's largest consumer electronic market" (Bensinger, 2007, p. 6) as measured in units sold. An estimated 990 million mobile telephone handsets were sold globally in 2006, up by more than 20% from the approximately 800 million sold in 2005. That figure represents more than four times the approximately 230 million computers sold around the world in 2006. About half of these handset sales went for upgrading phones, and the other half marked new wireless users. By April 2007, the number of wireless subscribers around the world reached 2.9 billion, a global penetration rate of approximately 44%.

Wireless phone penetration in the U.S. reached 77% by the end of 2006 (CTIA-The Wireless Association, as cited by Moorman, 2009). The number of subscribers in the United States numbered almost 242 million at that time, and the 28.8 million one-year increase from 213 million a year earlier marked the largest one-year subscriber growth in history with 80% of the approximately 300 million Americans using wireless phones (FCC, 2008c). The physical coverage of wireless service reached 75% of the American land mass. Excluding federal land, that figure reaches 85% of the country.

Significant numbers of American households began dropping wired telephone service to shift to wireless-only service by 2001 (FCC, 2008d). A survey by MediaMark Research (as cited by Mindlin, 2007) of about 13,000 households in April 2007 found that, for the first time, the proportion of American households with at least one mobile phone (86.2%) exceeded the proportion of households with landline-only phone service (84.5%). The company has been conducting such surveys since the mid-1980s. The penetration of wireless phones by the end of 2007 reached 84% and increased to 87% by the end of 2008. Between 1998 and 2008, the number of wireless phone subscribers increased by 69.2 million to exceed 270 million (CTIA-The Wireless Association, as cited by Moorman, 2009). The growth of the absolute number of wireless phones was continuing, even though the rate of growth had slowed.

Lenhart et al. (2010) reported that ownership of cell phones among teenagers and adults under 30 years of age was "nearly ubiquitous" (p. 4) in 2009. Fifty-eight percent of children aged 12 had cell phones; among teens, it was 75%, and among 18-29 year olds it was 93%.

Consolidation left the industry dominated by four national carriers (AT&T, Sprint Nextel, T-Mobile, and Verizon Wireless) that served 93% of American wireless phone subscribers (Moorman, 2009). The four major carriers purchased smaller regional companies to consolidate network coverage into national services. Faster network speeds, such as 3G, promoted the Web-based services featured on the more powerful handsets. In 2008, the Federal Communications Commission auctioned spectrum frequencies in the 700 MHz band that foreshadowed the development of 4G networks. A variety of applications running on a single device, including Web-based video, enhanced desirability of respective handset models in the eyes of customers.

In October 2009, Open Mobile Video Coalition announced a new standard that allowed television broadcasters to transmit high-definition signals to wireless devices (Hansell, 2009). The broadcasts were set to use the new set of frequencies allocated by Congress. Approximately 16 million Americans could watch video on their wireless phones, and the number was expected to reach 27.2 million by 2013 (IDC, as cited by Moorman, 2009). A survey in 2009 (IDC, as cited by Moorman, 2009) revealed that about 37% of respondents reported seeing at least one mobile video during the previous year. The availability of a variety of video forms (e.g., television shows, news, sports, and MTV videos) on phones helped push mobile video revenues from $1.2 billion in 2008 to projections of $1.4 billion by 2013 (Moorman, 2009).

Although wireless companies once competed for customers on the basis of price, competition shifted to focus on multi-function handsets (Moorman, 2009). Carriers began offering discounts on sophisticated handsets to subscribers, and the companies signed contracts with handset makers to offer exclusive deals. For example, AT&T partnered with Apple, Inc. to offer exclusive access to the iPhone. Once traditional discounts in the $100 range gave way to discounts of $200 per model, with the discounts subsidized by monthly service charges.

Apple, Inc. introduced the iPhone in the United States in June 2007, followed a year later by the iPhone 3G (third generation of wireless networks) (Kessler, 2009). By the end of 2008, the device was available in 70 countries, and Apple shipped 14 million iPhones that year. Apple announced in September 2009 that two billion downloads had been sold from the Apple store for the iPod and iPhone. The company followed in January 2010 by announcing that more than three billion applications had been sold (Stone, 2010).

Competing products emulated the iPhone operations, fostering an increase in a variety of mobile hardware and software. IDC (as cited by Kessler, 2009) projected a doubling of spending on mobile marketing and advertising "on a compounded annual basis for the foreseeable future, rising from $50 million in 2007 to $890 million in 2012" (p. 5).

A Pew study of teenagers (Lenhart et al., 2007) found that 35% talked on mobile phones every day. The average wireless subscriber used 472 minutes of wireless voice service per month in 2002. That figure increased annually to an average of 714 minutes per month in 2006, although the rate of increase began to slow by that time. This usage was more than four times that of Western Europe and Japan, where wireless service tended to be more expensive than in the United States. Users in those areas of the world have tended to use more text messages than Americans, but text messaging has gained popularity in America, too (FCC, 2008c).

In 2002, American wireless users sent an average of 1.02 billion text messages per month. Like voice messages, that figure increased annually to 18.71 billion monthly messages in 2006, but unlike voice messages, the rate of growth increased every year (FCC, 2008c). The Pew study (Lenhart et al., 2007) of teen media use reported that 28% of teens sent text messages daily, and nearly half of the substantial group of teens who were classified as multichannel teens sent text messages every day.

The age group spending the most time on mobile phones falls within the ages of 18 to 24. The data came from a 2007 survey by Telephia, Inc. (as cited by Jennings, 2007). The members of this group averaged 290 calls per month. Users from ages 13 to 17 sent the most text messages, an average 435 per month. People aged 45 to 54 placed an average of 194 monthly calls, but they used text messaging an average of only 57 times per month.

Other services used by wireless customers also showed increasing popularity. Multimedia messages, including photo messages, more than doubled from 2005 to 2006, growing from 1.1 billion messages to 2.7 billion (FCC, 2008c). By the end of 2005, about 44% of wireless subscribers owned cell phones that supported gaming. Jupiter Research (as cited by Leon & Kawaguchi, 2007) projected that 70% of American wireless phones would be gaming-capable by the end of 2006. Seven million Americans watched video via their wireless phones in 2007, and the number was expected to reach 24 million by 2010. Many more services will go wireless after the 2008 FCC auction of spectrum in the 700 MHz band that will support broadband wireless services (Kessler, 2007a).

Approximately 10.7% of American wireless users surfed the Internet during the first quarter of 2006, an increase of 9.9% over the comparable period in 2005. In 2005, 3.1 million wireless Internet capable devices were in use, and the figure grew to 21.9 million by the end of 2006. About 82% of Americans lived in census blocks served by at least one wireless Internet provider (FCC, 2008c).

Wireless telephone users paid about $0.11 per minute in 2002 for their service. The prices paid declined until 2005, when the cost per minute remained steady through 2006 at $0.07 per minute. Prepaid phone plans increased from 13% of wireless customers in 2005 to 15% in 2006 (FCC, 2008c).

The average monthly bill for local wireless service in 2002 was $48.40. The average local wireless bill of $50.64 in December 2004 represented a roughly flat trend since 1995, when the figure was $51, although monthly average prices in the interim fell as low as $39.43 in December 1998. Average monthly bills increased over the previous yearly average every year from 1998 through 2004 (FCC, 2005) when the year-end average was $50.64, nearly half of the 1987 average of $96.83 (FCC, 2007). However, the decline to $49.98 in 2005 reversed in 2006 to $50.56 per month (FCC, 2008c).

The FCC (2008d) reported that typical households spent $360 annually in 1981 for telephone service. The figure increased to $1,087 in 2006. Although the increase appears at first glance to be substantial, the FCC observed that consumer spending for telephone services, in terms of the proportion of all consumer spending, changed little over that 25-year period, despite all the development in telephones and services. The proportion of spending for telephone service remained at about 2%.

Spending among all American households that were billed for telephone service averaged $100 monthly in 1997, of which $60 went for wired service, and $40 went for wireless services. A decade later, the average telephone expenses among household billed for service reached $133 monthly, of which $48 was allocated for wired service, and $85 went for wireless uses (FCC, 2008d). By 2009, unlimited access plans for voice or voice and data ranged from $90 - $130 (Moorman, 2009).

Between 2001 and 2006, the number of wired home telephone lines in the United States fell from 161 million to 124 million. In 2006, nearly 7% of wired lines were dropped by consumers, many to be replaced by wireless service as the only home telephone, and 11.8% of adults lived in households with wireless phones but no wired phones. This trend applied particularly often with young adults, with half of such consumers under 30 years of age using wireless service only. Among adults aged 18 to 24, 25.2% lived in households with wireless-only service. The figure for adults aged 25 to 29 was 30%. However, as the users' ages increased, the proportion of wireless-only households dropped: 12.4% of adults 30 to 44; 6.1% for ages 45 to 64; and 1.9% of adults over 65 had wireless-only in 2006 (FCC, 2008c).

By December 2009, 83% of a sample of more than 2,000 adults reported owning a cell phone or another device that also functions as a cell phone (Rainie, 2010). That proportion was up from 75% just two years before. Among such users, 19% used these devices to send or receive email in 2007. In 2009, that proportion was up to 29%. For instant messaging, the proportion increased from 17% in 2007 to 31% in 2009. Using the Internet rose from 19% to 32%. Lenhart et al. (2010) reported the results of a 2009 Pew Research Center Survey that included the finding that 58% of 12-year olds owned a cell phone, up from 18% in 2004.

MOTION PICTURES

In the 1890s, George Eastman improved on work by and patents purchased from Hannibal Goodwin in 1889 to produce workable motion picture film. The Lumière brothers projected moving pictures in a Paris café in 1895, hosting 2,500 people nightly at their movies. William Dickson, an assistant to Thomas Edison, developed the kinetograph, an early motion picture camera, and the kinetoscope, a motion picture viewing system. A New York movie house opened in 1894, offering moviegoers several coin-fed kinetoscopes. Edison's Vitascope, which expanded the length of films over those shown via kinetoscopes and allowed larger audiences to simultaneously see the moving images, appeared in public for the first time in 1896. In France in that same year, Georges Méliès started the first motion picture theater. Short movies became part of public entertainment in a variety of American venues by 1900 (Campbell, 2002), and average weekly movie attendance reached 40 million people by 1922.

Average weekly motion picture theater attendance, as shown in Table 2.5 and Figure 2.7 on the companion Web site (www.tfi.com/ctu), increased annually from the earliest available census reports on the subject in 1922 until 1930. After falling dramatically during the Great Depression, attendance regained growth in 1934 and continued until 1937. Slight declines in the prewar years were followed by a period of strength and stability throughout the World War II years. After the end of the war, average weekly attendance reached its greatest heights: 90 million attendees weekly from 1946 through 1949. After the beginning of television, weekly attendance would never again reach these levels.

Although a brief period of leveling off occurred in the late 1950s and early 1960s, average weekly attendance continued to plummet until a small recovery began in 1972. This recovery signaled a period of relative stability that lasted into the 1990s. Through the last decade of the century, average weekly attendance enjoyed small but steady gains.

Box office revenues, which declined generally for 20 years after the beginning of television, began a recovery in the late 1960s. Box office revenues then began to skyrocket in the 1970s, and the explosion continued until after the turn of the new century. However, much of the increase in revenues came from increases in ticket prices and inflation, rather than from increased popularity of films with audiences. Total motion picture revenue from box office receipts declined during recent years, as studios realized increased revenues from television and home video (U.S. Department of Commerce/International Trade Association, 2000).

Motion picture attendance in terms of tickets sold displayed a steady upward trend from 1991 through 2002, with minor dips in 1995, 1999, and 2000. The 1.4 billion total motion picture theater admissions in 2008, however, marked the lowest number of annual admissions since 1997 (National Association of Theater Owners, 2010) and declined by 2.6% from the number of tickets sold in 2007. In 2008 and 2009, major film studios reduced the number of employees and the number of films released (Amobi, 2009).

Amobi (2009) cited data from the *Digital Entertainment Group*, a trade organization, showing that motion picture attendance dips were part of an overall trend in which revenues declined across a variety of entertainment sources, including DVD and digital rentals and purchases. Such revenues fell by 3.3% in 2007 to $23.3 billion and declined again in 2008 by 7.3% to $21.7 billion.

The total American motion picture box office receipts increased from about $6.9 billion in 1998 to about $9.8 billion in 2008 (U. S. Bureau of the Census, 2010). This increase in revenue occurred despite declining average weekly theater attendance during the same period. In 1998, about 28.5 million viewers went to the movies weekly, and that average fell to 26.2 million per week in 2008 (National Association of Theater Owners, 2010). The high point in 2003 was followed by a decline in average weekly attendance during every year through 2008 except 2006.

Consumer box office spending per person per year increased from $31.23 in 1998 (U.S. Bureau of the Census, 2005) to $38.16 in 2008 (U.S. Bureau of the Census, 2010). In the interim, the annual amount fluctuated, with the high year in 2002 at $39.59 (U. S. Bureau of the Census 2005). The average fell for three consecutive years after 2002 before increasing for three consecutive years through 2008.

The increase in ticket prices accounted for the total revenue gains while attendance was falling. Average ticket prices increased from $6.40 in 2005 to $6.58 in 2006, a gain of 2.6% (Amobi & Donald, 2007). Average ticket prices reached $7.16 by 2008 and grew by 4% to $7.45 by August 2009 (Amobi, 2009).

As shown in Table 2.5 on the companion Web site (www.tfi.com/ctu), American movie fans spent an average of 12 hours per person per year from 1993 through 1997 going to theaters. Although that average fluctuated between 12 and 14 hours during the years from 1998 through 2004, it stabilized at 12 hours per person per year spent in theaters during the period from 2005 through 2008 (U.S. Bureau of the Census, 2010).

In 2005, the most frequent purchasers of film tickets fell in the 12 to 20 year-old bracket. Members of that group purchased 27% of the tickets, although they accounted for only 15% of the population. The proportion of tickets purchased declined as ages grew higher, with people of ages 50 to 59 purchasing only 10% of the tickets, although they accounted for 15% of the population (Amobi & Donald, 2007). Americans purchased 1.4 billion theater tickets in 2008, an average of 4 million tickets per day (Amobi, 2009).

In the United States, six motion picture companies accounted for 80% of the box office revenues by 2009. Among approximately 39,000 theater screens in the country, 48% were owned by the top five chains (Amobi, 2009). These screens operated in about 6,300 locations (Nielsen EDI, as cited by Amobi, 2009).

In October 2008, three of the largest movie exhibitors signed long-term agreements with several Hollywood studios to make plans for showing 3-D films (Amobi, 2009). The studios agreed to produce such films and share the costs of setting up digital projection systems for nearly 20,000 screens over a three-and-a-half-year period beginning in 2009. Following a similar deal in March 2008 involving four major studios and as many as 10,000 screens, the economic recession interfered with these plans and slowed the program. By late 2009, fewer than 2,500 screens (less than 5% of North American screens) had been properly outfitted for 3-D. Nevertheless, several successful 3-D films earned strong audience responses in late 2009 and 2010, and one of them, *Avatar,* surpassed *Titanic* as the top grossing motion picture of all time at the box office (All time box office, 2010). However, after adjusting for ticket price inflation, *Avatar* ranked 14th in March 2010 on the list of top films, revealing the problem with measuring media performance with monetary standards.

The overseas box office revenues for American film studios reached $9.52 billion in 2007, up about 10% from 2006 (McNary & McClintock, 2008). In 2008, almost two-thirds of the $85 billion in global spending on American motion picture entertainment media (including box office receipts, DVDs, and other media) was spent outside the United States (Amobi, 2009).

Audio Recording

Thomas Edison expanded on experiments from the 1850s by Leon Scott de Martinville to produce a talking machine or phonograph in 1877 that played back sound recordings from etchings in tin foil. Edison later replaced the foil with wax. In the 1880s, Emile Berliner created the first flat records from metal and shellac designed to play on his gramophone, providing mass production of recordings. The early standard recordings played at 78 revolutions per minute (rpm). After shellac became a scarce commodity because of World War II, records were manufactured from polyvinyl plastic. In 1948, CBS Records produced the long-playing record that turned at 33-1/3 rpm, extending the playing time from three to four minutes to 10 minutes. *RCA* countered in 1949 with 45 rpm records that were incompatible with machines that played other formats. After a five-year war of formats, record players were manufactured that would play recordings at all of the speeds (Campbell, 2002).

The Germans used plastic magnetic tape for sound recording during World War II. After the Americans confiscated some of the tapes, the technology became a boon for Western audio editing and multiple track recordings that played on bulky reel-to-reel machines. By the 1960s, the reels were encased in cassettes, which would prove to be deadly competition in the 1970s for single song records playing at 45 rpm and long-playing albums playing at 33-1/3 rpm. At first, the tape cassettes were popular in 8-track players. As technology improved, high sound quality was obtainable on tape of smaller width, and 8-tracks gave way to smaller audio-cassettes. Thomas Stockholm began recording sound digitally in the 1970s, and the introduction of compact disc (CD) recordings in 1983 decimated the sales performance of earlier analog media types (Campbell, 2002). Figures 2.8 and 2.8A and Table 2.6 on the companion Web site (www.tfi.com/ctu) trace the rise and fall of the sales of audio recordings of these respective types.

This table and figure appeared in previous communication technology updates in this series and remain available to show the history of respective forms of shipping recorded music. Because of the declining shipments in some music genres, reported categories have recently been combined. Table 2.6A and Figures 2.8B and 2.8C show new categories that emerged to explain and illustrate these trends.

Table 2.6 and Figure 2.8 show that total unit sales of recorded music generally increased from the early 1970s through 2008. Figure 2.6A shows unit sales of physical units of music media from 1996 through 2008, more clearly illustrating recent trends in such media. The data show a brief recovery in 1995 through 1997, followed by steady declines except for a brief recovery in 2004 (Leeds, 2005) in total units sold.

During the decade after 1998, sales of vinyl singles managed to hang on, but cassette singles sales disappeared after 2000. In 2001 and 2002, more cassette singles were returned by retailers than the number of units sold, and other music cassettes moved closer to extinction each year. CD units sold rose every year from their introduction in 1983 until a downturn began in 2001. In the eight-year period that began that year, CD unit sales fell every year except in 2004. The decline between 2006 and 2008 approached 40%. By 2008, unit CD sales fell by more than half of their total in 1998. However, total unit music sales during that decade grew by about 65% because of the popularity of digital unit sales, which increased more than seven fold from 2004 through 2008.

Perhaps in response to economic hard times in 2008, album sales in that year fell by 14%, and CD unit sales dropped by 20% to below 400 million units. The Recording Industry Association of America (RIAA) reported that Americans spent $8.5 billion in 2008 for recorded music, two-thirds of which came from physical CDs and a third from digital downloads (Amobi, 2009).

The popularity of online single music track purchasing prompted the industry to create "track-equivalent albums" (TEA) (Amobi, 2009, p. 5) as a way of comparing sales performance in different time periods. Combined sales of TEA and physical albums declined by 9% in the first six months of 2009 to 235.8 million units (Nielsen SoundScan, as cited by Amobi, 2009). Album sales alone fell by 15% during the period to 174.5 million units, and CD sales declined by 21% to 135.7 units.

Digital Audio players, which transformed the way millions listen to music, celebrated their 10th anniversary in 2008 (Beaumont, 2008). In 2001, the Apple iPod brought the ability to store as many as 1,000 songs, and 150 million of them sold by 2008. Internet downloading of music, in its infancy in 2004, provided the source of about 19% of music sales by 2008. Mobile music (ringtones, ringbacks, full-length songs, etc.) accounted for nearly 10% of total music sales. From the launch of Apple's iTunes in 2003 through June 2009, consumers purchased about eight billion songs from the service, which replaced Wal-Mart as the world's largest music seller (Amobi, 2009).

Taking advantage of the popularity of social networking sites on the Internet, recording companies began contracting with such services as distribution mechanisms in 2008 (Amobi, 2009). After signing deals with four major music publishers and News Corp., MySpace Music began selling songs in September 2008 and grew by 190% in unique monthly visitors by June 2009. Competitors quickly began similar operations.

Radio

Guglielmo Marconi's wireless messages in 1895 on his father's estate led to his establishing a British company to profit from ship-to-ship and ship-to-shore messaging. He formed a U.S. subsidiary in 1899 that would become the American Marconi Company. Reginald A. Fessenden and Lee De Forest independently transmitted voice by means of wireless radio in 1906, and a radio broadcast from the stage of a performance by Enrico Caruso occurred in 1910. Various U.S. companies and Marconi's British company owned important patents that were necessary to the development of the infant industry, so the U.S. firms formed the Radio Corporation of America (*RCA*) to buy out the patent rights from Marconi.

The debate still rages over the question of who became the first broadcaster among KDKA in Pittsburgh, WHA in Madison (Wisconsin), WWJ in Detroit, and *KQW* in San Jose (California). In 1919, Dr. Frank Conrad of Westinghouse broadcast music from his phonograph in his garage in East Pittsburgh. Westinghouse's KDKA in Pittsburgh announced the presidential election returns over the airwaves on November 2, 1920. By January 1, 1922, the Secretary of Commerce had issued 30 broadcast licenses, and the number of licensees swelled to 556 by early 1923. By 1924, RCA owned a station in New York, and Westinghouse expanded to Chicago, Philadelphia, and Boston. In 1922, AT&T withdrew from RCA and started WEAF in New York, the first radio station supported by commercials. In 1923, AT&T linked WEAF with WNAC in Boston by the company's telephone lines for a simultaneous program. This began the first network, which grew to 26 stations by 1925. RCA linked its stations with telegraph lines, which failed to match the voice quality of the transmissions of AT&T. However, AT&T wanted out of the new business and sold WEAF in 1926 to the National Broadcasting Company, a subsidiary of RCA (White, 1971).

The 1930 penetration of radio sets in American households reached 40%, then approximately doubled over the next 10 years, passing 90% by 1947 (Brown, 2006). Table 2.7 and Figure 2.9 on the companion Web site (www.tfi.com/ctu) show the rapid rate of increase in the number of radio households from 1922 through the early 1980s, when the rate of increase declined. The increases resumed until 1993, when they began to level off.

By the end of 2006, the FCC reported that 11,020 commercial radio stations were broadcasting in the United States. In addition, 2,817 educational FM radio stations were on the air. Ownership of these stations is highly concentrated, with 20% of the total being owned by the largest 10 groups, accounting for about 45% of the radio broadcasting industry revenues (Amobi & Kolb, 2007). The number of licensed stations grew to 11,213 by the end of 2008, with 4,786 AM stations and 6,427 FM stations (Kolb & Amobi, 2009). The proportion of stations owned by the 10 largest groups swelled to 25%. The largest group, Clear Channel, owned stations reaching nearly 40% of the radio market.

Although thousands of radio stations were transmitting via the Internet by 2000, Channel1031.com became the first station to cease using FM and move exclusively to the Internet in September 2000 (Raphael, 2000). Many other stations were operating only on the Internet when questions about fees for commercial performers and royalties for music played on the Web arose. In 2002, the Library of Congress ruled by setting rates for such transmissions of sound recordings, a decision whose appeals by several organizations remained pending at the end of 2003 (U.S. Copyright Office, 2003). A federal court upheld the right of the Copyright Office to levy fees on streaming music over the Internet (*Bonneville v. Peters*, 2001).

In March 2001, the first two American digital audio satellites were launched, offering the promise of hundreds of satellite radio channels (Associated Press, 2001). Consumers were expected to pay about $9.95 per month for access to commercial-free programming that would be targeted to automobile receivers. The system included amplification from about 1,300 ground antennas. By the end of 2003, 1.621 million satellite radio subscribers tuned to the two top providers, XM and Sirius, up 51% from the previous quarter (Schaeffler, 2004). A market research firm, eMarketer, reported in November 2005 that the two firms combined, attracted 4.37 million subscribers in 2004 and 9.32 million in 2005 (Satellite radio, 2006). By the end of 2007, the combined audience for the two reached about 17.6 million subscribers, and the projected audience was estimated to reach 22 million by the end of 2008 (Amobi & Kolb, 2007). Most consumers paid about $13 per month for satellite radio subscriptions by 2005 (Siklos, 2005).

XM and Sirius satellite radio services merged in July 2008 to create Sirius XM Radio (Kolb & Amobi, 2009). Opponents of the merger contend that the deal would be anti-competitive, but the companies argued that the many competing media (e.g., portable digital audio players, the Internet, wireless phones) offer bountiful competition. By March 2009, the service reached 18.6 million subscribers, down by 2.1% from the number that were served by the combined services a year earlier. Meanwhile, the terrestrial digital radio service (HD radio) radio was not doing well, and some major providers stopped transmitting digital signals by 2009.

The estimated average number of hours of radio (broadcast and satellite combined) listening per person per year have been declining, according to recent publications by the U.S. Bureau of the Census (2010). The projected figure for 2008 back in 2006 was 1,120 hours per person per year, but the most current projected figure given (U.S. Bureau of the Census, 2010) is only 777 hours per person per year, a decline of more than 30%. During 2008, 93% of Americans of age 12 and older listened to radio at least once per week, and typical listeners tuned in for two hours daily (Kolb & Amobi, 2009). Nearly half of all week day radio listening occurred in vehicles, about 35% in homes, and just over 18% occurred at work or other places.

Television

Paul Nipkow invented a scanning disk device in the 1880s that provided the basis from which other inventions would develop into television. In 1927, Philo Farnsworth became the first to electronically transmit a picture over the air. Fittingly, he transmitted the image of a dollar sign. In 1930, he received a patent for the first electronic television, one of many patents for which RCA would be forced, after court challenges, to negotiate. By 1932, Vladimir Zworykin discovered a means of converting light rays into electronic signals that could be transmitted and reconstructed at a receiving device. RCA offered the first public demonstration of television at the 1939 World's Fair.

The FCC designated 13 channels in 1941 for use in transmitting black-and-white television, and the commission issued almost 100 television station broadcasting licenses before placing a freeze on new licenses in 1948. The freeze offered time to settle technical issues, and it ran longer because of U.S. involvement in the Korean War (Campbell, 2002). As shown in Table 2.8 on the companion Web site (www.tfi.com/ctu), nearly 4,000 households had television sets by 1950, a 9% penetration rate that would escalate to 87% a decade later. Penetration has remained steady at about 98% since 1980. Figure 2.9 illustrates the meteoric rise in the number of households with television by year from 1946 through the turn of the century.

From 1993 through 2003, the total number of U.S. commercial and noncommercial broadcast television stations grew by 13.7% to 1,733 (FCC, 2004b). By June 2004, the number of noncommercial and commercial U.S. television stations reached 1,747 and remained unchanged through June 2005. More than 15 million households, or 14% of all American television households, were still receiving broadcast television over the airwaves, not subscribing to any multichannel service (FCC, 2006a). At the end of 2008, 1,378 commercial television stations were licensed, and about 25% of them were owned or affiliated with the 10 largest station groups (Kolb & Amobi, 2009).

Television's popularity rebounded from declines early in the new century to new heights. Total television households increased by just more than 1% from the previous year to 109.6 million by June 2005. The FCC (2006a) cited data from Nielsen Media Research showing that typical American households kept television on for eight hours and 11 minutes daily during the 2004-2005 programming season, an increase of 12% over comparable statistics from a decade before. The new figures reached the highest viewing levels since the early days of television in the 1950s. Personal viewing set an all-time record by averaging four hours and 32 minutes daily.

By the first quarter of 2009, the typical American household watched television for 153 hours and 18 minutes each month (Nielsen Media Research, as cited by Amobi, 2009). This figure established a record high level since such monitoring began in the 1950s. The heaviest viewing occurred among people older than 54 years of age.

As important as programming success was to the television industry, perhaps technical standards were even more critical. American television standards set in the 1940s provided for 525 lines of information composing the picture. By the 1980s, Japanese high-definition television (HDTV) increased the potential resolution to more than 1,100 lines of data in a television picture. This increase enabled a much higher-quality image to be transmitted with less electromagnetic spectrum space per signal. In 1996, the FCC approved a digital television transmission standard and authorized broadcast television stations a second channel for a 10-year period to allow the transition to HDTV. As discussed in Chapter 6, that transition made all older analog television sets obsolete because they cannot process HDTV signals (Campbell, 2002).

The FCC (2002) initially set May 2002 as the deadline by which all U.S. commercial television broadcasters were required to be broadcasting digital television signals. Progress toward digital television broadcasting fell short of FCC requirements that all affiliates of the top four networks in the top 10 markets transmit digital signals by May 1, 1999.

The FCC (2006a) revised the schedule of transition from analog to digital services on June 9, 2005 by requiring that new sets and other receiving equipment, such as videocassette recorders (VCRs) and digital video recorders (DVRs) be capable of receiving digital transmissions. March 1, 2006 was subsequently set as the deadline by which all receivers including screens of 25 inches through 36 inches must contain digital tuners. By March 1, 2007, all sets with screens of 13 inches to 24 inches were required to meet that standard, and the same rules now apply to smaller screens. By October 2005, at least 1,537 television stations in the United States were broadcasting digital signals, including all of the 119 stations affiliated with the top four broadcast networks in the 30 largest television markets (FCC, 2006a). Congress eventually mandated that February 17, 2009 would be the last date for legal analog television broadcasts by full-power stations (FCC, 2008a), with that date eventually being pushed back to June 12, 2009.

Within the 10 largest television markets, all except one network affiliate had begun digital broadcasts including HDTV by August 1, 2001. By that date, 83% of American television stations had received construction permits for digital facilities or a license to broadcast digital signals (FCC, 2002). Despite broadcast digital and HDTV signals and having cable systems carrying HDTV programming available to more than 60 million households (FCC, 2004a), only about 1.5 million households were watching high-definition television by early 2004 (In-Stat/MDR, 2004). By the end of 2004, HDTV service was available to about 92 million households or 87% of homes with access to cable television. Among the 210 television markets, 184 included at least one cable system offering HDTV, and all 100 of the largest markets had the service (FCC, 2006a). Nielsen Media Research (as cited in Amobi & Kolb, 2007) estimated in October 2007 that 14% of American households, or nearly 16 million, had HDTV capable televisions.

The transition from analog to digital television received resistance from consumers over the need to purchase equipment capable of receiving the new signals. The average 1998 price of a digital television set of $3,147 fell to an estimated $1,043 in 2006. By that year, digital sets outsold analog sets by 66% (FCC, 2009a). As the digital transition progressed, converters making digital signals viewable on analog sets became available at around $60. Among the sources of educational information about DTV and HDTV, the FCC site at http://www.dtv.gov serves to inform consumers. By June 2009, HDTV penetration in the United States grew by 44% over that of the previous year to 44 million households (Consumer Electronics Association, as cited by Amobi, 2009).

In fall 2007, major broadcast television networks began offering primetime program episodes for free, supported by advertising, over the Internet via their own Web sites, as well as on syndicated Web sites operated by other distributors. Such shows could also be downloaded for fees from a variety of online sites (Amobi & Kolb, 2007). In the summer of 2009, Time Warner and Comcast began experimenting with TV Everywhere, a method of streaming full-length television shows and movies (Amobi, 2009). Online video sites had become popular by March 2009, led by such sites such as Google's YouTube, Fox Interactive Media (including MySpace), and Hulu (owned by News Corp., NBC Universal, and Disney).

By June 2009, the major broadcast networks (ABC, NBC, CBS, Fox, and CWTV) were streaming television shows via the Internet (Kolb & Amobi, 2009). Other shows were available through third-party video sites and as pay-per-view selections from a variety of sources. Hulu began providing full television shows and films in March 2008. Stelter (2010) described Hulu as the dominant online site for viewing of full television episodes, citing data from comScore as showing 1.01 billion views in December 2009, up from 580 million in September 2009. Hulu, having begun in 2007, averaged 44 million monthly viewers by early 2010.

Cable Television

Cable television began as a means to overcome poor reception for broadcast television signals. John Watson claimed to have developed a master antenna system in 1948, but his records were lost in a fire. Robert J. Tarlton of Lansford (Pennsylvania) and Ed Parsons of Astoria (Oregon) set up working systems in 1949 that used a single antenna to receive programming over the air and distribute it via coaxial cable to multiple users (Baldwin & McVoy, 1983). At first, the FCC chose not to regulate cable, but after the new medium appeared to offer a threat to broadcasters, cable became the focus of heavy government regulation. Under the Reagan administration, attitudes swung toward deregulation, and cable began to flourish. Table 2.9 and Figure 2.10 on the companion Web site (www.tfi.com/ctu) show the growth of cable systems and subscribers, with penetration remaining below 25% until 1981, but passing the 50% mark before the 1980s ended.

The rate of growth in the number of cable subscribers slowed over the last half of the 1990s. Penetration, after consistently rising every year from cable's outset, declined every year after 1997. The FCC reports annually to Congress regarding the status of competition in the marketplace for video programming, and the agency reported that, by 2001, the franchise cable operator share of multichannel video programming distributors (MVPDs) slipped from 80% in 2000 to 78% a year later (FCC, 2001). Continuing the slide, that figure reached 69.4% of the approximately 94.2 million MVPD households by June 2005 (FCC, 2006a). MVPD households accounted for almost 86% of the 109.6 million television homes in 2005. In June 2009, 85% of American households received either cable or satellite television, up from 56% in 1990 (Amobi, 2009).

During the decade beginning in 1994, the number of U.S. households passed by cable increased from 91.6 million to about 103.5 million in 2003. Cable systems passed 108.2 million homes with television in 2004, about 99% of homes that had television. The number of homes subscribing to cable fell in 2005 by 700,000 to 65.4 million subscribers. Despite that decline in penetration, cable revenue continued to increase because of additional services such as high-speed Internet access, digital channels, and higher basic subscription rates (FCC, 2006a).

Although the most popular broadcast networks continued to draw more viewers than the most popular cable television networks, audience share of cable television networks in primetime increased to 53% for the 2004-2005 season. Non-broadcast channels attracted a 53 share of primetime attention in 2004-2005, up from 52 a year earlier. Similar trends occurred across the entire viewing schedule, with non-broadcast channels growing from a 56 share the previous year to a 59 share during 2004-2005, reflecting the strength of cable programming (FCC, 2006a). By 2007-2008, 43 million households tuned to a typical evening broadcast while cable channels drew an average of 51 million (RPA, as cited by Stelter, 2009). The average audience reported by Nielsen Media Research for the 76 advertising-supported cable channels in 2008-2009 reached 56 million, compared with 43 million for broadcasting programming during the first half of the season.

During the decade beginning in 1993, the cost of cable television subscriptions grew by 53.1%—more than double the 25.5% increase in the consumer price index. The National Cable Television Association (NCTA) claimed that, although prices for cable were up, cost per viewing hour declined, as the public spent more time watching cable programming. Cable programming expenses grew by 10.6% from the end of 2003 to the end of

2004 to $12.68 billion. Average monthly cable revenue per subscriber increased from $66.22 in 2003 to $72.87 in 2004, and projected revenue per subscriber for 2005 was $80.33 (FCC, 2006a).

During 2005, the average subscriber monthly prices for cable television increased by 5.2% over the average for the previous year. The total average monthly price in 1995 for basic and expanded basic cable television was $22.35. In 2005, the figure rose to $43.04 per month, an increase of 92.6% in a decade (FCC, 2006b). In the five year period beginning in 2004, average monthly cable charges rose by 35% to $64 in 2009 (Leichtman Research, as cited by Quenqua, 2010).

At the end of 2000, 8.7 million households subscribed to digital cable. Within another six months, the estimated count reached 12 million (FCC, 2002). The total grew to 22.5 million at the end of 2003, and continued to 25.4 million in 2004, a 12.9% increase in a year. By June 2005, 26.3 million digital cable subscribers (FCC, 2006a) began receiving access on many cable systems to such options as digital video, video on demand, DVRs, HDTV, and telephone services.

The prevalence of digital services was an important factor in the FCC decision to eliminate analog broadcast television as of February 17, 2009. However, in September 2007, the FCC unanimously required cable television operators to continue to provide carriage of local television stations that demand it in both analog and digital formats for three years after the conversion date. This action was designed to provide uninterrupted local station service to all cable television subscribers, protecting the 40 million (35%) U.S. households that remained analog-only (Amobi & Kolb, 2007).

By 2008, the typical American household received 130 television channels, more than double the number received in 1998 (Lowry, 2009). The number of homes with television increased from about 101 million in 2000 to nearly 115 million in 2008. The average household owned 2.86 television sets, more than a set per person, up 18% since 2000. A decade before 2008, only 41% of households owned three or more sets, but more than half of American homes owned that many in 2008.

The FCC (2002) noted that video on demand (VOD) services showed signs of growing popularity by the end of 2001, when the services were estimated to have generated revenues exceeding $65 million. The service provides alternatives for digital cable customers to video rentals and was enabled in 19.5 million households by the end of 2004. By 2009, Comcast offered more than 1,000 choices for VOD selections to its cable subscribers (Kolb & Amobi, 2009).

By the end of 2004, 93% of homes passed by cable were offered high-speed Internet service (FCC, 2006a), and 38% were offered telephone services. In addition to the advantage of producing new revenue opportunities for cable operators, these services offered valuable options in competition with a variety of competitors (FCC, 2006a).

For years, some cable television operators offered circuit-switched telephone service, attracting 3.6 million subscribers by the end of 2004. Also by that time, the industry offered telephone services via voice over Internet protocol (VoIP) to 38% of cable households, attracting 600,000 subscribers. That number grew to 1.2 million by July 2005. In 2006, a consortium of cable companies formed a 20-year agreement with Sprint Nextel to offer enhanced wireless services, including voice and entertainment available to consumers using a single device (Amobi, 2005).

Although cable penetration dropped after 2000, as illustrated in Figure 2.10 on the companion Web site (www.tfi.com/ctu), estimated use of a combination of cable and satellite television increased steadily over the same period (U.S. Bureau of the Census, 2008). The combination of cable and satellite television serves about

84% of American households (Amobi & Donald, 2007). Consumers devoted 690 hours per person per year to MVPD services in 2000, and that figure reached 980 hours in 2005. Projections of such use continue to rise through 2010 (U.S. Bureau of the Census, 2008), although the number of cable systems fell to 6,391 by the end of 2007 (FCC, 2008b).

Ownership of cable systems in the United States is concentrated in the hands of the four largest multiple system operators (MSOs). These companies combined to serve about 75% of American subscribers and accounted for about 80% of the total cable revenues in 2007 (Amobi & Kolb, 2007).

MSOs have now upgraded their content delivery systems to enable them to concentrate less on expansion of infrastructure and more on new services, such as high-speed broadband Internet access to digital data and video transmissions. Telephone services provided by cable operators offer additional service opportunities, particularly with voice over Internet protocol (VoIP). MSOs offer bundles of telephone, cable television, and broadband Internet access services that help the companies reduce customer turnover or churn. VoIP offers several advantages over wired telephone systems. For example, VoIP enjoys low call routing costs that bypass regulatory toll charges, simplified maintenance, reduced operating costs from using a single network, and popular calling features, such as video voice conferencing, unified messaging, Web-based voicemail, file sharing, and voice-enabled chat (Bensinger, 2007). In the United States, nearly eight million VoIP subscribers were online by the end of 2006. Among these providers, the top three companies served nearly 70% of all the customers (Bensinger, 2007).

Direct Broadcast Satellite & Other Cable TV Competitors

Satellite technology began in the 1940s, but HBO became the first service to use it for distributing entertainment content in 1976 when the company sent programming to its cable affiliates (Amobi & Kolb, 2007). Other networks soon followed this lead, and individual broadcast stations (WTBS, WGN, WWOR, and WPIX) used satellites in the 1970s to expand their audiences beyond their local markets by distributing their signals to cable operators around the United States.

Competitors for the cable industry include a variety of technologies. Annual FCC reports distinguish between home satellite dish (HSD) and direct broadcast satellite (DBS) systems. Both are included as MVPDs, which include cable television, wireless cable systems called multichannel multipoint distribution services (MMDS), and private cable systems called satellite master antenna television (SMATV).

DBS attracted the second largest group of MVPD households after cable television, with a share of 27.7% of total MVPD subscribers by June 2005, up from 25.1% a year earlier. Total subscriptions to the combination of all other MVPD services declined from 2004 to 2005 to 2.9%, down from 3.3% in 2004 (FCC, 2006a). The three DBS providers attracted about 26.1 million American households in June 2005, representing growth in one year by 12.8% and approximately 27.7% of all American MVPD subscribers. Growth was stimulated in part by the increasing availability of local channels, with at least one local channel available to DBS subscribers in 167 of 210 television markets and 96% of all American homes. The Satellite Home Viewer Improvement Act of 1999 granted permission to DBS providers to carry local broadcast stations in their local markets, and the December 2004 Satellite Home Viewer Extension and Reauthorization Act of 2004 (SHVERA) extended for five more years many of the copyright and retransmission rights provisions of the original measure.

The two major providers of satellite television in 2001, DirecTV and EchoStar (under the DISH Network name), attracted about 16 million subscribers, an 18% market share (FCC, 2008b). Near the end of 2006, wired cable connections declined to a six-year low at the same time that alternatives were accounting for 24.5% of viewing households. The largest proportion of these alternatives was satellite television, which accounted for 28.1% of all television households in 2006 (Kingsport Times News, 2006). By late 2007, the two companies served 30 million subscribers, a 30% market share. During the same period, cable television subscribers fell by 4%, as DirecTV was growing by 54% and EchoStar was growing by 92% (FCC, 2008b).

By 2010 DirecTV served about 16.2% of MVPD subscribers in the United States, and DISH Network served about 13.01% (FCC, 2010a). As a major attraction to subscribers, DirecTV and DISH each offered more than 100 HD channels by June 2008 (Kolb & Amobi, 2009). Competitor Time Warner Cable offered more than 100 HD channels in some markets by mid-2009, and the largest cable operator, Comcast, doubled its number of HD channels to 50–60 channels in selected markets by that time.

C-band home satellite dishes in the early 1980s spanned six feet or more in diameter. Sales of dishes topped 500,000 only twice (1984 and 1985) between 1980 and 1995 (Brown, 2006), when home satellite system ownership apparently peaked before a steady decline in numbers. In 2003, the number of larger dish owners was less than 25% of the 1995 total. Conversely, smaller dish DBS subscribers have increased explosively every year since their numbers were first reported by census data in 1993, with the increase from 2004 to 2005 reaching 12.8%. Conversely, use of the larger home satellite dishes continued to decline through 2005 to slightly more than 200,000 households, a loss of 38.5% from 2004. By late 2007, 68,781 households were authorized to receive HSD services, which included about 350 free channels and 150 subscription-only channels over the C-band satellite transmissions (FCC, 2008b). Such declines characterized other forms of non-cable MVPD sources, as well.

MMDS, or wireless cable systems, peaked in popularity in 1996 (1.2 million households). However, only 100,000 homes used the services by 2005, a 50% decline in a year (FCC, 2006a). Major wireless telephone services began offering video programming through wireless phones by February 2005.

SMATV, or private cable, operations sometimes use their own facilities and sometimes partner with DBS companies to deliver video to consumers. SMATV systems often serve 3,000 to 4,000 subscribers, and larger operators serve up to 55,000 subscribers (FCC, 2008b). Although these systems do not report their operations to the FCC, 76 different providers of SMATV belonged to a trade association for their membership in late 2007. The total number of subscribers generally increased after 1993 until a 1998 decline, followed by a brief resurgence through 2002 (FCC, 2006a). Subscriptions declined every year thereafter. Table 2.10 and Figure 2.11 on the companion Web site (www.tfi.com/ctu) track trends of these non-cable video delivery types.

The FCC also considers several types of services as potential MVPD operators. These services include home video sales and rentals, the Internet, electric and gas utilities, and local exchange carriers (*LECs*). The latter category includes telephone service providers that were allowed by the *Telecommunications Act of 1996* to provide video services to homes, at the same time that the act allowed cable operators to provide telephone services. LECs use high-speed lines, including DSL (digital subscriber line) and fiber optic technology, to deliver video services to communities in 46 states, connecting 322,700 households. Verizon began offering multichannel video services in Texas in September 2005, and quickly opened similar services in Virginia and Florida (FCC, 2006a). By late 2007, the company served nearly one million video subscribers (FCC, 2008b).

In 2001, the FCC began reporting on a new category of video program distributor that began in 1998: broadband service providers (BSPs). These providers offer video, voice, and telephone capability over a single network to their customers. In that first year, such services passed 7.2 million households, but, by 2003, they were authorized by franchises to serve 17.7 million homes, with 1.4 million of those households subscribing, despite the obstacle of availability in only a few areas of the country (FCC, 2004a). By June 2005, BSPs served approximately 1.4 million subscribers or 1.5% of all MVPD households. Electric and gas utilities also provide MVPD and other services. At that time, 616 public power entities (serving about 14% of American households) offered some kind of broadband service (FCC, 2006a).

HOME VIDEO

Although VCRs became available to the public in the late 1970s, competing technical standards slowed the adoption of the new devices. After the longer taping capacity of the VHS format won greater public acceptance over the higher-quality images of the Betamax, the popularity of home recording and playback rapidly accelerated, as shown in Table 2.11 and Figure 2.12 on the companion Web site (www.tfi.com/ctu).

The annual FCC (2006a) report on competition in the video marketplace listed VCR penetration at about 90%, with multiple VCRs in nearly 46 million households. By 2004, approximately 100 million American households had VCRs, and about 80 million (about 72%) had DVD (digital videodisc) players. By the end of 2005, about 47,000 DVD titles were available, up from 30,000 in 2004. Rental spending for videotapes and DVDs reached $24.5 billion in 2004, far surpassing the $9.4 billion spent for tickets to motion pictures. DVD purchases accounted for $15.5 billion, up by 33% from 2003, and DVD rentals grew by 26% to more than $5.7 billion during the same period.

DVD sales rose in 2005 by 400% over the $4 billion figure for 2000 to $15.7 billion. The rate of growth, however, slowed by 2005 to 45%. By 2006, that rate continued declining by 2% to $15.9 billion, and VHS sales amounted to less than $300 million (Amobi & Donald, 2007). By 2008, DVD sales declined by 9% from the previous year to $14.5 billion, and the trend continued during the first half of 2009, when sales fell another 17% as compared with the same period a year before to $5 billion (Amobi, 2009).

Factors in the decline included growth in cable and satellite video-on-demand services, growth of broadband video availability, digital downloading of content, and the transition to Blu-ray format (Amobi, 2009). The competing new formats for playing high-definition content was similar to the one waged in the early years of VCR development between Betamax and VHS formats. Similarly, in early DVD player development, companies touting competing standards settled a dispute by agreeing to share royalties with the creator of the winning format. Until early 2008, the competition between proponents of HD-DVD and Blu-ray formats for playing high-definition DVD content remained unresolved, and some studios were planning to distribute motion pictures in both formats. Blu-ray seemed to emerge the victor in 2008 when large companies (e.g., Time Warner, Wal-Mart, Netflix) declared allegiance to that format.

Falling sales of DVDs were partially countered by the growth in popularity of Blu-ray discs (Amobi, 2009). During the first six months of 2009, Blu-ray disc sales revenues increased by 91% over the same period a year earlier to $407 million. Falling prices for Blu-ray players helped lead to establishing 11 million units in use. During the first half of 2009 player sales increased by 25% to more than 2 million Blu-ray units sold (Digital Entertainment Group, as cited by Amobi, 2009).

Although DVD sales struggled, the rental market thrived in an era of economic downturn. Rentrak Corporation, an audience measurement company, reported (as cited by Amobi, 2009) that home video rentals increased during the first half of 2009 by 8.3% over the same period in 2008 to $3.4 billion. The total 2008 home video expenditures remained about the same as in 2007 at $7.5 billion. Rentals of home videos benefitted from the popularity of $1 per night rental kiosks placed in a variety of retail locations. Coinstar Inc.'s Redbox emerged as the market leader with 15,000 kiosks by March 2009, with plans for 21,000 by the end of that year (Amobi, 2009). Netflix, Inc. served 10 million subscribers who received DVDs by mail and broadband transmissions by February 2009. Cable television video-on-demand, online services (e.g., Apple iTunes, Amazon Video on Demand), video game consoles (e.g., Xbox, Playstation III, Wii) that connected to the Internet expanded the means for home video consumption. Online digital distribution revenues grew by 21% during the first half of 2009 to $968 million.

Home entertainment rentals and sell-through spending totaled $13.3 billion in 1999 (Amobi, 2009). By 2008, the spending reached $22.4 billion, an increase of 68.4%. VHS rentals and sell through revenues disappeared by 2008 after earning $12.5 billion in 1999. High-definition and Blu-ray disks in this category began in 2007 with $300 million and jumped to $800 million in 2008.

In 2000, home video (VCR and DVD combined) accounted for an average of 43 hours per person per year. That figure rose through 2004 to 67 hours, but declined in 2005 to 63 (U.S. Bureau of the Census, 2008). DVD penetration (81.2%) in American households surpassed VCRs (79.2%) by 2006, but most homes still used both types of machines (FCC, 2009a).

Digital video recorders (DVRs, also called personal video recorders, PVRs) debuted during 2000, and about 500,000 units were sold by the end of 2001 (FCC, 2002). The devices save video content on computer hard drives, allowing fast-forwarding, rewinding, and pausing of live television; retroactive recording of limited minutes of previously displayed live television; automatic recording of all first-run episodes; automatic recording logs; and superior quality to that of analog VCRs. Dual-tuner models allow viewers to watch one program, even on satellite television, while recording another simultaneously.

DVR providers generate additional revenues by charging households monthly fees, and satellite DVR households tend to be less likely to drop their satellite subscriptions. Perhaps the most fundamental importance of DVRs is the ability of consumers to make their own programming decisions about when and what they watch. This flexibility threatens the revenue base of network television in several ways, including empowering viewers to skip standard commercials. Amobi (2005) cited potential advertiser responses, such as sponsorships and product placements within programming.

At the outset, consumers purchased their own set-top DVRs for connection with their television sets, and the leading seller (TiVo) commanded 3.6 million customers by July 2005 (FCC, 2006a). Satellite television providers began offering the service by early 2002, and EchoStar and DirecTV had 1.5 million of the 2.1 million customers using DVRs by 2003, a penetration rate of 2% (FCC, 2004a). By the end of 2004, 79% of homes were passed by cable television DVR services, and 1.8 million cable households purchased DVR service (FCC, 2004a). By July 2005, 8.3 million American households subscribed to DVR services.

Nielsen Media Research added DVR households to its ratings sample in late 2005 and began releasing reports in 2005 about shows viewed within 24 hours of recording. In 2006, the company planned reports about viewing within a week of recording on DVR, which Nielsen estimated to be in 7% of American households by early 2006, compared with 4% penetration during the previous year (Aspan, 2006). The DVR penetration of cable households reached 12% in 2006 (FCC, 2009a).

Amobi and Kolb (2007) estimated overall DVR penetration by the end of 2007 at 20%. During the 2007-2008 television season, major television networks and advertisers agreed that viewing is defined as watching a first-time broadcast on television or watching it within three days via DVR. A 2007 lawsuit by Hollywood studios against a network DVR service by Cablevision was declined for review by the U. S. Supreme Court in June 2009, clearing the way for the firm to offer network DVR services. By 2009, the penetration of network DVR services was greater than 30% (Amobi, 2009), and more than 20% of all viewing of scripted television programming in 2008 occurred at least one day later than the original air date (Lowry, 2009). Among satellite television customers, DVR penetration reached 40%, or 31.7 million households, by March 2009, and about half of new subscribers were ordering DVR (Kolb & Amobi, 2009). Cable households had a similar penetration rate among customers of the major cable providers.

The leading British pay-television provider, British Sky Broadcasting, began offering DVR service to its customers in 2001 as an expensive add-on at about $770 (U.S.). Sales reached 700,000 annual units in 2006, and the company announced total sales of more than two million by early 2007. These figures indicated an approximate penetration of 20% of households, suggesting a comparable rate of DVR usage with that in the United States, and surveys of usage revealed that 12.2% of viewing in homes with British Sky DVRs involved recorded programming. Such homes averaged 2 hours and 26 minutes of daily television viewing, compared with only 2 hours and 7 minutes in homes without DVRs. Sales in other European countries remained slower, although Sky Italia in Italy reportedly showed more vigorous reception of DVR technology. Both British Sky Broadcasting and Sky Italia are owned by the Rupert Murdoch media empire (Pfanner, 2007).

Personal Computers

The history of computing traces its origins back thousands of years to such practices as using bones as counters (Hofstra University, 2000). Intel introduced the first microprocessor in 1971. The MITS Altair, with an 8080 processor and 256 bytes of RAM (random access memory), sold for $498 in 1975, introducing the desktop computer to individuals. In 1977, Radio Shack offered the TRS80 home computer, and the Apple II set a new standard for personal computing, selling for $1,298. Other companies began introducing personal computers, and, by 1978, 212,000 personal computers were shipped for sale.

Early business adoption of computers served primarily to assist practices like accounting. When computers became small enough to sit on office desktops in the 1980s, word processing became a popular business use and fueled interest in home computers. With the growth of networking and the Internet in the 1990s, both businesses and consumers began buying computers in large numbers. Computer shipments around the world grew annually by more than 20% between 1991 and 1995 (Kessler, 2007b).

By 1997, the majority of American households with annual incomes greater than $50,000 owned a personal computer. At the time, those computers sold for about $2,000, exceeding the reach of lower income groups. By the late 1990s, prices dropped below $1,000 per system (Kessler, 2007b), and American households passed the 60% penetration mark in owning personal computers within a couple of years (U.S. Bureau of the Census, 2008). By 2006, prices dropped below $500 for desktops, with laptops selling for an average of about $700 (Kessler, 2007b), and 52% of adults with annual incomes under $30,000 reported being computer users (U.S. Bureau of the Census, 2008).

Factors other than prices that fueled computer purchases include both software and hardware upgrades. For example, operating systems such as Windows Vista and Windows XP and major applications such as new word processors and video editors stimulated demand for systems with more processing power. Computer peripherals such as color monitors and compact disc drives that replaced floppy disc drives, also motivated upgrades. The last major upgrade period occurred in 1999 when consumers feared the millennium bug. More recently, owners of hot-selling Apple iPods (digital music and video players introduced in 2001) and iPhones (introduced in 2007) often purchased new Apple computers to match their earlier purchases (Kessler, 2007b).

A decline in computer shipments occurred between 1995 and 1999 when worldwide shipments grew by 23% before slumping again (Kessler, 2007b). The first global decline in personal computer shipments since 1985 occurred in 2001, but growth returned in 2002 with a slight increase that jumped to 12% in 2003. During this period, lower prices and stronger computing power in laptop computers led to growth of more than 15% in both 2004 and 2005, although 2006 worldwide shipments grew by only 10%.

Table 2.12 and Figure 2.13 on the companion Web site (www.tfi.com/ctu) trace the rapid and steady rise in American computer shipments and home penetration. By 2003, 61.8% of American households owned personal computers, up from 42.1% in 1998 (U.S. Bureau of the Census, 2006). By 2006, an estimated 75 million computers were shipped annually in America, where about 29% of the more than 220 million worldwide computer shipments occurred. In that year, annual shipments of computers in the United States declined in the fourth quarter, but total worldwide shipments increased by 8.7%, thanks to growth in laptop computers that overcame the decline in desktops (Kessler, 2007b).

Princeton Survey Research Associates International (2009) conducted a survey for the FCC of more than 5,000 adults of ages 18 and older in late 2009. The results indicated that 81% of the respondents used computers in some location. Ownership of a desktop computer occurred among 66% of respondents, and 52% reported owning laptop computers.

A December 2009 survey (Rainie, 2010) reported that 46% of American adults owned a laptop computer. Lenhart et al. (2010) reported on the Pew Research Center 2009 survey that found that 66% of online 18-29 year-olds owned laptop computers or netbooks, and 53% owned desktop computers. No other age group reported greater laptop than desktop usage.

During 2009, global sales revenues for Netbooks, small laptop computers with displays of 10-inches or less, increased by 72% over 2008 amounts, despite declines in every other category of computer sales (Netbook 2009 revenues, 2009). In 2008, 16.4 million Netbooks were shipped world-wide, and the shipments increased in 2009 to 33.3 million units (Mini-note (Netbook) shipments grow, 2009). Global shipments of all portable computers increased from 146.1 to 169.6 million units from 2008 to 2009 (PC market rebounds, 2010).

In 2006, 234 million personal computers of all types were shipped, and that statistic increased in 2007 to 269 million units (Kessler, 2009). Global shipments of all computer types grew from 287.6 million units in 2008 to 294.2 million units in 2009 (PC market rebounds, 2010). Shipments in the United States during the fourth quarter of 2009 increased by more than 25% over the same 2008 period to 19.8 million units, the highest in the previous seven years.

INTERNET

The Internet began in the 1960s with ARPANET, or the Advanced Research Projects Agency (ARPA) network project, under the auspices of the U.S. Defense Department. The project intended to serve the military and researchers with multiple paths of linking computers together for sharing data in a system that would remain operational even when traditional communications might become unavailable. Early users, mostly university and research lab personnel, took advantage of electronic mail and posting information on computer bulletin boards. Usage increased dramatically in 1982 after the National Science Foundation supported high-speed linkage of multiple locations around the United States. After the collapse of the Soviet Union in the late 1980s, military users abandoned ARPANET, but private users continued to use it, and multimedia transmissions of audio and video became available. More than 150,000 regional computer networks and 95 million computer servers hosted data for Internet users (Campbell, 2002).

Penetration & Usage

Tables 2.13 and 2.14 Figures 2.14, 2.15, and 2.16 on the companion Web site (www.tfi.com/ctu) show trends in Internet usage in the United States. As of 2004, 61.4% of U.S. adults connected to the Internet either at home or at work within 30 days of being surveyed, and more than 60% of American households had Internet access (U.S. Bureau of the Census, 2006). The combination of cable modems, DSL, and other wired and wireless Internet access technologies reached 35.3 million households by the end of 2004 (FCC, 2006a).

By June 2005, 70.3 million American households had Internet access, and about 33.7 million of those homes enjoyed broadband access (FCC, 2006a). By the end that year, 44 million households had high speed Internet connections, including 58% in the form of cable modems, 40% DSL, and 2% other technologies (FCC, 2010b).

Internet penetration reached 71% of American households by 2006, and 57 million Americans enjoyed broadband access at home. That rate changed little in the next couple of years, reaching 71.9% of American adults in 2008, when about the same proportion of adults (71.6%) reported using the Internet within the previous 30 days (U.S. Bureau of the Census, 2010). The most common explanation given by Americans for buying a home computer was connection to the Internet (Kessler, 2007a).

The FCC (2010b) reported that cable modem subscribership increased by 14% to 41 million in 2008, and DSL connections grew by 3% to 30 million. Fiber connections increased by 56% to 3 million. Residential high-speed connections in 2008 included 70 million fixed-technology connections and 16 million wireless subscription plans for full Internet access. Among those 86 million residential connections, cable modems represented 46% of the total, DSL accounted for 31%, mobile plans made up 18%, and fixed fiber connections described 3%. All other technologies accounted for 1% of the residential Internet connections.

A national survey in April 2009 reported that 79% of English-speaking American adults used the Internet (Rainie, 2010). A similar survey in December 2009 with a sample of 2,258 adults expanded to include Spanish speakers and found that 74% of American adults used the Net. The latter report found that 60% of adults used broadband connections at home, and 55% used wireless connections. The survey found "little significant growth in the overall Internet user population since 2006" (p. 3). In 2004, a Pew survey of adult use of the Internet found that 27% reported using the Net several times daily. That figure rose to 38% by December 2009. Another Pew survey (Lenhart et al., 2010) in 2009 reported that 93% of teenagers and 93% of adults of ages 18-29 used the Internet. Among all Americans over age 18, 74% reported being online.

The FCC (2010b) reported 50,930,000 high-speed Internet connections in the United States at the end of 2005. The number more than doubled by December 2008 to just more than 102 million connections.

Connection Speeds Increase

In 2004, 36 million households in the United States, more than half of those with Internet access, connected to the network by means of a dial-up telephone connection (Belson, 2005). In the United States, cable modems offered the most commonly used (60.3%) means of broadband access, with 24.3 million American homes receiving access via cable modems by 2005. However, growing popularity of DSL high-speed connections (34.3% in 2003, up to 37.2% in 2004) deprived cable modems of market share, which fell from 63.2% in 2003. Although satellite broadband services exist, their installation and monthly charges tend to exceed those of other broadband technologies (FCC, 2006a).

In 2006, about 15 million American households were in rural areas that lacked wired access to the Internet. Satellite access to the Internet filled that void, but at quite expensive rates ($50 to $130 per month) that often double the cost of wired service. The monthly rates exclude the installation costs of the satellite dish (about $500, minus discounts) needed to deliver the connections. About 463,000 homes and businesses used these satellite connections in 2006, nearly 35% more than in 2005. One service reported that 80% of its customers were homes, not businesses (Belson, 2006). In 2007, the annual rate of increase in high-speed Internet access reached 17%, dropping to 10% in 2008 to 77 million connections to homes and businesses (FCC, 2010b).

By June 2007, high-speed Internet access via DSL was available to 82% of American households, and high-speed cable modem access was available to 96% of households with cable access (FCC, 2008d).

A 2009 survey for the FCC (Princeton Survey Research Associates International, 2009) of more than 5,000 adults of ages 18 and older found that 75% had home Internet access. Among those people (nearly 3,500), 87% had high-speed broadband connections, and 8% had low-speed access. The remainder seemed ignorant of what system they had. Among broadband users (nearly 3,000), 58% used cable modems for access, 44% had DSL, 44% used mobile wireless systems, 29% used fixed wireless systems, 10% used fiber optic connections, and 5% used T-1 lines. Another 12% offered the contradictory response that they used a dial-up connection to achieve broadband connection. Among respondents who used dial-up Internet access or did not know what kind of connection they had (567 respondents), 50% reported not obtaining broadband access because it was too expensive, and 29% reported that such service was not available at their home.

As more video content—including motion pictures—becomes available via the Internet, demand should increase for high-speed service. Perhaps broadband might enjoy even wider adoption if the service were not so expensive. Stross (2006) observed that consumers in Europe and Japan pay far less in monthly fees to access broadband content at higher speeds than are available in the United States.

The American Recovery and Reinvestment Act of 2009 (Recovery Act) was signed into law by President Obama on February 17th, 2009. The FCC is currently working in coordination with the National Telecommunications and Information Administration (NTIA) to perform the FCC's role under the Recovery Act. Specifically, in conjunction with the Broadband Technology Opportunities Program established by the Act, the FCC was tasked with creating a National Broadband Plan by February 17, 2010. The Recovery Act states that the National Broadband Plan shall seek to ensure all people of the United States have access to broadband capability and shall establish benchmarks for meeting that goal (FCC, 2009b)

Wireless Internet Access

Among the 45% of American adults who owned laptop computers in 2009, 83% used Wi-Fi Internet access, and 28% used wireless broadband access (Rainie, 2010). Among adults of ages 18-29, 81% were wireless Internet users in 2009 (Lenhart et al., 2010). That statistic fell to 63% among users of ages 30-49 and 34% for people aged 50 and older.

In May 2008, a consortium of large companies formed to create a nationally available WiMax network to offer wireless video access in the United States (Kolb & Amobi, 2009). The acronym represents "worldwide interoperability for microwave access," and it offered faster connections and better range than Wi-Fi (Kessler, 2009). By 2009, competing organizations emerged, and Sprint spent billions of dollars building a nationwide network of WiMax, beginning commercial service in 2008.

Social Networking

Internet access supports the formation of virtual communities or social networks on such services as MySpace and Facebook. Social networks do much more than support connections among member users by offering proprietary email, instant messaging, music, file sharing, video sharing, games, and other services. Negative consequences also emerge when Internet predators use social networks as a means to find victims.

Social networking also operates without computers through a variety of online services that allow individuals to use mobile phones to send out reports of daily activities. Users obtain software for their phones from Web sites. This software allows sending messages and photographs to receivers who use phones or computers accessing Web sites for reception (Stone & Richtel, 2007).

By mid-2008, the top seven social networking sites attracted 279 million unique worldwide visitors, representing a 51% annual growth rate. This constituency is equal to the combined number of users for the Google and Yahoo sites, which attracted approximately 140 million unique users each (Kessler, 2009). Among 8- to 18-year-olds surveyed by the Kaiser Family Foundation (2010), 25% of their recreational computer time was spent in 2009 with social networking.

Facebook, having opened its doors to all Internet users in September 2006, gathered an 11.5% share of American social networking traffic in that year. The social networking site attracted 52 million unique visitors in 2006. By July 2007, Facebook attracted 30 million users who visited the site at least monthly and increased its market share in North America to 68%. (Kessler, 2007a). The site overtook MySpace as the most popular social networking service in 2008, attracting 132 million unique visitors, a growth rate of 153% (comScore, as cited by Kessler, 2009). By March 2009, Facebook attracted 175 million visitors, giving it a population large enough to become the "sixth largest country in the world" (Kessler, 2009, p. 4).

MySpace captured nearly 80% of the social network connections in the United States in April 2007, and reported 114 million unique visitors by June of that year (Kessler, 2007a). By June 2008, the service attracted 118 million unique worldwide visitors (Kessler, 2009). Competing social networking sites included Hi5, which grew by 100% in 2008 to 56 million unique visitors; Friendster, which grew by 50% in 2008 with 37 million unique visitors; Orkut (Google), which grew by 41% in 2008 with 34 million unique visitors; Bebo, whch grew by 32% in 2008 with 24 million unique visitors; and Skyrock Network, which grew by 19% in 2008 with 21 million unique visitors.

Among online teenagers in 2009, 73% belong to social networking sites (Lenhart et al., 2010). The 2006 proportion was only 55%, rising to 65% by 2008. The proportion of online adults over age 18 who belonged to social networking sites reached 37% in 2008 and increased to 47% in 2009. Young adults (ages 18-29) used these sites almost as often, with the 2009 proportion at 72%. Among adults over 30 who were online in 2009, 40% were members of social networking sites.

Adult members of social networking sites were most likely in 2009 to belong to Facebook, with 73% maintaining such a profile, including 71% of users under 30 years of age and 75% of users over 30 (Lenhart et al., 2010). MySpace members included 48% of all online adults over 18 and 36% of adults over 30. Among all online adults, 14% belonged to Linkedin, a more professionally oriented site that attracted 19% of adults over 30 but only 7% of Internet users under 30. However, members under age 30 were more likely (66%) to belong to MySpace. These proportions should be interpreted with the knowledge that 52% of adults reported using multiple social networking sites, compared with 42% who did so in 2008.

The leading social network site in Europe in June 2007 was Bebo, which attracted a 63% share in its market. Friendster was the market leader in Asia with a share of 88% of its market, and Orkut led the Latin American market with 40%. MySpace is also available to members in Europe, Japan, Australia, and Latin America, and the company licensed itself in 2007 for operations in China where many local social networking competitors were already thriving (Kessler, 2007a).

A survey (Lenhart et al., 2007) of nearly 1,000 teenagers found that 21% send daily messages by means of social networking sites. A subset of teens using the Internet, instant messaging, text messaging, and social networking sites made up 28% of the survey sample and was given the label of "multichannel teens" (p. 4). Members of this group were even more invested in social networking, with 47% of them using the sites daily to send messages to friends.

Lenhart et al. (2010) reported from the results of a 2009 Pew Research Center survey that blogging declined after 2006 among young adults of ages 18-29 and teenagers and increased among older adults. Among teens, 14% of the 2009 respondents said that they blogged, compared with 28% in 2006. Also, 52% of teens reported commenting in 2009 on the blogs of their friends, relative to the 76% who so reported three years earlier. Pew surveys have reported a steady 10% of adult Internet users who engage in keeping online journals or blogs. The 2009 survey found that 11% of online adults over 30 years of age blogged, but only 15% of young adults from 18-29 did so.

Twitter, another service that takes advantage of the Internet, was created in 2006 by a group working at Odeo, Inc. (Sagolla, 2009). The group created Twitter while attempting to develop a technique of communicating short text messages by mobile phone. The messages, or tweets, consist of 140 characters. The 2009 Pew survey (Lenhart et al., 2010) of online use found that 19% of online adults used Twitter or similar tools to post short messages. However, only 8% of online teenagers reported using it. The heaviest users (33%) of Twitter came from the online users aged 18-29.

Internet Video

The growing penetration of broadband technology makes possible new video services such as video on demand via the Internet. The FCC (2006a) reported that, in January 2005, 14% of Americans had seen streaming video within the previous month. By mid-2006, 107 million Americans viewed online video, and about 60% of American Internet users had downloaded video. By the end of 2007, YouTube, an Internet video-serving site, used more bandwidth than was used by the entire Internet in 2000 (FCC, 2008b).

An FCC survey (Horrigan, 2010) of more than 5,000 adults in October and November 2009 revealed much about Internet use in the United States. Among Americans, 78% used the Internet in some location, and 74% had home access; 67% of households reported broadband access. Broadband, in this survey, included cable modem, DSL, satellite, mobile broadband access for computer or telephone, fiber optic cable, or T-1 line. Only 6% of households accessed the Internet with dial-up connections, and 6% accessed the Internet away from home but not at home. Having attended college raised the proportion of broadband users to 82% from only 46% of users whose highest earned diploma was from high school. Among households with annual incomes of less than $50,000, the proportion of broadband at home usage was 52%, rising to 87% among households with incomes greater than $50,000 yearly. For households earning less than $20,000 annually, the proportion of broadband adopters reached 40%. The average monthly broadband bill for survey respondents who knew the amount was $41, but half did not know how much they paid because their broadband service was part of a bundle of services. The average monthly bill among households not paying for a bundle of services was $46.25. The most popular uses for accessing the Internet were to contact friends and family (68%); keep current with news (39%); share content, including pictures, videos, and text (35%); shop online (24%); watch television shows, videos, and movies (10%); and play games online (9%).

Among Americans who responded to the FCC survey in 2009, three reasons dominated their explanations for not having broadband access at home (Horrigan, 2010). Cost (39%) was the most frequently named barrier. A substantial proportion (22%), particularly older respondents, named their lack of knowledge and comfort with using computers and digital tools as the main obstacle to broadband adoption. The proportion of respondents who said that the Internet lacks relevance or is a waste of time reached 19%.

The Kaiser Family Foundation (2010) surveyed more than 2000 8- to 18-year-olds, finding that 84% of them enjoyed home Internet access in 2009, up from 47% in 1999 and 74% in 2004. High-speed access increased from 31% in 2004 to 59% in 2009. No proportion was available in 1999. Access in their own bedrooms was available in 2009 to 33% of the respondents, up from 20% in 2004.

Lenhart et al. (2010) found that, among online adults of ages 18-29, 81% reported using wireless Internet access in 2009. About half (55%) of them connected with a laptop computer or mobile telephone, and about 25% had connected with a different device, such as an e-book reader or game player. Among Internet users of ages 30-49, 63% reported wireless Internet access in 2009, and among online users of 50 years or more, 34% used wireless access in 2009.

Outside the United States, DSL has an edge over cable access because of the much greater penetration of wired telephone lines relative to cable infrastructure. DSL attracted nearly 150 million subscribers in 2005, compared with just more than 50 million for cable. In 2006, DSL accounted for about 65% of the worldwide broadband Internet subscriptions. IDC (as cited by Bensinger, 2007) projected that the DSL growth rate would increase for several years, while the growth rate for cable Internet access would remain mostly stable.

DSL Forum (as cited by Bensinger, 2007), an industry consortium, estimated a global presence of 200 million DSL subscribers in mid-2007. Nine countries had more than five million DSL connections, with China holding 20% of the worldwide subscribers and the United States 15% (Bensinger, 2007).

Video Games

Competition for the attention of home entertainment audiences has included commercial video games since the 1970s, and research into the form began in the 1950s, as discussed in Chapter 14. Early versions were quite sedate, compared with modern versions that incorporate complex story lines, computer animation, and/or motion picture footage. Table 2.15 and Figure 2.17 trace trends in video game popularity, as measured by units purchased, spending per person, and time spent per person. Classifying games by media category will become increasingly difficult because they are available for dedicated gaming consoles that qualify as specialized computers, and both game software and hardware allow players to compete via the Internet. Since 1996, the number of home devices that play video games has more than doubled, and the amount of spending per person per year has more than tripled.

In 2004, console-based video gaming surpassed computer-based gaming. Surveys of gamers revealed that nearly 25% reported reduced television viewing, and 18% anticipated watching even less television in 2005. Weekly television viewing among gamers fell from 18 hours in 2004 to 16 in 2005. The number of households with video game consoles reached an estimated 62.6 million in 2005, 15% more than a year before. Homes using computer-based gaming were estimated at 56.6 million, an 8.2% gain over 2004. In all, about 76.2 million Americans engaged in video gaming by 2005, nearly 13% more than a year earlier (Ziff-Davis Media, 2005).

Bloomberg News (Video game, 2006) cited a report by the NPD Group that found that, during 2005, revenues from video games increased by 6% over sales in 2004. Revenues in 2005 reached $1.4 billion for portable game players alone, and the total sales increased to $10.5 billion for both games and hardware for playing them. That figure exceeded the previous record of $10.3 billion in 2002 and might have been even higher but for the late 2005 release of the XBox 360 console, for which few games were available when the new player arrived. Long lines of consumers waited in pre-dawn darkness for stores to open to allow the purchase of the new XBox 360. Nintendo had similar success with the Wii. For many months after the Wii console came on the market stores everywhere sold out, and consumers were forced to wait for the opportunity to purchase the system.

Among 8- to 18-year-olds, daily time spent playing games averaged one hour and 13 minutes in 2009, up from 26 minutes in 1999 and 49 minutes in 2004 (Kaiser Family Foundation, 2010). Those figures amounted to an increase of 88.5% from 1999 to 2004, 49% from 2004 to 2009, and 181% from 1999 to 2009. In 2009, boys spent nearly twice as much time daily playing games, averaging 97 minutes daily, with an average of 56 minutes on game consoles, 24 minutes on handheld players, and 17 minutes on cell phones. Girls divided their 48 daily minutes almost equally across the three types of players. Overall game play in 2009 was almost evenly divided between computers and video game consoles.

To measure online usage of these machines, Nielsen Media Research started Nielsen GamePlay Metrics in 2007. June 2007 data revealed average minutes played per online session of these consoles was 83 minutes for the PlayStation 3, 57 minutes for the Wii, and 61 minutes for XBox 360 (Kessler, 2007a).

Total revenues from online gaming reached $2.6 billion in 2006 and were projected in 2009 to rise to $14.9 billion by 2012 (IDC, as cited by Kessler, 2009). Subscriptions to online gaming sites generated $1.1 billion in 2007 and were expected by IDC to rise by six times in the successive five years. Consumers spent $734 million in 2007 to download games. Such revenues were projected by IDC to reach $34 billion by 2012.

The most profitable online games were called *MMORPGs* (massive multiplayer online role playing games) (Kessler, 2009). *World of Warcraft (WoW)* is the most popular game of that type, with nine million players in mid-2007 (Kessler, 2007a) and 11.5 million users by the end of 2008. (Kessler, 2009). *WoW* accounted for 62% of industry online gaming subscriptions by mid-2008, and its closest competitor achieved a market share of 8%. Sequels to the original *WoW* included *WoW: The Burning Crusade*, which sold 2.4 million on the date of its release in 2007. *WoW: Wrath of the Lich King* debuted in 2008, selling 2.8 million copies in the first 24 hours of availability.

The three best-selling gaming consoles all began providing online access that allowed viewing streaming movies in addition to online interactive gaming. The Wii, featuring its innovative, motion-sensor controller, sold 42 million players worldwide by December 2008. The XBox 360 sold 28 million units by December 2008, promoting online Xbox Live services, multi-player gaming, and in-game voice chat. Playstation 3 by that time sold 21 million by featuring always-on-online access, multi-player gaming, video messaging, voice chat, Internet downloads, and general Internet access (Kessler, 2009).

Gaming moved to mobile phones through simple games, such as *Solitaire*, *Brickbreaker*, and *Sudoku*. As mentioned earlier, nearly half of wireless phones included game playing by 2005. Worldwide revenues in 2006 for mobile games reached $2.9 million and were expected to soar to nearly $10 million by 2011 (Kessler, 2007a).

Synthesis

Horrigan (2005) noted that the rate of adoption of high-speed Internet use approximated that of other electronic technologies. He observed that 10% of the population used high-speed Internet access in just more than five years. Personal computers required four years, CD players needed 4.5 years, cell phones required eight years, VCRs took 10 years, and color televisions used 12 years to reach 10% penetration.

Early visions of the Internet (see Chapter 18) did not include the emphasis on entertainment and information to the general public that has emerged. The combination of this new medium with older media belongs to a phenomenon called "convergence," referring to the merging of functions of old and new media. The FCC (2002) reported that the most important type of convergence related to video content is the joining of Internet services. The report also noted that companies from many business areas were providing a variety of video, data, and other communications services.

Just as media began converging nearly a century ago when radios and record players merged in the same appliance, media in recent years have been converging at a much more rapid pace. Wireless telephones enjoyed explosive growth, and cable and telephone companies began offering competing personal communications opportunities. Electronic media are enticing consumers to switch from print media. Increasing proportions of the population are using laptop and tablet computers, personal digital assistants (PDA), mobile telephones with multimedia capability, and digital audio and video players that resemble small computers, all resulting in greater portability and convenience of online content. Electronic media content often contains materials that are not included in print media versions of the same titles, and consumers enjoy the ability to edit electronic materials and move them around to various playback devices (Peters & Donald, 2007).

Popularity of print media forms generally declined throughout the 1990s, perhaps, in part, after newspapers, magazines, and books began appearing in electronic and audio forms. After 2000, business remained strong in providing a variety of titles in both periodicals and books, although newspaper circulation continued to decline. Recorded music sales, including CDs, declined, although the controversies over digital music indicated no loss in the popularity of music listening. After debuting in 2001, satellite radio increased its subscribers elevenfold from 2003 to 2007, but subscription numbers have since fallen. Motion picture box office receipts remained steady, although theater attendance seems to be losing ground to home viewing. Television time shifting has become easier with the growing popularity of the DVR, a device that attracted such a strong following that advertisers changed their definition of television viewing to incorporate three days of recorded viewing. Video game competition for viewer attention strengthened over the period from 2002 to 2008. Game playing not only thrived at home on consoles that stand alone and interact over the Internet, but games expanded to mobile players and phones. The popularity of the Internet continued upward, particularly with the growth of high-speed broadband connections, for which adoption rates achieved comparability with previous new communications media. Consumer flexibility remains the dominant media consumption theme at the end of the first decade of the new century.

Princeton Survey Research Associates International (2009) reported heavy media use among respondents participating in a survey of more than 5,000 adults over age 18. For example, 80% had wired telephones at home, 86% had mobile phone devices, 65% had cable television, 29% had satellite television, 66% owned desktop computers, 52% owned laptop computers, and 75% had home Internet access. Internet users in this survey reported that 78% bought goods online, 76% get news online, 75% visited government Web sites, 63% conduct banking online, 57% retrieved job information, 52% used social networking sites, 47% downloaded music, 46% played games online, and 45% shared their created works (e.g., photos, videos, etc.).

The Pew Internet and American Life Project investigated how young people communicate and called teenagers "super communicators" (Lenhart et al., 2007, p. 5) because of the way they interact through media tools. Surprisingly, or not, their use of mobile telephones and social networking outweigh their face-to-face communication away from school. Among the most media-oriented teens, 70% talk on mobile phones every day, more than half send text messages every day, and more than half send instant messages every day. Although their seniors remain less likely to use these tools as often as do teens, the devices that support these activities are likely to become modus operandi for Americans, as they have more rapidly been adopted by residents of other countries.

The Kaiser Family Foundation (2010) found that media-use dominated the lives of 8- to 18-year-olds, with a total of 10 hours and 45 minutes of average daily use in 2009. Such a large amount of time became possible through multitasking, which accounted for 29% of the typical day among the sample group of more than 2,000 respondents to questions about recreational media use only. The average reflected an increase of 25.7% since 2004 (8 hours, 33 minutes) and 43.7% since 1999 (7 hours, 29 minutes). The rate of increase also grew, as the change from 1999 to 2004 amounted to only 14.3%. In 2009, electronic media far exceeded the level of interaction accounted for by print media, with average television use leading the way at 4 hours, 29 minutes of daily use. Music and audio garnered two hours and 31 minutes daily, followed by computers (1 hour, 29 minutes), video games (1 hour, 13 minutes), and movies finished last at only 28 minutes daily on average. Print media consumed an average of 38 minutes of daily use, down from 43 minutes in 2004, a decline of about 12%. Total media use among people in this group increased from 7 hours and 29 minutes in 1999 to 8 hours, 33 minutes in 2004.

Among the 8- to 18-year-olds studied by the Kaiser Family Foundation (2010), 76% owned iPods or other MP3 players, up from 18% in 2004; 66% owned cell phones, up from 39% in 2004; and 29% owned laptop computers, up from 12% in 2004. Respondents averaged talking on cell phones for 33 minutes daily and using cell phones for other activities (e.g., music, games, television) for 49 minutes daily in 2009.

The total average time spent with television increased by more than 16% from 2004 to 2009 and by more than 18% since 1999. Time spent watching live television declined from the amount reported in 2004 by an average of 29 minutes daily to 2 hours, 29 minutes. Embedded within the total 4 hours and 29 daily minutes of time spent with television was 22 minutes daily with time-shifted viewing, 32 minutes with viewing DVDs, 24 minutes with online programming, 16 minutes viewing television by iPod, and 15 minutes watching television content via cell phones (Kaiser Family Foundation, 2010).

The average time spent listening to music via media among 8-18-year-olds grew from one hour and 29 minutes in 1999 to 2 hours, 31 minutes in 2009 (Kaiser Family Foundation, 2010). Along the way, time listening to music fell by 4.6% between 1999 and 2004 before increasing by 45.2% between 2004 and 2009, most likely because of the explosion in popularity of iPods and other digital media players. The proportions of time spent listening to music by type of medium included 29% for iPods, 23% each for computers and radio, and 12% each for CDs and cell phones.

Computer use in 1999 averaged only 27 minutes daily among 8- to 18-year-olds, increasing by 130% to 62 minutes in 2004 (Kaiser Family Foundation, 2010). The average grew to one hour and 29 minutes by 2009, an increase of 43.5% over 2004 and 230% over 1999. Nearly half of computer time among the sample members was devoted to social interaction. Among respondents, 19% of their recreational computer time was spent in 2009 playing games, second only to the 25% devoted to social networking. Another 16% went for using video Web sites, 12% for non-video Web sites, 13% for instant messages, and 6% for email.

Among light (3 or fewer hours daily) users of media on a daily basis, 23% reported receiving fair or poor grades in school (Kaiser Family Foundation, 2010). Among moderate (3-16 hours daily) users, that statistic rose to 31%, and 47% of heavy (16 or more hours daily) users confessed to receiving fair or poor grades. Only 19% reported never using media while doing homework.

Convergence has arrived in a big way for both audio and video content. Music and video remain strong at home, but consumers now can also purchase packaged content *to go* from providers. Media fans can also record their own digital content and save it to such devices as computers, iPods, cell phones, DVD players, personal digital assistants, and other portable equipment for playback almost any time, anywhere. Understanding how people live requires knowing how they use media, and the remainder of this book explores the structure and use of these individual media.

Bibliography

All time box office. (2010). *Box Office Mojo*. Retrieved March 4, 2010 from http://boxofficemojo.com/alltime/adjusted.htm.

752 million. (2010, January 18) *Brandweek*, 51(3), 29. Retrieved February 08, 2010, from General OneFile via Gale.

Amobi, T. N. (2005, December 8). Industry surveys: Broadcasting, cable, and satellite industry survey. In E. M. Bossong-Martines (Ed.), *Standard & Poor's Industry Surveys*, 173 (49), Section 2.

Amobi, T. N. (2009). Industry surveys: Movies and home entertainment. In E. M. Bossong-Martines (Ed.), *Standard & Poor's Industry Surveys*, 177 (38), Section 2.

Amobi, T. N. & Donald, W. H. (2007, September 20). Industry surveys: Movies and home entertainment. In E. M. Bossong-Martines (Ed.), *Standard & Poor's Industry Surveys*, 175 (38), Section 2.

Amobi, T. N. & Kolb, E. (2007, December 13). Industry surveys: Broadcasting, cable, & satellite. In E. M. Bossong-Martines (Ed.), *Standard & Poor's Industry Surveys*, 175 (50), Section 1.

Aronson, S. (1977). Bell's electrical toy: What's the use? The sociology of early telephone usage. In I. Pool (Ed.). *The social impact of the telephone*. Cambridge, MA: The MIT Press, 15-39.

Aspan, M. (2006, January 16). Recording that show? You won't escape Nielsen's notice. *New York Times*. Retrieved January 21, 2006 from http://www.nytimes.com/2006/01/16/business/media/16delay.html.

Associated Press. (2001, March 20). Audio satellite launched into orbit. *New York Times*. Retrieved March 20, 2001 from http://www.nytimes.com/aponline/national/AP-Satellite-Radio.html?ex=986113045& ci=1&cn=7af33c7805ed8853.

Baldwin, T. & McVoy, D. (1983). *Cable communication*. Englewood Cliffs, NJ: Prentice-Hall.

Barr, C., & Harbison, C. (2009). Book title output and average prices. In D. Bogart (Ed.), *Library and book trade almanac* (pp. 504-513). Medford, NJ: Information Today, Inc.

Beaumont, C. (2008, May 10). Dancing to the digital tune As the MP3 turns 10. The Daily Telegraph, p. 19. Retrieved March 8, 2010 from LexisNexis Database.

Belson, K. (2005, June 21). Dial-up Internet going the way of rotary phones. *New York Times*. Retrieved June 21, 2005 from http://www.nytimes.com/2005/06/21/technology/21broad.html.

Belson, K. (2006, November 14). With a dish, broadband goes rural. *New York Times*. Retrieved November 11, 2006 from http://www.nytimes.com/2006/11/14/technology/14satellite.html?em&ex=1163826000&en=24bff61f6033f7c5&ei=5087%0A

Bensinger, A. (2007, August 2). Industry surveys: Communications equipment. In E. M. Bossong-Martines (Ed.), *Standard & Poor's Industry Surveys, 153* (31), Section 1.

Bonneville International Corp. et al. v. Marybeth Peters, as Register of Copyrights et al. Civ. No. 01-0408, 153 F. Supp.2d 763 (E.D. Pa., August 1, 2001).

Brown, D., & Bryant, J. (1989). An annotated statistical abstract of communications media in the United States. In J. Salvaggio & J. Bryant (Eds.), *Media use in the information age: Emerging patterns of adoption and consumer use.* Hillsdale, NJ: Lawrence Erlbaum Associates, 259-302.

Brown, D. (1996). A statistical update of selected American communications media. In Grant, A. E. (Ed.), *Communication Technology Update* (5th ed.). Boston, MA: Focal Press, 327-355.

Brown, D. (1998). Trends in selected U. S. communications media. In Grant, A. E. & Meadows, J. H. (Eds.), Communication Technology Update (6th ed.). Boston, MA: Focal Press, 279-305.

Brown, D. (2000). Trends in selected U. S. communications media. In Grant, A. E. & Meadows, J. H. (Eds.), *Communication Technology Update* (7th ed.). Boston, MA: Focal Press, 299-324.

Brown, D. (2002). Communication technology timeline. In A. E. Grant & J. H. Meadows (Eds.), *Communication technology update* (8th ed.) Boston: Focal Press, 7-45.

Brown, D. (2004). Communication technology timeline. In A. E. Grant & J. H. Meadows (Eds.). *Communication technology update* (9th ed.). Boston: Focal Press, 7-46.

Brown, D. (2006). Communication technology timeline. In A. E. Grant & J. H. Meadows (Eds.), *Communication technology update* (10th ed.). Boston: Focal Press. 7-46.

Brown, D. (2008). Historical perspectives on communication technology. In E. Grant & J. H. Meadows (Eds.), *Communication technology update* (11th ed.). Boston: Focal Press. 11-42.

Campbell, R. (2002). *Media & culture*. Boston, MA: Bedford/St. Martins.

Clifford, S. (2010). Newstand sales and circulation fall for magazines. *New York Times*. Retrieved February 9, 2010 from http://www.nytimes.com/2010/02/09/business/media/09mag.html?ref=media.

Federal Communications Commission. (2001, August). *Trends in telephone service.* Washington, DC: Industry Analysis Division, Common Carrier Bureau. Retrieved February 27, 2002 from http://www.fcc.gov/Bureaus/Common_Carrier/Reports/index.html.

Federal Communications Commission. (2002, January 14). *In the matter of annual assessment of the status of competition in the market for the delivery of video programming* (eighth annual report). CS Docket No. 01-129. Washington, DC 20554. Retrieved February 25, 2002 from http://www.fcc.gov/csb/.

Federal Communications Commission. (2004a). *In the matter of annual assessment of the status of competition in the market for the delivery of video programming,* 10th annual report. CS Docket No. 03-172. Retrieved February 26, 2004 from http://www.fcc.gov/mb/.

Federal Communications Commission. (2004b, February 24). *Broadcast station totals as of December 31, 1999.* Retrieved March 31, 2004 from http://www.fcc.gov/mb/audio/totals/bt031231.html.

Federal Communications Commission. (2005). *In the matter of Implementation of Section 6002(b) of the Omnibus Budget Reconciliation Act of 1993: Annual report and analysis of competitive market conditions with respect to commercial mobile services* (10th report). WT Docket No. 05-71. Retrieved March 9, 2006 from http://www.fcc.gov/oet/spectrum/FCC_Service_Rule_History_File.pdf.

Federal Communications Commission. (2006a). *In the matter of annual assessment of the status of competition in the market for the delivery of video programming,* 12th annual report. CS Docket No. 05-255. Retrieved March 6, 2006 from http://www.fcc.gov/mb/.

Federal Communications Commission. (2006b). *In the matter of implementation of the Cable Television Consumer Protection and Competition Act of 1992: Statistical report on average rates for basic service, cable programming service, and equipment.* Report on cable industry prices, MM Docket No. 92-266. Retrieved January 2, 2007 from http://hraunfoss.fcc.gov/edocs_public/attachmatch/FCC-06-179A1.doc.

Federal Communications Commission. (2007). *Statistical trends in telephony.* Retrieved February 15, 2008 from http://www.fcc.gov/wcb/iatd/trends.html.

Federal Communications Commission. (2008a). *Digital television—FAQ—Consumer corner.* Retrieved February 27, 2008 from http://www.dtv.gov/consumercorner.html.

Federal Communications Commission. (2008b). *Fourth report and order and further notice of proposed rulemaking.* Retrieved March 3, 2008 from http://hraunfoss.fcc.gov/edocs_public/Query.do?mode=advance&rpt=full.

Federal Communications Commission. (2008c). *In the matter of implementation of section 6002(b) of the* Omnibus Budget Reconciliation Act of 1993: *Annual report and analysis of competitive market conditions with respect to commercial mobile services* (12th report). WT Docket No. 07-71. Retrieved February 19, 2008 from http://wireless.fcc.gov/index.htm?job=cmrs_reports#d36e112.

Federal Communications Commission. (2008d). Trends in telephone service. Retrieved February 20, 2010 from www.fcc.gov/wcb/iatd/trends.html.

Federal Communications Commission. (2009a). *In the Matter of Annual Assessment of the Status of Competition in the Market for the Delivery of Video Programming* (13th report). WT Docket No. 06-189). Retrieved February 10, 2010 from http://www.fcc.gov/mb/.

Federal Communications Commission. (2009b). *What is broadband.* Retrieved March 12, 2010 from http://www.broadband.gov/about_broadband.html.

Federal Communications Commission. (2010a, January 20). *In the Matter of Review of the Commission's Program Access Rules and Examination of Programming Tying Arrangements.* MB Docket No. 07-198. Retrieved February 23, 2010 from http://hraunfoss.fcc.gov/edocs_public/attachmatch/FCC-10-17A1.doc.

Federal Communications Commission. (2010b, February). High-Speed Services for Internet Access: Status as of December 31, 2008. Retrieved March 12, 2010 from http://www.fcc.gov/wcb/iatd/recent.html.

Graham-Hackett, M. (2005, June 2). Global PC demand outlook losing steam. In E. M. Bossong-Martines (Ed.), *Standard & Poor's Industry Surveys, 173* (22), Section 1.

Grossman, L. (2010, January 18). A look at the nook. *Time, 175*(2), 61.

Hansell, S. (2009, October 16). Broadcasting to mobile gadgets. *New York Times.* Retrieved October 17, 2009 from http://bits.blogs.nytimes.com/2009/10/16/tv-stations-start-broadcasting-to-mobile-gadgets/?ref=technology

Hofstra University. (2000). *Chronology of computing history.* Retrieved March 13, 2002 from http://www.hofstra.edu/pdf/CompHist_9812tla1.pdf.

Horrigan, J. B. (2005, September 24). *Broadband adoption at home in the United States: Growing but slowing.* Paper presented to the 33rd Annual Meeting of the Telecommunications Policy Research Conference. Retrieved March 13, 2006 from http://www.pewinternet.org/PPF/r/164/report_display.asp.

Horrigan, J.B. (2010, February). *Broadband adoption and use in America: OBI Working Paper Series No. 1.* Washington, DC: Federal Communications Commission.

Huntzicker, W. (1999). *The popular press, 1833-1865.* Westport, CT: Greenwood Press.

IDC netbook & PC sales projection – 2008 through 2013. (2010, March 6). *TG Daily.* Retrieved March 15, 2010 from http://www.tgdaily.com/slideshows/index.php?s=200903062&p=1

Ink, G. & Grabois, A. (2000). *Book title output and average prices: 1998 final and 1999 preliminary figures,* 45th edition. D. Bogart (Ed.). New Providence, NJ: R. R. Bowker, 508-513.

In-Stat/MDR. (2004, April 5). *High-definition TV services finally establish a foothold.* Retrieved April 8, 2004 from http://www.instat.com/press.asp?ID=925&sku=IN0401241MB.

International Telecommunications Union. (1999). *World telecommunications report 1999.* Geneva, Switzerland: Author.

Jennings, A. (2007, August 4). What's good for a business can be hard on friends. *New York Times.* Retrieved August 4, 2007 from http://www.nytimes.com/2007/08/04/business/04network.html?_r=1&ref=technology.

Kaiser Family Foundation. (2010). Generation M2: Media in the lives of 8- to 18-year-olds, 2010. Retrieved March 11, 2010 from http://www.kff.org/entmedia/mh012010pkg.cfm.

Kessler, S. H. (2007a, September 20). Industry surveys: Computers: Consumer services & the Internet. In E. M. Bossong-Martines (Ed.), *Standard & Poor's Industry Surveys, 175* (38), Section 1.

Kessler, S. H. (2007b, August 26). Industry surveys: Computers: Hardware. In E. M. Bossong-Martines (Ed.), *Standard & Poor's Industry Surveys, 175* (17), Section 2.

Kessler, S. H. (2009). Industry surveys: Computer services and the Internet. In E. M. Bossong-Martines (Ed.), *Standard & Poor's Industry Surveys, 173* (49), Section 2.

Kingsport Times News. (2006, December 15). Wired cable TV penetration hits 6-year low in Tri-Cities, alternative delivery system posts big gains. Retrieved December 19, 2006 from http://www.timesnews.net/article.php?id=9000556.

Kolb, E. B., & Amobi, T. N. (2009). Industry surveys: Broadcasting, cable, & satellite. In E. M. Bossong-Martines (Ed.), *Standard & Poor's Industry Surveys, 177* (38), Section 2.

Lee, A. (1973). *The daily newspaper in America.* New York: Octagon Books.

Lee, J. (1917). *History of American journalism.* Boston: Houghton Mifflin.

Leeds, J. (2005, December 27). The net is a boon for indie labels. *New York Times.* Retrieved December 28, 2005 from http://www.nytimes.com/2005/12/27/arts/music/27musi.html.

Lenhart A., Purcell, K., Smith, A., & Zickuhr, K. (2010). *Social media & mobile Internet use among teens and young adults.* Pew internet & American Life Project.

Lenhart, A., Madden, M., Macgill, A. R., & Smith, A. (2007). *Teens and social media.* Pew Internet & American Life Project.

Leon, K., & Kawaguchi, K. (2007, March 22). Industry surveys: Telecommunications: Wireless. In E. M. Bossong-Martines (Ed.), *Standard & Poor's Industry Surveys, 175* (12), Section 1.

Lowry, B. (2009, December 9). Divergence over a decade. Daily Variety, 2. Retrieved March 8, 2010 from LexisNexis Database.

McNary, D. & McClintock, P. (2008, January 21). O'Seas B. O. nears $10 billion for year. *Variety, 409* (9), 16-17. Retrieved February 20, 2008 from General OneFile via Gale http://find.galegroup.com/itx/start.do?prodId=ITOF.

Mindlin, A. (2007, August 27). Cell phone-only homes hit a milestone. *New York Times.* Retrieved August 29, 2007 from http://www.nytimes.com/2007/08/27/technology/27drill.html?em&ex=1188532800&en=7e534d7ab44862If&ei=5087%0A.

Mini-note (Netbook) shipments grow 103% Y/Y in 2009; Revenues up 72%. (2009, December 22). DisplaySearch. Retrieved March 9, 2010 from LexisNexis Database.

Moorman, J. (2009). Industry surveys: Telecommunications: Wireless. In E. M. Bossong-Martines (Ed.), *Standard & Poor's Industry Surveys. 177* (38). Section 2.

Murray, J. (2001). *Wireless nation: The frenzied launch of the cellular revolution in America.* Cambridge, MA: Perseus Publishing.

National Association of Theater Owners. (2010). *Total U.S. admissions.* Retrieved February 15, 2010 from http://www.natoonline.org/statisticsadmissions.htm.

National Cable and Telecommunications Association. (2006). *Annual overview 2006.* Retrieved on May 9, 2006 from http://www.ncta.com.

Netbook 2009 revenues soar. (2009, December 23). TECHWEB. Retrieved March 9, 2010 from LexisNexis Database.

OECD. (2007). *OECD broadband statistics to December 2006.* Retrieved May 15, 2007 from http://www.oecd.org/document/7/0,2340,en_2649_34223_38446855_1_1_1_1,00.html.

PC market rebounds in Q4. (2010, January 14). TECHWEB. Retrieved March 9, 2010 from LexisNexis Database.

Peters, J., (2009). Industry surveys: Publishing. In E. M. Bossong-Martines (Ed.), *Standard & Poor's Industry Surveys. 176* (34). Section 1.

Peters, J., & Donald, W. H. (2007). Industry surveys: Publishing. In E. M. Bossong-Martines (Ed.), *Standard & Poor's Industry Surveys. 175* (36). Section 1.

Pfanner, E. (2007, January 8). The British like to control TV with their DVRs, too. *New York Times.* Retrieved January 8, 2007 from http://www.nytimes.com/2007/01/08/technology/08dvr.html?ref=technology.

Pfanner, E. (2009). Book sales in Europe are gaining in tough times. *New York Times.* Retrieved March 16, 2009 from http://www.nytimes.com/2009/03/16/business/worldbusiness/16books.html?ref=media.

Princeton Survey Research Associates International. (2009). Broadband service capability survey. Federal Communications Commission. Retrieved March 12, 2010 from http://hraunfoss.fcc.gov/edocs_public/attachmatch/DOC-296444A1.pdf.

Quenqua, D. (2010, March 10). Can a mouse cut the cable? New York Times. Retrieved March 11, 2010 from http://www.nytimes.com/2010/03/11/garden/11tv.html?ref=technology

Rainie, L. (2010). Internet, broadband, and cell phone statistics. *Pew Internet & American Life Project.*

Raphael, J. (2000, September 4). Radio station leaves earth and enters cyberspace. Trading the FM dial for a digital stream. *New York Times.* Retrieved September 4, 2000 from http://www.nytimes.com/library/tech/00/ 09/biztech/articles/04radio.html.

Rich, M. (2010, March 1). Math of publishing meets the E-book. *New York Times,* Retrieved March 1, 2010 from http://www.nytimes.com/2010/03/01/business/media/01ebooks.html?ref=technology.

Rich, M., & Stone, B. (2010, February 1). Publisher wins fight with Amazon over e-books. *New York Times.* Retrieved February 1, 2010 from http://www.nytimes.com/2010/02/01/technology/companies/01amazonweb.html?ref=technology.

Sagolla, D. (2009, January 30). 140 characters: How Twitter was born. Retrieved January 1, 2010 from http://www.140characters.com/2009/01/30/how-twitter-was-born/

Satellite radio hits its stride. (2006, February 7). *PC Magazine, 25* (2), 19.

Schaeffler, J. (2004, February 2). The real satellite radio boom begins. *Satellite News, 27* (5). Retrieved April 7, 2004 from Lexis-Nexis.

Siklos, R. (2005, December 11). Satellite radio: Out of the car and under fire. *New York Times.* Retrieved December 11, 2005 from http://www.nytimes.com/2005/12/11/business/yourmoney/11frenz.html.

Stellin, S. (2002, February 14). Cell phone saturation. *New York Times.* Retrieved February 14, 2002 from http://www.nytimes.com/pages/business/media/index.html.

Stelter, B. (2009). The upfront season this time won't be too upbeat. *New York Times.* Retrieved March 11, 2009 from http://www.nytimes.com/2009/03/11/business/media/11adco.html?ref=media

Stelter, B. (2010). Viacom and Hulu part ways. New York Times. Retrieved March 3, 2010 from http://www.nytimes.com/2010/03/03/business/media/03hulu.html?adxnnl=1&ref=technology&adxnnlx=1267625269-7LOKJ+wiTvnH0xceeIa5vg.

Stone, B. (2010, January 5). Apple's App Store tops three billion downloads. *New York Times.* Retrieved January 4, 2010 from http://bits.blogs.nytimes.com/2010/01/05/apples-app-store-tops-3-billion-downloads/?ref=technology.

Stone, B., & Rich, M. (2010, January 21). Apple courts publishers, while Kindle adds apps. *New York Times,* Retrieved January 21, 2010 from Retrieved January 21, 2010 from http://www.nytimes.com/2010/01/21/technology/21reader.html?ref=technology.

Stone, B. & Richtel, M. (2007, April 30). Social networking leaves the confines of the computer. *New York Times.* Retrieved May 1, 2007 from http://www.nytimes.com/2007/04/30/technology/30social.html?_r=1& ref=technology.

Stross, R. (2006, January 15). Hey, Baby Bells: Information still wants to be free. *New York Times.* Retrieved January 15, 2006 from http://www.nytimes.com/2006/01/15/business/yourmoney/15digi.html.

U.S. Bureau of the Census. (2003). *Statistical abstract of the United States: 2003* (123rd Ed.). Washington, DC: U.S. Government Printing Office.

U.S. Bureau of the Census. (2005). *Statistical abstract of the United States: 2005* (124th Ed.). Washington, DC: U.S. Government Printing Office. Retrieved February 6, 2006 from http://www.census.gov/prod/www/statistical-abstract.html.

U.S. Bureau of the Census. (2006). *Statistical abstract of the United States: 2006* (125th Ed.). Washington, DC: U.S. Government Printing Office. Retrieved February 6, 2006 from http://www.census.gov/prod/www/statistical-abstract.html.

U.S. Bureau of the Census. (2008). *Statistical abstract of the United States: 2008* (127th Ed.). Washington, DC: U.S. Government Printing Office. Retrieved January 31, 2008 from http://www.census.gov/compendia/statab/.

U.S. Bureau of the Census. (2010). *Statistical abstract of the United States: 2008* (129th Ed.). Washington, DC: U.S. Government Printing Office. Retrieved February 3, 2010 from http://www.census.gov/compendia/statab/.

U.S. Copyright Office. (2003). *106th Annual report of the Register of Copyrights for the fiscal year ending September 30, 2003.* Washington, DC: Library of Congress.

U.S. Department of Commerce/International Trade Association. (2000). *U.S. industry and trade outlook 2000.* New York: McGraw-Hill.

Video game sales up 6%. (2006, January 14). *Bloomberg News.* Retrieved January 14, 2006 from http://www.nytimes.com/2006/01/14/technology/14video.html.

White, L. (1971). *The American radio.* New York: Arno Press.

Ziff-Davis Media. (2005, August). Industry surveys: Digital gaming in America. In E. M. Bossong-Martines (Ed.), *Standard & Poor's Industry Surveys, 173* (38). Section 1.

3

Understanding Communication Technologies

Jennifer H. Meadows, Ph.D.[*]

Today, you can do dozens of things that your parents never dreamed of: surfing the Internet anytime and anywhere, watching crystal clear sports on a large high-definition television (HDTV) in your home, battling aliens on "distant worlds" alongside game players scattered around the globe, and "Googling" any subject you find interesting. This book was created to help you understand these technologies, but there is a set of tools that will not only help you understand them, but also understand the next generation of technologies.

All of the communication technologies explored in this book have a number of characteristics in common, including how their adoption spreads from a small group of highly interested consumers to the general public, what the effects of these technologies are upon the people who use them (and on society in general), and how these technologies affect each other.

For more than a century, researchers have studied adoption, effects, and other aspects of new technologies, identifying patterns that are common across dissimilar technologies, and proposing theories of technology adoption and effects. These theories have proven to be valuable to entrepreneurs seeking to develop new technologies, regulators who want to control those technologies, and everyone else who just wants to understand them. The utility of these theories is that they allow you to apply lessons from one technology to another or from old technologies to new technologies. The easiest way to understand the role played by the technologies explored in this book is to have a set of theories you can apply to virtually any technology you discuss. The purpose of this chapter is to give you those tools by introducing you to the theories.

The umbrella perspective discussed in Chapter 1 is a useful framework for studying communication technologies, but it is not a theory. This perspective is a good starting point to begin to understand communication technologies because it targets your attention at a number of different levels that might not be immediately obvious including hardware, software, organizational infrastructure, the social system, and, finally, the user. Understanding each of these levels is aided by knowing a number of theoretical perspectives that can help us understand the different levels of the umbrella for these technologies. Indeed, there are a plethora of theories that can be used to study these technologies. Theoretical approaches are useful in understanding the origins of the information-based economy in which we now live, why some technologies take off while others fail, the impacts and effects of technologies, and the economics of the communication technology marketplace.

---

[*] Professor, Department of Communication Design, California State University, Chico (Chico, California).

The Information Society and the Control Revolution

Our economy used to be based on tangible products such as coal, lumber, and steel. That has changed. Now, information is the basis of our economy. Information industries include education, research and development, creating informational goods such as computer software, banking, insurance, and even entertainment and news (Beniger, 1986). Information is different from other commodities like coffee and pork bellies, which are known as "private goods." Instead, information is a "public good" because it is intangible, lacks a physical presence, and can be sold as many times as demand allows without regard to consumption. For example, if 10 sweaters are sold, then 10 sweaters must be manufactured using raw materials. If 10 subscriptions to an online dating service are sold, there is no need to create new services: 10—or 10,000—subscriptions can be sold without additional raw materials.

This difference actually gets to the heart of a common misunderstanding about ownership of information that falls into a field known as "intellectual property rights." A common example is the purchase of a music compact disc (CD). The information, the music, is printed on a physical medium, the CD. A person may believe that because he or she purchased the CD, that purchase allows the copy and distribution of the music on the CD. Realizing the difference between the information (music), which has an inherent value, and the physical media that contains the information (the CD), is important.

Several theorists have studied the development of the information society, including its origin. Beniger (1986) argues that there was a control revolution: "A complex of rapid changes in the technological and economic arrangements by which information is collected, stored, processed, and communicated and through which formal or programmed decisions might affect social control" (p. 52). In other words, as society progressed, technologies were created to help control information. For example, information was centralized by mass media. In addition, as more and more information is created and distributed, new technologies must be developed to control that information. For example, with the explosion of information available over the Internet, search engines were developed to help users find it.

Another important point is that information is power, and there is power in giving information away. Power can also be gained by withholding information. At different times in modern history, governments have blocked access to information or controlled information dissemination to maintain power.

Adoption

Why are some technologies adopted while others fail? This question is addressed by a number of theoretical approaches including the diffusion of innovations, social information processing theory, and critical mass theory.

Diffusion of Innovations

The diffusion of innovations, also referred to as diffusion theory, was developed by Everett Rogers (1962; 2003). This theory tries to explain how an innovation is communicated over time through different channels to members of a social system. There are four main aspects of this approach. First, there is the innovation. In the case of communication technologies, the innovation is some technology that is perceived as new. Rogers defines characteristics of innovations: relative advantage, compatibility, complexity, trialability, and observability. So if someone is deciding to purchase a new iPod, characteristics would include the relative advantage over other digital audio players or even other ways to listen to music like CDs, whether or not the iPod is compatible with the existing needs of the user, how complex it is to use, whether or not the potential user can try it out, and whether or not the potential user can see others using the new iPod with successful results.

Information about an innovation is communicated through different channels. Mass media is good for awareness knowledge. For example, the new iPod has television commercials and print advertising announcing its existence and its features. Interpersonal channels are also an important means of communication about innovations. These interactions generally involve subjective evaluations of the innovation. For example, a person might ask some friends how they like their new iPods.

Rogers (2003) outlines the decision-making process a potential user goes through before adopting an innovation. This is a five-step process. The first step is knowledge. You find out there is a new iPod available and learn about its new features. The next step is persuasion when you form a positive attitude about the innovation. Maybe you like the new iPod. The third step is when you decide to accept or reject the innovation. Yes, I will get the new iPod. Implementation is the fourth step. You use the innovation, in this case, the iPod. Finally, confirmation occurs when you decide that you made the correct decision. Yes, the iPod is what is thought it would be; my decision is reinforced.

Another stage that is discussed by Rogers (2003) and others is "reinvention," the process by which a person who adopts a technology begins to use it for purposes other than those intended by the original inventor. For example, iPods were initially designed for music and other sound recording, but users have found ways to use them for a wide variety of applications ranging from alarm clocks to personal calendars.

Have you ever noticed that some people are the first to have the new technology gadget, while others refuse to adopt a proven successful technology? Adopters can be categorized into different groups according to how soon or late they adopt an innovation. The first to adopt are the innovators. Innovators are special because they are willing to take a risk adopting something new that may fail. Next come the early adopters, the early majority, and then the late majority, followed by the last category, the laggards. In terms of percentages, innovators make up the first 2.5% percent of adopters, early adopters are the next 13.5%, early majority follows with 34%, late majority are the next 34%, and laggards are the last 16%. Adopters can also be described in terms of ideal types. Innovators are venturesome. These are people who like to take risks and can deal with failure. Early adopters are respectable. They are valued opinion leaders in the community and role models for others. Early majority adopters are deliberate. They adopt just before the average person and are an important link between the innovators, early adopters, and everyone else. The late majority are skeptical. They are hesitant to adopt innovations and often adopt because they pressured. Laggards are the last to adopt and often are isolated with no opinion leadership. They are suspicious and resistant to change. Other factors that affect adoption include education, social status, social mobility, finances, and willingness to use credit (Rogers, 2003).

Adoption of an innovation does not usually occur all at once; it happens over time. This is called the rate of adoption. The rate of adoption generally follows an S-shaped "diffusion curve" where the X-axis is time and the Y-axis is percent of adopters. You can note the different adopter categories along the diffusion curve. Figure 3.1 shows a diffusion curve. See how the innovators are at the very beginning of the curve, and the laggards are at the end. The steepness of the curve depends on how quickly an innovation is adopted. For example, DVD has a steeper curve than VCR because DVD players were adopted at a faster rate than VCRs. Also, different types of decision processes lead to faster adoption. Voluntary adoption is slower than collective decisions, which, in turn, are slower than authority decisions. For example, a company may let its workers decide whether to use a new software package, the employees may agree collectively to use that software, or finally, the management may decide that everyone at the company is going to use the software. In most cases, voluntary adoption would take the longest, and a management dictate would result in the swiftest adoption.

Moore (2001) further explored diffusion of innovations and high-tech marketing in *Crossing the Chasm*. He noted there are gaps between the innovators and the early adopters, the early adopters and the early majority, and the early majority and late majority. For a technology's adoption to move from innovators to the early adopters the technology must show a major new benefit. Innovators are visionaries that take the risk of adopting something new such as 3-D televisions. Early adopters then must see the new benefit of 3-D televisions before adopting. The chasm between early adopters and early majority is the greatest of these gaps. Early adopters are still visionary and want to be change agents. They don't mind dealing with the troubles and glitches that come along with a new technology. Early adopters are likely to use a beta version of a new service like Google Wave. The early majority, on the other hand, are pragmatists and want to see some improvement in productivity; something tangible. Moving from serving the visionaries to serving the pragmatists is difficult; hence Moore's description of "crossing the chasm." This phenomenon could explain why Google Wave hasn't moved beyond the early adopter stage. Finally, there is a smaller gap between the early majority and the late majority. Unlike the early majority, the late majority reacts to the technical demands on the users. The early majority is more comfortable working with technology. So, the early majority would be comfortable using social networking like Facebook but the late majority is put off by the perceived technical demands. The technology must alleviate this concern before late majority adoption.

Figure 3.1
Innovation Adoption Rate

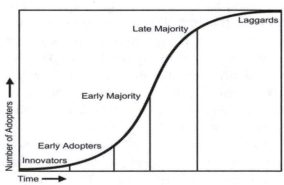

Source: Technology Futures, Inc.

Critical Mass Theory

Have you ever wondered who had the first e-mail address or the first telephone? Who did they communicate with? Interactive technologies such as telephony and e-mail become more and more useful as more people adopt these technologies. There have to be some innovators and early adopters who are willing to take the risk to try a new interactive technology. These users are the "critical mass," a small segment of the population that chooses to make big contributions to the public good (Markus, 1987). In general terms, any social process involving actions by individuals that benefit others is known as "collective action." In this case, the technologies become more useful if everyone in the system is using the technology, a goal known as universal access. Ultimately universal access means that you can reach anyone through some communication technology. For example, in the United States, the landline phone system reaches almost everywhere, and everyone benefits from this technology although a small segment of the population initially chose to adopt the telephone to get the ball rolling. There is a stage in the diffusion process that an interactive medium has to reach in order for adoption to take off. This is the "critical mass."

Another relatively new conceptualization of critical mass theory is the "tipping point" (Gladwell, 2002). Here is an example. The videophone never took off, in part, because it never reached critical mass. The videophone was not really any better than a regular phone unless the person you were calling also had a videophone. If there were not enough people you knew who had videophones, then you might not adopt it because it was not worth it. On the other hand, if most of your regular contacts had videophones, then that critical mass of users might drive you to adopt the videophone. Critical mass is an important aspect to consider for the adoption of any interactive technology.

Another good example is facsimile or fax technology. The first method of sending images over wires was invented in the '40s—the 1840s—by Alexander Bain, who proposed using a system of electrical pendulums to send images over wires (Robinson, 1986). Within a few decades, the technology was adapted by the newspaper industry to send photos over wires, but the technology was limited to a small number of news organizations. The development of technical standards in the 1960s brought the fax machine to corporate America, which generally ignored the technology because few businesses knew of another business that had a fax machine.

Adoption of the fax took place two machines at a time, with those two usually being purchased to communicate with each other, but rarely used to communicate with additional receivers. By the 1980s, enough businesses had fax machines that could communicate with each other that many businesses started buying fax machines one at a time. As soon as the "critical mass" point was reached, fax machine adoption increased to the point that it became referred to as the first technology adopted out of fear of embarrassment that someone would ask, "What's your fax number?" (Wathne & Leos, 1993). In less than two years, the fax machine became a business necessity.

Social Information Processing

Another way to look at how and why people choose to use or not use a technology is social information processing. This theory begins by critiquing rational choice models, which presume that people make adoption decisions and other evaluations of technologies based upon objective characteristics of the technology. In order to understand social information processing, you first have to look at a few rational choice models.

One model, social presence theory, categorizes communication media based on a continuum of how the medium "facilitates awareness of the other person and interpersonal relationships during the interaction (Fulk, et al., 1990, p. 118)." Communication is most efficient when the social presence level of the medium best matches the interpersonal relationship required for the task at hand. An illustration is that a person would break up with another person face to face instead of using a text message. Another rational choice model is information richness theory. In this theory, media are also arranged on a continuum of richness in four areas: speed of feedback, types of channels employed, personalness of source, and richness of language carried (Fulk, et al., 1990). Face-to-face communications is the highest in social presence and information richness. In information richness theory, the communication medium chosen is related to message ambiguity. If the message is ambiguous, then a richer medium is chosen. In this case, teaching someone how to dance would be better with a DVD that illustrates the steps rather than just an audio CD that describes the steps.

Social information processing theory goes beyond the rational choice models because it states that perceptions of media are "in part, subjective and socially constructed." Although people may use objective standards in choosing communication media, use is also determined by subjective factors such as the attitudes of coworkers about the media and vicarious learning, or watching others' experiences. Social influence is strongest in ambiguous situations. For example, the less people know about a medium, then the more likely they are to rely on social information in deciding to use it (Fulk, et al., 1987).

Think about whether you prefer a Macintosh or a Windows-based computer. Although you can probably list objective differences between the two, many of the important factors in your choice are based upon subjective factors such as which one is owned by friends and coworkers, the perceived usefulness of the computer, and advice you receive from people who can help you set up and maintain your computer. In the end, these social factors probably play a much more important role in your decision than "objective" factors such as processor speed, memory capacity, etc.

Impacts and Effects

Do video games make players violent? Do users seek out the World Wide Web for social interactions? These are some of the questions that theories of impacts or effects try to answer. To begin, Rogers (1986) provides a useful typology of impacts. Impacts can be grouped into three dichotomies: desirable and undesirable, direct and indirect, and anticipated and unanticipated. Desirable impacts are the functional impacts of a technology. For example a desirable impact of e-commerce is the ability to purchase goods and services from your home. An undesirable impact is one that is dysfunctional, such as credit card fraud. Direct impacts are changes that happen in immediate response to a technology. A direct impact of wireless telephony is the ability to make calls while driving. An indirect impact is a byproduct of the direct impact. To illustrate, laws against driving and using a handheld wireless phone are an impact of the direct impact described above. Anticipated impacts are the intended impacts of a technology. An anticipated impact of text messaging is to communicate without audio. An unanticipated impact is an unintended impact, such as people sending text messages in a movie theater and annoying other patrons. Often, the desirable, direct, and anticipated impacts are the same and are considered first. Then, the undesirable, indirect, and unanticipated impacts are noted later.

A good example of this is e-mail. A desirable, anticipated, and direct impact of e-mail is to be able to quickly send a message to multiple people at the same time. An undesirable, indirect, and unanticipated impact of e-mail is spam—unwanted e-mail clogging the inboxes of millions of users.

Uses and Gratifications

Uses and gratifications research is a descriptive approach that gives insight into what people do with technology. This approach sees the users as actively seeking to use different media to fulfill different needs (Rubin, 2002). The perspective focuses on "(1) the social and psychological origins of (2) needs, which generate (3) expectations of (4) the mass media or other sources, which lead to (5) differential patterns of media exposure (or engagement in other activities), resulting in (6) needs gratifications and (7) other consequences perhaps mostly unintended ones" (Katz, et al., 1974, p. 20).

Uses and gratification research surveys audiences about why they choose to use different types of media. For example, uses and gratifications of television studies have found that people watch television for information, relaxation, to pass time, by habit, excitement, and for social utility (Rubin, 2002). This approach is also useful for comparing the uses and gratifications between media, as illustrated by studies of the World Wide Web (WWW) and television gratifications that found that, although there are some similarities such as entertainment and to pass time, they are also very different on other variables such as companionship where the Web was much lower than for television (Ferguson & Perse, 2000). Uses and gratifications studies have examined a multitude of communication technologies including mobile phones (Wei, 2006), digital media players (Keeler & Wilkinson, in press), radio (Towers, 1987), and satellite television (Etefa, 2005).

Media System Dependency Theory

Often confused with uses and gratifications, media system dependency theory is "an ecological theory that attempts to explore and explain the role of media in society by examining dependency relations within and across levels of analysis" (Grant, et al., 1991, p. 774). The key to this theory is the focus it provides on the dependency relationships that result from the interplay between resources and goals. The theory suggests that, in order to understand the role of a medium, you have to look at relationships at multiple levels of analysis including the individual level—the audience, the organizational level, the media system level, and society in general. These dependency relationships can by symmetrical or asymmetrical. For example, the dependency relationship between audiences and network television is asymmetrical because an individual audience member may depend more on network television to reach his or her goal than the television networks depend on that one audience member to reach their goals.

A typology of individual media dependency relations was developed by Ball-Rokeach & DeFleur (1976) to help understand the range of goals that individuals have when they use the media. There are six dimensions: social understanding, self-understanding, action orientation, interaction orientation, solitary play, and social play. Social understanding is learning about the world around you, while self-understanding is learning about yourself. Action orientation is learning about specific behaviors, while interaction orientation is about learning about specific behaviors involving other people. Solitary play is entertaining yourself alone, while social play is using media as a focus for social interaction. Research on individual media system dependency relationships has demonstrated that people have different dependency relationships with different media. For example, Meadows (1997) found that women had stronger social understanding dependencies for television than magazines, but stronger self-understanding dependencies for magazines than television.

In the early days of television shopping (when it was considered "new technology"), Grant, et al. (1991) applied media system dependency theory to the phenomenon. Their analysis explored two dimensions: how TV shopping changed organizational dependency relations within the television industry and how and why individual users watched television shopping programs. By applying a theory that addressed multiple levels of analysis, a greater understanding of the new technology was obtained than if a theory that focused on only one level had been applied.

Social Learning Theory/Social Cognitive Theory

Social learning theory focuses on how people learn by modeling others (Bandura, 2001). This observational learning occurs when watching another person model the behavior. It also happens with symbolic modeling, modeling that happens by watching the behavior modeled on a television or computer screen. So, a person can learn how to fry an egg by watching another person fry an egg in person or on a video.

Learning happens within a social context. People learn by watching others, but they may or may not perform the behavior. Learning happens, though, whether the behavior is imitated. Reinforcement and punishment play a role in whether or not the modeled behavior is performed. If the behavior is reinforced, then the learner is more likely to perform the behavior. For example, if a student is successful using online resources for a presentation, other students watching the presentation will be more likely to use online resources. On the other hand, if the action is punished, then the modeling is less likely to result in the behavior. To illustrate, if a character drives drunk and gets arrested on a television program, then that modeled behavior is less likely to be performed by viewers of that program.

Reinforcement and punishment is not that simple though. This is where cognition comes in—learners think about the consequences of performing that behavior. This is why a person may play *Grand Theft Auto* and steal cars in the videogame, but will not then go out and steal a car in real life. Self-regulation is an important factor. Self-efficacy is another important dimension: learners must believe that they can perform the behavior.

Social learning/cognitive theory, then, is a useful framework for examining not only the effects of communication media, but also the adoption of communication technologies (Bandura, 2001). The content that is consumed through communication technologies contains symbolic models of behavior that are both functional and dysfunctional. If viewers model the behavior in the content, then some form of observational learning is occurring. A lot of advertising works this way. A movie star uses a new shampoo and then is admired by others. This message models a positive reinforcement of using the shampoo. Cognitively, the viewer then thinks about the consequences of using the shampoo. Modeling can happen with live models and symbolic models. For example, a person can watch another playing Wii bowling, a videogame where the player has to manipulate the controller to mimic rolling the ball. Their avatar in the game also models the bowling action. The other player considers the consequences of this modeling. In addition, if the other person had not played with this gaming system, watching the other person play with the Wii and enjoy the experience will make it more likely that he or she will adopt the system. Therefore, social learning/cognitive theory can be used to facilitate the adoption of new technologies and to understand why some technologies are adopted and why some are adopted faster than others (Bandura, 2001).

ECONOMIC

Thus far, the theories and perspectives discussed have dealt mainly with individual users and communication technologies. How do users decide to adopt a technology? What impacts will a technology have on a user? Theory, though, can also be applied to organizational infrastructure and the overall technology market. Here, two approaches will be addressed: the theory of the long tail that presents a new way of looking at digital content and how it is distributed and sold, and the principle of relative constancy that examines what happens to the marketplace when new media products are introduced.

The Theory of the Long Tail

Wired editor Chris Anderson developed the theory of the long tail. This theory begins with the realization that there are not any huge hit movies, television shows, and albums like there used to be. What counts as a hit TV show today, for example, would be a failed show just 15 years ago. One of the reasons for this is choice: 40 years ago viewers had a choice of only a few television channels. Today, you could have hundreds of channels of video programming on cable or satellite and limitless amounts of video programming on the Internet. You have a lot more choice. New communication technologies are giving users access to niche content. There is more music, video, video games, news, etc. than ever before because the distribution is no longer limited to the traditional mass media of over-the-air broadcasting, newspapers, etc. The theory states that, "our culture and economy is increasingly shifting away from a focus on a relatively small number of 'hits' at the headend of the demand curve and toward a huge number of niches in the tail" (Anderson, n.d.). Figure 3.2 shows a traditional demand curve; most of the hits are at the head of the curve, but there is still demand as you go into the tail. There is a demand for niche content and there are opportunities for businesses that deliver content in the long tail.

Figure 3.2
The Long Tail

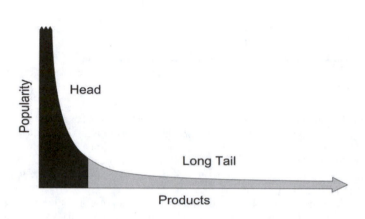

Source: Anderson (n.d.)

Both physical media and traditional retail have limitations. For example, there is only so much shelf space in the store. Therefore, the store, in order to maximize profit, is only going to stock the products most likely to sell. Digital content and distribution changes this. For example, Amazon and Netflix can have huge inventories of hard-to-find titles, as opposed to a bricks-and-motor video rental store, which has to have duplicate inventories at each location. All digital services, such as the iTunes store, eliminate all physical media. You purchase and download the content digitally, and there is no need for a warehouse to store DVDs and CDs. Because of these efficiencies, these businesses can better serve niche markets. Taken one at a time, these niche markets may not generate significant revenue but when they are aggregated, these markets are significant.

Anderson (2006) suggests rules for long tail businesses. Make everything available, lower the price, and help people find it. Traditional media are responding to these services. For example, Nintendo is making classic games available for download. Network television is putting up entire series of television programming on the Internet. The audience is changing, and expectations for content selection and availability are changing. The audience today, Anderson argues, wants what they want, when they want it, and how they want it.

The Principle of Relative Constancy

So now that people have all of this choice of content, delivery mode, etc., what happens to older media? Do people just keep adding new entertainment media, or do they adjust by dropping one form in favor of another? This question is at the core of the principle of relative constancy, which says that people spend a constant fraction of their disposable income on mass media over time. People do, however, alter their spending on mass media categories when new services/products are introduced (McCombs & Nolan, 1992). What this means is that, if a new media technology is introduced in order for adoption to happen, the new technology has to be compelling enough for the adopter to give up something else. For example, a person who signs up for Netflix may spend less money on movie tickets. A satellite radio user will spend less money purchasing music downloads or CDs. So, when considering a new media technology, the relative advantage it has over existing service must be considered, along with other characteristics of the technology discussed earlier in this chapter. Remember, the money users spend on any new technology has to come from somewhere.

Conclusion

This chapter has provided a brief overview of several theoretical approaches to understanding communication technology. As you work through the book, consider theories of adoption, effects, and economics and how they can inform you about each technology and allow you to apply lessons from one technology to others. For more in-depth discussions of these theoretical approaches, check out the sources cited in the bibliography.

Bibliography

Anderson, C. (n.d.). *About me.* Retrieved May 2, 2008 from http://www.thelongtail.com/about.html.

Anderson, C. (2006). *The long tail: Why the future of business is selling less of more.* New York, NY: Hyperion.

Ball-Rokeach, S. & DeFleur, M. (1976). A dependency model of mass-media effects. *Communication Research, 3,* 1 3-21.

Bandura, A. (2001). Social cognitive theory of mass communication. *Media Psychology, 3,* 265-299.

Beniger, J. (1986). The information society: Technological and economic origins. In S. Ball-Rokeach & M. Cantor (Eds.). *Media, audience, and social structure.* Newbury Park, NJ: Sage, pp. 51-70.

Etefa, A. (2005). *Arabic satellite channels in the U.S.: Uses & gratifications.* Paper presented at the annual meeting of the International Communication Association, New York. Retrieved May 2, 2008 from http://www.allacademic.com/ meta/p14246_index.html.

Ferguson, D. & Perse, E. (2000, Spring). The World Wide Web as a functional alternative to television. *Journal of Broadcasting and Electronic Media. 44* (2), 155-174.

Fulk, J., Schmitz, J., & Steinfield, C. W. (1990). A social influence model of technology use. In J. Fulk & C. Steinfield (Eds.), *Organizations and communication technology.* Thousand Oaks, CA: Sage, pp. 117-140.

Fulk, J., Steinfield, C., Schmitz, J., & Power, J. (1987). A social information processing model of media use in organizations. *Communication Research, 14* (5), 529-552.

Gladwell, M. (2002). *The tipping point: How little things can make a big difference.* New York: Back Bay Books.

Grant, A., Guthrie, K., & Ball-Rokeach, S. (1991). Television shopping: A media system dependency perspective. *Communication Research, 18* (6), 773-798.

Katz, E., Blumler, J., & Gurevitch, M. (1974). Utilization of mass communication by the individual. In J. Blumler & E. Katz (Eds.). *The uses of mass communication: Current perspectives on gratifications research.* Beverly Hills: Sage.

Keeler, J. & Wilkinson, J. S. (in press). iPods and God: Uses of mobile media to enhance faith. *Journal of Media and Religion* (in press; accepted for publication February 2008).

Markus, M. (1987, October). Toward a "critical mass" theory of interactive media. *Communication Research, 14* (5), 497-511.

McCombs, M. & Nolan, J. (1992, Summer). The relative constancy approach to consumer spending for media. *Journal of Media Economics,* 43-52.

Meadows, J. H. (1997, May). *Body image, women, and media: A media system dependency theory perspective.* Paper presented to the 1997 Mass Communication Division of the International Communication Association Annual Meeting, Montreal, Quebec, Canada.

Moore, G. (2001). *Crossing the Chasm.* New York: Harper Business.

Robinson, L. (1986). *The facts on fax.* Dallas: Steve Davis Publishing.

Rogers, E. (1962). *Diffusion of Innovations.* New York: Free Press.

Rogers, E. (1986). *Communication technology: The new media in society.* New York: Free Press.

Rogers, E. (2003). *Diffusion of Innovations, 3rd Edition.* New York: Free Press.

Rubin, A. (2002). The uses-and-gratifications perspective of media effects. In J. Bryant & D. Zillmann (Eds.). *Media effects: Advances in theory and research.* Mahwah, NJ: Lawrence Earlbaum Associates, pp. 525-548.

Towers, W. (1987, May 18-21). *Replicating perceived helpfulness of radio news and some uses and gratifications.* Paper presented at the Annual Meeting of the Eastern Communication Association, Syracuse, New York.

Wathne, E. & Leos, C. R. (1993). Facsimile machines. In A. E. Grant & K. T. Wilkinson (Eds.). *Communication technology update: 1993-1994.* Austin: Technology Futures, Inc.

Wei, R. (2006). Staying connected while on the move. *New Media and Society, 8* (1), 53-72.

4

The Structure of the Communication Industries

August E. Grant, Ph.D.[*]

T he first factor that many people consider when studying communication technologies is changes in the equipment and utility of the technology. But, as discussed in Chapter 1, it is equally important to study and understand all areas of the technology "umbrella." In editing the *Communication Technology Update* for the past 20 years, one factor stands out as having the greatest amount of change in the short term: the organizational infrastructure of the technology.

The continual flux in the organizational structure of communication industries makes this area the most dynamic area of technology to study. "New" technologies that make a major impact come along only a few times a decade. New products that make a major impact come along once or twice a year. Organizational shifts are constantly happening, making it almost impossible to know all of the players at any given time.

Even though the players are changing, the organizational structure of communication industries is relatively stable. The best way to understand the industry, given the rapid pace of acquisitions, mergers, start-ups, and failures, is to understand its organizational functions. This chapter addresses the organizational structure and explores the functions of those industries, which will help you to understand the individual technologies discussed throughout this book.

In the process of using organizational functions to analyze specific technologies, do not forget to consider that these functions cross national as well as technological boundaries. Most hardware is designed in one country, manufactured in another, and sold around the globe. Although there are cultural and regulatory differences that are addressed in the individual technology chapters later in the book, the organizational functions discussed in this chapter are common internationally.

---

* Professor, College of Mass Communications and Information Studies, University of South Carolina (Columbia, South Carolina).

What's in a Name? The AT&T Story

A good illustration of the importance of understanding organizational functions comes from analyzing the history of AT&T, one of the biggest names in communication of all time. When you hear the name "AT&T," what do you think of? Your answer probably depends on how old you are and where you live. If you live in Florida, you know AT&T as the new name of your local phone company. In New York, it is the name of one of the leading wireless telephone companies. If you are older than 55, you might think of the company's old nickname, "Ma Bell."

The Birth of AT&T

In the study of communication technology over the last century, no name is as prominent as AT&T. The company known today as AT&T is an awkward descendent of the company that once held a monopoly on long-distance telephone service and a near monopoly on local telephone service through the first four decades of the 20th century. The AT&T story is a story of visionaries, mergers, divestiture, and rebirth.

Alexander Graham Bell invented his version of the telephone in 1876, although historians note that he barely beat his competitors to the patent office. His invention soon became an important force in business communication, but diffusion of the telephone was inhibited by the fact that, within 20 years, thousands of entrepreneurs established competing companies to provide telephone service in major metropolitan areas. Initially, these telephone systems were not interconnected, making the choice of telephone company a difficult one, with some businesses needing two or more local phone providers to connect with their clients.

The visionary who solved the problem was Theodore Vail, who realized that the most important function was the interconnection of these telephone companies. As discussed in the following chapter, Vail led American Telephone & Telegraph to provide the needed interconnection, negotiating with the U.S. government to provide "universal service" under heavy regulation in return for the right to operate as a monopoly. Vail brought as many local telephone companies as he could into AT&T, which evolved under the eye of the federal government as a behemoth with three divisions:

◆ AT&T Long Lines—the company that had a virtual monopoly on long distance telephony in the United States.

◆ The Bell System—Local telephone companies providing service to 90% of U.S. subscribers.

◆ Western Electric—A manufacturing company that made equipment needed by the other two divisions, from telephones to switches. (Bell Labs was a part of Western Electric.)

As a monopoly that was generally regulated on a rate-of-return basis (making a fixed profit percentage), AT&T had little incentive—other than that provided by regulators—to hold down costs. The more the company spent, the more it had to charge to make its profit, which grew in proportion with expenses. As a result, the U.S. telephone industry became the envy of the world, known for "five nines" of reliability; that is, the telephone network was available 99.999% of the time. The company also spent millions every year on basic research, with its "Bell Labs" responsible for the invention of many of the most important technologies of the 20th century, including the transistor and the laser.

Divestiture

The monopoly suffered a series of challenges in the 1960s and 1970s that began to break AT&T's monopoly control. First, AT&T lost a suit brought by the "Hush-a-Phone" company, which made a plastic mouthpiece that fit over the AT&T telephone mouthpiece to make it easier to hear a call made in a noisy area (*Hush-a-phone v. AT&T*, 1955; *Hush-a-phone v. U.S.*, 1956). (The idea of a company having to win a lawsuit in order to sell such an innocent item might seem frivolous today, but this suit was the first major crack in AT&T's monopoly armor.) Soon, MCI successfully sued for the right to provide long-distance service between St. Louis and Chicago, allowing businesses to bypass AT&T's long lines (*Microwave Communications, Inc.*, 1969).

Since the 1920s, the Department of Justice (DOJ) had challenged aspects of AT&T's monopoly control, earning a series of consent decrees to limit AT&T's market power and constrain corporate behavior. By the 1970s, it was clear to the antitrust attorneys that AT&Ts ownership of Western Electric inhibited innovation, and the DOJ attempted to force AT&T to divest itself of its manufacturing arm. In a surprising move, AT&T proposed a different divestiture, spinning off all of its local telephone companies into seven new "Baby Bells," keeping the now-competitive long distance service and manufacturing arms. The DOJ agreed, and a new AT&T was born (Dizard, 1989).

Cycles of Expansion & Contraction

After divestiture, the leaner, "new" AT&T attempted to compete in many markets with mixed success; AT&T long distance service remained a national leader, but few people bought the overpriced AT&T personal computers. In the meantime, the seven Baby Bells focused on serving their local markets, with most of them named after the region they served. Nynex served New York and states in the extreme northeast, Bell Atlantic served the mid-Atlantic states, BellSouth served the southeastern states, Ameritech served the Midwest, Southwestern Bell served the south central states, U S West served a set of western states, and Pacific Telesis served California and the far western states.

Over the next two decades, consolidation occurred among these Baby Bells. Nynex and Bell Atlantic merged to create Verizon. U S West was purchased by Qwest Communication and renamed after its new parent, which was, in turn, acquired by CenturyTel as this book went to press in 2010. As discussed below, Southwestern Bell was the most aggressive Baby Bell, ultimately reuniting more than half of the Baby Bells.

In the meantime, AT&T entered the 1990s with a repeating cycle of growth and decline. It acquired NCR Computers in 1991 and McCaw Communications (at that time the largest U.S. cellular telephone company) in 1993. Then, in 1995, it divested itself of its manufacturing arm (which became Lucent Technologies) and the computer company (which took the NCR name). It grew again in 1998 by acquiring TCI, the largest U.S. cable television company, renaming it AT&T Broadband, and then acquired another cable company, MediaOne. In 2001, it sold AT&T Broadband to Comcast, and it spun off its wireless interests into an independent company (AT&T Wireless), which was later acquired by Cingular (a wireless phone company co-owned by Baby Bells SBC and BellSouth) (AT&T, 2008).

The only parts of AT&T remaining were the long distance telephone network and the business services, resulting in a company that was a fraction the size of the AT&T behemoth that had a near monopoly on the telephone industry in the United States just two decades earlier.

Under the leadership of Edward Whitacre, Southwestern Bell became one of the most formidable players in the telecommunications industry. With a visionary style not seen in the telephone industry since the days of Theodore Vail, Whitacre led Southwestern Bell to acquire Baby Bells Pacific Telesis and Ameritech (and a handful of other, smaller telephone companies), renaming itself SBC. Ultimately, SBC merged with BellSouth and purchased what was left of AT&T, then renamed the company AT&T, an interesting case comparable to a child adopting its parent.

Today's AT&T is a dramatically different company with a dramatically different culture than its parent, but the company serves most of the same markets in a much more competitive environment. The lesson is that it is not enough to know the technologies or the company names; you also have to know the history of both in order to understand the role that company plays in the marketplace.

Functions within the Industries

The AT&T story is an extreme example of the complexity of communication industries. These industries are easier to understand by breaking their functions into categories that are common across most of the segments of these industries. Let's start by picking up the heart of the "umbrella perspective" introduced in Chapter 1, the hardware and software. For this discussion, let's use the same definitions used in Chapter 1, with hardware referring to the physical equipment used and software referring to the content or the messages transmitted using these technologies. Some companies produce both equipment and content, but most companies specialize in one or the other.

The next distinction has to be made between "production" and "distribution" of both equipment and content. As these names imply, companies involved in "production" engage in the manufacture of equipment or content, and companies involved in "distribution" are the intermediaries between production and consumers. It is a common practice for some companies to be involved in both production and distribution, but, as discussed below, a large number of companies choose to focus on one or the other.

These two dimensions interact, resulting in separate functions of equipment production, equipment distribution, content production, and content distribution. As discussed below, distribution can be further broken down into national and local distribution. The following section introduces each of these dimensions, which are applied in the subsequent section to help identify the role played by specific companies in communication industries.

One other note: These functions are hierarchical, with production coming before distribution in all cases. Let's say you are interested in creating a new type of telephone, perhaps a "high-definition telephone." You know that there is a market, and you want to be the person who sells it to consumers. But you cannot do so until someone first makes the device. Production always comes before distribution, but you cannot have successful production unless you also have distribution—hence the hierarchy in the model. Figure 4.1 illustrates the general pattern, using the U.S. television industry as an example.

Hardware Path

When you think of "hardware," you typically envision the equipment you handle to use a communication technology. But it is also important to note that there is a second type of hardware for most communication industries—the equipment used to make the messages. Although most consumers do not deal with this equipment, it plays a critical role in the system.

Production

Production hardware is usually more expensive and specialized than other types. Examples in the television industry include TV cameras, microphones, and editing equipment. A successful piece of production equipment might sell only a few hundred or a few thousand units, compared with tens of thousands to millions of units for consumer equipment. The profit margin on each piece of production equipment is usually much higher than on consumer equipment, making it a lucrative market for electronics manufacturing companies.

Figure 4.1

Structure of the Broadcast TV Industry

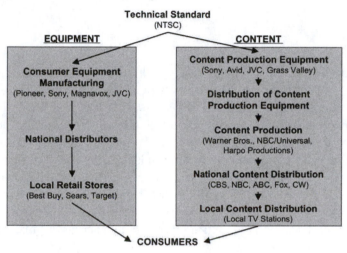

Source: Grant (2008)

CONSUMER HARDWARE

Consumer hardware is the easiest to identify. It includes anything from a digital video recorder (DVR) to a mobile phone or DirecTV satellite dish. A common term used to identify consumer hardware in consumer electronics industries is "CPE," which stands for "customer premises equipment." An interesting side note is that many companies do not actually make their own products, but instead hire manufacturing facilities to make products they design, shipping them directly to distributors. For example, Microsoft does not manufacture the Xbox 360; Flextronics, Wistron, and Celestica do. As you consider communication technology hardware, consider the lesson from Chapter I—people are not usually motivated to buy equipment because of the equipment itself, but because of the content it enables, from the pictures recorded on a camera to the conversations (voice and text!) on a wireless phone to the information and entertainment provided by a high-definition television (HDTV) receiver.

DISTRIBUTION

After a product is manufactured, it has to get to consumers. In the simplest case, the manufacturer sells directly to the consumer, perhaps through a company-owned store or a Web site. In most cases, however, a product will go through multiple organizations, most often with a wholesaler buying it from the manufacturer and selling it, with a mark-up, to a retail store, which also marks up the price before selling it to a consumer. The key point is that few manufacturers control their own distribution channels, instead relying on other companies to get their products to consumers.

Software Path: Production & Distribution

The process that media content goes through to get to consumers is a little more complicated than the process for hardware. The first step is the production of the content itself. Whether the product is movies, music, news, images, etc., some type of equipment must be manufactured and distributed to the individuals or companies who are going to create the content. (That hardware production and distribution goes through a similar process to the one discussed above.) The content must then be created, duplicated, and distributed to consumers or other end users.

The distribution process for media content/software follows the same pattern for hardware. Usually there will be multiple layers of distribution, a national wholesaler that sells the content to a local retailer, which in turn sells it to a consumer.

DISINTERMEDIATION

Although many products go through multiple layers of distribution to get to consumers, information technologies have also been applied to reduce the complexity of distribution. The process of eliminating layers of distribution is called disintermediation (Kottler & Keller, 2005); examples abound of companies that use the Internet to get around traditional distribution systems to sell directly to consumers. Netflix is a great example. Traditionally, DVDs (digital videodiscs) of a movie would be sold by the studio to a national distributor, which would then deliver them to hundreds or thousands of individual movie rental stores, which would then rent or sell them to consumers. (Note: The largest video stores buy directly from the studio, handling both national and local distribution.) Netflix cuts one step out of the distribution process, directly bridging the link from the movie studio and the consumer. (As discussed below, iTunes serves the same function for the music industry, simplifying music distribution.) The result of getting rid of one "middleman" is greater profit for the companies involved, lower costs to the consumer, or both.

Illustrations: HDTV & HD Radio

The emergence of digital broadcasting provides two excellent illustrations of the complexity of the organizational structure of media industries. HDTV and its distant cousin HD radio have had a difficult time penetrating the market because of the need for so many organizational functions to be served before consumers can adopt the technology.

Let's start with the simpler one: HD radio. As illustrated in Figure 4.2, this technology allows existing radio stations to broadcast their current programming (albeit with much higher fidelity), so no changes are needed in the software production area of the model. The only change needed in the software path is that radio stations simply need to add a digital transmitter.

The complexity is related to the consumer hardware needed to receive HD radio signals. One set of companies needs to make the radios, another has to distribute the radios to retail stores and other distribution channels, and stores and distributors have to agree to sell them. The radio industry is therefore taking an active role in pushing diffusion of HD radios throughout the hardware path. In addition to airing thousands of radio commercials promoting HD radio, the industry is promoting distribution of HD radios in new cars (because so much radio listening is done in automobiles). As discussed in Chapter 10, adoption of HD radio has begun, but has been slow because listeners see little advantage in the new technology. However, if the number of receivers increases, broadcasters will have the incentive to begin broadcasting the additional channels available with HD. As with FM radio, programming and receiver sales have to *both* be in place before consumer adoption takes place. Also, as with FM, the technology may take decades to take off.

Figure 4.2
Structure of HD Radio

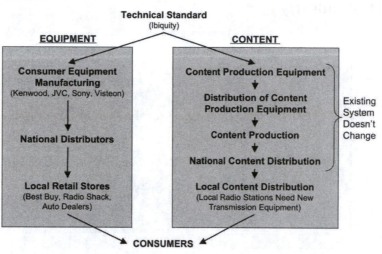

Source: Grant (2008)

The same structure is inherent in the adoption of HDTV, as illustrated in Figure 4.3. Before the first consumer adoption could take place, both programming and receivers (consumer hardware) had to be available. Because a high percentage of primetime television programming was recorded on 35mm film at the time HDTV receivers first went on sale in the United States, that programming could easily be transmitted in high-definition, providing a nucleus of available programming. (On the other hand, local news and network programs shot on video would require entirely new production and editing equipment before they could be distributed to consumers in high-definition. As of mid-2010, little local or syndicated programming is produced in HD.)

As discussed in Chapter 6, the big force behind the diffusion of HDTV and digital TV was a set of regulations issued by the Federal Communications Commission (FCC) that first required stations in the largest markets to begin broadcasting digital signals, then required that all television receivers include the capability to receive digital signals, and finally required that all full-power analog television broadcasting cease on June 12, 2009. In short, the FCC implemented mandates ensuring production and distribution of digital television, easing the path toward both digital TV and HDTV.

Figure 4.3
Structure of HDTV Industry

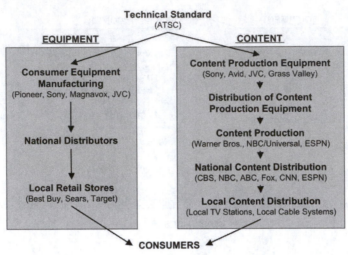

Source: Grant (2008)

From Target to iTunes

One of the best examples of the importance of distribution comes from an analysis of the popular music industry. Traditionally, music was recorded on CDs and audiotapes and shipped to retail stores for sale directly to consumers. At one time, the top three U.S. retailers of music were Target, Walmart, and Best Buy.

Once digital music formats that could be distributed over the Internet were introduced in the late 1990s, dozens of start-up companies created online stores to sell music directly to consumers. The problem was that few of these stores offered the top-selling music. Record companies were leery of the lack of control they had over digital distribution, leaving most of these companies to offer a marginal assortment of music. The situation changed in 2003 when Apple introduced the iTunes store to provide content for its iPods, which had sold slowly since appearing on the market in 2001. Apple obtained contracts with major record companies that allowed them to provide most of the music that was in high demand. Initially, record companies resisted the iTunes distribution model that allowed a consumer to buy a single song for $0.99; they preferred that a person have to buy an entire album of music for $13 to $20 to get the one or two songs they wanted. Record company delays spurred consumers to create and use file-sharing services that allowed listeners to get the music for free—and the record companies ended up losing lots of money. Soon, the $0.99 iTunes model began to look very attractive to the record companies, and they trusted Apple's digital rights management system to protect their music.

Today, as discussed in Chapter 16, iTunes is the number one music retailer in the United States. The music is similar, but the distribution of music today is dramatically different from what it was when this decade began. The change took years of experimentation, and the successful business model that emerged required cooperation from dozens of separate companies serving different roles in the production and distribution process.

Two more points should be made regarding distribution. First, there is typically more profit potential and less risk in being a distributor than a creator (of either hardware or software) because the investment is less and distributors typically earn a percentage of the value of what they sell. Second, distribution channels can become very complicated when multiple layers of distribution are involved; the easiest way to unravel these layers is simply to "follow the money."

Importance of Distribution

As the above discussion indicates, distributors are just as important to new communication technologies as manufacturers and service providers. When studying these technologies, and the reasons for success or failure, the distribution process (including the economics of distribution) must be examined as thoroughly as the product itself.

Diffusion Threshold

Analysis of the elements in Figure 4.1 reveals an interesting dimension—there cannot be any consumer adoption of a new technology until all of the production and distribution functions are served, along both the hardware and software paths. This observation adds a new dimension to Rogers' (2003) diffusion theory. The point at which all functions are served has been identified as the "diffusion threshold," the point at which diffusion of the technology can begin (Grant, 1990).

It is easier for a technology to "take off" and begin diffusing if a single company provides a number of different functions, perhaps combining production and distribution, or providing both national and local distribution. The technical term for owning multiple functions in an industry is "vertical integration," and a vertically integrated company has a disproportionate degree of power and control in the marketplace. Vertical integration is easier said than done, however, because the "core competencies" needed for production and distribution are so different. A company that is great at manufacturing may not have the resources needed to sell the product to end consumers.

Let's consider the newest innovation in radio, HD radio, again (also discussed in Chapter 10). A company such as JVC or Pioneer might handle the first level of distribution, from the manufacturing plant to the retail store, but they do not own and operate their own stores—that is a very different business. They are certainly not involved in owning the radio stations that broadcast HD radio music—that is another set of organizations.

In order for HD radio to become popular, one organization (or set of organizations) has to make the radios, another has to get those radios into stores, a third has to operate the stores, a fourth has to make HD radio transmitters and technical equipment for radio stations, and a fifth has to operate the radio stations. (Fortunately, the content is already available in the form of existing music or talk radio, or even more organizations would have to be involved in order for the first user to be able to listen to HD radio or see any value in buying an HD radio receiver.)

Most companies that would like to grow are more interested in applying their core competencies by buying up competitors and commanding a greater market share, a process known as "horizontal integration." For example, it makes more sense for a company that makes radio receivers to grow by making other electronics rather than by buying radio stations. Similarly, a company that already owns radio stations will probably choose to grow by buying more radio stations rather than by starting to make and sell radios.

The complexity of the structure of most communication industries prevents any one company from serving every needed role. Because so many organizations have to be involved in providing a new technology, many new technologies end up failing. The lesson is that understanding how a new communication technology makes it to market requires comparatively little understanding of the technology itself compared with the understanding needed of the industry in general.

A "Blue" Lesson

One of the best examples of the need to understand (and perhaps exploit) all of the paths illustrated in Figure 4.1 comes from the earliest days of the personal computer. When the PC was invented in the 1970s, most manufacturers used their own operating systems, so that programs and content could not easily be transferred from one type of computer to other types. Many of these manufacturers realized that they needed to find a standard operating system that would allow the same programs on content to be used on computers from different manufacturers, and they agreed on an operating system called CP/M.

Before CP/M could become a standard, however, IBM, the largest U.S. computer manufacturer—mainframe computers, that is—decided to enter the personal computer market. "Big Blue," as IBM was known (for its blue logo and its dominance in mainframe computers, typewriters, and other business equipment) determined that its core competency was making hardware, and they looked for a company to provide them an operating system that would work on their computers. They chose a then-little-known operating system known as MS-DOS, from a small start-up company called Microsoft.

IBM's open architecture allowed other companies to make compatible computers, and dozens of companies entered the market to compete with Big Blue. For a time, IBM dominated the personal computer market, but, over time, competitors steadily made inroads on the market. (Ultimately, IBM sold its personal computer manufacturing business in 2006 to Lenovo, a Chinese company.) The one thing that most of these competitors had in common was that they used Microsoft's operating systems. Microsoft grew…and grew…and grew. (It is also interesting to note that, although Microsoft has dominated the market for software with its operating systems and productivity software such as *Office*, it has been a consistent failure in most areas of hardware manufacturing. Notable failures include Microsoft's routers and home networking hardware, keyboards and mice, and WebTV hardware. The only major success Microsoft has had in manufacturing hardware is with its Xbox video game system, discussed in Chapter 14.)

The lesson is that there is opportunity in all areas of production and distribution of communication technologies. All aspects of production and distribution must be studied in order to understand communication technologies. Companies have to know their own core competencies, but a company can often improve its ability to introduce a new technology by controlling more than one function in the adoption path.

What Are the Industries?

We need to begin our study of communication technologies by defining the industries involved in providing communication-related services in one form or another. Broadly speaking, these can be divided into:

◆ Mass media, including books, newspapers, periodicals, movies, radio, and television.

◆ Telecommunications, including networking and all kinds of telephony (landlines, long distance, wireless, and voice over Internet protocol).

◆ Computers, including hardware and software.

◈ Consumer electronics, including audio and video electronics, video games, and cameras.

◈ *Internet*, including enabling equipment, network providers, content providers, and services.

These industries are introduced in Chapter 2 and individual chapters. At one point, these industries were distinct, with companies focusing on one or two industries. The opportunity provided by digital media and convergence enables companies to operate in numerous industries, and many companies are looking for synergies across industries. Figure 4.4 lists examples of well-known companies in the communication industries, some of which work across many industries, and some of which are (as of this writing) focused on a single industry. Part of the fun in reading this chart is seeing how much has changed since the book was printed in mid-2010.

Figure 4.4

Examples of Major Communication Company Industries, 2010

	TV/Film/Video Production	TV/Film/Video Distribution	Print	Telephone	Wireless	Internet
AT&T		•		•••	•••	••
Disney	•••	•••	•			••
Gannett		•••	•••			
Google		•			•	•••
News Corp.	•••	•••	•••			••
Sony	•••	•				•
Time Warner	•••	•••	•			••
Verizon				•••	•••	••
Viacom	•••	•••	•			••
Yahoo!						•••

The number of dots is proportional to the importance of this business to each company.   *Source:* Grant (2010)

There is a risk in discussing specific organizations in a book such as this one; in the time between when the book is written and when it is published, there are certain to be changes in the organizational structure of the industries. For example, as this chapter was being written in early 2010, Comcast had proposed a purchase of NBC/Universal from General Electric. By the time you read this, Comcast may have completed the purchase, or Comcast itself might be acquired by another company.

Fortunately, mergers and takeovers of that magnitude do not happen that often—only a couple a year! The major players are more likely to acquire other companies than to be acquired, so it is fairly safe (but not completely safe) to identify the major players and then analyze the industries in which they are doing business. As in the AT&T story earlier in this chapter, the specific businesses a company is in can change dramatically over the course of a few years.

Future Trends

The focus of this book is on changing technologies. It should be clear that some of the most important changes to track are changes in the organizational structure of media industries. The remainder of this chapter projects organizational trends to watch to help you predict the trajectory of existing and future technologies.

Disappearing Newspapers

For decades, newspapers were the dominant mass medium, commanding revenues, consumer attention, and significant political and economic power. As the second decade of the 21st century is beginning, however, newspaper publishers are reconsidering their core business. Noted newspaper researcher Philip Meyer (2006) has even predicted the demise of the newspaper, projecting (with a smile) that the last printed newspaper reader will disappear in the first quarter of 2043.

Before starting the countdown clock, it is necessary to define what we mean by a "newspaper publisher." If a newspaper publisher is defined as an organization that communicates and obtains revenue by smearing ink on dead trees, then Meyer's general prediction is more likely than not. If, however, a newspaper publisher is defined as an organization that gathers news and advertising messages, distributing them via a wide range of available media, then newspaper publishers should be quite healthy through the century.

The current problem is that there is no comparable revenue model for delivery of news and advertising through new media that approaches the revenues available from smearing ink on dead trees. It is a bad news/good news situation. The bad news is that traditional newspaper readership and revenues are both declining. Readership is suffering because of competition from the Web and other new media, with younger cohorts increasingly ignoring print in favor of other news sources. Advertising revenues are suffering for two reasons. The decline in readership and competition from new media are impacting revenues from display advertising. More significant is the loss in revenues from classified advertising, which at one point comprised up to one-third of newspaper revenues.

The good news is that newspapers remain profitable, at least on a cash flow basis, with gross margins of 10% to 20%. This profit margin is one that many industries would envy. But many newspaper companies borrowed extensively to expand their reach, with interest payments often exceeding these gross profits. Stockholders in newspaper publishers have been used to much higher profit margins, and the stock prices of newspaper companies have been punished for the decline in profits.

Some companies such as Belo reacted by divesting themselves of their newspapers in favor of TV and new media investments. Some newspaper publishers are using the opportunity to buy up other newspapers; consider McClatchy's 2006 purchase of the majority of Knight-Ridder's newspapers (McClatchy, 2008).

Gannett, on the hand, is taking the boldest, and potentially the riskiest, strategy by aggressively transforming both their newspaper and television newsrooms into "Information Centers," where the goal is to be platform agnostic, getting news out in any available medium as quickly as possible. According to Gannett CEO Craig Dubow, the goal is to deliver the news and content anywhere the consumer is, and then solve the revenue question later (Gahran, 2006). Gannett's approach is a risky one, but it follows the model that has worked for new media in the past—the revenue always follows the audience, and the companies that are first to reach an audience through a new medium are disproportionately likely to profit from their investments.

Advertiser-Supported Media

For advertiser-supported media organizations, the primary concern is the impact of the Internet and other new media on revenues. As discussed above, some of the loss in revenues is due to loss of advertising dollars (including classified advertising), but that loss is not experienced equally by all advertiser-supported media.

The Internet is especially attractive to advertisers because online advertising systems have the most comprehensive reporting of any advertising medium. For example, an advertiser using the Google AdWords system discussed in Chapter 1 gets comprehensive reports on the effectiveness of every message—but "effectiveness" is defined by these advertisers as an immediate response such as a click-through. As Grant and Wilkinson (2007) discuss, not all advertising is this type of "call-to-action" advertising. There is another type of advertising that is equally important—image advertising, which does not demand immediate results, but rather works over time to build brand identity and increase the likelihood of a future purchase.

Any medium can carry any type of advertising, but image advertising is more common on television (especially national television) and magazines, and call-to-action advertising is more common in newspapers. As a result, newspapers, at least in the short term, are more likely to be impacted by the increase in Internet advertising. Interestingly, local advertising is more likely to be call-to-action advertising, but local advertisers have been slower than national advertisers to move to the Internet, most likely because of the global reach of the Internet. This paradox could be seen as an opportunity for an entrepreneur wishing to earn a million or two by exploiting a new advertising market.

The "Mobile Revolution"

Another important trend that can help you analyze media organizations is the shift toward mobile communication technologies. Companies that are positioned to produce and distribute content and technology that further enable the "mobile revolution" are likely to have increased prospects for growth.

Areas to watch include mobile Internet access (involving new hardware and software, provided by a mixture of existing and new organizations), mobile advertising, new applications of GPS technology, and a host of new applications designed to take advantage of Internet access available any time, anywhere.

Consumers—Time Spent Using Media

Another piece of good news for media organizations in general is the fact that the amount of time consumers are spending with media is increasing, with much of that increase coming from simultaneous media use (Papper, et al., 2009). Advertiser-supported media thus have more "audience" to sell, and subscription-based media have more prospects for revenue. Furthermore, new technologies are increasingly targeting specific messages at specific consumers, increasing the efficiency of message delivery for advertisers and potentially reducing the clutter of irrelevant advertising for consumers. Already, advertising services such as Google's Double-Click and Google's AdWords provide ads that are targeted to a specific person or the specific content on a Web page, greatly increasing their effectiveness. Imagine a future where every commercial on TV that you see is targeted—and is interesting—to you! Technically, it is possible, but the lessons of previous technologies suggest that the road to customized advertising will be a meandering one.

Principle of Relative Constancy

On the other hand, the potential revenue from consumers is limited by the fact that consumers devote a limited proportion of their disposable income to media, the phenomenon discussed in Chapter 3 as the

"Principle of Relative Constancy." The implication is that emerging companies and technologies have to wrest market share and revenue from established companies. To do that, they cannot be just as good as the incumbents. Rather, they have to be faster, smaller, less expensive, more versatile, or in some way better so that consumers will have the motivation to shift spending from existing media.

Conclusions

The structure of the media system may be the most dynamic area in the study of new communication technologies, with new industries and organizations constantly emerging and merging. In the following chapters, organizational developments are therefore given a significant amount of attention. Be warned, however, between the time these chapters are written and published, there is likely to be some change in the organizational structure of each technology discussed in this book. To keep up with these developments, visit the *Communication Technology Update and Fundamentals* home page at www.tfi.com/ctu.

Bibliography

AT&T. (2008). *Milestones in AT&T history.* Retrieved May 4, 2008 from http://www.corp.att.com/history/ milestones.html.

Dizard, W. (1989). *The coming information age: An overview of technology, economics, and politics, 2nd ed.* New York: Longman.

Gahran, A. (2006). Gannett "Information Centers"—Good for daily journalism? *Poynter Online E-Media Tidbits.* Retrieved May 4, 2008 from http://www.poynter.org/dg.lts/id.31/aid.113411/column.htm.

Grant, A. E. (1990, April). *The "pre-diffusion of HDTV: Organizational factors and the "diffusion threshold.* Paper presented to the Annual Convention of the Broadcast Education Association, Atlanta.

Grant, A. E. & Wilkinson, J. S. (2007, February). *Lessons for communication technologies from Web advertising.* Paper presented to the Mid-Winter Conference of the Association of Educators in Journalism and Mass Communication, Reno.

Hush-A-Phone Corp. v. AT&T, et al. (1955). FCC Docket No. 9189. Decision and order (1955). 20 FCC 391.

Hush-A-Phone Corp. v. United States. (1956). 238 F. 2d 266 (D.C. Cir.). Decision and order on remand (1957). 22 FCC 112.

Kottler, P. & Keller, K. L. (2005). *Marketing management, 12th ed.* Englewood Cliffs, NJ: Prentice-Hall.

McClatchy. (2008). *About the McClatchy Company.* Retrieved May 7, 2008 from http://www.mcclatchy.com/100/story/ 179.html.

Microwave Communications, Inc. (1969). FCC Docket No. 16509. Decision, 18 FCC 2d 953.

Meyer, P. (2006). *The vanishing newspaper: Saving journalism in the information age.* Columbia, MO: University of Missouri Press.

Papper, R. E., Holmes, M. A., & Popovich, M. N. (2009). Middletown media studies II: Observing consumer interactions with media. In A. E. Grant & J. S. Wilkinson (Eds.) *Understanding media convergence: The state of the field.* New York: Oxford.

Rogers, E. M. (2003). *Diffusion of innovations, 5th ed.* New York: Free Press.

5

COMMUNICATION Policy & TECHNOLOGY

Lon Berquist, M.A.[*]

Throughout its history, U.S. communication policy has been shaped by evolving communication technologies. As a new communication technology is introduced into society, it is often preceded by an idealized vision, or Blue Sky perspective, of how the technology will positively impact economic opportunities, democratic participation, and social inclusion. Due, in part, to this perspective, government policymakers traditionally look for policies and regulations that will foster the wide diffusion of the emerging technology. At the same time, however, U.S. policy typically displays a light regulatory touch, promoting a free-market approach that attempts to balance the economic interests of media and communication industries, the First Amendment, and the rights of citizens.

Indeed, much of the recent impetus for media deregulation was directly related to communication technologies as "technological plenty is forcing a widespread reconsideration of the role competition can play in broadcast regulation" (Fowler & Brenner, 1982, p. 209). From a theoretical perspective, some see new communication technologies as technologies of freedom where "freedom is fostered when the means of communication are dispersed, decentralized, and easily available" (Pool, 1983, p. 5). Others fear technologies favor government and private interests and become technologies of control (Gandy, 1989). Still others argue that technologies are merely neutral in how they shape society. No matter the perspective, the purpose of policy and regulation is to allow society to shape the use of communication technologies to best serve the citizenry.

BACKGROUND

The First Amendment is a particularly important component of U.S. communication policy, balancing freedom of the press with the free speech rights of citizens. The First Amendment was created at a time when the most sophisticated communication technology was the printing press. Over time, the notion of "press" has evolved with the introduction of new communication technologies. The First Amendment has evolved as well, with varying degrees of protection for the traditional press, broadcasting, cable television, and the Internet.

Communication policy is essentially the balancing of national interests and the interests of the communications industry (van Cuilenburg & McQuail, 2003). In the United States, communication policy is often

---

[*] Telecommunications and Information Policy Institute, University of Texas at Austin (Austin, Texas).

shaped in reaction to the development of a new technology. As a result, policies vary according to the particular communication policy regime: press, common carrier, broadcasting, cable TV, and the Internet. Napoli (2001) characterizes this policy tendency as a "technologically particularistic" approach leading to distinct policy and regulatory structures for each new technology. Thus, the result is differing First Amendment protections for the printed press, broadcasting, cable television, and the Internet (Pool, 1983).

In addition to distinct policy regimes based on technology, scholars have recognized differing types of regulation that impact programming, the industry market and economics, and the transmission and delivery of programming and information. These include content regulation, structural regulation, and technical regulation. Content regulation refers to the degree to which a particular industry enjoys First Amendment protection. For example, in the United States, the press is recognized as having the most First Amendment protection, and there certainly is no regulatory agency to oversee printing. Cable television has limited First Amendment protection, while broadcasting has the most limitations on its' First Amendment rights. This regulation is apparent in the type of programming rules and regulations imposed by the Federal Communication Commission (FCC) on broadcast programming that is not imposed on cable television programming.

Structural regulation addresses market power within (horizontal integration) and across (vertical integration) media industries. Federal media policy has long established the need to promote diversity of programming by promoting diversity of ownership. The *Telecommunications Act of 1996* changed media ownership limits for the national and local market power of radio, television, and cable television industries; however, the FCC is given the authority to review and revise these rules. Structural regulation includes limitations or permissions to enter communication markets. For example, the *Telecommunications Act of 1996* opened up the video distribution and telephony markets by allowing telephone companies to provide cable television service and for cable television systems to offer telephone service (Parsons & Frieden, 1998).

Technical regulation needs prompted the initial development of U.S. communication regulation in the 1920s, as the fledgling radio industry suffered from signal interference while numerous stations transmitted without any government referee (Starr, 2004). Under FCC regulation, broadcast licenses are allowed to transmit at a certain power, or wattage, on a precise frequency within a particular market. Cable television systems and satellite transmission also follow some technical regulation to prevent signal interference.

Finally, in addition to technology-based policy regimes and regulation types, communication policy is guided by varying jurisdictional regulatory bodies. Given the global nature of satellites, both international (International Telecommunications Union) and national (FCC) regulatory commissions have a vested interest in satellite transmission. Regulation of U.S. broadcasting is exclusively the domain of the federal government through the FCC. The telephone industry is regulated primarily at the federal level through the FCC, but also with regulations imposed by state public utility commissions. Cable television, initially regulated through local municipal franchises, is regulated both at the federal level and the local municipal level (Parsons & Frieden, 1998). Increasingly, however, state governments are developing statewide cable television franchises, preempting local franchises (Eleff, 2006).

The Evolution of Communication Technologies

Telegraph

Although the evolution of technologies has influenced the policymaking process in the United States, many of the fundamental characteristics of U.S. communication policy were established early in the history of communication technology deployment, starting with the telegraph. There was much debate on how best to develop the telegraph. For many congressmen and industry observers, the telegraph was viewed as a natural extension of the Post Office, while others favored government ownership based on the successful European model as the only way to counter the power of a private monopoly (DuBoff, 1984). In a prelude to the implementation of universal service for the telephone (and the current discussion of a "digital divide"), Congress decreed that, "Where the rates are high and facilities poor, as in this country, the number of persons who use the telegraph freely, is limited. Where the rates are low and the facilities are great, as in Europe, the telegraph is extensively used by all classes for all kinds of business" (Lubrano, 1997, p. 102).

Despite the initial dominance of Western Union, there were over 50 separate telegraph companies operating in the United States in 1851. Interconnecting telegraph lines throughout the nation became a significant policy goal of federal, state, and local governments. No geographic area wanted to be disconnected from the telegraph network and its promise of enhanced communication and commerce. Eventually, in 1887, the *Interstate Commerce Act* was enacted, and the policy model of a regulated privately-owned communication system was initiated and formal federal regulation began. Early in the development of communication policy, the tradition of creating communications infrastructure through government aid to private profit-making entities was established (Winston, 1998).

Telephone

Similar to the development of the telegraph, the diffusion of the telephone was slowed by competing, unconnected companies serving their own interests. Although AT&T dominated most urban markets, many independent telephone operators and rural cooperatives provided service in smaller towns and rural areas. Since there was no interconnection among the various networks, some households and businesses were forced to have dual service in order to communicate (Starr, 2004). As telephone use spread in the early 1900s, states and municipalities began regulating and licensing operators as public utilities, although Congress authorized the Interstate Commerce Commission (ICC) to regulate interstate telephone service in 1910. Primarily an agency devoted to transportation issues, the ICC never became a major historical player in communication policy. However, two important phrases originated with the commission and the related *Transportation Act of 1920*. The term, common carrier, originally used to describe railroad transportation, was used to classify the telegraph and eventually the telephone (Pool, 1983). Common carriage law required carriers to serve their customers without discrimination. The other notable phrase utilized in transportation regulation was a requirement to serve the "public interest, convenience, or necessity" (Napoli, 2001). This nebulous term was adopted in subsequent broadcast legislation, and continues to guide the FCC even today.

As telephone use increased, it became apparent that there was a need for greater interconnection among competing operators, or the development of some national unifying agreement. In 1907, AT&T President Theodore Vail promoted a policy with the slogan, "One system, one policy, universal service" (Starr, 2004, p. 207). There are conflicting accounts of Vail's motivations: whether it was a sincere call for a national network available to all, or merely a ploy to protect AT&T's growing power in the telephone industry (Napoli, 2001). Eventually, the national network envisioned by Vail became a reality, as AT&T was given the monopoly power, under strict regulatory control, to build and maintain local and long distance telephone service throughout the nation. Of course, this regulated monopoly was ended decades ago, but the concept of universal service as a significant component of communication policy remains today.

Broadcasting

While U.S. policymakers pursued an efficient national network for telephone operations, they developed radio broadcasting to primarily serve local markets. Before the federal government imposed regulatory control over radio broadcasting in 1927, the industry suffered from signal interference and an uncertain financial future. The *Federal Radio Act* imposed technical regulation on use of spectrum and power, allowing stations to develop a stable local presence. Despite First Amendment concerns about government regulation of radio, the scarcity of spectrum was considered an adequate rationale for licensing stations. In response to concerns about freedom of the press, the *Radio Act* prohibited censorship by the Radio Commission, but the stations understood the power of the commission to license implied inherent censorship (Pool, 1983). In 1934, Congress passed the *Communication Act of 1934*, combining regulation of telecommunications and broadcasting by instituting a new Federal Communications Commission.

The *Communication Act* essentially reiterated the regulatory thrust of the 1927 *Radio Act*, maintaining that broadcasters serve the public interest. This broad concept of "public interest" has stood as the guiding force in developing communication policy principles of competition, diversity, and localism (Napoli, 2001; Alexander & Brown, 2007). Rules and regulations established to serve the public interest for radio transferred to television when it entered the scene. Structural regulation limited ownership of stations, technical regulation required tight control of broadcast transmission, and indirect content regulation led to limitations on station broadcast of network programming and even fines for broadcast of indecent material (Pool, 1983). One of the most controversial content regulations was the vague Fairness Doctrine, established in 1949, that required broadcasters to present varying viewpoints on issues of public importance (Napoli, 2001). Despite broadcasters' challenges to FCC content regulation on First Amendment grounds, the courts defended the commission's ability to limit network control over programming (*NBC v. United States*, 1943) and the Fairness Doctrine (*Red Lion Broadcasting v. FCC*, 1969). In 1985, the FCC argued the Fairness Doctrine was no longer necessary given the increased media market competition, due in part to the emergence of new communication technologies (Napoli, 2001).

Historically, as technology advanced, the FCC sought ways to increase competition and diversity in broadcasting with AM radio, UHF television, low-power TV, low-power FM, and more recently, digital television.

Cable Television and Direct Broadcast Satellite

Since cable television began simply as a technology to retransmit distant broadcast signals to rural or remote locations, early systems sought permission or franchises from the local authorities to lay cable to reach homes. As cable grew, broadcasters became alarmed with companies making revenue off their programming, and they lobbied against the new technology. Early on, copyrights became the major issue, as broadcasters complained that retransmission of their signals violated their copyrights. The courts sided with cable operators, but Congress passed compulsory license legislation that forced cable operators to pay royalty fees to broadcasters (Pool, 1983). Because cable television did not utilize the public airwaves, courts rebuffed the FCC's attempt to regulate cable.

In the 1980s, the number of cable systems exploded and the practice of franchising cable systems increasingly was criticized by the cable industry as cities demanded more concessions in return for granting rights-of-way access and exclusive multi-year franchises. The *Cable Communications Act of 1984* was passed to formalize the municipal franchising process while limiting some of their rate regulation authority. The act also authorized the FCC to evaluate cable competition within markets (Parsons & Frieden, 1998).

After that, cable rates increased dramatically. Congress reacted with the *Cable Television Consumer Protection and Competition Act of 1992*. With the 1992 Cable Act, rate regulation returned with the FCC given authority to regulate basic cable rates. To protect broadcasters and localism principles, the act included "must carry" and "retransmission consent" rules that allowed broadcasters to negotiate with cable systems for carriage (discussed in more detail in Chapter 7). Although challenged on First Amendment grounds, the courts eventually found that the FCC had a legitimate interest in protecting local broadcasters (*Turner Broadcasting v. FCC*, 1997).

To support the development of direct broadcast satellites (DBS), the 1992 act prohibited cable television programmers from withholding channels from DBS and other prospective competitors. As with cable television, DBS operators have been subject to must-carry and retransmission consent rules. The *1999 Satellite Home Viewers Improvement Act* (SHIVA) required and, more recently, the *Satellite Home Viewer Extension and Reauthorization Act* (SHVER) reconfirmed that DBS operators must carry all local broadcast signals within a local market if they choose to carry one (FCC, 2005). DBS operators challenged this in court, but as in *Turner Broadcasting v. FCC*, the courts upheld the FCC rule (Frieden, 2005).

Policies to promote the development of cable television and direct broadcast satellites have become important components of the desire to enhance media competition and video program diversity, while, at the same time, preserving localism principles within media markets.

Convergence and the Internet

The *Telecommunications Act of 1996* was a significant recognition of the impact of technological innovation and convergence occurring within the media and telecommunications industries. Because of that recognition, Congress discontinued many of the cross-ownership and service restrictions that had prevented telephone operators from offering video service and cable systems from providing telephone service (Parsons & Frieden, 1998). The primary purpose of the 1996 Act was to "promote competition and reduce regulation in order to secure lower prices and higher-quality service for American telecommunications consumers and encourage the rapid deployment of new telecommunications technologies" (*Telecommunications Act of 1996*). Competition was expected by opening up local markets to facilities-based competition and deregulating rates for cable television and telephone service to let the market work its magic. The 1996 Act also opened up competition in the local exchange telephone markets and loosened a range of media ownership restrictions.

In 1996, the Internet was a growing phenomenon, and some in Congress were concerned with the adult content available online. In response, along with passing the act, Congress passed the *Communication Decency Act* (CDA) to make it a felony to transmit obscene or indecent material to minors. The Supreme Court struck down the CDA on First Amendment grounds in *Reno v. ACLU* (Napoli, 2001). Congress continued to pursue a law protecting children from harmful material on the Internet with the *Child Online Protection Act* (COPA), passed in 1998; however, federal courts have found it, too, unconstitutional due to First Amendment concerns (McCullagh, 2007). It is noteworthy that the courts consider the Internet's First Amendment protection more similar to the press, rather than broadcasting or telecommunications (Warner, 2008).

Similarly, from a regulatory perspective, the Internet does not fall under any traditional regulatory regime such as telecommunications, broadcasting, or cable television. Instead, the Internet is considered an "information service" and therefore not subject to regulation (Oxman, 1999). There are, however, policies in place that indirectly impact the Internet. For example, section 706 of the *Telecommunications Act of 1996* requires the FCC to "encourage the deployment on a reasonable and timely basis of advanced telecommunications capability to all Americans;" with advanced telecommunications essentially referring to broadband Internet connectivity (Grant & Berquist, 2000).

Recent Developments

Network Neutrality

In 2005, AT&T CEO Edward Whitacre, Jr. created a stir when he suggested Google and Vonage should not expect to use his pipes for free (Yang, 2005). Internet purists insist the Internet should remain open and unfettered, as originally designed, and decried the notion that broadband providers might discriminate by the type and amount of data content streaming through their pipes. Users of Internet service are concerned that, as more services become available via the Web such as video streaming and voice over IP (VoIP), Internet service providers (ISPs) will become gatekeepers limiting content and access to information (Gilroy, 2007).

In 2007, the FCC received complaints accusing Comcast of delaying Web traffic on its cable modem service for the popular file sharing site BitTorrent (Kang, 2008). Because of the uproar among consumer groups, the FCC held hearings on the issue and ordered Comcast to end its discriminatory network management practices (FCC, 2008). Although Comcast complied with the order and discontinued interfering with peer-to-peer traffic like BitTorrent, it challenged the FCC's authority in court. In April 2010, the U.S. Court of Appeals for the D.C. Circuit determined that the FCC had failed to show it had the statutory authority to regulate an Internet service provider's network practices and vacated the order (*Comcast v. FCC*, 2010). Because broadband service is an unregulated information service, the FCC argued it had the power to regulate under its broad "ancillary" authority highlighted in Title I of the Telecommunications Act. The court's rejection of the FCC argument has disheartened network neutrality proponents who fear the court's decision will encourage broadband service providers to restrict network data traffic, undermining the traditional openness of the Internet.

Media and Communication Ownership

The *Telecommunications Act of 1996* requires the FCC to periodically review broadcast ownership rules under Section 202, and determine if the rules continue to serve the public interest and are necessary as a result of competition. In 2003, the FCC completed its *2002 Biennial Review Order* after completing a series of studies on broadcast ownership and program diversity (FCC, 2003). The order loosened ownership rules in such a significant way that a single entity could own a newspaper, a cable television system, three television stations, and eight radio stations within a single market (Watson & Chang, 2008). Media activists and civic groups criticized the report for lacking public input, while scholars questioned the methodology of the studies supporting the report conducted primarily by FCC staff (Rice, 2008).

Many of the groups objecting to the FCC order formed a coalition, the Prometheus Radio Project, to challenge the FCC in court. The result was a rejection of the FCC order by the Third Circuit Court of Appeals in June 2004 (*Prometheus v. FCC*, 2004). The court opinion was critical of the FCC's empirical basis for the ownership changes, and the FCC has responded with revised research of media ownership issues, although Congress has changed the Section 202 review period from two to four years.

As part of its 2006 Quadrennial Review of media ownership, the FCC revisited the longstanding ban on newspapers owning a broadcast station within the same market and reviewed national cable system ownership. Responding to the growth of cable giant Comcast Communication, they reconfirmed the rule that no one entity can control more than 30% of cable systems nationwide. The other determination, which proved more controversial, relaxed newspaper/broadcast cross-ownership within the top 20 markets allowing a company to operate both a newspaper and a television or radio station in the same market (Labaton, 2007).

While the courts have often reversed FCC rulemaking, Congress, too, has exerted its power by revisiting broadcast ownership statutes. In 2003, when the FCC raised the national television ownership limit to 45% of the national market, Congress responded by initially restoring it to the previous 35% limit. However, in final form, the statute set the limit at 39% of the national market. As critics of the new cap pointed out, the 39% level protected the existing market share for Viacom (38.8%) and News Corporation (37.7%), thereby shielding incumbent media corporations from violating the rule (Watson & Chang, 2008).

Broadband

In response to a weakening U.S. economy, Congress passed the American Recovery and Reinvestment Act (ARRA) of 2009. Stimulus funds were appropriated for a wide range of infrastructure grants, including broadband, to foster economic development. Congress earmarked $7.2 billion to encourage broadband deployment, particularly in unserved and underserved regions of the country. The U.S. Department of Agriculture Rural Utility Service (RUS) was provided with $2.5 billion to award Broadband Initiatives Program (BIP) grants, while the National Telecommunications and Information Administration (NTIA) was funded with $4.7 billion to award Broadband Technology Opportunity Program (BTOP) grants. In addition, Congress appropriated funding for the Broadband Data Improvement Act, legislation that was approved during the Bush Administration in 2008, but lacked the necessary funding for implementation. Finally, as part of ARRA, Congress directed the FCC to develop a *National Broadband Plan* that addressed broadband deployment, adoption, affordability, and the use of broadband to advance healthcare, education, civic participation, energy, public safety, job creation, and investment.

In preparing the *National Broadband Plan*, the FCC commissioned a number of studies to determine the current state of broadband deployment in the United.States. In analyzing U.S. broadband adoption, the FCC determined 65% of U.S. adults use broadband (Horrigan, 2010); however, researchers forecast regions around the country, particularly rural areas, will continue to suffer from poor broadband service due to lack of service options or slow broadband speeds (Atkinson & Schultz, 2009). In examining foreign broadband markets and their success with broadband deployment and enhanced bandwidth capability, the Berkman Center for Internet and Society (2009) suggested U.S. policymakers should consider open-access policies adopted throughout Asia and Europe, to foster competition among U.S. broadband service providers.

The Berkman Center report used international broadband data from the Organisation for Economic Co-operation and Development (OECD) to determine the United States ranked 15th among developed nations for broadband penetration (see Table 5.1). Other OECD reports show the United States ranked a lowly 23th for average advertised download speed (14.6 Mb/s), with top- ranked Japan offering significantly greater broadband speed (107.7 Mb/s), followed by Portugal (103.7 Mb/s), France (54.6 Mb/s), Korea (52.8), and Netherlands (33.7 Mb/s) (OECD, 2009). In terms of price, the U.S. average cost of $49.25/month for broadband ranked 20th according to OECD data, with Greece offering the lowest average price at $31.60.

The *National Broadband Plan* highlights a number of strategies and goals to connect America to broadband, which is defined as "the great infrastructure challenge of the 21st century" (FCC, 2010, p.3). Among the strategies are plans to:

◈ Design policies to ensure robust competition.

◈ Ensure efficient allocation and use of government-owned and government-influenced assets

◈ Reform current universal service mechanisms to support deployment of broadband.

◈ Reform laws, policies, standards and incentives to maximize the benefits of broadband for government priorities, such as public education and health care.

The targeted goals of the plan through 2020 include 1) at least 100 million homes should have affordable access to download speeds of 100 Mb/s and upload speeds of 50 Mb/s, 2) the United States should lead the world in mobile innovation with the fastest and most extensive wireless network in the world, 3) every American should have affordable access to robust broadband service, and the means and skills to subscribe, 4) every American community should have affordable access to at least 1 Gb/s broadband service to schools, hospitals, and government buildings, 5) every first responder should have access to a nationwide, wireless, interoperable broadband public safety network, and 6) every American should be able to use broadband to track and manage their real-time energy consumption (FCC 2010).

The most far reaching components of the plan include freeing 500 MHz of wireless spectrum, including existing television frequencies, for wireless broadband use; and reforming the current telephone Universal Service Fund to support broadband deployment.

Table 5.1
International Broadband Penetration

Country	Broadband Penetration*
Netherlands	38.1
Denmark	37.0
Norway	34.5
Switzerland	33.8
Korea	32.8
Iceland	32.8
Sweden	31.6
Luxembourg	31.3
Finland	29.7
Canada	29.7
Germany	29.3
France	29.1
United Kingdom	28.9
Belgium	28.4
United States	26.7

* Broadband access per 100 inhabitants   *Source:* OECD (2009)

Factors to Watch

As technology continues to converge, it is apparent that the traditional policy regimes may no longer be so easily distinguished, leading to a convergence of policy (van Cuilenburg & McQuail, 2003). The *Telecommunications Act of 1996* was a first attempt at rearranging policy and regulation around new communication technologies, more than 60 years after the initial *Communication Act of 1934.* Over 10 years have passed since enactment of the 1996 law, and technologies are significantly more advanced while policies and regulation have remained stagnant. It is unlikely that Congress will wait another 60 years to revisit the *Communications Act,* and some legislators (Watson & Chang, 2008) as well and telecommunications firms (Poirier, 2010) have called for revisiting the 1996 legislation.

As the FCC pursues the *National Broadband Plan,* it is mindful of the U.S. Court of Appeals decision that has limited its authority for regulating broadband service. Some industry observers suggest the FCC should reclassify broadband service as a common carrier, subject to Title II regulation under the Telecommunications Act (Schatz & Sheth, 2010). Broadcasters are concerned about spectrum reserved for television being reclaimed by the FCC for wireless broadband services, and Congress has questioned the appropriateness of the provision in the plan (Eggerton, 2010). The FCC's *National Broadband Plan* was authorized by Congress, and the final direction of any significant broadband policy will be guided by Congressional action. Still, the plan offers one of the most significant communication policy plans in the history of the FCC, and the interaction of Congress, the FCC, and the communications industry will ultimately determine its fate.

The FCC has already issued a Public Notice to consider whether a Notice of Inquiry (NOI) should be issued to explore the appropriate policies to facilitate and respond to the transition from traditional public switched telephone network (PSTN) technology and services to an Internet Protocol (IP) based communications environment. As the notice states, "No longer is broadband simply another service—it is a growing platform over which the consumer accesses a multitude of services, including voice, data, video in an integrated way across applications and providers" (FCC, 2009, p. 1).

As communication policy is reshaped to accommodate new technologies, policymakers must continue to explore ways to serve the public interest. Despite the limitations of communication policy and regulation in promoting communication technologies, the successful diffusion of technologies is evident in the wide range of technologies presented in this book.

Bibliography

Alexander, P. J. & Brown, K. (2007). Policy making and policy tradeoffs: Broadcast media regulation in the United States. In P. Seabright & J. von Hagen (Eds.). *The economic regulation of broadcasting markets: Evolving technology and the challenges for policy.* Cambridge: Cambridge University Press. *American Recovery and Reinvestment Act of 2009,* Pub. L. No. 111-5, 123 Stat. 115 (2009). Retrieved April 7, 2010 from http://www.gpo.gov/fdsys/pkg/PLAW-111publ5/pdf/PLAW-111publ5.pdf.

Atkinson, R.C. & Schultz, I.E. (2009). Broadband in America: Where it is and where it is going (according to broadband service providers). Retrieved April 7, 2010 from http://broadband.gov/docs/Broadband_in_America.pdf.

Berkman Center for Internet and Society. (2009). Next generation connectivity: A review of broadband Internet transitions and policy from around the world. Retrieved April 7, 2010 from http://www.fcc.gov/stage/pdf/Berkman_Center_Broadband_Study_13Oct09.pdf.

The Broadband Data Improvement Act of 2008, Pub. L. 110-385, 122 Stat. 4096 (2008). Retrieved April 7, 2010 from http://www.ntia.doc.gov/advisory/onlinesafety/BroadbandData_PublicLaw110-385.pdf.

Comcast v. FCC. No. 08-1291 (D.C. Cir., 2010). Retrieved April 12, 2010 from http://hraunfoss.fcc.gov/edocs_public/attachmatch/DOC-297356A1.pdf.

DuBoff, R. B. (1984). The rise of communications regulation: The telegraph industry, 1844-1880. Journal of Communication, 34 (3), 52-66.

Eggerton, J. (2010, April 14). Boucher: Broadband plan should not force broadcasters off spectrum. *Broadcasting & Cable.* Retrieved April 15, 2010 from http://www.broadcastingcable.com/article/451469-Boucher_Broadband_Plan_Should_Not_Force_Broadcasters_Off_Spectrum.php.

Eleff, B. (2006, November). *New state cable TV franchising laws.* Minnesota House of Representatives Research Department. Retrieved April 6, 2008 from http://www.house.leg.state.mn.us/hrd/pubs/cablelaw.pdf.

Federal Communications Commission. (2003, July). *2002 biennial regulatory review—Review of the commission's broadcast ownership rules and other rules adopted pursuant to Section 202 of the* Telecommunications Act of 1996. Retrieved April 6, 2008 from http://hraunfoss.fcc.gov/edocs_public/attachmatch/FCC-03-127A1.pdf.

Federal Communications Commission. (2005, September 8). *Retransmission consent and exclusivity rules: Report to Congress pursuant to section 208 of the* Satellite Home Viewer Extension and Reauthorization Act of 2004. Retrieved April 8, 2008 from http://hraunfoss.fcc.gov/edocs_public/attachmatch/DOC-260936A1.pdf.

Federal Communications Commission. (2008, August 20). *Memorandum opinion and order* (FCC 08-183). Broadband Industry Practices. Retrieved April 8, 2008 from http://hraunfoss.fcc.gov/edocs_public/attachmatch/FCC-08-183A1.pdf.

Federal Communications Commission. (2009). Comment sought on transition from circuit-switched network to all-IP network (NBP Public Notice #25). Retrieved April 10, 2010 from http://hraunfoss.fcc.gov/edocs_public/attachmatch/DA-09-2517A1.pdf.

Federal Communications Commission. (2010). *Connecting America: National broadband plan.* Retrieved April 9, 2010 from http://hraunfoss.fcc.gov/edocs_public/attachmatch/DOC-296935A1.pdf.

Fowler, M. S. & Brenner, D. L. (1982). A marketplace approach to broadcast regulation. University of Texas Law Review 60 (207), 207-257.

Frieden, R. (2005, April). *Analog and digital must-carry obligations of cable and satellite television operators in the United States.* Retrieved April 8, 2008 from http://ssrn.com/abstract=704585.

Gandy, O. H. (1989). The surveillance society: Information technology and bureaucratic control. Journal of Communication, 39 (3), 61-76.

Gilroy, A. A. (2007, Dec. 20). Net neutrality: Background and issues. *CRS Reports to Congress.* CRS Report RS22444. Retrieved April 3, 2008 from http://assets.opencrs.com/rpts/RS22444_20071220.pdf.

Grant, A. E. & Berquist, L. (2000). Telecommunications infrastructure and the city: Adapting to the convergence of technology and policy. In J. O. Wheeler, Y, Aoyama, & B. Wharf (Eds.). *Cities in the telecommunications age: The fracturing of geographies.* New York: Routledge.

Horrigan, J. (2010). *Broadband adoption and use in America* (OBI Working Paper No. 1). Retrieved April 1, 2010 from http://hraunfoss.fcc.gov/edocs_public/attachmatch/DOC-296442A1.pdf.

Kang, C. (2008, March 28). Net neutrality's quiet crusader. *Washington Post,* D01.

Labaton, S. (2007, December 19). FCC reshapes rules limiting media industry. *New York Times,* A1.

Lubrano, A. (1997). *The telegraph: How technology innovation caused social change.* New York: Garland Publishing.

McCullagh, D. (2007, March 22). Net porn ban faces another legal setback. *C/NET News.* Retrieved April 10, 2008 from http://www.news.com/Net-porn-ban-faces-another-legal-setback/2100-1030_3-6169621.html.

Napoli, P. M. (2001). *Foundations of communications policy: Principles and process in the regulation of electronic media.* Cresskill, NJ: Hampton Press.

National Broadcasting Co. v. United States, 319 U.S. 190 (1949).

Organisation for Economic Co-operation and Development. (2010). *OECD broadband portal.* Retrieved April 15, 2010 from http://www.oecd.org/document/54/0,3343,en_2649_34225_38690102_1_1_1_1,00.html.

Oxman, J. (1999). *The FCC and the unregulation of the Internet.* OPP Working Paper No. 31. Retrieved April 8, 2008 from http://www.fcc.gov/Bureaus/OPP/working_papers/oppwp31.pdf.

Parsons, P. R. & Frieden, R. M. (1998). *The cable and satellite television industries.* Needham Heights, MA: Allyn & Bacon.

Poirier, J. (2010, April 5). FCC forms strategy to defend broadband powers. *Reuters.com.* Retrieved April 15, 2010 from http://www.reuters.com/article/idUSTRE6341CB20100405.

Pool, I. S. (1983). *Technologies of freedom.* Cambridge, MA: Harvard University Press.

Prometheus v. FCC. No. 03-3388 (3rd Cir., 2004). Retrieved April 8, 2008 from http://www.fcc.gov/ogc/documents/opinions/2004/03-3388-062404.pdf.

Red Lion Broadcasting Co. v. Federal Communications Commission, 395 U.S. 367 (1969).

Rice, R. E. (2008). Central concepts in media ownership rules and research and regulation. In Rice, R. E. (Ed.), *Media ownership research and regulation.* Creskill, NJ: Hampton Press.

Schatz, A. & Sheth, N. (2010, April 8). FCC seeks new web plan. *Wall Street Journal,* B1.

Starr, P. (2004). *The creation of the media.* New York: Basic Books.

Telecommunications Act of 1996, Pub. L. No. 104-104, 110 Stat. 56 (1996). Retrieved April 10, 2008 from http://www.fcc.gov/Reports/tcom1996.pdf.

Turner Broadcasting System, Inc. v. FCC, 512 U.S. 622 (1997).

van Cuilenburg, J. & McQuail, D. (2003). Media policy paradigm shifts: Toward a new communications policy paradigm. *European Journal of Communication, 18* (2), 181-207.

Warner, W. B. (2008). Networking and broadcasting in crisis. In R. E. Rice (Ed.), *Media ownership research and regulation.* Creskill, NJ: Hampton Press.

Watson, D. E. & Chang, S. H. (2008). Politics of legislating media ownership. In R. E. Rice (Ed.), *Media ownership research and regulation.* Creskill, NJ: Hampton Press.

Winston, B. (1998). *Media technology and society: A history from the telegraph to the Internet.* New York: Routledge.

Yang, C. (2005, December 26). At stake: The net as we know it. *Business Week,* 38-39.

Electronic Mass Media

6

Digital Television & Video

Peter B. Seel, Ph.D. & Michel Dupagne, Ph.D.*

Digital television and video are increasingly ubiquitous technologies in global societies. Digital video recording capability is now a standard feature in almost every mobile phone or music player sold. While video image quality varies greatly in these devices, Moore's law has made high-definition (HD) recording capability commonplace in video cameras. The combination of HD-quality CCD sensors, video image-processing chipsets, and inexpensive solid-state storage has produced pocket-sized video cameras such as the $150 Flip UltraHD (see Figure 6.1). The pocket camera features a fold-out USB port which can be plugged into any computer for fast downloading of the acquired video. Once edited with the embedded software, the completed program can be uploaded to the Internet with a single click. The democratization of "television" production generated by the explosion in the number of devices that can process digital video has created a world where 20 hours of video are uploaded every minute on the YouTube.com site ("Broadcasting Ourselves," 2009).

While most YouTube videos are unlikely to win an Emmy® award, the online distribution of digital video and television programming is an increasingly disruptive force to established broadcasters and program producers. They have responded by making their content available online for free or via subscription as increasing numbers of viewers seek to "pull" digital television content on request rather than watch at times when it is "pushed" as broadcast programming. Television news programs routinely feature video shot by bystanders, such as the 2009 emergency landing of an airliner in the Hudson River in New York. The increasing ubiquity of digital video recording capability bodes well for the global free expression and exchange of ideas via the Internet. The expanding "universe" of digital television and video is being driven by improvements in high-definition video cameras for professional production and the simultaneous inclusion of higher-quality video capture capability in mobile phones and pocket cameras such as the Flip.

Another important trend is the current global conversion from analog to digital television (DTV) technology. The United States completed its national conversion to digital broadcasting on June 12, 2009, Japan will complete their transition in July 2011, most European nations by 2012, and China plans to do so in 2015 (Careless, 2009). At the outset of high-definition television (HDTV) development in the 1980s, there was hope that one global television standard might emerge, easing the need to perform format conversions for international program distribution. However, as Table 6.1 demonstrates, there are now multiple competing DTV standards based on regional affiliations and national political orientation. In many respects, global television has reverted to a "Babel" of competing digital formats reminiscent of the advent of analog color television.

---

* Peter B. Seel is Associate Professor, Department of Journalism and Technical Communication, Colorado State University (Fort Collins, Colorado). Michel Dupagne is Associate Professor, School of Communication, University of Miami (Coral Gables, Florida).

Figure 6.1
Contemporary High-Definition Television Cameras

Professional $150,000 Sony CineAlta video camera used to shoot motion pictures and television programs.

Consumer $150 pocket Flip UltraHD camera used to shoot 720p HD videos for "broadcast" on the Internet.

Sources: Sony and P.B. Seel

DTV programming in the widescreen 16:9 aspect ratio is now a commonplace sight in nations that have made the conversion. The good news for consumers is that digital television displays have become commodity products with prices dropping rapidly each year. As of mid-2010, a United States consumer can purchase a 32-inch LCD digital television for $320—reaching the $10 per diagonal inch benchmark for the first time.

The global conversion to digital has also facilitated the development of new technologies, such as mobile DTV and 3-D TV, that are being tested in Asia, North America, and Europe. In fact, the development of new digital variants, such as 3-D TV, is related to price plunges for conventional digital television sets. As DTV display prices have plummeted, manufacturers are seeking new higher-end technologies that can command premium prices. Panasonic's 50-inch 3-D plasma televisions are on sale for $2,500 (compared with $1,300 for the same size non-3-D 1080p model), and the special electronic glasses needed with the sets cost $150 a pair—beyond the single pair that are included with each display (personal retail survey, and "Panasonic schedules 3DTV rollout," 2010). In April 2010, BSkyB launched the first European 3-D channel (Sky 3D) by broadcasting via satellite 3-D soccer matches to more than a thousand pubs in the United Kingdom (Bonnett, 2010).

Table 6.1
Global DTV Standards and Switch-Off Dates of Analog Terrestrial Television

Asia/Oceania	Year	Standard	Europe	Year	Standard	Americas	Year	Standard
Taiwan	2010	DVB-T	Netherlands	2006	DVB-T	United States	2009	ATSC
Japan	2011	ISDB-T	Sweden	2007	DVB-T	Canada	2011	ATSC
South Korea	2012	ATSC	Germany	2008	DVB-T	Mexico	2022p	ATSC
New Zealand	2012	DVB-T	Switzerland	2009	DVB-T	Panama	N.D.	DVB-T
Australia	2013	DVB-T	Spain	2010	DVB-T	Columbia	N.D.	DVB-T
Philippines	2015p	DVB-T	France	2011	DVB-T	Brazil	2016p	SBTVD
China	2015p	DMB-TH	United Kingdom	2012	DVB-T	Peru	N.D.	SBTVD

p = projected date. N.D. = No analog termination date set. The SBTVD standards used in Brazil and Peru are variants of the Japanese ISDB-T terrestrial DTV standard. DMB-TH is a unique DTV standard developed in China.

Sources: DigiTAG and TV Technology

The global conversion from analog to digital technology is the most significant change in television broadcast standards since color images were added in the 1960s. Digital television combines higher-resolution image quality with improved multi-channel audio and the ability to seamlessly integrate Internet-delivered "television" content into the displays. The digital television transition will facilitate the merger of computer technology with that of television in ways that will transform traditional concepts of broadcasting. New DTV models now include the capability of receiving and displaying Internet Protocol Television (IPTV) programs, in addition to the more traditional broadcast, cable-cast, and satellite-transmitted programming. IPTV providers, such as AT&T's U-Verse and Verizon's FiOS, have greatly increased their HDTV programming since 2008 (Cotriss, 2010).

As discussed in this chapter, DTV refers primarily to native digital programming produced by terrestrial broadcasters, even though it may be retransmitted to a majority of homes by cable or satellite operators. In the U. S., the Federal Communications Commission (FCC, 1998) defines DTV as "any technology that uses digital techniques to provide advanced television services such as high-definition TV (HDTV), multiple standard definition TV (SDTV) and other advanced features and services" (p. 7420). One key attribute of digital technology is "scalability"—the ability to produce audio-visual quality as good (or as bad) as the viewer desires (or will tolerate). This feature does not refer to program content quality—that factor will still depend on the creative ability of the writers and producers.

HDTV represents the highest image and sound quality that can be transmitted through the air. It is defined by the FCC in the United States as a system that provides image quality approaching that of 35 mm motion picture film, that has an image resolution of approximately twice that (1080i or 720p) of analog television, and has a picture aspect ratio of 16:9 (FCC, 1990) (see Table 6.2). At this aspect ratio of 1.78:1 (16 divided by 9), the television screen is wider in relation to its height than the 1.33:1 (4 divided by 3) of NTSC. Figure 6.2 compares a 16:9 HDTV aspect ratio with that of a 4:3 NTSC display. Note that the wider screen of an HDTV display more closely matches that of a motion picture than the conventional television screen. Computer displays are also expanding their aspect ratios in a similar manner to accommodate widescreen content—another example of the merger between television and computing.

SDTV, or standard-definition television, is another type of digital television technology that can be transmitted *along with,* or *instead of,* HDTV. Digital SDTV transmissions offer lower resolution (480 lines) than HDTV, and it is available in both narrowscreen and widescreen formats. Using digital video compression technology, it is feasible for U.S. broadcasters to transmit up to five SDTV signals instead of one HDTV signal within the allocated 6 MHz digital channel. The development of multichannel SDTV broadcasting, called "multicasting," is an approach that broadcasters at national and local levels have adopted, especially the local affiliate stations of the Public Broadcasting Service (PBS) in the United States. Many PBS stations broadcast two children-oriented SDTV channels in the daytime along with educational channels geared toward adults. Most public and commercial networks reserve true HDTV programming for evening prime-time hours.

Figure 6.2
LCD Television Aspect Ratios

52-inch LCD displays on sale in a retail electronics store.

Comparison of 4:3 display of analog television and widescreen 16:9 display of most digital televisions.

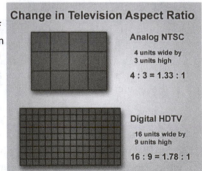

Source: P. B. Seel

Digital television programming can be accessed via over-the-air (OTA) fixed and mobile transmissions, through cable or satellite multichannel video program distributors, and through broadband IPTV connections from Internet sites. IPTV is a "pull' technology in that viewers seek out a certain program and watch it in a video stream or as a downloaded file (discussed in more detail in Chapter 8). Over-the-air (OTA) broadcasting is a "push" technology that transmits a digital program to millions of viewers at once. IPTV, like other forms of digital television, is a scalable technology that can be viewed as lower quality, highly compressed content or programs can be accessed in HDTV quality on sites such as Vimeo.com. IPTV is a rapidly growing method of accessing digital television programming as more viewers seek to watch their favorite shows on demand.

Background

In the 1970s and 1980s, Japanese researchers at NHK (Japan Broadcasting Corporation) developed two related analog HDTV systems: an analog "Hi-Vision" *production* standard with 1125 scanning lines and 60 fields (30 frames) per second; and an analog "MUSE" *transmission* system with an original bandwidth of 9 MHz designed for satellite distribution throughout Japan. Japanese HDTV transmissions began in 1989 and steadily increased to a full schedule of 17 hours a day by October 1997 (Nippon Hoso Kyokai, 1998).

The decade between 1986 and 1996 was a significant era in the diffusion of HDTV technology in Japan, Europe, and the United States. There were a number of key events during this period that shaped advanced television technology and related industrial policies:

◆ In 1986, the Japanese Hi-Vision system was rejected as a world HDTV production standard by the CCIR, a subgroup of the International Telecommunication Union (ITU). By 1988, a European research and development consortium, EUREKA EU-95, had created a competing system known as HD-MAC that featured 1250 widescreen scanning lines and 50 fields (25 frames) displayed per second (Dupagne & Seel, 1998).

◆ In 1987, the FCC in the United States created the Advisory Committee on Advanced Television Service (ACATS), charged with investigating the policies, standards, and regulations to facilitate the introduction of advanced television (ATV) services in the U. S (FCC, 1987).

◆ U.S. testing of analog ATV systems by ACATS was about to begin in 1990 when General Instrument Corporation announced it had perfected a method of digitally transmitting a high-definition signal. The other participants in the ACATS competition soon developed digital systems that were submitted for testing. Ultimately, the three competitors (AT&T/Zenith, General Instrument/MIT, and Philips/Thomson/Sarnoff) merged into a consortium known as the Grand Alliance and developed a single digital broadcast system for ACATS evaluation (Brinkley, 1997).

The FCC adopted a number of key decisions during the ATV testing process that defined a national transition process from analog NTSC to an advanced digital television broadcast system:

◆ In 1990, the Commission outlined a *simulcast* strategy for the transition to an ATV standard (FCC, 1990). This strategy required that U.S. broadcasters transmit *both* the new ATV signal and the existing NTSC signal concurrently for a period of time, at the end of which all NTSC transmitters would be turned off.

◆ The Grand Alliance system was successfully tested in the summer of 1995, and a U.S. digital television standard based on that technology was recommended to the FCC by the Advisory Committee (Advisory Committee on Advanced Television Service, 1995).

◆ In May 1996, the FCC proposed the adoption of the *ATSC Digital Television (DTV) Standard* that specified 18 digital transmission variations as outlined in Table 6.2 (FCC, 1996a). Stations would be able to choose whether to transmit one channel of HDTV programming, four to six channels of SDTV programs during various dayparts, or a mixture of HDTV and SDTV programs. The Commission approved the DTV standard in December 2006 (FCC, 1996b).

Table 6.2
U.S. Advanced Television Systems Committee (ATSC) DTV Formats

Format	Active Lines	Horizontal Pixels	Aspect Ratio	Picture Rate*
HDTV	1080 lines	1920 pixels/line	16:9	60i, 30p, 24p
HDTV	720 lines	1280 pixels/line	16:9	60p, 30p, 24p
SDTV	480 lines	704 pixels/line	16:9 or 4:3	60i, 60p, 30p, 24p
SDTV	480 lines	640 pixels/line	4:3	60i, 60p, 30p, 24p

*In the picture rate column, "i" indicates interlaced scan in television *fields*/second with two fields required per frame and "p" is progressive scan in *frames*/second.   *Source:* ATSC

U.S. broadcasters decided to produce and transmit HDTV in the 16:9 aspect ratio with either 720p or 1080i picture rates, but many television stations still produce news programs in 4:3 SDTV formats. The Advanced Television Systems Committee (ATSC) standard also specified the adoption of the Dolby AC-3 six-channel audio system that can replicate a theatrical environment in the home with six surround-sound speakers.

In April 1997, the FCC defined how the United States would make the transition to DTV broadcasting and set December 31, 2006 as the target date for the phase-out of NTSC broadcasting (FCC, 1997). In 2005, after it became clear that this deadline was unrealistic due to the slow consumer adoption of DTV sets, the deadline was reset at February 17, 2009 for the cessation of analog full-power television broadcasting (*Deficit Reduction Act*, 2005). The legislation also defined the DTV spectrum to include only channels 2 through 51. The spectrum in the 700 MHz range outside these allocations was auctioned off early in 2008 (mainly to wireless communication providers), and these auctions raised $19.6 billion for the U.S. Treasury (Dickson, 2008; Hansell, 2008). The United States government had a significant vested economic interest in these auctions and was a primary stakeholder in speeding the national transition to digital broadcasting.

The Act also included a provision to allocate a total of $990 million from the U.S. Treasury for the issuance of two $40 coupons per household for the purchase of digital-to-analog converter boxes for households with older analog television sets (*Deficit Reduction Act*, 2005). These boxes down-convert DTV signals so that homes with analog sets could still watch broadcast television after the analog shut-off date.

As the February 17, 2009 deadline approached, millions of over-the-air television households had not purchased the converter boxes needed to continue watching broadcast television. Cable and satellite customers would not be affected as provisions were made for the digital conversion at the cable headend or with a satellite set-top box. Neither the newly inaugurated Obama administration nor members of Congress wanted the invite the wrath of millions of disenfranchised analog television viewers, so the shut-off deadline was moved by an Act of Congress 116 days to June 12, 2009 (*DTV Delay Act*, 2009). In the year leading up to the prior February shut-off date, a nationwide public awareness campaign had been conducted by the FCC and the

National Telecommunications and Information Administration (NTIA) in partnership with the Consumer Electronics Association (CEA) and the National Association of Broadcasters. The campaign was highly visible in the form of graphic "crawls" across the bottom of television screens and with point-of-sale posters in electronics stores.

As shown in Table 6.3, the percentage of households that were unready for the DTV transition decreased by 50% from February 15 (4.4%) to June 14, 2009 (2.2%). Therefore, the extension of the February 17 deadline was a shrewd political maneuver by the Obama administration. But despite the massive public relations campaign by government and industry, the Nielsen Company estimated that 2.8 million U.S. households were still unprepared by June 10, 2009—two days before the final analog switch-off (Nielsen, 2009). In addition, important ethnic and age differences in level of unreadiness persisted during the last months of the digital transition and beyond. After a Providence, Rhode Island television station shut down its analog transmitter, a viewer called to ask, "Why didn't they tell us this was going to happen?" Referring to this case, a broadcaster responded to a reporter, "I don't know where this person's been. Maybe on Mars?" (O'Neal, 2009a, p. 6). According to the NTIA (2009), viewers requested 64.1 million coupons to defray the cost of converter boxes and redeemed 34.9 million of these coupons between January 2008 and December 2009, a redemption rate of 54.4%.

Table 6.3
Percentage of Households Completely Unready For DTV*

Date	Overall	White	African-American	Hispanic	Asian	Under Age 35	Over Age 55
August 30, 2009	0.6	0.5	1.0	1.3	0.4	1.6	0.2
July 26, 2009	1.1	0.8	2.2	1.6	1.3	2.7	0.4
June 14, 2009	2.2	1.6	4.6	3.6	3.2	4.4	1.1
May 24, 2009	2.7	2.1	5.4	4.7	3.2	5.0	1.5
April 26, 2009	3.1	2.4	5.9	5.0	4.1	5.7	1.7
March 15, 2009	3.6	2.9	6.6	6.1	4.4	6.5	2.0
February 15, 2009	4.4	3.6	7.5	7.4	5.1	8.1	2.6
January 18, 2009	5.7	4.6	9.9	9.7	6.9	8.8	4.0
December 21, 2008	6.8	5.6	10.8	11.5	8.1	9.9	5.2

*A completely unready household refers to one that has no television set capable of receiving digital broadcast television signals through a digital-to-analog converter box, a built-in digital tuner, or a multichannel video programming distribution provider (e.g., cable operator). Estimates based on the National People Meter panel data.

Source: Nielsen

RECENT DEVELOPMENTS

Despite the delay in the cut-off of analog broadcasting in the U.S. from February 17 to June 12 in 2009, there were still significant transition problems for some over-the-air viewers. Some OTA households simply had not connected or tested their converter boxes before the June 12th deadline, and the FCC reported that their DTV-transition hotline fielded over 900,000 calls in the days surrounding the analog transmission shut-off (FCC, 2009). In some markets the digital broadcast footprint was smaller than that of analog transmissions, and some viewers at the edge of the footprint lost their over-the-air service on some channels. Analog television signals will fade to snowy images at the edge of the broadcast contour, but digital television provides all or nothing results at the edge of OTA reception. To restore service to these areas, some broadcast stations will need to add digital signal repeaters.

Since the 2009 termination of analog broadcasting in the United States, the most significant digital developments concern the advent of *mobile* DTV service and the development of new electronic 3-D television systems. The creation of a national mobile standard for digital television broadcasting in the United States was proposed by the industry consortium Open Mobile Video Coalition (OMVC) in 2007, and the same ATSC organization that codified the DTV standard in 1995 assumed a similar role for a mobile standard (Advanced Television Systems Committee, 2009). After two years of testing in the lab and in the field, the A/153 ATSC Mobile DTV Standard (mDTV) was approved on October 15, 2009 by a vote of the ATSC membership (O'Neal, 2009b).

Mobile DTV

The mDTV standard uses the same 8VSB modulation scheme as the DTV terrestrial broadcast standard, but incorporates decoding technology specifically added to improve mobile reception. Local television broadcasters can include these mobile signals along with their regular DTV transmissions. One unique aspect of the new mobile standard is that it allows an Internet-based return path from devices, such as mobile phones, for viewer voting and other interactive services (O'Neal, 2009b).

Adoption of the new mDTV standard by U.S. broadcasters is accelerating, and manufacturers of mobile phones, laptops, netbooks, and small portable TV sets are incorporating mDTV receiver chips in them. A National Association of Broadcasters' 2009 study predicted $2 billion in incremental revenue for broadcasters once the technology was available nationwide (Johnston, 2009). Mobile DTV reception was tested in 2009 in Washington, DC, Seattle, Washington, and Atlanta, Georgia (O'Neal, 2009b). Tests of the technology by WRAL-TV in Raleigh, North Carolina, on the local bus system indicated that the transmission technology was robust and functioned effectively. Local U.S. broadcasters are expected to embrace the technology as the $100,000 investment required to transmit mDTV signals is relatively small compared to the cost of the DTV conversion, and there is significant advertising revenue potential in reaching affluent mobile television viewers. One aspect that is rarely discussed is that mDTV adoption strengthens the case for local television broadcasters to retain their allotted DTV spectrum in the face of FCC interest in reclaiming part of it for other mobile broadband applications. Broadcasters can claim with accuracy that they are providing new advertiser-supported digital mobile content to consumers, at no charge.

3-D DTV

3-D TV is the other recent development in digital television technology. In 2009, both Sony and Panasonic conducted live demonstrations of their 3-D production and display systems at the National Association of Broadcasters conference in Las Vegas (Ankeny, 2009). There are two primary 3-D technologies that apply to television: anaglyphic and electro-optical. Most filmgoers are familiar with anaglyphic projection where both left-eye and right-eye information is projected on the screen at the same time. The screen looks blurry and out of focus to the naked eye, but when polarized glasses are donned, the lens polarization provides slightly offset information to each eye. The brain processes the slightly askew 2-D visuals as an illusion of three dimensions. This 3-D technology dates back to the advent of 3-D films in the 1950s (Hayes, 1989). The polarized glasses provide much improved color rendition compared to the cardboard "glasses" from that era with red and blue plastic "lenses." The anaglyphic system was used on television during the 2010 Grammy® awards where a tribute to Michael Jackson aired in 3-D as auditorium and home audiences donned cardboard glasses to watch the segment.

The *active* electro-optical systems developed by Panasonic, Sony, and other manufacturers are a significant improvement over *passive* anaglyphic technologies. These active systems use special battery-powered glasses with liquid-crystal lenses that open and close 60 times a second in sync with the alternate left-eye and right-eye frames displayed on the screen (Tabuchi, 2009). As the left-eye frame is presented, the left-eye shutter on the glasses opens and then quickly closes, then the right-eye shutter opens with the right-eye frame, and so on. What is remarkable about this system is that the display is cycling at 120 frames per second and maintaining perfect sync with the glasses. The 3-D illusion created on a large HDTV display is breathtaking (see Figure 6.3).

Figure 6.3
Electro-Optical 3-D Viewing Equipment

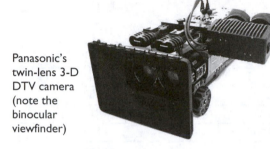

Panasonic's twin-lens 3-D DTV camera (note the binocular viewfinder)

NAB 2009 exhibit attendee watches a Panasonic promotional video in 3-D. He is wearing the active-shutter electronic glasses the electro-optical display.

Source: Panasonic Corporation

What will purchasers of these sets be able to watch? One primary type of 3-D content viewable on a home system will be films produced in 3-D and viewed on Blu-ray discs. There has been a significant increase in 3-D film production in the past three years, especially for animated films. Seven films released in 3-D in 2009 broke the $100 million mark in gross box office receipts (Tilley, 2010). Of *Avatar's* record-breaking $2 billion box office gross in the United States, 80% came from audiences who donned glasses to see it in 3-D. The sale of the first telecast rights to *Avatar* (in 2-D and 3-D versions) to the FX cable network is estimated to have earned the film's producers between $25 and $35 million (Weprin, 2010). Consumer electronics companies have studied these box office returns and see a significant audience for 3-D home viewing of these films and other television programs.

Sony and Panasonic will pay networks to produce and telecast 3-D programs in 2010 and 2011. Panasonic will sponsor DirecTV's creation of three satellite-delivered 3-D channels by June 2010. Programs in 3-D for the DBS channels will be provided by CBS, NBC, MTV, AEG, HDNet, and Fox Sports. Sony will underwrite ESPN's 3-D telecasts of 85 live sporting events in 2010, starting with the FIFA World Cup match between Mexico and South Africa in June (Grossman & Dickson, 2010). Network executives have indicated that they will not pay for the added expense of telecasting in 3-D and expect television manufacturers to foot the bill (Grossman & Dickson, 2010). This situation is similar to the roll-out of digital television programming when Mitsubishi subsidized CBS's first season of DTV programming in 1999, and Panasonic underwrote the DTV simulcast of *Monday Night Football* and the Super Bowl on ABC in 2000 (Seel & Dupagne, 2000).

CURRENT STATUS

United States

Receiver Sales. According to the CEA, 141.9 million DTV sets and displays were sold to dealers between 1998 and 2009 (Table 6.4). CEA has forecast that digital TV shipments will reach about 38 million units in 2010. According to SNL Kagan, U.S. HDTV sales totaled 29 million in 2009, a substantial increase from the

26.2 million units sold in 2008 (Winslow, 2009a). Some of this increase can be attributed to the shutdown of analog broadcasting in June 2009, but consumers have also purchased second and third HDTV sets for home use as prices dropped during that period. The Leichtman Research Group (2009) found that 38% of HDTV owners had more than one HDTV receiver at home in October 2009. Table 6.4 shows that the average price of a DTV receiver has fallen by 80% to $631 in 2009. Table 6.5 also reports that the average retail prices of LCD and plasma TV sets have dropped steadily from 2005 to 2009 for a variety of screen sizes. Sales of LCD and plasma HDTV displays have become a commodity market as prices decline and set sizes increase. Manufacturers have responded to this marketing challenge by developing new high-end technologies, such as 3-D DTV.

Table 6.4
Sales of Digital TV Sets & Displays to Dealers, 1998-2010*

Year	Units Sales in Thousands	Dollar Sales in Millions	Average Unit Price
1998	14	$43	$3,147
1999	121	$295	$2,433
2000	625	$1,422	$2,275
2001	1,460	$2,648	$1,812
2002	2,535	$4,280	$1,688
2003	4,102	$6,521	$1,590
2004	8,002	$12,300	$1,537
2005	10,719	$15,043	$1,403
2006	22,366	$22,696	$1,015
2007	24,966	$24,519	$982
2008	31,153	$25,931	$832
2009e	35,808	$22,579	$631
2010p	37,708	$22,133	$587

*This category includes digital direct-view TV receivers, flat panel (LCD and plasma) TVs and displays, projection TVs (e.g., DLPs), combination TVs (e.g., DVD/VCR/TV), and OLED displays. e = estimated. p = predicted.

Source: Consumer Electronics Association

Table 6.5
Average Prices of LCD & Plasma TV Sets for Various Screen Sizes, 2005-2009

Top Selling Flat-Panel Screen Sizes Based on Unit Volume	Average Retail Price in 2005	Average Retail Price in 2007	Average Retail Price in 2009
32-inch LCD TV	$1,354	$745 (720p)	$424 (720p)
37-inch LCD TV	$2,096	$963 (720p)	$596 (1080p)
40-inch LCD TV	$3,014	$1,200 (720p)	$709 (1080p)
46-inch LCD TV	n/a	$2,300 (720p)	$1,293 (1080p)
52-inch LCD TV	n/a	$3,000 (720p)	$1,575 (1080p)
42-inch Plasma TV	$2,034	$900 (720p)	$600 (720p) $800 (1080p)
50-inch Plasma TV	$3,574	$1,555 (1080p)	$900 (720p) $1,300 (1080p)

720-line progressively scanned displays (720p) are typically less expensive than higher resolution 1080-line (1080p) systems. n/a = not available

Sources: Personal retail surveys by one of the authors for 2009 and 2007 data and NDP Group for 2005 data.

HDTV Penetration. While it is undisputed that penetration of HDTV sets has dramatically increased since 2008, estimating such penetration rate is affected by definitional and methodological variations. The Nielsen-based penetration data, which are reproduced in Table 6.6, prove this point. Depending on whether survey respondents live in HD receivable homes, HD capable homes, or HD display capable homes, HDTV penetration rates in February 2010 would reach 46%, 49%, or 56%, respectively, and would fluctuate by as much as 21%. Therefore, it is critical to take into account the exact wording of the survey question when determining the level of HDTV ownership. Whereas a more conservative assessment including HDTV programming would suggest that HDTV was available in 46% of U.S. households in February 2010, a less conditional approach would raise this estimate to 56%. Regardless of the definitional category, HDTV has now quickened the pace of diffusion beyond innovators and early adopters and is becoming widely available in U.S. homes.

Table 6.6

Household Penetration of HDTV, 2007-2010

Date	HD Receivable*	HD Capable**	HD Display Capable***
July 2007	10.1%	12.2%	18.9%
December 2007	13.6%	16.8%	24.9%
July 2008	19.8%	24.8%	34.0%
December 2008	24.5%	30.4%	39.3%
July 2009	36.9%	39.4%	47.2%
December 2009	42.9%	46.0%	52.7%
February 2010	46.2%	49.3%	55.7%

*An HD receivable home is a home that has a high-definition television (HDTV) set and tuner and receives at least one network or station in high definition.
**An HD capable home is a home that has an HDTV set and tuner capable of receiving signals in high definition.
***An HD display capable home is a home that has an HDTV set capable of displaying content in high definition.

Source: Nielsen data reported by the Television Bureau of Advertising

HDTV Adoption and Viewing. Consistent with diffusion theory, HDTV owners tend to have higher incomes, be more educated, and be younger than non-owners (Leichtman Research Group, 2009; Nielsen, 2008). As HDTV adoption progresses toward saturation, these demographic differences are expected to dwindle. Marketing studies also reported that HDTV owners do not always take advantage of available HDTV programming. For instance, a 2009 survey from Frank N. Magid Associates revealed that "Only two-thirds [66%] of those who say they own an HDTV set subscribe to an HD service" (Winslow, 2009b, p. 14). More intriguing is the finding from the Leichtman Research Group (2009) indicating that about 14% of HDTV survey respondents believed they were watching HDTV programs when in fact they were not. These results suggest that consumer education from retailers and multichannel video programming distributors is still not optimal.

Two 2009 studies—from the Council for Research Excellence and from Knowledge Networks—found an increase in (HDTV) viewing among HDTV households (Winslow, 2009b). Only time will tell whether availability of HDTV programming will produce a permanent upward shift in TV viewing habits for one or more demographic groups. The Magid survey also reported that two-thirds of cable subscribers were satisfied with the number of HDTV channels accessible on cable (Winslow, 2009b). According to Nielsen (2007, 2008), sports and movies remain the most popular television genres among HDTV owners.

Display Types. Consumers have many options for digital television displays, and many new sets sold today offer Internet connectivity, higher-resolution screens (1080p vs. 720p), and more interactive features. Research firm iSupply stated that 27% of all new digital televisions sold in January 2010 included an Internet connection capability, and predicted that 85 million of these "NeTVs" would be in use worldwide by 2013 (Putman, 2010).

◆ *Liquid Crystal Display (LCD) models*—LCDs work by rapidly switching color crystals off and on. Early LCD displays needed to be viewed head on, but newer displays can be viewed from wider angles. LCD displays use less electrical power than plasma displays of similar screen sizes. A variant technology uses LEDs (light emitting diodes) as the light source instead of Cold Cathode Fluorescent (CCFL) backlighting. The use of LEDs for screen backlighting provides higher image contrast ratios with richer blacks and brighter highlights than CCFL models (Silva, 2010).

◆ *Organic Light Emitting Diode (OLED)*—The Sony Corporation developed remarkably bright and sharp "OLED" televisions in 2008 that had a display depth of 3 mm–about the thickness of three credit cards. The suggested retail price in Japan for the ultra-thin 11-inch model was $2,200. The company decided in 2010 that the sets would be too expensive to manufacture and have discontinued production (Uranaka, 2010). One irony is that the Samsung mDTV-capable "Mythic" mobile phone has an OLED screen, so this display technology is not dead, but it may be confined to small cell phone screens where its high resolution is an asset.

◆ *Plasma displays*—Plasma gas is used in these sets as a medium in which tiny color elements are switched off and on in milliseconds. Compared with early LCD displays, plasma sets offered wider viewing angles, better color fidelity and brightness, and larger screen sizes, but these advantages have diminished over the past decade. The high power demand of plasma displays, especially for the largest set sizes, is a factor for consumers to consider. Many manufacturers have stopped making plasma sets in favor of LCD models, but Panasonic is the exception.

◆ *Digital Light Processing (DLP) projectors*—Developed by Texas Instruments, DLP technology utilizes hundreds of thousands of tiny micro-mirrors mounted on a 1-inch chip that can project a very bright and sharp color image. This technology is used in a three-chip system to project digital versions of "films" in movie theaters. For under $3,000, a consumer can create a digital home theater with a DLP projector, a movie screen, and a multichannel surround-sound system.

Programming. All network and cable channel programming in the United States is now produced in widescreen HDTV. There are many legacy 4:3 productions still being telecast (and there will be for years to come given each network's extensive analog archives), but it is typically being shown on widescreen displays with pillarbox graphics at the left and right side of the screen. Most cable operators have provided space on their systems for additional HD-quality channels and eventually (10-15 years) will phase out the down-converted 4:3 channels for subscribers with older analog sets. This move will free up a great deal of bandwidth, now occupied by narrow-screen simulcasts of HDTV programs, on most cable systems. Satellite multichannel video program providers, such as DIRECTV and the DISH Network, are each competing to see how many HDTV channels they can provide, and each now offers more than 150 (Greczkowski, 2010).

Japan

Japan continues to prepare for the 2011 DTV satellite and terrestrial conversion deadlines. BS satellite-delivered analog HDTV transmission ceased in September 2007, and analog SD satellite broadcasting is scheduled to end in July 2011 (Moriyama, 2009). (Digital high-power (BS) satellite broadcasting started in 2000.)

Using the Integrated Services Digital Broadcasting-Terrestrial (ISDB-T) standard (see Table 6.7), Japanese broadcasters began digital terrestrial television (DTT) service in three major cities by December 2003 and rolled it out nationwide by the end of 2006. Analog NTSC broadcasting should be terminated in July 2011. The Ministry of Internal Affairs and Communications will spend ¥220 billion ($2.33 billion as of April 2, 2010) on a transition plan to subsidize the distribution of antennas and digital-to-analog converter boxes to low-income households ("Ministry," 2008). But as the United States did, Japan is facing consumer-related challenges to meet the digital switch-over deadline. By mid-2008, about one third of viewers did not know that analog terrestrial TV broadcasts would end in July 2011 ("Ministry," 2008). To address this awareness concern, Japanese TV broadcasters are airing public service announcements to alert viewers about the impending switch-off of analog terrestrial television (S. Moriyama, personal communication, March 23, 2010). As of September 2009, 70% (34.75 million) of Japanese households had at least one digital device (e.g., receiver, tuner) to receive over-the-air digital signals (Ministry of Internal Affairs and Communications, personal communication, January 26, 2010). However, this household penetration rate missed the planned target of 72% established by the Ministry by that month ("70% of Families," 2009). In December 2008, the cheapest DTV receiver cost ¥50,000 ($529 as of April 2, 2010) (Brasor, 2008).

🌍 Sustainability 🌍

With the completion of the U.S. digital television (DTV) transition on June 12, 2009, approximately 200 million analog television sets were rendered obsolete. Of course, many such receivers can still be used with a digital converter box or hooked up to cable or satellite services. However, most of these older sets have CRT screens with heavy glass tubes infused with lead to limit radiation exposure to viewers (e.g., children) sitting close to the set. The tubes have the potential to leak this lead into landfills if they are not disposed of properly. The circuit boards in older television sets, VCRs, DVD players, and computers contain toxic metals that also require proper disposal. In 2007, 77% of an estimated 27 million television sets were discarded without proper recycling procedures (Rosenwald, 2009).

For this reason, many states and local landfills prohibit the dumping of consumer electronics items and require their recycling or proper disposal. By September 2009, 18 states required consumer electronics manufacturers to help pay for the recycling of their products (Rosenwald, 2009). Some retailers, such as Best Buy, will recycle many electronic products for free, but they charge $10 to recycle televisions that are smaller than 32 inches diagonal (Best Buy, 2010). Earth911.com is a useful Web site that provides online information about the nearest approved disposal options for home electronics.

Another environmental concern is the notoriously high energy consumption of large-screen digital televisions, especially large plasma displays. In November 2009, California became the first state to mandate energy efficiency standards for all new HDTV sets (up to 58 inches) to curtail energy consumption by one-third on January 1, 2011. More stringent standards taking effect in 2013 are expected to reduce television-related power consumption by 50% in the state. Nationwide, television-related power usage has tripled in 10 years to 10 billion kilowatt hours each year, or 10% of residential energy consumption (Lifsher & Chang, 2009). Manufacturers are developing new DTV models that use less power, and the ideal choice for energy-efficiency is a LCD model with LED backlighting (see chapter for detailed description), as these are bright displays with vivid colors that use less energy than conventional LCD sets.

One common problem with consumer electronics is that some devices draw power even when supposedly off. The situation is known as "vampire power," a reference to the energy consumption occurring when people are asleep. Set-top boxes and digital video recorders are typical culprits. One simple solution is to put multiple electronic items on a single power strip and use that switch to completely power them down when not in use. Not only are these simple energy conservation steps good for the environment (fewer new power plants needed), but they will save consumers money each month in utility bills.

Table 6.7
Primary International Terrestrial DTV Standards

System	ISDB-T	DVB-T	ATSC DTV
Region	Japan	Europe	North America
Modulation	OFDM	COFDM	8-VSB
Aspect Ratio	1.33:1, 1.78:1	1.33:1, 1.78:1, 2.21:1	1.33:1, 1.78:1
Active Lines	480, 720, 1080	480, 576, 720, 1080, 1152	480, 720, 1080*
Pixels/Line	720, 1280, 1920	varies	640, 704, 1280, 1920*
Scanning	1:1 progressive, 2:1 interlace	1:1 progressive, 2:1 interlace	1:1 progressive, 2:1 interlace*
Bandwidth	6-8 MHz	6-8 MHz	6 MHz
Frame Rate	30, 60 fps	24, 25, 30 fps	24, 30, 60 fps*
Field Rate	60 Hz	30, 50 Hz	60 Hz
Audio Encoding	MPEG-2 AAC	MUSICAM/ Dolby AC-3	Dolby AC-3

*As adopted by the FCC on December 24, 1996, the ATSC DTV image parameters, scanning options, and aspect ratios were not mandated, but were left to the discretion of display manufacturers and television broadcasters (FCC, 1996b).

Source: M. Dupagne

NHK remains a committed advanced television innovator and has been developing the next-generation HDTV system called Super Hi-Vision (SHV) in its Science & Technical Research Laboratories since 1995. SHV's technical characteristics include: a video format resolution of 4,320 (V) x 7,680 (H) pixels, an aspect ratio of 16:9, a progressive scanning frequency of 60 frames, and a 22.2 multichannel audio system with a top layer of nine channels, a middle layer of 10 channels, a bottom layer of three channels, and two low-frequency effects channels (Shishikui, Fujita, & Kubota, 2009; Sugawara, 2008). All in all, SHV has 16 times as many pixels as HDTV—about 33 million pixels per frame. Beyond the pixel count, this advanced technology "produces three-dimensional spatial sound that augments the sense of reality and presence" (Shishikui et al., 2009, p. 1). At IBC 2008, NHK and European broadcasters demonstrated two international live transmissions: one over two satellite transponders between Turin, Italy, and Amsterdam, the Netherlands, and another over an ultra-broadband IP network between London and Amsterdam. The native 24 Gbps SHV signal was compressed to 140 Mbps and 600 Mbps for satellite and IP delivery, respectively. While regular SHV broadcasting is unlikely to start before 2020 in Japan, NHK plans to improve the compression techniques for satellite transmission in 2010 and develop a full-resolution SHV camera by 2011 (Shishikui et al., 2009).

Europe

By the end of 2009, seven European countries had ceased analog TV broadcasts, and nine planned to complete the digital switch-over in 2010 and 2011 (see Table 6.8). Consistent with the Commission of the European Communities' (2005) proposed deadline, most of the terrestrial broadcasters in the European Union should turn off their analog television transmitters by 2012. Key factors that affect the pace of the DTT switch-over in the European markets include the number of OTA homes, spectrum availability, and extent of DTT penetration and coverage (DigiTAG, 2008). Countries with a limited number of households that rely on OTA reception to watch television will be able to shut off analog broadcasting more quickly than those with a large base of OTA households. Countries with fewer OTA frequencies will be less likely to simulcast analog and digital programs and will be forced to switch to DTT more quickly than those with greater spectrum availability.

But the time frame of the digital transmission conversion will also depend on how fast consumers adopt the necessary equipment to receive DTT signals and how available these DTT signals are to viewers throughout the country (DigiTAG, 2008).

It is worth noting from Table 6.8 that European countries that launched DTT service between 2005 and 2010 tend to rely on the newer MPEG-4 AVC encoding technology instead of the conventional MPEG-2 format. MPEG-4 could produce compression gains as high as 50% compared to MPEG-2 (Louis & Roger, 2008), thereby creating greater bandwidth efficiency and providing a palatable upgrade path to HD DTT for broadcasters. We should also point out that, unlike the United States, European countries frequently count digital cable and satellite homes along DTT homes in their DTV universe. For instance, the DTV household penetration in the United Kingdom reached nearly 90% by the third quarter of 2009, with digital satellite accounting for 38% of the digital take-up, DTT for 38%, digital cable for 12%, and other platforms for about 1% (Ofcom, 2009).

Using the Digital Video Broadcasting-Terrestrial (DVB-T) standard (see Table 6.7), European broadcasters have focused for many years on delivering SDTV programs to provide more viewing options to their audiences. But by the mid-2000s, they realized the long-term inevitability of HDTV services, the demand of which has been driven in large part by the growing popularity of flat-panel displays and Blu-ray disc players in Europe (DigiTAG, 2007). Both consumer electronics devices can be viewed as complementary goods for HDTV.

Screen Digest reported that the (unduplicated) number of HDTV channels distributed on satellite, cable, terrestrial, and IPTV platforms in 28 European countries rose from one (Belgium-based Euro1080) in 2004 to 173 in 2008 ("High-Definition Television," 2009). These HDTV channels are primarily subscription-based and available via satellite. The TV household penetration of HD-ready display sets in 26 European countries climbed from 5% in 2006 to 26% in 2008 and is predicted to reach 52% in 2010 ("High-Definition Television," 2009). Estimating the percentage of HDTV homes is as challenging a task in Europe as it is in the United States because of the way HDTV households are identified. The 2008 percentage of TV households that were HD-enabled (i.e., owned an HD-ready set and an HD set-top box to receive HDTV programming) was only 2% in Europe, compared to 25% (HD receivable) in the United States (see Table 6.6). In 2008, a 42-inch LCD HD-ready set cost €1,000 ($1,350 as of April 2, 2010) ("High-Definition Television," 2009).

In a few short years, the United Kingdom has taken the lead in HDTV broadcasting initiatives and may represent a valuable country case study for the future of HDTV in Europe. BSkyB's Sky+HD service, which was introduced in April 2006, supplied nearly 40 HDTV satellite channels for £10 ($15 as of April 2, 2010) as of April 2010. As an example of aggressive marketing strategy, the company decided to offer the first Sky+HD set-top box for free. All these HDTV channels are encoded using MPEG-4 AVC and transmitted in 1080i format. Sky+HD totaled 1.6 million subscriptions by the third quarter of 2009 (Ofcom, 2009).

In December 2009, Freeview, the U.K. DTT platform that offers 50 digital TV channels and is used in 18 million homes, rolled out HD service. By the end of April 2010, the BBC, ITV, and Channel 4 should each have an HD DTT channel available on Freeview HD. Assuming that they own an aerial antenna and an HD-ready receiver, Freeview viewers only need to purchase a £99 ($151 as of April 2, 2010) set-top box to receive HDTV signals (Midgley, 2010). Freeview HD channels are transmitted in 1080i using MPEG-4 compression technology and the new DVB-T2 terrestrial transmission standard. HDTV channels are also available on Freesat (satellite), Virgin Media (cable), and BT Vision (IPTV). Consistent with U.S. survey findings, U.K. HDTV viewer respondents reported watching more television, especially movies and sports programs (Ofcom, 2007). The HD broadcasts of the FIFA World Cup matches on the BBC and ITV in Summer 2010 could stimulate interest in HDTV programming and ownership and accelerate the diffusion of this technology in the United Kingdom.

Table 6.8
Switch-Off Dates of Analog Terrestrial Television in 22 European Countries (2010)

Country	Launch Date	Compression Format	Switch-Off Date
Netherlands	2003	MPEG-2	2006
Sweden	1999	MPEG-2	2007
Finland	2001	MPEG-2	2007
Germany	2002	MPEG-2	2008
Switzerland	2001	MPEG-2	2008
Denmark	2006	MPEG-2/MPEG-4 AVC	2009
Norway	2007	MPEG-4 AVC	2009
Spain	2000/2005	MPEG-2	2010
Estonia	2006	MPEG-4 AVC	2010
Austria	2006	MPEG-2	2010
Latvia	2009	MPEG-4 AVC	2010
France	2005	MPEG-2/MPEG-4 AVC	2011
Czech Republic	2005	MPEG-2	2011
Slovenia	2006	MPEG-4 AVC	2011
Hungary	2008	MPEG-4 AVC	2011
Croatia	2009	MPEG-2	2011
United Kingdom	1998	MPEG-2	2012
Italy	2004	MPEG-2	2012
Lithuania	2008	MPEG-4 AVC	2012
Portugal	2009	MPEG-4 AVC	2012
Slovakia	2009	MPEG-2	2012
Ireland	2010	MPEG-4 AVC	2012

Source: DigiTAG

In 2008, the Digital Video Broadcasting (DVB) Project adopted the technical parameters for the second-generation terrestrial transmission system called DVB-T2. In 2009, the European Telecommunications Standards Institute approved the specification as a standard. DVB-T2 "incorporates the latest developments in modulation and error-protection to increase the bit-rate capacity and improve signal robustness" (DigiTAG, 2009, p. 5). The outcome is that DVB-T2 is at least 30% and possibly up to 65% more efficient than its predecessor. With a DVB-T2 capacity of 40 Mbps, a DTT multiplex (digital channels sharing the bandwidth previously assigned to a single analog channel) could provide viewers with 4-6 HDTV channels or 15-20 SDTV channels (DigiTAG, 2009). Unfortunately, DVB-T2 is not backward compatible with DVB-T and will require broadcasters and consumers to acquire new equipment. Besides the United Kingdom, Finland plans to launch DVB-T2 services in 2010, and other European countries are conducting DVB-T2 trials. But extensive deployment of DVB-T2 transmission technology will probably have to wait until 2012—when most European countries will have completed their digital switch-over (Mouyal, 2009).

Factors to Watch

The global diffusion of DTV technology will evolve over the second decade of the 21st century. In the United States, the future inclusion of mDTV receivers and HD-quality video recording capability in most mobile phones will enhance this diffusion on a personal and familial level. Most still cameras will be able to capture high-quality videos on their storage chips and the inclusion of HD-quality CCD chips in video cameras will mean that any single frame of video can be printed as sharp enlarged still images.

On a global scale, the more developed nations of the world will phase out analog television transmissions as they transition to digital broadcasting. As Table 6.1 demonstrated, a significant number of nations will complete the digital transition by 2015. In the process, DTV will influence what people watch, especially as it will offer easy access to the Internet and other forms of entertainment that are more interactive than traditional television.

The following issues are likely to emerge between 2010 and 2015:

◆ *3-D DTV*—The initial high cost ($2,000 and up) of 3-D televisions that use electro-optical technology will limit their adoption by consumers who have just upgraded their analog sets to HDTV. While consumer electronics manufacturers are buoyed at the prospect of 3-D DTV receiver sales (e.g., Panasonic predicts selling 1 million 3-D televisions worldwide by March 2011), some retailers are more circumspect and have expressed concerns at compatibility issues (e.g., 3-D glasses) ("Dealers Doubt 3DTV," 2010; Wakabayashi, 2010). In addition, the limited number of 3-D television programs and film programs will also be an inhibiting factor in consumer purchasing decisions. However, if television manufacturers include 3-D display capability in HDTV sets at a modest price premium, it may boost sales and encourage more television production in 3-D. This parity in pricing may not occur until 2015 or later. Future 3-D television technologies may not require the use of glasses, another key inhibiting factor in consumer adoption.

◆ *The Next Analog Deadline*—As part of the conversion to DTV, the FCC required in 2007 that U.S. cable television operators either provide a set-top converter box that will down-convert digital programming for display on older analog televisions, or continue to distribute the analog signals of all channels carried (in addition to the digital versions) for a three-year period starting February 18, 2009 (FCC, 2007). This three-year period effectively started on the revised analog shut-down date of June 12, 2009 and now extends to June 12, 2012. For most U.S. cable systems, there are incentives to make this conversion occur before the deadline as there are significant amounts of bandwidth to be recovered by ending dual carriage of networks in both analog and digital versions. For satellite systems the conversion will be easier as each of their set-top boxes is already a digital-to-analog converter.

◆ *Mobile DTV*—Given the relatively modest investment ($100,000) needed by local stations to transmit mDTV, it is expected that this technology will become a service that all U.S. broadcasters can be expected to offer. The investment will be offset by increased revenue from advertising targeted to mobile DTV viewers. As noted above, the wide adoption of mDTV by local U.S. broadcasters may assist in their efforts to retain the spectrum assigned for DTV broadcasting in the face of recent FCC efforts to reclaim it for wireless broadband services.

◆ *HD Video Streaming*—This derivative technology encodes high-definition video into a streaming file, which can be viewed by online users without prior downloading (Dupagne & Grinfeder, 2009). In effect, it is the equivalent of HDTV in the Internet environment. But the encoded bit rate of HD video streaming is substantially lower than that of broadcast HDTV to accommodate slower broadband connections. It can often be 2.5 Mbps or less, compared to up to 19.4 Mbps for terrestrial HDTV (Dupagne & Grinfeder, 2009). Although the amount of HD video streaming viewing is difficult to ascertain, it is clear that more Web sites are offering HD programs or clips (e.g., ABC, CBS, Fox, Hulu, Vimeo, YouTube). On the other hand, the recent decisions taken by some broadband service providers to implement bandwidth caps and usage-based billing could adversely affect the growth of HD video streaming, especially if content becomes less compressed.

◆ *HD News* —Even though the DTV transition is now complete in the United States, many TV stations still need to upgrade their news operations to HD. The pace of these upgrades was relatively brisk in 2006 and 2007, but slowed down in 2008 and 2009 due to the recession and its impact on capital budgeting. By October 2009, it was projected that no more than 20% of local TV newsrooms, generally in larger markets, had upgraded their studio facilities to HD; the percentage was even smaller for field news operations (Kaufman, 2009). According to Mark Siegel, president of the system integrator company Advanced Broadcast Solutions, a TV station in a top 25 market will have to invest between $3 and $5 million to upgrade all facilities from SD to HD (Kaufman, 2009). Given these cost estimates and the economic climate, it is not surprising that some engineering departments are considering cheaper HD cameras for electronic news gathering.

◆ *Multicasting*—The use of multiple SDTV channels will remain in the mind of many broadcasters in the years to come. But whether multicasting can generate significant additional revenue is still open to debate (Malone, 2009), especially if the economic recovery in 2010 and 2011 continues to proceed with sluggishness. As of April 2010, an estimated 615 full-power commercial television stations were multicasting channels within their allocated 6 MHz spectrum (C. Webster, BIA/Kelsey, personal communication, April 5, 2010). Genres of multicast networks are plentiful, ranging from Spanish-language programs (e.g., *LATV*) to sports (e.g., *Untamed Sports*) to entertainment (e.g., *This TV*). Revenue is generally based on a sharing agreement between the multicast network and its affiliates. For instance, based on a 50-50 barter split, an affiliate with *This TV* could earn more than $1 million per year (Malone, 2009).

Digital video and television are omnipresent in modern society. Television viewers are watching DTV programs on home widescreen displays that have remarkable image clarity, color accuracy, and audio fidelity. Some will be watching television news and weather on their netbooks as they commute to work. They are shooting HD video with their mobile phones, editing it on their laptops, and uploading their mini-movies to online sites for sharing with friends and family. It represents a new era in television broadcasting and video production, where content is scalable to any size display, is increasingly personal, has anytime access anywhere, and may provide the illusion of three dimensions in the near future.

Bibliography

Advanced Television Systems Committee. (2009, October 15). A/153: ATSC mobile DTV standard, parts 1 – 8. Washington, DC: Author.

Advisory Committee on Advanced Television Service. (1995). Advisory Committee final report and recommendation. Washington, DC: Author.

Ankeny, J. (2009, May 15). Sony looks to bring 3-D into the living room. TV Technology, 27, 11.

Balanced Budget Act of 1997, Pub. L. No. 105-33, § 3003, 111 Stat. 251, 265 (1997).

Best Buy. (2010). Frequently asked questions for electronics recycling program. Retrieved April 2, 2010, from http://www.bestbuy.com/site/null/null/pcmcat174700050009.c?id=pcmcat174700050009

Bonnett, T. (2010, April 3). Fans cheer football's new TV dimension. *Sky News.* Retrieved April 3, 2010, from http://news.sky.com/skynews/Home/Technology/Sky-3D-TV-Manchester-United-Vs-Chelsea-Shown-In-3D-In-Over-1000-Pubs-Around-Country/Article/201004115592773?f=rss

Brasor, P. (2008, December 28). Critics switched off over digital-TV plans. *The Japan Times.* Retrieved April 2, 2010, from http://search.japantimes.co.jp/cgi-bin/fd20081228pb.html

Brinkley, J. (1997). *Defining vision: The battle for the future of television.* New York: Harcourt Brace & Company.

Broadcasting Ourselves. (2009, May 20). *YouTube Blog.* Retrieved April 2, 2010, from http://youtube-global.blogspot.com/2009/05/zoinks-20-hours-of-video-uploaded-every_20.html

Careless, J. (2009, July 22). Latin America goes its own way on DTV. *TV Technology, 27,* 16.

Commission of the European Communities. (2005, May 24). *Communication from the Commission to the Council, the European Parliament, the European Economic and Social Committee and the Committee of the Regions on accelerating the transition from analogue to digital broadcasting.* COM(2005) 204 final. Brussels: Author. Retrieved April 2, 2010, from http://eur-lex.europa.eu/LexUriServ/LexUriServ.do?uri=COM:2005:0204:FIN:EN:PDF

Cotriss, D. (2010). High-definition slowly coming to IPTV. *IPTV Daily.* Retrieved April 2, 2010, from http://www.dailyiptv.com/features/high-definition-iptv-031908

Dealers doubt 3DTV. (2010, March 31). *Television Broadcast.* Retrieved April 2, 2010, from http://www.televisionbroadcast.com/article/97564

Deficit Reduction Act of 2005, Pub. L. No. 109-171, § 3001-§ 3013, 120 Stat. 4, 21 (2006).

Dickson, G. (2008, March 23). Spectrum auction concludes: $19.6B. *Broadcasting & Cable.* Retrieved April 2, 2010, from http://www.broadcastingcable.com/article/112950-Spectrum_Auction_Concludes_19_6B.php

DigiTAG. (2007). *HD on DTT: Key issues for broadcasters, regulators and viewers.* Geneva: Author. Retrieved April 2, 2010, from http://www.digitag.org/HDTV_v01.pdf

DigiTAG. (2008). *Analogue switch-off: Learning from experiences in Europe.* Geneva: Author. Retrieved April 2, 2010, from http://www.digitag.org/ASO/ASOHandbook.pdf

DigiTAG. (2009). *Understanding DVB-T2: Key technical, business, & regulatory implications.* Geneva: Author. Retrieved April 2, 2010, from http://www.digitag.org/DTTResources/DVB-T2_Handbook.pdf

DTV Delay Act of 2009. Pub. L. No. 111-4, 123 Stat. 112 (2009).

Dupagne, M., & Grinfeder, K. (2009). Availability and characteristics of high-definition video streaming content. *Feedback, 50*(4), 33-40. Retrieved April 2, 2010, from http://www.beaweb.org/Content/ContentFolders/Journals2/feed50v4.pdf

Dupagne, M., & Seel, P. B. (1998). *High-definition television: A global perspective.* Ames: Iowa State University Press.

Federal Communications Commission. (1987). Formation of Advisory Committee on Advanced Television Service and Announcement of First Meeting, 52 Fed. Reg. 38523.

Federal Communications Commission. (1990). Advanced Television Systems and Their Impact Upon the Existing Television Broadcast Service (*First Report and Order*), 5 FCC Rcd. 5627.

Federal Communications Commission. (1996a). Advanced Television Systems and Their Impact Upon the Existing Television Broadcast Service (*Fifth Further Notice of Proposed Rule Making*), 11 FCC Rcd. 6235.

Federal Communications Commission. (1996b). Advanced Television Systems and Their Impact Upon the Existing Television Broadcast Service (*Fourth Report and Order*), 11 FCC Rcd. 17771.

Federal Communications Commission. (1997). Advanced Television Systems and Their Impact Upon the Existing Television Broadcast Service (*Fifth Report and Order*), 12 FCC Rcd. 12809.

Federal Communications Commission. (1998). Advanced Television Systems and Their Impact Upon the Existing Television Broadcast Service (*Memorandum Opinion and Order on Reconsideration of the Sixth Report and Order*), 13 FCC Rcd. 7418.

Federal Communications Commission. (2007). Carriage of digital television broadcast signals: Amendment to Part 76 of the Commission's Rules (Third Report and Order and Third Further Notice of Proposed Rule Making), 22 FCC Rcd. 21064.

Federal Communications Commission. (2009, June 15). *FCC continues DTV outreach across the nation* (Press release). Retrieved April 2, 2010, from http://hraunfoss.fcc.gov/edocs_public/attachmatch/DOC-291400A1.pdf

Greczkowski, S. (2010, February 11). The new DISH HD is up for many. *Multichannel News.* Retrieved April 2, 2010, from http://www.multichannel.com/blog/The_Satellite_Dish/30776-The_New_DISH_HD_Is_Up_For_Many.php

Grossman, B., & Dickson, G. (2010, January 11). 3D hype brings out the skeptics. *Broadcasting & Cable, 140,* 4, 6.

Hansell, S. (2008, January 31). Spectrum auction: C Block hits reserve price. *The New York Times* (Bits blog). Retrieved April 2, 2010, from http://bits.blogs.nytimes.com/2008/01/31/spectrum-auction-c-block-hits-reserve-price/?st=cse&sq=spectrum+auction&scp=3

Hayes, R. M. (1989). *3-D movies: A history and filmography of stereoscopic cinema.* Jefferson, NC: McFarland & Company.

High-definition television in Europe. (2009, March). *Screen Digest, 450,* 77-84.

Johnston, C. (2009, May 15). Mobile DTV still packs a room. *TV Technology, 27,* 11.

Kaufman, D. (2009, October 1). Stations moving HD news off back burner. *TVNewsCheck.* Retrieved April 2, 2010, from http://www.tvnewscheck.com/articles/2009/10/01/daily.3/

Leichtman Research Group. (2009, November 30). *Nearly half of U.S. households have an HDTV set* (Press release). Retrieved April 2, 2010, from http://www.leichtmanresearch.com/press/113009release.html

Lifsher, M., & Chang, A. (2009, November 19). State mandates power-saving TVs. *The Los Angeles Times*, p. B1. Retrieved April 2, 2010, from LexisNexis Academic database.

Louis, A., & Roger, M. (2008, Q1). The roll-out of DTT in France. *EBU Technical Review*, 1-10. Retrieved April 2, 2010, from http://www.ebu.ch/fr/technical/trev/trev_2008-Q1.pdf

Malone, M. (2009, June 22). Digi-channels enjoy brave new post-DTV world. *Broadcasting & Cable, 139,* 16.

Midgley, N. (2010, February 26). Want HD digital TV? *The Daily Telegraph*, Business section, p. 4. Retrieved April 2, 2010, from LexisNexis Academic database.

Ministry budgets ¥220 billion for digital TV transition in 2011. (2008, July 20). *The Japan Times*. Retrieved April 2, 2010, from http://search.japantimes.co.jp/cgi-bin/nn20080720a9.html

Moriyama, S. (2009, November 26). *Heading for switchover in Japan*. Retrieved April 2, 2010, from http://web.pts.org.tw/~web01/2009digital/download/day1-04.pdf

Mouyal, N. (2009, October). Interest for DVB-T2 in Europe. *DigiTAG Web Letter*. Retrieved April 2, 2010, from http://www.digitag.org/WebLetters/2009/External-Oct2009.html

National Telecommunications and Information Administration. (2009, December 9). *TV converter box coupon program: Final status update*. Retrieved April 2, 2010, from http://www.ntia.doc.gov/dtvcoupon/reports/NTIA_DTVWeekly_120909.pdf

Nielsen. (2007, October 3). *HDTV customers are happy with picture quality, less enthusiastic about programming options, Nielsen finds* (News release). Retrieved April 2, 2010, from http://en-us.nielsen.com/etc/medialib/nielsen_dotcom/en_us/documents/pdf/press_releases/2007/october.Par.77242.File.pdf

Nielsen. (2008, December 22). HD TV households skew upscale, educated, younger. *Nielsen Wire*. Retrieved April 2, 2010, from http://blog.nielsen.com/nielsenwire/media_entertainment/hd-tv-households-skew-upscale-educated-younger/

Nielsen. (2009, June 10). 2.8 million homes still unready for DTV transition on June 12. *Nielsen Wire*. Retrieved April 2, 2010, from http://blog.nielsen.com/nielsenwire/media_entertainment/28-million-homes-still-unready-for-dtv-transition-on-june-12/.

Nippon Hoso Kyokai. (1998). *NHK factsheet '98*. Tokyo: Author.

Ofcom. (2007). *Communications market report*. Retrieved April 2, 2010, from http://www.ofcom.org.uk/research/cm/cmr07/cm07_print/cm07_1.pdf

Ofcom. (2009). *The communications market: Digital progress report (Digital TV, Q3 2009)*. Retrieved April 2, 2010, from http://www.ofcom.org.uk/research/tv/reports/dtv/dtv_2009_q3/dtv_2009_q3.pdf

O'Neal, J. E. (2009a, March 4). Are we there yet? *TV Technology, 27,* 6.

O'Neal, J. E. (2009b, November 4). Mobile DTV standard approved. *TV Technology, 27,* 23.

Panasonic schedules 3DTV roll-out in Japan. (2010, March 3). *TV Technology, 28,* 5.

Pay TV benefits from DTV transition. (2009, July 22). *TV Technology, 27,* 16.

Poor, A. (2010, February 17). HDTV Almanac - Sony pulls plug on OLED TV in Japan. *HDTV Magazine*. Retrieved April 2, 2010, from http://www.hdtvmagazine.com/columns/2010/02/hdtv_almanac_sony_pulls_plug_on_oled_tv_in_japan.php

Putman, P. (2010, April 7). NetTVs really are the 'next big thing.' *TV Technology. 28,* 8.

Rosenwald, M. S. (2009, September 19). Left in the flat-screen dust. *The Washington Post*, p. A01. Retrieved April 2, 2010, from LexisNexis Academic database.

Seel, P. B., & Dupagne, M. (2000). Advanced television. In A. E. Grant & J. H. Meadows (Eds.), *Communication Technology Update* (7th ed., pp. 75-88). Boston: Focal Press.

70% of families have digital TV receiver. (2009, November 7). *The Japan Times*. Retrieved April 2, 2010, from http://search.japantimes.co.jp/cgi-bin/nb20091107a6.html

Shishikui, Y., Fujita, Y., & Kubota, K. (2009, January). Super Hi-Vision – The star of the show! *EBU Technical Review*, 1-13. Retrieved April 2, 2010, from http://www.ebu.ch/en/technical/trev/trev_2009-Q0_SHV-NHK.pdf

Silva, R. (2010). LED TVs – the truth about 'LED" Televisions. *About.com*. Retrieved April 2, 2010 from, http://hometheater.about.com/od/televisions/qt/ledlcdtvfacts.htm

Sugawara, M. (2008, Q2). Super Hi-Vision – Research on a future ultra-HDTV system. *EBU Technical Review*, 1-7. Retrieved April 2, 2010, from http://www.ebu.ch/fr/technical/trev/trev_2008-Q2_nhk-ultra-hd.pdf

Tabuchi, H. (2009, October 10). Seeing the future in 3-D television. *The New York Times*, p. B3.

Tilley, S. (2010, February 3). Will 'Avatar' boost 3D TV sales? *Toronto Sun*. Retrieved April 2, 2010, from http://www.torontosun.com/life/gadgets/2010/02/03/12727671.html

Uranaka, T. (2010, February 16). Sony pulls plug on OLED TV in Japan. Reuters. Retrieved April 2, 2010 from, http://www.reuters.com/article/idUSTRE61F0ZO20100216.

Wakabayashi, D. (2010, March 8). Panasonic to launch its 3-D push in U.S. *The Wall Street Journal*, p. B6. Retrieved April 2, 2010, from ProQuest database.

Weprin, A. (2010, January 8). 'Avatar' fuels 3D hype and hope. *Broadcasting & Cable*. Retrieved April 2, 2010, from http://www.broadcastingcable.com/blog/BC_Beat/29852-_Avatar_Fuels_3D_Hype_and_Hope.php

Winslow, G. (2009a, October 7). Kagan: HDTV sales to rebound in late '09. *Multichannel News*. Retrieved April 2, 2010, from http://www.multichannel.com/article/357142-Kagan_HDTV_Sales_To_Rebound_In_Late_09.php

Winslow, G. (2009b, December 14). Mixed pictures; High-def penetration up, but confusion persists. *Multichannel News*, p. 14. Retrieved April 2, 2010, from LexisNexis Academic database.

7

Multichannel Television Services

Jennifer H. Meadows, Ph.D.[*]

Just several decades ago, people would sit down for an evening of television and have a choice of two to five channels. Nowadays, most people have so many channels to choose from that they have to use interactive program guides to help them decide which program to watch. Who would think there would be channels devoted to food, auto racing, and jewelry shopping? Multichannel television services deliver this programming and more.

Multichannel television services include cable television, direct broadcast satellite (DBS) services, and pay television services. (Internet protocol television services (IPTV) are also considered multichannel television services, but they will be discussed in Chapter 8.) With cable television services, television programming is delivered to the home via a coaxial cable or a hybrid system combining fiber optics and coaxial cable. The subscriber either uses a set-top box or connects the cable directly into the television. DBS customers receive programming using a small, pizza-sized satellite dish and a set-top receiver connected to a television.

Pay television services are available on both cable and DBS systems and include premium channels, pay-per-view (PPV), near video on demand (NVOD), and video on demand (VOD). Premium channels are programming channels for which subscribers pay a monthly fee above the regular cable or DBS subscription fee. These channels usually contain a mix of movies, events, and original programming without commercials. HBO and Starz are examples of premium channels. Pay-per-view is a program such as a movie, concert, or boxing match that is ordered and then played at a specific time. Near video on demand is like pay-per-view except that there are many available starting times. Video on demand is programming that is available at any time. Users also have control over the program so the program can be paused, rewound, and fast-forwarded. VOD can be available for a one-time charge. For example, a movie can be ordered for a set fee. VOD can also be offered for a monthly fee. For example, subscription video on demand (SVOD) is a slate of programming offered on demand for a monthly charge. Many premium channels offer SVOD included in their monthly subscription rate. Finally, free VOD is available; its programming is varied, and offerings range from children's shows to fitness videos to broadcast network programming.

This chapter will discuss the origins of multichannel television services as well as recent developments such as new interactive services, retransmission consent battles, and the changing regulatory landscape.

---

[*] Professor, Department of Communication Design, California State University, Chico (Chico, California).

Background
The Early Years

Many people do not realize that cable television has been around since the beginning of television in the United States. Cable television grew out of a need to sell television sets. People were not going to purchase television sets if they had nothing to watch. It has not been established who was first, but communities in Oregon, Pennsylvania, and Arkansas have claimed to be the first to establish Community Antenna Television (CATV). These communities could not get over-the-air programming with regular television antennas because of geographical limitations. Antennas were erected on top of hills and mountains to receive signals from nearby cities, and then homes in the community were connected via coaxial cable. Appliance stores could sell televisions, and people who bought them had programming to watch (NCTA, n.d.).

Figure 7.1
Traditional Cable TV Network Tree & Branch Architecture

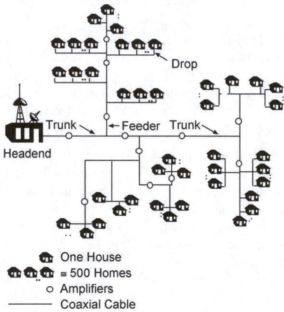

Source: Technology Futures, Inc.

Soon CATV operators began to offer customers distant channels since their antennas could pick up other stations besides those in the local market. These new channels threatened local broadcast stations, and the FCC responded by limiting the importation of distant channels. Continuing into the early 1970s the FCC responded to concerns of broadcasters and the film industry by limiting cable's ability to offer any programming other than that offered by local broadcast channels (for example, sports and movies). There was not much growth in cable during this time.

The situation changed in 1972 when the FCC began to deregulate cable, and previous restrictions on cable programming were loosened. Also in the early 1970s, "the Open Skies" policy was established that allowed private companies into satellite communications (NCTA, n.d.). In 1972, HBO, the first premium channel, began as a local microwave service in Pennsylvania, and was offered to cable companies around the country via satellite.

A few years later, Ted Turner put his small independent television station from Atlanta on the same satellite carrying the HBO service, giving cable companies another "free channel" and establishing the first "Superstation," WTBS. Use of satellites to deliver programming soon facilitated the creation of many cable networks that are still popular today including ESPN, A&E, CNN, and MTV.

This use of satellites was also key to the development of DBS services. Chances are, if you lived in a rural area in the 1970s, your community was not wired for cable television. With a television receive only satellite dish (TVRO), people could receive television programming delivered via satellite. In 1977, Taylor Howard, a professor at Stanford University, who worked with satellite technology, may have been the first to build a satellite dish to receive HBO programming at his home. This marked the beginning of TVRO satellites. The technology has limitations, though. First, it used the low-power C-band (3.7 GHz to 4.2 GHz) frequencies, which meant the dishes were large and unattractive. Some communities even banned the dishes because of their appearance. They were also expensive to install and complicated to operate. Finally, programming networks began to scramble their signals so TVRO users had to purchase decoding boxes and pay to unscramble the signals (Museum of Broadcast Communication, n.d.).

The Growth Years

Deregulation continued into the 1980s, allowing cable systems to accelerate their growth. The *Cable Communications Act of 1984* amended the *Communications Act of 1934* with regulations specific to cable. The most important change made by this act was that it removed the rights of a local franchising authority to regulate cable TV rates unless the area was served by fewer than three broadcast signals. When a cable company operates in a community, it has to have a franchising agreement with the community. This agreement covers issues such as public access requirements, subscriber service and renewal standards, and a franchise fee; it is negotiated between the franchising agency and the cable company. With the passage of the 1984 Act, cable companies were allowed to increase rates without government approval, and rates grew—and grew. At the same time, deregulation and rising rates allowed cable companies to raise capital to expand their services and upgrade their technology. However, cable customers found their cable rates rising significantly, with the average rate more than doubling from 1984 to 1992 as service standards dropped.

At the same time, new satellite television services and wireless cable companies were struggling to be established. Direct-to-home satellite service in the 1980s used the medium-power Ku-band (11.7 GHz to 12.2 GHz) and offered customers a limited amount of "cable" programming. The service was not successful for a number of reasons. First, the service only offered a limited number of channels. Second, the operators were unable to obtain the programming that customers wanted—popular cable programming networks. In addition, the service was expensive and performed poorly in bad weather (Carlin, 2006).

Another attempt at satellite television was made in 1983 when the International Telecommunications Union and the World Administrative Radio Conference established that the high power Ku-band (12.2 GHZ to 12.7 GHz) would be used for direct broadcast satellite service and assigned orbital positions and frequencies for each country. In the United States, the FCC established eight orbital positions and accepted eight applications for the slots. The applicants had to prove due diligence, which meant they had to begin constructing a satellite within a year and have the service operational within six years. All of those applicants failed. The FCC collected a new group of applicants in 1989, and those companies also failed to begin service by 1992. The services could not take off for two reasons. First, they could not transmit enough channels because there was no acceptable digital video compression standard. Without digital video compression, these satellite services could only broadcast a very limited amount of channels, nowhere close to what cable systems were offering at the time. Digital video compression would allow several channels worth of programming to be squeezed into the space of one analog channel. Second, there needed to be a way for satellite services to get access to popular cable programming channels. Cable companies, at the time, were using their power to prevent any programming deals with the competition (DBS), leaving satellite providers with a small number of channels that few people wanted to watch.

These problems were solved in the early 1990s. First, the MPEG-1 digital video compression standard was approved in 1993, followed by the broadcast-quality MPEG-2 format in 1995. This standard allowed eight channels to be compressed into the space of one analog channel. Second, the *Cable Television Consumer Protection and Competition Act* (a.k.a. The Cable Act of 1992) forced cable programming companies to sell to other video distribution outlets for terms comparable to cable. Now, DBS had the channel capacity and the programming to adequately compete with cable. DirecTV (Hughes) and USSB (Hubbard) were the first to launch service in 1994. EchoStar launched their DISH service in 1996. Other DBS applicants failed to launch their services, and DirecTV and EchoStar obtained some of their channels. Rainbow DBS launched in 2003 and was used for the short-lived VOOM HD service.

Not to be outdone, the cable industry entered the satellite television service market with Primestar. This medium-power KU-band service offered only a limited number of channels, so as to not compete with local cable systems. The consortium of cable systems involved in Primestar included Cox, Comcast, Newhouse, TCI, and Time Warner. Primestar eventually adopted digital video compression to offer more channels and directly compete with DirecTV. They highlighted the fact that subscribers did not have to buy the equipment; rather, they rented it just like a cable set-top box.

Primestar was eventually purchased, along with USSB, by DirecTV, making it the largest DBS service in the United States. EchoStar eventually took over the VOOM channels from Rainbow DBS and took over the orbital positions of DBS applicant MCI. Finally, one last DBS service was launched in 1999: Sky Angel, which offers religious programming. Due to satellite problems in 2006, the service moved to IPTV (Sky Angel, n.d.).

Consolidation within the satellite television market sparked a price war between DirecTV and DISH and between the DBS companies and cable. Subscribers no longer had to pay for equipment as DBS services began to offer free installation and hardware and even multiple room receivers. Cable still had a major advantage over DBS, because DBS subscribers could not get local broadcast stations through their satellite service. This was due to the *Satellite Broadcasting Act of 1988*, which prohibited the distribution of local broadcast stations over satellite to subscribers who lived in the coverage area of the station. This meant that DBS subscribers had to set up an antenna or subscribe to basic cable to get local channels. This problem was solved with the *Satellite Home Viewer Improvement Act of 1999*, which allowed DBS companies to offer those local channels to their customers. The issue then was for DBS companies to have enough space on their satellites available to offer local channels in all markets in the United States. The *Satellite Home Viewer Extension and Reauthorization Act* (SHVERA) extended SHVIA in 2004 (FCC, n.d.-b).

Cable television at this time was reacting to its first real competition. After the boom years brought about, in part, by the deregulation of the *Cable Act of 1984*, the cable industry was perhaps a little complacent, raising prices and disregarding service. These complaints eventually led to the *1992 Cable Act* discussed earlier, which re-regulated basic cable rates. One of the most important provisions of the Act gave broadcasters negotiating power over cable companies. Broadcasters had for years been complaining about how cable operators were retransmitting their signals and collecting money for them, with none of the money coming back to broadcasters. The "must-carry" and "retransmission consent" provision of the *1992 Act* let broadcasters decide if the cable system must carry their signal or an agreement had to be reached between the cable company and the broadcaster for retransmission consent. This consent could "cost" anything from money to time. The concept of "must-carry" would come back to haunt both cable operators and broadcasters as the digital television transition neared. As discussed in Chapter 6, broadcasters can transmit one HDTV and up to five SDTV channels. Broadcasters argue that, under must-carry, cable operators should be forced to carry all of those channels. Cable operators, on the other hand, say they should only have to carry the stations' primary signal. The Federal Communications Commission (FCC), thus far, has sided with the cable operators saying that multi-channel must-carry would be an unnecessary burden to cable operators under the dual must-carry ruling.

While cable and DBS services were growing and developing quickly at this time, the same was not true for pay television services. Premium channels were popular, especially HBO and its main competitor, Showtime, but pay-per-view had failed to gain major success. The limitations of PPV are numerous and mostly outweigh the advantages. First, PPV programs had a very limited number of available start times. The programs could not be paused, rewound, or fast-forwarded. There was only a limited amount of programming available. Users needed to call the cable company to order the program and had to have a cable box to get them. By the time a movie was available in PPV, it had already been available for sale and rental at home video stores. Often times, as well, the price was higher for PPV than rental. The only real advantages of PPV were no late fees, you did not have to leave your house, and sometimes it was the only way to get certain special events such as championship boxing.

DBS solved some of these problems with near video on demand. Instead of having only a few channels devoted to PPV, DBS providers could have many channels of PPV and could offer programs at staggered start times so the viewer had more choice. The buy rates for movies on NVOD were higher than PPV (Adams, 2005). DBS services have since moved away from NVOD. While they often offer more channels of PPV than cable, DBS providers such as DirecTV offer VOD services with a DVR receiver and a broadband connection. The program is ordered and delivered to the DVR over the Internet connection.

Digital Upgrades

As cable television systems upgraded their networks from analog to digital, new services and features began to roll out. For example, cable systems began to upgrade their networks from coax to hybrid fiber/coax (see Figure 7.2). This upgrade allowed cable systems to offer new services such as high-definition programming, DVR services, VOD, SVOD, broadband Internet access, and telephony. Video programming, broadband Internet access, and telephony make up the cable "triple play," which is one feature that the cable industry uses to differentiate its service from DBS. (For more on DVRs, see Chapter 15, and for more on cable Internet, see Chapter 21.)

The digital upgrades helped advance pay television services. First, the upgraded digital networks allowed cable systems to carry more channels of programming. Premium channels took advantage of this additional bandwidth by offering multiplexed versions of their services. So, for example, instead of just getting one HBO channel, a subscriber also gets different versions or "multiplexes" of HBO including HBO2, HBO Signature, HBO family, etc. Most premium channels now offer a package of multiplexed channels to subscribers including Starz, Showtime, and Cinemax. Even "regular" cable programming channels are multiplexing. For instance, sports fans can now watch ESPN, ESPN2, ESPN Classic, ESPN U, and ESPN News. More advanced pay television services were also introduced, including subscription VOD. HBO was the first to offer HBO on Demand in 2001 that allows HBO subscribers with digital cable to access a selection of HBO programs on demand. These programs include original series, movies, and events. HBO even experimented with the service by making episodes of *The Wire* available first on On Demand before airing on HBO (Kaufman, 2007).

Figure 7.2
Hybrid Fiber/Coax Cable TV System

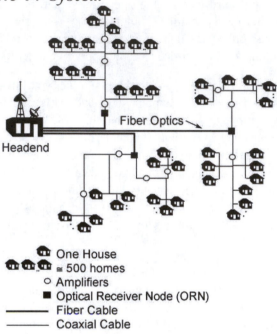

Headend

Fiber Optics →

🏠 One House

🏠🏠🏠 ≅ 500 homes

○ Amplifiers

■ Optical Receiver Node (ORN)

———— Fiber Cable

———— Coaxial Cable

Source: Technology Futures, Inc.

Video on demand was the next service to be rolled out by cable companies. VOD has been tested for the last three decades, with the largest test being Time Warner's Full Service Network in Orlando (Florida) from 1994 to 1997. The Full Service Network eventually failed because of numerous factors including cost and technological limitations. The VOD feature of the service was popular with customers, though.

Video on demand is now offered to digital cable subscribers by the major cable multiple system operators (MSOs) including Comcast, Cox, Time Warner, and Cablevision. Subscribers have access to a variety of programming including new movies for a one-time charge. The fee usually entitles the viewer 24-hour access to the program. Free older movies are available as well as a selected number of television shows from broadcast and cable networks. Finally, special VOD only channels and programs have developed and are available by choosing from a menu of "channels" such as Comcast's Life and Home, News and Kids, and the Cutting Edge (On demand menu, n.d.).

High-Definition Programming

When it comes to high-definition programming, DBS services have been the most aggressive in developing and marketing the service. DirecTV started the battle when it announced that it would be offering 100 channels of HD content by 2008 (Berger, 2007). DISH also quickly added HD channels. Both services use MPEG-4 AVC video compression for HD programming. The compression allows the companies to squeeze two channels of HD into the space formerly used by one. The biggest problem with the move to MPEG-4 AVC is that customers with older DirecTV and DISH MPEG-2 boxes had to upgrade to a new box to get the new HD channels (Patterson & Katzmaier, 2008).

Cable television companies are also bulking up their HD offerings, especially in response to competition from DBS. Not only do cable MSOs offer HD channels, but they are also able to offer HD VOD and HD SVOD. The local HD channels are a different issue. As discussed earlier, under the must carry and retransmission consent rules of the *Cable Act of 1992*, broadcasters can decide if the cable company must carry their channel. With the digital transition, broadcasters can offer their primary signal in HD and several other digital multicast channels. Broadcasters want must-carry to apply to all of their digital channels, not just the primary channel. Then FCC chairman, Kevin Martin, was a supporter of multicast must carry, but the commission as a whole was not. Martin had to pull a vote on the subject in June 2006 (Hearn, 2007). The FCC did vote that cable operators must carry the local broadcaster's signals in digital and analog form ("dual must-carry") for three years after the 2009 digital transition date.

The FCC also issued a ruling on "plug-and-play" in 2003. The ruling requires that properly equipped digital television sets be able to receive digital cable without a set-top box by inserting a "CableCARD" into the set. With first generation CableCARD, though, users can only get one-way information, so using advanced services such as VOD is impossible with a CableCARD (FCC, n.d.-a). To get around this, subscribers can also insert CableCARDs into set-top boxes and DVRs like TiVo. This development is interesting, since the Cable-CARD was supposed to help eliminate the set-top box.

Another advantage of the CableCARD is that the technology allows people to purchase set-top boxes from retailers and then get a CableCARD from the cable provider. An FCC rule went into effect on July 1, 2007 that required cable operators to remove certain security technology from their systems to allow for the use of outside boxes.

Regulation

A la carte. Arguing that cable customers are charged too much for channels that they do not even watch, then FCC Chairman Martin (2005-2009) pushed for "a la carte." With a la carte, customers would choose what channels they wanted instead of purchasing programming in bundled tiers. Martin also argued that parents like a la carte because they could avoid channels that are not family friendly. Cable responded to that concern with the establishment of family tiers. Spanish-speaking viewers, argued Martin, would also benefit by not having to pay for English language programming. The cable industry is vehemently against a la carte. They argue that a la carte would raise prices, limit diversity, and lower revenue for the development and expansion of new services. Under current regulations, the FCC cannot force the cable companies to break up their programming tiers. A la carte remains an issue for many consumer groups but as of March 2010 there have been no new developments from the FCC.

Video franchising order. Cable companies are facing competition from telephone companies, which are rolling out IPTV (Internet protocol television) services using advanced fiber optic network technology with services including AT&T's U-Verse and Verizon's FiOS (discussed in more detail in Chapter 8). One of the difficulties of starting a new video service is the negotiation of franchising agreements, those agreements between the community and the video service provider. AT&T and Verizon argued that franchising agreements were hampering their efforts to roll out these new services and lobbied for national and statewide franchising agreements. Many states passed these. The FCC became involved when it ruled that local governments only have 90 days to negotiate a franchising agreement, and, if no agreement is reached, then the franchise would be granted. This procedure would allow the telephone company to avoid good faith negotiations and just wait until the deadline passed. Then, these companies could build out their systems as they please, perhaps avoiding lower income neighborhoods or rural areas (Bangeman, 2007). The same franchising rules are not applicable to cable.

Recent Developments

Since 2008 there have been some major changes in multichannel television services. New services have been introduced, and new ways to deliver programming are being developed and deployed. The regulatory environment is changing and fights over programming carriage contracts and retransmission consent have left customers without their favorite channels.

Policy Issues: Retransmission Consent, Carriage Contracts, Mergers & Set-Top Boxes

In early 2010, movie fans in New York with Cablevision service didn't know whether they could watch the *Academy Awards* on WABC. The issue was retransmission content. *The Cable Act of 1992* requires that multichannel television providers negotiate with broadcasters to carry their channels. As discussed earlier in this chapter, broadcasters can choose to make cable systems carry their channel (must carry) or negotiate some kind of payment (retransmission consent) (Peers, 2010; Ovide, 2010). In the 1990s, broadcasters were not successful at negotiating cash payments but the tide has turned in favor of broadcasters in the past few years. Broadcasters are aware that cable companies pay as much at $4.00 per month per subscriber to carry specific channels. Because they are losing advertising revenue as more and more viewers turn to other sources of video, broadcasters want to have the same dual revenue stream that cable channels such as Discovery and ESPN have. These cable channels get revenue from advertising and carriage fees. In 2009 and 2010 there were several high profile standoffs between broadcasters and cable companies. Disney/ABC (which owns WABC in New York) and Cablevision settled at the last minute, with viewers only missing the opening of the 2010 *Oscars*. Time Warner and Fox had a similar impasse prior to some 2010 college bowl games (Schatz, 2010b). In all of these cases, the cable company agreed to compensate the broadcaster for the right to retransmit the station's programming.

With all of the disputes mentioned above, it is the customers who lose the most when they cannot watch anticipated events. Indeed, the FCC is getting involved. As of mid-2010, the Commission is studying whether to force broadcasters to keep their channels on cable systems during retransmission consent negotiations. Multichannel television providers support this idea, but broadcasters see it as taking away a negotiation tool (Eggerton, 2010a; Eggerton, 2010b; Eggerton, 2010c).

Multichannel TV subscribers do not like it when their favorite channels are no longer available. Just as broadcast channels have been pulled over retransmission disputes, other channels have been pulled over carriage contract disputes. For example, in January 2010, Scripps Interactive pulled the Food Network and HGTV from Cablevision systems. Scripps Interactive wanted Cablevision to increase their carriage fee of $.25 per month per subscriber for both channels to $.75. The channels were restored after three weeks and many angry customer communications. Although the settlement wasn't released, Scripps Interactive did get an increase, estimated at $.45 (Wilkerson, 2010; Siriwardane, 2010). This type of dispute is expected to occur more frequently. Time Warner is set to begin negotiations with Disney in mid 2010. Disney owns the popular and expensive EPSN programming channels and is expected to further its pressure on multichannel programming providers to increase carriage fees.

Some multichannel television providers own programming channels. For example, Comcast owns E! and Versus, and Cablevision partly owns the Sundance Channels and AMC. One concern is that these companies may withhold their programming from other multichannel television providers. The FCC ruled that cable operators must sell rivals' programming. Comcast and Cablevision challenged this ruling in 2010 in the U.S. Court of Appeals. The Court denied the challenge, upholding the FCC's rule (McQuillen & Shields, 2010).

This ruling became even more important when Comcast and NBC Universal agreed in early 2010 to a merger. The Comcast NBCU deal is under scrutiny by the Department of Justice, Congress, and the FCC as of mid 2010. Comcast has stated that it will maintain free over-the-air NBC service. With this merger Comcast would own popular cable channels including Bravo, USA and The Weather Channel. The ruling discussed above becomes important because, with the merger, Comcast becomes owner of two of the top 10 cable channels: USA and The Weather Channel. Rival multichannel television services are concerned. DirecTV and Versus just recently settled a carriage dispute. DirecTV wanted to move Versus to a higher tier package that would reach fewer subscribers. In the end, Versus stayed in the same tier and came back on before the Stanley Cup Playoffs and a major UFC event. This trend suggests that the battles between programming providers and service providers will continue (Wyshynski, 2010; Schatz 2010b; Weprin, 2010; Eggerton, 2009).

Another concern with the proposed merger is on-line video. Comcast has Fancast Xfinity, and NBC jointly owns Hulu; two popular on-line video services that offer full length programs. House and Senate members worried that the merged corporation would have too much control over online video. For example, would Comcast limit access to NBC content online? If the merger is approved, there would be a number of conditions to deal with any potential problems. Both the FCC and the Justice Department are expected to make a final decision on the merger by the end of 2010 (Schatz, 2010a; Eggerton, 2010d).

Many consumers want to access their programming in multiple forms. For example a person can watch *The Daily Show* on television, online or on a mobile device. It is becoming easier to move online content to the television with a number of devices such as Apple TV and advanced televisions. One key feature of multichannel television services is the set-top box. The set-top box connects your television to the network. As discussed earlier, the FCC's Plug and Play mandate required that users could access cable services without a set-top box, instead using a CableCARD. The FCC hoped that this mandate would encourage a market for independent set-top boxes but as of March 2010 this effort has not been successful (Eggerton, 2010e). The FCC's 2010 broadband plan advocates use of a "gateway" device that could deliver broadband and television but multichannel television providers have a mixed reaction. The idea of an "all-MVPD" box is supported by cable but disliked by others services such as DirecTV which uses its own boxes (Eggerton, 2010e).

Some set-top boxes also contain DVRs. TiVo is one of the pioneers in DVR technology and still makes stand alone DVRs. DISH was one of the first multichannel video providers that offered customers a set-top box with a DVR. TiVo sued DISH's parent company Echostar for patent infringement and won in 2006. The case was upheld in Federal Court in 2010. TiVo will receive $300 million in damages and sanctions. DISH has had to devise a workaround with their DVRs so as to not infringe on TiVo's patents (Kendall, 2010).

New Services: 3-D, Interactive & Online

New 3-D television technology seemingly came out of nowhere in 2009. Although children's movies had been released in 3-D and were popular, it wasn't until *Avatar* was released that a wide cross section of Americans experienced 3D without those annoying red and blue glasses. Many in the television industry believe that the next frontier for 3-D is the home. Companies including Panasonic and Samsung are selling flat screen 3D televisions. But if people are going to buy these televisions there has to be something 3-D to watch. You can only watch *Cloudy with a Chance of Meatballs* so many times. Cable and DBS companies are looking to offer 3D programming. Comcast is experimenting with 3-D sports along with CBS. The 2010 Masters golf tournament was broadcast in 3-D and made available to Comcast subscribers for free with 2 hours of 3-D coverage available each day (Dickson, 2010b). Cablevision offered a professional hockey game in 3-D to its subscribers in March 2010.

ESPN is scheduled to introduce a new 3-D network, ESPN 3D, in June 2010. The company is planning to offer about 85 events per year in 3-D including World Cup Soccer, the X Games, and college football and basketball. DirecTV was the first service to commit to carrying the channel and will launch it with three of its own 3-D channels including one called N3D that will be sponsored by Panasonic. To watch the 3-D programming, subscribers will need both a 3-D television and 3-D glasses (Spangler, 2010c; Dickson, 2010a).

Along with 3-D programming, multichannel television providers are expanding their selection of interactive services. These services include widgets to deliver horoscopes, weather and news. Comcast is working with the television shopping channel HSN to deploy the HSN Shop by Remote app. The service allows viewers to purchase items for sale with a push of a button. As of March 2010 about 12 million Comcast customers could get the app, which has an astounding 10% sales-conversion rate (Spangler, 2010a; Farrell, 2009). (For more on interactive television, see Chapter 9.)

Cablevision is launching a trial of a service called PC to TV Media Relay in June 2010 that allows subscribers to its broadband and television service to watch online content on their television on a dedicated channel (Worden, 2010). Other cable companies are using different strategies to keep their customers from switching to Internet only viewing. Comcast has expanded its online service Fancast Xfinity TV. The service offers programming from 27 networks including HBO, CBS, Hallmark and the Travel Channel. The service is free to Comcast broadband and television subscribers (Spangler, 2009). Subscribers, though, only have access to networks they get through their cable service.

HBO is also reaching out to subscribers on the Internet. HBO GO was released in early 2010. The online service gives subscribers access to over 600 hours of programming. The service was first available to Verizon FiOS customers. Only regular HBO subscribers have access to HBO GO. Comcast subscribers won't get HBO GO because they already have access through Fancast Xfinity. HBO GO is looking into offering the service to subscribers who use mobile devices (HBO Go, n.d.; Schechner, 2010).

Mobile Services

With the growing popularity of mobile devices such as smartphones, multichannel programming providers are looking to expand their reach to include those devices. Mobile phone users can access this programming several ways. First they can access programs through their mobile phone provider. An example of this would be Verizon's V-Cast Mobile TV service. V-Cast users can watch "cable" channels including the Food Network, Comedy Central, and MTV. Other providers including AT&T and Sprint also offer these television services. They all use MediaFlo technology that uses the UHF television band to deliver video to mobile phones.

Downloading is another way users can get "cable" programming on mobile devices. Popular programming is available to download to mobile devices such as BlackBerry handsets and iPhones. So if a person missed last night's *South Park*, he or she could go to iTunes and buy the episode, and it could be watched on an iPod, iPhone, iPad, or a computer. Premium channels are using smartphone apps to gain new customers. For example, Showtime's free iPhone app has clips, games, and sneak previews. Of course, users can also order Showtime with the app.

Competition from Broadcast TV?

One of the more interesting developments since the switch to digital broadcast television is the number of people dropping basic cable and/or discovering the variety of over-the-air programming. With free over-the-air television, stations can broadcast multiple channels of programming. So viewers in markets that had only five over-the-air analog channels could now receive 15 different over-the-air digital channels. Most markets give viewers up to 30 different channels. In Los Angeles, viewers can get 70 channels. Another plus is that the image quality of digital broadcast channels is often better than on cable or satellite. About 11 million households rely on over-the-air television and not just because of cost. You could argue that many of those new channels don't have compelling programming but broadcast television can now offer high quality competition to basic cable. Of course, a good antenna is always important (Welch, 2010). (For more on digital television see Chapter 6.)

CURRENT STATUS

Figure 7.3 and Table 7.1 show the market share and top ten Multichannel Television Providers in the United States as of September 2009. Cable still leads with the greatest share but over the years their market share has dropped significantly with greater competition from DBS and IPTV.

Figure 7.3
Multichannel TV Market Share

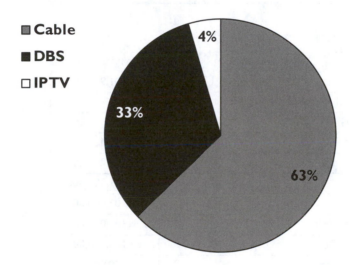

■ Cable
■ DBS
□ IPTV

Source: NCTA (2010)

U.S. Cable

According to the NCTA, cable penetration as of December 2009 is 49.3% of total television households. That adds up to 62.1 million subscribers. As of December 2009, there were 42.6 million digital cable customers, 41.8 million cable Internet customers, and 22.2 million cable voice/phone customers (NCTA, 2010).

Comcast is the largest cable MSO in the United States with 23.8 million subscribers as of September 2009. Time Warner is second with 13 million subscribers, followed by Cox Communications with 5.3 million, and Charter Communications with 4.9 million subscribers (NCTA, 2010).

Table 7.1

Top 10 MVPDs as of September 2009

MSO	Subscribers
Comcast Cable Communications	23,759,000
DirecTV	18,441,000
Dish Network Corporation	13,851,000
Time Warner Cable, Inc.	12,964,000
Cox Communications, Inc.	5,274,000
Charter Communications, Inc.	4,897,000
Cablevision Systems Corporation	3,066,000
Verizon Communications, Inc.	2,708,000
Bright House Networks LLC	2,283,000
AT&T, Inc.	1,817,000

Source: NCTA (2010)

Table 7.2

Top 10 Programming Networks as of 2009

Network	Subscribers
TBS	101,900,000
The Weather Channel	101,700,000
Discovery	101,500,000
Nickelodeon	101,400,000
USA Network	101,200.000
TNT	101,000,000
CNN	101,000,000
Food Network	101,000,000
HGTV	100,900,000
Lifetime Television	100,900,000

Source: NCTA (2010)

TBS is the U.S. programming channel with the greatest number of subscribers with an estimated 101.9 million. Table 7.2 shows the top 10 programming networks in 2009 (NCTA, 2010).

U.S. DBS

DISH Network had 14.1 million subscribers in the United States as of March 2010. DirecTV had 18.4 million subscribers as of the first quarter of 2010. DirecTV reported strong growth, especially in subscriptions to HD service. For comparison, DirecTV added 460,000 new subscribers in the first quarter of 2009 while DISH lost 94,000. One problem for DISH is their reliance on re-sellers. Their deal with AT&T ended in 2009 and about one million of their customers were from AT&T. AT&T now offers their U-Verse IPTV service (DBSTrak, 2009). Things began to look up for DISH at the end of 2009 when they added 249,000 new subscribers (Paul & Adegoke, 2010). Both services offer programming and service packages that start at $29.99 per month and go up depending on the number of channels, HD programming, premium channels, special sports packages, and DVR services you want.

U.S. Pay Television Services

HBO and Cinemax have the most premium channel subscribers with over 40 million in the United States. HBO on Demand is the leading SVOD service (Time Warner, n.d.). Starz is second with 16.9 million subscribers. In the past, Starz differentiated itself from HBO and Showtime by focusing on movies rather than original series, but is now producing original series such as *Spartacus* (About Starz, n.d.). Showtime is in third place with around 17 million subscribers (Stelter, 2009), and is now aggressively pursuing HBO's core audience with original programming such as *Nurse Jackie*.

PPV has done surprisingly well lately with events, particularly sports, but not with movies. UFC (mixed martial arts) events had six of the top ten buy rates of 2009 with July 2009's UFC 100: Brock Lesnar vs. Frank Mir getting 1.6 million buys. Boxing events were the other four with the Pacquiao vs. Cotto fight bringing in 1.25 million buys (Meltzer, 2010; Reynolds & Umstead, 2009).VOD did not experience expected gains from 2008 to 2010, with VOD using falling behind both DVR use and live television viewing. Online video even has a lead over VOD. One study by Frank N. Magid Associates found that although 21% of respondents watched VOD frequently or occasionally, 43% watched online video. This is not to say that VOD is not used. Over half of homes that have VOD use it monthly to watch an average of 18 programs (Winslow, 2009).

⊕ Sustainability ⊕

The greening of multichannel television services is happening in three areas: the set-top box, distribution, and programming.

The Set-top Box—Energy Star (2010) reports that set-top boxes combined with televisions and related devices such as VCRs and DVD players use almost 10% of total household energy consumption. Although technology users are encouraged to unplug their devices when not in use, doing so can be difficult with many multichannel television set-top boxes. Set-top boxes with DVRs send and receive information such as schedules even when the box is "turned off." Power down the satellite receiver and the box will have to completely re-set itself taking up to 15 minutes to check satellite settings and load the schedule. So unplugging these devices is often more of a hassle for the user. Instead set to boxes and receivers are becoming more energy efficient. For example, UPC has developed a set-top box that uses only 5.5 Watts per day in standby mode. Users can choose to operate the box in full functionality, eco-mode (where it goes into low power standby mode when not in use), "hot standby," and "cold standby" (lower power consumption but taking longer to start up) (Boran, 2009).

In the United States, Energy Star qualified set-top boxes must be 30% more energy efficient than older models. If all set-top boxes in the US were Energy Star qualified that would save $2 billion in energy costs per year and be equivalent to cutting the green house gas emissions of 2.5 million vehicles (Energy Star, 2009).

Distribution—DBS shines in this area because satellite transmission is solar powered. Cable and IPTV on the other hand are using their broadband networks to allow for energy savings in smart energy distribution, and green technologies for home and business such as avoiding business travel with video conferencing and reducing local travel with e-commerce (Grace, 2010).

Content—A plethora of programming content is now available that explores sustainability issues. In July 2008, Discovery Networks launched Planet Green "the first and only 24-hour eco-lifestyle television network with a robust online presence and community. (About Planet Green, n.d.)" The channel is available to 50 million homes and offers 250 hours of original programming.

Factors to Watch

Multichannel television services are continuing to evolve. Changes will most likely occur in the way people get their services. Other things to look for include the results of the Comcast NBCU merger, and the continued fights over carriage contracts and retransmission consent.

Broadband distribution. Increasingly we have choices in how we get our television programming. Not only can people turn to cable and DBS services for their favorite programming, but also the Internet and mobile devices. These services are discussed in more detail in Chapters 8 and 9. Look for cable programming providers and multichannel television providers to use the combination of the Internet and television delivery to create new types of content and interactive services like HBO Go.

Cross-platform multichannel television services. Multichannel television service subscribers and television viewers in general have shown that they like to control their media. They timeshift with DVRs and they watch content on computer screens, television screens, and mobile device screens. Look for all of the major multichannel television services to offer more cross platform access to their content, but also expect that the content will come with a price. The popular online video service Hulu may be charging for content soon. Fancast Xfinity users are already paying through their Comcast subscription fees.

Increasing fights over retransmission consent and carriage contracts. As advertising dollars decrease, programming providers and broadcast networks are looking for ways to increase revenues. The battles between Cablevision and ABC, DirecTV and Versus, and between Cablevision and Scripts Interactive are only the beginning. Look for these disputes to heat up as carriage contacts come up for renewal. How the FCC is going to protect the consumer during these disputes remains to be seen.

Comcast NBCU merger. The merger of the largest multichannel television provider with one of the major content providers and U.S. broadcasters leaves many uncomfortable. It will be interesting to see the results of the FCC and Justice Department deliberations of the merger. The impact of the merger could be felt across multiple distribution networks including cable, satellite, online, mobile, and across multiple content providers.

Multichannel television services are bringing the consumer more choice. Sometimes that choice can be overwhelming. Most people only watch a few of the channels available to them, but people still want a wide variety of choices (Neuendorf, Atkin & Jeffres, 2001). Digital technologies are enabling multichannel television providers to offer more programming choice and more control over that programming. New delivery options, including broadband Internet and mobile networks, are creating even more competition in the multichannel television service market although mergers may limit this choice in the future. Companies are looking for new ways to monetize their content, and consumers may have greater choice in delivery method and programming but all of the choice might come at a cost. Paying that cost could be difficult for those who have become used to free online video, creating an incentive for even more opportunities for multichannel programming delivery.

Bibliography

About Planet Green. (n.d.). *Planet Green*. Retrieved April 7, 2010 from http://planetgreen.discovery.com/about.html

About Starz (n.d.). Retrieved March 22, 2010 from http://www.starz.com/about

Adams, T. (2005). Video on demand: The future of media networks. *Screendigest*. Retrieved May 2, 2008 from http://www.screendigest.com/reports/vid_on_demand_us/readmore/view.html.

Bangeman, E. (2007). Telecoms get a break with new FCC franchise rules. *Ars Technica*. Retrieved April 30, 2008 from http://arstechnica.com/news.ars/post/20070306-telecoms-get-a-break-with-new-fcc-franchise-rules.html.

Berger, R. (2007). DirecTV's 100 channel promise. *TVtechnology.com*. Retrieved May 2, 2008 from http://www.tvtechnology.com/pages/s.0082/t.8585.html.

Boran, M. (2009). UPC greens the set-top box. *Gadget Republic*. Retrieved April 7, 2010 from http://www.gadgetrepublic.com/news/item/1272/

The Cable Communications Act of 1984. (1984). *Public Law 98-549*. Retrieved May 2, 2008 from http://www.publicaccess.org/cableact.html.

Carlin, T. (2006). Direct broadcast datellites. In A. Grant & J. Meadows (Eds.). *Communication technology update, 10th edition*. Boston, Focal Press.

DBSTrak (2009). Subscriber gap widens between DirecTV and Dish. *One Touch Intelligence, LLC*.

Dickson, G. (2010a). ESPN Declares 2D/3D Production a Success. Test may spur more cost-effective 3D techniques. *Broadcasting & Cable*. Retrieved March 22, 2010 from http://www.broadcastingcable.com/article/450008 ESPN_Declares_2D_3D_Production_a_Success.php

Dickson, G. (2010b, March 15). The Masters Takes 3D Leap. 3D coverage to be distributed by Comcast. *Broadcasting & Cable*. Retrieved March 22, 2010 from http://www.broadcastingcable.com/article/450259-The_Masters_Takes_3D_Leap.php

Eggerton, J. (2009, December 3). Comcast-NBCU: Opposition Lines Up. Comcast outlines promises to make deal more palatable to regulators. *Broadcasting & Cable*. Retrieved March 19, 2010 from http://www.broadcastingcable.com/article/407448-Comcast_NBCU_Opposition_Lines_Up.php?rssid=20068

Eggerton, J. (2010a, March 10). Broadcasters Counter Cable With Retrans Letter NAB argues that Congress and the FCC have reviewed the playing field and found it level. *Broadcasting & Cable*. Retrieved March 20, 2010 from http://www.broadcastingcable.com/article/449980-Broadcasters_Counter_Cable_With_Retrans_Letter.php

Eggerton, J. (2010b, March 10). Cable, Satellite Ops Seek Congressional Review of Retrans. Top multichannel providers say there is current imbalance in favor of broadcasters. *Broadcasting & Cable*. Retrieved March 20, 2010 from http://www.broadcastingcable.com/article/449949-Cable_Satellite_Ops_Seek_Congressional_Review_of_Retrans.php

Eggerton, J. (2010c, March 11). FCC: Retrans Framework Under Review. Genachowski says retrans framework under "active consideration" since New Year's Day. *Broadcasting & Cable*. Retrieved March 19, 2010 from http://www.broadcastingcable.com/article/450074-FCC_Retrans_Framework_Under_Review.php

Eggerton, J. (2010d, March 11). Senate Commerce Committee Holds Comcast-NBCU Hearing Genachowski, Roberts, Wells, others testify on Capitol Hill in toned-down affair. *Broadcasting & Cable*. Retrieved March 15, 2010 from http://www.broadcastingcable.com/article/450073-Senate_Commerce_Committee_Holds_Comcast_NBCU_Hearing.php

Eggerton, J. (2010e, March 16). FCC Broadband Plan: NCTA Critiques Set-Top Statements. *Broadcasting & Cable*. Retrieved March 20, 2010 from http://www.broadcastingcable.com/article/450357-FCC_Broadband_Plan_NCTA_Critiques_Set_Top_Statements.php

Energy Star (2010). Set-top Boxes and Cable Boxes. Retrieved April 7, 2010 from http://www.energystar.gov/index.cfm?fuseaction=find_a_product.showProductGroup&pgw_code=ST

Farrell, M (2009, October 27). TAM Summit 2009: VOD, Mobile Apps Dominate Cable's Future Plans Interactive Advertising, Internet Among Top Concerns. *Multichannel News*. Retrieved March 18, 2010 from http://www.multichannel.com/article/366579-CTAM_Summit_2009_VOD_Mobile_Apps_Dominate_Cable_s_Future_Plans.php

Federal Communications Commission. (n.d.-a). *Compatability of cable TV and digital TV receivers "plug-and-play."* Retrieved April 30, 2008 from http://www.fcc.gov/cgb/consumerfacts/plugandplaytv.pdf.

Federal Communications Commission. (n.d.-b). *Satellite Home Viewer Extension and Reauuthorication Act* (SHVERA). Retrieved April 8, 2008 from http://www.fcc.gov/mb/policy/shvera.html.

Grace, L. (2010). National Broadband Plan on Energy & Environment: Green, Lean and Mean. *The Cable Pipeline*. Retrieved April 7, 2010 from http://www.thecablepipeline.com

HBO Core statistics (n.d.). Retrieved March 22, 2010 from http://www.timewarner.com/corp/businesses/detail/hbo/index.html

HBO GO about (n.d.). Retrieved March 22, 2010 from http://www.hbogo.com/#about/

Hearn, T. (2007). FCC: Dual carriage will last three years. *Multichannel News*. Retrieved May 2, 2008 from http://www.multichannel.com/index.asp?layout=article&articleid=CA6478706.

Kaufman, D. (2007, July 22). HBO On Demand: "The Wire." *TV Week*. Retrieved May 2, 2008 from http://www.tvweek.com/news/2007/07/the_wire_hbo_on_demand.php.

Kendall, B. (2010, March 4). 2nd UPDATE:US Court Affirms EchoStar-Dish Contempt Sanction In TiVo Case. *The Wall Street Journal*. Retrieved March 22, 2010 from http://online.wsj.com/article/BT-CO-20100304-715501.html?mod=crnews

McQuillen, W and Shields, T. (2010). Comcast, Cablevision Lose Challenge to Sharing Rule. *Bloomberg*. Retrieved March 20, 2010 from http://www.bloomberg.com/apps/news?pid=newsarchive&sid=ah5pVEyGctrI

Meltzer, D. (2010, February 15). UFC remains king of PPV hill. *Yahoo! Sports*. Retrieved March 22, 2010 from http://sports.yahoo.com/mma/news?slug=dm-ppvbiz021510&prov=yhoo&type=lgns

The Museum of Broadcast Communications. (n.d.). *Scrambled signals*. Retrieved May 2, 2008 from http://www.museum.tv/archives/etv/S/htmlS/scrambledsig/scrambledsig.htm.

National Cable and Telecommunications Association. (n.d.). *History of cable television*. Retrieved March 31, 2008 from http://www.ncta.com/About/About/HistoryofCableTelevision.aspx.

National Cable and Telecommunications Association. (2010). *Operating Metrics*. Retrieved March 22, 2010, from http://www.ncta.com/StatsGroup/operatingmetric.aspx.

Neuendorf, K, Atkin, D. & Jeffres, L. (2001). Reconceptualizing channel repertoire in the Urban Cable Environment. *Journal of Broadcasting and Electronic Media*. Retrieved April 28, 2010 from http://findarticles.com/p/articles/mi_m6836/is_3_45/ai_n25037083/?tag=content;col1

On demand menu. (n.d.). *Comcast*. Retrieved April 30, 2008 from http://images.tvplanner.net/comcast_menuGuide.pdf.

Ovide, S. (2010, March 2). New York ABC Station May Go Dark For Cablevision Customers. *The Wall Street Journal*. Retrieved March 22, 2010 from http://online.wsj.com/article/SB10001424052748704125804575096320101246524.html?mod=dist_smartbrief

Patterson, B. & Katzmaier, D. (2008). HDTV programming compared. *C/NET News*. Retrieved April 30, 2008 from http://www.cnet.com/4520-7874_1-5108854-3.html.

Paul, F & Adegoke, Y (2010, March 1). Update 4-Dish Network rev rises on subscriber additions. *Reuters*. Retrieved April 28, 2010 from http://www.reuters.com/article/idUSN0124011120100301

Peers, M. (2010, March 3). The ABC's of Cablevision's Dispute Over Television Fees. *The Wall Street Journal*. Retrieved March 22, 2010 from http://online.wsj.com/article/SB10001424052748704548604575097823903723394.html?KEYWORDS=interactive+television

Reynolds, M. and Umstead, R. (2009, November 20). Pacquiao-Cotto Jabs 1.25 Million Buys, $70 Million In PPV Revenue Bout Follows Mayweather-Marquez To Score As Only Back-To-Back Boxing PPV Cards To Surpass 1 Million Buys. *Multichannel News*. Retrieved March 20, 2010 from http://www.multichannel.com/article/390040-Pacquiao_Cotto_Jabs_1_25_Million_Buys_70_Million_In_PPV_Revenue.php

Schatz, A. (2010a, February 25). House Weighs Comcast-NBC Deal. *The Wall Street Journal*. Retrieved March 22, 2010 from http://online.wsj.com/article/SB10001424052748704479404575087830555689508.html?KEYWORDS=comcast

Schatz, A. (2010b, March 11). FCC to Examine Rules for TV Fee Disputes. *The Wall Street Journal*. Retrieved March 22, 2010 from http://online.wsj.com/article/SB10001424052748703625304575115641586979572.html?KEYWORDS=comcast

Schechner, S. (2010, February 17). HBO Shows Online Video Service HBO GO. *The Wall Street Journal*. Retrieved March 22, 2010 from http://blogs.wsj.com/digits/2010/02/17/hbo-shows-online-video-service-hbogo/?KEYWORDS=comcast

Siriwardane, V. (2010, January 1). Food Network, HGTV channels to be restored to 3.1M Cablevision customers in N.J., N.Y., Conn. *The Star-Ledger*. Retrieved March 22, 2010 from http://www.nj.com/news/index.ssf/2010/01/food_network_hgtv_channels_to.html

Sky Angel History and Timeline (n.d). *Sky Angel*. Retrieved March 20, 2010 from http://www.skyangel.com/About/CompanyInfo/Timeline/

Spangler, T. (2009, December 15). Comcast Keeps 'Beta' Tag On Online TV Service. Top Cable Operator Hedging Against Kinks, Ad Models, Windowing. *Multichannel News*. Retrieved March 17, 2010 from http://www.multichannel.com/article/440472-Comcast_Keeps_Beta_Tag_On_Online_TV_Service.php?rssid=20063

Spangler, T (2010a, March 9). Comcast: ITV Ready For 50 Networks Later This Year MSO Targets 100% Deployment of EBIF in Motorola Footprint by Midyear. *Multichannel News*. Retrieved March 22, 2010 from http://www.multichannel.com/article/449858-Comcast_ITV_Ready_For_50_Networks_Later_This_Year.php

Spangler, T. (2010b, March 17). Verizon Files Patent Complaints Against Cablevision Telco Accuses Cablevision of Infringing Set-Top Patents in ITC Action. *Multichannel News*. Retrieved March 19, 2010 from http://www.multichannel.com/article/450370-Verizon_Files_Patent_Complaints_Against_Cablevision.php

Spangler, T. (2010c, March 29). DirecTV Puts On ESPN's 3D Glasses. Satellite Operator to Carry 3D Telecasts of 25 World Cup Matches and Other Events. *Multichannel News*. Retrieved March 29, 2010 from http://www.multichannel.com/article/450791-DirecTV_Puts_On_ESPN_s_3D_Glasses.php

Stelter, B. (2009, March 18). Starz Has High Hopes for Its Original Shows. *The New York Times*. Retrieved March 20, 2010 from http://www.nytimes.com/2009/03/19/arts/television/19starz.html

Time Warner. (n.d.). *Home Box Office overview*. Retrieved April 29, 2008 from http://www.timewarner.com/corp/ businesses/detail/hbo/index.html.

Welch, C. (2010). After Digital Switch, Basic TV Offers Cable Alternative. *NPR*. Retrieved March 12, 2010 from http://www.npr.org/templates/story/story.php?storyId=124056416

Weprin, A. (2010). DirecTV, Versus Settle Carriage Dispute. Sports network will be available on satellite carrier after six and a half month dispute. *Broadcasting & Cable*. Retrieved March 20, 2010 fromhttp://www.broadcastingcable.com/article/450282-DirecTV_Versus_Settle_Carriage_Dispute.php

Wilkerson, D. (2010, January 4). Dispute keeps Food Network, HGTV off Cablevision systems. Cable carrier, Scripps Interactive point fingers as signals go dark. *MarketWatch*. Retrieved March 17, 2010 from http://www.marketwatch.com/story/fee-spat-keeps-food-network-hgtv-off-cablevision-2010-01-04?dist=WSJfeed&siteid=WSJ

Winslow, G. (2009, July 13). Cover Story: Failure To Lift Off. VOD Posts Solid Growth, But It's No 'Killer App'. *Multichannel News*. Retrieved March 20, 2010 from http://www.multichannel.com/article/314874-Cover_Story_Failure_To_Lift_Off.php

Worden, N. (2010, February 25). Cablevision Plans Service to Display Web Content on TV. *The Wall Street Journal*. Retrieved March 22, 2010 from http://online.wsj.com/article/SB10001424052748704240004575085041422759152.html?mod=loomia&loomia_si=t0:a16:g2:r1:c0.072994:b31108870

Wynshynski, G. (2010, March 15). Versus, DirecTV deal done; satellite fans get their playoff hockey. *Yahoo! Sports*. Retrieved March 22, 2010 from. http://sports.yahoo.com/nhl/blog/puck_daddy/post/Versus-DirecTV-deal-done-satellite-fans-get-th?urn=nhl,228103

8

IPTV: Streaming Media

Jeffrey S. Wilkinson[*]

We have entered the age of ubiquitous digital video (Bell and Bull, 2010; Unickow, 2010). Televisions have Ethernet jacks, iPhones and Android smart phones can post directly to YouTube, and freely-downloaded high definition video clips are easily found on consumer Web sites. Whether by cable or telco set-top box or streamed through the Internet, video is so common that the question now is how best to pay for it all. Roughly 15 years ago the term "streaming" was coined to describe moving audio and video files across the Internet and playing them back on a computer. Back then (and until recently), most of the content was free. But the choices were few, resolution was slow, and constant buffering made it a game for the patient.

But streaming has changed, and the economics of the Internet have changed. We are in a new commercial world where Internet broadband video and television have merged to give us IPTV—Internet protocol television—that delivers content to television home theaters, computers, mobile telephones, and anything else in our digital technology repertoire.

IPTV is defined by the International Telecommunications Union as "multimedia services such as television/video/audio/text/graphics/data delivered over IP-based networks managed to support the required level of quality of service (QoS)/quality of experience (QoE), security, interactivity, and reliability" (ITU-T Newslog, 2009). IPTV provides a more personalized interactive experience and the types of services are only limited by your imagination. As second-generation IPTV systems are launched around the world, virtually all forms of content can be provided on demand.

It is more complicated than it seems because all the services and content involving video, the PC, and the television use the term "IPTV." IPTV can involve streaming, satellite delivery of audio and video, wireline delivery of audio and video, and wireless delivery of audio and video. IPTV services are designed to work seamlessly on "the three screens"—television, computer, and mobile telephone. It is difficult to find marketing material that does *not* use the term.

Regardless of what it is, there is an ongoing battle among media companies and service providers to bring digital services into the home. There is a lot of money at stake as consumers globally look for video on demand. Whether it is through a dish or fiber optic cable, a myriad of companies all claim to provide it through IPTV. In the United States, satellite companies such as DirecTV and DISH, cable companies such as Comcast, telcos such as AT&T, and even Google are jumping into the fray. What is a customer to do? This chapter hopes to sort out the confusion about IPTV and provide a glimpse as to where it's going.

---

[*] Acting Dean and Professor, United International College (Zhuhai, China).

Background

Two basic and distinct forms of IPTV have emerged (Light & Lancefield, 2007). One is centered around distribution via the PC (Web television) and the other one through a set-top box (STB). The term "streaming" is still used to describe the former, while those who market the latter use a closed network broadband connection (commonly advertised as IPTV). Bringing video through an STB harkens to traditional pay-TV models while video to the PC uses a vastly different approach. Compare Verizon's FiOS with YouTube in terms of content and cost. Each has its own history and perspective and need to be addressed separately. First we'll take a look at streaming media.

In 1995, Progressive Networks launched RealAudio and immediately streaming audio and video became an interesting add-on to computers (along with gaming, e-mail, word processing, and simple surfing). After a brief partnership with Progressive Networks, Microsoft launched Windows Media Player, and not long after that, Apple launched Quicktime, an MPEG-based architecture/codec. In 1999, Apple introduced QuickTime TV, using Akamai Technologies' streaming media delivery service. A few years later came Flash, DIVX, MPEG players, and others. As the technology improved and bandwidth increased, new applications sprang up. Sports highlights, news, and music clips became increasingly popular. Napster made (illegal) file-sharing a household phrase, and YouTube heralded the beginning of a new age, redefining forever what media professionals and audiences considered to be content.

Types of Streaming

Probably the most common distinctions are "live," "time-shifted," and "on demand." Among media companies and professional business applications, on-demand streamed video content is more common than live streamed content (delivering live video via videoconferencing and webcams constitutes a different type of technology; see Chapter 22). To offer on-demand streaming, you must use a streaming server with enough capacity to hold your content that can be configured to enable a sufficient number of simultaneous users (unlike broadcasting, the number of simultaneous users is limited to server capacity). To do professional *live* streaming, you need all of the above and the addition of a dedicated computer (called a "broadcaster" or "encoder") to create the streams from the live inputs (such as a microphone or camera) by digitizing, compressing, and sending out the content to the streaming server. Most of the commercial Web video services offer content that is on-demand.

From the perspective of the consumer, true streaming is not downloading, but occurs when the content takes a few seconds to buffer before playing. Nothing is actually stored on your hard drive. True streaming is enabled when the provider employs a special streaming server (such as Real's Helix server, Apple's Xserve, Microsoft's Silverlight Streaming, or Adobe's Flash Media Rights Management Server). For several years the protocols of choice were RSTP and RTMP, but in 2009 most of the large distributors and providers of content moved to HTTP (Ozer, 2010), because HTTP is simpler for providers to use because it's more firewall-friendly and more cache-efficient. A notable exception is the Apple streaming server, which still uses open-source RTP/RTSP.

The advantages of streaming are speed, (host) control, and flexibility. Streamed material is played back quickly—almost instantaneously. Control is maximized for the host, because the original content remains on the server, and access can be controlled using password, digital rights management (DRM), registration, or some other security feature. Finally, since streamed segments are placed individually on a host server and can be updated or changed as needed, there is tremendous flexibility. Increasingly, thanks to broadband, content can be found that is in high-definition. Both Apple and Windows Media Video Web sites offer HD clips that can be downloaded at resolutions of 720p and 1080p.

Streaming Platforms

There are several player-platforms for providing and playing streaming video. For a decade, the main streaming players were from Real, Windows, and Apple. The ubiquitous Flash plug-in used by YouTube is technically a browser plug-in, not a streaming player, because consumers cannot operate the player independently of the browser, save and manipulate files, or create playlists.

According to Weboptimization.com, Nielsen Online has tracked the changes of the four most widely adopted players over the past six years. The players are Windows Media Player (Microsoft), Real (RealNetworks), QuickTime (Apple), and iTunes (Apple). Each has some technical differences, each has its merits, and all are regularly upgraded. Table 8.1 shows the number of unique users of the popular streaming players from January 2004 to January 2009. While Windows media player continues to be the most popular player, the growth in iTunes users is noteworthy.

Table 8.1
Streaming Media Player Growth in Unique Users (in Thousands)

Month	iTunes	Apple QuickTime	iTunes+QuickTime	RealPlayer	Windows Media Player
Jan-04	1,118	15,458	16,576	28,593	51,056
Jan-05	5,370	13,136	18,506	28,182	60,782
Jan-06	18,568	12,817	31,385	28,687	71,112
Jan-07	27,396	13,934	41,330	31,309	72,510
Jan-08	35,269 (23.6%)	12,531	47,800 (32%)	25,800	75,810 (50.7%)
Jan-09	44,764 (27.8%)	13,832	58,596 (36.4%)	20,709	81,795(50.7%)

Source: Nielsen Online cited in Website Optimization.com

RealNetworks. The early dominance of RealNetworks has been attributed to it having been the first on the scene and having the foresight to give away players rather than sell them. Since 1995, several generations of improvements have been made in its products. The overall pricing structure for Real services has remained stable, and the basic player is a free download (new models with tech support are offered for a price). For those wishing to deliver video and audio, Real offers a wide variety of servers and other products, as streaming applications/needs expand. The Web site offers a variety of free and trial versions of RealProducer and the Helix line of servers. Real has also diversified to offer content such as music, movies, and gaming services.

Microsoft Windows. Shortly after RealNetworks began streaming audio, Microsoft partnered with them and afterward released Windows Media Player as a free plug-in to all Windows users. Since then, improved versions of Windows Media Player have been regularly released, and WMP remains the most-installed player in the world (see Table 8.1). The latest version (WMP 12) has been positively reviewed and remains a standard for online video. In addition, Microsoft has moved ahead with HTTP "smooth streaming" with Silverlight. Silverlight is a cross-browser, cross-platform plug-in for "creating rich media applications and business applications for the Web, desktop, and mobile devices" (Microsoft Web site, "what is silverlight?" 2010). Silverlight is compatible across platforms because it is based on the commonly accepted MPEG-4 file format, while WMP continues to be the proprietary Microsoft format.

Apple/QuickTime/iTunes. In 1999, Apple began offering a streaming application with the QuickTime 4 platform. QuickTime has been popular because it plays on both PC and Macintosh computers and delivers virtually any kind of file from your Web server. The QuickTime file format is an open standard and was adopted as part of the MPEG family of standards. Apple has a few types of servers (such as Xserve and Mac OSX server). To produce live events, Apple provides QuickTime Broadcaster. Most recently, Apple has been marketing and providing content and services to take advantage of the combined applications of iPhone, iTunes, iPod, and Apple TV.

Adobe/Adobe Media Player/Flash. In December 2005, Adobe acquired Macromedia and has since enjoyed great success with the Flash platform. In May 2008, Adobe announced the Open Screen Project. Supported by companies such as Cisco, Intel, Marvell, Motorola, Nokia, Samsung, Sony Ericsson, Toshiba, and Verizon Wireless, the project seeks to provide "rich Internet experiences across televisions, personal computers, mobile devices, and consumer electronics" (Adobe, 2008). Content providers such as BBC, MTV Networks, and NBC Universal are also involved. The Open Screen project employs the Adobe Flash Player (and in the future, Adobe AIR) to allow developers and designers to publish content and applications across desktops. In so doing, Adobe surpassed Microsoft in the area of media support, particularly H.264/Advanced Audio Coding (AAC) audio and full HD video playback.

Podcasting

A relative of video streaming, podcasting, remains an important aspect of IPTV. Podcasting refers to various types of online audio on demand programs (Webster, 2009). Podcasts are common on the Web, and are typically programs such as a talk show, hosted music program, or commentary. They are commonly pulled by the user as an automatic download via RSS (really simple syndication) through a service such as iTunes. According to Edison Media Research, in 2009 around 22% of Americans had ever listened to a podcast, and around 27 million had listened to a podcast in the past month (Webster, 2009). Because online video use exceeds online radio, radio stations need to use video on their Web sites in order to stay competitive (Webster, 2009) (for more on podcasting, see Chapter 16).

Proprietary Platforms

The streaming platforms mentioned above are quite different from those provided by the so-called "traditional media" companies. As we are witnessing in the convergence of computers, television, and digital applications, traditional content providers also seek to find their place in the new media environment. To stay relevant (and profitable), the race is on for distribution, what cable companies used to call "the last mile." As discussed in Chapter 21 a host of acronyms are now used: FTTB (fiber-to-the-building), FTTC (fiber-to-the-curb or the cabinet), FTTH (fiber-to-the-home), FTTN (fiber-to-the-node), and FTTP (fiber-to-the-premises). It is truly all about *the* connection and what companies will be able to use IPTV to supply all a person's information, entertainment, and communication needs. Information now means not only news, but also banking, security, weather, and politics. Entertainment includes a variety of live and recorded experiences involving music, sports, and dramatic, comedic, and theatrical performances. Communication through technology can now involve all one-way or two-way interactions with family, friends, classmates, colleagues, and strangers.

The fight for who is chosen to deliver the triple-play is ongoing between telephone companies, cable companies, satellite companies, and even Internet companies (Google). Fresh from a decade of dominance (having surpassed traditional TV networks as the primary means of bringing information into the home), cable companies seem to be in the best position. But telephone companies are also pushing to provide services. In spring 2008, telephone company Verizon made headlines with its FiOS digital TV service, using a high-capacity, fiber optic network. In 2009, Verizon raised the connection speed of its entry-level FiOS Internet service from 10/2 megabits per second (Mbps) to 15/5 Mbps, and raised the connection speed of its popular mid-tier offering from 20/5 Mbps to 25/15 Mbps. (The first number is the download speed; the second is the upload speed.) In New York City and its suburbs, FiOS Internet has a new entry-level connection speed of 25/15 Mbps, and a new mid-tier offering of 35/20 Mbps (Lee and Henson, 2009).

IPTV via STB

Gartner (2008) defines IPTV as "the delivery of video programming (either broadcast or on-demand) over a carrier's managed broadband network to a customer's TV set. It does not include streaming media over the Internet to a PC." (p. 5). According to Gartner, the importance of IPTV is that it is not a single service; it is a new carrier distribution platform over which several communication and entertainment services can be offered.

The ongoing argument is whether the appeal of IPTV is about the TV or the IP (Reedy, 2008). Most television watching is still relatively passive. Added services sound good to consumers, but not everyone is ready to migrate to services such as surveillance and security (home, video, and banking). While it is important to bundle services, the foot in the door is still the TV experience. Many customers may still not care whether the provider is a telephone, cable, or satellite company. So, perhaps bundling HD content may still be the best means of differentiating services (Reedy, 2008). Generally, AT&T's U-verse is slower but also noticeably less expensive than Verizon FiOS. According to Focus editors at focus.com, there are currently three top IPTV providers in the U.S.:

AT&T. U-Verse TV offers up to 300 channels including majors like HBO, Showtime, Cinemax, and Starz. Features include DVR, VOD, and HD. Packages range from $59 to $119 per month, and custom packages are also available. HD service costs an extra $10. U-verse can provide up to 10 Mb/s downstream and up to 1.5 Mb/s upstream. Service is available in various cities in California, Texas, Connecticut, Wisconsin, and Indiana.

Verizon. FiOS TV offers up to 200 channels including all the majors plus international channels. Features include VOD, HD, and Multi-Room DVR (control and watch DVR programs from multiple rooms). Pricing is generally $39.99 per month but varies depending on location. Some popular cable channels involve additional costs. Service is available in various cities in several states.

SureWest. This IPTV service offers 260 channels including international programming. Features include VOD, HD, and TiVO service. VOD service provides unlimited viewing with a 24-hour window, where you can watch as many times as wanted with full DVR functionality. Pricing varies and involves extra costs for some popular channels. Service is only available in Sacramento, CA at the moment but is expected to expand.

IPTV via P2P

While cable, telephony, and satellite are working to deliver the highest quality (and most expensive) programs and services into the home, the "other" delivery form of IPTV is also making inroads. So-called "P2P" or peer-to-peer networking became famous through Napster and associated with illegal file-sharing, so some prefer to call it "distributed streaming media" (Miller, 2007, p. 34). Either way, P2P is far less expensive than the STB approach. Some believe that delivery of high-definition video may need to use P2P in order to be cost-effective.

Well-known providers of content via P2P include BitTorrent and Azureus, and content owners such as Fox, Viacom, and Turner use P2P to publish and distribute content. The basic concept is that P2P moves digital content through several paths before reaching the user's (destination) computer. While STB systems need to purchase several servers to dedicate bandwidth and deliver programs, P2P becomes more efficient (and less expensive) as more clients join the distributed network. This is because the content can be drawn in pieces from multiple sources. This type of network tends to be less concerned with copyright and more about sharing popular files. Obscure or less common content will take longer to pull together because there will be fewer sources to draw from. As of early 2010, the BitTorrent Web site stated they had 160 million clients to send content to users (BitTorrent.com Web site, 2010). In February, 2010, Twitter was said to be seeking help from BitTorrent to deploy files across its servers in order to be more efficient (Torrentfreak, 2010).

One of the factors influencing the STB-P2P debate is digital rights management. Controlling access to the content is a key element for STB providers, and they argue it is the only/best way to maintain appropriate (monetized) use. P2P providers such as BitTorrent and Abacast suggest that a more passive approach to DRM will win the heart and wallet of the consumer. In other words, they suggest marking the file so everyone knows where it came from, but then let it go.

Recent Developments

FiOS Versus U-verse…Versus Google?

In July, 2009, Verizon's FiOS TV services announced it had over 2.5 million subscribers (Spangler, 2009a). During the period from January 2008 to then, the company managed to add an average of almost 100,000 new subscribers per month. In April 2009, AT&T announced the U-verse service grew by 284,000 during the quarter (over 90,000 per month), boosting their overall numbers above 1.3 million TV subscribers (Spangler, 2009b). In January, 2010, U-verse announced they had 2.1 million subscribers (Spangler, 2010).

In March 2010, Google made things interesting by announcing they were looking for communities to be part of an experiment for its own 1-Gigabit-per-second, fiber-to-the-home network. More than 600 communities applied for the chance, and Google said it hoped to reach between "50,000 and up to 500,000 people with the FTTH project" (Spangler, 2010). It had set Friday, March 26, as the deadline for proposals. Afterward Google revealed it had received more than 600 proposals and over 190,000 responses from individuals. The Internet giant said it would meet with local officials before deciding where the networks would be built.

Interoperable Players

For a decade, there was a struggle among Real, Microsoft, Apple, Adobe, and others to try to be the primary viewing platform for online video. In those early days, compatibility was a factor, and consumers pretty much needed to install all the players. With recent product launches by Microsoft, Adobe, Real, and Apple, it seems the long-expressed goal of interoperability has, for the most part, been achieved. Each company is finding other ways to differentiate itself and find its own niche. Microsoft for example, is pushing its Silverlight player into the living room. In April, 2010, the company announced that "a full version of Silverlight on a chip will be available to Intel and Broadcom-based set-top and Blu-ray device makers later this fall (2010), bringing the full Silverlight experience to the TV" (Dreier, 2010).

Universities, Content, and Fair Use

After halting the streaming of copyrighted video to students in late 2009, UCLA started the service back up again (Riismandel, 2010). In accordance with negotiations UCLA had suspended streaming copyrighted video to students in response to complaints from the Association for Information and Media Equipment (AIME) (Riismandel, 2010). The authors of a brief by the Library Copyright Alliance (LCL) noted that courts had extended Fair Use to print works that were "repurposed and recontextualized" online. The argument is being extended that uploading a feature film to a course website for student use is a similar form of repurposing. As of publication, this suit is unresolved.

On another front, Yale University alumni released a 16 minute viral video aimed at boosting admissions to the school. The video's humorous-yet-informative approach took the Web by storm and by March, 2010, had recorded over 400,000 views (Riismandel, 2010).

Mobile Apps

All the major platforms are jumping into delivering video via the Web to cell phones. In March 2010, Real announced a new mobile video service to help entertainment and wireless companies reach consumers. The service is aimed at making it easier to produce video applications across platforms (including Verizon and AT&T). Real supports live or on-demand video via iPhone, Android, Windows Mobile, BlackBerry, and Java, as well as the mobile Web (Duryee, 2010).

CURRENT STATUS

To read the market surveys, it is fast becoming an IPTV world. Globally, IPTV—providing video services over managed IP networks to consumers' televisions—has been rapidly rising since its commercial introduction in 2002. In 2007, the number of IPTV subscribers was estimated between 10 million and 13 million (Spangler, 2008). By the end of the end of the first quarter of 2009, that estimate now stands at 24 million (IPTV news, 2009). Almost half the IPTV customers are in Western Europe (over 11 million), and the greatest growth was reported in Eastern Europe (21% over 3 months, total around 1.2 million subscribers). As noted earlier, in the U.S., FiOS and U-verse subscribers together number around five million.

In contrast to podcasts, online video use continues to grow rapidly in the U.S. Nielsen announced in February 2010 that the number of Americans watching online video had increased over 10% from the previous year and numbered over 140-million unique viewers (Lewin, 2010). Another report put the number of online video viewers at 173 million (comScore, 2010). Nielsen data estimates that on average, each viewer watches around 3 hours of online video per month, watching on average 73 different streams (Lewin, 2010). According to comScore, viewers of YouTube watched 93 videos on average during the month of January, 2010 (comScore, 2010).

Who is Watching Online

Consuming video content online—not surprisingly—correlates (negatively) with age. The largest audience group for online movies and television content is young adults. According to research by Pew, almost 90% of young adults watch video online and over a third (36%) say they watch on a typical or average day (Madden, 2009).

In older groups, viewing tends to drop off but it is still growing with each year. For those between the ages of 30 and 49, 67% say they use online video sites, and only 16% say they watch online video 'on a typical day.' For those 50-64, daily online viewing is less common (41%), and above 65 even less (27%). But the general direction is up substantially from 2008 as all demographic groups increasingly look online for video content (Madden, 2009).

In terms of gender, men still tend to watch more online video than women, but the gap is narrowing. In 2009, 65% of men said they had watched video online compared to 59% of women. The year before, 57% of men and 46% of women said they had watched online video (Madden, 2009).

Who's Going Where for Video

By far the most popular source for online video is YouTube. YouTube has been the change agent for cultures, countries, and the label used for an entire generation. The site has been credited for allowing other companies to test the waters and survive even as analysts have speculated how unprofitable YouTube itself has been for parent Google. But Google CEO Eric Schmidt is now predicting YouTube will turn a profit in 2010 (Parrack, 2010).

Even as YouTube has begun to offer so-called 'premium content' (Parrack, 2010), so also full-length movies and TV shows are consistently among the most viewed content on the major video sharing sites (Lewin, 2010). Many movies and television shows are also widely available on peer-to-peer networks and BitTorrent sites.

For example, major television networks now provide more full-length episodes of primetime television shows for free online. ABC's *Lost* and *Desperate Housewives* were among the first free offerings, and many other shows from all the networks soon followed. There are a number of ways to find and watch favorite programs online, the most popular source by far is YouTube, followed by Hulu.

But there are countless other video Web sites including FreeTVonline and Veoh. Professional or amateur, long-form or clips, high-definition or low-grade and grainy—consumers can find what they want, the way they want it. Veoh, for example, provides several channels and programs but few network shows. Another video online site, FreeTVonline, does not actually host programs on its servers, but instead simply mirrors freely and publicly available video links from other sites. Table 8.2 shows a comparison of the most popular online video sources from September 2009 and January 2010 (some September 09 data was not available for the January Top 10).

In the past two years, the top two online video sites have solidified their lead in terms of consumer traffic. YouTube, of course, continues to be the monster site that revolutionizes the world. It has been so effective that some countries have blocked the site (including China, which has blocked YouTube for over a year). The second most popular online video site is Hulu, the joint venture between NBC Universal, News Corporation, and Disney that was launched in March 2007. Hulu is free (ad-supported) with selections from more than 50 content providers including NBC, Fox, MGM, Sony Pictures Television, Warner Brothers, and Lionsgate. The site offers both clips and full-length features. Some network TV shows are offered the day after being broadcast (*The Simpsons, The Office*). The site also offers older "classics" such as *Miami Vice* and *Buffy the Vampire Slayer*. Table 8.3 lists the 'stickiest' online video sites. By far Hulu tops the list with viewers averaging 244 minutes (Nielsen, 2010).

Table 8.2

Top 10 Online Video Sources (Thousands)

Rank	Brand	Total Streams Jan 2010	Unique Viewers (000) Jan 2010	Total Streams Sept 2009	Unique Viewers (000) Sept 2009
1	YouTube	6,622,374	112,642	6,688,367	106,180
2	Hulu	635,546	15,256	437,407	13,519
3	Yahoo!	221,355	26,081	228,494	30,084
4	MSN/WindowsLive/Bing	179,741	15,645	180,104	18,109
5	Turner Sports and Entertainment Digital Network	137,311	5,343	123,665	6,062
6	MTV Networks Music	131,077	5,949	116,839	9,647
7	ABC Television	128,510	5,049		
8	Fox Interactive Media	124,513	11,450	139,634	14,342
9	Nickelodeon Kids and Family Network	117,057	5,004	127,654	5,303
10	Megavideo	115,089	3,654		

Source: Nielsen Online (2009)

Table 8.3

Top Online Brands, Ranked by Time Spent Viewing per Viewer (250K Unique Viewer Minimum)

Video Brand	Time per Viewer (min)	MOM Time % Growth
Hulu	244.8	4.3%
ABC Family	203.3	10.8%
Youku	195.6	2.1%
Liquid Compass	183.2	-14.6%
Megavideo	160.0	-13.5%
Cwtv.com	127.0	102.9%
Tudou.com	110.8	-6.8%
YouTube	108.0	-3.6%
Justin.tv	104.3	-35.4%
Internet Archive	95.1	426.0%

Source: The Nielsen Company

Mobile Video

The integration of streaming services with home entertainment and mobile broadband has also helped drive up consumer adoption of smart phones to 30% of the estimated 52 million mobile phones predicted to be sold in the U.S. in 2010 (Siglin, 2010) (for more on Mobile Telephones, see Chapter 18; for more on broadband networks, see Chapter 21).

Television stations have announced they are now using the mobile digital television (DTV) standard, A/153, to begin sending their signals to cell phones. According to Siglin (2010), the LA Times reported that 80 TV stations covering 38% of U.S. households predicted they will broadcast DTV signals to cell phones by the end of the year.

The rise in smart phone sales is also changing what kind of video audiences have searched for in the past. In 2007, news was the top category, but in 2008, Nielsen reported that for mobile video, comedy was the solid number one (Covey, 2009). Music, films, news, weather, sports, and user-generated content represent other highest-viewed categories. Top mobile video sites listed in Table 8.4 reflect greater diversity in viewer share than overall online video viewing in Table 8.2.

Table 8.4
Mobile Video: What They're Watching
Top Channels Q3 2009

Rank	Channels	Unique Audience (000s)	Share of Mobile Video Viewers
1	YouTube	5,337	33.9%
2	Fox	4,737	30.1%
3	The Weather Channel	4,507	28.6%
4	CBS	4,276	27.2%
5	Comedy Central	4,037	25.6%
6	ABC	3,964	25.2%
7	MTV	3,658	23.2%
8	ESPN	3,415	21.7%
9	NBC	3,345	21.2%
10	E!	3,178	20.2%

Source: The Nielsen Company. Q3 2009 Mobile Video Report

As more people adopt smart phones, overall use and influence of mobile video will also rise. It may be that preference for short, entertaining video content simply reflects acceptance (and use) of mobile video content to pass short periods of inactivity. The brief periods when people are in transit or waiting for others, for example, are opportune times for a short burst of video entertainment.

FACTORS TO WATCH

Converged Television

According to Graham (2009), we are rapidly heading toward a place where consumers will want converged television. This perspective championed by many from the cable/telco industry, sees consumers as ultimately wanting to be able to 'personalize' their television experience and merge it with the other communication and media devices in the house. People will be able to "get the content they want, where they want, and how they want" (Branet, cited by Graham, 2009, p.15).

Graham posits the following conclusions for consumers and IPTV:

A. Consumers want an environment that can be personalized. Analogous to customizing a car interior. Volume, PIP, channel lineup/favorites, on-screen notification (such as for caller ID).

B. Consumers want services to be independent of their location or device. People recognize that video quality is affected by bandwidth (cell phone display demands are different from HDTV), but even recognizing this, they want any and all services available regardless whether they're at home or on the go.

C. Consumers want their TV integrated with other services. ALL other services. Convergence includes the synchronization of Web, TV, telephone, security cameras, music playlists, etc.

D. Consumers want 'wide and deep' programming choices on demand. People want to be able to access any written, audio or visual content ever produced. The so-called "long tail" of what's available via the Internet.

This somewhat utopian view is popular among industry insiders. We believe we know what people want, and what they want is every possible array of gadget and service we have to offer…for as much as we can charge ($100, $200, $300 per month?). But this view has to be balanced with the reality about technology. We have to remember that 20 years ago most people could not set the time on their VCRs. The IPTV multi-service multi-screen time-shifting global-interactive experience may simply overwhelm most consumers. In tough economic times, people may opt for watching old favorites for free on Hulu.

Low Cost Bandwidth & HD File Sizes

Video file sizes have always been extremely large, but engineers have been hard at work to reduce file size, and this is not the barrier it once was. Originally, content providers were compressing video files for dial-up (56K) lines. Many still remember small windows, low resolution, and constant re-buffering from these dial-up connections. But the cost of bandwidth has dropped dramatically the past decade. Unickow (2010) notes that "today Netflix pays about 5 cents to stream a movie over the Internet. If Netflix tried to do this in 1998 at the same quality it's doing it today, it would have cost the company $270 per movie." According to Rayburn (2010), in 1998, the average video was streamed at 37 Kbps, but today we talk in terms of delivering Mb, Gb or even Tb.

So the stream of content is now a river, and each of the most popular streaming platforms (Real, Adobe, Microsoft, and Apple) offer HD video clips on their Web sites. In general, broadband users need at least 6 Mb/s to 10 Mb/s service in order to enjoy HD video (Gubbins, 2007). Both Verizon and AT&T's fiber-based services are sufficient to provide full-length films in HD as are a number of cable broadband services. ABC.com has been offering streams of selected shows like *Lost* and *Ugly Betty* in HD since 2007.

Trans Border Content Flow

Globally, nations will have to think about the invisible border around our consuming audiences. Regarding HD, for example, the constraints are not physical, but regulatory. Since the Web is global, European or Asian content providers can compete with domestic companies for market share. In the United States, there are a number of ways for consumers to purchase services from content providers in other countries. The current does not always run both ways, however, and protectionism manifests itself in many forms. Many providers whose content (or advertising) is targeted at users in one country can be programmed to refuse to deliver streams to users in other countries, using the IP address of the user to identify the user's location.

Regions of Growth

Projections for the future vary, but all are upbeat about IPTV. According to a report by Multimedia Research Group (MRG), the number of global IPTV subscribers is expected to grow from 28 million in 2009 to 83 million by 2013 (International Television Expert Group, 2009).

Furthermore, global IPTV market revenues are forecasted to grow from US$12 billion to US$38 billion during that same period. This same study suggested that the greatest growth would be in Europe, followed by Asia (Smith, 2009).

European IPTV providers are generally telecommunications companies, and they don't face the degree of competition from cable TV as in the U.S. The incumbent operators there have direct broadband access to millions of subscribers. Top IPTV providers in Western Europe include Deutsche Telekom, Belgacom, France Telecom, Telecom Italia, British Telecom, Telefonica, and Swisscom (Focus Editors, 2010).

While most or all of these companies are firmly entrenched in their home country, services are also offered across borders in some cases. France Telecom offers service to Poland and Spain, and Telecom Italia also offers service to France, Germany, and the Netherlands.

In Asia, a number of industry watchers see China Telecom and China Unicom as having the largest potential. Japanese telecommunications company NTT as well as KT (Korea Telecomm) in Korea are seen as having large potential IPTV markets (Focus Editors, 2010).

Growth of Online Video Ads

The stability of video online enabled by broadband has resulted in huge growth in video advertising online (IAB, 2010). According to the Interactive Advertising Bureau, digital video advertising grew almost 40% in 2009 over 2008. Presumably this is because of the stability, maturity of streaming technologies and broadband. Video works very well online and ad dollars for video advertising.

Projections are continuing to be positive for online video ads, as illustrated in Figure 8.6 (eMarketer, December 11, 2009). Even though overall online advertising was down in 2009, video ad revenue increased from $734 million to over $1 billion. Video ad spending growth is also expected to outpace any other online format, running in the 34% to 45% range from 2009 through 2014. These extremely high growth rates "are the result of video ads moving from the sidelines to center stage, becoming the main form of brand advertising in the digital space." (eMarketer, 2009).

Consumer-Generated Content

The joker in the deck regarding IPTV is the effect or influence of consumer-generated content. YouTube has changed the video landscape forever. From now on, Viacom and the BBC must compete with piano playing pets and dancing ninjas for audience share. Human beings are resourceful, and we have not exhausted the possible genres or types of video content. How new forms of expression and creativity will influence future generations cannot be known, but media companies and providers of "professional" (paid-for) content will remain vigilant to adopt "the next big thing" in entertainment, information, or communication.

Program creators in the industry will continue to rely on standard program lengths (22 minutes for TV shows, for example) but probably experiment with other lengths and formats. User-generated content posted on YouTube does not have a standard length or narrative format, which is both a strength and a weakness from a marketing perspective. This unpredictability so far inhibits the revenue potential from sponsorship, product placement, or other means of generating revenue.

Table 8.5
U.S. Online Advertising Spending, by Format, 2008–2014 (millions)

	2008	2009	2010	2011	2010	2013	2014
Search	$10,546	$10,782	$11,422	$12,172	$13,641	$14,694	$15,810
Banner ads	$4,877	$4,765	$4,923	$5,090	$5,411	$5,630	$5,800
Classifieds	$3,174	$2,215	$2,030	$1,915	$1,981	$2,077	$2,176
Lead Generation	$1,683	$1,521	$1,628	$1,739	$1,868	$1,984	$2,108
Rich Media	$1,642	$1,476	$1,558	$1,688	$1,868	$2,046	$2,142
Video	$734	$1,029	$1,440	$1,966	$2,858	$3,844	$5,202
Sponsorships	$387	$313	$316	$328	$351	$372	$388
E-mail	$405	$268	$283	$302	$323	$353	$374
Total	$23,448	$22,370	$23,600	$25,200	$28,300	$31,000	$34,000

Note: Numbers may not add up to total due to rounding

Source: eMarketer, December 2009

🌍 Sustainability 🌍

IPTV is considered to be one of the more sustainable technologies explored in this book. It will remain so for some time because the demand for content—high quality video that is interesting, entertaining, or both—is rapidly increasing rather than decreasing. Some aspects of this demand present implications that are worth noting, because they relate to how people use the technology and perceive it as having benefits and/or consequences.

With IPTV, once the initial setup is completed (involving computer and access to the Internet), the delivery of video content in electronic form to the consumer eliminates the need to use any additional paper, plastic, or fuel to move the content from the manufacturer to the user.

Computers do use electricity, however, computers also generate heat, which in the winter time can be useful but in the summer months may require additional air conditioning.

The availability of high-quality content that can be viewed in a home theater can reduce the need to use fuel to see a movie or experience other, similar content. This factor may be more important for adults, who increasingly may be concerned about travel time and competing with other viewers. This is not so much a factor for younger age groups, as movie going is more of a group socialization ritual and even "courting experience" for teens and young adults.

Conversely, the economics can shift very quickly. Content providers are always searching for ways to generate higher revenues and greater return from consumers. Whether consumers will shift to micropayments or pay-per-click models or stay with traditional one-time rental charges, IPTV providers will find a way to go deeper into the wallet or purse of each consumer.

IPTV reflects the cacophony of the digital marketplace. With hundreds of channels, thousands of programs, and millions of clips and excerpts, it is easier than ever for individuals to create their own unique and personal media experiences.

The next stage may be mobile broadband high-definition video. No one really knows when or how it will pay for itself. Consumers may find it too inconvenient on a crowded bus or a noisy bar to warrant the cost. Or they may find it too dangerous in wind, rain, or snow to even sample the experience.

We can now vaguely see the time when we will be able to watch whatever we want, wherever we want, whenever we want. On any screen size. If we can afford it, our lives may simply be the spare moments we allow to happen between watching and being entertained.

Bibliography

Adobe.com. (2008, May 1). *Adobe and industry leaders establish open screen project.* Retrieved March 25, 2010 from http://www.adobe.com/aboutadobe/pressroom/pressreleases/200804/050108AdobeOSP.html.

Apple Streaming media players target Microsoft (2009, March 13). *WebSiteOptimization.com.* Retrieved March 12, 2010 from http://websiteoptimization.com/bw/0903/.

Bell, L., & Bull, G. (2010). Digital video and teaching. *Contemporary Issues in Technology and Teacher Education, 10*(1). Retrieved April 28, 2010 from http://www.citejournal.org/vol10/iss1/editorial/article1.cfm

comScore, Inc. (2010, March 8). comScore releases January 2010 U.S. online video rankings: Average YouTube viewer watched more than 93 videos in January, up 50 percent vs. year ago. comScore.com. Retrieved April 12, 2010

from http://www.comscore.com/layout/set/popup/Press_Events/Press_Releases/2010/3/comScore_Releases_January_2010_U.S._Online_Video_Rankings.

Covey, N. (2009, January). Tuned in … to your hand? Mobile video use in the U.S. *Nielsen.com/Consumer insight.* Retrieved March 12, 2010 from http://www.global-mediainsight.com/media/consumerinsight-mobilevideo.pdf.

Davidson, E. (2008, April/May). Wanted: Sexy HDTV that connects to the Internet and services all DVRs. *Streaming Media,* 86-94.

Dreier, T. (2010, April 8). Microsoft previews NAB demos, Silverlight advances. *Streamingmedia.com.* Retrieved April 14, 2010 from http://www.streamingmedia.com/Articles/News/Featured-News/Microsoft-Previews-NAB-Demos-Silverlight-Advances-66477.aspx.

Duryee, T. (2010, March 23). Realnetworks offers new way to mass produce mobile video apps. Moconews.net. Retrieved March 24, 2010 from http://moconews.net/article/419-realnetworks-takes-the-kinks-out-to-mass-produce-mobile-video-apps-/.

eMarketer.com (2009, December 11). US Online ad spend turn the corner. eMarketer.com. Retrieved March 4, 2010 from http://www.emarketer.com/Article.aspx?R=1007415.

Focus Editors (2010, March 18). Top IPTV providers. Focus.com. Retrieved March 22, 2010 from http://www.focus.com/fyi/unified-communications/top-iptv-providers/.

Gartner.com (2008, March 28). Gartner says worldwide IPTV subscribers will reach 48.8 million by 2010. *Gartner.com.* Retrieved April 29, 2010 from http://www.gartner.com/it/page.jsp?id=496291.

Graham, B. (2009, June). IPTV: Converged Television. White paper, Occam Networks. Retrieved March 5, 2010 from http://www.iptv-news.com/__data/assets/file/0007/145429/OCC_-_IPTV_White_Paper_6_09.pdf

Gubbins, E. (2007, August 27). Akamai: HD over the Web is here. *Telephony Online.* Retrieved April 17, 2008 from http://www.telephonyonline.com/home/news/hd_web_video_082707/index.html.

Interactive Advertising Bureau (2010, April 7). Internet ad revenues reach record quarterly high of $6.3 billion in Q4 '09. *IAB.com.* Retrieved April 29, 2010 from http://www.iab.net/about_the_iab/recent_press_releases/press_release_archive/press_release/pr-040710.

ITU-T Newslog (2009, February 3). New IPTV standard supports global rollout. Retrieved March 21, 2010 from http://www.itu.int/ITU-T/newslog/CategoryView,category,QoS.aspx.

International Television Expert Group (2009, November). Global IPTV market. *ITVE.org.* Retrieved April 14, 2010 from http://www.international-television.org/tv_market_data/global-iptv-forecast-2009-2013.html.

IPTV-news (2009, June 16). Global IPTV market nears 24m subs, Europe leads growth. *IPTV news.* Retrieved March 26, 2010 from http://www.iptv-news.com/iptv_news/june_09_2/global_iptv_market_nears_24mn_subs,_europe_leads_growth.

Lee, C., and Henson, B. (2009, June 22). Verizon amps up FiOS Internet with increased two-way speeds and launches free netbook/camcorder promotion. *Verizon.com.* Retrieved March 25, 2010 from http://newscenter.verizon.com/press-releases/verizon/2009/verizon-amps-up-fios-internet.html.

Lewin, J. (2010, March 13). Online video growth slows to 10.5%. *Podcasting news*. Retrieved March 20, 2010 from http://www.podcastingnews.com/2010/03/13/online-video-growth-slows-to-10-5/.

Light, C., and Lancefield, D. (2007). Strategies for success in IPTV. IPTV-news.com. Retrieved April 28, 2010 from http://www.iptv-news.com/__data/assets/pdf_file/0011/51140/iptv_strategies_for_success_pwc_final.pdf.

Madden, M. (2009, July). The audience for online video-sharing sites shoots up. *Pew Internet & American Life Project*. Retrieved March 17, 2010 from http://fe01.pewinternet.org/Reports/2009/13--The-Audience-for-Online-VideoSharing-Sites-Shoots-Up.aspx.

Miller, R. (2007, June/July). Cookin' with P2P: Recipe for success or flash in the pan? *Streaming Media*, 32-38.

The Nielsen Company (2009, October 12). Nielsen announces September U.S. online video usage data. *Nielsen.com*. Retrieved March 12, 2010 from http://en-us.nielsen.com/main/news/news_releases/2009/october/nielsen_announces.

The Nielsen Company (2010, March 12). February online video usage up more than 10% over last year. *Nielsen Wire*. Retrieved March 27, 2010 from http://blog.nielsen.com/nielsenwire/online_mobile/february-online-video-usage-up-more-than-10-over-last-year/

Ozer, J. (2010, February 9). The Player's the thing...but so is the codec, format, and protocol. *Streamingmedia.com*. Retrieved February 27, 2010 from http://streamingmedia.com/article.asp?id=11666.

Parrack, D. (2010, January 22). YouTube redesign arrives, profits to follow? *WebTV wire*. Retrieved March 25, 2010 from http://www.webtvwire.com/youtube-redesign-arrives-profits-to-follow/.

Rayburn, D. (2010, February 9). CDN News Roundup: 2009 Content Delivery year in review. *Streamingmedia.com*. Retrieved March 12, 2010 from http://streamingmedia.com/article.asp?id=11662.

Reedy, S. (2008, March 17). The view from the living-room couch. *Telephony Online*. Retrieved March 26, 2010 from http://www.telephonyonline.com/iptv/news/telecom_view_livingroom_couch/index.html.

Riismandel, P. (2010, February 24). Video.edu: Library alliance defends streaming, Yale admissions goes viral. *Streamingmedia.com*. Retrieved March 12, 2010 from http://streamingmedia.com/article.asp?id=11735.

Siglin, T. (2010, January 7). CES 2010: Streaming leads consumer electronics growth. Streamingmedia.com. Retrieved February 27, 2010 from http://streamingmedia.com/article.asp?id=11569.

Smith, R. (2009, December 7). Global IPTV forecast exceeds 2009 prediction by 2M subscribers. Multimedia Research Group press release. Retrieved April 14, 2010 from http://www.mrgco.com/press_releases.html#gf1109.

Spangler, T. (2008, March 20). IPTV to grow 52% annually through 2012: Study. *Multichannel News*. Retrieved March 26, 2010 from http://www.multichannel.com/article/CA6544163.html.

Spangler, T. (2009, April 26). Verizon nets another 299,000 FiOS TV customers. *Multichannel News*. Retrieved March 26, 2010 from http://www.multichannel.com/article/210036-Verizon_Nets_Another_299_000_FiOS_TV_Customers.php.

Spangler, T. (2009, July 27). FiOS TV cracks 2.5 million customers. *Multichannel News*. Retrieved March 26, 2010 from http://www.multichannel.com/article/316458-FiOS_TV_Cracks_2_5_Million_Subscribers.php.

Spangler, T. (2010, January 28). AT&T: U-verse revenue nears $3 billion annually. *Multichannel News*. Retrieved March 26, 2010 from http://www.multichannel.com/article/446516-AT_T_U_verse_Revenue_Nears_3_Billion_Annually.php.

Spangler, T. (2010, March 26). Google's fiber-to-the-home offer attracts 600-plus communities. *Multichannel News*. Retrieved March 26, 2010 from http://www.multichannel.com/article/450780-Google_s_Fiber_To_The_Home_Offer_Attracts_600_Plus_Communities.php.

Torrentfreak.com. (2010). *Twitter uses BitTorrent for server deployment*. Retrieved March 22, 2010 from http://torrentfreak.com/twitter-uses-bittorrent-for-server-deployment-100210/

Unickow, J. (2010, February 9). Publisher's Note: The Revenge of Online Video. Streamingmedia.com. Retrieved March 12, 2010 from http://streamingmedia.com/article.asp?id=11656.

Viscusi, S. (2007, October 5). Report: 489 million IPTV subscribers worldwide by 2016. IPTV: A community and resource center. *TMC Net*. Retrieved March 25, 2010 from http://www.tmcnet.com/scripts/print-page.aspx?.

Webster, T. (2009, April). The infinite dial 2009: Radios digital platforms. *Edison Media Research*. Retrieved March 3, 2010 from http://www.edisonresearch.com/home/archives/2007/03/ 2007_podcast_statistics_analysis.php.

What is BitTorrent? (2010). Retrieved April 29, 2010 from http://www.bittorrent.com/btusers/what-is-bittorrent.

What is Silverlight. (2010). Retrieved April 29, 2010 from http://www.microsfot.com/silverlight/what-is-silverlight/.

9

INTERACTIVE TELEVISION

Cheryl D. Harris, Ph.D. *

Television as an idea and experience is facing obsolescence due to the proliferation of mobile and personal media delivery platforms. Replacing TV is a plethora of programming available either on-demand or at a scheduled time, and on a variety of electronic devices, allowing the viewer to interact with them by requesting more information, making a purchase, expressing an opinion, or contributing other content. The types of response permitted vary depending on the input device: available inputs on a cell phone are likely different than those available on a large-screen home theater system complete with elaborate remotes and keyboards. Interactive inputs include handsets, touch screens, keyboards, mice, gesture recognition, and other feedback technologies. Nearly every news day reveals an innovative, new input option, as well as a new usage envisioned for interactive media. One can imagine interactive television (ITV) as a continuum where any content delivered "on demand" constitutes one end of the spectrum, and runs all the way through applications that allow the viewer to fully shape the content to be delivered, as in interactive storytelling. Shopping applications, where the user responds to embedded tags or content to permit browsing and purchasing, falls somewhere in the middle of this continuum. Interestingly, the huge market for ITV shopping predicted in the past decade has cooled. Many experts have come to feel that ITV's potential is to realize pent-up audience desire to customize their viewing experience as much as possible, rather than being able to click and buy "Rachel's sweater" while watching it (the reference is to the character on the 1990's American sitcom, *Friends*, often mentioned as the touchstone of ITV shopping desires) (Baker, 2009).

Interactive television is a term used to describe the "convergence of television with digital media technologies such as computers, personal video recorders, game consoles, and mobile devices, enabling user interactivity. Increasingly, viewers are moving away from a 'lean back' model of viewing to a more active, 'lean forward' one" (Midgley, 2008; Lu, 2005). Interactive television is increasingly dependent on an Internet delivery system for advanced digital services (and in this case, also referred to as Internet protocol TV or IPTV). Another frequently used technical definition of a delivery system describes the process as slicing a signal into packets, "sending the packets out over a secure network…" and reassembling them at the endpoint (Pyle, 2007, p. 18). This process sounds similar to what is used to send e-mail across the network, but requires a highly layered and complex architecture to achieve it.

The potential of ITV has long been discussed and continues to enjoy its share of hyperbole: "It will seem strange someday that I cannot chat with a friend on a show we're both watching…" or "that I can't get to my sports team with a few clicks of a button to see how the game is going currently" (Reedy, 2008).

---

* Director of Communications at University of California, San Diego, and CIO of the research firm, Decisive Analytics.

"Imagine a television viewing experience so intuitive and interactive that a set-top box recognizes which viewer is watching and adapts to meet his or her entertainment needs" (Reedy, 2008). Many viewers are beginning to understand what video delivered over the Internet might provide, and their imaginations have already broken free of their living rooms. Multi-platform initiatives and mobile ITV have been added to the strategic planning of many key players in the ITV industry. In fact, some multichannel television operators, such as Verizon, have begun to develop "app" stores such as that offered by Apple for its iPhone platform, in the hope that layering applications on top of programming will not only transform passive viewing into a "conversation" but also provide a launchpad for future targeted offers (Hansell, 2009). Video delivered to the mobile phone, although at present a frequently unsatisfying experience due to bandwidth limitations, small screen size, and other factors, is expected to increase both in offerings and in consumer demand. Interactive features for mobile video are expected to be part of the deployment (Schuk, 2010).

Perhaps the most promising development in the ITV viewing experience is the marriage of programming with social media platforms that allow viewers to "co-view" and comment, even though not physically co-located (Vance, 2010; Porges, 2007). Examples include NBC Universal's Hulu service, Verizon's Facebook and Twitter connections tied to FiOS subscriptions, and startups such as Justin.tv. Justin.tv viewers swap more than 100 million messages per month while watching video, and in a single month in late 2009, watched 50 million hours of video together (Vance, 2010). BuddyTV and Joost launched with streaming chat. (Harboe et al., 2008). The Oxygen network has also begun to integrate chat streams in its programming (*Bad Girls Club*), and this is also a popular feature on the Bravo network (*Watch what Happens Live*) (Swedlow, 2010). Industry opinion is that audiences are increasingly seeking shared, "clickable moments" in their interactions with media and that there will ultimately be a significant marketplace for those who offer them (Elliott, 2208).

Researchers have indeed begun scrutinizing the characteristics and outcomes of "virtual co-viewing" in which millions of people may interactively watch programming together and share a variety of commentary, impressions, and critiques. One claim is that "the final goal of social interactive television is to provide the users an enriched shared experience" and that traditional non-interactive media forms will ultimately fall by the wayside (Cesar & Jensen, 2008). Young people between 16-24 years of age seem to be the "most avid adopters" of new forms of media consumption and the most likely to engage with media through a wider variety of devices than adults (Ursuet al., 2008; Obrist et al., 2008).

The past several years have been a proving ground in Europe, Asia, and North America in terms of whether or not audiences will accept and demand ITV in the long run, once the novelty effect has worn off, and whether currently-understood ITV business models would be feasible (Porges, 2007; Burrows, 2007; Dickson, 2007; Harris, 1997). Notably, Microsoft shifted its ITV strategy both in the United States and overseas. In the United States, even small, rural "Tier III" telcos with a few thousand customers are using IP-based networks and advanced MPEG-4 compression to launch ITV services by teaming with satellite service providers and providing a range of services similar to those of much larger players such as AT&T (Dickson, 2007).

Some question whether advertising-supported programming in the ITV era can survive, especially since Internet users have become abundantly accustomed to content being "free." With DVR usage expected to hit 50% of households in the U.S. by late 2010 and nearly 32 million DVR units expected to ship worldwide each year by 2011 (InStat, 2008) "unbundled" and "on demand" programming is predicted to bring about the demise of the television business models as we have known them in the United States. In late 2009, Park Associates estimated that by 2014, U.S. addressable, interactive TV advertising revenue would exceed $4.3 billion, although that would require a very steep growth pattern from the current level of $133 million predicted for 2010 (Parks Associates, 2010.) However, compared to the annual TV advertising marketplace of approximately $70 billion, it is clear that ITV advertising has a long way to go before it can displace the conventional TV ad market.

For nearly 70 years, the notion of "watching television" has emphasized the centrality of the "television set" in the home as an important source of ad-supported news, information, and entertainment. Our ideas of what constitutes an "audience" and how to measure viewership have stuck rather closely to the iconographic status of that centralized, home-based television set. Many of those assumptions have been challenged as multi-set households, out-of-home viewing, and portable video/TV delivery devices have proliferated. Already, programming can be watched anywhere and on a multitude of devices such as PDAs (personal digital assistants), cell phones, iPods, seatback screens on an airplane, or mesmerizing big-screen monitors in home "entertainment centers." It has been widely reported that media delivery is tending to become more portable (untethered from a specific location) and personalized. Portability threatens the ability to adequately measure media exposure, at the same time as it opens new opportunities for targeting. Personalization and customizability are perhaps more of a concern to the media industry because of the propensity for audiences who can customize media delivery to choose to strip out advertising messages and to shift programming out of the carefully constructed "programming schedules" so cherished by network executives.

Television broadcasting is in the latter stages of its transition to digital broadcasting. The move to digital television is taking place at the same time as the number of subscribers to broadband Internet access has reached 83 million U.S. households and 466.9 million worldwide by the end of 2009 (Vanier, 2010), with 64% of U.S. households now subscribing to a broadband service. One obstacle to IPTV growth in the U.S.—as indeed in much of the world—is the unequal access to broadband services, which is concentrated in urban over rural areas, and tends to be associated with higher incomes. For example, in the U.S., 89% of households with annual incomes over $150,000 have broadband in the home, compared to just 29% with incomes of $15,000 or less. Minorities also tend to have less access to broadband (Tessler, 2010). The social and cultural implications of unequal access could be profound over time and require further study.

Wider availability of broadband service, coupled with digital program delivery, has long been considered a key condition in promoting interactive television in the United States. It should be noted, however, that U.S. broadband access is still considered to be costlier, less available, and offered at slower speeds than in several Asian countries, especially Japan (Berman, et al., 2006; McChesney & Podesta, 2006). At least in theory, search services and Internet browsing have put audiences in the habit of seeking interactivity, something the ITV platform can build on (Stump, 2005). Google, for example, may well prove to be a leader in combining its search, profiling, and advertising delivery services to provide highly customized ITV offerings. Google's highly-publicized acquisition of YouTube in 2006 for $1.65 billion, and the subsequent introduction of a nascent "video search" service which allows viewers to search video content by keywords, may eventually allow powerful data-mining of huge repositories of video content and the ability to proactively and intelligently match viewer interests with video materials (Google Press Release, 2006; Lenssen, 2007).

Some have said that a "critical mass" of consumer interest to pave the way for ITV in the United States was required, and that stage has now been reached. Examples cited include the observation that popular TV shows such as *American Idol* are explicitly interactive and involve millions of voting viewers (Mahmud, 2008; Loizides, 2005). The number of users of on-demand video has steadily increased since 2004, and experiments by interactive agencies such as Ensequence and the company Visible World have proven that dynamic, addressable advertising is viable (Parks Associates, 2010; Mahmud, 2008).

It must be noted, however, that despite the forward momentum of interactive content and advertising services, there are still questions about whether personalized content is inherently more appealing or persuasive for viewers than content that is not customized. At least one study that examined this assumption reported "mixed results" and also found that too much choice diminished impact (Varan, 2004). Audience research has not yet definitively proven that we understand either the nature of interactivity or the perceived value of personalization. However, work is being done in developing a conceptual framework for how ITV (and any advertising associated with ITV) might be processed cognitively and emotionally, and how this might differ (if it does) from patterns associated with conventional television viewing or from other forms of video delivery (Bellman, et al., 2005).

Despite this uncertainty, various types of content are under development for the forthcoming two-way digital delivery system, including interactive games, video on demand, and enhancements to programming that provide "t-commerce" (the ability to learn more about products or even purchase a product directly). Some of these enhancements take the form of product placement (that, on mouseover, for example, could be purchased) or even other types of interactive and embedded advertising within programs to encourage longer "dwell-time" in the interactive advertising environment (Lee, 2005).

There are several capabilities that are considered to be critical components of a native ITV application (Reedy, 2008; Damásio & Ferreira, 2004). These include:

◈ Multichannel delivery.

◈ Time-shifting capabilities.

◈ Content personalization (intelligent agent/dynamic delivery).

◈ Content enhancements.

◈ User interaction (including user-to-user and user-to-content).

◈ Content on demand (content alerts, search, and converged services).

There are still a number of other, unpredictable factors. Mike Ramsay, the cofounder of DVR (digital video recorder) and interactive programming guide company TiVo, speculates that connecting the Internet to video delivery could turn the 500-channel cable TV universe into "50 million channels" via Internet protocol television (Levy, 2005). Since programming is likely to be delivered primarily upon demand, there is also the problem of learning what is available and being able to efficiently select programs. To do so, a wealth of collaborative filtering agents (or bots) and other personalization software tools that go beyond the traditional interactive program guide (IPG, sometimes called the EPG) are likely to be needed by audiences and offered by inventive entrepreneurs. Such tools could study a user's preferences, behaviors (such as what has been watched in the past), and other information to customize a "microchannel" to the user. It is also worth noting that many experts believe that viewers will be more interested in interacting with *content* than with *advertising* in this new ITV environment, which presents a challenge to the traditional model of ad-supported video delivery (Meskauskas, 2005).

Background

The history of interactive television in the United States, to date, has been one of experimentation and, often, commercial failure. Conspicuous investments in various forms of interactive television ranged from the 1977 Qube TV service offered by Warner Amex in Columbus (Ohio), Dallas, and Pittsburgh to Time Warner's much-publicized FSN (Full Service Network) in Orlando in 1994-1997. An earlier, 1960s era effort called "Subscription TV (STV)," which debuted in Los Angeles and San Francisco and offered cultural events, sports, and even an interactive movie channel, fizzled out (Schwalb, 2003). Microsoft joined the fray with its purchase of

WebTV in 1997, which, after three years, "topped out at about a million users before descending into marketing oblivion" (Kelly, 2002). Although MSN spent hundreds of millions of dollars to finance speculative programming (such as $100 million on the Web show *474 Madison*), it did not find an audience to support its programming. Meanwhile, throughout 2006, a small, (then) anonymous crew using a cramped, makeshift room made to look like a teenager's bedroom, and an unknown volunteer actress, posted a series of videos on YouTube under the pseudonym "LonelyGirl15" and drew millions of obsessive viewers who posted streams of commentary, speculation, and blog postings throughout the Internet. Is this non-professional, user-generated content the future of the 500-million channel ITV universe (McNamara, 2006)?

Not surprisingly, the success of ventures such as YouTube, coupled with the apparent willingness of audiences to interact and contribute to these venues, have resulted in considerable investor interest. Nearly every week there is a new story in the press about the rise to "instant fame" of a YouTube contributor. Amateur Web videos are frequently shown on network news shows, and some YouTube creators have earned considerable income from ads placed alongside their video channels in the site. The number of online video viewers is expected grow by more than two-thirds to 941 million in 2013, up dramatically from 563 million viewers reported in 2008 , and may reach 941 million viewers by 2013 (ABI Research, 2008).

While ITV efforts in the United States were having difficulty finding audiences in the last decade, European and U.K. ITV initiatives continued to be developed and, in some cases, flourish. As a result, American hardware and content providers have had the rare opportunity to watch and learn from several well-funded ITV applications abroad, such as BSkyB and the BBC's "Red Button" service (Warman, 2009). Interactive commercials are already commonplace in the United Kingdom.; BSkyB , Britain's biggest satellite television service, "already plies 9 million customers with interactive ads" and that response in terms of clickthrough rates and conversions are much higher than Web-delivered ads (3-4% vs. .3%) (*The Economist*, 2009). Some European operators have found that gambling and gaming (not advertising) comprise a larger part of their revenue (Shepherd & Vinton, 2005).

Recent Developments

By 2005, EchoStar Communications' DISH Network and DirecTV had already rolled out ITV platforms in the United States, with a combined audience of about 25 million viewers (Morrissey, 2005). A majority of cable TV companies are currently offering video on demand (VOD) services or will in the near future, and, as previously mentioned, providers such as Verizon are beginning to layer applications such as Facebook, Twitter, etc. on top of their programming. Microsoft has made a large commitment to IPTV services, but with a multi-platform strategy involving converged services focusing on the "MediaRoom" environment (Porges, 2007). Bill Gates announced that the next generation of "interactive television services completely blows open any of the limitations that channels used to create" and has abolished the previous video platform in favor of IPTV (InformITV, 2006a). Microsoft has had agreements in place to provide IPTV services to major corporations in Europe, Asia, and the United States; companies include Deutsche Telekom, Swisscom, Telecom Italia, BellSouth, Bell Canada, and Reliance Infocomm, among others (Burrows, 2007; Jones, 2008; InformITV, 2006a; InformITV, 2006b).

Access to digital television services worldwide jumped from just 16% in 2006 to 28% in 2009, and is predicted to reach 40% by 2012. (Global Digital Media, 2009). Parks Associates reported the number of telco/IPTV households worldwide grew by nearly 80% in 2008 to exceed 20 million. The growth rate was expected to reach 40 million by the end of 2009. (Parks Associates, 2009).

Figure 9.1
IPTV Subscribers Worldwide

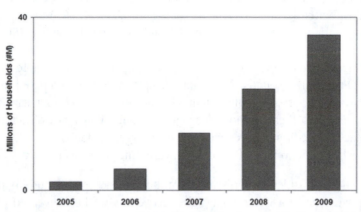

Source: Digital Living Forecast Workbook—Global, 2009 Parks Associates

What could hold up ITV's progress? The technology underlying ITV delivery is complex, and several key problems have yet to be solved, particularly those related to packet processing and security. The transport network supporting Internet services such as voice over IP (VoIP), video, and all the regular Internet traffic is described as "limited" in its ability to provide an adequate "quality of experience" from a user-perspective. Adding the heavy burden of almost unlimited video on demand to this infrastructure is proving worrisome to the engineers developing the means of managing all of these signal streams (Tomar, 2007). The introduction of Mobile ITV services is likely to further complicate the picture (Tong-Hyung, 2009).

A positive development was the announcement in January 2008 by the International Telecommunications Union of the first set of global standards for IPTV, built with technical contributions from service providers and technology manufacturers as well as other stakeholders. This group has committed to regular ongoing meetings so that these standards will continue to evolve (Standards for Internet Protocol TV, 2008).

CURRENT STATUS

Media Buying/Planning

Confusion about how to buy or sell advertising on IPTV and ITV is rampant, even years after its introduction. Traditional television networks circulate content proposals to media buyers a year or more in advance, while newer video forms provide little lead time for buyers to make decisions. Viewers claim to be interested in interacting with advertising targeted to their interests: a surprising 66% said they were looking for an opportunity to do so. Apparently, the interest crosses content genres and is not limited to reality shows, at least according to the data released to date (Mahmud, 2008; Krihak, 2006). Agencies and advertisers will need to come to an agreement concerning how to treat the market for ITV product, both during the transitional period and when ITV is fully implemented. There is also concern that consumer-generated content (CGC)—content that individuals provide that include blogs (with/without RSS [really simple syndication]), podcasts, vblogs (blogs with video content), animations, newsletters, content "traces," and other information—will continue to be a rising trend. These media offerings may compete for the same advertiser dollars as affiliated networks, but outside of the traditional media planning framework.

Media Measurement

An upheaval in media measurement practices and accepted standards is currently underway, fueled in part by advertiser demand to better account for new technologies such as DVR, VOD, and portable media devices. The Nielsen Company continues to adhere to client demand to "follow the video" (Story, 2007; Whiting, 2006) but by early 2010 had introduced no comprehensive plan for doing so. Other media measurement players such as Integrated Media Measurement, Inc. (IMMI) proposed using cell phones adapted to measure consumer media exposure by sampling nearby sounds. The sound samples are then compared, and the database matches them to media content. This approach could potentially track exposure to compact discs, DVDs (digital video-discs), video, movies seen in a theater, and videogames, among other types of media. No clear winner in the race to provide satisfactory media measurement has yet emerged. Established online ratings providers ComScore and NetRatings will also be well positioned to deliver ratings or measurement services to ITV.

However, there will be considerable pressure to produce an acceptable and highly accountable system for measuring media exposure and for determining ad effectiveness in the converged media environment. Some experts believe that the field of Web analytics, already relatively sophisticated after more a decade of development, may offer some solutions. In a converged media environment with Internet-delivered content as the primary focus, all exposure from all users could conceivably be tracked, without reliance on panel-based measurement schemes. Data mining models could then be used to profile and extract program and ad exposure information, as well as what audience members then did in response to exposure.

Lessons learned from this kind of data could eventually allow advertisers and content providers to apply powerful behavioral targeting techniques that would further customize media delivery.

🌐 Sustainability 🌐

Interactive television technology has the potential to play an important role in educating people about how their behaviors affect their communities, their carbon footprint, and the environment in general. The National Cable Television Association (NCTA) provided a "My World" showcase at its 2010 Cable Show in Los Angeles that explored a myriad of ways that cable companies are attempting to improve the way that consumers live, work, and play (Spangler, 2010, March 23).

One of the most promising parts of the exhibit from a sustainability perspective was Time Warner Cable's *Connect a Million Minds* interactive television application, which is designed to help children find after-school programs in science, technology, engineering, and math. The application is a five-year, $100 million program funded by Time Warner Cable to help make American children more competitive globally (Spangler, 2010b).

If this program is successful, it should lead to the development and implementation of other applications, games, and information sources that will leverage the power of interactive television to achieve pro-social goals.

Factors to Watch

Business Models

All the content delivery options now in play and expected to be available in the future create a number of questions for new business and revenue models that may support the content infrastructure. In competition for both viewers and advertising dollars will be contenders such as the download services (iTunes, Google, Yahoo), TV networks and producers, Web sites containing video offerings, and specialty programming targeted to devices such as cell phones. There is also the continuing threat from peer-to-peer or file-sharing networks that swap content, much of it illegally obtained, and without anyone getting paid. Some believe that content providers, including television networks and movie studios, should put ads in their programming and give them away for free. Others believe the best value proposition is to emphasize the value of content over advertising and sell episodes or films directly, advertising-free, at a higher price than ad-supported media products. At the same time, numerous content providers can cite past failed experiments with a "pay wall" model in which users are expected to pay for content (which may have been previously offered for free), but refuse to do so. It is not clear if ITV/IPTV will manage to support itself through advertising revenue, bundled e-commerce, a micropayment or subscription system, or perhaps a combination of all of these (Deloitte Touche Tomatsu, 2010).

Consultants are piling up with theories about how to win in the emerging marketplace. IBM recently released an influential report revealing their thinking about how ITV will stack up. First, analysts predict a "generational chasm" between baby boomers in early retirement or nearing retirement age who are accustomed to decades of passive media usage and the younger Generation X and Millennials. Described as in the "lean back" category, baby boomers may have splurged on a flat screen TV and DVR, but have not greatly modified their TV viewing habits in many years. Their children are likely to be much more media-evolved and more likely to be "multi-platform" media users, looking to smart phones, P2P (peer-to-peer) services, VOD—whatever improves convenience and access.

At a further remove, teenagers have been exposed to (and immersed in) high-bandwidth networks and services from very early ages and experiment unflinchingly with media and platforms. Mobile devices and multitasking behaviors are central to their lives. It is second nature for them to rip and share content and have different definitions of both privacy and piracy, ones perhaps unrecognizable to their parents. They expect—and have many of the tools to obtain—total control of media content (Berman, et al., 2006).

In the same report, the pronouncement that "the mass market will stop always, trumping the niche market" is made to stunning effect (Berman, et al., 2006, p. 5). The point is that the so-called "long-tail theory" popularized by Chris Anderson of *Wired* fame suggests that a convergent marketplace is one that ITV is perfectly positioned to exploit (Anderson, 2006).

When programming tied to a schedule is no longer supported, pre-release content may command a premium price. It is not clear, however, what happens to any of the former television pricing models when the idea of a "fixed schedule" of programming is truly out the window. Some question remains as to whether or not *any* content needs to be offered live or "real-time" in the future. Sporting events, news, and even election results may have more value to viewers if under their control, but these types of live content may have even more need for immediacy when viewers are getting instant updates from real-time, social networking applications including Twitter, Facebook, and even the ESPN Score Center App. These issues have yet to be put to the test. Interestingly, although Apple's business venture of offering individual recordings at an average of $.99 through its iTunes Store has been a huge success in its first few years (and has reportedly brought the traditional music business "to its knees"), its related video business over iTunes has not performed as well. By 2008, more than 5 billion songs had been sold through iTunes, but only 18 million videos/movies (NPD Group, 2009; Barnes, 2007).

New forms of content are also emerging, including efforts by companies interested in porting existing content to various alternative devices, and even those solely dedicated to developing new content for devices such as mobile phones. Ad formats that are in consideration for the support of content delivery include on demand ads delivered to match stated interests:

◆ *Vertical ads* that link the viewer to topical information and related products.

◆ *Opt-in ads* accepted in exchange for free or discounted programming.

◆ *Hypertargeted ads* delivered with localization or profiled matching criteria.

◆ *Embedded advertising*, the digital equivalent of product placement.

◆ *Sponsored content*, longer-form programming sponsored by an advertiser, similar to the early sponsorship models of 1950s-era television (Kiley & Lowrey, 2005; Brightman, 2005).

Consumer-Generated Content

There is little doubt that the Internet has provided a powerful means of disintermediation (the process of businesses communicating or dealing directly with end users rather than through intermediaries). More than one observer has noted that the "blog" or Weblog has afforded everybody a printing press at little or no cost. Similarly, video programming can be created, distributed, and sold online without the assistance of the traditional media gatekeepers. Consumer-generated content is endemic online, ranging in quality from the primitive to the highly polished. Even seasoned television and film producers as well as news correspondents are said to be producing their own shows for online distribution and sale outside of the network and studio system (Hansell, 2009; 2006).

Few people are asking, however, whether or not there will really be an audience for all the available content in a future ITV environment. In the "50 million channel universe," how many of those channels will be able to survive and endure?

According to The Nielsen Company—and this finding is consistent over time—households receiving more than 60 channels tend to watch only about 15 of them on a regular basis (Webster, 2005). Will we see a similar concentration of interest once the novelty of ITV wears off? How will we effectively navigate such a vast universe of content?

Piracy and Digital Rights

Consumer-generated content, which is generally free of charge to those who wish to view it, is certainly a threat to established television business models, although a relatively small problem. However, the threat from file-sharing sites such as BitTorrent or YouTube, which may facilitate the distribution of copyright-restricted content, is much greater. Such sites account for half the daily volume of data sent via the Internet by some estimates (Wray, 2008; Kiley & Lowrey, 2005) and may be even more since many file-sharing networks have effectively gone "underground" in the past few years. Industry analysts assume that billions of dollars are already lost each year to copyright theft and outright piracy (Brightman, 2005). In an all-digital content world, sharing content becomes much easier, and many file-sharing consumers do not see their actions as theft or piracy. Adding insult to injury, few encryption schemes hold up to the concerted—and sometimes well-coordinated—efforts of crackers (Tomar, 2007).

Media Delivery Options Proliferate

Devices through which media might be delivered are likely to proliferate in the coming years, assuming consumer demand for increased portability and personalized media delivery continues. Some of these devices might be entirely new in form, and others might be examples of converging functions in single devices. The extent to which personalization might be taken as a result of consumer interest in customizing media experiences is still unclear. Early experiments in alternative interactive media suggest that there may be many ways of determining consumer interest and preferences, such as bioreactive devices, and consequently, our ideas of what constitutes interactive television or media, today, might not bear much resemblance to what might be considered "interactive" in a decade or less.

Bibliography

ABI Research. (2008, December 12.) As Online Video viewing shifts from PC to TV Screen, Viewers will Number Nearly One Billion by 2013. Retrieved February 15, 2010 from http://www.abiresearch.com/press/1327-As+Online+Video+Viewing+Shifts+From+PC+to+TV+Screen,+Viewers+Will+Number+Nearly+One+Billion+by+2013

Anderson, C. (2006). *The long tail: Why the future of business is selling less of more.* New York: Hyperion.

Baker, J. (2009). Interactive TV allows viewers to shop remotely. National Public Radio. September 30. Retrieved January 22, 2010 from: http://npr.org/templates/story/storyId=11331598

Barnes, B. (2007, August 31). NBC will not renew iTunes contract. *New York Times.* Retrieved from http://www.nytimes.com/2007/08/31/technology/31NBC.html.

Bellman, S., Schweda, A., & Varan, D. (2005). *Interactive television advertising: A research agenda.* ANZMAC 2005 Conference on Advertising/Marketing Communication Issues.

Berman, S., Duffy, N., & Shipnuck, L. (2006). The end of TV as we know it. *IBM Institute for Business Value executive brief.* From http://www-935.ibm.com/services/us/index.wss/ibvstudy/imc/a1023172?cntxt=a1000062.

Brightman, I. (2005). *Technology, media & telecommunications (TMT) trends: Predictions, 2005.* Retrieved January 2008 from http://www.deloitte.com/dtt/section_node/0%2C1042%2Csid%25253D1012%2C00.html.

Burrows, P. (2007, November 7). Microsoft IPTV: At long last, progress. *Business Week Online.*

Business Wire. (2005). Kagan projects interactive TV revenues from gaming, t-commerce and advertising will reach $2.4 billion by 2009. *Business Wire.* From http://www.businesswire.com/portal/site/google/index.jsp?ndmViewId=news_view&newsId=20051004005902&newsLang=en.

Business Wire. (2006). Tuning in with IPTV? Early adopters see value in interactive services. *Business Wire.* Retrieved March 13, 2006, from http://home.businesswire.com/portal/site/google/index.jsp?ndmViewId=news_view&newsId=20060313005761&newsLang=en.

Cesar, P. & Jensen, J. (2008). Social Television and User Interaction. *ACM Computers in Entertainment,* 6 (1), May, Article 4.

Clark, D. (2006, April 6). Ad measurement is going high-tech. *Wall Street Journal,* 2.

Damásio, C. & Ferreira, A. (2004). Interactive television usage and applications: The Portuguese case study. *Computers & Graphics,* 28, 139-148.

Deloitte Touche Tohmatsu. Media Predictions 2010.

Dickson, G. (2007, November 5). IPTV hits the heartland. *Broadcasting & Cable,* 137 (44), 24.

Dorrell, E. (2008, April 3). Online TV broadcasters fight to control content, *New Media Age.* Retrieved from http://www.nma.co.uk/Page=/Articles/37483/Online+tv+broadcasters+fight+to+control+content.html

Dvorak, J. (2007, December 25). Understanding IPTV. *PC Magazine,* 56.

Edwards, C. (2007a, November 19). I want my iTV. *Business Week.* Special Report, 54.

Edwards, C. (2007b, December 3). The long wait for tailor-made TV. *Business Week,* 77.

Elliott, S. (2008, June 16). Remote Clicks that do more than just change channels. *The New York Times.* C:8.

Global Digital Media (2009). Global Digital Media Trends and Statistics, Paul Budde Communication, PTY, Ltd.

Google, (2006, October 9.) Google to Acquire YouTube for $1.65 Billion in Stock. Google Press Release, Retrieved March 30, 2010 from: http://www.google.com/intl/en/press/pressrel/google_youtube.html

Hanekop, H. & Schrader, A. (2007). Usage patterns of mobile TV. *German Online Research 2007,* Leipzig. Unpublished Paper.

Hansell, S. (2006, March 12). As Internet TV aims at niche audiences, the Slivercast is born. *New York Times.* Retrieved March 14, 2006 from http://www.nytimes.com/2006/03/12/business/ourmoney/12sliver.html.

Hansell, S. (2009, September 7). Getting people to do more than just sit and watch: Cable TV operators see iPhone as model for viewer interactivity. *The International Herald Tribune.*

Harboe, G., Massey, N., Metcalf, C., Wheatley, D., Romano, G. (2008). The Uses of Social Television. *ACM Computers in Entertainment,* 6 (1), May, Article 8.

Harris, C. (1997, November). Theorizing interactivity. *Marketing and Research Today,* 25 (4), 267-271.

InformITV. (2006a). *Bill Gates' vision for next generation television.* Retrieved January 5, 2006 from http://informiTV.com/articles/2006/01/05/billgatesvision/.

InformITV. (2006b). *Deutsche Telekom calls on Microsoft for IPTV services.* Retrieved March 21, 2006, from http://informiTV.com/articles/2006/03/21/deutschetelekomcalls/.

InStat (2008). Long Term Prospects Bright for PVR Market. Retrieved March 14, 2010 from: http://www.in-stat.com/press.asp?Sku=IN0703640ME&ID=2193

Jones, K. (2008, April 1). Streaming media to draw $70 billion in revenue before 2014; Internet, IPTV, networks, mobile handsets will increase revenue. *Information Week.* Retrieved from http://www.informationweek.com/ story/showArticle.jhtml?articleID=207001008.

Kelly, J. (2002). Interactive television: Is it coming or not? *Television Quarterly, 32* (4), 18-22.

Kiley, D. & Lowrey, T. (2005, November 21). The end of TV (as you know it). *Business Week,* 40-44.

Krihak, J. (2006). Video, video everywhere. *Media Post Online Video Insider.* Retrieved February 20, 2006 from http://publications.mediapost.com/index.cfm?fuseaction=Articles.showArticle&art_aid=39978.

Lee, J. (2005). An A-Z of interactive TV. *Campaign,* 13.

Lenssen, P. (2007). Google Video now a Video Search Engine. Retrieved April 1, 2010 from: http://blogoscoped.com/archive/2007-06-14-n62.html

Levy, S. (2005, May 23). Television reloaded. *Newsweek.* Retrieved from http://www.newsweek.com/id/49954/.

Loizides, L. (2005). Interactive TV: Dispelling misconceptions in the media. *ACM Computers in Entertainment, 3* (1), 7a.

Lu, K. (2005). *Interaction design principles for interactive television.* Unpublished Master's Thesis, Georgia Institute of Technology.

Macklin, B. (2008). Broadband services: VoIP and IPTV trends. *eMarketer.* Retrieved from http://www.emarketer.com/ Reports/All/Emarketer_2000393.asp.

Mahmud, S. (2008, January 25). Viewers crave TV ad fusion. *AdWeek Online.* http://www.adweek.com/aw/ content_display/news/media/e3i9c26dcb46eda7449d1197b0419feb7a1.

Martin, K. (2006, April 2). Why every American should have broadband access. *Financial Times.* Retrieved from http://www.ft.com/cms/s/2/837637ee-c269-11da-ac03-0000779e2340.html.

McChesney, R. & Podesta, J. (2006, January/February). Let there be Wi-Fi: Broadband is the electricity of the 21st century, and much of America is being left in the dark. *Washington Monthly.* Retrieved from http://www.washingtonmonthly.com/features/2006/0601.podesta.html.

McNamara, M. (2006). LonelyGirl15: An online star is born. *CBS News Online.* Retrieved from http://www.cbsnews.com/ stories/2006/09/11/blogophile/main1999184.shtml.

Midgley, N. (2008). Do you lean forward or lean back? August 14, *The Telegraph* (UK).

Meskauskas, J. (2005). Digital media converges. *iMediaConnection.com.* Retrieved June 1, 2005 from http://www.imediaconnection.com/content/6013.asp.

Morrissey, B. (2005, March 28). Can interactive TV revive the 30-second spot? *Adweek Online.* Retrieved from http://www.adweek.com/aw/esearch/article_display.jsp?vnu_content_id=1000855874.

NPD Group. (2009). Digital Music Increases Share. Retrieved February 22 2010 from: http://www.npd.com/press/releases/press_090818.html

Obrist, M. Bernhaupt, R., Tscheligi, M. (2008). Interactive TV for the Home: An Ethnographic Study on user's Requirements and Experiences. *International journal of Human-Computer Interaction.* 24(2), 174-196.

Omniture introduces new video measurement. (2008, March 5). *Editor & Publisher.* Retrieved from http://www.editorandpublisher.com/eandp/departments/online/article_display.jsp?vnu_content_id=1003719631.

Parks Associates, (2010, March 23). Addressable, Interactive TV Revenue Predicted to Reach 133 million in 2010. Retrieved April 5, 2010 from: http://parksassociates.blogspot.com/2010/03/addressable-interactive-tv-advertising.html

Parks Associates. (2009, July 21). Telco/IPTV subscribers to total almost 40 million households worldwide in 2009. Retrieved February 5, 2010 from: http://newsroom.parksassociates.com/article_display.cfm?article_id=5170

Porges, S. (2007, December 4). The future of Web TV. *PC Magazine,* 19.

Pyle, K. (2007, November 5). What is IPTV? *Telephony, 247* (18).

Reedy, S. (2008, March 17). To IPTV and beyond. *Telephony, 248* (4). Retrieved from http://telephonyonline.com/ iptv/news/telecom_iptv_beyond/.

Schwalb, E. (2003). *ITV handbook: Technologies and standards.* Saddle River, NJ: Prentice Hall.

Schuk, C. (2010, January 4.) Predictions for Mobile TV in 2010. *Broadcast Engineering.*

Shepherd, I. & Vinton., M. (2005, May 27). ITV report: Views from the Bridge. *Campaign,* 4.

Spangler, T. (2010a, March 23). NCTA showcase highlights intersection of entertainment, technology. *Multichannel News.* Retrieved May 10, 2010 from http://www.multichannel.com/article/450658-Cable_Show_2010_It_s_My_World_After_All.php

Spangler, T. (2010b, May 4). Interactive social media application a first for corporate social responsibility program. *Multichannel News.* Retrieved May 10, 2010 from http://www.multichannel.com/article/452237-Cable_Show_2010_TWC_To_Show_Connect_A_Million_Minds_Pro_Social_ITV_App.php

Standards for Internet protocol TV. (2008, January 8). *Computer Weekly,* 151.

Story, L. (2007, June 28). Nielsen adds to cell phone tracking. *New York Times.* Retrieved from http://www.nytimes.com/ 2007/06/28/business/media/28adco.html?_r=1&scp=2&sq=nielsen+june+28%2C+2007&st=nyt&oref=slogin.

Stump, M. (2005, October 31). Interactive TV unchained: How Web-created habits are stoking interest in participatory TV—finally. *Multichannel News*, 14.

Swedlow, T. (2010, April 5.) Ikea is first company to sponsor Oxygen's Two-Screen Social/Interactive TV Service, OxygenLive. Interactive TV Today. Retrieved April 5, 2010 from http://www.itvt.com/story/6589/ikea-first-company-sponsor-oxygens-two-screen-socialinteractive-tv-service-oxygenlive

Tessler, J. (2010, February 16). U.S. Broadband Figures show 40% Lack Broadband, *The Huffington Post.* Retrieved April 22, 2010 from: http://www.huffingtonpost.com/2010/02/16/us-broadband-figures-show_n_463849.html

The Economist (2009, October 10). Shop after you Drop. Interactive Television Advertising. U.S. edition.

Tomar, N. (2007, December 10). IPTV redefines packet processing requirements at the edge. *Electronic Engineering Times*, 31.

Tong-Hyung, K. (2009, November 26). Mobile TV to Become Interactive. *Korea Times.*

Ursuet, M., Thomas, M., Kegel, I., Williams, D., Tuomola, M., Lindsted, I., Wright, T. (2008). Interactive TV Narratives: Opportunities, Progress, and Challenges. ACM *Transactions on Multimedia Computing*, Communications and Applications, 4(4), Article 25.

Vance, A. (2010, January 4). Watching TV Together, Miles Apart. The New York Times, B:1.

Vanier, F. (2010, March). World broadband statistics report Q4 2009. Point Topic. Retrieved February 10, 2010 from: http://www.point-topic.com/content/

Varan, D. (2004). *Consumer insights associated with interactive television.* Retrieved March 10, 2006 from http://www.broadcastpapers.com/whitepapers/Consumer-Insights-Associated-with-Interactive-Television.cfm?objid=32&pid=576&fromCategory=44.

Warman, M. (2009, May 2.) Ten years of pressing red: Matt Warman celebrates a decade of interactive TV, and looks at the future of the BBC Service. *The Daily Telegraph.*

Webster, J. (2005). Beneath the veneer of fragmentation: Television audience polarization in a multichannel world. *Journal of Communication, 55* (2), 366–382.

Whiting, S. (2006, March 1). To our clients. In N. M. R. Clients (Ed.). New York: Nielsen Media Research.

Wray, R. (2008, February 22). Filesharing law unworkable. *The Guardian.* Retrieved from http://www.guardian.co.uk/technology/2008/feb/22.

10

Radio Broadcasting

Gregory Pitts, Ph.D.[*]

> Our research shows that 92% of Americans believe radio is important in their daily lives. But while it is valued, radio is also taken for granted. Because it is so pervasive, radio is sometimes overlooked, just like water or electricity (National Association of Broadcasters, 2008).

> Radio is the last analog medium. To not face the digital evolution and join it, to ignore it and remain complacent will put analog radio where the 45-RPM record and cassette tapes are today (Kneller, 2010).

Radio technology spent its first 80 years in sedate existence. Its most exotic innovation—beyond improvements in the tuner itself—was the arrival of FM stereo broadcasting in 1961. Today, audiences are redefining the term "radio." Satellite-delivered audio services from Sirius-XM, streaming audio options, and audio downloads (both music and full-length programming) are allowing consumers to think anew about the meaning of the word *radio*. Radio is just as likely to refer to personal audio media—multiple selections and formats of audio content provided by a variety of sources—beyond FM and AM radio. Radio is becoming a generic term for audio entertainment supplied by terrestrial broadcast frequency, satellite, Internet streaming, cell phones, and portable digital media players—via podcasts, some of which come from traditional radio companies and still others that are the product of technology innovators (Green, et al., 2005). Today, broadcast radio comprises only half (51%) of the audio day for men and women (The Nielsen Company, 2009).

The latest effort by the AM and FM radio industry to add technological sizzle comes from digital over-the-air radio broadcasting (called HD Radio, HD2, and HD3), an effort by the radio industry to promote new technological competition but not create new competitors to the radio industry. HD Radio is the brand name for new digital AM and FM radio technology developed by iBiquity Digital to allow existing radio stations to stream digital content simultaneously with their analog FM and AM signals. Existing station owners, after licensing the new technology, may simulcast an existing station's programming or offer multiple channels of programming in addition to an existing AM or FM radio station. For the consumer, no subscription fee must be paid to receive the program (unlike satellite programming) but there is also no option to download program podcasts, only a few receivers allow listeners to pause content as do most online sites and, of course, listeners need an HD radio receiver. The primary advantage of HD Radio is cleaner, clearer sound when compared to AM or FM radio.

---

[*] Professor, Department of Communications, University of North Alabama (Florence, Alabama).

The National Association of Broadcasters has not ignored radio innovation. NAB identifies five initiatives that promote radio technology and program availability. These include:

◆ *NAB's Flexible Advanced Services for Television and Radio On All Devices (FASTROAD)*, to help accelerate deployment of new technologies.

◆ *The National Radio Systems Committee (NRSC)* a jointly sponsored NAB and Consumer Electronics Association (CEA) committee to recommend technical standards for radio receivers.

◆ *The Radio Data System (RDS)* that allows analog FM stations to provide digital data services, such as song title and artist or traffic information.

◆ *HD Radio*, the in-band-on-channel digital radio broadcasting system developed by iBiquity Digital Corporation.

◆ *Radio Heard Here*, the consumer promotional phase of the Radio 2020 campaign to remind consumers and the media industry of radio's value (NAB, n.d.).

Radio remains an important part of the daily lives of millions of people. Personality and promotion driven radio formats thrust themselves into the daily routines of listeners. Radio station ownership consolidation has led to greater emphasis on formats, format branding, and promotional efforts designed to appeal to listener groups and, at the same time, yield steady returns on investments for owners and shareholders through the sale of advertising time. But advertising loads and the availability of personal choice technology, such as portable digital media players and personalized online audio, are driving listeners to look for other options.

Critics have been quick to point to the malaise brought upon the radio industry by consolidated ownership and cost-cutting but the previous ownership fragmentation may never have allowed today's radio to reach the point of offering HD radio as a competitor to satellite and streaming technologies. Through consolidation, the largest owner groups have focused their attention on new product development to position radio to respond to new technological competition. There have been technology stumbles in the past:

◆ *FM broadcasting*, which almost died because of lack of support from AM station owners and ultimately took more than 35 years to achieve 50% of all radio listening in 1978.

◆ *Quad-FM* (quadraphonic sound) never gained market momentum.

◆ *AM stereo*, touted in the early 1980s as a savior in AM's competitive battle with FM.

These technologies did not fail exclusively for want of station owner support, but it was an important part of their failure. Large ownership groups have an economic incentive to pursue new technology. HD radio best exemplifies the economy of scale needed to introduce a new radio technology. Whether consumers will view HD radio as a technological offering worthy of adoption when they can subscribe to satellite services or download digital music to various portable media players is not yet clear. HD Radio may be a technology that has arrived too late to satisfy consumers.

This chapter examines the factors that have redirected the technological path of radio broadcasting. The most important technological improvement for AM and FM radio is the implementation of digital terrestrial audio broadcasting capable of delivering near-CD-quality audio and a variety of new data services from song/artist identification, to local traffic and weather, to subscription services yet to be imagined.

Background

The history of radio is rooted in the earliest wired communications—the telegraph and the telephone—although no single person can be credited with inventing radio. Most of radio's "inventors" refined an idea put forth by someone else (Lewis, 1991). Although the technology may seem mundane today, until radio was invented, it was impossible to simultaneously transmit entertainment or information to millions of people. The radio experimenters of 1900 or 1910 were as enthused about their technology as are the employees of the latest tech startup. Today, the Internet allows us to travel around the world without leaving our seats. For the listener in the 1920s, 1930s, or 1940s, radio was the only way to hear live reports from around the world.

Probably the most widely known radio inventor/innovator was Italian Guglielmo Marconi, who recognized its commercial value and improved the operation of early wireless equipment. The one person who made the most lasting contributions to radio and electronics technology was Edwin Howard Armstrong. He discovered regeneration, the principle behind signal amplification, and invented the superheterodyne tuner that led to a high-performance receiver that could be sold at a moderate price, thus increasing home penetration of radios. In 1933, Armstrong was awarded five patents for frequency modulation (FM) technology (Albarran & Pitts, 2000). The two traditional radio transmission technologies are amplitude modulation and frequency modulation. AM varies (modulates) signal strength (amplitude), and FM varies the frequency of the signal.

The oldest commercial radio station began broadcasting in AM in 1920, with the technology advantage of being able to broadcast over a wide coverage area. AM signals are low fidelity and subject to electrical interference. FM, which provides superior sound, is of limited range. Commercial FM took nearly 20 years from the first Armstrong patents in the 1930s to begin significant service and did not reach listener parity with AM until 1978 when FM listenership finally exceeded AM listenership.

FM radio's technological add-on of stereo broadcasting, authorized by the Federal Communications Commission (FCC) in 1961, along with an end to program simulcasting (airing the same program on both AM and FM stations) in 1964, expanded FM listenership (Sterling & Kittross, 1990). Other attempts, such as Quad-FM (quadraphonic sound), ended with disappointing results. AM stereo, touted in the early 1980s as the savior in AM's competitive battle with FM, languished for lack of a technical standard because of the inability of station owners and the FCC to adopt an AM stereo system (FCC, n.d.-a; Huff, 1992). Ultimately, consumers expressed minimal interest in AM stereo.

Why have technological improvements in radio been slow in coming? One obvious answer is that the marketplace did not want the improvements. Station owners invested in modest technological changes; they shifted music programming from the AM to the FM band. AM attracted listeners by becoming the home of low-cost talk programming. Another barrier was the question of what would happen to AM and FM stations if a new radio service were created? Would existing stations automatically be given the first opportunity to occupy new digital space, as an automatic grant, eliminating the possibility that new competition would be created? What portion of the spectrum would a new digital service occupy? Were listeners ready to migrate to a new part of the spectrum? New radio services would mean more competitors for the limited pool of advertising revenue. Radio listeners expressed limited interest in new radio services at a time when personal music choice blossomed through the offering of 45-RPM records, followed by 8-track and then cassette tapes, and then CDs and portable digital media players. If radio owners were reluctant to embrace new technology offerings, consumers were not reluctant. Radio remained important because it was free and familiar. The consumer electronics industry focused on other technological opportunities, including video recording and computer technology, rather than new forms of radio.

The change in thinking for the radio industry came when iBiquity Digital was formed in August 2000 by the merger of USA Digital Radio and Lucent Digital Radio (iBiquity, n.d.-c). Some of the largest radio groups at that time were investors in the company. The investors' goal was to support the creation of a new digital radio service that would allow the use of existing FM and AM frequencies, thus lessening the potential for the creation of new competitors and likely ensuring existing broadcasters with first claims to the new service. The new digital service came to be called in-band, on-channel (IBOC).

The Changing Radio Marketplace

The FCC elimination of ownership caps mandated by the *Telecommunications Act of 1996* set the stage for many of the changes that have taken place in radio broadcasting in the last decade. Before the ownership limits were eliminated, there were few incentives for broadcasters, equipment manufacturers, or consumer electronics manufacturers to upgrade the technology. Outside of the largest markets, radio stations were individual small businesses. (At one time, station owners were limited to seven stations of each service. Later, the limit was increased to 18 stations of each service, before deregulation eventually removed ownership limits.) Analog radio, within the technical limits of a system developed nearly 90 years ago, worked just fine. The fractured station ownership system ensured station owner opposition to FCC initiatives and manufacturer efforts to pursue technological innovation.

The compelling question today is whether anyone cares about the technological changes in terrestrial radio broadcasting. Or, are the newest changes in radio coming at a time when public attention has turned to other sources and forms of audio entertainment? The personal audio medium concept suggests that *local* personality radio may not be relevant when listeners can access both mega-talent personalities and local stars through satellite services, online, and with podcasting.

RECENT DEVELOPMENTS

There are four areas where technology is affecting radio broadcasting:

1) New digital audio broadcasting transmission modes that are compatible with existing FM and AM radio.

2) Delivery competition from satellite digital audio radio services (SDARS).

3) New voices for communities: low-power FM service.

4) New technologies that offer substitutes for radio.

New Digital Audio Broadcasting Transmission Modes

Most free, over-the-air AM and FM radio stations may still be broadcasting in analog, but their on-air and production capabilities and the audio chain, from music and commercials to the final program signal delivered to the station's transmitter, is digitally processed and travels to a digital exciter in the station's transmitter where the audio is added to the carrier wave. The only part of the process that remains analog is the final transmission of the over-the-air FM or AM signal.

AM and FM radio made the critical step toward digital transmission in 2002, when the FCC approved the digital broadcasting system proposed by iBiquity Digital (marketed as HD radio). The first HD radio receiver was sold about two years later in January 2004 in Cedar Rapids (Iowa). The FCC calls stations providing the new digital service hybrid broadcasters because they continue their analog broadcasts (FCC, 2004). This should not be confused with iBiquity's identification of "HD" as only a marketing label not a reference to the FCC's station classification. By 2010, the FCC database listed 1,541 FM HD Radio stations and 292 AM HD Radio stations. Almost one-third are non-commercial radio stations affiliated with National Public Radio (author calculation from the FCC database). As of mid-2010, iBiquity claimed nearly 2,000 HD Radio stations and about 1,000 HD2 or HD3 channels covering 90% of the population (iBiquity, n.d.-a). As a percentage of licensed stations, either number represents less than 15% of the more than 15,000 licensed radio stations in the United States.

The HD Radio digital signal eliminates noise and multipath distortion, provides better audio quality—including surround sound, and provides digital information delivery, including traffic information, song tagging, and other forms of consumer information. IBOC technology consists of an audio compression technology called perceptual audio coder (PAC) that allows the analog and digital content to be combined on existing radio bands, and digital broadcast technology that allows transmission of music and text while reducing the noise and static associated with current reception. The system does not require any new spectrum space, as stations continue to broadcast on the existing analog channel and use the new digital system to broadcast on the same frequency. As illustrated in Figure 10.1, this digital audio broadcasting (DAB) system uses a hybrid in-band, on-channel system that allows simultaneous broadcast of analog and digital signals by existing FM stations through the use of compression technology, without disrupting the existing analog coverage. The FM IBOC system is capable of delivering near-CD-quality audio and new data services including song titles, and traffic and weather bulletins. A similar system for AM IBOC provides FM stereo quality signals from AM station broadcasts. The so-called killer application to attract consumers to HD radio is the ability to offer a second, third or fourth audio channel. For example, KIMN in Denver airs Hot AC on the analog FM channel but Best of the 80s on HD2 and Holy Hits on HD3 (iBiquity, n.d.-a).

Terrestrial digital audio broadcasting involves not only regulatory procedures, but also marketing the technology to radio station owners, broadcast equipment manufacturers, consumer and automotive electronics manufacturers and retailers, and most important, the public. iBiquity Digital markets the new technology to consumers as HD radio, a static-free service without hiss, fading, or pops and available without a monthly subscription fee. As with satellite radio's earliest efforts to attract subscribers, receiver availability is a significant consumer barrier. Receiver choices, while increasing, remain limited; prices have declined but cost between $49 and $400 for portable, home or automotive tuners. They are often difficult to tune in, sometimes requiring several seconds to lock on a frequency (Boehret, 2010). Receiver sales may be increasing but overall market penetration is minimal. As of mid-2010 the number of digital radio receivers in the U.S. is estimated at well over one million, compared to more than 800 million conventional (analog) FM receivers in the U.S. (Kneller, 2010; FCC, 2004).

There is no current plan to eliminate analog FM and AM broadcasts, and the HD radio transmissions will not return any spectrum to the FCC for new uses. Thus, there are questions as to whether consumers want the new service, given the expense of new receivers, the abundance of existing receivers, and the availability of other technologies including subscriber-based satellite-delivered audio services, digital media players with audio transfer and playback, and competition from digital television. As was true with satellite radio, gaining the interest of the automotive industry to offer HD radio as an optional or standard audio feature is crucial. Unlike satellite radio, no automotive manufacturers are investors in iBiquity Digital, although car manufacturers are beginning to add the service.

Figure 10.1
Hybrid and All-Digital AM & FM IBOC Modes

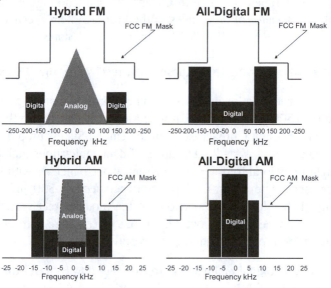

Source: iBiquity

For broadcasters, digital audio broadcasting is more than just a new broadcast technology. HD radio will allow one-way wireless data transmission similar to the radio broadcast data system (RBDS or RDS) technology that allows analog FM stations to send traffic and weather information, programming, and promotional material from the station for delivery to smart receivers. HD radio utilizes multichannel broadcasting by scaling the digital portion of the hybrid FM broadcast. IBOC provides for a 96 Kb/s (kilobits per second) digital data rate, but this can be scaled to 84 Kb/s or 64 Kb/s to allow 12 Kb/s or 32 Kb/s for other services, including non-broadcast services such as subscription services.

iBiquity Digital's HD radio also gives listeners, who are used to instant access, one odd technology quirk to get used to. Whenever an HD radio signal is detected, it takes the receiver approximately 8.5 seconds to lock onto the signal. The first four seconds are needed for the receiver to process the digitally compressed information; the next 4.5 seconds ensure robustness of the signal (iBiquity, 2003). The hybrid (analog and HD) operation allows receivers to switch between digital and analog signals, if the digital signal is lost. Receivers compensate for part of the lost signal by incorporating audio buffering technology into their electronics that can fill in the missing signal with analog audio. For this approach to be effective, iBiquity Digital recommends that analog station signals operate with a delay, rather than as a live signal. Effectively, the signal of an analog FM receiver, airing the same programming as an HD receiver, would be delayed at least 8.5 seconds. As a practical matter, iBiquity Digital notes, "Processing and buffer delay will produce off-air cueing challenges for remote broadcasts..." (iBiquity, 2003, p. 55).

While trying to promote marketplace adoption of receivers and multi-cast channels, stations have been faced with weak signal coverage. The FCC approved a blanket power increase for HD Radio stations in 2010. FM radio stations may voluntarily increase digital power levels up to ten percent of analog power levels, subject to resolving any interference problems this might create. Practically speaking, most FM stations are permitted to increase their digital power by 6 dB, a four-fold power increase (FCC, 2010-a).

A different form of DAB service is in operation in a number of countries. The Eureka 147 system broadcasts digital signals on the L-band (1452-1492 MHz) or a part of the spectrum known as Band III (around 221 MHz) and is in operation or experimental testing in Canada, the United Kingdom, Sweden, Germany, France, and about 40 other countries. Because of differences in the Eureka system's technology, it is not designed to work with existing AM and FM frequencies. Broadcasters in the United States rejected the Eureka 147 system in favor of the "backward and forward" compatible digital technology of iBiquity Digital's IBOC that allows listeners to receive analog signals without having to purchase a new receiver for the DAB system (FCC, 2004).

The World DAB Forum, an international, non-government organization to promote the Eureka 147 DAB system, reports that more than 500 million people around the world can receive the 1,000 different DAB services (World DAB, n.d.). As with digital broadcasting in the United States, proponents of Eureka 147 cite the service's ability to deliver data as well as audio. Examples of data applications include weather maps or directional information that might be helpful to drivers or emergency personnel. As with the iBiquity Digital projections, the Eureka numbers seem impressive until put into perspective: 500 million people can potentially receive the signal, but only if they have purchased one of the required receivers. Eureka 147 receivers have been on the market since the Summer 1998; about 325 models of commercial receivers are currently available and range in price from around $55 to more than $1,000 (World DAB, n.d.).

Two new services, DAB+ and digital multimedia broadcasting (DMB), offer the potential for DAB to leap beyond ordinary radio applications. DAB+ is based on the original DAB standard, but uses a more efficient audio codec. It provides the same functionality as the original DAB radio services including services following traffic announcements and PAD multimedia data (dynamic labels such as title artist information or news headlines, complementary graphics, and images) (World DAB, n.d.).

As with HD radio technology, both DAB+ and DMB require new receivers if consumers are to use the content. For consumers to adopt the technology, there must be sufficient rollout of the services to create enough consumer interest in the products. DMB, with eight million devices sold, is reaching less than 2% of the 500 million potential users.

An early effort by iBiquity Digital and its broadcast equipment manufacturing partners introduced HD Radio to other countries, particularly in Europe. While the technology attracted some attention, it does not appear to be gaining station or regulatory converts.

Competition from Satellite Radio

The single biggest competitive challenge for free, over-the-air radio broadcasting in the United States has been the introduction of competing subscriber-based satellite radio service, a form of out-of-band digital "radio," launched in the United States in 2001 and 2002 by XM Satellite Radio and Sirius Satellite Radio, respectively. The competition with HD Radio intensified in July 2008 when the two companies merged to become Sirius-XM.

Satellite service was authorized by the FCC in 1995 and, strictly speaking, is not a radio service. Rather than delivering programming primarily through terrestrial (land-based) transmission systems, each service uses geosynchronous satellites to deliver its programming (see Figure 10.2). (Terrestrial signals do enhance reception in some fringe areas, such as tunnels.) Daily reach of satellite radio is small when compared with broadcast radio, 15.3% reach for satellite versus 77.3% for broadcast radio (The Nielsen Company, 2009). But the newly combined company saw an increase in revenue in 2009 and positive cash flow of $463 million, a $599 million improvement over 2008 (Sirius XM, 2010). Users pay a monthly subscription fee of between $10 and $14 and must have a proprietary receiver to decode the transmissions.

Figure 10.2
Satellite Radio

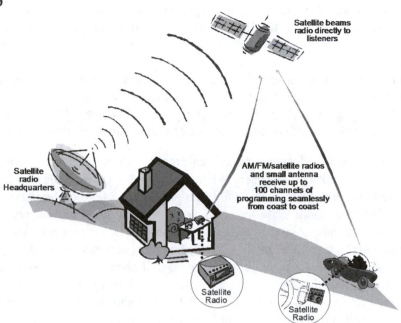

Source: J. Meadows & Technology Futures, Inc.

There is a willingness among consumers to pay for audio service; Sirius-XM finished the first quarter of 2010 with 18.944 million subscribers, reflecting a net addition of 171,441 subscribers during the first quarter. The cost to attract and add each new subscriber remains high; the conversion rate from trial subscriptions improved to 45.2% (Radio Business Reports, 2010).

Helping the growth of satellite radio has been an array of savvy partnerships and investments, including alliances with various automobile manufacturers and content relationships with personalities and artists, including Howard Stern, Martha Stewart, Oprah Winfrey, Rosie O'Donnell, Jamie Foxx, Barbara Walters, and Opie & Anthony. Sirius-XM Radio is the "Official Satellite Radio Partner" of the NFL, Major League Baseball, NASCAR, NBA, NHL,PGA Tour, and major college sports.

New Voices for Communities: Low-Power FM Service

The FCC approved the creation of a controversial new classification of noncommercial FM station in January 2000 (Chen, 2000). LPFM, or low-power FM, service limits stations to a power level of either 100 watts or 10 watts (FCC, n.d.-b). The classification was controversial because existing full-power stations were afraid of signal interference. The service range of a 100-watt LPFM station is about a 3.5-mile radius. LPFM stations do not have the option of adopting HD Radio but they do provide free analog programming to supplement existing FM broadcasts. As of mid-2010, the number of licensed LPFM stations in the U.S. is 864 (FCC, 2010-b).

New Competition—Internet Radio, Digital Audio Files, and Podcasts

Listening to portable audio devices and streaming audio are becoming mainstream practices. Online listening may include content originating from over-the-air stations, including HD Radio or FM stations, begging the question of which distribution venue will be more valuable to consumers in the future. The average reach of these services is about 10% but together they constitute 12.8% of the daily share of all audio listening (The Nielsen Company, 2009). High-speed Internet connectivity—wired or wireless—and the accompanying smart devices, phones, netbooks, and the iPad, are technological challengers for terrestrial radio. These sexier technologies offer more listener choice and they lure consumer dollars to the purchase of these technologies instead of HD Radio receivers. (For more information on digital audio and Internet connectivity, see Chapters 16 and 21.) The opportunity to control music listening options and to catalog those options in digital form presents not just a technological threat to radio listening, but also a lifestyle threat of greater magnitude than listening to tapes or CDs. Listeners have thousands of songs that can be programmed for playback according to listener mood, and the playback will always be commercial-free and in high fidelity. As digital audio file playback technology migrates from portable players to automotive units, the threat to radio will increase.

For nearly a decade, cellular telephones have been predicted to become the leading delivery vehicle for mobile entertainment (Borzo, 2002). Consumers in Europe, Japan, the United States, and Australia already use cell phones to receive music files, video clips, and video games. Missing from the latest generation of smartphones is an FM or AM tuner, once again fostering an environment where consumers grow up without the choice of broadcast radio listening. Apple, after substantial lobbying by the broadcast industry, has finally added a conventional FM tuner to some iPod models. HD Radio tuners were not included, although the less popular Microsoft Zune does have an HD radio option. Whether cell phones are used for audio playback, mobile video applications, or personal television viewing, they are competitors to radio stations. They occupy listener time and consume financial resources that are not committed to radio or the purchase of HD radio receivers. HD Radio, DAB+ and DMB proponents all seem to forget that the newly developing wireless technologies offer the advantage of two-way communication and access to greater amounts of content.

Nearly three-fourths of radio listening takes place in cars. Automobiles no longer come with simple radios; they are equipped with sophisticated audio systems. The latest generation of car audio systems allows for the integration of consumer smartphones and other devices, bringing a host of new capabilities to the car (Cheng, 2010). Included in the features are the ability to run mobile programs such as Internet audio programs from Pandora, Stitcher, and Twitter's OpenBeak Internet audio service as well as providing consumers with a seamless access to their own content from personal audio files.

Internet radios and mobile devices offer access to thousands more online audio/radio services than any FM tuner ever could (Taub, 2009). *Streamingradioguide.com* is a Web guide listing more than 14,000 online stations. Excluding LPFM stations, this number is roughly equal to the total number of commercial and non-commercial radio stations in the U.S. By comparison, local over-the-air reception usually provides access to fewer than 100 stations. Internet radios are comparably priced to HD and other receivers, starting at about $100.

New Legislation

For over 70 years, radio stations contend that they have offered recording artists and record companies valuable on-air promotion in exchange for right to broadcast the music the stations have played. The only parties receiving compensation for the songs aired are the individuals who actually wrote the song—not the performers. This situation may change. Congress is considering a law that would establish additional performance royalties on radio stations on behalf of artists and record companies that own the recordings. Performance royalties are already collected for songs played on satellite and online radio. Other countries collect such royalties from broadcasters, but they do not pay U.S. performers because the U.S. does not require payment of a performance royalty. The amount of the performance royalty will still need to be negotiated if the law is passed, but broadcasters are fighting the law to avoid the additional expense (Plambeck, 2010). Estimates of the total cost for broadcasters are in the range of hundreds of millions of dollars per year for an industry with already declining advertising revenue. For broadcasters, the royalty represents a business disincentive to innovate. Even if the royalty is levied on individual stations and not on individual radio companies, there is a potential disincentive to offer multiple programming streams on HD Radio services or even to launch HD Radio. Meanwhile, radio's competitors see the royalty as simple fairness. For example, Pandora Internet radio earned slightly more than $40 million in revenue but is expected to pay about $30 million in license fees in 2009 (Wingfield, 2010). Perhaps more significant than the royalty is the lobbying battle the broadcasters stand to lose.

CURRENT STATUS

Terrestrial broadcast radio remains a big part of the lives of most people. Each week, more than 239 million people hear the nearly 15,284 FM, LPFM, and AM radio stations in the U. S. Advertisers spent $16 billion on radio advertising in 2009—a substantial amount but a decrease of 18% from 2008. The decline resulted from the soft economy as well as advertising shifts to other media, including online sources (FCC, 2010b; RAB, n.d.-a & U.S. Bureau of the Census, 2008). Radio listening statistics are impressive but a closer examination shows persistent radio industry declines, ranging from declining ad revenue to a daily drop in listeners.

The FCC estimates there are nearly 800 million radios in use in U.S. households, private and commercial vehicles, and commercial establishments (FCC, 2004). All of these radios will continue to receive analog signals from radio stations even after the stations commence HD radio broadcasts. An HD Digital Radio Alliance funded survey optimistically found that 77% of radio listeners were aware of HD radio and that 31% were interested in the service (iBiquity, n.d.-c). In 2008, industry observers estimated that fewer than 500,000 HD Radios had been sold (Fisher, 2008). By 2010, the estimate was more than one million in the marketplace but this growth came after iBiquity and radio groups aired $680 million in promotional spots to promote iBiquity from 2006-2008 (Butcher, 2008). The lack of consumer interest may be reflected by the fact that almost $1000 worth of promotional spots were aired for each HD radio sold, and it took more than five years to sell the first million HD radio receivers. By contrast, on the first sales day Apple sold more than 300,000 iPads and application downloads have exceeded one million (Graham, 2010).

🌍 Sustainability 🌍

Radio is often the leading communications medium in transitional countries in Africa and Asia for the same reasons that radio remains popular in the United States. Radio receivers are relatively cheap, they are easy to use, and in transitional countries, radio messages can overcome transportation logistical issues (no roads or poor roads that make newspaper delivery difficult), and country literacy problems. You don't have to know how to read to understand a speaker on the radio. Further more, the U.S. Agency for International Development (USAID) has promoted the distribution of wind-up and solar radio receivers that don't require economically disadvantaged listeners to buy batteries and thus produce the waste of discarded batteries. Similar wind-up radios are marketed in the U.S., though primarily as emergency radios. In the United States, there are some novel examples of radio stations using solar energy to power transmitters. Radio station KATO in Taos, New Mexico, has used solar panels to power the station for about 20 years (KATO, n.d.) A community radio station in Tucson also recently unveiled a solar panel array to generate part of the station's power needs.

Radio has the ability to make significant contributions to social and environmental sustainability, if listeners will take the time to actually listen to the messages. Throughout its history, radio stations filled mostly unsold airtime with public service announcements to inform and educate listeners. The business model of most radio station owners seems to have shifted most campaigns towards self-interest efforts (on-air self-promotions including the industry's efforts to fight performance royalties with broadcast announcements) but radio still commands a substantial listening audience. Should radio stations decide to focus on delivering a sustainability message, they could foster a new level of listener and regulator goodwill.

Table 10.1

Radio in the United States at a Glance

Number of Radios

Households with radios	99%
Average number of radios per household	8
Number of radios in U.S. homes, autos, commercial vehicles and commercial establishments	800 million

Source: U.S. Bureau of the Census (2008) and FCC (2004)

Radio Station Totals

AM Stations	4,790
FM Commercial Stations	6,479
FM Educational Stations	3,151
Total 14,420	
FM Translators and Boosters	6,155
LPFM Stations	864

Source: FCC (2010-b)

Radio Audiences

Persons Age 12 and Older Reached by Radio:	
Each week:	93.2% (About 239 million people)
Daily Reach	71% (About 183 million people)
Persons Age 12 and Older Radio Reach by Daypart:	
6–10am	77%
10–3pm	82.5%
3–7pm	81.8%
7–12 Mid.	57.4%
12 Mid–6am	25.8%
Where Persons Age 12 and Older Listen to the Radio:	
At home:	28.8% of their listening time
In car:	73% of their listening time
At work or other places:	16.2% of their listening time
Daily Share of Time Spent With Various Media:	
Broadcast Radio	77%
TV/Cable	95%
Newspapers	35%
Internet/Web	64%
Magazines	27%

Source: Radio Advertising Bureau Marketing Guide (n.d.-b)

Satellite Subscribers

SIRIUS-XM Satellite Radio	18,944,199

Source: Sirius-XM Satellite Radio (2010)

FACTORS TO WATCH

    Radio stations have been in the business of delivering music and information to listeners for nearly a century. Public acceptance of radio, measured through listenership more than any particular technological aspect, has enabled radio to succeed. Stations have been able to sell advertising time based on the number and perceived value of their audience to advertising clients. Technology, when utilized by radio stations, focused on improving the sound of the existing AM or FM signal or reducing operating costs.

Digital radio technology has modest potential to return the radio industry to a more relevant status among consumers. The plethora of alternative delivery means suggests that radio may be entering the competitive arena too late to attract the attention of consumers. Chris Andersen (2006), writing in *Wired*, promotes the notion of *The Long Tail*, where consumers, bored with mainstream media offerings, regularly pursue the digital music road less traveled. As *Business Week* noted, "Listeners, increasingly bored by the homogeneous programming and ever-more-intrusive advertising on commercial airwaves, are simply tuning out and finding alternatives" (Green, et al., 2005). Satellite audio holds the promise to create multiple revenue streams: the sale of the audio content, sale of commercial content on some programming channels, and possible delivery of other forms of data. Regulatory barriers to these new technologies are not the issue. Appropriate timing for the introduction of new delivery technologies, consumer interest in the technologies, perfecting the technology so that it is as easy to use as traditional radio broadcasting has always been, marketing receivers at affordable prices, and delivering content that offers value will determine the success of any new technologies (including HD Radio) that are attempting to take audiences from analog radio.

Consumer ability to easily store and transfer digital audio files to and from a variety of small personal players that have a pricing advantage over HD radio receivers will be another determining factor in the success of HD radio. Listeners desiring only entertainment will find little compelling advantage to purchasing a digital receiver. Eclectic or narrowly programmed formats might be attractive in the short term to encourage audiences to consider purchasing an HD receiver, but the desire by radio companies to attract the largest possible audience will result in a contraction of format offerings. And, consumer ability to use other devices to program personal eclectic program content supersedes the value of HD Radio. The competitive nature of radio suggests that the battle for listeners will lead to fewer format options and more mass appeal formats, as stations attempt to pursue an ever-shrinking radio advertising stream.

Localism—the ability of stations to market not only near-CD-quality audio content but also valuable local news, weather, and sports information—has been cited as the touchstone for the terrestrial radio industry. In his farewell address in 2005, retiring NAB President Eddie Fritts presented this challenge: "Our future is in combining the domestic with the digital. Localism and public service are our franchises, and ours alone" (Fritts farewell, 2005, p. 44). But even radio localism is under attack by newspapers and television stations as these competitors attempt to offer micro-local content through Internet and smart device delivery. Why wait for the radio station to provide weather, traffic or sports scores when the content is available on your mobile phone as text, audio or video. But ease of access and use of radio technology that requires only a receiver and no downloading or monthly fees may keep radio relevant for a core group of listeners unwilling to pay for new services and new technologies.

Bibliography

Albarran, A. & Pitts, G. (2000). *The radio broadcasting industry*. Boston: Allyn and Bacon.

Anderson, C. (2006). *The long tail: Why the future of business is selling less of more*. New York: Hyperion.

Boehret, K. (2010, January 27). Reaching for the height of radio. *The Wall Street Journal*, p. D8.

Borzo, J. (2002, March 5). Phone fun. *Wall Street Journal*, R8.

Butcher, D. (2008, July 2). Clear Channel, CBS Radio promote HD Radio via mobile. Retrieved May 1, 2010 from
    http://www.mobilemarketer.com/cms/news/messaging/1259.html

Chen, K. (2000, January 17). FCC is set to open airwaves to low-power radio. *Wall Street Journal*, B12.

Cheng, R. (2010, April 28). Car phones getting smarter. *The Wall Street Journal*, p. B5.

Federal Communications Commission. (n.d.-a). *AM stereo broadcasting.* Retrieved May 1, 2010 from http://www.fcc.gov/mb/audio/bickel/amstereo.html.

Federal Communications Commission. (n.d.-b). *Low-power FM broadcast radio stations.* Retrieved May 1, 2010 from http://www.fcc.gov/mb/audio/lpfm.

Federal Communications Commission. (2004). In the matter of digital audio broadcasting systems and their impact on the terrestrial radio broadcast services. *Notice of proposed rulemaking.* MM Docket No. 99-325. Retrieved April 20, 2010 from http://hraunfoss.fcc.gov/edocs_public/attachmatch/FCC-04-99A4.pdf.

Federal Communications Commission. (2007). *Third report and order and second further notice of proposed rulemaking.* MM Docket No. 99-25 Retrieved February 21, 2008 from http://www.fcc.gov/mb/audio/lpfm/index.html.

Federal Communications Commission. (2010-a, January 29). Digital Audio Broadcasting Systems and Their Impact on the Terrestrial Radio Broadcast Service. Retrieved on April 2, 2010 from http://www.fcc.gov/mb/audio/digital.html.

Federal Communications Commission. (2010-b, February 26). *Broadcast station totals as of December 31, 2009.* Retrieved March 23, 2010 from http://www.fcc.gov/mb/audio/totals/index.html.

Fisher, Marc (2008, February 10). HD Radio: If a Tree falls & No One Hears It…. *The Washington Post.* Retrieved April 19, 2010 from http://www.washingtonpost.com/wp-dyn/content/article/2008/02/08/AR2008020801035_pf.html

Fritts' farewell: Stay vigilant, stay local. (2005, April 25). *Broadcasting & Cable*, 44.

Graham, Jefferson (2010, April 15) Apple sells 300,000 iPads in first day. *USA Today.* Retrieved from http://www.usatoday.com/tech/products/2010-04-04-apple-ipad-sales_N.htm on April 26, 2010.

Green, H., Lowry, T., & Yang, C. (2005, March 3). The new radio revolution. *Business Week Online.* Retrieved February 15, 2006 from http://yahoo.businessweek.com/technology/content/mar2005/ tc2005033_0336_tc024.htm.

Huff, K. (1992). AM stereo in the marketplace: The solution still eludes. *Journal of Radio Studies*, 1, 15-30.

iBiquity Digital Corporation. (n.d.-a). Find HD Radio Stations Near You. Retrieved April 10, 2010 from http://www.ibiquity.com/hd_radio/hdradio_find_a_station

iBiquity Digital Corporation. (n.d.-b). Radio Companies Kick Off First Phase of $200 Million Ad Campaign for HD Digital Radio. Retrieved April 17, 2010 from http://hdradio.com/press_room.php?newscontent=23

iBiquity Digital Corporation. (n.d.-c). HD Digital Radio Alliance Marks Three Successful Years. Retrieved April 19, 2004 from http://hdradio.com/press_room.php?newscontent=309.

iBiquity Digital Corporation. (2003). *Broadcasters marketing guide, version 1.0.* Retrieved March 10, 2006 from http://www.ibiquity.com/hdradio/documents/BroadcastersMarketingGuide.pdf.

KATO. (n.d.) About KATO. Retrieved May 2, 2010, from http://www.ktao.com/.

Kneller, H. (2010, January 18). Nautel responds to "HD Radio in Brazil" article. *Radio Business Reports.* Retrieved April 22, 2010 from http://www.rbr.com/radio/ENGINEERING/95/20134.html?print

Lewis, T. (1991). *Empire of the air: The men who made radio.* New York: Harper Collins.

National Association of Broadcasters. (2008, June 27). Rehr Delivers Keynote During Conclave Learning Conference. Retrieved April 23, 2010 from http://www.nab.org/documents/newsRoom/pressRelease.asp?id=1633

National Association of Broadcasters. (n.d.). *Innovation in Radio.* Retrieved April 23, 2010 from http://www.nab.org/radio/innovation.asp

Plambeck, J. (2010, March 7). Dispute heats up over proposed new fees for playing songs on the radio. *The New York Times.* Retrieved May 2, 2010 from http://www.nytimes.com/2010/03/08/business/media/08royalty.html?scp=1&sq=radio+performance+tax&st=nyt

Radio Advertising Bureau. (n.d.-a). *Radio revenue trends.* Retrieved March 2, 2010 from http://rab.com/public/pr/yearly.cfm.

Radio Advertising Bureau. (n.d.-b). *Radio Marketing Guide.* Retrieved March 2, 2010 from http://www.rab.com/public/marketingGuide/rabRmg.html.

Radio Business Reports. (2010, April 20). Analysts expecting strong Q1 from Sirius XM. Retrieved April 23, 2010 from http://www.rbr.com/radio/23490.html.

Sirius XM Radio. (2010, April 14). SIRIUS XM Adds Over 171,000 Net Subscribers in the First Quarter. Retrieved April 15, 2010 from http://investor.sirius.com/releasedetail.cfm?ReleaseID=458949.

Sterling, C. & Kittross, J. (1990). *Stay tuned: A concise history of American broadcasting.* Belmont, CA: Wadsworth Publishing.

Taub, E. A. (2009, December 30). Internet radio stations are the new wave. *The New York Times.* Retrieved May 2, 2010 from http://www.nytimes.com/2009/12/31/technology/personaltech/31basics.html?_r=1&scp=3&sq=internet%20radio%20receivers&st=Search

The Nielsen Company. (October 29, 2009) *How U.S. Adults Use Radio and Other Forms of Audio.* Retrieved April 22, 2010 from http://www.researchexcellence.com.

U.S. Bureau of the Census. (2008). *Statistical abstract of the United States.* Washington, DC: U.S. Government Printing Office.

Wingfield, B. (2010, January 8). Radio Royalties Fight Heats Up In Washington *Forbes.* Retrieved May 2, 2010 from http://www.forbes.com/2010/01/08/radio-internet-royalties-business-beltway-radio.html

World DAB: The World Forum for Digital Audio Broadcasting. (n.d.). DAB/DAB+/DMB Receivers. Retrieved March 11, 2010 from http://www.worlddab.org/products_manufacturers

11

Digital Signage

Janet Kolodzy, M.S.J.*

Most people have experienced digital signage technology without thinking twice about it. It can be as big as the digital billboards on Times Square or as simple as a digital photo frame displayed in a reception area or waiting room. Digital signage is being used to alert passengers to the next subway train, to inform students about the speaker at the campus center, or to provide cooking tips to a supermarket shopper. Digital signage can involve an LED or plasma screen display, a touch screen kiosk, or a mobile phone screen. It can present text, video, and graphics. It is a growing industry that is attracting audio-visual suppliers, electronic integrators, network developers, marketers, and the like who see it as a new medium for any message. Digital signage proponents argue that anything a paper sign once did, a digital sign can do in a timelier, more uniform, more efficient and more available fashion (Little, 2010). Paper and digital signs are compared in Table 11.1.

The Digital Signage Association defines digital signage as "the use of electronic displays or screens (such as LCD, LED, plasma or projection) to deliver entertainment, information and/or advertising in public or private spaces, outside of home" (Digital Signage FAQs, 2010). But others involved in the industry indicate a more focused use for business communication "where a dynamic messaging device is used to take the place of, or supplement, other forms of messaging" (Yackey, 2009).

In the forward of Keith Kelsen's *Unleashing the Power of Digital Signage*, digital signage is referred to as an "experience medium, a place that engages people in the experience" (Kelsen, 2010). The future of digital signage is in its capacity to engage and connect with individuals on each person's terms, anywhere, anyhow, and any time. Kelsen maintains that the use of networks and mobile devices in conjunction with a screen display will create new layers of "connectedness" of media, messages, and audiences. Digital signage, like mobile devices, allows for audiences to "opt in" *but* in places where audiences want to opt in. Digital signage "is technology that meets viewers in their environment with potentially the right message at the right time" (Kelsen, 2010, p. xiii).

Retailers and marketers have adopted the use of digital signage in greater proportion than other industries, but its potential use in educational, health care, and internal business communication has led to consistent annual predictions of steady growth amid tough economic times in other aspects of communication. Digital signage involves the marriage of certain hardware, software, and content. New developments providing easier, cheaper, and more energy-efficient offerings in each of these areas indicate future growth in digital signage.

However, issues of distraction and intrusion are arising as digital signage expands beyond limited pockets of usage to national networked displays. Those in the digital signage industry are examining ways to develop a

---

* Associate Professor, Department of Journalism, Emerson College (Boston, Massachusetts).

standard system of both measurement of digital signage impact and of operation or presentation. Digital signage providers are also developing an independent trade association.

Table II.1

Paper versus Digital Signage

Traditional/Paper Signs	Digital Signage
◆ Can display a single message over several weeks	◆ Can display multiple messages in several hours
◆ No audience response available	◆ Can allow for interactivity with audience
◆ Requires hours, days for changing content	◆ Can change content quickly and easily
◆ Two-dimensional presentation	◆ Can mix media = text, graphics, video, pictures
◆ Lower initial costs	◆ High upfront technology investment costs

Source: Janet Kolodzy

Background

Digital signage emerged from a variety of ancestors: audio-visual equipment, outdoor advertising billboards, trade show displays, television and computer monitors, video recorders, and media players. Its precursors range from Turner Broadcasting's Checkout Channel, which aired news and information for those waiting in the checkout line, to the electronic displays on New York's Times Square. Yet, digital signage truly came to the fore within the past decade with the rise of flexible flat display screens and multimedia players with a variety of content files (documents, digital pictures, videos, animation, etc.) that can be controlled, updated, and enhanced via content management systems by users and not just by suppliers.

In fact, even the term "digital signage" has had dozens of variations and interpretations before it became a generally accepted term in the industry. Terms such as "Captive Audience Networks" and "Digital Signage Broadcasting" to "Dynamic or Digital Out-Of-Home (DOOH)" and "Digital Displays" now sit under the digital signage umbrella (Schaeffler, 2008). A digital signage resource directory now lists integrators, installers, networks, content services, displays, media players, and control systems among businesses connected to the industry.

Lars-Ingemar Lundstrom, author of *Digital Signage Broadcasting* and a Swedish digital signage manager indicated "Digital signage is very different from most other kinds of media because it is really a combination of existing technologies" (Lundstrom, 2008, p. xii). In many ways, digital signage is a combination of Internet and broadcasting designed to present information. It can present images and information in real-time or live via broadcast or from stored memory via the Internet. The technology can arrange that presentation in a variety of ways, with a screen devoted solely to one image or divided up into several segments using video, still images, and text (either moving continuously via a "crawl" or stationary in a graphic). "Digital signage systems allow automatic content storage at several locations en route to the viewer. The stored content may also be updated at any time" (Lundstrom, 2008, p. 5).

The development of durable and flexible displays, of software and content management systems, and now Internet and wireless networks to connect screens in multiple locations has opened up a range of uses for digital signage. The rise of an Internet Protocol TV (IPTV) format provides the basis for this new communication medium (Schaeffler, 2008).

Technology needs: hardware and software. As illustrated in Figure 11.1, typical digital signage involves a screen, a media player, content, and a content management system. A TV set connected to a VCR playing a videotape in a store was a raw form of digital signage. Add an antenna or connect it to cable, and that TV could be considered part of a network.

Figure 11.1
Digital Signage System

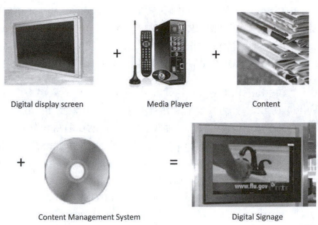

Digital display screen   Media Player   Content

Content Management System   Digital Signage

Source: Janet Kolodzy

Today, the options and variations in digital signage in hardware, software, and networking are as vast as the types of display screens, media players, and digital images available in the consumer market.

Plasma screens, Liquid Crystal Display (LCD) monitors, Light Emitting Diode (LED) screens, and projection screens are part of the digital signage hardware display options. Environmental conditions such as rain, heat, dust, and even kitchen grease for digital signs in cafeterias have led to modifications in digital signage display screens compared to display screens for the consumer electronics market. Innovations in not only screen size but resolution, brightness, and eliminating image retention are being seen in improving digital signage. Alan C. Brawn, in *Digital Signage* magazine, noted that displays are now available that are nearly four time brighter than a typical 40-inch LCD flat panel (Brawn, 2009). A plasma or LCD screen used for digital signage could cost 10 to 20 times as much as a typical consumer grade television or computer screen but it is designed to run for more hours, dissipate more heat and be more secure (Digital Signage FAQ, n.d.). An LED screen for a digital billboard can use up to 50,000 LED tubes but modifications are being made to make them burn brighter and longer and use less electricity.

When it comes to software and servers, digital signage software experts are split into two camps: 1) premise-based systems, which involve in-house servers and software or 2) Software as a Service (SaaS), which is like cloud computing, with off-site servers and applications accessed via the Web. The difference is the equivalent of the debate over whether Excel software on your own computer is better than using the Google Docs spreadsheet application.

Jeff Collard, of Omnivex, which provides digital signage software, noted in *Digital Signage* magazine that a premise-based system provides better solutions to security concerns and greater flexibility in uploading and distributing real-time data, particularly if designed for in-house communication (Collard, 2009). The new Dallas Cowboys stadium uses a premise-based system by Cisco systems that connects its video, digital content, and interactive fan services and involves nearly 3,000 displays (Cisco, 2009).

SaaS systems are often the choice of businesses making an initial venture into digital signage. Rather than installing a server in-house, a software provider will host the server and/or the software for the digital signage system, eliminating the need for extensive in-house technical support. Computing could be done in "the cloud," in a manner similar to Google applications like Google Sites and Google Docs.

Digital signage also offers a mix of in-house and off-site software, servers and support. When Boston's Brigham and Women's Hospital decided to upgrade its internal communication system with digital signage at its campus, it turned to Smithcurl Communications to set up a system using media players and a dedicated server. The hospital uses Carousel media players and a software application for creating, storing, and then displaying bulletins about hospital activities. The dedicated server is a part of the hospital's "server farm." The system's set-up has some elements of a premise-based system since its own servers are used, but is also a SaaS since software updates and servicing is provided by an off-site firm (Connolly, 2010).

The media players used for digital signage and what they actually present to audiences also figure into the technology configuration. When digital signage was first making inroads, media players were often limited in presenting one form of media (video or DVD player, MP3 files, jpgs). Today, most personal computers are set up to present multiple forms of media, and media players for digital signage can do the same. Memory cards and flash drives can be used to store and present content on displays with minimal need for updating. Also, the development of wireless networks has expanded the reach of media players, allowing presentation of the same material on different screens in either the same way or in different configurations

Types of digital signage. Keith Kelsen, author of *Unleashing the Power of Digital Signage* and broadcast and digital signage entrepreneur, referred to digital signage as "the fifth screen" for communication. He points out that the movie screen was the first screen, television the second, the computer monitor the third, and the mobile phone screen the fourth screen used in presenting messages to audiences (Kelsen, 2010). This fifth screen can be found in a variety of locations, ranging from a price display in a retail store to a large sports screen or outdoor billboard. Kelsen has identified three environments suited for this fifth screen: point of sale, point of wait (where people are in a waiting area or mode like a doctor's office or elevator), and point of transit (where people are in transit like at an airport) (Kelsen, 2010).

Digital signage has expanded exponentially at points of sale. At the multiplex movie theater, the refreshment stand uses several screens to display its snack options and run ads for soft drinks. Restaurants and food stands are using digital signage as menu boards, often allowing chain restaurants to update and revise daily specials and offerings at multiple locations. In the mall, digital screens will provide weather and fashion updates, along with ads for certain items that can be found in stores in the mall. In supermarkets, digital screens can be found in certain sections, such as the deli, with recipe demonstrations and information for certain items such as hummus or dinner rolls that may be featured in the recipes. A Digital Signage Association survey found two-thirds of 1,200 respondents reported using digital signage for brand messaging and marketing. Less than a fourth were running ads on their screens (Bickers, 2009).

Digital signs at transit hubs such as airports, train stations, and subway stops as well as displays in buses, subway cars, and taxicabs represent point-of-transit uses of digital signage. Digital signs supplying transit information can be found at transit stops and most airports in the U.S., as well as in major international hubs, which feature digital signage for providing passengers with travel information. Digital signs can provide "wayfinding," basically providing navigational tools to get people to the place they want to be.

Digital signs also present advertising and entertainment within modes of transportation, such as taxis in New York City and the subway in Beijing, China. New York taxi riders can watch ads as well as news updates on screens embedded in the backs of the taxi's front seat. During the 2008 Olympics, Beijing subway riders were offered public transit etiquette reminders, food ads, and Olympic highlights on screens built into the sides of the subway cars.

Digital billboards also represent point-of-transit digital signage. Some digital billboards have been used to disseminate information, such as national AMBER Alerts on missing children, but mostly they are seen as a more modern version of roadside advertising. Local governments that have placed restrictions on traditional paper or vinyl billboards have done the same with digital versions. The U.S. government also has begun setting standards on brightness of the signs and acceptable content (such as restricting moving, flashing, intermittent, and other fast-moving visuals) (Schaeffler, 2008).

A three-year-old digital mural display by WGBH, Boston's public television station and the producer of extensive PBS children's programming, illustrates the social and political dilemmas being faced in the use of digital signage. The 30-foot by 45-foot LED display at the station's studios hangs over a key east-west highway, the Massachusetts Turnpike, and was the first digital signage of its kind in the city (see Figure 11.2). Two governmental agencies, the Turnpike Authority and the Boston Redevelopment Authority, as well as community groups, all played a role in approving the display that WGBH personnel refer to as a "gift to the community" showcasing WGBH and community activities (Bruner, 2010). Although it has all the aspects of a digital billboard because of the size and placement of the display, WGBH's Vice President for Communication and Government Relations Jeanne Hopkins said the very restrictive use standards placed on the display has led to it being viewed "more like public art." She added, "our intention is to say this is WGBH and here are images of what we do and to connect with Boston" (personal communication, March 2010).

Figure 11.2
WGBH Digital Billboard

Only two or three images a day are rotated through like a slide show on the 30-by-45-foot LED digital mural on the WGBH public television station's Allston-Brighton headquarters.

Source: WGBH.

Unlike digital billboard advertising that may want video, animation, and multiple changes or views for the driving audience, the WGBH mural displays at most three still images in sequence over a 30-second time frame. "We wanted the pace to be slow from the beginning," said Cynthia Broner, the station's director of constituent community. The images do not contain wording or phone numbers to keep driving distractions minimal for the estimated half-million vehicles that pass it weekly. "Safety is our No. 1 prerequisite," she said, adding

"We don't want anyone puzzling out what's displayed." Until recently, not even the WGBH logo was on the mural. The images, which change daily, only run from 6:30 a.m. to 7 p.m. At night, a night sky image is displayed. Community events and activities from the Boston Marathon to the return of James Levine to the conducting podium of the Boston Symphony have been featured, as well as key news events, such as the August 2009 death of Senator Ted Kennedy. Promotional art of WGBH's children's programming tends to be very popular, Broner and Hopkins said, especially displayed on weekends (Bruner, 2010). Turnpike Authority studies have shown no correlation between the mural and accidents by distracted drivers (Irons, 2009). Concerns about intrusion have not materialized. Those issues, however, are coming to the fore as more digital billboards start appearing on roadsides.

Recent Developments

The areas of most intense growth and discussion in digital signage involve the development of networks and greater delineation and control of content. The two are pushing digital signage in new directions, creating both growth and tension and raising concerns about distraction and intrusion.

Accu-Weather and the Associated Press have all had a part in digital signage broadcasting. *The New York Times* has decided to go digital beyond the computer screen and the mobile telephone. Starting in March 2010, *New York Times* content is being delivered to some 850 digital screens in business district restaurants and cafes in five major U.S. cities: New York, Los Angeles, Boston, Chicago, and San Francisco. Thanks to a networking set-up by RMG Networks, *New York Times* content (short-form text, photos, and videos) is pulled every 30 seconds for updating, with different *Times*' sections (such as Health, Business, Technology, Movies, Travel, and Best Sellers) being featured in informational loops that run in a seven-minute programming wheel (Boyer, 2010), illustrated in Figure II.3.

Advertising, in full-screen flash or video, is placed to run between the different featured sections, but will relate to content in that section (Boyer, 2010). The digital screens also provide mobile phone connections so viewers interested in reading a full story or downloading it will be linked via www.NYT2day.com. RMG indicates this new collaboration will "connect" six million mobile professionals with NYTimes.com content" (RMG Networks, 2010). "This platform is a great opportunity to expose our brand to new audiences in a medium that is quickly expanding," said Murray Gaylord of The New York Times Media Group (RMG Networks, 2010). The screens feature *Times*' content but RMG provides the network. RMG's Donna Boyer, vice president and general manager of the NYTimes Today network, added that the signage network displays may boost the *Times'* regional presence in San Francisco and Chicago, as well as sales and subscriptions in that region (Boyer, 2010). The interactivity of the collaboration, providing mobile users the ability to download the *Times'* full story content, provides an example of where the digital signage industry expects expansion. Nearly 38% of the 1,200 respondents to the 2009 State of the Digital Signage Industry survey for the Digital Signage Association identified interaction with mobile phones as the technology that will impact digital signage the most in the next five years (Bickers, 2009).

Preliminary examination of download rates and consumer interaction from digital signage versus a computer find a higher percentage (3%) for mobile phones compared to less than 1% for computers (Kelsen, 2010). That rate jumps to 30% if mobile phones are set to a discoverable mode, enabling better haphazard recognition of messages transmitted from digital signage. "Currently we have all these isolated media channels," said Keith Kelsen (2010), digital signage expert and innovator. But he added that digital signage will be able to use different media platforms to reach different audiences any time and any place and with continuity. He said digital signage connections with mobile phones will allow for interactivity and engagement with consumers as they can use phones to respond to contests or even buy a product via the mobile phone (Kelsen, 2010).

Interactivity and connectivity have additional commercial and political implications. NEC Corp. and others have been developing digital signage with sensors that would enable the signage messages to be more tailored toward individuals who come within the range of the signs. The NEC system, called the Next Generation Digital Signage Solution, will use cameras to figure out the age and gender of someone nearby and then provide an ad more suited to someone of that gender and within that age range. Some refer to this system as the realization of the science-fiction advertising system in the 2002 film *Minority Report* with Tom Cruise (McGlaun, 2010). This is referred to as gesture technology and takes the technology used in touch screens for interactivity a step further as a system of cameras and computer can engage individuals differently based on gestures.

Figure 11.3
New Work Times Digital Cafe Delivery

The New York Times has teamed with RMG Networks to provide Times' text, pictures and video on 800 digital screens in cafes in five major US cities.

Source: RMG Networks.

While interactive digital signage is just now being developed and may lead to future questions about intrusion, the growing use of digital signage displays in outdoor advertising has spurred new government examination of its use. Billboard firms have been arguing for acceptance of the signs with community leaders from Toronto, Ontario to St. Petersburg, Florida. In Toronto, Astral Media Outdoor wanted to convert 10 traditional billboards to a digital format operating 24 hours a day (Moloney, 2009). In St. Petersburg, Florida, the outgoing mayor in late 2009 tried to clear a deal with Clear Channel Outdoor to replace 10% of its traditional signs with digital ones (DeCamp, 2010). Lawmakers in Michigan and Minnesota plan hearings for a moratorium on digital billboards to provide time to study their safety and efficacy (Richtel, 2010). Homeowners in Los Angeles have complained after a 2006 city billboards deal has led to some 92 digital billboard conversions of the estimated 6,200 billboards in the city (Reston, 2009).

All of the governmental discussions raise questions of driving distractions, despite three studies, commissioned by outdoor signage industry, finding digital billboards as "safety neutral" (Bachman, 2009). The Federal Highway Administration is expected to weigh in with its report on the distraction safety issue sometime in 2010 (Richtel, 2010).

While digital signage has great potential as a communication medium, thanks to technological advances which provide interactivity, greater attention is now being placed on the content on digital signage and what works and does not work. Numerous experts in the industry have noted broadcast or print-designed ads do not translate well to digital signage. Content design for digital signage must be designed for the environment in which they are placed. A 15-second or 30-second television ad often is too long for digital billboards or retail signs.

Also, digital screens are being divided into sectors to allow for different messages to be projected to different audiences. One area might be devoted to a video display, while another might be just text of weather and time, while another part could be a still-image ad. Kelsen (personal interview, March 9, 2010) said content needs to be relevant to the consumer so they don't get confused with a "hodgepodge" of ads, indicating that there is a "symbiotic relationship" between digital signal technology and content. Whereas technology can be a one-time decision, he noted, content requires perpetual work to ensure it is responsive.

CURRENT STATUS

The growth in digital signage is charted by the number of display screens in that are being bought for use outside the home and the rise of video advertising networks. PQ Media, a Connecticut-based advertising and media research firm, showed digital out-of-home advertising spending increased to $2.47 billion in 2009 in the United States. Worldwide digital signage expenditures in 2009 were estimated to be $6.69 billion (PQ Media, 2009). PQ Media forecasts Asia, particularly China and India, as the hottest area for digital signage growth, estimating $2.18 billion will be spent there in 2009 (PQ Media, 2009). An estimated 1.6 million LED and plasma screens were shipped for digital signage use last year and another 300,000 screens are expected to be added to that number in 2010 (PQ Media, 2010a).

Digital billboards, now undergoing greater government scrutiny, have seen and are expected to see the largest growth. The Outdoor Advertising Association of America estimates about 15% of the nation's 450,000 billboards may become digital in between 2010 and 2013. As of early 2010, about 2,000 are (Richtel, 2010). However, only about 400 digital billboards were counted in 2007. While revenues for outdoor advertising were down in 2008 and 2009, digital billboard spending equaled $502 million in 2009 and more than 10% growth was forecast in 2010 (PQ Media, 2009).

Various industry estimates indicate more than 1 million unique advertising spots played on digital signage displays in the U.S. and Canada during 2009 (Bunn, 2009). The Out-of Home Video Advertising Bureau (OVAB) membership accounts for more than 400,000 dynamic, location-based video/digital displays, and there are nearly 200 ad-based video networks operating in the United States (Bunn, 2010a) (Bunn, 2010b). Bunn estimates more than 20,000 people are employed as content producers for digital signage (Bunn, 2010b).

FACTORS TO WATCH

Networking. More than three-fourths of the 1,200 digital signage firms in the Fall 2009 industry survey are not providing their messages on extensive networks. More than half of those surveyed also are not managing their digital display screens remotely, through a central network. Instead they are manually inserting flash cards or DVDs to update their messages. Digital signage use and networking is expected to grow as digital signage is increasingly a part of new construction of business space. Some 240 firms participating in the survey plan to spend from $48 million to $240 million in the next two years to expand and upgrade digital signage offerings.

🌐 Sustainability 🌐

The ability to use the same displays while updating and changing messages for up to 100,000 hours of display time spurs digital signage proponents to argue it is more environmentally friendly than paper and vinyl displays. Rather than printing and buying a new paper sign every time a changed is needed, digital signage can translate into a lot less paper. Yet, digital signage media players, servers and display screens consume electrical power and contain "e-waste" materials. Some companies are developing ways to reduce the amount of power for and the toxic materials in media players and display screens while others are working on ways to increase digital signage displays' lifespan and brightness.

One media player manufacturer for digital signage, SpinetiX has built a player that consumes only two watts of power annually compared to 50 to 100 watts for an industrial or standard PC (SpinetiX, 2010). To improve the efficiency of displays, manufacturers have been building LCD screens that use edge or side lighting over backlighting and LEDs instead of fluorescent bulb backlighting.

The development of Organic Light Emitting Diode (OLED) screens is being touted by screen makers as a "greener" alternative to LCD and plasma screens. OLEDs are thin flexible plastic sheets that use less power because OLEDs do not require backlighting to brighten the image. Since the diodes are made from hydrogen and carbon, they are "organic." But those components also make OLEDs susceptible to deterioration. OLEDs have a lifespan 5 to 10 times shorter that some LCD displays. They have yet to be built in large formats, with sizes measured less than 20 inches, so they are now being tried out for use in mobile phones. Televisions with OLEDs are beginning to hit the consumer market (Jones, 2009). However, one 30-inch OLED television costs $10,000 (Katzmaier, 2010).

Another new technology, Laser Phosphor Display by Prysm, Inc. is designed for large-format displays and promises a small carbon footprint. A Prysm brochure states its displays can consumer fewer watts than a standard home light bulb, or about 100 watts per square meter of display (Prysm, Inc, 2010).

Finally, a 2009 study by MediaZest, a market media research firm, and co-sponsored by Cisco and Panasonic looked at the carbon footprint of digital and conventional signage. It found the carbon consumption of a digital display is 7.5% lower than a traditional poster display over a period of three years (MediaZest Plc, 2009). The study compared all aspects of use from installation to shutdown, examining use of electricity, paper and ink.

Expansion of digital signage outside of retail. Health care, education, and internal business communication provide fertile ground for growing use of digital signage.

Boston's Brigham and Women's Hospital uses more than two dozen monitors for its digital signage display in more than a half-dozen buildings comprising its main campus, one of which is illustrated in Figure 11.4. BWH's David Connolly said the initial impetus for use of digital signage was to reduce clutter, as well as present a more cutting-edge presentation of information to hospital employees. Five years ago, special events and lectures were announced via poster board and key lobby areas could be littered with more than a half-dozen posters on easels, Connolly said. Today, on any given day, the digital signage network cycles through some 35 still-frame messages and video covering topics ranging from hand washing to weekly rounds to National Nutrition Month activities. About 50 hospital employees have been trained on the content management system to submit postings. The communications department publishes the submissions, updating the rotation daily. The submissions are saved as jpg files and are uploaded on the hospital's Intranet system, should people need more time to view the messages.

Figure II.4
Traditional & Digital Signs at Boston's Brigham & Women's Hospital

Main lobbies and waiting areas at Boston's Brigham and Women's Hospital are equipped with digital signage of hospital activities, replacing many poster board signs.

Source: Janet Kolodzy

In the meantime, more digital signage networks are being used at the hospital's clinics and sites in other parts of metropolitan Boston. Video presentations about key health issues, such as flu shots, are extending the use to more than a digital bulletin board. St. Joseph Hospital in Orange County, California has been using digital signage to coordinate its operating facility involving information on treatment rooms, pre-operative activities, and patient readiness (Collard, 2010). BWH's Connolly and others indicate digital signage provides a useful tool in hospital accreditation work.

Colleges and universities have been installing digital signage to improve emergency messaging. However, some schools also are seeing digital signage displays are useful interactive classroom devices. Education and conference rooms represented the top two applications of touch-screen digital signage purchases in 2009 (PQ Media, 2010b). Sanju Khatri, a principal analyst on digital signage with the media research firm PQ Media noted, "These whiteboards make it easy for teachers to enhance presentation content by integrating a wide range of material into a lesson, such as an image from the Internet, a graph from a spreadsheet, or text from a Microsoft Word file, in addition to student and teacher annotations on these objects." (PQ Media, 2010b).

Government study, regulation, and standardization. Federal transportation studies on the effect of digital signage on driver attention are expected to be presented in 2010 and will have an impact on the debate in several states and cities about regulating digital billboards, especially as the outdoor advertising industry moves for more conversion from traditional billboards. The industry also is trying to develop greater standardization to measure the effects of digital signage on consumers.

Digital signage has the potential to become one of the most ubiquitous communication technologies. If so, the growth of this medium will create new markets for hardware and networking services, but the most important new opportunities may be for those who will create the messages that appear on digital signage. These messages will draw from existing media, but the ultimate form and content of ads may be as different from today's media as Internet Web sites are different from broadcast and print.

Bibliography

Bachman, K. (2009, November 20). Digital Billboards Safe, Another Study Says. Adweek.com.

Bickers, J. (2009). The State of the Digital Signage Industry Survey. Retrieved February 11, 2010, from http://www.digitalsignagetoday.com/white_paper.php?id=79

Boyer, D. (2010, March 11). VP and General Manager, NYTimes.com Today Network for RMG Networks. (S. a. Hughes, Interviewer)

Brawn, A. C. (2009, November). The World is Flat. Digital Signage, 5 (5), p. 17.

Bruner, C. a. (2010, March 5, 12). WGBH director of constituent communication. (J. Kolodzy, Interviewer)

Bunn, L. (2009, September). 1,000,000+ ads now playing on North America's Digital-Out-of-Home networks. Retrieved March 14, 2010 frin http://lylebunn.com/PapersandArticles.aspx

Bunn, L. (2010a, January). 2010—The Year of Choice. Retrieved March 13, 2010, from http://lylebunn.com/documents/2010 Choices for DS sourcing.pdf

Bunn, L. (2010b, March). Content is gaining "stride" and growing fast. Retrieved March 14, 2010, from lylebunn.com.

Cisco (2009, June 19). Retrieved March 12, 2010, from http://newsroom.cisco.com/dlls/2009/prod_061709.html

Collard, J. (2010, January 29). Aligning healthcare organizations and staff through digital signage. Retrieved March 12, 2010, from Digital Signage Today: http://digitalsignagetoday.com/article.php?id=23679

Collard, J. (2009, July/August). On-Premise, For Robust Data-Mining Solutions. Digital Signage, 5 (4), pp. 18-21.

Connolly, D. (2010, March 5). BWH Internal Communications Mgr. (J. Kolodzy, Interviewer)

DeCamp, D. (2010, February 26). Bay Buzz, Political News of Tampa Bay. St. Petersburg Times, tampabay.com edition.

Digital Signage Association. (2010, February 11). Retrieved February 11, 2010, from digitalsignageassociation.org: http://www.digitalsignageassociation.org/faws

Digital Signage Frequently Asked Questions. (n.d.). Retrieved February 11, 2010, from digitalsignageassociation.org: http://www.digitalsignageassociation.org/FAQs

Irons, M. (2009, May 19). WGBH mural aglow once more; Problems had plagued the giant LED. Boston Globe, p. B4.

Jones, P. (2009, July 08). Global OLEDs market starts to pick up. Retrieved March 18, 2010, from http://www.icis.com: http://www.icis.com/Articles/2009/07/13/9230899/global-oleds-market-starts-to-pick-up.html

Katzmaier, D. (2010, January 13). CES post-show wrap-up: HDTV. Retrieved March 17, 2010, from cnet.com: http://ces.cnet.com/8301-19167_1-10140707-100.html?tag=mncol

Keene, D. (Ed.). (2009,). Digital Signage Resource Directory Listinfs. Digital Signage Magazine (8th annual), p. 4.

Kelsen, K. (2010). Unleashing the Power of Digital Signage. Burlington, MA: Focal Press.

Little, D. (2010, Feb 11). DSA The Perspective. Retrieved February 11, 2010, from digitalsignageassociation.org/the-perspective: http://www.digitalsignageassociation.org/the-perspective

Lundstrom, L.-I. (2008). Digital Signage Broadcasting; Broadcasting, Content Management and Distribution Techniques. Burlington, MA : Focal Press.

McGlaun (2010, March 11). NC Develops "Minority Report" Advertising System. Retrieved March 12, 2010 from http://www.dailytech.com/NEC+Develops+Minority+Report+Advertising+System/article17876.htm

MediaZest Plc. (2009, April 14). Digital Signage: A Sustainable Advantage. Retrieved March 15, 2010, from http://www.mediazest.com/index-home.html: http://www.mediazest.com/cms/uploads/2bf2c3287731984c41c9abfd0ca1427/MediaZestGreenStudy.pdf

Moloney, P. (2009, April 28). Signs are a-chang' maybe: Billboard firm lobbies councillors to support switch to digital format . Toronto Star, p. GT03.

Prysm, Inc. (2010,). Enable Immersive Experiences. Retrieved March 17, 2010, from prysm.com: http://www.prysm.com/Prysm_CompanyBrochure_011210_hr_opt.pdf

PQ Media. (2010a, March 2). Surging digital signage market attracts interest of IT firms. Retrieved March 14, 2010, from http://www.isuppli.com/News/Pages/Surging-Digital-Signage-Display-Market-Attracts-Interest-of-IT-Firms.aspx

PQ Media. (2010b, January 12). Touch Screens Score Touchdown in Signage and Professional Displays. Retrieved March 14, 2010, from pqmedia.com: http://www.isuppli.com/News/Pages/Touch-Screens-Score-Touchdown-in-Signage-and-Professional-Displays.aspx

PQ Media. (2009, November 10). Third Annual PQ Media Digital OHH FOrecast. Retrieved March 12, 2010, from pqmedia.com: http://www.pqmedia.com/about-press-20091110-dooh2009.html

Reston, M. (2009, December 27). Homeowners fight the glare of digital billboards. Los Angeles Times, p. A41.

Richtel, M. (2010, March 2). Roadside Marquee. The New York Times, p. B1.

RMG Networks, The New York Times launch DOOH network. (2010, March 1). Retrieved March 3, 2010, from digitalsignagetoday.com: http://digitalsignagetoday.com/article.php?id=23891

Schaeffler, J. (2008). Digital Signage: Software, Networks, Advertising, and Displays: A Primer for Understanding the Business. Focal Press.

SpinetiX. (2010). Energy cost savings in Europe with the SpinetiX HMP100 device. Retrieved March 17, 2010, from spinetix.com: http://www.spinetix.com/files/SpinetiX_Energy_Cost_Savings.pdf

Yackey, B. (2009, July 28). A beginner's guide to digital signage. Retrieved Feb 11, 2010, from digitalsignagetoday.com.

12

Cinema Technologies

Jillian Neal, Stephanie Warren, & Natasha Whitling[*]

From the first time someone put their eye up to a Kinetoscope or slipped a coin in a nickelodeon and saw an image flicker, we have been fascinated with moving pictures. A billion dollar international industry was spawned from those humble machines, and viewing films has become a cherished activity that provides us with social interaction, entertainment, and another way to learn. Who could have imagined that from black and white silent pictures could be born massive movie spectacles like *Titanic*?

Background

The invention of the technology that created the film industry cannot be traced back to one individual or innovation, but rather a series of technological inventions that combined to bring about the projection of moving pictures. In the 1870s, advances in still photography and the invention of celluloid set into place the "preconditions that were necessary for the projection of moving pictures" (Chapman, 2003, p. 52). Other inventions including the zoopraxiscope, which was a lantern that produced the illusion of movement with photos printed on rotating glass; plastic, electricity and incandescent light bulbs were all instrumental in making it possible to project moving pictures (Kindersley, 2006).

The movie industry is experiencing many changes with the digital revolution, and new technologies that advance every aspect of movie making, including production, distribution, and exhibition. Production looks at the steps involved in making the film and is divided into pre-production, production, and post-production. In pre-production, the proposal, script, storyboard, budget and production schedule prepare the project for its production stage. During production, setup and rehearsals begin in preparation for filming. Character and camera blocking determine the movement of the actors and the placement of the cameras in preparation for filming. Post-production starts once recordings of visual images and sound has been captured. "The post-production stage ties together the audio and visual elements of production and smoothes out all the rough edges" (Kindem & Musburger, 2005, pg. 3).

After production, distribution takes the finished movie and delivers it to the theaters and other viewing outlets. The distribution step also encompasses the marketing and advertising that occurs for a film. The final step is exhibition which refers to the showing of films in theaters, including their projection method and the environment of the theater. For example, concessions are a huge portion of a theaters' income and are a part of

---

[*] Graduate Students, School of Journalism & Mass Communications, University of South Carolina (Columbia, South Carolina).

the exhibition category. The exhibition process does not stop at the theaters though, but is continued through other methods described later in this chapter.

Unlike many industries that are regulated by the government, the movie industry took it upon itself to regulate its' trade. The Motion Picture Association of America was established in 1922, and one of its first methods of self-regulation was requiring members to submit their movies for approval before they could be distributed. The 1960s saw a threat of government censorship as content began pushing boundaries. In 1968, a voluntary movie rating system was put into place during a time when the country was experiencing dramatic social change. Unlike its previous system, "the movie industry would no longer 'approve or disapprove' the content of films. Instead, an independent ratings body would give advance cautionary warnings to parents to help them make informed decisions about…movie-going" (The Movie Rating System, n.d.).

The first movies depicted everyday life because the technology was such that people would go to see a movie just for the experience. Soon, though, audiences began expecting more regarding the subject, stories, and techniques employed to create films.

Realizing that motion pictures could appeal to a paying audience, Thomas Edison created the Kinetoscope in 1894, a coin-operated viewing device that people could peep inside to see short films. Two French inventors, Louis and Auguste Lumiere, followed up Edison's invention with the Cinematographe, which allowed projection onto a screen. This development made it possible for multiple people to see a movie at the same time. Thought by many people to be the 'birthday of cinema,' December 28, 1895 marked the Lumiere brothers' first projection of a film to a paying audience. Edison followed in 1896 with the Vitascope, which also projected film images onto screens (Chapman, 2003).

Production

The Motion Picture Patents Company, consisting of six individual equipment manufacturers, was formed in 1908. The Eastman Kodak Company contracted with the company to only sell raw film to their licensees. Producers could still create any films they choose to and distribute them through any channel they liked. Distribution licenses were granted to 116 exchanges, and they could distribute the films only to licensed exhibitors who paid a projection license of two dollars per week. One difficult situation with the system was that it was connected to one reel films, which only ran 15 minutes, so it took eight reels to show a two-hour film. Unlicensed producers and exchanges continued to be a problem, so in 1910 the Patents Company created the General Film Company to distribute their films. This development proved to be highly profitable and "was…the first stage in the organized film industry where production, distribution and exhibition were all integrated, and in the hands of a few large companies" (Jowett, 1976, p. 34).

Early attempts to combine sound with films had failed, however in the 1910s AT&T's research branch, Bell Labs, "produced prototypes of loudspeakers and sound amplifiers" (Campbell, Martin and Fabos, 2011, p. 222). It was in conjunction with these developments that Warner Brothers produced the first full-length feature film, *The Jazz Singer*, to include sound.

Early color processes included methods like hand tinting and the Kinemacolor process. The idea was that when projected at about 30 pictures per second, a viewer's eye blends the colors together so that they appear natural. "In order to produce three-color motion pictures, three separate color records had to be recorded and projected simultaneously in precise registration or consecutively with sufficient speed to fuse the three images into one multiple color scene through persistence of vision" (Kindem, 1981, p. 6). These processes were time consuming and projection errors, particularly with Kinemacolor, were common. It was the development of the CinemaScope process for photography in 1939 that allowed color films to become more widely available. The

Technicolor process came about in 1922, but was restricted by its patent owners until the 1950s. By the 1960s, the majority of films were in color.

Even with all the technological advances audiences were seeing in films, with the invention of television, movie theaters had to create viewing experiences that could not be achieved at home. Milton Gunzberg obtained the rights to a three-dimensional process in the 1940s and released *Bwana Devil*, a 'dreadful' film that drew in audiences and surprisingly broke box office records (Jowett, 1976). Although 3-D along with "smellies" did not stick around, 3-D exhibition has seen a comeback in recent times (Jowett, 1976). Following 3-D came Cinerama, a process that required filming with a three-lens camera and projecting in three screens with synchronized projectors. This viewing was meant to mimic the curve of the retina and fill a viewer's entire peripheral vision. "Cinerama arrived at a moment when movies needed to stir interest" (Phipps, 2008. But Cinerama fared no better than early 3-D.

Distribution

The overwhelming popularity and profit movie houses were seeing in the early 1900s allowed for the growth of a more efficient distribution process. For a "trivial investment in a projection machine and a few chairs anyone could become a showman and prosper" (Jowett, 1976, p. 30). Expensive conversion of buildings was not necessary; rather "success lay in cheap conversion and a constant supply of new films which held the audience's attention" (Jowett, 1976, p. 30). The permanent establishments created reliable clients for distribution companies, which were in continual need for a change in product, for distribution companies.

Since theaters could only show one picture at a time and large cities had dozens of theaters, it became important for theaters to be the first to show the most entertaining films. These films would "command ten to twenty times the rental it could at a later showing" (Jowett, 1976, p. 33). The demand for rental films led to the creation of somewhere between 125 and 150 film exchanges in the US by 1907 (Jowett, 1976).

Exhibition

To correspond with the social activities of the times, films were shown as part of festivals, vaudeville theatre, and other traveling acts or in spaces like church halls, rented stores, or tents. This worked well in the beginning with the shorter features, but as the length and complexity of films increased in the early 1900s, there became a need for permanent cinemas. Cinemas also gave the industry a better hold on consumers because of their accessibility and inexpensive admission, along with the fact that they were not seasonal, made them more popular than other forms of entertainment (Chapman, 2003).

In an effort to control from whom movie houses got their films, projection manufacturers often would have a clause in the contracts that their exhibitors signed allowing them only to use films from that company. Distributors were unable to strictly monitor this condition, and companies did not have enough films to meet the demands of a movie house. Also, with the similarities in equipment from cameras to projectors to film, the end product was interchangeable across many systems. This meant that exhibitors would acquire films from other distributors, despite these clauses.

The 1920s brought about the introduction of sound to the movies. Edison and Lee DeForest had both spent many years working on their devices, Edison's Kinetophone and DeForet's Phonofilm process, but it was the Vitaphone Company that would produce the first sound shorts in 1926. The introduction of sound also created changes in the production process where some silent film actors could not transition into the "talkies" because of the voice requirements. Sound added the need for both recording during the film, as well as editing sounds in post-production. The talking pictures would revolutionize the industry, and by the end of the 1920s, more than 40% of theaters were wired for sound (Kindersley, 2006). Initially sound was viewed as a novelty and not expected to be a permanent addition to movies, while others thought films with sound would be for the mass audience and silent films would continue for people "able to appreciate its values" (Jowett, 2003, p. 196).

Projection systems evolved as the century progressed. Until the 1970s, movie theaters required a trained "projectionist" who "knew about luminance, film formats and machine maintenance" (Haines, 2003, p. 94). There was a push for automation, which included attaching cue tape to the edge of the film at a specific location. When the tape passed over the electrical contact, it acted as a switch turning off the first projector and sound while starting the second projector. The reasoning behind automation was said to get rid of the human error, but "it appeare[d] the real agenda was to save money in exhibition" (Haines, 2003, p. 96).

Another concept that changed the way we view movies was the move from one-screen theaters to cineplexes. The first multi-theater house was built in the 1930s with two theaters, and by the late 1960s, there were venues that had four to six theaters. What these theaters lacked was the atmosphere that the early theaters had. While some put effort into the appearance of the lobby and concessions area, in most cases the "actual theater was merely functional" (Haines, 2003, p. 91). Continuing to grow the number of theaters in one location, 1984 marked the opening of the first 18-plex theater in Toronto (Haines, 2003). More recently, the addition of stadium seats have offered attendees a better experience with unobstructed views of the screen ("EPS Geofoam", n.d.). Although the number of screens in a location continues to increase, many theaters today are working on the atmosphere they offer attendees. From bars and restaurants to luxury theaters with a reserved $29 movie ticket, many theater owners are once again working to make the moviegoing experience something you can't get at home (Gelt and Verrier, 2009).

In 1999 *Star Wars: The Phantom Menace* was the first release to have digital projection in a four theater experiment. To avert any problems that might occur, a 35 mm version of the film was set up to run simultaneously with the digital projection, and in the event the system failed, it would change to film projection. To make it easier to integrate special effects into some scenes from the movie, portions of the film were shot on digital video (Campbell, Martin, and Fabos, 2011). Although it pushed boundaries technologically, viewers were not always impressed by what they saw. The "grain structure in color pixels" and its effect on a viewer's sense of depth was a change (Haines, 2003, p. 187). "Despite its sharpness and color…digital imagery often has a flat, artificial appearance," leaving some audience members disappointed (Haines, 2003, p. 187).

When box office revenues faltered in 2005, a push began to convert to digital projection and distribution. Not only would it give moviegoers a "newer and better experiences," but it would make "movie distribution simpler, faster and cheaper" (Tryon, 2009, p. 60)

RECENT DEVELOPMENTS

Production

Celluloid film is quickly becoming an endangered medium for making movies as more and more filmmakers are using digital cameras that are capable of creating high quality images without the time, expense and chemicals required to shoot and process on film (Straubhaar & LaRose, 2008). Large, heavy 16-mm and 35-mm film cameras are being put on the shelf in favor of the much smaller and lighter digital cameras. Digital production also presents a significant savings for low-budget and independent filmmakers. Production costs using digital cameras and computerized editors are a fraction of the costs of film production, sometimes as little as a few thousand dollars (Campbell, Martin, & Fabos, 2011). The 2009 horror film *Paranormal Activity* was shot for around $15,000 and raked in close to $200 million worldwide (Campbell et al, 2010).

Digital technology is also changing how things are done in postproduction. Editing film used to be a very labor-intensive process that involved cutting and splicing long lengths of celluloid film in order to get the "final cut" (Straubhaar & LaRose, 2008). Now editors can do what is called nonlinear editing and simply work from the digital raw footage which has been "transferred to computer media where they can be accessed at random and spliced with the click of a mouse" (Straubhaar & LaRose, 2008, p. 204).

Figure 12.1
Cinema History Highlights

	Film	People	Technologies	Other
1880s	*Monkeyshines No. 1*	Thomas Edison	1884 – Thomas Edison opens the first kinetoscope parlors	
1890s	1894 – *Fred Ott's Sneeze*	Auguste and Louis Lumière	Cinématograph	
1900s	1902 – *Le Voyage Dans La Lune*	Edwin S. Porter	First animated film short	The first permanent movie house built in L.A.
1910s	1915 – *The Birth of a Nation*	Charlie Chaplin	Kinemacolor	Max Factor created the first makeup formulated especially for film
1920s	1922 – *Nosferatu*	Cecil B. DeMille	First feature-length "talkie" *The Jazz Singer*	The *Academy Awards* are handed out for the first time.
1930s	1939 – *Gone with the Wind* and *The Wizard of Oz* (color)	Frank Capra	Bosko, The Talk-Ink Kid – The first synchronized talking animated short/cartoon	Double features emerged
1940s	1942 – *Casablanca*	Walt Disney	Introduction of television leads to massive drop in attendance	The Hollywood Ten are jailed for contempt against Congress
1950s	1955 – *Rebel Without a Cause*	Alfred Hitchcock	CinemaScope; 3-D	
1960s	1965 – *The Sound of Music*	Stanley Kubrick	Smell-O-Vision	1967 – The MPAA introduces a rating system
1970s	1977 – *Star Wars*	George Lucas	IMAX	The first movies are released on home video
1980s	1981 – *Raiders of the Lost Ark*	Steven Spielberg	1983 – THX	The first Blockbuster Video store opened
1990s	1997 – *Titanic*	James Cameron	*Star Wars Episode I—The Phantom Menace*, first film shot and projected digitally	The MPAA introduces the NC-17 rating
2000s	2009 – *Avatar*	Judd Apatow	Digital conversion begins; first digital 3-D movie *Chicken Little*	Advertising in pre-show becomes popular

Source: Neal, Warren & Whitling. *Images*: © 2010, Jupiterimages Corporation

DIGITAL 3-D

The first digital 3-D film released was Disney's *Chicken Little* which was shown on Disney Digital 3-D (PR Newswire, 2005). About 100 theaters in the 25 top markets were outfitted by Dolby Laboratories with Dolby(R) Digital Cinema systems in order to screen the film.

The idea of actually shooting a film in digital 3-D did not become a reality until the creation of the Fusion Camera, a collaborative invention by director James Cameron and Vince Pace (Hollywood Reporter, 2005).The camera fuses two Sony HDC-F950 HD cameras "2½ inches apart to mimic the stereoscopic separation of human eyes" (Thompson, 2010). The camera was used to film 2008's *Journey to the Center of the Earth* and 2010's *Tron Legacy*.

Cameron used a modified version of the Fusion Camera to shoot 2009's blockbuster *Avatar*. The altered Fusion allows the "director to view actors within a computer-generated virtual environment, even as they are working on a 'performance-capture' set that may have little apparent relationship to what appears on the screen" (Cieply, 2010). Another breakthrough technology born from *Avatar* is the swing camera. For a largely animated world such as the one portrayed in the film, the actors must perform through a process called motion capture which records 360 degrees of a performance but with the added disadvantage that the actors do not know where the camera will be (Thompson, 2010). Likewise, in the past, the director had to choose the shots desired once the filming was completed. Cameron tasked virtual-production supervisor Glenn Derry with creating the swing camera which "has no lens at all, only an LCD screen and markers that record its position and orientation within the volume relative to the actors" (Thompson, 2010). An effects switcher feeds back low-resolution CG images of the virtual world allowing the director to move around shooting the actors photographically or even capturing other camera angles on the empty stage as the footage plays back (Thompson, 2010).

Of course filming movies in 3-D is a fairly novel production method. Many films, such as Tim Burton's 2010 *Alice in Wonderland* are shot in 2-D and later converted. IMAX is the leader in 2-D to 3-D conversion but is facing some competition from smaller companies like Prime Focus Ltd. (Georgiades, 2010). The cost of 3-D conversion has decreased significantly from around $25-30 million to around $5 million (Georgiades, 2010).

CGI (COMPUTER-GENERATED IMAGERY)

It's very difficult to find a blockbuster within the last decade that did not employ computer-generated imagery, or CGI. Since the first use of CGI in 1976's *Futureworld*, the technology has continued to progress through decades from the spectacular explosion of the Death Star in *Star Wars* to the digitally-created hordes of Orcs in the *Lord of the Rings* trilogy (Vivian, 2011). CGI use has grown exponentially and hand-in-hand with the chunk of a film's budget it occupies. Creating the CGI wonders to which film-goers have become accustomed is both labor and cost intensive. A frame of CGI can take anywhere from 2 to 20 hours to render (Vivian, 2011).

Cameron's *Avatar* ushered in a new era of computer generated imagery which he used to create his other-worldly creatures—the Na'vi. One of the greatest obstacles to CGI is effectively capturing facial expressions. In order to overcome this final hurdle, Cameron brought to life a technology he dreamed up in 1995, a tiny camera on the front of a helmet that was able to "track every facial movement, from darting eyes and twitching noses to furrowing eyebrows and the tricky interaction of jaw, lips, teeth and tongue" (Thompson, 2010). The camera generates a digital framework of the actors face then transfers it to the face of their virtual character.

Distribution

The conversion to digital exhibition which will be discussed later in this chapter has had a profound effect on how movies are distributed. Traditionally 35-mm film canisters were produced, shipped around the world and back, and later stored—a high-cost process. With digital distribution there is no need to make bulky 35-mm reels. Instead movies can be distributed on optical disks, hard drives or via satellite. The potential savings to studios has been estimated to be around $568 million per year in just transportation and handling (Vivian, 2011).

However, there are some concerns about digital distribution and film preservation. Even though celluloid reels take up a lot of space, if properly stored they can last for hundreds of years. Digital presents its own loss risks. "…digital formats can be lost as storage formats fail and devices become obsolete" (Campbell, Martin, & Fabos, 2011). Studios are currently still producing films in both formats but only until the digital conversion is complete.

ONLINE DISTRIBUTION

With the advent of digital distribution of films via the Internet, it wasn't long before filmmakers began to look for ways to distribute their work via the Web, thereby bypassing traditional lines of distribution. In the past studios have struck deals with distribution companies to be in charge of releasing their films and taking a cut of the profits. Now several companies offer direct distribution via the Internet such as iTunes and Cinema-Now. CinemaNow chooses films via a submission process, placing them on the Web site for download, purchase, or rent (Film Specific, 2009). Amazon.com's CustomFlix works like on-demand book publishing by creating a DVD for each individual order.

Exhibition

THE DIGITAL CONVERSION

In the never-ending quest to lure consumers back into theater seats, all entities in the cinema food chain continue to look toward a complete digital conversion as a way to streamline production, distribution, and exhibition by eliminating actual film.

The digital conversion allows studios and distributors to forgo the cost of making and transporting 35mm film in favor of hard drives, discs, and streaming of live events. In 2007, Digital Cinema Implementation Partners was formed by exhibition companies AMC Entertainment Inc., Cinemark USA, Inc., and Regal Entertainment Group (Digital Cinema Implementation Partners). Once the group was formed it became imperative to bring the studios on board to help provide incentives for exhibitors to take on the massive cost of conversion from film projection to digital projection systems.

Early adopters of the digital systems numbered about 5,000 between 2005 and 2006 (Mead, 2008). But the largest exhibitors which later formed the DCIP were in the second wave. There are three main ways for the digital conversion to be financed: distributors, exhibitors, or the government. The first model has been most prevalent in the U.S. with distributors paying a virtual print fee which is paid to a third party company that has allowed exhibitors to finance the digital conversion to be paid back over the course of 10-15 years (Screen Digest, 2006). Digital conversion is estimated to cost about $70,000 per screen, which doesn't include the long term maintenance and replacement costs that aren't associated with traditional film projectors. In April 2009, Sony Pictures joined Walt Disney, Viacom. Paramount Pictures, News Corp's Twentieth Century Fox, General Electric's Universal Pictures, and Lions Gate Entertainment to partner with the DCIP on a plan to convert 20,000 U.S. and Canadian cinema screens. The price tag for the conversion is estimated to be more than $1 billion.

Digital conversion was further impacted by the financial crisis and credit crunch of October 2008 and was revived in late 2009 early 2010 with the release of the high-grossing 3-D film *Avatar*. (Screen Digest, 2010). Analysts agree that it could take close to a decade to complete a full digital conversion. As of March 2010, there were 16,405 digital screens worldwide, about 14.8% of the modern cinemas, and 9,000 of those were equipped for 3-D (Screen Digest, 2010).

3-D EXHIBITION

Gone are the days when 3-D movie goers were expected to don cheap paper glasses with blue and red lenses. RealD has been at the forefront of revolutionizing how 3-D movies are exhibited. In the past, 3-D movies were displayed using a different projector for each eye. RealD developed a new technology that uses "a liquid crystal adaptor that attaches to a single digital projector, synchronizing left and right eye images 144 times per second" (Verrier, 2009). RealD also developed lightweight plastic glasses with gray lenses that look more like sunglasses. As of 2009, RealD's products account for approximately 90% of the U.S. 3-D exhibition market (Verrier, 2009). RealD premiered its new 3-D technology on 88 digital 3-D screens with Disney's 2005 animated film *Chicken Little*. By 2007, RealD's technology was used on over 900 screens domestically for Paramount's *Beowulf* (Film Journal International, 2008).

According to some sources, 3-D digital movies bring in from two times to four times the box office revenue of traditional 2-D movies, (Mead, 2008) and studios have been investing heavily in the format in hopes of increasing revenue. The pressure to make blockbuster movies is high for studios. The top movies released in 2009, *Transformers: Revenge of the Fallen*, *Avatar*, and *Harry Potter and the Half-Blood Prince* each cost between $210-$250 million to make and an additional $100 million in marketing expenses (Young, J. Gong, & and Van der Stede, 2010).

CINEMA ADVERTISING & ALTERNATIVE PROGRAMMING

The digital conversion also allows for increased opportunities for advertising revenue in the cinema. The digital switch "…will not only boost niche films, thanks to lower distribution costs, in turn broadening advertising opportunities, but also improve targeting" (Media: Cinemas Digital Dream, 2009, p.30). Companies such as ScreenVision and Cinemedia offer digital pre-shows that incorporate national and local advertising (What's new at the pre-show, 2009).

According to the U.S. Cinema Advertising Council, total screen advertising revenues were $571.4 million in 2008, an increase of 5.8% over 2007. 76.5% of all revenues came from national or regional sales, and 23.5% were generated from local sales (Screen Digest, 2009).

These companies can also marry advertising with alternative programming such as sporting events. The British company Digital Cinema Media took advantage of this and built an onscreen campaign for Nike. Nike sponsored the screening of games from the 2006 World Cup in addition to two short films about two popular England players. (Hancock, 2009)

AUDIO

There's no mistaking the gut-rumbling crescendo associated with THX. It's nearly as recognizable as its patron's famous *Star Wars* theme. Developed by George Lucas' Lucasfilms, THX is not a cinema sound format, rather a standardization system that strives to "reproduce the acoustics and ambience of the movie studio, allowing audiences to enjoy a movie's sound effects, score, dialogue and visual presentation with the clarity and detail of the final mastering session" (THX, 2010). THX debuted in 1983 with Lucas' *Star Wars Episode VI: Return of the Jedi* and spread across the industry. Only movie theaters that meet clear specifications can be certified THX. As of early 2010, there were close to 2,000 THX certified theaters worldwide (THX, 2010).

While THX sets the standards, Dolby Digital 5.1—Surround Sound is one of the leading audio delivery technologies in the cinema industry. Dolby 5.1 uses "five discrete full-range channels—left, center, right, left surround, and right surround—plus a sixth channel for low-frequency" (Dolby, 2010). Dolby also offers Dolby Digital Surround EX, a technology developed in partnership with Lucasfilm's THX that places a speaker behind the audience to allow for a "fuller, more realistic sound for increased dramatic effect in the theatre" (Dolby, 2010).

One of the latest movements in cinema sound is 3-D sound. The technology is pioneered by Iosono, which was founded by founded by Karlheinz Brandenburg, a contributor to MP3 compression sound technology. Iosono's 3-D employs over 600 speakers and eliminates theater "hot spots" or places in the theater where the sound is better (Taub, 2009). It creates "the illusion that sound is filling the room, or even occurring outside the theater".

Only a handful of theaters, including Hollywood's Mann Theaters, are equipped with 3-D sound. The cost is prohibitive as an installation can cost about $100,000 and the sound mixes can add about $200,000 to a film's budget (Taub, 2009).

CURRENT STATUS

As of 2008, the average cost to a major studio to make and promote a feature length film was $109 million: $72 million in production, and an additional $37 million in promotion. From this hefty initial investment, there are six major windows of exhibition where studios hope to turn a profit: domestic box office (theaters), home video, pay-per-view (PPV)/video on demand (VOD), premium pay channels, network and cable TV, and syndication (Young, Gong, & Van der Stede, 2010).

In 2009, domestic theatrical box office receipts reached $10.6 billion – an all-time high. Home video is the next window of exhibition, when the film is released onto DVD and Blu-ray discs and in digital form for sale or rental. Standard & Poor's reported that in 2008, DVD sales and rentals generated $23.7 billion: $16.2 billion in sales and $7.5 billion in rentals. However, due to a combination of the high price of DVDs, the recession, and the growing popularity of DVD rental sites, DVD sales are declining (Young, Gong, and Van der Stede, 2010).

PPV/VOD, the next window of exhibition, enables cable or satellite TV subscribers to "order movies directly through a joint venture that licenses the films from all the major studios" (Young, Gong, & Van der Stede, 2010, p. 38). While initially this window opened approximately seven months after the initial theatrical release in order to prevent conflicts with video release, since the 1990s studios have released DVDs sooner. Today, some movies are released for PPV/VOD on the same day as home video but many cable and satellite providers still complain that movies are received too late to compete with DVDs. Thus, this stream of revenue has not proven to be as lucrative as hoped. Following PPV/VOD, movies are released to premium pay TV channels. The licensing fee for a movie is calculated based on domestic box office figures. Fees range anywhere from $2 to $25 million per film (the average is $7 million) (Young, Gong, & Van der Stede, 2010).

Network and cable TV follows with networks and cable stations vying to obtain the rights to broadcast a film. Typically, the rights run anywhere from $3 to $15 million, again, depending on box office figures as well as the number of times the movie will be run (Young, Gong, & Van der Stede, 2010). Finally, movies are passed on to syndicated TV, where local stations bid for the rights to air the movie. Local stations can pay anywhere from a few hundred dollars up to $5 million in large markets for the right to broadcast a successful movie (Young, Gong, & Van der Stede, 2010).

In addition to the domestic process described above, this same process may be repeated at an international level. Since the 1960s, revenue generated by international box office has accounted for a little less than half of the total income for major studios. In 2008, international box office numbers reached $18 billion for American movies, about half of which is kept by the exhibitors. The U.K., Japan, Germany, France, Spain, Australia, and New Zealand are the largest consumers of American movies. International TV networks also have an interest in buying the rights to American movies. Studios will sell movies to foreign networks in packages of six to ten movies with the licensing fee spread across the films at the studio's judgment. In 2003, the TV licensing for American movies overseas accounted for approximately $1.76 billion (split equally between broadcast stations and networks and pay TV.) Standard & Poor's predicts that by 2011, overseas revenues from American movies will grow to $41.6 billion (Young, Gong, & Van der Stede, 2010).

Table 12.1
Movie Distribution Windows

Distribution Window	Length of Time	Typical U.S. Revenue Generated
Domestic Box Office	Three weeks–eight months	$10.6 billion (2009)
Home video	Six weeks before Pay-Per-View	$23.7 billion (2008)
Pay-Per-View (PPV) Video on Demand (VOD)	Two-six weeks before premium channels	
Premium Pay Channels	Up to 18 months before network/cable TV	$7 million for the average movie
Network and cable TV	12-18 months before syndication	$3 - $15 million per movie
Syndication	60 months on network/cable	Up to $5 million for a successful movie in a large market
International Box Office		$18 billion (2008)
International licensing for broadcast station, networks, and pay TV		$1.76 billion (2003)

Source: Neal, Warren, & Whitling

2009 was a big year for the movie industry—first with an all-time high for domestic box office revenue ($10.6 billion) (Young, Gong, & Van der Stede, 2010) and then with the Academy Awards expanding the Best Picture category to include 10 movies instead of the usual five. The biggest surprise may have been when the year's biggest financial success, *Avatar*, did not earn Best Director or Best Picture. The coveted Best Director award went to Kathryn Bigelow, director of *The Hurt Locker* (Edgar, 2010). While an isolated example, this shows that cinema is an evolving industry where economic success is not the only kind recognized and celebrated.

For cinema in general, there has been a steady increase in ticket price from 2007 to 2010. The same cannot be said for theater revenues or ticket sales. In 2007, the average price of a ticket was $6.88. 1.4 billion tickets were sold for 631 movies in that year, grossing $9.7 billion for movie theaters—an increase in revenue from the previous year, but a very slight decrease in ticket sales from the previous year. 2008 saw a decrease in both revenue and ticket sales, with yearly revenue dipping down to $9.6 billion earned by 1.3 billion tickets sold for 606 movies at an average price of $7.18 a ticket. 2009 saw an increase for both revenue and ticket sales with theaters grossing $10.6 billion on 1.4 billion tickets sold to 520 movies. The average ticket price for 2009 was $7.50. 2010 has seen another increase in ticket price up to $7.61 per ticket (Movie box office, 2010).

Gallup conducts surveys periodically to ascertain American movie-attending habits. The last survey Gallup conducted on this subject was in 2005, so the data may well have changed over the past five years. However, in 2005, Americans saw an average of four movies in a movie theater in the past 12 months. Of the people surveyed, 33% reported that they had not seen a movie in a theater, 42% saw between one and four movies, and 24% had seen five movies or more. By age, younger Americans were much more likely to see a movie in theaters with the average American between the ages of 18 and 29 attending seven movies or more. For 30- to 49-year-olds, this number dipped to four. The average 50- to 64-year-old saw three movies a year and for Americans 65 or older, the average saw only two. Not surprisingly, household income influenced movie attendance with Americans living in higher-income households being more likely to go to the movies than those in lower-income households. Members of households earning less than $30,000 a year on average saw two movies. In households with an income of $30,000 to $75,000, that number increased to three and for households earning more than $75,000 annually, the number doubled to six. There was no difference between men and women's movie attendance, however Americans in rural areas were less likely to go to the movies than those living in urban or suburban communities. Rural Americans saw an average of two movies a year, while urban and suburban Americans saw an average of four movies (Carroll, 2005).

One of the biggest changes in the movie-going experience is the slow but steady growth of IMAX theaters. IMAX technology involves specific projection and audio systems combined with special theater geometry and designated screens which seek to offer an immersive experience to audience members ("IMAX.com corporate," 2010). With steadily increasing ticket prices, it may not be a surprise that in the second quarter of 2009, IMAX started to see its first financial improvements for the first time in three years. IMAX's profit for that quarter was $2.6 million as compared to the previous year which reported a loss of $12.2 million. The company also enjoyed a 94% revenue increase to $41 million. There are a variety of reasons for these improvements including increased presence in theaters as well as a strategy that involves focusing on "lower-cost digital projection systems and us[ing] DMR (Digital Re-Mastering) technology to convert 35mm film into digital form" (McNary, 2009). Another reason for IMAX's newfound financial success is the achievement of a few key movies IMAX has distributed (McNary, 2009).

Films such as 2009's *Avatar* and 2008's *The Dark Knight*, have helped IMAX become one of the leading exhibition formats, with 403 screens in 44 countries. In 2004, IMAX enjoyed financial success with Warner Brother's *The Polar Express*, earning $71 million due in part to a number of holiday re-releases of the film. IMAX's next cash cow was the 2008 release of another Warner Brother's film, *The Dark Knight*. This film grossed $66 million in the IMAX format and was also the company's highest grosser until 2009's *Avatar*. The new highest grosser, *Avatar*, earned $120.1 million domestically at 179 IMAX screens and $80.2 million at 84 international IMAX screens after only three months (Stewart, 2010).

2009 saw box office revenue for 3-D movies increase three-fold from 2008, growing from $307 million to $1.3 billion. Domestically, Disney/Pixar's *Up* raked in $293 million. With an additional $390 million internationally, the worldwide total for the movie was $683 million. The next highest grossing 3-D movie domestically was DreamWorks Animation/Paramount's *Monsters vs. Aliens* which garnered an impressive $198.4 million and another $183.1 million internationally to reach $381.5 million in total. Additional 3-D movies that achieved more than $100 million domestically included Disney's *A Christmas Carol*, Sony's *Cloudy With a Chance of Meatballs*, and Disney's *G-Force*. Fox's *Ice Age: Dawn of the Dinosaurs* grossed $687.1 million internationally and $196.6 million domestically to reach a worldwide total of $883.7 million (McClintock, 2009). While many of the movies released in 3-D in 2009 were children's movies, *Avatar* (2009), *Clash of the Titans* (2010), and others have shown Hollywood's intention to start introducing a greater variety of movies in this format.

RealD has emerged as the market leader when it comes to outfitting movie theaters for 3-D exhibition. As of the end of 2009, RealD estimated that 100 million moviegoers had experienced their technology. This statistic is not surprising, given that RealD partners with 19 of the 20 top exhibitors in the world with "9,500 screens under contract, and 4,800 screens installed in 48 countries with 300 exhibition partners" (McClintock, 2009). Besides RealD, two other major suppliers of 3-D cinema technology include Dolby 3-D Digital Cinemas and IMAX Theaters. While the average 3-D ticket costs two to three dollars more than a regular ticket, some markets average even higher and IMAX Theaters typically charge higher ticket prices (McClintock, 2009).

🌐 Sustainability 🌐

The most visible sustainability effort in the movie industry may be the many actors out promoting green efforts, but the reality is that the industry has not been aggressive in taking steps to have a smaller impact on the environment. With that said, the digital revolution is making the film industry more eco-friendly by eliminating the use of film, which produces harmful chemicals when it is produced and stored. Digital distribution also reduces the carbon footprint of the industry by doing away with the need to ship and deliver films since they can be transmitted to the theater instead. Even small efforts by movie theaters discounting concessions prices for popcorn to viewers who bring their own container are a step in the right direction to a greener industry.

The film industry is not like manufacturing industries in that each time the process of filming a movie occurs the end product is not the same. Locations, sets, props, casts, all vary from film to film. "Those who believe the industry is unique are more likely to feel that the planning, construction, disposal and energy-efficiency approaches that work in more traditional industries can...not work in the motion picture industry" (Sustainability in the Motion Picture Industry, 2006, p. 73). Although this statement may be true, others feel like the industry should adopt some general guidelines for environmental practices. Another issue is that studios want to put the burden of green practices on producers so they don't have the expense involved. It will be interesting to see where the industry goes from here and where the push for greener practices will come from in the future, whether it be actors, patrons, or the government requiring it.

FACTORS TO WATCH

From 2008 to 2009, movie attendance rose 10%. The decrease during the preceding years can be explained by increasing entertainment options (video games, music, television, and user-generated content) as well as the increase in formats and methods of delivery of this content. Still, the 2008 to 2009 increase may be due to the recession and the public's need to escape their financial woes, if only for a few hours. To gauge the continued success and even survival of cinema technologies, it will be imperative to watch not only movie attendance, but also the aforementioned rise in ticket prices. Movie piracy is another important factor, with the Motion Picture Association estimating that more than $6.1 billion in revenue was lost due to the practice. Piracy is a growing problem, given the rise and ease of use of file-sharing sites (Young, Gong, & Van der Stede, 2010).

In the continued adoption of a digital format to film, as always, cost plays a major role. On the one hand, the digital format enables "instant and dirt-cheap distribution" as well as the ability to provide the "targeted distribution of independent films, distinct versions for unique audiences, subtitles, and dubbing" (Serwer, 2009, p. 181). Many foresee the digital transition as enabling those involved in the film industry to save billions of dollars by eliminating print and shipping expenses since the digital format of film can simply be downloaded. However, on the other hand, there is the initial investment involved in upgrading to digital in the first place. Digital projectors cost upwards of $65,000 per screen (O'Connor, 2010). The number of digital screens in the U.S. has increased from ten in 1999 to more than 5,000 in 2009 (Serwer, 2009). As of 2010, 7,600 of the country's 39,380 movie screens are digital (O'Connor, 2010).

With the recent success of 3-D movies such as *Avatar* and *Up*, theater owners must wrestle with the decision of whether to upgrade not only to a digital system, but perhaps even a 3-D digital system. While the aforementioned transition to digital costs about $65,000 per screen, the upgrade to 3-D digital costs approximately $100,000 per screen. Also, of the 7,600 of the digital movie screens in the country as of mid 2010, 3,400 of those are 3-D. Given the current economic climate, the major concern for theater owners is who will finance upgrades. Although many theater owners would like to upgrade to 3-D, some have not even upgraded to digital yet. Some distributors seek to foot the bill for equipment costs by paying a "virtual print fee" to the theaters showing their movies. In 2009, Paramount Pictures paid said fee to some theaters that showed digital versions of their movies *Star Trek* and *Monsters vs. Aliens*. Others, such as AMC, Regal, and Cinemark, have tried to lower costs by buying equipment in bulk from providers such as the Digital Cinema Implementation Partners. However, the credit crisis had a chilling effect on upgrades and left many theater owners looking to upgrade to finance their own transition (O'Connor, 2010).

Online ticketing is another field in flux. Currently, there are two major players in the field—Movietickets.com and Fandango. Movietickets.com is owned by theater chains and media companies including National Amusements, Marcus, and AMC much like larger competitor, Fandango, which is owned by another group of movie theaters including Regal and Carmike as well as a few venture capital firms (Serwer, 2009). In 2008, Comcast's Fandango acquired Disney's Movies.com. Movies.com started its life as a joint venture with Fox and was meant to be a video-on-demand platform but had instead developed into an entertainment news depository (Garrett, 2008). For the future of online ticketing, it will be important to track mergers and acquisitions such as this.

Bibliography

Bansal, R. (2009, December 2) 3D 'Avatar' promises edge-of-seat special effects. Retrieved March 15, 2010 from http://blog.taragana.com/e/2009/12/02/3d-avatar-promises-edge-of-seat-special-effects-66328/

Campbell, R., Martin, C., & Fabos, B. (2011). *Media & Culture: An Introduction to Mass Communication*. Boston: Bedford/St. Martin's.

Carroll, J. (2005, December 20). Movie attendance: Americans saw average of four movies in last year. *Gallup*, Retrieved February 22, 2010 from http://www.gallup.com/poll/20521/Movie-Attendance.aspx

Chapman, J. (2003). *Cinemas of the World*. London: Reaktion Books Ltd.

Cieply, M. (2010, January 13). For All Its Success, Will "Avatar" Change the Industry? *The New York Times* , C1.

Deprez, E. and Son, H. (2010, February 1) "'Avatar' Tops Box Office, Passes $2 Billion in Worldwide Sales." *Entertainment daily*. Retrieved March 16, 2010 from http://www.businessweek.com/news/2010-02-01/-avatar-tops-box-office-passes-2-billion-in-worldwide-sales.html

Digital Cinema Implementation Partners. (n.d.). *About Us*. Retrieved 2010, March 1 from Digital Cinema Implementation Partners: http://www.dcipllc.com/aboutus.xml

Dolby. (2010). *Dolby Digital Details.* Retrieved March 18, 2010 from
http://www.dolby.com/consumer/understand/playback/dolby-digital-details.html

Edgar, C. (2010, March 11). Academy awards results shock the public. *The Arrow,* Retrieved March 16, 2010 from
http://media.www.capahaarrow.com/media/storage/paper768/news/2010/03/11/ArtsEntertainment/Academy.Awar
ds.Results.Shock.The.Public-3888238.shtml

EPS Geofoam Raises Stockton Theater Experience to New Heights. Retrieved March 15, 2010 from
http://www.falcongeofoam.com/Documents/Case_Study_Nontransportation.pdf

Espejo, R. (2009), *The film industry* (pp. 181-183). Farmington Hills, MI: Greenhaven Press.

Film Journal International. (2008, January 22). *RealD Results: 3D Global Cinema Platform Creates Robust Market Opportunity.* Retrieved April 25, 2010 from http://www.reald.com/Content/mediaRoom.aspx

Film Specific. (2009). *Distribution School: The Beginner's Crash Course in Independent Film Distribution.* Retrieved 2010 йил 8-March from Film Specific: http://www.filmspecific.com/public/130.cfm

Fuchs, A. (2008). The Neural effect: THX brings surround impact to pre-show sound. *Film Journal International.*

Gelt, J. and Verrier, R. (2009, December 28) "Luxurious views: Theater chain provides upscale movie-going experience." *The Missoulian.* Retrieved March 16, 2010 from http://www.missoulian.com/busi ness/article_934c08a8-f3c3-11de-9629-001cc4c03286.html

Garrett, D. (2008, June 22). Fandango buys movies.com. *Variety,* Retrieved February 22, 2010 from
http://www.variety.com/article/VR1117987926.html?categoryid=13&cs=1&query=Fandango

Georgiades, A. (2010 March 1). *Imax's Status In 2D/3D Conversion Challenged By Competitors.* Retrieved March 14, 2010
http://online.wsj.com/article/BT-CO-20100301-711081.html

Haines, R. W. (2003). *The Moviegoing Experience, 1968-2001.* North Carolina: McFarland & Company, Inc.

Hancock, D. (2009). Digital has potential to broaden screen advertisers' business. *Film Journal International,* 35.

Hollywood Reporter. (2005, September 15). *Future of Entertainment.* Retrieved March 7, 2010 from
http://www.hollywoodreporter.com/hr/search/article_display.jsp?vnu_content_id=1001096307

IMAX.com - corporate - technology. (2010). Retrieved April 21, 2010 from
http://www.IMAX.com/corporate/profile/technology/

Jowett, G. (1976). *Film: The Democratic Art.* United States: Little, Brown & Company.

Kindem, G. (1981, Spring). The Demise of Kinemacolor: Technological, Legal, Economic, and Aesthetic Problems in Early Color Cinema History. *Cinema Journal,* 20(2), 3-14. Retreived March 15, 2010 from
http://www.jstor.org/stable/1224830

Kindem, G. A. & Musburger, R. B. (2005). *Introduction to media production: the path to digital media production* (3rd ed.). Boston: Focal Press.

Kindersley, D. (2006). *Cinema Year by Year 1894-2006.* DK Publishing.

McClintock, P. (2009, December 14). 3D pays off at box office. *Variety,* Retrieved February 22, 2010 from
http://www.variety.com/article/VR1118012750.html?categoryid=3762&cs=1&query=3D+cinema

McNary, D. (2009, August 6). IMAX swings to second-quarter profit. *Variety,* Retrieved February 22, 2010 from
http://www.variety.com/article/VR1118007002.html?categoryid=13&cs=1&query=IMAX

Mead, B. (2008). The rollout rolls on: U.S. digital conversions nearing critical mass. *Film Journal International,* 40.

Media: Cinema's digital dream. (2009). *Marketing,* 30.

Movie box office results by year, 1980-present. (2010). Retrieved February 22, 2010 from http://boxofficemojo.com/yearly/

Movie Rating System (n.d.) National Association of Theatre Owners. Retrieved February 22, 2010 from
http://www.natonline.org/ratingsabout.htm

O'Connor, C. (2010, January 24). The future is now: digital and 3-D as 'Avatar' speeds up the revolution, northeast Ohio movie-theater owners wonder how to pay for the transition. *Plain Dealer,* E1.

Phipps, K. (2008, November 11) Imagine Seeing John Wayne in IMAX: That's sort of what watching *How the West Was Won* is like. Retrieved April 25, 2010 from http://www.slate.com/id/2204189/

PR Newswire. (2005 , June 27). *The Walt Disney Studios and Dolby Bring Disney Digital 3-D(TM) to Selected Theaters Nationwide With CHICKEN LITTLE.* Retrieved March 27, 2010 from
http://www.prnewswire.co.uk/cgi/news/release?id=149089

Reuters, T. (2009, April 16). *Sony joins other studios in digital conversion deal.* Retrieved March 7, 2010 from
http://www.reuters.com/assets/print?aid=USTRE53F5Y520090416

S. Mark Young, J. J. (2010). The Business of Making Money with Movies. *Strategic Finance ,* 35-36.

Screen Digest. (2010, March 3). *Digital Cinema Building Momentum as 3-D Drives Market.* Retrieved March 7, 2010 from http://www.screendigest.com/press/releases/pdf/PR-DigitalCinemaand3D-03032010.pdf

Screen Digest. (2006). *Digital Cinema: Rollout, Business Models and Forecast to 2010.* Screen Digest.

Screen Digest. (2009). US screen ad growth slowing in difficult market. *Screen Digest, 252.*

Serwer, A. (2009). Movie theaters are adapting to changes in the film industry. In R. Espejo (Ed.), *The film industry* (pp. 181-183). Farmington Hills, MI: Greenhaven Press.

Solutions, D. C. (n.d.). *About Us.* From http://www.dcipllc.com/aboutus.xml

Straubhaar, J., & LaRose, R. (2008). *Media Now: Understanding Media, Culture, and Technology.* Belmont: Thomson Wadsworth.

Stewart, A. (2010, February 22). 'Avatar' sets IMAX record. *Variety,* Retrieved February 22, 2010 from http://www.variety.com/article/VR1118015615.html?categoryid=1009&cs=1

Sustainability in the Motion Picture Industry. (2006, November). UCLA Institute for the Environment and Integrated Waste Management Board.

Taub, E. A. (2009, October 27). *Will Sound Be Cinema's Killer App?* Retrieved February 25, 2010 from http://gadgetwise.blogs.nytimes.com/2009/10/27/will-sound-be-cinemas-killer-app/

The Movie Rating System: Its History, How It Works and Its Enduring Value.(n.d.) Retrieved March 16, 2010 from http://www.filmratings.com/filmRatings_Cara/downloads/pdf/about/cara_about_voluntary_movie_rating.pdf

Thompson, A. (2010, January). How James Cameron's Innovative New 3D Tech Created Avatar. *Popular Mechanics* Retrieved May 8, 2010 from http://www.popularmechanics.com/technology/digital/visual-effects/4339455.

THX. (2010). *THX Certified Cinemas.* Retrieved 2010 йил 17-March from THX: http://www.thx.com/professional/cinema-certification/thx-certified-cinemas/

Tryon, C. (2009). *Reinventing cinema: Movies in the age of media convergence.* New Brunswick, N.J.: Rutgers University Press.

Verrier, R. (2009, March 26). 3-D Technology Firm RealD Has Starring Role at Movie Theater. *Los Angeles Times*

Vivian, J. (2011). *The Media of Mass Communication.* Boston: Pearson.

What's new at the pre-show. (2009). *Film Journal International, 37.*

Young, S. M., Gong, J. J., & Van der Stede, W. (2010). The Business of making money with movies. *Strategic Finance,* 35-40.

Computers & Consumer Electronics

13

Personal Computers

Chris Roberts, Ph.D.[*]

Fast food remained a fairly new concept during much of McDonald's Corporation's first four decades, so the world's largest burger maker occasionally updated store signs to highlight its ever-rising count of the billions of sandwiches sold. That chore ended in 1994, when the company tired of buying new signs and instead posted the generic "Billions and Billions Served" phrase on store signs (Ruch, 2001).

McDonald's and the personal computer industry have plenty of parallels: Both sell products that were once uncommon but now are a commodity. Both started in the United States and blossomed internationally. Both have sold billions. And both have fundamentally changed the world.

The computer industry, halfway into its fourth decade since the first "personal computer" was sold in 1975, topped its billionth worldwide sale during 2006 (Computer Industry Almanac, 2007). Computer companies shipped nearly 306 million units in 2009, the most ever (Gartner, 2010a).

Just as the majority of young Americans have never known life without a nearby McDonald's, they've never known life without computers. More than a third of the U.S. population is under 24 (U.S. Bureau of the Census, 2008), meaning more than 100 million Americans are "digital natives" whose lives, cultures, and identities are bound with computer-mediated communication. They may have started with desk-bound machines, but many now carry their computers with them in the guise of notebooks, netbooks, and telephones. Since PCs became a household word, consider that:

◆ Computer sales keep rising. The 305.8 million units shipped worldwide in 2009 was a 5% increase from 2008, rising despite a worldwide recession. Annual sales have jumped nearly 11,000% since 1983, the year the industry shipped 2.8 million PCs and Time magazine named the computer its "Machine of the Year" (Friedrich, 1983),

◆ In the United States there are nearly 90 computers in use for every 100 Americans (Computer Industry Almanac, 2009). By 2013, the United States may have more working computers than residents.

◆ Nearly 80% of Americans had online access in late 2009, a rate roughly unchanged since 2006 but nearly double the percentage of 1998 (Whitney, 2009a). The average American with Web access is online 17 hours per week (University of Southern California, 2009), although time online ranges wildly by age group and skews highest for younger users. While not all Internet use

---

[*] Assistant Professor of Journalism, University of Alabama (Tuscaloosa, Alabama).

involves a personal computer, PCs remain the key device for delivery of online content. See Figure 13.1 for an overview of online use during the past 15 years.

Figure 13.1
Americans Online

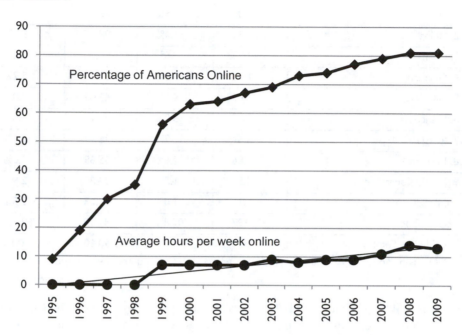

Source: Harris Interactive

◆ Americans ages 8 to 18 averaged nearly 90 minutes a day on a computer in 2009, triple the time spent a decade earlier (Lewin, 2010).

◆ More households have computers, and more households have more computers. A University of Southern California (2009) study found 86% of U.S. households had at least one computer, and nearly a quarter have at least three computers.

◆ We're consuming more "bytes" of information on computers. Americans in 2008 consumed 9.6 exabytyes of information on computers not including game playing (Bohn & Short, 2009). That is roughly the amount of storage needed to store audio copies of every phone call made in America each year.

◆ The world's "digital divide" is narrowing. In 2008, about 22% of the world's PCs were in America. A decade earlier, it was more than one-third (Computer Industry Almanac, 1997). While 72% of all computers are in use in just 15 countries—a figure that has not changed in the past decade— the world's number of PCs in use has tripled during the same time period. Although the gap between the digital haves and have-nots remains wide, PCs are common in many more nations. See Table 13.1 for details.

Table 13.1

PC Use by Country

Country	1996		2008	
	No.	Share	No.	Share
1. U.S.	108	35.5%	264.1	22.2%
2. China	4.34	1.4%	98.67	8.3%
3. Japan	23.3	7.6%	86.22	7.2%
4. Germany	16.2	5.3%	61.96	5.2%
5. UK	14.5	4.8%	47.04	4.0%
6. France	11.7	3.9%	43.11	3.6%
7. Russia	3.64	1.2%	36.42	3.1%
8. Italy	7.86	2.6%	35.69	3.0%
9. South Korea	4.57	1.5%	34.87	2.9%
10. Brazil	3.15	1.0%	33.3	2.8%
Top 15 Total	197	64.8%	741.38	62.3%
Worldwide Total	305	100%	1,190.10	100%

* No. is millions of PCs in use. Share is percentage of all computers in use worldwide.

Source: Computer Industry Almanac, Inc.

◆ The United States' "digital divide" still exists as the percentage of computer users starts to plateau. The biggest divides in computer use involve educational attainment and income: while nearly 95% of college graduates use computers, the rate is nearly half that for adults with less than a high school education. While 95% of people use computers in households earning at least $75,000 a year, the percentage falls to 56% among households with an annual income of less than $30,000. While 78% of whites used computers in 2006, the rate was 66% for blacks—wider than the gap of four percentage points in 1995 (U.S. Bureau of the Census, 2009). The gender gap has closed: 78% of men and 77% of women used computers in 2009; men held a seven percentage point advantage in 1995.

◆ Computer chip capacity and speeds continue to grow, even as chips become smaller. In 1983, the fastest processing chip made by industry giant Intel ran at 12 million cycles per second (Oldcomputers.com, n.d.). In early 2010, Intel's top chip for traditional personal computers included four independent processors, each running at more than 3.3 billion cycles per second (Intel, 2010a).

◆ Few commodities in the history of manufacturing have seen such increases in quality and declines in prices. Take, for example, IBM's 5150, the "personal computer" that sold 200,000 units within a year of its August 1981 introduction and had much to do with jump-starting the computer revolution. The original business-focused machine ran at a mere 4.77 megahertz and had a monochrome, text-only display. Its built-in memory held 64,000 bytes—not quite enough to hold all the characters in this chapter. There were no hard drives; the business version shipped with a single floppy disc drive. The cost: about $3,000 (IBM, n.d.), or $7,000 in current dollars after adjusting for inflation. Today, a PC that runs thousands of times faster and holds billions of more pieces of data sells for a few hundred dollars.

◈ Nearly every other technology in this book is tied to a computer in its design and use.

This chapter provides a brief history of computers, describes the current state of technology, and offers some insight into what may be coming next.

Background

A Brief History of Computers

As America grew in geography and population grew during the late 1800s, the U.S. Bureau of the Census was overwhelmed by the constitutional mandate to conduct a decennial headcount. The Bureau needed seven years to compile 1880 data, too late for useful decision making. The agency turned to employee Herman Hollerith, who built a mechanical counting device based on how railroad conductors punched tickets of travelers. The punched-card tabulation device helped the agency compile its 1890 results in about three months (Campbell-Kelly & Aspray, 1996) and was the first practical use of a "computer."

Hollerith, whose company later became a founding part of International Business Machines Corporation, owed a debt to 1800s British inventor Charles Babbage. While his "difference engine" was never built, Babbage's idea for a computer remains a constant regardless of the technology: Data is input into a computer's "memory," processed in a central unit, and the results output in a specified format.

Early computers were first called "calculators," because "computers" were people who solved math equations. The early machines were built to tackle a specific task—counting people, calculating artillery firing coordinates, or forecasting weather. The first general-purpose computers emerged at the end of World War II in the form of ENIAC, the "electronic numerical integrator and computer" (Brown & Maxfield, 1997). The next technological leap was Sperry-Rand's UNIVAC, or "UNIVersal Automatic Computer," which reached the market in 1950.

IBM quickly controlled the market, and competing computer makers were known as the "Seven Dwarfs" compared to IBM, which controlled two-thirds of the market when personal computers debuted in 1975. That year saw the introduction of the MITS Altair 8800, which was the first practical PC on the market. It used an Intel chip and later software designed by a new company called Microsoft (Freiberger & Swaine, 2000). An assembled box started at $600, or $2,600 in current dollars. A year later in California, Apple demonstrated its Apple I computer—which, unlike the Altair, came with a keyboard. The company's Apple II machine hit the market in 1977, and the company owned half of the personal computer market by 1980. The early 1980s were marked by a Babel of personal computing formats, but a standard emerged after the August 1981 arrival of the IBM PC. The machine was powered by an Intel chip and MS-DOS (Microsoft-Disk Operating System), the programs that manage all other programs in a computer (Campbell-Kelly & Aspray, 1996).

The two early powers behind the IBM PC took different paths. IBM's influence faded as competitors delivered machines with lower prices and higher performance. IBM controlled less than one-fourth of the computer market share in 1985 and in 2004 sold its PC business to Lenovo to focus on its server-based systems (Lohr, 2004). Microsoft, however, soon controlled the market for text-based operating systems and held off competitors (including IBM) in the transformation to operating systems with graphical user interfaces (GUI), which harness a computer's graphics capability to make the machine simpler and more intuitive. Apple in 1984 debuted the Macintosh, which like it 1983 predecessor, the Lisa, was built upon a GUI that had an ease-of-use advantage over text-based systems and a premium price. Microsoft's began selling a GUI operating system in late 1985, but its Windows software did not reach widespread adoption until its third version shipped in mid-1990. The mass acceptance of Windows gave Microsoft further dominance in the business of selling operating systems, and the company leveraged that power by selling applications based on the Windows platform. A Microsoft operating system ran on 92% of all PCs that accessed the Internet in January 2010 (Netmarketshare, 2010).

How Computers Work

The elements that make up a computer can be divided into two parts—hardware and software. Hardware describes the physical parts of a computer, such as the central processing unit, power controllers, memory, storage devices, input devices such as keyboards, and output devices such as printers and video monitors. "Software" is the term that describes the instructions regarding how hardware manipulates the information (data) (Spencer, 1992). This definition of software differs from Chapter 1's Umbrella Perspective on Communication Technology, which defines software as the "messages communicated through a technology system." Under the Umbrella Perspective, the content of a word-processing document would be considered "software," while the word-processing program would be defined as part of the hardware.

The most important piece of hardware is the central processing unit (CPU), also known as the microprocessor. The CPU is the brain of the computer, and it performs math and logic tasks according to given information. To do its work, the CPU's memory holds the data and instructions. The memory is based upon a series of switches that, like a light switch in a house, are flipped on or off.

The original memory devices required vacuum tubes, which were expensive, bulky, easily broken, and generated a great deal of heat. The miniaturization of computers began in earnest after December 23, 1947, when scientists perfected the first "transfer resistor," better known as a "transistor." Nearly a decade later, in September 1958, Texas Instruments engineers built the first "integrated circuit"—a collection of transistors and electrical circuits built on a single "crystal" or "chip." CPUs once the size of buildings became the size of wafers. Today, circuit boards hold the CPU and the electronic equipment needed to connect the CPU with other components. The "motherboard" is the main circuit board that holds the CPU, sockets for random access memory, expansion slots, and other devices. "Daughterboards" attach to the motherboard to provide additional components, such as extra memory or cards to accelerate graphics.

The CPU needs two types of memory: random access memory (RAM) and storage memory. RAM is the silicon chip (or collection of chips) that holds the data and instruction set to be dealt with by the CPU. Before a CPU can do its job, the data are quickly loaded into RAM—and that data are eventually wiped away when the work is done. RAM is measured in "megabytes" (the equivalent of typing a single letter of the alphabet one million times) or, increasingly, in "gigabytes" (roughly one billion letters). Microsoft's Windows 7 operating system claims to function with as little as 1 gigabyte of RAM (Microsoft, 2009). Only the cheapest netbook PCs sold in 2010 ship with less than 1 gigabyte of RAM, with standard consumer-aimed computers shipping with 2 or 4 gigabytes.

Think of RAM as "brain" memory, a quick but volatile memory that clears when a computer's power goes off or when a computer crashes. Think of storage memory as "book" memory—information that takes longer to access but stays in place even after a computer's power is turned off. Storage memory devices use magnetic or optical media to hold information. Major types of storage memory devices include:

> ◆ *Hard drives*, which are rigid platters that hold vast amounts of information. The platters spin at speeds of 5,400 to 15,000 revolutions per minute, and "read/write" heads scurry across the platters to move information into RAM or to put new data on the hard drive. The drives, which

can move dozens of megabytes of information each second, are permanently sealed in metal cases to protect the sensitive platters. A drive's capacity is measured in gigabytes, and only the most basic desktop computers today ship with less than 250 gigabytes of hard-drive capacity. The drives almost always hold the operating system for a computer, as well as key software programs (PC World, 2007). Although nearly every computer has a built-in hard drive, external drives that plug into computers using universal serial bus (USB) or other ports are increasingly common. Many external drives are powered through the USB port, meaning the drive does not need to be plugged into a traditional electrical socket.

Laptop hard drives often are smaller in size and capacity. The highest-end laptops use flash memory—a solid-state storage device with no moving parts—instead of the spinning platters. Solid-state drives can make laptops weigh less, use less energy and run more quietly—but at an additional cost of $500 or more (McClatchy-Tribune News Services, 2010). Laptop makers also like solid-state drives because they can load software faster, which moves the industry closer to the goal of instant-on computers (Kanellos, 2006).

❖ *Keydrives* (also called flashdrives or thumbdrives) are tiny storage devices that earned the name because they are the size of a thumb and can attach to a keychain. They use flash memory and plug into a computer using the USB port, which also powers the drive. Some larger-capacity keydrives hold 128 gigabytes of data, and capacity improvements are continual. Prices have plunged, with 2 GB devices selling for less than $10 as of mid 2010.

❖ *Other flash memory devices* can be connected to a computer. Most personal computers ship with devices that can access the small memory cards used in digital cameras, music players, and other devices. Storage capacities and access speeds are also increasing, driven by their use in cameras and camcorders.

❖ *Compact discs.* Introduced more than 25 years ago, these 12-centimeter wide, one-millimeter thick discs hold nearly 700 megabytes of data or more than an hour of music. They ship in three formats: CD-ROM (read-only memory) discs that come filled with data and can be read from but not copied to; CD-R discs that can be written to once; and CD-RW discs that, like a floppy diskette, can be written to multiple times. Most computers ship with CD drives capable of recording ("burning") CDs.

❖ *DVDs*, known as "digital versatile" or "digital video" discs, continue to replace CDs as the storage medium of choice. They look like CDs but hold much more information—typically 4.7 gigabytes of computer data, which is more than six times the capacity of a conventional CD. DVD players and burners are becoming standard equipment with new computers, because DVD video has reached critical mass acceptance and because DVD players and burners are backward-compatible with CDs. As illustrated in Table 13.2, DVD technology includes multiple formats, not all of which are compatible with each other. The newest format is Blu-ray, which beat Toshiba's HD DVD format in 2008 and currently ships with a top double-layer capacity of 50 GB (Fackler, 2008). Many computer companies sell machines with devices that can read from and write to typical DVDs and CDs but can only read data from Blu-ray discs.

Table 13.2
DVD Formats

Format	Storage Size*	Pros	Cons
DVD-ROM	4.7 to 9.4 GB	Works in set-top DVD players and computers	Read-only
DVD-R	4.7 to 9.4 GB	Works in most set-top DVD players and computers	Can be written to only once; may not work in DVD+R drives
DVD-RAM	2.6 to 9.4GB	Is rewritable many times	Works only in a DVD-RAM drive
DVD-RW	4.7 to 9.4 GB	Can be written to up to 1,000 times; used in most DVD players/computers	DVD-RW discs may not play back on some older systems
DVD+R	4.7 to 9.4 GB	Works in most set-top DVD players and computers equipped with DVD-ROM drives	Can be written to once; may not work in DVD-R drives.
DVD+RW	4.7 to 9.4 GB	Works in most set-top DVD players and computers equipped with DVD-ROM drives	DVD+RW discs may not play back on some older or entry-level DVD systems
Blu-ray	23.3 to 27 GB	Became industry standard in 2008.	Limited ability to write to this format

* Assumes single-side storage only.

Source: Roberts (2010)

Another key category of hardware is known as input and output devices. Input devices—named because they deliver information to the computer—include keyboards, mice, microphones, and scanners. Output devices that deliver information from the computer to users include monitors and printers. Other devices that let computers communicate with the outside world are modems (modulator/demodulators that translate the digital data of a computer into analog sound that can travel over telephone lines), network cards that let computers send and receive high-speed digital data signals through computer networks, and hardware that lets computers access wireless networks. Fewer computers ship with modems because broadband or network-accessed data connections have become more common, reducing the need to connect over a phone line. Also becoming more common are computers that use Bluetooth, a protocol that uses short range wireless technology to connect computers to input and output devices.

Software

Computers need software—the written commands and programs that load in the computer's random access memory and are performed in its central processing unit. The most important software is the operating system, which coordinates with hardware and manages other software applications. The operating system controls a computer's "look-and-feel," stores and finds files, takes input data and formats output data, and interacts with RAM, the CPU, peripherals, and networks. Microsoft's Windows operating systems reigns supreme in sales against competing operating systems such as Apple's OS X, UNIX, and various versions of GNU/Linux.

Operating systems provide the platform for applications—programs designed for a specific purpose for users. Programmers have created tens of thousands of applications that let users write, make calculations, browse the Web, create Web pages, send and receive e-mail, play games, edit images, download audio and video, and program other applications.

Programs designed to improve computer performance are known as utilities. The best-known utility programs improve how data is stored on hard drives and stop malicious computer code (such as viruses, worms, or Trojan horses) designed to destroy files, slow computer performance, or let outsiders surreptitiously take control of a computer. Software that identifies and sorts unsolicited commercial "spam" e-mail messages is also popular, as is software that removes "pop-up" advertising from Web sites.

Recent Developments

Hardware

The key to the hardware business remains as it ever was: Making CPUs that are more capable, smaller, and don't overheat. Companies are making smarter and faster CPUs through the principle of "parallelism," in which computing tasks are divided among the multiple CPUs on chip that have multiple cores able to run multiple threads. While the newest CPUs for servers can run eight cores (Franco, 2010), most consumer-aimed chips include two or four CPU "cores." Coming soon will be consumer-focused machines running with six cores, with CPU prices of at least $1,000 (Chen & Tsai, 2010). Both Intel and Advanced Micro Devices (AMD) will add additional cores as they continue their battle for CPU supremacy, which Intel continues to lead by a whopping margin.

Chip transistors are becoming tinier every day. Chips are now shipping with 45-nanometer transistors, allowing chipmakers to pack more transistors onto chips than the previous mass-market PC chips with 65-nanometer transistors. (One inch equals 25.4 million nanometers.) Next up are servers built with 32 nanometer transistors (Morgan, 2010a) and 25 nanometer technologies that will allow greater storage on flash memory devices (Intel, 2010b).

As chips acquire more cores with smaller transistors, they are also being built to address more information at once. Many new processors can manipulate binary numbers that are 64 zeroes and ones long, and they can work with up to 16 quintillion (that is, 16 billion billion) bytes of RAM—far more than the four billion bytes of RAM that were all a 32-bit processor could handle (Markoff, 2003). Major chipmakers introduced 64-bit chips in 2003. The first consumer-aimed operating system that had 64-bit capabilities was Apple's Mac OS X 10.3 operating system, introduced in 2003; it offered full 64-bit capabilities with its 2009 OS X 10.6 system. Microsoft's Vista operating system included a 64-bit version with its 2007 debut, and its 2009 Windows 7 included a 64-bit version that also is designed to work with multi-core chips.

The introduction of multi-core chips has breathed new life into Moore's Law. The 1965 prediction by Intel engineer Gordon E. Moore states that the number of transistors on a computer chip would double every two years, meaning computing power roughly doubles along with it (Intel, n.d.). Moore's statement remains prescient after more than four decades (see Table 13.3), but Moore now says the law is within 10 or 15 years of ending because "we'll hit something fairly fundamental"—such as the physical size of atoms (Martell, 2007). The response of CPU makers is to add more technology onto fewer chips to keep Moore's law alive (Crothers, 2009). The greater issue continues to be ways to dissipate the heat generated by CPU chips. Heat is the chief enemy of a CPU; most chips come with "heat sinks" and small fans designed to draw heat away from the chip. New computer technologies are designed to solve heat issues by cutting power use, spreading the heat across multiple chips, and powering down when not in use (Morgan, 2010).

Table 13.3
Moore's Law

Microprocessor	Introduced in:	Transistors
4004	1971	2,300
8008	1972	2,500
8080	1974	4,500
8086	1978	29,000
286	1982	134,000
386	1985	275,000
486	1989	1,200,000
Pentium	1993	3,100,000
Pentium II	1997	7,500,000
Pentium III	1999	9,500,000
Pentium 4	2000	42,000,000
Itanium	2001	25,000,000
Itanium 2	2003	220,000,000
Itanium 2 (9 MB cache)	2004	592,000,000
Core i7 (Quad core)	2008	731,000,000
Xeon (Six cores)	2008	1,900,000,000
Tukwila (Quad core)	2010	2 billion
Xeon Nehalem-EX (8 cores)	2010	2.3 billion

Source: Intel

Heat and size are special considerations for laptop computers, which began outselling desktops in 2005 (Singer, 2005) and in 2009 made up two of every three computers sold worldwide (Agence France-Presse, 2009). Computer makers are focusing on machines that deliver performance that is similar to desktop models, but at a fraction of the weight and size and for a higher cost on comparable models. Laptop sales remained a bright (or, at least a less-dark) spot for the computer industry during the past few years, as the global recession cut into total revenue. Laptop makers sold nearly 170 million machines during 2009 in the United States, up 17% from the previous year (Whitney, 2009b).

At the same time, some computer makers are prospering by selling cheaper, smaller, lighter, and less-powerful laptops called "netbooks." The machines are underpowered compared to traditional laptops, with screens of less than 10 inches, less RAM, slower processors, smaller hard drives (although some use solid-state flash drives), and without CD or DVD drives. Chinese computer maker Asus in 2007 released the first netbook, which was an immediate hit and led other computer companies to produce netbook lines even as sales ate into traditional laptop sales. Netbook sales nearly doubled in the United States in 2009, to 33 million machines worth $11 billion, even as total notebook revenue fell by 7% (Whitney, 2009b).

Other computer makers are focusing on machines that are not traditional portable computers at all. In April 2010, Apple debuted its iPad, a touch screen computer that uses the iPhone operating system and has a 9.7-inch color screen and virtual keyboard. While touch screen portable computers are nothing new—Windows

3.1 had "pen" support for laptops in the 1990s—the iPad garnered a great deal of attention as it seeks its niche between cellphones and laptops, and amid e-book devices such as Amazon's Kindle, Sony' Reader, and Barnes & Noble's Nook.

Still other computer companies are focused on machines with even smaller screens—those found on smartphones, which are both telephones and computers. Competitors among operating systems include the Symbian (which runs about half of all smartphones worldwide), iPhone OS for Apple devices (which runs about half the smartphones in the United State), Microsoft's Windows Mobile, Blackberry, and the Android system introduced by Google in 2009 (Hamblen, 2009). While companies sold 1.2 billion mobile phones in 2009, about 14% were smartphones. By 2013, the penetration rate is predicted to reach 38% worldwide (Gartner, 2009a).

Flash memory continues to fall in price and grow in storage size. While solid state drives of 128 GB to 256 GB still sell at a premium on laptops, prices for devices that require less flash memory are falling. Related to this sort of flash memory are SD (secure digital) cards, the postage-stamp sized devices that record images in cameras and camcorders and then transfer the data to computers. The original SD standard is being replaced by the SDHC (secure digital high capacity) format, which can hold up to 32 GB and move data faster than the original format. Coming next is the SDXC (extended capacity) format that can hold up to 2 terabytes (or 2,000 megabytes) and move data even faster (Grunin, 2010). Some of the newer cards can transfer information wirelessly.

While the storage capacity of flash drives is growing, it is still far behind the capacity of traditional hard drives. Prices for 1 terabyte hard drives dipped below $100 for the first time in 2009, and 2 terabyte drives sold for less than $200 in early 2010. Falling prices and rising capacities have allowed more home office/small office users to buy networked hard drives, which provide both backup abilities and the ability to access information over the Internet. Some newer network drives also work wirelessly.

Newer printers work wirelessly, too. While network printers are nothing new, in 2008 manufacturers began producing more consumer-focused inkjet and laser printers that do not have to be physically connected to a network or computer in order to work. Nearly all of these computers are known as "multifunction" printers because they come with scanners and facsimile technology. Despite the technological improvements, printer sales fell worldwide in 2009 because of the sour economy (Gartner, 2009b).

In 2005, flat-panel monitors began outselling heavier cathode-ray based monitors, and prices for flat panels continue to fall as size increases. The lines between "televisions" and "monitors" are blurring as more desktop and laptop computers come with HDMI (High-Definition Multimedia Interface) output, providing uncompressed digital data to be sent to monitors. Also, some computer companies are making it easier to add multiple monitors to a single computer, a feature that is especially useful as more people replace desktop machines with laptops.

Computer Software

If it's possible to sell hundreds of millions of copies of a product that is deemed a flop, Microsoft managed the feat with its Vista operating system (McAllister, 2008). Vista ran on nearly 400 million computers worldwide following its January 2007 debut, but many users (including corporate users, who generate a bulk of Microsoft's sales) opted to stay with Windows XP, which first began selling in 2001.

The company's response was Windows 7, which began selling in October 2009 and recorded triple the sales of Vista during their initial releases (Whitney, 2009c). By early 2010, within a few months of its release, nearly 10% of computers were running Windows 7 (Fried, 2010) through sales of new computers and as holdouts bypassed Vista and went from Windows XP to Windows 7. Throughout the life of Vista, Microsoft continued to sell Windows XP to people who didn't want to make the Vista leap, and also for netbooks that could run an operating system with smaller hardware requirements.

While Microsoft software powers most PC systems, it is not without competitors with new operating systems. Its most notable for-profit competitor is Apple, whose Macintosh OS X 10.6 operating system, dubbed "Snow Leopard," was released in August 2009 and holds a single-digit portion of the market. The new version was an incremental upgrade of previous versions, which are based on UNIX (Apple, n.d.). Mac systems come with Boot Camp software that made it compatible with Windows-based systems, including Windows 7 (AppleInsider.com, 2010).

Rarely found on personal computers—but more likely found on servers—are various flavors of UNIX-based operating systems beyond the Mac OS. The most common are Linux-based operating systems, which also hold single-digit shares of the personal computer market and are usually free or sold at little cost. Linux-based systems have less available software and can require more technically proficient users, but it saw a boost in the past few years in "One Laptop Per Child" systems and some notebook models. See Figure 13.2 for a look at how market share is divided among operating systems.

Another challenge to Microsoft's dominance was announced by Google, which announced plans to release its new Google Chrome operating system during 2010. The Linux-driven system is designed to run on netbooks or smaller devices, boot quickly, and focus on "cloud computing," in which users' programs and data are stored on Web servers and access over the Internet (Helft, 2009).

🌍 Sustainability🌍

Computer companies for years have been thinking of ways to cut energy use, and the result has been computers that run faster but use less energy and generate less heat. This has been done through manufacturing techniques, new hardware technologies, and software designed to cut a machine's energy use. An example is the widespread replacement of cathode-ray monitors, which use much more energy (and take up more space) than the more efficient liquid-crystal display monitors. While improvements in cutting energy use and heat are occurring on all PC fronts, it is especially important on laptop machines, where heat and weight are a particular nuisance.

Gartner (2010b) predicts that by 2012, nearly three-fifths of a PC's greenhouse gas emissions will occur during the production and transportation of a new PC. Currently, it's about 80% for a PC, which "consumes 10 times its own weight in fossil fuel." Gartner says more businesses are asking PC makers to supply information related to the power use and carbon dioxide emissions used in making and running a PC. Companies such as Apple have made "green" a part of their marketing efforts.

The U.S. Environmental Protection Agency (2008) reports that less than 20% of computer products are recycled; in 2006-07, it meant 48.2 million PCs, monitors and other computer-related products were recycled. State and local governments also are stepping up efforts to reduce "e-waste" by recycling computers and other electronic devices. At least 20 states have rules designed to boost recycling, and at least another dozen states are considering recycling laws (Electronics TakeBack Coalition, 2010).

Figure 13.2
The World's Top PC Makers, 2006-2009

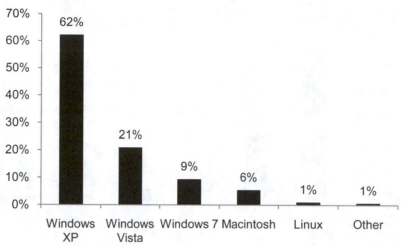

Source: StatCounter, February 2010

Just as Windows dominates its category despite free competitors, Microsoft's Office also holds a wide lead in the market for business application suites. The company released a new Windows version of Office in January 2007, and that version (plus previous versions) helped it maintain a market share of more than 80% (Montalbano, 2009). It also released a new Macintosh version in 2008. In all, Microsoft claims 97 cents of every $1 in sales of business application suites (Gonsalves, 2007). About 60% of the company's $20 billion in 2009 operating income (a measure of profitability) came from Office suite sales (Microsoft, 2010).

Not every user buys from Microsoft, however. OpenOffice, partially funded by Sun Microsystems, is a free suite that was downloaded 100 million times in the year after its third version was released in October 2008 (Openoffice.org, 2009). OpenOffice is an example of open-source software, in which the code is freely available to the public to use and improve. Some businesses and governments adopted OpenOffice to save money (or make a statement against Microsoft) and sought "open document" formats that will let word processing files, spreadsheets, and presentation files work regardless of the program used to create them.

Microsoft's other suite competitor is Google, which in September 2007 released its "Google Docs" system that includes a free (and online) software similar to other office suites. Users have a free gigabyte of storage on Google servers and can buy more storage (Google, 2010) each year. This is an example of "software as a service," in which users pay fees to use software or storage for a period of time. Microsoft has a similar product named Office Live that competes with similar Google products, and the Microsoft Office suite to be released during 2010 will include online versions of its major programs (Muchmore, 2010).

Google, Microsoft, Apple, and others also compete in another type of widely used software—Web browsers. Google in 2008 released its Chrome browser, which by early 2010 trailed Microsoft's Internet Explorer and the open-source Firefox browsers in market share. (See Figure 13.3 for details.) While all of these companies give away their browsing software for free, some of the companies make money by selling space to search engines—and Google and Microsoft seek to drive traffic to their search engines through their browsers. Microsoft's antitrust agreement with the European Union required it to give users a choice of browsers to download; the result has been a decline in Internet Explorer use (Mah, 2010).

Figure 13.3
Operating System Market Share

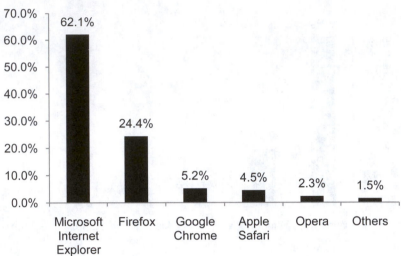

Source: NetMarketshare, February 2010

And a challenge to Microsoft and other "traditional" software companies is the boom in sales of mobile phone applications. The industry sold $9.4 billion in phone "apps" during 2009, and Apple had a hand in nearly all of them through its app store, which opened in July 2008 in conjunction with the introduction of its iPhone 3G (Foresman, 2010). Microsoft announced plans to upgrade its phone software during 2010 in hopes of competing. (For more on smartphones and "apps," see Chapter 18.)

Current Status

Americans bought about $162 billion in computers in 2009 and spent $354 billion on software in 2008 (the most recent year available). All told, these two add up to about 4% of the nation's Gross Domestic Product, or the value of all goods and services produced (U.S. Bureau of Economic Analysis, 2010).

Intel remains the leader in computer chip sales, snagging 79.7% of all CPU sales in late 2009 (Hachman, 2010) but struggling with antitrust charges across the globe (Lohr & Kanter, 2009). AMD was second with 20.1% of all processor sales but has struggled in the past few years for profitability as they work to make technology that has an advantage over Intel's. AMD earned a 2009 profit, its first in three years, after Intel paid it $1.25 billion to settle an antitrust charge.

In computer sales, Dell has fallen from the top in 2005 to third. Hewlett-Packard took the lead from Dell after 2006, and HP sells nearly one in five computers sold worldwide (Gartner, 2010a). Acer leapfrogged Dell in 2009, thanks to Acer's early move into netbook computers.

Microsoft remains the world's largest software seller. It reported sales of $58.7 billion and profits of $16.3 billion for the year ending December 2009, and its profit margin was nearly 28%. The introduction of Windows 7 boosted its late 2009 sales, but sales have not been rising for the company as they had in previous decades.

FACTORS TO WATCH

How will PC sales do? The computer industry's revenues suffered during the past few years but had no control over some factors, such as the recession. In addition, sales of netbooks and continued adoption of open-source software cut into revenues. Forrester Research (2010) predicts that computer purchases will rise 8% in 2010 over the previous year, a faster pace than the rest of the economy.

Will netbooks fade away? Among the biggest trends in the past two years has been the rise in sale of cheap but good-enough netbooks, but some industry watchers say netbooks are a passing fancy as laptops and other portable computer-like devices offer more power (or another useful benefit) for the same price (Ward, 2009).

What happens to "One Laptop per Child?" The rise of the netbook may be one reason for the decline in the "One Laptop per Child" initiative of the past decade. The nonprofit's goal was to deliver a $100 notebook with inexpensive hardware and free software to developing nations, but the cost was closer to $188 when production began in late 2007. While 1.5 million of these inexpensive laptops have been delivered to 30 nations (Hernandez, 2010), the program has been undercut by the netbook, the economy, and efforts by commercial competitors such as Intel who have shipped 2 million of its competing Classmate PCs since 2006 (Takahashi, 2010). The One Laptop initiative has fewer workers but still has plans for a newer system to be released in 2011 and a tablet PC for 2012 (One Laptop, 2009).

Will tablets take off? The arrival of the Apple's iPad created a great deal of attention to the topic of small, touch screen computers, but many other companies offered such products during the Consumer Electronics Show 2010 (Gizmodo.com, 2010) and more are on the way. The question is whether tablets can find a sweet spot between their heavier laptop brethren and much-smaller smartphones, and whether users can survive without keyboards.

How quickly will phones overtake PCs as the way to reach the Web? Gartner (2010b) says it will happen by 2013, when the world will have slightly more smartphones than PCs. The question is whether Web designers will continue to use programming languages and techniques that are not conducive to phone-based browsing.

How does Microsoft respond to Google? The world's largest software company continues to hold dominate market shares with its operating systems and office suite, but its key threat is Google. The two currently compete with office suite technology, search engines, and mobile operating systems, and the competition could grow with Google's upcoming Chrome OS.

How does Google respond to Microsoft? The company seems well positioned to make a run at Microsoft's OS and office applications, but only if users decide they are comfortable working in "cloud" environments in which they use the Internet to access applications and data. Gartner (2010b) predicts that 20% of companies will not own any information technology assets by 2012, instead relying on the "cloud" for services.

What's up with viruses? Concerns about evil people who write malware that use the Internet to steal access and files from computers remain with us, and this could factor into acceptance of "cloud" computing. While most virus writers aim at Microsoft-designed systems because they dominate the desktop, Apple software and the Firefox browser also are targets.

What does Apple do next? The company's iPhones are a runaway best seller, with at least a quarter of the U.S. smartphone market, but its computer market share remains in single digits. In fact, Windows 7 needed a little more than three months in the marketplace to top the Mac operating system's slice of the market (Prota-linksi, 2010). Apple is known for its reticence to discuss future plans, making it unclear what plans the company has for its lines of desktops and laptops even as it makes news with its iPhone and iPad systems.

What's next with chips? Intel remains the industry leader by its sheer size and plans to continue shipping faster and more efficient chips during the coming years, but competitors remain on the horizon. The New York Times (Vance, 2010) notes a rise in demand for a competing type of chip called ARM that is used in phones but is making its way into computers. It's also worth noting that Apple's iPad runs on ARM technology created by Apple (Shah, 2010).

What's next with flash memory? While solid-state hard drives remain a high-priced luxury on personal computers, it's possible that technological breakthroughs and economies of scale will boost adoption and lower prices of flash devices. But some predict that some forms of flash memory will reach their growth limits by 2015 or so because the memory cannot be made any denser. Some companies are already researching the next technology to let users store more information in smaller spaces without the use of spinning discs (Mearian, 2010).

Will computers load faster? A perennial complaint about personal computers is that, unlike television sets and many mobile devices, it takes minutes for a PC to load its operating system. Some PC makers added components or secondary operating systems that give users Internet access while the machine boots, but the main OS still takes time. Some universities are working on hardware solutions that could lead to "instant-on" computers, but no PC maker has yet introduced the technology (Ganapati, 2009).

Will piracy ebb? More than 40% of business software used in the world during 2008 was pirated, up from about a third in 2006 and representing a loss of $53 billion for software companies (Business Software Alliance, 2009). The industry trade group notes that emerging nations buy 45% of the world's PCs but less than 20% of the software. Companies continue to find a sweet spot between making piracy easy and making registration and copy-protection schemes too onerous for users; the move to "cloud" computing might cut piracy, too.

Will peripheral speeds increase? Nearly all personal computers ship with the ability to handle Universal Serial Bus (USB) peripherals such as computers, mice, and keyboards. The USB 2 standard is a decade old. The first peripherals able to handle the USB 3 standard, which can move information many times faster than USB 2, are expected to be released in 2010. The original Windows 7 did not support the standard, and USB 3 controllers have yet to be put in a mainstream PC chipset, so it is unclear how quickly devices able to handle the faster speeds will be available (Graham-Smith, 2010).

Will TVs and PCs continue to merge? Computer companies for years have sought to move the PC out of the home study and into the entertainment room. Early efforts failed, but PC companies are encouraged by better hardware, digital video recorders, wireless home networks, flat-panel monitors that double as TV sets, and the movement of entertainment software onto digital formats. This movement could lead to a continued decline in DVD sales, and new revenue streams for PC-based delivery of entertainment (Wortham, 2010). New versions of operating systems—not to mention the burgeoning number of online services that deliver TV-like content to computers—are putting more faces in front of computer screens than ever. Meanwhile, new TVs are able to access computers and the Internet in order to play stored media. Researchers note that the fundamental differences between computers and televisions make it difficult for one technology to be used as the other (one example: computer users sit much closer to the screen than television users) (Morrison & Krugman, 2001).

What's next for monitors? Monitor makers saw fundamental changes in the past five years as tube monitors faded and flat-panel monitors took over. The next steps may be wireless displays (Ackerman, 2010), or monitors that can handle three-dimensional images (Franklin, 2010). Although high prices and few uses make these novelties today, it's worth remembering that, like other PC-related technologies, a novelty one year can lead to mass acceptance another year.

Bibliography

Ackerman, D. (2010, January 7). CES 2010 people's voice award: Intel wireless display. *Cnet.* Retrieved February 10, 2010, from http://ces.cnet.com/best-of-ces.

Agence France-Presse. (2009, January 8). Electronic sales may slow down. Retrieved January 8, 2010, from www.taipeitimes.com/News/biz/archives/2009/01/08/2003433191.

AppleInsider.com. (2010, January 19). Apple updates Boot Camp with Windows 7 support. Retrieved February 8, 2010, from www.appleinsider.com/articles/10/01/19/apple_updates_boot_camp_with_windows_7_support.html.

Apple (n.d.) Mac OS X. Retrieved February 8, 2010, from www.apple.com/macosx.

Bohn, R.E., & Short, J.E. (2009). How much information? 2009 report on American consumers. Global information industry center, University of California, San Diego. Retrieved February 7, 2010, from http://hmi.ucsd.edu/pdf/HMI_2009_ConsumerReport_Dec9_2009.pdf.

Brown, C. & Maxfield, C. (1997). *Bebop bytes back: An unconventional guide to computers.* Madison, AL: Doone Publications.

Business Sofware Alliance. (2009, May). Sixth annual BSA-IDC global software piracy study. Retrieved February 10, 2010 from http://global.bsa.org/globalpiracy2008/index.html.

Campbell-Kelly, M. & Aspray, W. (1996). *Computers: A history of the information machine.* New York: Basic Books.

Chen, M. & Tsai, J. (2010, January 29). AMD and Intel preparing to launch six-core processors. *DigiTimes.* Retrieved February 8, 2010, from www.digitimes.com/news/a20100129PD216.html.

Computer Industry Almanac, Inc. (2007, September 27). PCs in-use reached nearly 1B in 2006: USA accounts for over 24% of PCs in-use. Retrieved February 25, 2008 from http://www.c-i-a.com/pr0907.htm.

Computer Industry Almanac, Inc. (2009, January 14). PCs in-use nearly 1.2 B in 2008. Retrieved February 7, 2010, from http://www.c-i-a.com/pr0109.htm.

Computer Industry Almanac, Inc. (1997, November 12). Top 25 countries with the most computers. Retrieved February 25, 2008, from http://www.c-i-a.com/pr1197.htm.

Crothers, B. (2009, September 13). Intel Forum preview: Moore's Law expressed as fewer chips. *Cnet.com.* Retrieved February 8, 2010, from http://news.cnet.com/8301-13924_3-10351519-64.html.

Electronics TakeBack Coalition (2010). State legislation. Retrieved February 10, 2010, from www.computertakeback.com/legislation/state_legislation.htm.

Fackler, M. (2008, February 20.) Toshiba concedes defeat in the DVD battle. *New York Times,* C2.

Foresman, C. (2010, January 18). Apple responsible for 99.4% of mobile app sales in 2009. Retrieved February 10, 2010, from http://arstechnica.com/apple/news/2010/01/apple-responsible-for-994-of-mobile-app-sales-in-2009.ars.

Forrester Research (2010, January 29). Predictions 2010: The tech industry rebounds faster than the overall economy. Retrieved February 10, 2010, from www.forrester.com/rb/Research/predictions_2010_tech_industry_rebounds_faster_than/q/id/56287/t/2

Franco, J. (2010, February 8). IBM launches next generation Power 7 CPU, servers. Techspot.com. Retrieved February 8, 2010, from www.techspot.com/news/37845-IBM-launches-next-generation-Power-7-CPU-servers.html.

Franklin, E. (2010, January 11). ViewSonic makes second foray into 3D. *Cnet.* Retrieved February 10, 2010, from http://ces.cnet.com/?categoryId=9830921.

Freiberger, P., & Swaine, M. (2000). Fire in the valley: The making of the personal computer. New York: McGraw-Hill.

Fried, I. (2010, February 2). Windows 7 market share tops 10 percent. Cnet. Retrieved February 8, 2010, from http://news.cnet.com/8301-13860_3-10445776-56.html.

Friedrich, O. (1983, January 3). Machine of the year: The computer moves in. *Time,* 142, 14.

Ganapati, P. (2009, April 22). Lab breakthrough brings instant-on computers closer. *Wired.* Retrieved February 10, 2010, from www.wired.com/gadgetlab/2009/04/instant-on-comp/

Gartner, Inc. (2009a, December 15). Gartner says worldwide mobile device sales on pace for flat growth in 2009. Retrieved February 8, 2010, from www.gartner.com/it/page.jsp?id=1256113.

Gartner, Inc. (2009b, August 25). Gartner says worldwide printer, copier and multifunctional product market declined 20 per cent in first half 2009. Retrieved February 8, 2010, from http://www.gartner.com/it/page.jsp?id=1146512.

Gartner, Inc. (2010a, January 13). Gartner says worldwide PC shipments in fourth quarter of 2009 posted strongest growth rate in seven years. Retrieved February 8, 2010, from www.gartner.com/it/page.jsp?id=1279215.

Gartner, Inc. (2010b, January 13). Gartner highlights key predictions for it organizations and users in 2010 and beyond. Retrieved February 10, 2010, from www.gartner.com/it/page.jsp?id=1278413.

Gizmodo.com (2010, January 8). Tablet coverage. Retrieved February 8, 2010, from http://gizmodo.com/tag/ces2010/tablets.

Gonsalves, A. (2007, February 14). Office 2007 doubles the sales of Office 2003 in launch week. *InformationWeek.* Retrieved March 12, 2008 from http://www.informationweek.com/management/showArticle.jhtml?articleID= 197006187.

Google.com (2010, January 12). Upload and store your files in the cloud with Google Docs. Retrieved February 10, 2010, from http://googledocs.blogspot.com/2010/01/upload-and-store-your-files-in-cloud.html.

Graham-Smith, D. (2010, February 9). USB 3: The future arrives. *PCAuthority.com.* Retrieved February 10, 2010, from www.pcauthority.com.au/GroupTests/166792,usb-3-the-future-arrives.aspx.

Grunin, L. (2010, January 10). CES wrap-up: Cameras and camcorders. *Cnet.* Retrieved February 8, 2010, from http://ces.cnet.com/8301-31045_1-10432211-269.html.

Hachman, M. (2010, January 26). IDC puts Intel on top again in 2009 CPU sales. *PCMag.com* Retrieved February 8, 2010, from www.pcmag.com/article2/0,2817,2358434,00.asp.

Hamblen, M. (2009, October 6). Android to grab No. 2 spot by 2012, says Gartner. *Computerworld.com.* Retrieved February 8, 2010, from www.computerworld.com/s/article/9139026/Android_to_grab_No._2_spot_by_2012_says_Gartner.

Helft, M. (2009, November 19). Google offers peak at operating system, a potential challenge to Windows. *New York Times*, B4. Retrieved February 10, 2010, from http://www.nytimes.com/2009/11/20/technology/companies/20chrome.html.

Hernandez, C. (2010, February 8). Computers in Haiti and Afghanistan: One Laptop Per Child expands its reach. *Smartplanet.com.* Retrieved February 8, 2010, from www.smartplanet.com/people/blog/pure-genius/computers-in-haiti-and-afghanistan-one-laptop-per-child-expands-its-reach/1813.

Intel Corporation. (n.d.). Moore's Law. Retrieved April 10, 2008 from http://www.intel.com/technology/mooreslaw/.

Intel Corporation. (2010a, February). Intel core i7 desktop professor family. Retrieved February 7, 2010 from http://ark.intel.com.

Intel Corp. (2010b, February 1). Intel, Micron introduce 25-nanometer NAND. Retrieved February 8, 2010, from www.intel.com/pressroom/archive/releases/2010/20100201comp.htm.

International Business Machines, Inc. (n.d.). The IBM PC's debut. Retrieved February 28, 2008 from http://www-03.ibm.com/ibm/history/exhibits/pc25/pc25_intro.html.

Kanellos, M. (2006, January 4). Bye-bye hard drive, hello flash. *C/NET News.* Retrieved March 11, 2008 from http://www.news.com/Bye-bye-hard-drive,-hello-flash/2100-1006_3-6005849.html.

Lewin, T. (2010, January 20). If your kids are awake, they're probably online. *New York Times*, A1. Retrieved January 20, 2010, from www.nytimes.com/2010/01/20/education/20wired.html.

Lohr, S. (2004, December 8). Sale of IBM PC unit is a bridge between companies and cultures. *New York Times*, A1.

Lohr, S. & Kanter, J. (2009, November 12). A.M.D.-Intel settlement won't end their woes. *New York Times*, B1. Retrieved February 8, 2010, from www.nytimes.com/2009/11/13/technology/companies/13chip.html.

Mah, P. (2010, March 23). Internet Explorer's market share in EU takes a tumble. *TechWatch.* Retrieved 23, 2010, from www.fiercecio.com/techwatch/story/internet-explorers-market-share-eu-takes-tumble/2010-03-23.

Markoff, J. (2003, August 18). How an extra 32 bits can make all the difference for computer users. *New York Times*, C4.

Martell, D. (2007, September 20). Intel pioneer's law nearing end. *Toronto Star*, B7.

McAllister, N. (2008, January 21). Tech's all-time top 25 flops. *InfoWorld.com.* Retrieved February 8, 2010, from www.infoworld.com/t/platforms/techs-all-time-top-25-flops-558.

McClatchy-Tribune News Service (2010, February 2). Solid-state hard drives are faster, quieter, but costly. *Montreal Gazette.* Retrieved February 7, 2010, from www.montrealgazette.com/technology/Solid+state+hard+drives+faster+quieter+costly/2513830/story.html.

Mearian, L. (2010, February 4). Is NAND flash about to hit a dead end? *Computerworld.com.* Retrieved February 10, 2010, from www.computerworld.com/s/article/9151659/Is_NAND_flash_about_to_hit_a_dead_end_.

Microsoft (2010). Microsoft Corp. fiscal year 2009 annual report 10-K. Retrieved February 10, 2010, from www.microsoft.com/msft/download/FY09/MSFT_10K_2009.docx.

Microsoft. (2009). Windows 7 system requirements. Retrieved February 7, 2010, from www.microsoft.com/windows/windows-7/get/system-requirements.aspx.

Morgan, T.P. (2010a, February 3). Intel sneak peeks Westmere EP server silicon. *The Register.* Retrieved February 8, 2010, from www.theregister.co.uk/2010/02/03/intel_westmere_ep_preview.

Montalbano, E. (2009, June 4). Forrester: Microsoft Office in no danger from competitors. NetworkWorld.com. Retrieved February 10, 2009, from http://www.networkworld.com/news/2009/060409-forrester-microsoft-office-in-no.html.

Morgan, T.P. (2010, February 8). Brace yourself for a bevy of server chip announcements. *ITJungle.com.* Retrieved February 8, 2010, from www.itjungle.com/tfh/tfh020810-story08.html.

Morrison, M. & Krugman, D. (2001). A look at mass and computer mediated technologies: Understanding the roles of television and computers in the home. *Journal of Broadcasting & Electronic Media*, 45 (1), 135-161.

Muchmore, M. (2010, February 3). Microsoft presents Office 2010 RC to select few. *PCMag.com.* Retrieved February 10, 2010, from www.pcmag.com/article2/0,2817,2358760,00.asp.

Netmarketshare. (2010, January). Operating system market share. Retrieved Feb. 7, 2010, from http://marketshare.hitslink.com/operating-system-market-share.aspx?qprid=8.

Old-computers.com. (n.d.). PC-XT Model 5160. Retrieved April 11, 2008, from http://www.old-computers.com/museum/ computer.asp?st=1&c=286.

One Laptop Per Child. (2009, December 31). New Year's newsletter: 2009 in review. Retrieved February 8, 2010, from http://blog.laptop.org/2009/12/30/new-years-newsletter.

Openoffice.org. (2009, October 29). OpenOffice.org clocks up one hundred million downloads. Press release. Retrieved February 10, 2010, from http://www.prweb.com/releases/ooo/centomilioni/prweb3108474.htm.

PC World. (2007, July 23). How to buy a hard drive. *PC World.* Retrieved February 29, 2008 from http://www.pcworld.com/article/id,125778-page,3/article.html.

Protalinski, E. (2010, January 22.) Windows 7 growing faster than Vista, overtakes Mac OS X. Arstechnica.com. Retrieved February 10, 2010, from http://arstechnica.com/microsoft/news/2010/01/windows-7-growing-faster-than-vista-overtakes-mac-os.ars

Ruch, J. (2001, October 4.) Stupid question. Retrieved February 7, 2009, from http://archives.stupidquestion.net/sq10401.html.

Shah, A. (2010, January 29). Apple's A4 chip could find a home in iPhones. *MacWorld.* Retrieved February 10, 2010, from www.macworld.com/article/146008/2010/01/a4chip_iphone_ipad.html.

Singer, M. (2005, June 3). PC milestone—notebooks outsell desktops. *Cnet.* Retrieved February 8, 2010, from http://news.cnet.com/PC-milestone--notebooks-outsell-desktops/2100-1047_3-5731417.html.

Spencer, D. (1992). *Webster's new world dictionary of computer terms,* 4th ed. New York: Prentice Hall.

Takahashi, D. (2010, January 15). Intel makes progress with Classmate PC for the world's kids. *Venturebeat.com.* Retrieved February 10, 2010, from http://venturebeat.com/2010/01/15/intel-makes-progress-with-classmate-pc-for-the-worlds-kids.

U.S. Bureau of Economic Analysis. (2010). Prices and outputs for information and communication technologies. Retrieved February 20, 2010, from www.bea.gov/national/info_comm_tech.htm.

U.S. Bureau of the Census. (2008). American Community Survey three-year population estimates. Retrieved February 7, 2010, from http://factfinder.census.gov/servlet/STTable?_bm=y&-geo_id=01000US&-qr_name=ACS_2008_3YR_G00_S0101&-ds_name=ACS_2008_3YR_G00_.

U.S. Bureau of the Census. (2009). Statistical abstract of the United States, 129 ed. Washington, DC: U.S. Government Printing Office. Retrieved February 8, 2010, from www.census.gov/compendia/statab/.

U.S. Environmental Protection Agency (2009). Statistics on the management of used and end-of-life electronics. Retrieved February 10, 2010, from www.epa.gov/waste/conserve/materials/ecycling/manage.htm.

University of Southern California Center for the for Digital Future (2009, April 29). Annual Internet survey by the Center for the Digital Future finds large increases in use of online newspapers. Retrieved February 8, 2010, from http://www.digitalcenter.org/pdf/2009_Digital_Future_Project_Release_Highlights.pdf.

Vance, A. (2010, January 14). Intel's bet on innovation pays off in faster chips. *New York Times,* B1. Retrieved February 10, 2010, from www.nytimes.com/2010/01/15/technology/companies/15chip.html.

Ward, M. (2009, December 31). Technology changes "outstrip" netbooks. BBC. Retrieved February 10, 2010, from http://news.bbc.co.uk/2/hi/technology/8421491.stm.

Whitney, L. (2009a, December 23). Average Net use now online 13 hours a week. *Cnet.* Retrieved February 7, 2010, from http://news.cnet.com/8301-1023_3-10421016-93.html.

Whitney, L. (2009b, December 23). 2009 sales of Netbooks rise, but notebooks fall. Cnet.

Whitney, L. (2009c, November 5). Windows 7 sales outshine Vista. *Cnet.* Retrieved February 8, 2010, from http://news.cnet.com/8301-10805_3-10391484-75.html.

Wortham, J. (2010, January 1). Five tech themes for 2010. *New York Times.* Retrieved February 8, 2010, from http://bits.blogs.nytimes.com/2010/01/01/five-web-predictions-for-2010.

14

Video Games

Brant Guillory[*]

Video gaming has expanded from a small university time-waster to a multibillion dollar industry that includes a variety of hardware and software, as well as multiple delivery and distribution models. The 'culture' of video gamers has served as the subtext for successful online comics such as *Penny Arcade* and television shows including *The Big Bang Theory*.

In monetary terms, video games are easily competitive with the largest media. The opening day sales of *Call of Duty: Modern Warfare 2* exceeded $310 million in the US, UK, and Canada alone, easily exceeding the largest-ever weekend movie gross (*The Dark Knight*) and the first-day sales of the final Harry Potter book (Zabek, 2008; Thorsen, 2009). Additionally, videogame franchises are themselves becoming hot media properties, with such series as *Resident Evil*, *Bioshock*, *Fallout*, *HALO*, and *Mass Effect* spawning multiple sequels, Web sites, videos, downloadable games, and physical content ranging from action figures to comic books to coffee mugs.

"Video games" as a catch-all terms includes games with a visual (and usually audio) stimulus, played through a digitally-mediated system. Video games are available as software for other digital systems (home computers, cell phones), standalone systems (arcade cabinets), or software for gaming-specific systems (platforms). There have been tentative forays into games delivered through set-top boxes and digital integration with offline games.

A video game system will have some form of display, a microprocessor, the game software, and some form of input device. The microprocessor may be shared with other functions in the device. Input devices have also evolved in sophistication from simple one-button joysticks or keyboards to replicas of aircraft cockpits and race cars, as well as new controllers integrating haptic feedback (enabling users to "feel" aspects of a game).

Background

Video gaming has advanced hand-in-hand with the increases in computing power over the past 50 years. Some might even argue that video games have pushed the boundaries of computer processors in their quest for ever-sharper graphics and increased speed in gameplay. From their early creation on large mainframe computers, video games evolved through a variety of platforms, including standalone arcade-style machines, personal computers, and dedicated home gaming platforms.

---

[*] M.M.C., Ph.D. Candidate, Ohio State University (Columbus, Ohio).

Figure 14.1
Video Game Genres

Sports

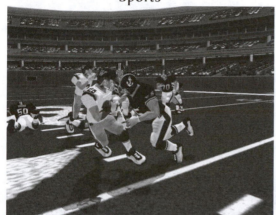

Space

Military

History

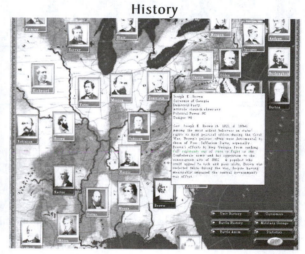

Source: Matrix Games

As media properties, video games have shared characters, settings, and worlds with movies, novels, comic books, non-digital games, and television shows. In addition to a standalone form of entertainment, video games are often an expected facet of a marketing campaign for new major movie releases. The media licensing has become a two-way street, with video game characters and stories branching out into books and movies as well. As video gaming has spread throughout the world, the culture of video gaming has spawned over two dozen magazines and countless Web sites, as well as industry conventions, professional competitions, and a cottage industry in online "farming" of in-game items in massive multiplayer online role-playing games (MMORPGs).

Although some observers have divided the history of video games into seven, nine, or even 14 different phases, many of these can be collapsed into just a few broader eras, as illustrated in Figure 14.2, each containing a variety of significant milestones. Most histories of video games focus on the hardware requirements for the games, which frequently drove where and how the games were played. However, it is equally possible to divide the history of games by the advances in software (and changes in the style of gameplay), the diffusion of games among the population (and the changes in the playing audience), or the increases in economic power wielded by video games, measured by the other industries overtaken through the years. Regardless of the chosen path, as the history of video games developed, however, it became increasingly fragmented into specialty niches.

Figure 14.2
Video Game Chronology

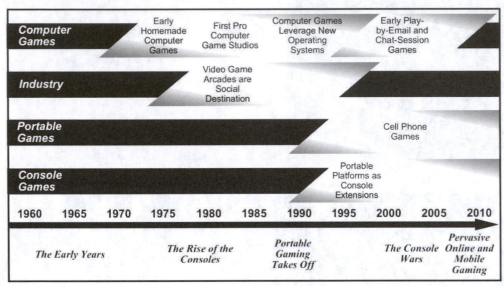

Source: Guillory (2008)

Most industry observers describe the current generation of home gaming consoles as the seventh generation since the release of the first-generation Magnavox Odyssey. Handheld consoles are often said to be on their fourth generation. No one has yet attempted to assign "generations" to computer gaming software, in large part, because console "generations" are hardware-based and released in specific waves, while computer hardware is continually evolving, and major computer milestones are the releases of new operating systems (Windows Vista, Mac OS X, etc).

The early years of video gaming were marked by small hobby programs, many developed on large university and corporate mainframes. Willy Higenbotham, a nuclear physicist with the Department of Energy, had experimented with a simple tennis game for which he had developed a rudimentary analog computer (Anderson, 1983). A team of designers under Ralph Baer developed a variety of video game projects for the Department of Defense in the mid-1960s, eventually resulting in a hockey game, which left their military sponsors nonplussed (Hart, 1996). Baer also led another team that developed *Chase*, the first video game credited with the ability to display on a standard television set. In the early 1960s, *SpaceWar* was also popular among the graduate students at MIT and inspired other work at the Pentagon. Although many different treatises have been written arguing over the invention of the video game, it is still unclear how much, if at all, any of the early video game pioneers even knew of each others' work; it is completely unknown if they drew any inspiration from each other.

In the early 1970s, dedicated gaming consoles began to appear, starting with the Magnavox Odyssey in 1972. Built on switches, rather than a microprocessor, the Odyssey included a variety of "analog" components to be used in playing the video portions of the game, such as dice, play money, and plastic overlays for a common touchpad. The first home video game product built on a microprocessor was a home version of the popular coin-operated *Pong* game from Nolan Bushnell's Atari. Although it contained only one game, *Pong*, hard-coded into the set, it would be a popular product until the introduction of a console that could play multiple games by swapping out software (Hart, 1996).

The second generation of video gaming began approximately in 1977 with the rise of consoles. The Atari 2600 led the market for home video game sales, in which consumers would purchase a standard console and insert cartridges to play different games. While Colecovision and Intellivision (two other consoles) were popular in the market, nothing could compare with the market power wielded by Atari (which was eventually purchased by Warner Communications) from 1977 to 1982, during which an estimated $4 billion of Atari products were sold (Kent, 2001). During this time, Atari also pioneered the media license tie-in with other Warner Communications products, such as the popular movie licenses for *E.T. The Extra-Terrestrial* and *Raiders of the Lost Ark*. Atari's success also led to the formation of Activision, a software company founded by disgruntled Atari game programmers. Activision became the first major game studio that designed their games exclusively for other companies' consoles, thus separating the games and consoles for the first time.

After a brief downturn in the market from 1981 to 1984, mostly as a result of business blunders by Atari, home video game consoles began a resurgence. Triggered by the launch of the Sega Master System in the mid-1980s and the Nintendo Entertainment System (NES) shortly thereafter, home video game sales continued to climb for both the games and the hardware needed to play them. The inclusion of 8-bit processors closed the gap between the performance of large standalone arcade machines and the smaller home consoles with multiple games and signaled the start of the decline of the video game arcade as a game-playing destination. By 1987, the NES was the best-selling toy in the United States (Smith, 1999).

During this time, video games also began to appear in popular culture not as mere accessories to the characters, but as central plots around which the stories were built. *Tron* (1982), *War Games* (1983), and *The Last Starfighter* (1984) all brought video gaming into a central role in their respective movie plots.

Computer games were also developing alongside video game consoles. Catering to a smaller market, computer games were seen as an add-on to hardware already in the home, rather than the primary reason for purchasing a home computer system. However, the ability to write programs for home computers enabled consumers to also become game designers and share their creations with other computer users. Thus, a generation of schoolkids grew up learning to program games on Commodore PET, Atari 800, and Apple II home computers.

The commercial success of the Commodore 64 in the mid-1980s gave game publishers a color system for their games, and the Apple Macintosh's point-and-click interface allowed designers to incorporate the standard system hardware into their game designs, without requiring add-on joysticks or other special controllers. Where console games were almost exclusively graphics-oriented, early computer games included a significant number of text-based adventure games, such as *Zork* and *Bard's Tale*, and a large number of military-themed board games converted for play on the computer by companies such as SSI (Falk, 2004). In 1988, the first of several TSR-licensed games for *Dungeons & Dragons* appeared, and SSI's profile continued to grow. Other prominent early computer game publishers included Sierra, Broderbund, and Infocom, among others. Nevertheless, home computer game sales continued to lag behind console game sales, in large part, because of the comparatively high cost and limited penetration of the hardware.

With video games ensconced in U.S. and Japanese households and expanding worldwide, it was only a matter of time before portable consoles began to rival the home siblings in quality and sophistication, and thus began the third phase in the history of video games.

Portable video games proliferated in the consumer marketplace beginning in the early 1980s. However, early handhelds were characterized by very rudimentary graphics used for one game in each handheld. In fact, "rudimentary" may even be generous in describing the graphics—the early Mattel handheld *Electronic Football* game starred several small red "blips" on a one-inch-by-three-inch screen in which the game player's avatar on the screen was distinguished only by the brightness of the blip.

Atari released the Lynx handheld game system in 1987. Despite its color graphics and relatively high-speed processor, tepid support from Atari and third-party developers resulted in its eventual demise. In 1989, Nintendo released Game Boy, a portable system whose controls mimicked the NES. With its low cost and stable of well-known titles ported from the main NES, the Game Boy became a major force in video game sales (Stahl, 2003). Although technically inferior to the Lynx—black-and-white graphics, dull display, and a slower processor—the vast number of Nintendo titles for the Game Boy provided a major leg up on other handheld systems, as audiences were already familiar and comfortable with Nintendo as a game company. Sega's Gamegear followed within a year. Like the Lynx before it, superior graphics were not enough to overcome Nintendo's catalog of software titles or the head start in the market the Game Boy already had. By the mid-1990s, most families that owned a home game console also owned a handheld, often from the same company.

Although the portable revolution did not (yet) migrate to computer gaming, it was hardware limitations, rather than game design, that prevented the integration of computer games into portable systems. The release of the Palm series of handheld computers (Hormby, 2007) gave game designers a new platform on which they could develop that was not tied to any particular company. This early step toward handheld computing would include early steps toward handheld computer gaming.

The third and fourth generations of video game history begin to overlap as the console wars included the handheld products of various console manufacturers, coinciding with the release of Windows 95 for Intel-powered PC computers, which gave game designers a variety of stable platforms on which to program their games. The console wars of the late 1990s have continued to today, with independent game design studios developing their products across a variety of platforms.

As Nintendo began to force Sega out of the platform market in the mid-1990s, another consumer electronics giant, Sony, was preparing to enter the market. With the launch of the Playstation in 1995, Sony plunged into the video game platform market. Nintendo maintained a close hold on the titles it would approve for development on its system, attempting to position itself primarily as a "family" entertainment system. Sony developers, however, had the ability to pursue more mature content, and their stable of titles included several whose graphics, stories, and themes were clearly intended for the 30-year-old adults who began playing video games in 1980, rather than 13-year-old kids (Stahl, 2003). Sony and Nintendo (and to a lesser extent, Sega) continued their game of one-upmanship with their improvements in hardware over the next several years.

As the graphical processing power of consoles increased, and games gained greater notoriety in the press as they pushed the edges of storytelling and explicit graphics, the Interactive Digital Software Association finally caved to public pressure and instituted a rating system for games, which sought to better inform consumers about the target ages for games, as well as the reasons for the ratings. The ISDA became the ESA in 2004 (ESRB, 2009), and the ratings for computer-based games have become a standard feature of every game, both console and computer. More granular than movie ratings, computer software ratings break down into more than a half-dozen age categories and more than twenty content descriptors. Controversies have (predictably) ensued; unlike movies, video games can easily incorporate alternate, hidden, or add-on content which might alter their ratings. Among the most famous ratings controversies was the "Hot Coffee" content in *Grand Theft Auto*, in which downloaded patches opened up sexually explicit and violent content (BBC, 2005).

By early 2001, Sega admitted defeat in the hardware arena and focused instead on software. The next salvo in the platform wars was about to be launched by Microsoft, which debuted the Xbox in late 2001. With built-in networking and a large hard drive, Microsoft's Xbox began to blur the lines between computer video gaming and platform-based video gaming. Additionally, building their console on an Intel processor eased the transition for games from PC to Xbox, and many popular computer titles were easily moved onto the Xbox. Around the same time, Sony entered the handheld arena to challenge Nintendo's Game Boy dominance with the PSP: PlayStation Portable. Capable of playing games as well as watching movies and (with an adapter) having online access, the PSP was intended to show the limitations of the Game Boy series with its greater number of features. Although the platform wars continue today, every one of them supports networked gaming, the cusp of the fifth generation of video gaming.

With high-speed data networks proliferating throughout North America, Japan, Korea, Western Europe, and (to a lesser extent) China and Southeast Asia, online gameplay has become a major attraction to many video gamers, especially through MMORPGs. These pervasive worlds host shared versions of a variety of different games, including sports, military, and sci-fi and fantasy games. MMORPGs are most commonly accessed through computer platforms rather than game consoles. Since its launch in 2004, *World of Warcraft* has grown to exceed 10 million simultaneous subscribers at any one time, though their rate of subscriber turnover continues to be high. MMORPGs have highly-developed in-game economies, and those economies have begun to spill over into the "real world." Web sites and online classified listings offer game-world items, money, and characters for sale to players seeking an edge in the game but are reluctant to sacrifice the time to earn the rewards themselves. Fans' reactions have not been universally positive to these developments, and some have started petitions to ban such behavior from the games (Burstein, 2008).

Wireless networking has also extended the ability to participate in online-based games to handhelds, both dedicated to gaming (Nintendo DS) and consumer-oriented (personal digital assistants and cell phones). Moreover, many software-specific companies have designed their online game servers such that the players' platforms are irrelevant, and thus gamers playing on an Xbox might compete against other gamers online who are using PCs.

The 2006 release of Nintendo's Wii game console drew a new audience by attracting large numbers of older users to the motion-based games enabled by the Wii's motion-sensitive remote. Not long after its release, the Wii began to appear on the evening network news as a new activity in senior citizens homes and in stories about children and grandparents sharing the game (Potter, 2008). Although graphically inferior to the Xbox or PS3, the Wii has developed an audience of players who had never tried video gaming before.

RECENT DEVELOPMENTS

By some estimates, video games may be in their seventh, tenth, or twelfth generation. Those generations have been collapsed into five for this chapter: the early years, the rise of the consoles and computer games, portable gaming, the console wars, and pervasive online gaming. Computer gaming roughly followed this same trajectory, although the introduction of portable computer gaming lags behind for hardware reasons. While the fourth generation described above is still ongoing, it seems as though the market has stabilized in that the three current major players in the console market (Nintendo, Microsoft, and Sony) appear likely to remain in the market for the long term. Similarly, with three major computer platforms (Windows, Macintosh, and UNIX/Linux), computer gamers are expected to have a variety of choices for the foreseeable future as well.

The availability of broadband connections has resulted in many software companies selling games online directly to the consumer (especially for computer gaming), with manuals and other play aids available as printable files for those players who wish to do so. Steam, from Valve Corporation, is a download site that boasts over 25 million accounts (Steam, 2010) and delivers downloadable games directly to computer platforms. Matrix Games sells virtually every title as a download directly to their customers, and many other software makers sell their software directly or through online stores. These sales are *not* simply mail-orders of physical copies, but actual direct-to-PC downloads. This direct-to-consumer sales route has reduced the dependence on local computer software stores for computer games; these stores have reacted by stocking more console games.

Regulatory Environment—Continuing Legislative Efforts to "Protect the Children"

The legislative landscape continues to be hostile to video games, continuing to treat them as a child-oriented medium as though the average videogame player was ten years old. However, these laws, once challenged in the courts, have continually been struck down. In 2009, the Ninth Circuit Court upheld a ruling that a California law was too restrictive and violated free speech rights (Walters, 2010).This case was then appealed to the Supreme Court of the United States, which has agreed to hear the case during the 2010-2011 session (Stohr, 2010). Nonetheless, 2009 saw six other bills seeking to restrict access to videogames pending in various legislatures (Walters, 2010).

Console-Based Music Games—Better Than Karaoke!

Beginning with the release of *Guitar Hero* in 2005, console-based music games have skyrocketed from 'non-existent' to among the most popular games available. Based on a late-90s Japanese game called *Guitar-Freaks*, *Guitar Hero* featured a guitar-shaped controller that was used to interact with an on-screen scroll of notes. Since the release of the original *Guitar Hero*, a competing franchise (*Rock Band*) has been introduced, as well as controllers for drums and keyboards and integration of vocals for both series of games.

In addition, the musical videogame genre has seen the release of multiple versions branded with particular artists, such as The Beatles (*Rock Band*), Aerosmith (*Guitar Hero*), and Metallica (*Guitar Hero*). Support for the musical videogame genre also includes downloadable music tracks to add to the games. *Rock Band* downloads exceeded 2 million within the first 8 weeks of their availability (Bruno, 2008).

Pervasive Mobile Gaming

With the increase in computing power available in handsets, mobile gaming has split along two lines. First, Nintendo and Sony both have handheld game platforms with wireless capability built in, allowing for head-to-head gameplay with other nearby systems, as well as shared gameplay through an Internet connection, where available. Platforms such as Nintendo's DS line and Sony's PSP machines are capable of establishing local networks for head-to-head gaming without any wireless service.

In addition, mobile phone handsets have sufficient computing power to allow for a variety of gaming. Nokia's N-Gage phone, while critically panned, showed that handheld multipurpose systems—such as a mobile smart phone—possessed sufficient memory and processor speed for true gaming (Carnoy, 2006). The release of Apple's iPhone and iPod Touch, in conjunction with Apple's App Store, opened a new market for games on portable devices. The success of Apple's App Store has spawned several imitators, including Google's Android platform, with application stores that include a wide variety of videogames for use on mobile phones and associated devices. Most important, the portability of gaming, whether on a cell phone, a PDA, or a dedicated handheld platform, ensures that gamers have the ability to play regardless of their locations.

Broadband-Enabled Downloads for Consoles

In a manner similar to the Steam download service, console manufacturers have integrated online participation and downloadable content through their consoles. Not only can networks of players compete cooperatively or head-to-head around the world, but broadband networking has enabled the push of content through storefronts including the Xbox Live Marketplace and the Nintendo Wii Virtual Console.

Xbox Live Marketplace includes not only games, but movies from major studios. Nintendo's Virtual Console has seen competition from WiiWare (Chan, 2010) for the download market on the Wii consoles. Sony's Playstation network is integrating connections to popular online destinations such as Facebook (Thorpe, 2009) and NetFlix (Kennedy, 2009), further blurring the delivery lines between computers and other Internet-enabled devices.

Get Off the Couch!—Physical Videogame Interaction

Following in the footsteps of the Wii, the idea of physical interaction with videogames has expanded to other consoles as well. Microsoft's Project Natal (see more below) has incorporated recognition of physical characteristics. Apple's iPhone and iPod Touch leverage multi-touch-based screens and accelerometers to enable physical feedback in a portable machine. New physical interfaces for the Wii have also appeared, including balance boards, skateboards, and steering wheels.

CURRENT STATUS

No new platforms have been released since late 2006, although the three major platforms have all received upgrades to their current configurations. Because consoles are primarily dependent on their software to maintain customer interest, constant hardware upgrades may not be as necessary, and in fact might be considered detrimental to sales if the consoles are not backward-compatible with older games in the same product family. Computer-based games are not as dependent on regular hardware updates, and software continues to appear daily for computer-based videogamers.

In 2009, global sales of video games totaled nearly $77 billion, with an additional $30 billion in console sales. By the end of 2009, the Nintendo Wii had overwhelmed the competition with 47% of global console revenue, followed by Microsoft's Xbox with 35% and 18% for Sony's PS3 (Graft, 2010). Given the multi-function nature of desktop and laptop computers, counting the hardware for computer game sales makes little sense.

Figure 14.3
TOP-SELLING VIDEO GAMES OF 2009

Title	Global Sales (millions)	US Sales (millions)
Call Of Duty: Modern Warfare 2	11.86	8.82
Wii Sports Resort	7.57	4.54
New Super Mario Bros. Wii	7.41	4.23
Wii Fit Plus	5.8	3.53
Wii Fit	5.44	3.6

Source: NPD Group

Advergames had proven to be both successful and controversial for a variety of reasons, such as the supposed targeting of impressionable youth and glorification of violence. They have also been adopted by a variety of questionable organizations, such as the game *Special Force*, which is used as a recruiting tool by Hezbollah in Lebanon. These games have also become the subject of interest for several researchers, who have sought to understand and describe the potential effects on game players (Moon, et al., 2006). The proliferation of in-game advertising has resulted in a set of video game advertising guidelines being released by the Interactive Advertising Bureau, with guidelines for how to measure ads, their exposure, and the audience (Zabek, 2009).

"Gamer parents" continue to be a phenomenon of interest. Often used as a buttress against the argument that "video games are for kids," gamer parents are those game players that grew up with a game console in their households and are now raising their own children with consoles. The average game player is 35 years old and has been playing for over 12 years (ESA, 2009). Although legislative action has often been touted as a remedy for inhibiting access to video games that legislators feel is inappropriate, gamer parents have repeatedly noted that they are intimately familiar with video games and capable of making informed choices about their children's access to video games. In addition, gamer parents tend to take the lead in game purchases for their households, thus making them a valuable target for the corporate marketing machines. In fact, 92% of all game players under age 18 note that their parents are present when they purchase or rent their games (ESA, 2009).

As noted above, legislative action against video games continues in multiple venues. Not every legislative action is opposed by industry trade groups, however. The Entertainment Software Association has consistently supported measures designed to prohibit access to sexually explicit games by minors, as well as supporting legislation that increases access to ratings information for consumers (Walters, 2008). However, laws intended to severely limit games access to a large segment of the population have yet to stand up to judicial scrutiny.

🌍 Sustainability 🌍

The video game industry seems to have a bi-polar approach to sustainability. On one hand, numerous games exist to promote sustainability, environmentalism, and Earth-friendly action. On the other hand, consoles and computers are full of dangerous metals, extracted in way profoundly unfriendly to the environment, and rarely recycled.

Columbite-tantalite, a rare mineral mined in conflicted areas of Africa (Vick, 2001), is used in the manufacture of many electronics components, including game consoles. Dubbed the "Playstation War" by some media outlets (Peckham, 2008), Congo's conflict showed that the demand for electronic components had serious environmental ramifications.

Meanwhile, video games have been used by different organizations to capture the attention of younger game players in an attempt to instill environmental lessons in the audience. Sponsored by organizations including the UN and IBM, these games have gained some wide attention, with IBM's *PowerUp* being selected as the official game of the Earth Day Network in 2008 (Libby, 2009).

Finally, more attention is now being drawn to video game consoles and computers as "vampire devices" that continue to drain power even when not in use. Comparisons of the three most popular consoles show that the Wii uses dramatically less power than either the Xbox or PS3, but that all of them continue to draw power even in standby mode (Troast, 2009). Similarly, the rate of recycling of consoles and their related peripherals continues to lag compared to other industries, and is potentially more damaging to the environment than other household discards due to the high quantity of toxic metals used in the hardware. Greenpeace has ranked Nintendo and Microsoft as two of the worst manufacturers of electronic components (Greenpeace, 2010).

Sustainability in the video game industry remains elusive at best, and outright ignored at worst. Although there have been forays by individual game companies into environmentalism in the form of consciousness-raising games, the manufacturing processes and power consumption of video game consoles continue to pose significant environmental challenges.

Factors to Watch

Industry-watchers have looked to Microsoft for almost half of a decade in anticipation of an expected foray into mobile, handheld gaming to compete with platforms from Nintendo (Game Boy / DS series) and Sony (PSP). An expected handheld product from 2006 turned out to be the Zune music player and, as of mid-2010, Microsoft has not yet announced a mobile gaming device, and no credible rumors seem to exist to the contrary.

While the industry was watching Microsoft in anticipation of a yet-to-appear handheld device, Apple's iPhone has excited a variety of developers with its motion sensors, multi-touch screen, microphone, and haptic feedback (Schramm, 2008). Apple has come under some criticism for its strict licensing of software development kits to developers and their tight controls on software to consumers. Developers, however, seem willing to work within Apple's constraints to create software.

The early-2010 release of Apple's iPad also bears watching. A large-screen touchpad that leverages the interface of the iPhone and iPod Touch, the iPad uses a variety of multi-touch gestures and accelerometers to allow users to interact with games, some of which are direct ports from the iPhone. The iPad's screen is much larger than those of any other portable game platform, and opens up many possibilities for interface design than would be challenging on a smaller screen or a non-touchscreen device.

Microsoft's Project Natal for Xbox 360 will bring motion-based gaming (until now limited to Nintendo's Wii and limited other games) to another major console. Unlike the Wii, which relies on a remote control, Project Natal relies on a camera that recognizes gestures, facial features, and body motion (Archibald, 2009). The ability to recognize motion will free game-players from at least part of the needed hardware for gameplay.

Nintendo seems to have moved on beyond motion-sensitive controllers to incorporate two other new technologies into their handheld DS line. The DSi incorporates digital cameras that can be integrated into gameplay, beyond merely replicating video-conferencing. *Ghostwire* is a game that interacts with camera images of the game-player's real environment, inserting ghosts and paranormal images into the local scenery (Ha, 2009). Nintendo has also announced a new 3-D version of their DS platform that supposedly allows viewing of 3-D images without any special glasses (Tabucki, 2010). With the advances in 3-D television technology that are appearing on larger-screen devices, it remains to be seen if Nintendo's software will work equally well when (or if) it is ever brought to a larger screen, or if it is reliant on the small-screen handheld.

The growth in the numbers of women playing video games is expected to continue to accelerate. 40% of the game-playing public are women, a 2% increase from 2008; adult women represent a greater share of the market (34%) than young males under 17 (18%) (ESA, 2009). The online titles favored by women are dependent not only on the continued diffusion of the software, but also on the continued diffusion of the high-speed Internet access needed to enable the online environment.

Government funding of new projects with video game developers will also continue as sponsors search for projects applicable to their specific fields. The U.S. Army established an office specifically designed to leverage video game technology for training purposes (Peck, 2007) and is expanding the use of commercial off-the-shelf (COTS) games for a variety of teaching purposes. The U.S. Marine Corps' success with VBS-2—and the integrated language modules built for it that allow for voice-recognition interaction—has led the US Army to adopt it as their standard training platform for the future, in spite of their investment of over $10 million in *America's Army* and over $40 million invested in DARPA's *Real World* (Nichols, 2010).

Despite years of video game legislation being rejected by the courts, legislators will continue to react to media coverage of parental concern about video game content. Overwhelming demographic data shows that video gamers are typically adults, and 25% of them are over age 50. Nonetheless, many news outlets and legislators continue to view video games as toys for kids, and make no distinction in subject matter between mature-themed games and games clearly targeted at children. Legislative efforts are further complicated by legal precedents being established in cases about online distribution of content, which is increasingly relevant as Internet-enabled consoles are connected to broadband networks.

All three major consoles and many computer games allow for collaborative online play. Expect to see two developments in this area. First, as game titles proliferate across platforms, expect to see more games capable of sharing an online game across those platforms, allowing a player on the Xbox to match up against an opponent on a PC system, as both players communicate through a common back-end server. Second, many of these online systems, such as the Xbox Live, already allow voice conversations during the game through a voice over Internet protocol system. (VoIP is discussed in more detail in Chapter 18.) As more digital cameras are incorporated into consoles, either as an integrated component or an aftermarket peripheral, expect these services to start offering some form of videoconferencing, especially for players involved in games such as chess, poker, or other "tabletop" games being played on a digital system.

Bibliography

Archibald, A. (2009). Project Natal 101. *Seattle Post-Intelligencer.* Retrieved March 4, 2010 from
http://blog.seattlepi.com/digitaljoystick/archives/169993.asp

Anderson, J. (1983). Who really invented the video game. *Creative Computing Video & Arcade Games 1* (1), 8. Retrieved February 28, 2008 from http://www.atarimagazines.com/cva/v1n1/inventedgames.php.

Associated Press. (2007a). Microsoft to spin off Bungie Studios, creators of "Halo" game series. *International Herald Tribune.* Retrieved January 12, 2008 from http://www.iht.com/articles/ap/2007/10/05/business/NA-FIN-US-Microsoft-Halo-Spinoff.php.

Associated Press. (2007b). Singapore bans Microsoft Xbox video game "Mass Effect" over lesbian love scene. *Associated Press Financial Wire.* Accessed April 10, 2008 through www.lexisnexis.com.

Azzoni, T. (2008, April 10). Brazil Judge bans video game "Bully." *Associated Press Online.* Accessed April 10, 2008 through www.lexisnexis.com.

BBC. (2005). Hidden sex scenes hit GTA rating. *BBC News.* Retrieved April 11, 2010 from
http://news.bbc.co.uk/2/hi/technology/4702737.stm

Bruno, A. (2008). *Rock Band, Guitar Hero* drive digital song sales. *Reuters.* Retrieved March 3, 2010 from
http://www.reuters.com/article/idUSN1934632220080120

Burstein, J. (2008). Video game fan asks court to ban real sloth and greed from *World of Warcraft. Boston Herald.* Retrieved April 11, 2008 from http://www.bostonherald.com/business/technology/general/view.bg?articleid= 1086549.

Carnoy, D. (2006). Nokia N-Gage QD. *C/NET News.* Retrieved April 9, 2008 from http://reviews.cnet.com/cell-phones/nokia-n-gage-qd/4505-6454_7-30841888.html.

Cendrowicz, L. (2008, January 17). EU wants taught kids TV regs. *The Hollywood Reporter.* Accessed April 10, 2008 through www.lexisnexis.com.

Chan, T. (2010). WiiWare Market Grows to Nearly $60M USD in 2009. *Nintendo Life.* Retrieved March 4, 2010 from
http://www.nintendolife.com/news/2010/02/wiiware_market_grows_to_nearly_usd60m_usd_in_2009

Entertainment Software Association. (2009). *Industry Facts.* Retrieved March 4, 2010 from http://www.theesa.com/facts/index.asp

Entertainment Software Rating Board. (2009). *Chronology of ESRB Events.* Retrieved April 11, 2010 from
http://www.esrb.org/about/chronology.jsp

Falk, H. (2004). *Gaming Obsession Throughout Computer History Association.* Retrieved March 15, 2008 from
http://gotcha.classicgaming.gamespy.com.

Graft, K. (2010). Report: Wii Holds 47 Percent Of Global Console Revenue. *Gamasutra.* Retrieved April 11, 2010 from
http://www.gamasutra.com/view/news/27932/Report_Wii_Holds_47_Percent_Of_Global_Console_Revenue.php

Greenpeace. (2010). How The Companies Line Up. *Guide to Greener Electronics.* Retrieved April 13, 2010 from
http://www.greenpeace.org/international/en/campaigns/toxics/electronics/how-the-companies-line-up/

Ha, P. (2009). Nintendo DSi to become ghost hunter. *CrunchGear*. Retrieved April 11, 2010 from http://www.crunchgear.com/2009/05/25/nintendo-dsi-to-become-ghost-hunter/

Harnden. (2004). Video games attract young to Hizbollah. *The Telegraph*. Retrieved March 10, 2008 from http://www.telegraph.co.uk/news/main.jhtml?xml=/news/2004/02/21/whizb21.xml.

Hart, S. (1996). A brief history of home video games. *Geekcomix*. Retrieved March 11, 2008 from http://geekcomix.com/vgh/.

Hormby, T. (2007). History of Handspring and the Treo (Part III). *Silicon User*. Retrieved March 13, 2008 from http://siliconuser.com/?Q=node/19.

Kennedy, S. (2009). Netflix Officially Coming to PS3. *1up.com*. Retrieved March 4, 2010 from http://www.1up.com/do/newsStory?cId=3176634

Kent, S. (2001). *The ultimate history of video games: From Pong to Pokemon—The story behind the craze that touched our lives and changed the world.* New York: Patterson Press.

Libby, B .(2009). Sustainability-Themed Computer Games Come to the Classroom. *Edutopia*. Retrieved April 11, 2010 from http://www.edutopia.org/environment-sustainability-computer-games

Linde, A. (2008). PC games 14% of 2007 retail games sales; World of Warcraft and Sims top PC sales charts. *ShackNews*. Retrieved March 14, 2008 from http://www.shacknews.com/onearticle.x/50939.

Microsoft. (2008). Beyond games. *Xbox*. Retrieved April 9, 2008 from http://www.xbox.com/en-US/hardware/ beyondgames101.htm.

Moon, I., Schneider, M., & Carley, K. (2006). Evolution of player skill in the America's Army game. *Simulation*. *82* (11).

Nintendo. (2008). *What is Wii?*. Retrieved April 9, 2008 from http://www.nintendo.com/wii/what.

Nichols, P. (2010). Personal communication with the author.

Nystedt, D. (2007, September 26). Microsoft's "Halo 3" breaks first-day sales records. *PC World*. Retrieved April 27, 2008 from http://www.pcworld.com/article/id,137737-c,games/article.html.

Peck, M. (2005). Navy video game targets future sailors. *National Defense*. Retrieved March 12, 2008 from http://www.nationaldefensemagazine.org/issues/2005/dec1/Navy_Video.htm.

Peck, M. (2007). Constructive progress. *TSJOnline.com*. Retrieved January 11, 2008 from http://www.tsjonline.com/ story.php?F=3115940.

Peckham, M. (2008). Did Rare Metallic Ore Fuel African "Playstation War"? *PCWorld*. Retrieved April 11, 2010 from http://blogs.pcworld.com/gameon/archives/007340.html

Potter, N. (2008). Game on: A fourth of video game players are over 50. *ABC News*. Retrieved January 19, 2008 from http://abcnews.go.com/WN/Story?id=4132153.

Price, M. (2007, Sept 18). Federal judge strikes down Okla.'s violent video game law. *The Journal Record*.

Schramm, M. (2008). EA Mobile prez: iPhone is hurting mobile game development. *TUAW.com*. Retrieved March 22, 2008 from http://www.tuaw.com/2008/01/08/ea-mobile-prez-iphone-is-hurting-mobile-game-development/.

Smith, B. (1999). Read about the following companies: Nintendo, Sego, Sony. *University of Florida Interactive Media Lab*. Retrieved March 7, 2008 from http://iml.jou.ufl.edu/projects/Fall99/SmithBrian/aboutcompany.html.

Sony. (2008). *About PlayStation 3—Specs*. Retrieved April 9, 2008 from http://www.us.playstation.com/ps3/about/specs.

Stahl, T. (2003). Chronology of the history of videogames. *The History of Computing Project*. Retrieved April 18, 2008 from http://www.thocp.net/software/games/games.htm.

Steam (2010). Steam Realizes Extraordinary Growth in 2009. Press release retrieved March 4, 2010 from http://store.steampowered.com/news/3390/

Stohr (2010). Violent Video Game Law Gets Top U.S. Court Hearing. *Bloomberg BusinessWeek*. Retrieved May 1, 2010 from http://www.businessweek.com/news/2010-04-26/violent-video-game-law-gets-top-u-s-court-hearing-update1-.html

Tabucki, H. (2010). Nintendo to Make 3-D Version of Its DS Handheld Game. *New York Times*. March 23, 2010.

Thorpe, J. (2009). PlayStation 3 Firmware (v3.10) Update Preview. *Playstation.blog*. Retrieved March 4, 2010 from http://blog.eu.playstation.com/2009/11/17/playstation-3-firmware-v3-10-update-preview/

Thorsen, T (2009). Modern Warfare 2 Sells 4.7 million in 24 hours. *GameSpot*. Retrieved February 18, 2010 from http://www.gamespot.com/news/6239789.html

Troast, P. (2009). Vampire Power Check: Comparing the Energy Use of Xbox and Wii. *Energy Circle*. Retrieved April 13, 2010 from http://www.energycircle.com/blog/2009/12/29/vampire-power-check-comparing-energy-use-xbox-and-wii

Vick, K. (2001). Vital Ore Fuels Congo's War. *Washington Post*. March 19, 2001, Pg A01

Wai-Leng, L. (2007, November 16). MDA lifts ban on game with same-sex love scene. *The Straits Times*. Retrieved April 9, 2008 from http://www.straitstimes.com/Latest%2BNews/Singapore/STIStory_177468.html.

Walters, L. (2008). Another one bites the dust. *GameCensorship.com*. Retrieved April 14, 2008 from http://www.gamecensorship.com/okruling.html.

Walters, L. (2010). (untitled page). *GameCensorship.com*. Retrieved March 4, 2010 from http://www.gamecensorship.com/legislation.htm.

Zabek, J. (2009). In-Game Advertising Guidelines Created. *Wargamer.com*. Retrieved March 4, 2010 from http://www.wargamer.com/news/6176/In-Game-Advertising-Guidelines-Created.

15

Home Video

Steven J. Dick, Ph.D.[*]

A t one time, home video limited people to watching live, over-the-air programs. The evolution of home video from simple reception devices to the media centers of today marks a tremendous investment for consumers and media companies alike. Each change in home video has given audiences more power and control, yet at a cost: frequently, old equipment has been abandoned in favor of a new generation of devices.

Background

As technology has improved, it is not enough to simply *receive* video. Increasingly, we have begun to *manipulate* video through storage and editing systems. Finally, *displays* have grown dramatically in quality and picture size. Consumers have aggressively adopted television. Since the 1970s, 97% to 98.9% of U.S. households have owned a television. In addition, the number of televisions per household continues to increase (see Figure 15.1), with an average of 2.8 televisions per household in 2008 (Television Bureau of Adverting, n.d.).

Like so many parts of the communication process, home video involves hardware (e.g., the display and DVD player), software (content), and distribution. The way the consumer receives media content has a great deal to do with business models and media options. There are three basic ways for a home to receive an electronic signal: by air, by conduit, and by hand.

Reception by Air

U.S. commercial television began in 1941 when the Federal Communications Commission (FCC) established a broadcasting standard. Over-the-air television stations were assigned six megahertz (MHz) of bandwidth in the very-high-frequency (VHF) band of the electromagnetic spectrum. Video is encoded using amplitude modulation (same as AM radio), but sound is transmitted the same as it is for FM radio (frequency modulation). Television development virtually stopped during World War II, with only six stations continuing to broadcast. Post-war confusion led to more delays as the FCC was inundated with new applications. After granting 107 licenses with 700 more to process, the FCC initiated a freeze on television applications in 1948 (Whitehouse, 1986). Initially, it was a short pause in processing but the technical demands were daunting. Thus, from 1948 to 1952, there were only about 100 stations on the air nationally.

[*] Media Industry Analyst, Modern Media Barn (Youngsville, Louisiana). The author wishes to gratefully acknowledge the support of the University of Louisiana at Lafayette and Cecil J. Picard Center for Child Development and Lifelong Learning.

Figure 15.1
Televisions per Household

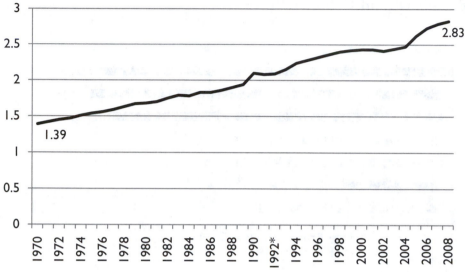

* Adjusted for 1990 Census

Source: Compiled from TVB.org

In 1952, the freeze was over and the FCC formally accepted a plan to add ultra-high-frequency (UHF) television. UHF television transmissions were encoded the same way as VHF, but on a higher frequency. Existing television sets needed a second tuner to receive the new band of frequencies, and new antennas were often needed. This put UHF stations in a second-class status that was almost impossible to overcome. It was not until 1965 that the FCC issued a *final* all-channel receiver law, forcing set manufacturers to include a second tuner for UHF channels. Initially, television was broadcast in black-and-white. In 1953, color was added to the signal by adding color information to the existing (luminance) signal. This meant that color television transmissions were still compatible with black-and-white televisions or what is called reverse compatibility.

Today, around 10% of U.S. households still receive television from traditional terrestrial broadcasting alone. Yet, traditional broadcast networks are an essential part of the media landscape. The four top broadcast networks each still receive a weekly cume audience of 70% to 75% which is approximately double the top cable networks (Television Bureau of Adverting, n.d., See Figure 15.2).

Reception by Conduit

A combination of factors, including the public's interest in television, the FCC freeze on new stations, and the introduction of UHF television, created a market for a new method of television delivery. As discussed in Chapter 7, cable television's introduction in 1949 brought video into homes by wire conduit. At first, cable simply relayed over-the-air broadcast stations. In the 1970s, cable introduced a variety of new channels and expanded home video capability.

Figure 15.2
Weekly Cume Percent
For Top Broadcast and Cable Networks

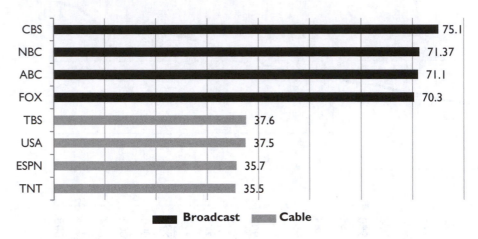

Source: TVB.org

As a closed, wired system, cable television is less prone to interfering with other radio communications. Thus, it can use more frequencies than can be delivered over the air. For example, there is a large gap between VHF channels six and seven. Over-the-air, the gap is used for FM radio stations, aircraft communication, and other purposes. Cable TV companies use the same frequencies for channels 14 through 22 (Baldwin & McVoy, 1986). Other cable channels are generally placed immediately above the over-the-air VHF channels. At first, a set-top box was used to receive the extra channels. Then the industry promoted the creation of "cable-ready" television sets that allowed reception of cable channels. However, the "cable box" has returned as new technology is introduced (e.g., DVR, digital signals).

As capacity grew, program providers answered with new channels for delivery. An analysis of FCC data reveals that a total of 105 national and regional programming networks started operation prior to 1992. The *Cable Consumer Protection and Competion Act of 1992* stimulated growth in multichannel services. By 2002, the number of program networks more than tripled to 344 with the biggest increase (111) between 1997 and 1999 (McDowell & Dick, 2003). From 1996 to 2005, the number of satellite delivered programming networks increased from 145 to 565 (NCTA, 2007).

Reception by Hand

At first, television had to be either live or on film. After Ampex developed videotape for the broadcast industry in 1956, the next logical step was to develop a version of the same device for the home. Sony introduced an open videotape recorder for the home in 1966. Open reel tape players were difficult to use and expensive. Then Sony went on to develop the videocassette recorder (VCR) in 1969. Videocassettes eliminated the need to touch the tape since they allowed the machine to thread it, creating a consumer-friendly, easy-to-handle box for the tape. The first VCRs were expensive, had little to no content, and had a short recording time.

1977 saw the introduction of practical VCRs with competing standards. Sony debuted the Betamax, and JVC introduced a competing standard called VHS. By 1982, a full-blown price and technology war existed between the two formats, and, by 1986, 40% of U.S. homes had VCRs. The two formats competed over available record time and content. Video distributers were forced to distribute content in both formats for a while. Eventually, the VHS format became the standard, and Betamax owners were left with incompatible machines.

VCRs gave consumers new power for on demand programming. They could either rent tapes or record programs off the air. This record capability became the subject of a lawsuit (*Sony v. Universal Studios*, 1984, commonly known as the "Betamax" case), as a wary film industry attempted to protect its rights to control content. However, the U.S. Supreme Court determined that the record and playback capability in the home (time-shifting) was a justifiable use of the VCR. This decision legalized the VCR for home use and helped force the eventual legitimization of the video sales and rental industry. VCR penetration quickly grew from 10% in 1984 to 79% 10 years later. In 2006, the FCC estimated that 90% of television households had at least one VCR (FCC, 2006).

While videotapes were well accepted by consumers, they could be easily damaged and often suffered in quality. In the 1980s, VCRs received a major challenge from two incompatible videodisc formats. RCA's "Selectavision" videodisc player used vinyl records with much smaller grooves to accommodate the larger signal. MCA and Philips introduced a more sophisticated "Discovision" format in 1984 that used a laser to read an optical disc. Selectavision sold a half million units in the first six months and Discovision was sold to Pioneer and renamed "Laserdisc." Despite the higher quality signal, the discs were never accepted in the consumer market. RCA withdrew Selectavision rather quickly. "Laserdisc" was marketed as a high-end video solution. Well over one million players were sold by Pioneer before the format was abandoned in the late 1990s in the face of the emerging DVD format.

Based on the compact audio disc (CD), the DVD (digital videodisc or digital versatile disc) was introduced in 1997 as a mass storage device for all digital content. Bits are recorded in optical format within the plastic disc. Unlike earlier attempts to record video on CDs (called VCDs), the DVD had more than enough capacity to store an entire motion picture in television quality. The first DVDs were disadvantaged by the lack of a record capability. However, they were lighter and more durable than VHS tapes. The nonlinear capability of the DVD made it good for gaming and computer programs while the mass storage allowed motion picture companies to include extra content on the discs such as better quality video, multiple language tracks, and trailers. DVD penetration grew from 6.7% in 1999 to 81.2% by the third quarter of 2006, eclipsing VCR penetration (79.2%) (Gyimesi, 2006). Today, the DVD player is also an easy way to move home video content out of the home as mobile players are more common.

The transition to a high-definition DVD player resulted in an all-out format battle reminiscent of the Beta/VHS competition in consumer videocassettes. Two standards were introduced in 2001. The first, called Blu-ray, was supported by Sony, Hitachi, Pioneer, and six others. The second, called HD-DVD, was supported by Toshiba, NEC, and Microsoft (HDDVD.org, 2003). Unlike the Beta/VHS battle, Sony's product could hold more content (50 GB compared to 30 GB for HD-DVD and 9 GB for standard DVDs). The initial cost for the players was around $500, but fell dramatically into the $250 range as the format war continued (Ault, 2008). Both groups created exclusive deals with major film studios. Warner Brothers delivered a surprising blow at the 2008 Consumer Electronics Show by switching from HD DVD to Sony's Blu-ray. Without content from a major studio like Warner Brothers, HD-DVDs were not going to succeed. Other studios, unhappy with multiple formats soon followed suit. While Toshiba initially vowed to continue to fight, the company gave up within a month.

Video Manipulation

The first manipulation technology was the home video camera. If you track home video back to film, home cameras are much older than television itself. The first practical home camera was introduced in 1923 in the 16-millimeter "Cine Kodak" camera and the "Kodascope Projector" (Eastman Kodak, n.d.). Fifty years later, video manipulation became more practical with the introduction of VCRs. But one big impediment to home video cameras was the image sensor. Professional quality cameras used an expensive and fragile vacuum pick-up tube as the image sensor.

Replacing the pickup tube with a photosensitive chip reduced camera size and fragility and increased reliability. JVC introduced two such cameras in 1976. The cameras weighed just three pounds, but were attached to an outside VCR (at least 16 pounds). In 1982, JVC and Sony introduced the combination "Camcorder," and the true home video industry was born (Consumer Electronics Association, n.d.). Panasonic and Sony introduced the Mini DV camcorder in 1995. The combination of digital video, smaller tapes, flat LCD screens, and chips rather than tubes for optical pickup resulted in smaller, sturdier cameras.

The ultimate downsizing of the camera came in the late 1990s with solid state record devices. Like the MP3 players, this new generation of camera used a small internal memory card. At first, the required memory cards were too small and expensive for effective video recording. Over the next 10 years, the capacity of memory cards increased and prices dropped and home video cameras became more ubiquitous. Since 2005, the greatest growth in the home video market resulted when the video/still camera became a part of the cell phone and online video sharing sites proliferated (see more in Chapter 8).

These cameras also offer easy digital video transfer to personal computers for editing and DVD authoring. Advances made in home video cameras and multimedia computers have been matched by software developments. Both Microsoft (MovieMaker) and Apple (iMovie) have joined a growing field of companies distributing simple to use software designed for home video editing. Amateur content has become more important with online video distribution systems. A growing *prosumer* market, gathering talent between traditional media professionals and amateurs, has had a market impact.

Display

As a fixture in American homes, the history of the television set itself deserves some discussion. The television "set" is appropriately named because it includes *tuner(s)* to interpret the incoming signals and a *monitor* to display the picture. Tuners have changed over the years to accommodate the needs of consumers (e.g., UHF, VHF, cable-ready). Subprocessors were later added to the tuners to interpret signals for closed captioning, automatic color correction, and the V-chip.

The first type of television monitor was the cathode ray tube (CRT). The rectangular screen area of a CRT is covered with lines of phosphors that correspond to the picture elements (pixels) in the image. Color monitors use three streams of electrons, one for each color channel (red, blue, and green). The phosphors glow when struck by a stream of electrons sent from the back of the set. The greater the stream, the brighter the phosphor glows. The pixels combine to form an image.

The first United States color television standard was set by the National Television Standards Committee (NTSC), which called for 525 lines of video resolution with interlaced scanning. Interlacing means that the odd numbered video lines are transmitted first, and then the display transmits the even numbered lines. The whole process takes one-thirtieth of a second (30 frames of video per second). Interlaced lines ensured even brightness of the screen and a better feeling of motion (Hartwig, 2000).

Recent Developments

The most important recent development has been the transition to digital broadcasting (discussed in Chapter 6). While the 2009 economic downturn affected the media industry as much as any other industry, the transition combined with the exciting new digital displays created a perceived need to buy. The Consumer Electronics Association (CEA) reported an industry-wide 7.7% decrease in revenue in 2008 (CEA, 2009), but the penetration of HD displays grew dramatically even if programming was not available (see Figure 15.3). HD displays grew from below 20% penetration in mid-2007 to over 55% in January, 2010. Still, in late 2008, nearly 15% of U.S. households who owned HD displays did not have the ability to receive a single HD channel. Further, it is apparent that consumers chose to purchase a display to add rather than replace. The rush to meet the digital transition deadline corresponded with a growth in multi-set households. Multiset homes increased by 8.7 million from 1996 to 2002 then another 13.8 million from 2003 to 2009.

Figure 15.3
HD Display Sales and HD Displays Lacking Content

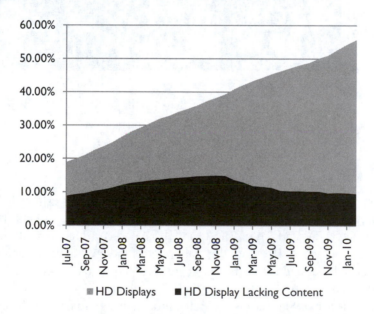

■ HD Displays   ■ HD Display Lacking Content

Source: Compiled from TVB.org

As consumers faced with new equipment choices, competing parts of the multichannel delivery industry attempted to earn a place in their homes. DBS systems began to make serious inroads following the 1992 Cable Act. Then, the Telecommunications Act of 1996 also allowed for a new entrant into the market delivered by telephone companies (Telcos). These newer systems took time to grow and had to work harder for custormers and it was reflected in satifaction surveys. According to the findings of J.D. Power, AT&T U-verse TV and Verison's FIOS TV earned highest customer satisfaction ratings (Spangler, 2009). The new telephone and satellite multichannel providers have consistently outperformed cable television in customer satisfaction. Traditional cable television reached a pentration high of 71% in February of 2001, alternative multichannel services (mainly DBS) grew to 29.3% with all multichannel delivery services reaching 91% by Novemeber of 2009.

In 2006, the International Telecommunications Union set 2015 as a global target for conversion to digital television (ITU, 2006). International manufacturers are working to meet the world's needs. The top manufactures are from Korea and Japan. In 2007, Samsung earned the top position with a 17.7 share in value and 13.3 share of units sold. Second and third place went to Japan's Sony Corporation and Korea's LG Electronics, with market shares of 10.8% and 9.6%, respectively (Lee, 2007).

Figure 15.4

Multichannel Services Penetration

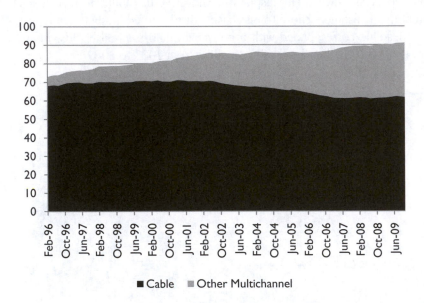

■ Cable   ■ Other Multichannel

Source: Compiled from TVB.org

Digital video recorders (DVRs) have grown from having a fairly small but extremely loyal following to become an important supplemental service for satellite and cable television subscribers. Initial units were marketed under the names ReplayTV and TiVo. The heart of a DVR is a high-capacity hard drive capable of recording 40 or more hours of video. However, the real power of the DVR is the computer brain that controls it. The DVR is able to search out and automatically record favorite programs. Since it is a nonlinear medium, the DVR is able to record and playback at the same time. This ability gives the system the apparent ability to pause (even rewind) live television. Since users can watch programming even as it is being recorded, they have the option to move start times from minutes to days. DVRs increase the ability to skip commercials. As a nonlinear medium, the user can even simply skip ahead 30 seconds. In 2007, 65% of DVR users said they always skip commercials compared with 52% in 2006 (Solutions Research Group, 2007).

In order to identify and record programming, DVRs must be continuously updated with channel lineups and program schedules. As a result, most DVRs are offered as a service that includes a subscription to the program schedules, at a cost that ranges between $5 and $20 a month. However, as it downloads data, the DVR can also upload consumer use data. Use data, such as which shows have been watched and where users have manipulated the programs (e.g., paused or rewound a program), have already been collected, analyzed, and shared by TiVo.

CURRENT STATUS

As the digital market has grown, consumers have more choices than ever when they select a new television. While most digital sets will at least attempt to produce a picture for all incoming signals, some will be better able to than others. CEA suggests five steps in the decision process (CEA, 2007b):

1) Select the right size.

2) Choose an aspect ratio.

3) Select your image quality.

4) Pick a display style.

5) Get the right connection.

New sets are larger than ever, and it is easy to buy too large or small. Even with a high-definition set, if you sit too close, you see too much grain. If you sit too far away, you lose picture quality. The rule of thumb is to measure the distance from the picture to the seat. Divide that distance by three. The product is the smallest set for the room. Divide the distance by two and the product is the largest set for the room (see Figure 15.5).

Figure 15.5
Choosing the Correct Size Television

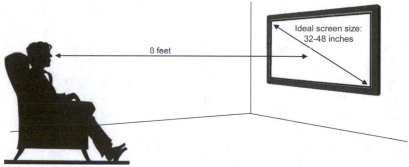

Selecting the right size set for a room is easy using this simple calculation: 1. Measure distance from TV to sitting position. 2. Divide by 2 and then by 3 to get ideal screen size range. The resulting numbers will be the ideal screen sizes. **Example:** Distance = 8 feet (or 96 inches), 96 / 2 = 48" set, 96 / 3 = 32" set, and Ideal set is 32" to 48".

Source: Technology Futures, Inc.

The aspect ratio is changing for high-definition content. Standard definition sets have an aspect ratio of 4:3 or four inches wide for every three inches tall. The new widescreen format is 16:9. Most televisions will attempt to fill the screen with the picture, but the wrong image for the screen distorts or produces a "letterbox" effect. In addition, picture size is a measure of the diagonal distance, and wider screens have proportionally longer diagonals. For example, a 55-inch diagonal set with a 4:3 aspect ratio has 1,452 square inches of picture space. The same 55-inch set with a 16:9 aspect ratio has only 1,296 square inches of picture space. Thus, it is misleading to compare the diagonal picture size on sets with different aspect ratios.

Image quality may be one of the most important choices. People spending more money on a television are expecting a better image. This assumes, however, that content is available in the image quality selected. As digital television content becomes available, there is an increasing variety of resolutions. It is not always easy for a set to display a lower-quality image. CEA has established three quality levels:

◈ *Standard definition* uses 480 lines interlaced. It is most like analog television, but contains the circuitry to convert higher-quality images down to the lower-resolution screen.

◈ *Enhanced definition* sets use 480p or higher. The image more smoothly presents high-definition content because of the progressive scan; it meets the quality of standard DVDs.

◈ *High-definition* pictures are at resolutions of 720p or better. They can display HD content and HD DVDs at full resolution.

While the natural temptation is to assume that 1,080 lines of resolution is better that 720, that may not be the case. There are additional considerations. Signals come in from broadcasters, cablecasters, and others each encoded to various broadcast/production "standards." (See Chapter 6 for more on digital broadcast standards.) The modern video monitor must be able to quickly interpret and display several incoming formats. The monitor is designed to display certain signals best. These are called "native resolutions." All other signals are converted. If a monitor has only 720 lines of resolution, it cannot display 1,080 lines native, and the signal must be converted. Furthermore, due to differences in technologies, even native resolutions can be displayed with unequal clarity. Non-native resolutions can be even worse. *Consumer Reports* indicates some monitors with 720 lines of resolution are better than 1,080 (Consumer Reports, 2008). The key is to choose a set based on the kind of content watched in your home or business. Fast-moving, highly-detailed content (e.g., sports) looks better on some screens, while others are more attuned to movies with brilliant pictures and high contrast.

The major display styles are CRT, plasma, LCD, and projection. Although CRT screens tend to be smaller, they remain the most affordable choice for a bright picture and a wide viewing angle. LCD (liquid crystal display) and plasma are the new flat screen technologies. They take up less floor space and can be mounted like a picture on the wall. LCD displays tend to have a brighter image but a narrower viewing angle. Plasmas have a wider viewing angle but the shiny screens more easily reflect images from the room. Front or rear projection systems offer the best value for very wide images but use an expensive light bulb that must be replaced periodically. Projection systems are best in home theater installations.

Finally, the right connections are essential to transmitting the highest quality image into the set. Analog video connecters will move an image to the monitor, but can severely limit quality. Depending on your video accessories, sets should ideally come with an HDMI input, or IEEE-1394 (Firewire) and/or component jacks. Given the growth of Internet video, a connection to your computer may be desirable.

Most blamed the high-definition DVD format war for the lagging sales in newer DVD systems. Despite the creation of the de facto Blu-ray standard in 2008, DVD sales have not rebounded. The number of Blu-ray players is continuing to rise with Blu-ray player prices having dropped to a level near that of DVD players and Blu-ray playback capability included in all Sony PS3 game consoles. Still, 2009 was the first year since 2002 that people spent more money at the movie theater or on other forms of entertainment acquisition (McBride, 2010). The profitable home video market is clearly being threatened but it is not that bad. First, while the $9.9 billion spent at the theaters is larger than DVD sales or rentals, it is not larger than the $16.9 billion spent on the two combined. In addition, 2009 was the year of expensive technology in the theaters. *Avatar*, the box office smash, claimed the role as the highest grossing movie of all time. However, as Corliss (2010) points out, *Avatar* made 80% of its domestic gross from more expensive 3-D and IMAX tickets.

Figure 15.6
Consumer Spending on Movies (Billions)

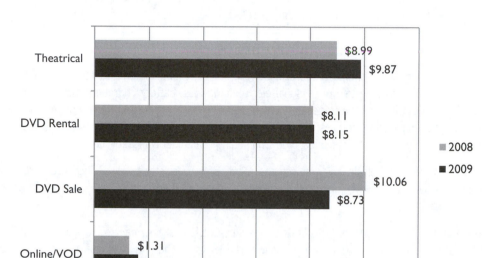

Source: McBride, 2010

In addition, video on demand and other content services are becoming more popular. By the end of 2005, all major multiple system operators (MSOs) were offering VOD services. VOD was offered to digital cable subscribers with some to most of the content free of charge (FCC, 2006). In 2006, Time Warner COO Jeffrey Bewkes challenged cable operators to make all networks available on free, ad-supported VOD in the following year. Bewkes maintained, "I think that the record is clear for 20 years on pay-per-view that that is not the way to maximize usage. It's not really what consumers want" (Farrell, 2006). For more on VOD, see Chapter 7.

Redbox: The relatively new entrant in the home video marketplace; the DVD kiosk is having a huge impact on the market. Strategically placed machines give consumers the opportunity to easily rent the most popular movies for a low nightly rate. It is go to the video store for a large selection and pay $4.95 or the kiosk for one dollar a night. The largest in this sector, Redbox, started in 2002 and claimed 24,000 kiosks in place by the end of 2009. The typical Redbox contains nearly 700 DVDs with up to 200 titles. Customers are charged a dollar a night for the first 25 nights. After that, the DVD is considered sold. Redbox also holds patents on two valuable enhancements. One, allows the user to rent from one Redbox and return to another. The second allows users to reserve movies online or the phone. (Redbox, n.d.)

Redbox pays about $18 for each DVD and rents them up to 15 times. Average revenue from each rental is about two dollars. Currently, it can sell about half of the DVDs back to the wholesaler for about $4 and a small percentage to customers for $7. In addition, there is the cost of the kiosk (close to $1000 for the high tech machine), maintenance, credit card fees, and commission to the store (Vending.com, n.d.). Like everything else in the media, some titles will sell better than others. Many of the DVDs will cycle out of the machine before reaching their necessary 15 rentals. New deals with movie studios will require that Redbox destroy more DVDs rather than selling them, but it is expected that some payment will replace the lost revenue.

Video Kiosks such as Redbox face two major issues, distribution windows and new competition. The movie industry, always trying to earn the most money per movie, is giving preference to DVD sales and more profitable rentals (i.e., Blockbuster, and VOD). At the beginning of 2010, Redbox agreed with most studios to a 28 day delay for its distribution. Competition has entered the market as Redbox has proven the kiosk business model. Most notably, Blockbuster is replacing some of its less performing stores with kiosks of its own – up to 10,000 are promised by the end of 2010 (Lieberman, 2009).

🌍 Sustainability 🌍

The annual energy cost for a single family home is approximately $2,200 and home electronics account for 4% of that cost (EnergyStar, n.d.) . However, the growing use of personal electronic devices, battery chargers, power supplies, and instant-on capability is driving up electric use. The transition to high definition has encouraged the adoption of larger flat screen televisions. As the diagonal dimension doubles, the powered space of the television grows by 4 (geometrically). Three factors determine the amount of electricity used: size; type; and setting (Katzmaer & Moskovciak, 2009).

- Size: While newer televisions are more efficient, larger screens requires more electricity. A 32 inch LCD screen uses about half the electricity as a 52 inch. However, the screen size nearly triples so there it is not a proportional advantage for the smaller screen.

- Type: Plasmas use nearly twice as much electricity as LCDs. In tests by CNET.com (Katzmaer & Moskovciak, 2009), the average LCD uses 176 watts of power while the average plasma uses 338 watts. The projected energy costs of matched 52 inch sets would be $27 for an LCD and $63 for a plasma. In addition, new technology is increasing the efficiency. Most LCDs use a florescent backlight (see section on technology). Some newer LCDs have adopted an array of more efficient light emitting diodes (LED). The LEDs not only use less power than the florescent, LEDs can be turned down dynamically in dark scenes. The most advanced sets use "local dimming" to reduce light use in dark parts of the screens. Local dimming not only saves electricity, it improves reproduction of black and shadow detail (Norton, 2010).

- Settings: It is not surprising that the brighter the screen the more the power. Thus, energy conservation can be achieved by controlling both the physical setting and picture setting. A darker room will allow the set to function at lower light setting and saves power. At least, the set should be placed in a location that avoids direct exposure to either natural or artificial light. Beyond location, picture should be set to the lowest needed brightness and contrast. Other features such as dynamic lighting control (for room light or scene brightness), energy saver modes, and instant on controls can save energy as well. However, all these changes used too aggressively can reduce image fidelity and convenience.

- An Energy Star qualified set means that the television uses about 30% less than standard sets of similar size. The smart buyer should keep aware of the Energy Star standard year. The 2008 standard has scheduled revisions in May of 2010 and 2012.

FACTORS TO WATCH

The future of home video will continue to highlight choices. Digital broadcasting is creating more choices than ever before in display devices. Delivery methods and content choices are also expanding at an equal pace. Content owners are continuing to tweak distribution windows to force extra revenue from the product. At the same time, lower-cost distributers such as Netflix and Redbox kiosk fight, sometimes in court, for the best content as early as possible (Mike, n.d.).

Content distribution has been caught in a nexus of theoretical approaches that may be driving some distribution business models including.

◆ *The Long Tail* (Anderson, 2006) a concept that the virtually unlimited space of the Internet or mail-to-order distribution systems will increase the value of the less popular content. In effect, the mass of less popular content can be more profitable than the major hits.

◆ *Channel repertoire* (Ferguson & Perse, 1993) despite how many choices a person has, consumers tend to return to the same channel selection pattern. It is similar to the double jeopardy effect (McDowell & Dick, 2005) in which consumers are most loyal to the most popular channels, limiting sampling.

Services such as Netflix, and YouTube are favoring a long tail approach. The Netflix Web site boasts more than 100,000 titles for mail delivery and 17,000 for streaming. The long tail model seems justified given the fortunes of brick-and-mortar store competitor Blockbuster, which posted a $435 million loss for the fourth quarter of 2009 (Reisinger, 2010). Blockbuster has failed to succeed with the more limited titles in the physical store and in Netflix virtual environment. As of early 2010, its plan is to close nearly a thousand stores and open kiosks similar to the Redbox kiosks.

Meanwhile, there is reason to believe that consumers select programming in a more limited fashion. First, the Television Bureau of Adverting (n.d.) reports that there is not a direct correlation between channel use and the number of channels subscribed. Based on Nielsen People Meter sample, multichannel subscribers use between 16 and 18 channels no matter how many channels their subscription gives them (see Figure 15.7). In addition, a 2009 study from the Wharton School of Business (Tan & Netessine, n.d.) is being quoted in industry circles (Peoples, 2009). In it, data from Netflix put the Long Tail model in question. The authors conclude that the long tail model is not supported and that hits still drive the rental marketplace.

Figure 15.7
Video Channels Received vs. Channels Used

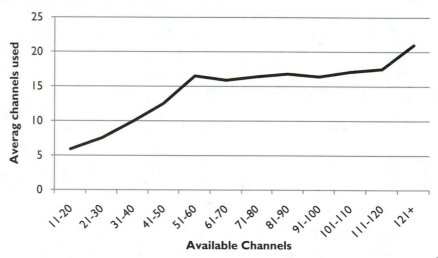

Source: TVB.org

The high definition display is more than ever a significant investment for many households. Differences in technology (discussed above) are only the beginning. Manufacturers are working hard to differentiate their products. Given that HD displays are so much better than previous analog systems, it is difficult to show (much less explain) differences such as shadow detail, refresh rate, and viewing angle. For video enthusiasts new features include:

◆ New interpolation schemes: Higher quality displays create video frames that bridge the motion between existing video frames. From an original 60 hertz frame rate, the system will create additional video frames to make the motion more smooth and reduce perceived flicker. These sets are then marketed as 120 or 240 hertz sets. For presentation of motion pictures shot at 24 frames per second, the display can adapt to that frame rate at/or double it to 48 hertz – reducing flicker or a "video-like" image.

◆ LCD backlight change from florescent to LED: LCD screens require a backlight. Traditional florescent backlights efficiently illuminate the whole screen evenly. The change to LED illumination allows for both brighter and more energy efficient backlighting and (on some displays) local dimming. Local dimming creates better contrast between light and dark areas of the image.

◆ Four color technology: Yellow is a difficult color to produce for the standard red, blue, green color system. Some manufacturers are now marketing an additional yellow channel that they claim allows for better color reproduction.

Other features are easier to communicate but are less about picture quality such as wireless connection, Internet connectivity, personal picture, and music playback. At the 2010 Consumer Electronics Show (CES), the product that made the biggest splash was 3-D TV. The basic concept of 3-D images is to take advantage of the mind's natural ability to process two images (interocular parallax)—one in each eye and knit together a three dimensional representation in the mind. The trick is getting separate images to each eye. This new breed of televisions uses a wireless communication system to synchronize shuttered lens glasses to the television signal. The glasses will shutter fast enough that it is barely noticeable to the user.

Several manufacturers (Sony, Samsung, LG, and Toshiba) displayed 3-D television sets at the CES and one from Panasonic won overall "Best in Show" from CNET.com (Katzmaier, 2010). Cable networks have announced content produced for the new 3-D televisions. Although 3-D television sounds like another potential fad, the International Telecommunications Union (2010) has created a detailed plan for the introduction of 3-D television. The displays introduced at the 2010 CES represent the first-generation out of four planned.

Figure 15.8
Monthly Use of Time Shifted Content (Hours)

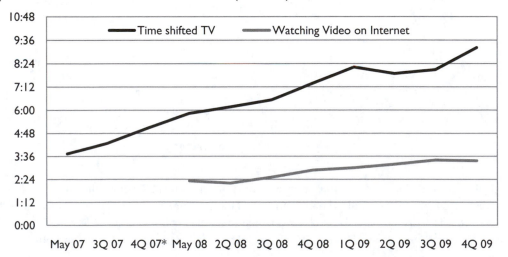

Compiled From: Nielsen 2008, 2009, 2010

The distribution of home video has become hopelessly mixed with the distribution of mobile video. From car DVD players to the new mobile subscription television from Flo TV, the alternate delivery systems are taking up an ever increasing amount of viewing. From May 2007 to the fourth quarter of 2009, consumers use of time shifted content nearly tripled (see Figure 15.8). In addition, Internet viewing increased from about an hour a month. The ultimate goal would be video content that follows its viewer from device to device and location to location. The most active users of online video are people ages 18-24 with an average of nearly six hours a month (5:57). While much of the online viewing is short form (e.g., YouTube, movie trailers), there is a growing consumption of program length content. The inauguration of Barack Obama (and celebration) drew more than 10 million streams (Akamai, 2010). The term "catch up programming" has been attached to online consumption of program length content. The term refers to people using the Internet to see old episodes of shows they missed. Akamai (2010) identifies five areas where online content falls short of broadcast.

- ❖ *Physical* context: computer screen is not as comfortable as home television.

- ❖ Interface: it is not as easy to access online content or change from one program to another.

- ❖ Content: programs are offered after they air on broadcast station or not at all.

- ❖ Image quality: HD is not as available.

- ❖ Performance: the content stops, pauses, or loses quality.

If these issues can be addressed, online media can become much more important in the years to come.

Conclusion

Options are just too enticing as a new generation of home video technologies comes of age. The industry is reading for an age of multiple platforms from the very large home theater to the small mobile device. Which devices and markets will become a success is up to consumers and producers alike. The consumer must accept the platform and the producer must create a business model that will work for everyone.

Bibliography

Akamai. (2010). Akamai Live HD Event, Retrieved March 10, 2010 from http://wwns.akamai.com/hdnetwork/flash/post.hml

Anderson, C. (2006). *The Long Tail: Why the Future of Business Is Selling Less of More.* New York:Hyperion.

Ault, S. (2008, January 21). The format war cost home entertainment in 2007. *Video Business.* Retrieved February 17, 2008 from http://www.videobusiness.com.

Baldwin, T. & McVoy, D. (1986). *Cable communications,* 2nd edition. Englewood Cliffs, NJ: Prentice-Hall.

Consumer Electronics Association. (n.d.). *Camcorders.* Retrieved April 1, 2004 from http://www.ce.org/publications/books_references/digital_america/history/camcorder.asp.

Consumer Electronics Association. (2007). DTV—Consumer buying guide. Retrieved February 17, 2008 from http://www.ce.org/Press/CEA_Pubs/1507.asp.

Consumer Electronics Association. (2009). Retrieved February 22, 2010 from http://www.ce.org/Research/Sales_Stats/default.asp.

Consumer Reports. (2008, March). TV stars. *Consumer Reports,* 18-31.

Corliss, R. (2010). Avatar Ascendant. *Time International* (Atlantic Edition), 175(5), 42-43. Retrieved March 1, 2010 from Academic Search Complete database.

Eastman Kodak Company. (n.d.). Super 8mm film products: History. Retrieved April 4, 2004 from http://www.kodak.com/US/en/motion/super8/history.shtml.

EnergyStar. (n.d.). Televisions for Consumers. Retreived March 10, 2010 from
	http://www.energystar.gov/index.cfm?fuseaction=find_a_product.showProductGroup&pgw_code=TV.

Farrell, M. (2006). Bewkes offers up a free-VOD challenge. *Multichannel News*. Retrieved April 13, 2006 from
	http://www.multichannel.com/article/CA6324236.html?display=Breaking+News.

Federal Communications Commission. (2006). Annual assessment of the status of competition in the market for the delivery of video
	programming. Retrieved March 4, 2006 from http://www.fcc.gov/mb/csrptpg.html.

Ferguson, D., & Perse, E. (1993). Media and audience influences on channel repertoire. Journal of Broadcasting and Electronic Media,
	37Retrieved March 10, 2010 from EBSCO Publishing Citations database.

Gyimesi, K. (2006, December 19). Nielsen study shows DVD players surpass VCRs. Nielsen Media Research. Retrieved March 12, 2008
	from http://www.nielsenmedia.com/.

Hartwig, R. (2000). *Basic TV technology: Digital and Analog*, 3rd edition. Boston: Focal Press.

HDDVD.org. (2003). The different formats. Retrieved April 4, 2004 from http://www.hddvd.org/hddvd/ difformatsblueray.php.

International Telecommunications Union. (2006). Press release on digital terrestrial broadcasting. Retrieved February 17, 2008 from
	http://www.itu.int/newsarchive/press_releases/2006/11.html.

International Telecommunications Union. (2010). Has 3D TV Come of Age? *ITU News*. Retrieved March 1, 2010 from
	http://www.itu.int/net/itunews/issues/2010/02/04.aspx.

Katzmaier, D & M. Moskovciak. (2009). The basics of TV Power. *CNET Reviews*. Retrieved February 10, 2010 from
	http://reviews.cnet.com/green-tech/tv-power-efficiency/.

Katzmaier, D. (2010). Panasonic Makes 3D HD Official with VT25 Plasma TV Series. *CNET.com*. Retrieved March 1, 2010 from
	http://ces.cnet.com/8301-31045_1-10427983-269.html?tag=mncol.

Lee, S. (2007, November 16). Samsung leads in global LCD TV sales. *The Korea Herald*. Retrieved March 15, 2008 from LexisNexis.

Lieberman, D. (2009). DVD kiosks like Redbox have rivals seeing red. *USA Today* updated 8/13/2009. Downloaded April 25, 2010
	from http://www.usatoday.com/tech/products/2009-08-11-rental-dvd-redbox_N.htm.

McBride, S. (2010, January 4). Cinema Surpassed DVD Sales in 2009. *Wall Street Journal - Eastern Edition*, p. B3. Retrieved March 22,
	2010 from Academic Search Complete database.

McDowell, W & Dick, S (2003). Has Lead-in Lost its Punch? *The International Journal on Media Management, Vol. 5*, no. IV. pp.
	285-293.

McDowell, W & Dick, S.(2005). Revealing a Double Jeopardy Effect in Radio Station Audience Behavior. *Journal of Media Econom-
	ics*,18(4),271.

Mike, S. (n.d). Blu-ray is the silver lining among dwindling DVD sales. USA Today, Retrieved from Academic Search Complete data-
	base 3/20/2010.

National Cable and Telecommunications Association. (2007). *National video programming*. Retrieved February 18, 2008 from
	http://www.ncta.org/Statistic/Statistic/NationalVideoProgramming.aspx

Nielsen. (2008). A2/M2 Three Screen Report: 3rd Quarter 2008. Retrieved March 1, 2010 from http://en-
	us.nielsen.com/sitelets/landing/a2m2/a2m2_h.html.

Nielsen. (2009). A2/M2 Three Screen Report: 3rd Quarter 2009. Retrieved March 1, 2010 from http://en-
	us.nielsen.com/sitelets/landing/a2m2/a2m2_h.html.

Nielsen. (2010). A2/M2 Three Screen Report: 1st Quarter 2010. Retrieved March 20, 2010 from http://en-
	us.nielsen.com/sitelets/landing/a2m2/a2m2_h.html.

Norton, T.J. (2010). Flat-Panel HDTVs. Home Theater: 2010Buyer's Guide. Pp6-8.

Peoples, G. (2009). Research Conflicts with 'Long Tail." *The Hollywood Reporter*. Retrieved March 20, 2010 from
	http://www.hollywoodreporter.com/hr/content_display/technology/news/e3i87c96b4228796e1d8b1edfbcc98a4738.

Redbox.com (n.d.). History of Redbox. Download April, 24, 2010 from
	http://redboxpressroom.com/factsheets/TheHistoryofRedbox.pdf.

Reisinger, D. (2010). Trouble Ahead: Blockbuster posts $435 million loss. *Cnet News*. Retrieved March 20, 2010 from
	http://news.cnet.com/8301-13506_3-10459637-17.html?part=rss&subj=news&tag=2547-1_3-0-20

Spangler, T. (2009). Satellite, Telcos Beat Cable on TV Satisfaction, *Multichannel News*. Retrieved March 10, 2010 from
	http://www.multichannel.com/article/357001-Satellite_Telcos_Beat_Cable_On_TV_Satisfaction_J_D_Power.php.

Solutions Research Group. (2007). Digital life America. Retrieved March 1, 2008 from http://www.srgnet.com/us/ programs.html.

Television Bureau of Adverting. (n.d.). Media Trends Track. Retrieved February 20, 2010 from http://tvb.org/nav/build_frameset.aspx.

Tan, T & S. Netessine. (n.d.). Is Tom Cruise Threatened? Using Netflix Prize Data to Examine Long Tail Commerce. Retrieved March
	15, 2010 from http://opim.wharton.upenn.edu/~netessin/TanNetessine.pdf.

Vending.com (n.d.). Vending Machine Business. Downloaded April 25th, 2010 from
	http://www.vending.com/Business_Outlook/Vending_Machine_Business/ and related pages.

Whitehouse, G. (1986). *Understanding the new technologies of mass media*. Englewood Cliffs, NJ: Prentice-Hall.

16

Digital Audio

Ted Carlin, Ph.D.[*]

n her report, *The State of Music Online: Ten Years after Napster*, Mary Madden of the Pew Internet and American Life Project sums up today's digital consumer,

> As more and more Internet users acquire smart phones and high-speed wireless connectivity improves, music consumers get ever closer to the "celestial jukebox" dream of any song at any time that started during the days of Napster. For now, quality and reliability are still an issue, but the march of technology will quickly stomp out that minor hurdle. Ultimately, whether you're storing a library of music files on your home computer or streaming songs through your iPhone, it all becomes the same: instant access to the music you want (Madden, 2009, p. 16).

The last few years have included technological developments that have given consumers compelling reasons to buy products that enhance their passion for listening to music—the passion that launched the hi-fi industry in the 1950s. From digital media player/wireless phone convergence to solid-state disk (SSD) devices, audio innovation is creating a new breed of audio consumer. Today, most audio consumers listen to music as background in the home while engaged in other activities, and serious music listening is more likely to be done in the car or on-the-go outside the car and home. In addition, thousands of theatrical DVDs and hundreds of electronic games exist in surround- and high-quality sound (Dolby Labs, 2010).

As a result, convenience, portability, and sound quality, re-energized the audio industry for the 21st century. Competition, regulation, innovation, and marketing will continue to shape and define this exciting area of communication technology.

Background

Analog Versus Digital

Analog means "similar" or "a copy." An analog audio signal is an electronic copy of an original audio signal as found in nature, with a continually varying signal. Analog copies of any original sound suffer some degree of signal degradation, called generational loss, and signal strength lessens and noise increases for each

---

[*] Professor, Department of Communication/Journalism, Shippensburg University (Shippensburg, Pennsylvania).

successive copy. However, in the digital domain, this noise and signal degradation can be eliminated (Watkinson, 1988).

Encoding. In a digital audio system, the original sound is encoded in binary form as a series of 0 and 1 "words" called bits. The process of encoding different portions of the original sound wave by digital words of a given number of bits is called "pulse code modulation" (PCM). This means that the original sound wave (the modulating signal, i.e., the music) is represented by a set of discrete values. In the case of music CDs using 16-bit words, there are 2^{16} word possibilities (65,536). The PCM tracks in CDs are represented by 2^{16} values, and hence, are digital. First, 16 bits are read for one channel, and then 16 bits are read for the other channel. The rest are used for data management. The order of the bits in terms of whether each bit is on (1) or off (0) is a code for one tiny spot on the musical sound wave (Watkinson, 1988). For example, a word might be represented by the sequence 1001101000101001. In a way, it is like Morse code, where each unique series of dots and dashes is a code for a letter of the alphabet (see Figure 15.1).

Sampling and quantizing. Digital audio systems do not create exact bit word copies of the entire original continuous sound wave. Instead, depending on the equipment used to make the digital copy, various samples of the original sound wave are taken at given intervals using a specified sampling rate to create a discrete digital wave (Alten, 2010). The established sampling rates for digital audio are:

◆ 32 kHz for broadcast digital audio.

◆ 44.1 kHz for CDs.

◆ 48 kHz for digital audiotape (DAT) and digital videotape (mini-DV and DV).

◆ 96 kHz or 192.4 kHz for DVD-audio and BD-ROM (Blu-ray disc) audio.

◆ 2.8224 MHz for SACD (Super Audio CD) and DSD (Direct Stream Digital).

These samples are then quantized at a specific bit level (16-bit, 32-bit, etc.); the higher the bit level, the higher the quality of the digital reproduction.

Figure 15.1
Analog Versus Digital Recording

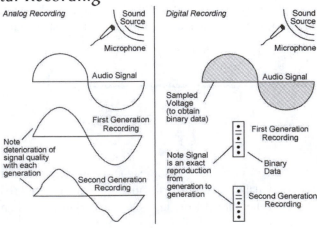

Source: Focal Press

File formats and codecs. Once the signal is digitized, sampled, and quantized, the digital signal can be subjected to further processing—in the form of audio data compression—to reduce the size of the digitized audio file even further. This is similar to "zipping" a text file to more easily send it as an attachment to an e-mail. However, there are file formats that do not require reduction and remain uncompressed. These include audio files stored on CDs and DV tape, as well as audio files stored as .AIFF or .WAV. Some file formats, including QuickTime and DVD-Audio, can be compressed or uncompressed.

Audio compression algorithms are typically referred to as *audio codecs*. As with other specific forms of digital data compression, there exist many "lossless" and "lossy" formulas to achieve the compression effect (Alten, 2010). Lossless compression works by encoding repetitive pieces of information with symbols and equations that take up less space, but provide all the information needed to reconstruct an exact copy of the original. As file storage and communications bandwidth have become less expensive and more available, the popularity of lossless formats has increased, as people are choosing to maintain a permanent archive of their audio files. The primary users of lossless compression are audio engineers, audiophiles, and those consumers who want to preserve the full quality of their audio files, in contrast to the quality loss from lossy compression techniques such as MP3.

Lossy compression works by discarding unnecessary and redundant information (sounds that most people cannot hear) and then applying lossless compression techniques for further size reduction. With lossy compression, there is always some loss of fidelity that becomes more noticeable as the compression ratio is increased. (That is why the audio quality of MP3s and other file formats are compared to the lossless audio quality of CDs.) The goal then becomes producing sound where the losses are not noticeable, or noticeable but not annoying. Unfortunately for consumers, there is no one standard audio codec. As is discussed later in this chapter, several companies are battling it out in the marketplace. Table 16.1 provides a list of the major codecs in use in 2010.

Copyright Legislation, Cases & Actions

With this ever-increasing ability to create and distribute an indefinite number of exact copies of an original sound wave through digital reproduction comes the incumbent responsibility to prevent unauthorized copies of copyrighted audio productions and safeguard the earnings of performers and producers. Before taking a closer look at the various digital audio technologies in use, a brief examination of important legislative efforts and resulting industry initiatives involving this issue of digital audio reproduction is warranted.

AUDIO HOME RECORDING ACT OF 1992

The *Audio Home Recording Act (AHRA) of 1992* exempts consumers from lawsuits for copyright violations when they record music for private, noncommercial use and eases access to advanced digital audio recording technologies. The law also provides for the payment of modest royalties to music creators and copyright owners, and mandates the inclusion of the Serial Copying Management Systems (SCMS) in all consumer digital audio recorders to limit multigenerational audio copying (i.e., making copies of copies). This legislation also applies to all future digital recording technologies, so Congress is not forced to revisit the issue as each new product becomes available (HRRC, 2000).

Table 15.1
Popular Audio Codecs

Codec	Developer	Date	Compression Type
AAC	MPEG	2002	lossy
AACplus or HE-ACC	MPEG	2003	lossy
AIFF	Electronic Arts/Apple	1985	uncompressed
ALAC	Apple	2004	lossless
AU	Sun	1992	uncompressed
FLAC	Xiph.org	2003	lossless
LAME	Cheng/Taylor	1998	Lossy
Monkey's Audio	M. Ashland	2002	lossless
MP3	Thomson/Fraunhofer	1992	lossy
MP3 Pro	Thomson/Fraunhofer	2001	lossy
MP3 Surround	Thomson/Fraunhofer	2004	lossy
Musepak	Buschmann/Klemm	1997	lossy
SDII (Sound Designer II)	Digidesign	1997	lossless
SHN (Shorten)	T.Robinson/W. Stielau	1993	lossless
Speex	Xiph.org	2003	lossy
Vorbis (Ogg Vorbis)	C. Montgomery/Xiph.org	2002	lossy
TTA (True Audio)	Alexander Djourik	2007	lossless
VoxWare MetaSound	A. Penry	2004	lossy
WavPack	D. Bryant	1998	lossless
WMA (Windows Media Audio)	Microsoft	2000	lossy
WMA Lossless	Microsoft	2003	lossless

Source: T. Carlin

Multipurpose devices, such as personal computers, CD-ROM drives, or other computer peripherals, are not covered by the AHRA. This means that the manufacturers of these devices are not required to pay royalties or incorporate SCMS protections into the equipment. It also means, however, that neither the manufacturers of the devices, nor the consumers who use them, receive immunity from copyright infringement lawsuits (*AHRA*, 1992).

THE DIGITAL PERFORMANCE RIGHT IN SOUND RECORDINGS ACT OF 1995

This law (*Digital Performance Right in Sound Recordings Act*, 1996) allows copyright owners of sound recordings to authorize certain digital transmissions of their works, including interactive digital audio transmissions, and to be compensated for others. This right covers, for example, interactive services, digital cable audio services, satellite music services, commercial online music providers, and future forms of electronic delivery. Most non-interactive transmissions are subject to statutory licensing at rates to be negotiated or, if necessary, arbitrated.

Exempt from this law are traditional radio and television broadcasts and subscription transmissions to businesses. The bill also confirms that existing mechanical rights apply to digital transmissions that result in a specifically identifiable reproduction by or for the transmission recipient, much as they apply to record sales.

NO ELECTRONIC THEFT LAW (NET ACT) OF 1997

The *No Electronic Theft Law* (the NET Act) states that sound recording infringements (including by digital means) can be criminally prosecuted even where no monetary profit or commercial gain is derived from the infringing activity. Punishment in such instances includes up to three years in prison and/or $250,000 in fines. The NET Act also extends the criminal statute of limitations for copyright infringement from three to five years.

Additionally, the NET Act amended the definition of "commercial advantage or private financial gain" to include the receipt (or expectation of receipt) of anything of value, including receipt of other copyrighted works (as in MP3 trading). Punishment in such instances includes up to five years in prison and/or $250,000 in fines. Individuals may also be civilly liable, regardless of whether the activity is for profit, for actual damages or lost profits, or for statutory damages up to $150,000 per work infringed (*NET Act*, 1997).

DIGITAL MILLENNIUM COPYRIGHT ACT OF 1998

On October 28, 1998, the *Digital Millennium Copyright Act* (DMCA) became law. The main goal of the DMCA was to make the necessary changes in U.S. copyright law to allow the United States to join two new World Intellectual Property Organization (WIPO) treaties that update international copyright standards for the Internet era.

The DMCA amends copyright law to provide for the efficient licensing of sound recordings for Webcasters and digital subscription audio services via cable and satellite. In this regard, the DMCA:

◆ Makes it a crime to circumvent anti-piracy measures (i.e., digital rights management technology) built into most commercial software.

◆ Outlaws the manufacture, sale, or distribution of code-cracking devices used to illegally copy software.

◆ Permits the cracking of copyright protection devices, however, to conduct encryption research, assess product interoperability, and test computer security systems.

◆ Provides exemptions from anti-circumvention provisions for nonprofit libraries, archives, and educational institutions under certain circumstances.

◆ In general, limits Internet service providers from copyright infringement liability for simply transmitting information over the Internet. Service providers, however, are expected to remove material from users' Web sites that appear to constitute copyright infringement.

◆ Limits liability of nonprofit institutions of higher education—when they serve as online service providers and under certain circumstances—for copyright infringement by faculty members or students.

◆ Calls for the U.S. Copyright Office to determine the appropriate performance royalty, retroactive to October 1998.

◆ Requires that the Register of Copyrights, after consultation with relevant parties, submit to Congress recommendations regarding how to promote distance education through digital technologies while maintaining an appropriate balance between the rights of copyright owners and the needs of users (U.S. Copyright Office, 2010).

The DMCA contains the key agreement reached between the Recording Industry Association of America (RIAA) and this coalition of non-interactive Webcasters (radio stations broadcasting on the Web), cablecasters (DMX, MusicChoice, Muzak), and satellite radio service (Sirius XM). It provides for a simplified licensing system for digital performances of sound recordings on the Internet, cable, and satellite. This part of the DMCA provides a compulsory license for non-interactive and subscription digital audio services with the primary purpose of entertainment. Such a compulsory licensing scheme guarantees these services access to music without obtaining permission from each and every sound recording copyright owner individually, and assures record companies an efficient means to receive compensation for sound recordings. This is similar to ASCAP and BMI compulsory licensing for music used on radio and television stations.

The U.S. Copyright Office designated a nonprofit organization, SoundExchange, to administer the performance right royalties arising from digital distribution via subscription services. Once rates and terms are set, SoundExchange collects, administers, and distributes the performance right royalties due from the licensees to the record companies (SoundExchange.com, 2010). Of the performance royalties allocated to the record companies, the DMCA states that half of the royalties are distributed to the copyright holder of the song. The other half must be distributed to the artists performing the song. SoundExchange only covers performance rights, not music downloads or interactive, on-demand Internet services. These are governed by the reproduction rights in sound recordings of the Copyright Act, are not subject to the DMCA compulsory license, and must be licensed directly from the copyright owner, usually the record company or artist.

All of this now leaves an artist with three types of copyright protection to consider for one piece of music, depending on how it is used:

◆ Traditional compulsory license via ASCAP, BMI, or SESAC for music broadcast on AM and FM radio stations.

◆ DMCA compulsory license via SoundExchange for music digitally distributed on Webcasts and cable or satellite subscription services.

◆ Voluntary (or direct) license via an individually-negotiated agreement for music to be downloaded on the Internet from a Web site or an Internet jukebox; used in a movie, TV program, video, or commercial; or used in a compilation CD.

DIGITAL RIGHTS MANAGEMENT

Digital rights management (DRM), as mentioned in the *Digital Millennium Copyright Act*, is the umbrella term referring to any of several technologies used to enforce predefined policies controlling access to software, music, movies, or other digital data. In more technical terms, DRM handles the description, layering, analysis, valuation, trading, and monitoring of the rights held over a digital work (U.S. Copyright Office, 2010). Some digital media content publishers claim DRM technologies are necessary to prevent revenue loss due to illegal duplication of their copyrighted works. However, others argue that transferring control of the use of media from consumers to a consolidated media industry will lead to loss of existing user rights and stifle innovation in software and cultural productions.

The two most prominent digital audio DRM technologies are Apple's Fairplay (for iBook e-books and non-music iTunes content) and Microsoft's Windows Media DRM (WMDRM). Some of the other popular DRM technologies in use today include Advanced Access Content System (AACS) used by Blu-ray discs, Content Protection for Prerecorded Media (CPPM) used in DVD-Audio, High-Bandwidth Digital Content Protection (HDCP), and OpenMobile Alliance (OMA) for mobile phones (Wilson, 2009).

MGM VERSUS GROKSTER

Although there has been a constant debate in all three of these copyright areas, it is the copyright protection pertaining to Internet music downloading that has led to the most contentious arguments. On June 27, 2005, the U.S. Supreme Court ruled unanimously against peer-to-peer (P2P) file-sharing service providers Grokster and Streamcast Networks (developers of Morpheus). The landmark decision in *MGM Studios, Inc. v. Grokster, Ltd.* (545 U. S. 125 S. Ct. 2764, 2005) was a victory for the media industry and a blow to P2P companies. At the same time, the decision let stand the main substance of the Supreme Court's landmark "Beta-max" ruling (*Sony Corp. of America v. Universal City Studios*, 1984), which preserved a technologist's ability to innovate without fear of legal action for copyright infringement, and which the media industry sought to overturn.

The Supreme Court found that technology providers should be held liable for infringement if they *actively promote* their wares as infringement tools. Writing for the court, Justice David Souter stated, "We hold that one who distributes a device with the object of promoting its use to infringe copyright, as shown by clear expression or other affirmative steps taken to foster infringement, is liable for the resulting acts of infringement by third parties" (*MGM Studios, Inc. v. Grokster, Ltd.*, 2005, p. 1).

The decision created a new theory of secondary infringement liability based on "intent to induce" infringement, which now extends the existing theory of contributory liability (knowingly aiding and abetting infringement). This inducement concept is derived from an analogous and established theory in patent law (Kalinsky & Sebald, 2005). Again, technology inventors must promote the illegal use of the product to be found liable:

> ...mere knowledge of infringing potential or of actual infringing uses would not be enough here to subject a [technology] distributor to liability.... The inducement rule, instead, premises liability on purposeful, culpable expression and conduct, and thus does nothing to compromise legitimate commerce or discourage innovation having a lawful promise (*MGM v. Grokster*, 2005, p. 19).

The effect of this decision on illegal P2P downloading has been mixed. The decision remanded the case back to the Ninth Circuit Court of Appeals and cleared the way for a trial that could have lasted years. However, both Grokster and StreamCast reached out-of-court settlements with the record companies. Grokster agreed to end operations and pay a $50 million settlement, while StreamCast agreed to a $100 million settlement and to the installation of filters that prevent music file sharing by Morpheus users (Mark, 2006).

Overall, this decision does not mean that P2P services have shut down altogether—as of mid-2010, Morpheus is still active, and many P2P services without previous marketing efforts are flourishing on the Internet, including The Pirate Bay, Oink, LimeWire, BearShare, and eDonkey.

U.S. DEPARTMENT OF JUSTICE OPERATIONS & RIAA LAWSUITS

The DOJ's Computer Crimes and Intellectual Property Section (CCIPS) is responsible for coordinating and investigating violations of the *U.S. Copyright Act*, the *Digital Millennium Copyright Act*, and other cyber laws discussed earlier in this chapter. The CCIPS, along with the Federal Bureau of Investigation's (FBI's) Cyber Division and numerous state Attorneys General, have been actively monitoring and investigating illegal operations associated with digital audio and copyright violations since 2004, namely through *Operation Buccaneer* ("warez" group copyright piracy), *Operation Fastlink* (international intellectual property piracy), *Operation Phish Phry* (phishing for personal information), *Operation Digital Gridlock* (P2P copyright piracy), and *Operation Site Down* (international intellectual property and organized crime).

In February 2010, the DOJ created a new Task Force on Intellectual Property as part of its initiative to crack down on the growing number of domestic and international intellectual property crimes. The purpose of the task force is to help prosecutors implement a "multi-faceted strategy" that involves federal, state and international law enforcement agencies (Department of Justice, 2010). The task force is expected to increase the department's focus on the international aspect of intellectual property law enforcement, particularly the links between intellectual property crime and organized crime. It will work closely with the recently established Office of the Intellectual Property Enforcement Coordinator (IPEC), housed in the Office of the President. The IPEC has been charged with drafting an administration-wide strategic plan on intellectual property enforcement.

The RIAA and several of its member record companies provide assistance to the DOJ and FBI in their investigations. The legal issues surrounding digital audio are not limited to file sharing networks. The RIAA assists authorities in identifying music pirates and shutting down their operations. In piracy cases involving the Internet, the RIAA's team of Internet specialists, with the assistance of a Danish-based anti-piracy firm, DtecNet, helps stop Internet sites that make illegal recordings available.

Based on the *Digital Millennium Copyright Act*'s expedited subpoena provision, the RIAA sends out information subpoenas as part of an effort to track and shut down repeat offenders and to deter those hiding behind the perceived anonymity of the Internet. Information subpoenas require the Internet service provider (ISP) providing access to or hosting a particular site to provide contact information for the site operator. Once the site operator is identified, the RIAA takes steps to prevent repeat infringement. Such steps range from a warning e-mail to litigation against the site operator. The RIAA then uses that information to send notice to the operator that the site must be removed. Finally, the RIAA requires the individual to pay an amount designated to help defray the costs of the subpoena process (RIAA, 2010).

Digital Audio Technologies

DIGITAL AUDIOTAPE

Digital audiotape (DAT) is a recording medium that spans the technology gulf between analog and digital. On one hand, it uses tape as the recording medium; on the other, it stores the signal as digital data in the form of numbers to represent the audio signals. DAT has not been very popular outside of professional and semi-professional audio and music recording, although the prospect of perfect digital copies of copyrighted material was sufficient for the music industry in the United States to force the passage of the *Audio Home Recording Act of 1992*, creating the "DAT tax" (Alten, 2010).

COMPACT DISC

In the audio industry, nothing has revolutionized the way we listen to recorded music like the compact disc. Originally, engineers developed the CD solely for its improvement in sound quality over LPs and analog cassettes. After the introduction of the CD player, consumers became aware of the quick random-access characteristic of the optical disc system. In addition, the size of the 12-cm (about five-inch) disc was easy to handle compared with the LP. The longer lifetime of both the medium and the player strongly supported the acceptance of the CD format. The next target of development was the rewritable CD. Sony and Philips jointly developed this system and made it a technical reality in 1989. Two different recordable CD systems were established. One is the write-once CD named CD-R, and the other is the re-writable CD named CD-RW (Alten, 2010).

MP3

Before MP3 came onto the digital audio scene, computer users were recording, downloading, and playing high-quality sound files using an uncompressed codec called .WAV. The trouble with .WAV files, however, is their enormous size. A two-minute song recorded in CD-quality sound uses about 20 MB of a hard drive in the .WAV format. That means a 10-song CD would take more than 200 MB of disk space.

The file-size problem for music downloads has changed, thanks to the efforts of the Moving Picture Experts Group (MPEG), a consortium that develops open standards for digital audio and video compression. Its most popular standard, MPEG, produces high-quality audio (and full-motion video) files in far smaller packages than those produced by .WAV. MPEG filters out superfluous information from the original audio source, resulting in smaller audio files with no perceptible loss in quality. On the other hand, .WAV spends just as much data on superfluous noise as it does on the far more critical dynamic sounds, resulting in huge files (Alten, 2010).

Since the development of MPEG, engineers have been refining the standard to squeeze high-quality audio into ever-smaller packages. MP3—short for MPEG 1 Audio Layer 3—is the most popular of three progressively more advanced codecs, and it adds a number of advanced features to the original MPEG process. Among other features, Layer 3 uses entropy encoding to reduce to a minimum the number of redundant sounds in an audio signal. The MP3 codec can take music from a CD and shrink it by a factor of 12, with no perceptible loss of quality (Digigram, 2010).

To play MP3s, a computer-based or portable digital audio player is needed. Hundreds of portable digital audio players are available, from those with 512 MB flash drives to massive 160 GB hard drive-based models. They are sold by manufacturers such as Apple, Archos, Creative, Microsoft, and Philips. The amount of available disc space is most relative to the way a person uses the portable player, either as a song selector or song shuffler. Song selectors tend to store all of their music on players with larger drives and select individual songs or playlists as desired, whereas song shufflers are more likely to load a group of songs on a smaller drive and let the player shuffle through selections at random.

Dozens of computer-based digital audio players are available for download. Winamp, still the most popular, sports a simple, compact user interface that contains such items as a digital readout for track information and a sound level display. This user interface can be customized by using "skins," small computer files that let the user change the appearance of the digital audio player's user interface.

Another intriguing part of the MP3 world is the CD ripper. This is a program that extracts—or rips—music tracks from a CD and saves them onto a computer's hard drive as .WAV files. This is legal as long as the MP3s created are solely for personal use, *and* the CDs are owned by the user. Once the CD tracks have been ripped to the hard drive, the next step is to convert them to the MP3 format. An MP3 encoder is used to turn .WAV files into MP3s.

All the copyright laws that apply to vinyl records, tapes, and CDs also apply to MP3s. Just because a person is downloading an MP3 of a song on a computer rather than copying it from someone else's CD does not mean he or she is not breaking the law. Prosecution of violators, through the efforts of the RIAA, is the recording industry's main effort to prevent unauthorized duplication of digital audio using MP3 technology.

The first era in Internet audio has undeniably belonged to the MP3 codec, the audio standard codified by MPEG 14 years ago. France's Thomson and Germany's Fraunhofer Institute for Integrated Circuits IIS, the companies that hold the patents for the MP3 technology, have long been licensing and collecting royalties from software and hardware companies that use the codec (Thomson, 2010).

Competing with MP3, Microsoft, with its own digital audio codec, Windows Media Audio (WMA), has been a beneficiary of a similar type of interoperability. WMA is being used in hundreds of different devices and by AOL MusicNow, Musicmatch, Napster, PassAlong, Wal-Mart, and other distributors (Microsoft, 2010).

In April 2004, Apple Computer incorporated MPEG-4 Advanced Audio Coding (AAC) into QuickTime, iTunes, and iPod portable music players. AAC was developed by the MPEG group that includes Dolby, Fraunhofer, AT&T, Sony, and Nokia. The AAC codec builds upon signal processing technology from Dolby Laboratories and brings true variable bit rate (VBR) audio encoding to QuickTime and the iPod, which will now support AAC, MP3, MP3 VBR, Audible, AIFF, and WAV codecs.

This created a struggle—or opportunity for collaboration—among the primary players in the digital download arena. However, rather than develop a universal standard under the SDMI banner, companies have been taking their technology to the marketplace to let consumers decide (Hydrogenaudio, 2008). The big winner, without a doubt, continues to be Apple. For example, with sales of its iPod music players at 10.2 million in the fourth fiscal quarter of 2009, Apple reported the highest quarterly revenue ($9.87 billion) in the company's history. Apple shipped more than 22 million iPods during this period (Apple, 2009). Much of the credit has been given to the iPhone and the diversity of iPod models introduced since 2005, including the iPod touch, video iPods, and lower priced iPod shuffles.

WIRELESS DIGITAL MEDIA

Another interesting digital audio development has been the development of the wireless digital media player. The first use for a wireless digital media player was fairly obvious: transferring music without physically connecting the player to a computer. This change is certainly convenient, but as wireless connections become common for MP3 players, the sky is (literally) the limit in terms of where your music can come from.

Mobile phone companies, looking to extend their reach even further, are taking the wireless digital media concept to the next level. In March 2009, Europe's largest mobile phone operator, Vodafone, joined forces with the world's largest record companies (Universal Music Group, Sony Music Entertainment and EMI Music) to offer DRM-free digital music tracks and albums across Vodafone markets for both mobile phones and computers. A key feature of the Vodafone service is that customers will be able to buy and play music bought from these three labels via the Vodafone Music store without any limit to the type of device used (Grill, 2009). More than one million music tracks are currently available for download through agreements with these music labels.

In the United States, Verizon offers its V CAST Music Service, an online music store where customers can download DRM-free MP3s and WMA songs directly to their V CAST-enabled phones. Additionally, by subscribing to V CAST Music Service with Rhapsody (at $14.99/month) Verizon customers can purchase and synch new songs or albums from the V CAST Music with Rhapsody music catalog (Verizon Wireless, 2010).

HARD-DISK JUKEBOX DIGITAL MEDIA PLAYERS

With computer hard drive prices steadily falling since 2002, and with computer technology becoming more crash-resistant and portable, manufacturers are rapidly producing portable digital players that use expansive hard drives (1.5 GB to 160 GB) as their recording media. The number of companies offering these multimedia jukeboxes rose from 30 in 2004 to more than 150 in 2010, with the leaders being the Apple iPod, the Microsoft Zune, and the Creative Nomad Zen (Hard drive MP3, 2008). Storing music in MP3, AAC, or WMA, these devices archive both video and audio, accessible by album title, song title, artist name, or music genre.

Some of the players include modems to download music from Web sites without the assistance of a PC. Some deliver streaming audio content from the Web to connected AV systems. For superior sound quality, the devices can be connected to broadband modems. Some hard-drive players also come with a built-in CD player, making it possible to rip songs from discs for transfer to the hard drive. Next-generation jukeboxes from Archos and Cowon are marketed as portable media players (PMPs) capable of displaying MPEG and MPEG-4 video, streamed video content, JPEG pictures, MP3, MP3Pro, and WMA audio files (MP3.com, 2010).

PODCASTING

Podcasting is the distribution of audio or video files, such as radio programs or music videos, over the Internet using RSS (really simple syndication) for listening on mobile devices and personal computers (Podcast Alley, 2010). A podcast is basically a Web feed of audio or video files placed on the Internet for anyone to download or subscribe to. Podcasters' Web sites may also offer direct download of their files, but the subscription feed of automatically delivered new content is what distinguishes a podcast from a simple download or real-time streaming. A quick search of the Internet will uncover a myriad of content that is available—and accumulating daily.

Recent Developments

Copyright Legislation, Cases & Actions

Not waiting for Congress to act, several record companies, supported by the RIAA, filed a lawsuit, *Atlantic Recording Corporation et al. v. XM Satellite Radio, Inc.* (2007), in U.S. District Court of Southern New York. The lawsuit claimed that XM Radio was operating as both a broadcaster and a digital download subscription service by allowing devices such as the Pioneer Inno to record blocks of XM Radio programming, which then could be sorted through, reorganized, and listened to by users at a later time. It argued that XM Radio was not authorized to "distribute" music in this "disaggregation" method under its license agreement, and that XM Radio was actually competing unfairly with the music companies in the sale of digital music downloads. The suit contended that XM's "librarying function…does not have substantial or commercially significant *non-infringing uses*" that might protect it under *AHRA* and *MGM v. Grokster* (*Atlantic Recording*, 2007, p. 18).

After a failed attempt to have the lawsuit dismissed, XM Radio initiated discussions with the record companies to settle the dispute. By 2009, the four major record labels (EMI, Sony BMG Music, Universal Music

Group, Warner Brothers Records) participating in the lawsuit reached multi-year settlement agreements with XM Radio to allow its programming to be disaggregated by users on compatible devices (Kawamato, 2008).

The *Performance Rights Act*, a bill sponsored by Rep. John Conyers (D-MI), was successfully voted out of committee to the full House of Representatives in May 2009 (GovTrack.us, 2010a). The bill proposes to amend federal copyright law to grant performers of audio recordings equal rights to compensation from terrestrial AM/FM broadcasters. In effect, this bill would allow artists to be paid for all performance venues – broadcast, satellite, Internet/digital. The companion bill in the Senate, *S.379*, was proposed by Sen. Patrick Leahy (D-VT) and was also successfully passed out of committee to the full Senate (GovTrack.us, 2010b).

While making progress in this broadcast area, the record companies and the RIAA are still pursuing illegal P2P downloaders. As has been the case since 2006, the RIAA continues to pursue illegal downloaders, but it is relying on new partnerships with ISPs to track down pirated online content in place of the "John Doe" lawsuits used in the past. In the new enforcement system, known as "graduated response," the RIAA alerts an ISP that a customer appears to be file sharing. The ISP will then notify the person that he or she appears to be file sharing. If the behavior by the customer does not change, more e-mails/letters are sent. If the customer ignores these, then the ISP may choose to limit, suspend or terminate the person's service (Sandoval, 2009). ISPs including AT&T, Comcast, Verizon are participating in these anti-piracy efforts, but no new lawsuits have yet to emerge.

Digital Audio Technologies

DRM-FREE MUSIC

Although buying practices are rapidly changing, much of the music sold in the world is still sold on compact discs. CDs have no encryption. They are DRM-free and can play on any CD player, including computer drives. CDs also provide high-quality digital content that can easily be ripped to a digital file, copied, or shared (legal issues notwithstanding) at the discretion of the buyer.

Digital downloads, in contrast, are accessible online at any time, making their purchase convenient. Often sold as singles and not full albums, they are economical as well. That convenience comes at the cost of quality and, especially, portability. Smaller digital files appropriate for downloads mean that the purchaser gets the music with lesser sound quality. Because the major labels insisted (until 2007) that downloadable music be encrypted with DRM, and there was no universal, open-standard for that encryption, the music could only play on devices capable of decrypting the specific DRM encryption the music was encoded with (as opposed to universally on any digital media player).

One of the biggest developments in digital audio technologies was the 2008 announcement by the Big Four record companies, Amazon.com, Apple, and others to offer DRM-free music tracks over the Internet (Holahan, 2008). For years, DRM was simply a way to protect the rights of the artists and record labels whose music was being illegally distributed. Most in the music industry believed that the technology was a necessary evil that needed to be put in place for content creators to make sure that they were being fairly compensated for their work. However, as mentioned earlier in the chapter, DRM wraps music tracks in a copy-protection code that is not only restrictive but also confusing for many potential users. Very few consumers wanted to purchase music on one service using a specific DRM, only to find out later that they cannot play it on this MP3 player, that computer, or this operating system.

The good news is that the negative attitude toward DRM kept nearly every independent label from utilizing the technology, and it pressured the Big Four labels into backing out of the restriction-laden model. One reason was the increasing popularity of iTunes, as music labels made no secret of wanting to wrest power away from Apple in the wake of its success in the early years of the music download market (Holahan, 2008). While not all DRM-free music can be played back on every single device, taking DRM out of the equation makes things considerably easier for the consumer This means there are now ever-increasing options for legally acquiring DRM-free music (for an updated list of DRM-free services, see the CTU Web site: www.tfi.com/ctu).

However, DRM-free does not mean consumers are free from having to purchase the music. And, unlike the mid-2000s, where providers offered music tracks (or albums) for a single price, the 2010s have ushered in the era of variable pricing and limited-time discounts by many providers, including Amazon, iTunes, Rhapsody and Wal-Mart. For example, rather than static track pricing of 99-cents each, iTunes began offering tracks at $0.69, $0.99 or $1.29 depending on the age and popularity of the track (Ankeny, 2010). To further entice consumers, limited-time promotional offers—such as release date discounts or holiday specials—have become a standard marketing approach as well.

WIRELESS DIGITAL MEDIA

Blackberry and Puretracks. Toronto-based Puretracks, the leading Canadian digital music service, provides a DRM-free mobile music store and service for BlackBerry smart phones. The Puretracks Mobile Edition music store for BlackBerry is a digital music service developed exclusively for wireless handsets using DRM-free AAC/AAC+ file formats. The files are the same AAC format used by iTunes, which offers higher quality at smaller file sizes than MP3. This digital format is only half the size of MP3 files, significantly reducing the download time and storage capacity required while maintaining CD quality sound—both important qualities for time-based wireless services. Puretracks Mobile Edition has over 3.4 million available tracks from all of the Big Four music companies and several indie labels (Puretracks.com, 2010).

AT&T Wireless and Napster/e-music.. AT&T Wireless has also joined the music download business in a partnership with Napster and e-music (AT&T Wireless, 2010). Selecting from over seven million available music tracks, AT&T Wireless customers can purchase five song Track Packs from either service for $7.49 or individual tracks for $1.99 (Napster only). A unique artist and title searching feature, MusicID, is included for an additional $2.99/month. AT&T Wireless also provides access to MobiRadio, a streaming radio station, as well as 25 XM Satellite radio channels and streaming music videos from MTV and VHI. It is interesting to note that the e-music per track cost is almost five times that of e-music's most expensive $0.33 rate for non-wireless customers who subscribe to its regular download service. It appears that AT&T Wireless, like most other U.S. wireless providers, will continue to charge more for impulse, on-the-go purchases.

On the international side, Napster has also been a leader in wireless MP3 subscription services. Partnering with Chilean provider Entel PCS and Ericsson phones, Napster established the first mobile music service in Latin America. Partnering again with Ericsson in Europe, Napster teamed up with Italy's Telecom Italia, Switzerland's Swisscom Mobile, and the United Kingdom's O2 UK to create Napster Mobile services in those countries. In Japan, Napster expanded its music subscription service to NTT DoCoMo wireless phone customers through partnerships with nine different phone manufacturers (Ericsson, 2010).

Sprint Power Vision. The first music service to utilize wireless phones to download music over the air, Sprint's Music Store offers tracks at $0.99, and customers receive two copies of the song—one for their phone and another for their PC. Customers can also burn their music to a CD using Windows Media Player. To use the Digital Lounge to preview and purchase any of the two million available tracks at the Sprint Music Store, a phone enabled for the Sprint Power Vision network is required. A monthly Power Vision data plan, as part of the customer's wireless calling plan, is also required (Sprint, 2010).

SUBSCRIPTION-BASED SERVICES

With the evolution of track-based DRM-free Internet and wireless downloading, only three subscription-based online music services remain active in mid-2010: Napster, Rhapsody, and Zune Pass.

Napster. With over nine million DRM-free MP3tracks, Napster is available in three subscription levels: $5/month annual pass, $5/month 3-month pass and $7/month 1-month pass. Subscribers can access their account and copy their library of downloaded songs on up to three computers. If a subscriber decides to terminate a subscription, downloaded music will no longer be playable at the end of final billing period. Subscribers can choose to pay additional per track fees to permanently purchase music. Only these purchased tracks can be burned to CD or transferred to WMA-compatible devices. Subscribers can also sign up for Napster to Go service to be able to transfer these purchased MP3s to Napster-compatible portable devices (Napster, 2010).

Rhapsody. Rhapsody, which is jointly owned by MTV and RealNetworks, offers two types of subscription services: Rhapsody to Go and Rhapsody Unlimited. Rhapsody to Go, available on Windows PCs only for $14.99 per month, allows subscribers to listen to all available music (over five million tracks) and transfer this music to supported MP3 players, such as the Sansa e200R Rhapsody. Rhapsody Unlimited, available on Windows, Mac, and Linux computers for $12.99 per month permits subscribers to listen to unlimited music just on the download computer. Like Napster, the downloaded music is unavailable after subscription termination, and tracks must be purchased separately to permit CD burning. Two unique features are the ability of subscribers to add downloaded music to their Facebook site and for any non-member consumer to listen to 25 free tracks per month (Rhapsody, 2010).

Zune Pass. From Microsoft, Zune includes digital audio players, client software, and the Zune Marketplace online music store. The Zune devices come in five styles, all of which play music and videos, display pictures, and receive FM and HD radio broadcasts. They can share files wirelessly only with other Zunes and via USB (universal serial bus) with Microsoft's Xbox 360, and can sync wirelessly with Windows PCs. The Zune software allows users to manage files on the player, rip audio CDs, and buy songs at the online store. The Zune Pass subscription is similar to the other two subscription services and allows subscribers to download as many songs as they like from Zune Marketplace and listen to them while their subscription is current, on up to three PCs. Like Napster, songs downloaded via a Zune Pass do not include burn rights, which only be obtained through the purchase of Microsoft Points (Zune, 2010).

P2P MUSIC FILE SHARING

The music industry's anti-piracy efforts appear more and more futile as CD sales continue to decline and illegal P2P file sharing networks continue to proliferate. Digital rights management, long touted as a solution, has been all but abandoned by the Big Four music companies and most legal music download services. Although the RIAA is said to have threatened or taken action against some 20,000 suspected file sharers over the last several years, the market-research firm NPD Group reports that there was actually a 25% decline in illegal downloading in the United States via P2P sites during 2009 (Sandoval, 2010).

However, the music industry is still concerned. Having failed to stop piracy by suing Internet users, the RIAA has been considering a file sharing surcharge that Internet service providers would collect from users and place into a pool that would be used to compensate songwriters, performers, publishers, and music labels. A collecting agency would divide the money according to artists' popularity on P2P sites, just as ASCAP and BMI pay songwriters for broadcasts and live performances of their work (Rose, 2008). Also in consideration is the concept of adding an ISP-based (and monitored) music service that is locked to the subscriber's ISP account. Once the subscriber leaves his ISP for another one, the accumulated music would be unavailable (Van Buskirk, 2010).

Even one of the most conspicuous file sharing services, the BitTorrent indexer The Pirate Bay, has managed to survive. After being found guilty of contributory copyright infringement by a Swedish court in April, 2009, the service has managed to continually relocate its servers while it fights the shutdown ruling via an appeal hearing in 2010 or 2011. In addition to jail time, the defendants were ordered to pay damages of $3.6 million to various entertainment companies, including Sony Music Entertainment, Warner Bros, EMI and Columbia Pictures, for the infringement of 33 specific movie and music properties tracked by investigators (Kiss, 2009).

CURRENT STATUS

CEA Sales Figures

In the latest version of the Consumer Electronics Association's *Digital America* report, CEA President and CEO Gary Shapiro reinforces the continued strength of the consumer electronics industry amidst the economic recession of the last few years,

> *"While not without serious challenges, the U.S. CE industry grew by more than five percent in 2008 to a new high of $172 billion in sales, a seventh consecutive year of growth. The devices and services our industry produces have historically done well in even the most difficult economic times going back to the emergence of radio during the Great Depression. Consumers recognize the tremendous value inherent in CE devices and have come to rely on them as an integral part of everyday life. With the typical American household now featuring some two dozen electronics products for work, communication and entertainment, the products our industry delivers have become a hallmark of life in the 21st century"* (CEA, 2010a, p. 1).

Details on the current state of the digital audio marketplace from the *Digital America* report included:

◈ Portable audio products, led by Digital Media players, will outsell home audio products for the fifth consecutive year in 2009, according to CEA forecasts.

◈ Total home audio sales slipped in 2008 by only 1.3% at the factory level to $3.78 billion and remained flat in 2009 despite the worst recession in a quarter century. Sales include component audio, audio systems, clock and tabletop home radios and MP3 player docking speaker systems.

◈ The MP3/portable media player (PMP) market enjoyed years of triple and double-digit percentage growth, but factory-level unit and dollar sales dipped for the first time in 2008 and will again in 2009, CEA forecasts.

◈ The household penetration rate of MP3/PMPs hit 46% in January 2009, up from 20% in January 2006.

◈ The music industry's embrace of the unrestricted, DRM-free MP3 format promises to further accelerate sales of authorized music downloads. (CEA, 2010b)

    i. Nielsen SoundScan Data

Nielsen SoundScan, the sales source for the Billboard music charts, tracks sales of music and music video products throughout the United States and Canada. Sales data is collected weekly from over 14,000 outlets, including brick and mortar merchants, online retailers, and performance venues. SoundScan data from 2009 was compiled in the Nielsen Company Year-End Music Industry Report. Some of the report's most interesting findings:

◆ Music purchases in 2009 reached the 1.5 billion mark, making it the fifth consecutive year music sales have exceeded 1 billion: 1.5 billion (2008), 1.4 billion (2007), 1.2 billion (2006), and 1.01 billion (2005) .

◆ Digital music accounted for 40% of all music purchases in 2009; up from 32% in 2008.

◆ Digital track sales broke the one billion sales mark for the 2nd straight year with 1,160,000 digital track sales in 2009. The previous record was 1,070,000 digital track purchases during 2008; an increase of 8% over 2008.

◆ Digital album sales reached an all-time high with more than 76 million sales up from 65 million in 2008; an increase of 16% over the previous year.

◆ Digital album sales accounted for 20% of total album sales in 2009 compared to 15% in 2008, 10% in 2007 and 5.5% in 2006.

◆ Eighty-nine digital songs exceeded the one million sales mark in 2000 compared to 71 digital songs in 2008, 41 in 2007, 22 in 2006, and only two digital songs in 2005. (Nielsen, 2010).

IFPI Digital Music Report

The International Federation of the Phonographic Industry (IFPI) is the organization that represents the interests of the recording industry worldwide. IFPI is based in London and represents more than 1,450 record companies, large and small, in 75 different countries. IFPI produces an annual report on the state of international digital music, and the *Digital Music Report 2010* also provides some interesting information on the current state of the global digital music industry:

◆ Music companies' revenues from digital channels (27%) are proportionately more than double that of films (5%), newspapers (4%) and magazines (2%) combined.

◆ The digital music business has huge growth potential. In the US, only 18% of Internet users aged 13 and over regularly buy digital music. In Europe, digital adoption is even less widespread – only 8% of Internet users in the top five EU markets frequently buy music digitally.

◆ Despite the successes, digital is not offsetting the overall decline. Digital sales grew 940% since 2004, but the overall music market fell by around 30% in that period. Sales were down 12% in the first half of 2009 and the full year figure is likely to show a similar trend.

◆ In Spain, a culture of state-tolerated apathy towards illegal file-sharing has contributed to a dramatic slump in the music market. Spain has the worst piracy problem of any major market in Europe. Illegal file-sharing in Spain, at 32% of Internet users, is more than double the European rate of 15%.

◆ Illegal file-sharing has a negative net impact on music purchasing. In the UK, research from Harris Interactive in 2009 highlighted that nearly one in four P2P file-sharers (24%) typically spend nothing on music, while finding an overlap of legal and illegal downloading among some file-sharers.

◆ P2P network file-sharing remains the most damaging form of piracy, but the last two years have also seen a sharp rise in non-P2P piracy, such as downloading from hosting sites, mobile piracy, stream ripping, instant message sharing and downloading from forums and blogs. According to Jupiter Research in 2009, about one in five Internet users across Europe's top markets (21%) are engaged in frequent unauthorized music-sharing. P2P piracy is still the biggest source of this (IFPI, 2010).

🌍 Sustainability 🌍

A 2009 study financed by Intel and Microsoft and conducted by research teams from Carnegie Mellon University, Lawrence Berkeley National Laboratory, and Stanford University concluded that downloading music cuts energy consumption and carbon dioxide emissions significantly in comparison to shopping at your local music retailer. The study shows that purchasing digital music downloads results in a 40-80% reduction in energy use and carbon emissions compared to distributing CDs. The study took into consideration the energy used to download the files over the Internet.

The study compared four different ways of obtaining and keeping music. The least energy intensive way of acquiring music is to download it and listen to it digitally. Downloading and then burning a CD of the music wastes more energy, purchasing a CD online wastes even more energy, and purchasing a CD at a retail store wastes the most energy. And, if you have to drive to the store to buy music in person, you waste even more energy. In effect, the advantage for downloading is largely because CDs must be manufactured, packaged and transported over long distances.

However, there is room for debate. The high carbon cost associated with visiting the store, for example, rises when a customer makes the trip by car. If a consumer walks to the store instead, then buying a CD is "nearly equivalent" in carbon terms, the study says, to downloading the music and burning it onto a CD.

Large file transfer sizes can reduce the carbon advantage of downloads due to the "increased Internet energy use required for downloading." The study also concedes that in some instances, the downloading and purchasing of hard copies are not perfect substitutes. Some consumers, for example, pursue albums for reasons beyond the music — say, for the album's artwork.

To access the study's findings, go to http://download.intel.com/pressroom/pdf/CDsvsdownloadsrelease.pdf.

FACTORS TO WATCH

By the end of 2010, the factors to watch in digital audio will be:

Apple. How will the industry leader react to the developing DRM-free services of Amazon, Rhapsody, and others? Will new entries into the U.S. marketplace, such as Spotify and Mog, create new directions for Apple? Will new versions of the iPhone and Apple iPod Touch help to extend Apple's device dominance? Will Apple's efforts overseas with EMI, Virgin, and other partners bolster its efforts? Will Apple's iPad have any impact on digital media content and consumer use of this content? Will variable pricing remain, or become even more variable in the future? Apple purchased Lala.com, the first free fully licensed service to instantly provide anywhere Web access to consumers' existing digital music library on their PC or Apple computer. Instead of uploading MP3 files from a PC, totally Web-based Lala uses a licensed technology to instantly match songs from consumers' personal music libraries with Lala's Web-based catalog of over 8 million tracks from the major record labels and thousands of independent artists. On lala.com, users can sample any full song or complete album for free, then can add tracks to their Web collection for only 10 cents or buy DRM-free MP3 downloads to use on any device for 79 cents or more (Lala, 2010). Apple has already incorporated Lala's Web-based track sampling into its iTunes Charts application, and analysts speculate that Apple may be creating a Web-based version of iTunes, which would store your music purchases online rather on your computer (Ionescu, 2010). This prediction may be true because on May 1, 2010 Apple announced they are shutting down Lala on May 31st, 2010 (Bloomberg, 2010).

Spotify and Rdio. Will Europe's Spotify make a successful transition to the U.S. from Europe? Will Rdio be a Skype-like success? Spotify uses a legal, proprietary P2P system in which users store music in cache folders on their computers and stream that music to others when requested. If no users have the music, Spotify feeds it from its servers in Ogg Vorbis format. Spotify is trying to secure U.S. agreements with record labels to be able to launch in 2010. It would be available in two versions – a free, ad-supported version and a premium, subscription version (McElhearn, 2009). Janus Friis and Niklas Zennstrom, the creators of Kazaa and Skype, are developing their own subscription service called Rdio. Unlike Spotify, Rdio will be Web-based rather than application-based. This means that unlike their other two major creations, Rdio will lack a P2P component. Rdio, too, is seeking record label deals here in the U.S. in preparation of a 2010 launch (Stone, 2009).

Social music and playlist services. After nearly a decade of plunging music sales, the record labels are trying to overhaul their traditional business. Instead of just selling recorded music, they can use music to sell a range of related extras, from online advertising to mobile phones packed with music. The new business model puts the Internet at the heart of the industry in an attempt to transform artist Web sites from promotional vehicles into money-making enterprises. In addition to these newly-renovated and socially-linked music label Web sites, an ever growing number of social media sites are evolving to bring labels, artists, advertisers and consumers together on the Web. From sharing user-created playlists to enabling reviews and comments, social media sites keep music fans up to date on the music business and each other at the same time. In addition to the now familiar MySpace Music and Facebook, here's a few of the popular social media Web sites vying for attention: Finetune, Hype Machine, iLike, iMeem, Mog, and Playlist.com.

File sharing. The Big Four record labels and the RIAA have sued thousands of P2P users, and file sharing is up. The labels beat The Pirate Bay and other P2P networks in court, and file sharing is up. The labels proposed dozens of laws to thwart it, and file sharing is up. The labels successfully closed P2P applications and sites, and file sharing is up. The labels have formed several successful DRM-free pay services to make legal downloading easier and more portable for all. What happened? File sharing is up. This trend is certain to continue (IFPI, 2010). The two factors to watch here are:

1) The impact of The Pirate Bay appeal case on future lawsuits and interventions by government and copyright holders into P2P activities.

2) The increased involvement of ISPs. ISP monitoring of customer activities (via software like Cview) is gaining support domestically and internationally, and is being pushed by the RIAA and the recording industry. Also, an ISP tax appears to be gaining momentum in many countries, especially in France and Spain, where illegal downloading is prevalent. Both initiatives would signify a fundamental shift toward achieving accountability at a different point in the puzzle, the ISP level.

Expect to see continued innovation, marketing, and debate in the next few years. Which technologies and companies survive will largely depend on the evolving choices made by consumers, the courts, and the continued growth and experimentation with the Internet and digital technology. Consumers seem to be very willing to move forward with the convenience and enjoyment being afforded by the new technologies of digital audio even in troubling economic times.

Bibliography

Alten, S. (2010). *Audio in media, 9th edition.* Belmont, CA: Wadsworth.

Ankeny, J. (2010, February 10). iTunes variable pricing cited for slowing WMG music sales. Retrieved March 12, 2010 from http://www.fiercemobilecontent.com/story/itunes-variable-pricing-cited-slowing-wmg-music-sales/2010-02-10.

Apple Computer, Inc. (2009, October 19). Apple reports fourth quarter results. Retrieved March 11, 2010 from http://www.apple.com/pr/library/2009/10/19results.html.

Atlantic Recording Corporation, et al. v. XM Satellite Radio, Inc. (2007, January 19). 06 Civ. 3733-DAB, S.D.N.Y.

AT&T Wireless. (2010, March 12). AT&T mobile music. Retrieved March 12, 2010 from http://www.wireless.att.com/source/music/mobilemusic/.

Audio Home Recording Act of 1992, 17 U.S.C. §§ 1001–10 (1992).

Audiotools.com. (2005, September 27). *DAT.* Retrieved March 14, 2006 from http://audiotools.com/dat.html.

Bloomberg. (2010, May 1). Apple to shut down its Lala online music site this month. Retrieved May 10, 2010 from http://www.sfgate.com/cgi-bin/article.cgi?f=/g/a/2010/05/01/bloomberg1376

Consumer Electronics Association. (2010a). *Digital America 2009: Introduction.* Retrieved March 12, 2010 from http://www.ce.org/PDF/DigitalAmerica2009_abridged.pdf.

Consumer Electronics Association. (2010b). *Digital America 2009: Audio overview.* Retrieved March 12, 2010 from http://www.ce.org/PDF/DigitalAmerica2009_abridged.pdf.

Department of Justice. (2010, February 12). Justice Department Announces New Intellectual Property Task Force as Part of Broad IP Enforcement Initiative. Retrieved March 11, 2010 from http://www.justice.gov/opa/pr/2010/February/10-ag-137.html.

Digital Performance Right in Sound Recordings Act, Pub. L. No. 104-39, 109 Stat. 336 (1996).

Digigram. (2010, March 11). About world standard ISO/MPEG audio. Retrieved March 11, 2010 from http://www.digigram.com/support/library.htm?o=getinfo&ref_key=282.

Dolby Labs. (2010, March 13). Digital cinema solution. Retrieved March 13, 2010 from http://www.dolby.com/professional/solutions/cinema/digital-cinema.html

Ericsson. (2010). Corporate information. Retrieved March 12, 2010 from http://www.ericsson.com/ericsson/corpinfo/index.shtml.

Geutskens, Y. (2009, August 28). FAQ. *SA-CD.net.* Retrieved March 11, 2010 from http://www.sa-cd.net/faq.

Geutskens, Y. (2010, March 11). SACD titles. Retrieved March 11, 2010 from http://www.sa-cd.net/titles.

GovTrack.us. (2010a). *H.R. 848: Performance Rights Act.* Retrieved March 11, 2010 from http://www.govtrack.us/congress/bill.xpd?bill=h111-848.

GovTrack.us. (2010b). *S.379: Performance Rights Act.* Retrieved March 11, 2010 from http://www.govtrack.us/congress/bill.xpd?bill=s111-379.

Grill, A. (2009, March 12). Music to my ears now Vodafone comes with music. Retrieved March 11, 2010 from http://andrewgrill.com/blog/index.php/2009/03/music-to-my-ears-now-vodafone-comes-with-music/.

Hard-drive MP3 players. (2008, March 14). *C/NET News.* Retrieved March 14, 2008 from http://reviews.cnet.com/4244-6497_7-0-1.html?query=jukebox&tag=cat_2.

Holahan, C. (2008, January 4). Sony BMG plans to drop DRM. *Business Week.* Retrieved March 16, 2008 from http://www.businessweek.com/technology/content/jan2008/tc2008013_398775.htm.

Home Recording Rights Coalition. (2000, April). HRRC's summary of the *Audio Home Recording Act.* Retrieved April 3, 2002 from http://www.hrrc.org/ahrasum.html.

Hydrogenaudio. (2008, March 14). Lossless comparison. Retrieved March 14, 2008 from http://wiki.hydrogenaudio.org/index.php?title=Lossless_comparison.

IFPI. (2010, January 21). *IFPI digital music report 2010.* Retrieved March 13, 2010 from http://www.ifpi.org/content/section_resources/dmr2010.html.

Ionescu, D. (2010, January 7). Apple puts Lala music service to work. Retrieved March 13, 2010 from http://www.pcworld.com/article/186183/apple_puts_lala_music_service_to_work.html?loomia_ow=t0:s0:a38:g26:r17:c0.000360:b29239486:z0.

Kalinsky, R. & Sebald, G. (2005, August). Supreme Court's inducement theory in Grokster creates uncertainty. *IP Today.* Retrieved March 16, 2005 from http://www.iptoday.com/pdf_current/Kalinsky_Sebald_Final.pdf.

Kawamato, D. (2008, June 10). *EMI and XM Satellite Radio reach settlement.* Retrieved March 11, 2010 from http://news.cnet.com/8301-10784_3-9964615-7.html.

Kiss, J. (2009, April 17). *The Pirate Bay trial: guilty verdict.* Retrieved March 13, 2010 from http://www.guardian.co.uk/technology/2009/apr/17/the-pirate-bay-trial-guilty-verdict.

Lala. (2010). *How it works.* Retrieved March 13, 2010 from http://www.lala.com/#howitworks.

Madden, M. (2009, June). The State of Music Online: Ten Years after Napster. Retrieved March 11, 2020 from http://www.pewinternet.org/Reports/2009/9-The-State-of-Music-Online-Ten-Years-After-Napster.aspx.

Mark, R. (2006, July 27). KaZaa settles up. *Internetnews.com.* Retrieved March 14, 2008 from http://www.internetnews.com/bus-news/article.php/3622991/Kazaa+Settles+Up.htm.

McElhearn, (2009, November 3). *Is Spotify the future of music listening? MacWorld.* Retrieved March 13, 2010 from http://www.macworld.com/article/143615/2009/11/spotify.html.

MGM v. Grokster. (2003, April 25). Retrieved March 15, 2004 from http://www.cacd.uscourts.gov/CACD/ RecentPubOp.nsf/bb61c530eab091lc882567cf005ac6f9/b0f0403ea8d6075e88256d13005c0fdd? OpenDocument.

Metro-Goldwyn-Mayer Studios, Inc., et al. v. Grokster, Ltd., et al. (2005, June 27). 545 U. S. 125 S. Ct. 2764.

Microsoft. (2010, March). Create and distribute audio using Windows media technology. Retrieved March 11, 2010 from http://www.microsoft.com/windows/windowsmedia/forpros/AudioProd.aspx.

Mitchell, B. (2008). Top 10 free P2P file sharing programs—Free P2P software. *About.com.* Retrieved March 16, 2008 from http://compnetworking.about.com/od/p2ppeertopeer/tp/p2pfilesharing.htm.

MP3.com. (2010, March 11). *Hard-drive.* Retrieved March 11, 2010 from http://www.mp3.com/hardware/hard/hardwa re.hml.

Napster. (2010). Napster customer support FAQs. Retrieved March 12, 2010 from http://napsterus.custhelp.com/cgi-bin/napsterus.cfg/php/enduser/std_alp.php?p_sid=-DgoAHWj.

Nielsen. (2010, January 7). *The Nielsen Company 2009 Year-End Music Industry Report.* Retrieved March 13, 2010 from http://blog.nielsen.com/nielsenwire/wp-content/uploads/2010/01/Nielsen-Music-2009-Year-End-Press-Release.pdf.

No Electronic Theft (NET) Act, Pub. L. No. 105-147, 111 Stat. 2678 (1997).

Podcast Alley. (2010). What is a podcast? Retrieved March 11, 2010 from http://www.podcastalley.com/what_is_a_podcast.php.

Puretracks.com. (2010). Puretracks music store. Retrieved March 12, 2010 from http://corporate.puretracks.com/music.htm.

Recording Industry Association of America. (2010, March 11). About music copyright notices. Retrieved March 11, 2010 from http://riaa.org/ispnoticefaq.php.

Rhapsody. (2010). Get to know Rhapsody. Retrieved March 12, 2010 from http://www.rhapsody.com/rhapsody_faqs.

Rose, F. (2008, March 13). Music industry proposes a piracy surcharge on ISPs. *Wired.* Retrieved March 16, 2008 from http://www.wired.com/entertainment/music/news/2008/03/music_levy.

Sandoval, G. (2010, March 1). P2P music use down; users may be stuffed. Retrieved March 12, 2010 from http://news.cnet.com/media-maverick/?keyword=The+NPD+Group.

Sandoval, G. (2009, December 23). *A year out, where's RIAA's promised ISP help? CNET.* Retrieved March 11, 2010 from http://news.cnet.com/8301-31001_3-10420803-261.html.

Sony Corp. of America v. Universal City Studios, Inc., 464 U.S. 417. (1984). Retrieved March 14, 2008 from http://caselaw.lp.findlaw.com/scripts/getcase.pl?navby=CASE&court=US&vol=464&page=417.

SonyMusic.com. (2006, March 14). *SACD FAQ.* Retrieved March 14, 2006 from http://www.sonymusic.com/store/ SACD.htm.

SoundExchange.com. (2010, March 11). FAQ. Retrieved March 11, 2010 from http://soundexchange.com/category/faq/.

Sprint. (2010). Sprint Power Vision network. Retrieved March 12, 2010 from http://www1.sprintpcs.com/explore/ueContent.jsp?scTopic=music100.

Stone, B. (2009, October 14). Pair plan venture to sell music subscriptions. Retrieved March 11, 2010 from http://www.nytimes.com/2009/10/14/technology/internet/14music.html?_r=1.

Thomson. (2010). *Royalty rates.* Retrieved March 11, 2010 from http://www.mp3licensing.com/royalty/.

U.S. Copyright Office. (2010). *The Digital Millennium Copyright Act of 1998: U.S. Copyright Office summary.* Retrieved March 11, 2010 from http://lcweb.loc.gov/copyright/legislation/dmca.pdf.

Van Buskirk, Eliot. (2010, February 4). *Locking music to ISPs could earn ISPs hundreds of millions: study.* Retrieved March 12, 2010 from http://www.wired.com/epicenter/2010/02/locking-music-to-isps-could-earn-isps-hundreds-of-millions-study/.

Verizon Wireless. (2010, March 11). Answers to FAQ. Retrieved March 11, 2010 from http://support.vzw.com/clc/faqs/V%20CAST%20Music/faq.html.

Watkinson, J. (1988). *The art of digital audio.* London: Focal Press.

Wilson, Jonathan (2009, March 14). It's just not rock 'n' roll. *Engineering & Technology,* Vol. 4, Issue 5, pp. 32-33.

Zune. (2010). Zune learning center. Retrieved March 12, 2010 from http://www.zune.net/en-us/products/learningcenter/default.htm.

17

Digital Imaging & Photography

Michael Scott Sheerin, M.S.[*]

> I don't believe photography can change the world,
> But it can show the world changing.
> —Elliot Erwitt (Hopkinson, 2010)

Sales of digital still cameras (DSCs) in the U.S. market are expected to reach 24.8 million in 2010, the lowest number since the 20.5 million DSCs sold in 2005. One reason for the decline is the economy, but the major reason is the market saturation of the DSC. It is projected that 81.3% of all U.S. households will own a DSC by the end of 2010, a slightly less than 4% increase from the previous year (PMA, 2010). Because of this market saturation, industry forecasters conclude that DSC sales in the next few years will be driven mostly by the purchase of replacement DSCs. According to PMA Marketing Research, the average replacement period for a DSC is 3.8 years (Clairmont, 2010). Meanwhile traditional film camera sales continue to plummet: only 200,000 units are projected for 2010, the lowest total since 1995 (PMA, 2010). In fact, since 2003, DSCs have outsold traditional still cameras, prompting industry giant Eastman Kodak, in 2004, to stop selling their traditional 35mm still cameras and their Advanced Photo Systems (APS) cameras in the U.S., Canadian, and Western European markets. Even the iconic Kodachrome slide film was discontinued in 2009 after 74 years. As of mid-2010 only one Kodachrome processing house in the world, Dwayne's Photo Service of Kansas, still exists. However, they plan to shut down their processing services on December 31, 2010. (Kodak, 2010). You can follow the year long tribute celebration to Kodachrome at the The Kodachrome Project Web site, kodachromeproject.com.

From the point of view of what happens after you snap a picture, we find that an estimated 30.4 billion digital images will be taken (and saved) in 2010 (compared to only 2.5 billion images taken, processed, and printed from film). However, of that 30.4 billion, an estimated 22.5 billion, or 74% of the digital images saved, will not be printed (see Figure 17.1) (PMA, 2010). Due to the "jump to screen" phenomenon, we will instead view, transfer, manipulate, and post these images on high-definition televisions (HDTV) and computer screens, Web pages, and social media sites. We will send them in e-mails, post them in collaborative virtual worlds, and take, transfer, and view them on cell phones and other handheld devices, including DSCs. The digital image has allowed the photo industry to fully converge with the computer industry, thus changing the way we utilize

---

[*] Assistant Professor, School of Journalism and Mass Communications, Florida International University (Miami, Florida).

images. Unlike the discovery of photography, which happened when no one alive today was around, this sea change in the industry is happening right in front of us; in fact, we are all participating in it. This chapter will look at some of the implications for our society as digital images leave the old boundaries of camera and photographic paper, jump to screen, and enter seamlessly into all our media.

Figure 17.1

Saved Digital Images—Printed vs. Not Printed (Billions of Images)

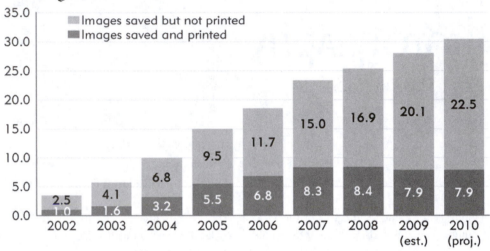

Source: PMA Marketing Research (2010)

BackgRound

With digital imaging, images of any sort, from family photographs to medical X-rays, are now treated as data. This ability to take, scan, manipulate, disseminate, or store images in a digital format has spawned major changes in the communication technology industry. From the photojournalist in the newsroom to the magazine layout artist to the vacationing tourist, digital imaging has changed media and how we view images. The ability to manipulate digital images has grown exponentially with the addition of imaging software, but photomanipulation dates back to the film period. Images have been manipulated as far back as 1906, when a photograph taken of the San Francisco Earthquake was said to be altered as much as 30% according to forensic image analyst George Reid. In 1910, the Martin Postcard Company published an image of a man riding a giant fish (Pictures that lie, 2010). More humorous than deceitful, the same cannot be said of the 1984 *National Geographic* cover photo of the Great Pyramids of Giza, in which the two pyramids were moved closer together to fit the vertical layout of the magazine (Ritchin, 2008). In fact, repercussions stemming from the ease with which digital photographs can be manipulated caused the National Press Photographers Association (NPPA), in 1991, to update their code of ethics to encompass digital imaging factors (NPPA, 2010). Here is a brief look at how the captured, and now malleable, digital image got to this point.

The first photograph ever taken is credited to Joseph Niepce, and it turned out to be quite pedestrian in scope. Using a technique he derived from experimenting with the newly-invented lithograph process, Niepce was able to capture the view from outside his Saint-Loup-de-Varennes country house in 1826 in a camera obscura (Harry Ransom, University of Texas at Austin, 2010). The capture of this image involved an eight-hour exposure of sunlight onto bitumen of Judea, a type of asphalt (Lester, 2006). Niepce named this process heliography, which is Greek for sun writing. Ironically, this was the only photograph of record that Niepce ever shot, and it still exists as part of the Gernsheim collection at the University of Texas at Austin (Lester, 2006).

The next 150 years included significant innovation in photography. Outdated image capture processes kept giving way to better ones, from the daguerreotype (sometimes considered the first photographic process) developed by Niepce's business associate Louis Daguerre, to the calotype (William Talbot), wet-collodion (Frederick Archer), gelatin-bromide dry plate (Dr. Richard Maddox), and the now slowly disappearing continuous-tone panchromatic black-and-white and autochromatic color negative films. Additionally, exposure time has gone from Niepce's eight-hour exposure to 1/500th of a second or less.

Cameras themselves did not change that much after the early 1900s until digital photography came along. A modern 35mm single lens reflex (SLR) camera works in principle like an original Leica, the first 35mm SLR camera introduced in 1924. Based on a relationship between film's sensitivity to light, the lens aperture (the size of the opening that lets light in, also known as the "f-stop"), and the shutter speed (time of exposure), the SLR camera allows photographers, both professional and amateur, to capture images using available light.

All images captured on these traditional SLR cameras had to be processed after the film's original exposure to light in order to see the image. Instant photography changed all that. Edwin Land invented the first instant photographic process in 1947. It produced a sepia colored print in about 60 seconds (Sheerin, 2008). This first Polaroid camera, called Model 95, was sold in November 1948 at Jordan Marsh in Boston for $89.75 (Sheerin, 2008). Polaroid's innovations in instant photography peaked in 1972, when the SX-70 camera was introduced. Using Time-Zero film, this SLR camera was "fully automated and motorized, ejecting self-developing, self-timing color prints" that could instantly be shared with others (Sheerin, 2008).

The first non-film camera produced analog, not digital, images. In 1981, Sony announced a still video camera called the MAVICA, which stands for magnetic video camera (Carter, 2010a). It was not until nine years later, in 1990, that the first DSC was introduced. Called the Dycam (manufactured by a company called Dycam), it captured images in monochromatic grayscale and had a resolution that was lower than most video cameras of the time. It sold for a little less than $1,000 and had the ability to hold 32 images in its internal memory chip (Aaland, 1992).

In 1994, Apple released the Quick Take 100, the first mass-market color DSC. The Quick Take had a resolution of 640 × 480, equivalent to a NTSC TV image, and sold for $749 (PCMAG.com, 2010). Complete with an internal flash and a fixed focus 50mm lens, the camera could store eight 640 × 480 color images on an internal memory chip and could transfer images to a computer via a serial cable. Other mass-market DSCs released around this time were the Kodak DC-40 in 1995 for $995 (Carter, 2010b) and the Sony Cyber-Shot DSC-F1 in 1996 for $500 (Carter, 2010c).

A DSC works in much the same way as a traditional still camera. The lens and the shutter allow light into the camera based on the aperture and exposure time, respectively. The difference is that the light reacts with an image sensor, usually a charge-coupled device (CCD) sensor, a complementary metal oxide semiconductor (CMOS) sensor, or the newer, live MOS sensor. When light hits the sensor, it causes an electrical charge. The size of this sensor and the number of picture elements (pixels) found on it determine the resolution, or quality, of the captured image. The number of thousands of pixels on any given sensor is referred to as the megapixels. The sensors themselves can be different sizes. A common size for a sensor is 18 × 13.5mm (a 4:3 ratio), now referred to as the Four Thirds System (Four Thirds, 2010). In this system, the sensor area is approximately 25% of the area of exposure found in a traditional 35mm camera.

The pixel, also known in digital photography as a photosite, can only record light in shades of gray, not color. In order to produce color images, each photosite is covered with a series of red, green, and blue filters, a technology derived from the broadcast industry. Each filter lets specific wavelengths of light pass through, according to the color of the filter, blocking the rest. Based on a process of mathematical interpolations, each pixel is then assigned a color. Because this is done for millions of pixels at one time, it requires a great deal of computer processing. The image processor in a DSC must "interpolate, preview, capture, compress, filter, store, transfer, and display the image" in a very short period of time (Curtin, 2010). This intensive processing issue, often referred to as shutter lag, has been one of the major drawbacks in digital photography, although it has been mostly eliminated in some of the newer, high-end digital single lens reflex (DSLR) cameras. In traditional photography, when the photographer pushes the button to take a picture, the film is immediately exposed, based on the shutter speed setting. In digital photography, there is a latent computer processing time that delays the actual exposure from happening when the user pushes the capture button, especially if the camera uses auto focus and/or a built-in flash. With many compact DSCs, what you think you are shooting, especially moving subjects, may be slightly different than what you actually capture. A 2010 Consumer Electronics reports states that "the only digital cameras these days that eliminate shutter lag are expensive DSLRs, used by camera aficionados and professional photographers" (Mandle, 2010).

Recent Developments

New trends in the imaging industry show that hardware innovations in digital imaging, though still important, are no longer the lead story when discussing the industry. In keeping with Saffo's 30-year rule, we are entering the third decade, or the "So what? It's just a standard technology and everyone has it" phase (Fidler, 1997, p. 9). In fact, in a statement that has further reaching implications than just the digital imaging industry, Saffo states, "the electronics revolution is over" (Saffo, 2010). If that is so, DSCs made great strides during the revolution, going from low-resolution black-and-white images to high-resolution lifelike images in a quarter of a century. It has been written, "Unlike the evolution of other types of media, the history of photography is one of declining quality" (Pavlik & McIntosh, 2004, p. 104). Images shot with large format cameras in the 1880s were superior to the digital images of only a decade ago. However, the "declining quality" trend is no longer, as many of us now capture digital images of superior quality to that of 35mm film. Furthermore, high-end medium format digital cameras, such as the Hasselblad H4D 60, with a 60 megapixel image sensor that is twice as large as any 35mm sensor, have matched and surpassed the image resolution of the 19th century large format cameras (Hasselblad, 2010). Roger N. Clark concludes in his study of digital still versus film resolution that the resolution obtained from an image sensor of 10 megapixels or more is equal to or greater than the resolution of 35mm film (Clark, 2010). Most mid-range DSLRs on today's market are 12 megapixels or greater. In fact, many of the point and shoot DSCs are available today with 10 megapixels (or more) image sensors, with many priced under $200.

i. Workflow & Post-Production

Professional photographer Brad Tuckman thinks that the biggest change in the industry is what occurs after the image capture. Tuckman states that the workflow and the post-production process are just as critical to producing quality digital images as the capture process itself, and that workflow continues to evolve (Tuckman, personal communication, March 8, 2010). Due to the Wi-Fi ability found in many new DSCs, content can be instantaneously uploaded to software platforms designed to enhance, manipulate, distribute, and store the digital images. Professional photographers can re-touch photos "on-the-fly" in digital image software programs like Capture One 5.1 PRO (Tuckman, personal communication, March 8, 2010). Clients can view images from the shoot while the photographer works, as the RAW workflow of the PRO version offers tethered shooting with Live Preview, multiple monitor support, and editing tools such as Focus Mask, Enhanced Colour Editor, Lens Correction Tool and Metadata editing (Phase One, 2010). Adobe's Photoshop Camera Raw 2.3 plug-in, also found in their Lightroom 2 application, supports many RAW formats found on leading DSLRs as well as the Digital Negative (DNG) format (Adobe, 2010a). RAW digital image formats are usually based on specifications that are proprietary for each DSLR manufacturer, so the publicly available archival format DNG offers an open standard solution, assuring RAW file accessibility in the future (Adobe, 2010b). RAW and DNG are increasingly popular formats for professionals because the data saved from the digital camera or imaging device is minimally processed and lossless, unlike the more popular JPEG format, which is compressed and lossy.

Tuckman's observations allude to a point made earlier in the chapter: that of the digital image leaving the boundaries of the camera and photographic paper. Although this chapter has dealt mainly with DSCs, more images are captured worldwide on camera phones than on DSCs (see figure 17.2) (PMA, 2010). The ever increasing number of images taken and saved with either a DSC or camera phone creates new markets in storage and dissemination, as well as in manipulation and enhancement software. Like the workflow described earlier, consumers can just as easily emulate the professionals by adding a WiFi enabled flash memory card, such as Eye-Fi Pro X2, an 8 GB card that can upload RAW image files. Images from your DSC can instantly and automatically be sent to one of over 25 popular image sharing sites, including Flickr, snapfish, Picasa, Youtube, and Facebook. Google offers a free 4 GB Eye-Fi card if you sign up for 200 GB of storage with them (Eye-Fi, 2010). All these software, hardware, and camera phone applications allow for the photograph to indeed "jump to the screen." Add in the ubiquitous nature of the camera phone and "the world has become like a stage, transformed into a photo-opportunity—a parallel universe owing its existence largely to the shutter's release" (Ritchin, 2008).

Figure 17.2
Camera Phone versus Digital Camera Use (2009 Statistics)

	Household penetration	Units per household	Total units in use (millions)	Pictures per units
Digital Cameras	78%	1.3	122	230
Camera Phones	62%	1.9	141	28

Source: PMA Marketing Research (2010)

Convergence of Equipment

This "jump to the screen" trend in digital imaging is obviously a result of convergence of the cell phone, computer, camera, and video camera. A fast growing trend is the use of the DSLR (and to a lesser extent, the compact DSCs) as a video camera. New flash memory cards that adhere to the Class 10 specification allow for 30 Mb/s read/write speeds and more, allowing for HD video recording. *Studio* magazine, a popular resource for professional videographers, runs a DSLR short film competition via their studiodaily.com site. Only shorts recorded with a DSLR camera, like the D90 from Nikon that can shoot 24fps at 720p, are allowed to be entered, suggesting a mediamorphosis in the use of the DSC. Technological convergence is further illustrated by the hardware/software development of touch screen technology found on new DSCs. Many new point and shoot DSCs have added touch screen controls, following the innovations found in cell phones, computers, and handheld devices such as the Blackberry. The convenience of selecting what you want the lens to focus on by touching the subject on the screen is a unique and useful tool. Some DSCs, like the Nikon S70 and the Samsung TL225, allow you to focus and shoot via the touch screen interface (Goldman, 2010). Options such as writing on an image (photo-tagging), flipping through the captured images, or saving copies are available in touch screen playback mode on some models. Drawbacks to the new technology are the added cost of the touch screen hardware, as well as the additional drain on the battery. Camera lens technology is also changing for compact DSCs. Recently, the Four Thirds system announced their new Micro Four Thirds System standard for interchangeable lens type digital camera systems. This standard works "by enabling dramatic reductions in size and weight" that will make it "possible to develop ultra-compact interchangeable lens type digital camera systems unlike anything seen before" (Four Thirds, 2010).

The number and variety of image editing tools and updated plug-ins has increased, offering users more features than ever before. Fred Ritchin, in his essay "Of Other Times and Places" in *Aperture* magazine, says these programs are "taking advantage of this malleability and the pervasiveness of the photographic image on the Internet in powerful and potentially very exciting ways" (Ritchin, 2008, p. 80). Examples are Topaz Adjust 4, which "uses unique technology that automatically adapts to different image conditions like light, detail, and color (BusinessWire, 2010a), Melancholytron from Nova Scotia, "a vignetting software that lets you subdue hue and focus, directing the viewer to the photograph's main subject" (Farace, 2010), and STOIK Imagic, which allows the user to "easily organize, browse, search and edit photos and video including automated corrections and HDR support" (*BusinessWire*, 2010b). You can even manipulate and share your images from your camera phone, as Adobe's **Photoshop.com** Mobile app is available for many of the newer camera phone models (**Photoshop.com**, 2010).

The ability to manipulate the digital image discussed in this chapter so far deals with the single user. But when the image jumps to screen, it enters the metaverse, defined as "the convergence of virtually enhanced physical reality and physically persistent virtual space" (Smart et al, 2007). Thus, it is subject to areas such as crowdsourcing and data-based algorithmic manipulations. Studies in computational photography have brought us many interesting applications that further stretch the usage and malleability aspect of the digital image. One such application is Sketch2Photo. Similar to the computational photographic applications Photo Clip Art (PCA) and Scene Completion that came out of Carnegie-Mellon in 2007, Sketch2Photo is described as an Internet image montage. It "composes a realistic picture from a simple freehand sketch annotated with text labels" (Sketch2Photo, 2010). The resulting composite image is made by "seamlessly stitching several photographs in agreement with the sketch and text labels" from images found on the Internet (Sketch2 Photo, 2010). Microsoft's Live Labs has come up with three applications that draw "from the collective memory" of all digital image contributors, resulting in an "immensely rich virtual model" of the world (Arcas, 2010a). The first of this trio is Seadragon. Seadragon and the newer Seadragon Ajax library technology "enables web experiences where graphics and photos are smoothly browsed, regardless of the amount of data or the bandwidth of the network" (Seadragon, 2010). The second application is Photosynth. This software "allows you to stitch digital photos together into comprehensive 3D models and enables others to virtually explore them in vivid detail" (Microsoft, 2010). These two applications, along with geo-mapping image technology are now being used together, as seen in the December 2009 release of the Bing Maps application. The Silverlight application runs the rich mapping search engine, and it offers a bird's eye view, as well as a street view of a location (Streetside), based on high resolution images. A green camera icon appears on the Streetside map if "photosynths" of the area have been created, and you can dive in and explore these user created 3-D worlds. These worlds are made up of geo-registered images from the Flickr data base. A beta version of Bing Maps includes the ability to integrate geo-registered video, carried over a 4G network, into a photosynth, as well as a view of the sky (from Worldwide Telescope feeds), integrated into the map (Arcas, 2010b).

Sorting of Data

As the sheer number of images posted on Flickr and other image data bases grow, the need to sort and make sense of it all increases. The third and newest application from Live Labs, Pivot, does just that. Pivot presents data in the form of a collection of images accompanied by textual data (Naone, 2010). By working in tandem with Seadragon, users can tease out patterns from large sets of imaging data. "You can interact with the data in a way that's not quite browsing and not quite searching," says Gary Flake, founder and director of the lab (Flake, 2010). A similar data visualization application is IBM's many eyes, currently in beta production. Founder Martin Wattenberg writes that he wants to "democratize visualization, enabling anyone on the internet to publish powerful interactive visualizations and start their own data conversations" (many eyes, 2010). Sorting through all the image data found in the metaverse by developing computational photographic algorithms and more sophisticated mathematical techniques is the goal. "What is the standard deviation of a collection of images?" he says. "That question doesn't even make sense" (Naone, 2010). Swiss company start-up Kooaba has joined the fray, offering an image recognition API. With a library of over 10 million images, Kooaba aims to "provide access to all that precious data via the cloud" by simply capturing the image via a mobile Kooaba app-enhanced camera phone (Wauters, 2010). Want to learn more about that band you see in the magazine ad, or info about a CD? Simply open the free Kooaba app on your camera phone and snap an image of the content you want to know more about. "In an instant, you receive everything, from purchasing info, to trailers and tickets, directly on your mobile phone" (YouTube, 2010). Mobile Acuity's Spellbinder is similar to Kooaba, only it works on more of a 3-D plane, associating digital content with real places. Spellbinder software allows for "new location based services and games where graphical digital content is precisely located in the real world" (Sci-Fun, 2010). Mobile Acuity also offers other "visual interactivity" applications such as Visual Product Search, Face Finder and Colour ID that can be used with a camera phone (Mobile Acuity, 2010).

Role of Social Media

Social media sites play an active role in the proliferation of the digital image in the metaverse. In addition to the aforementioned image-based consumer sites (Flickr, Picasa, Shutterfly, etc.), there are also professional photojournalism news aggregator sites such as Daylife, Tumblr, Boston Globe's The Big Picture and BBC's In Pictures. Perhaps the best use of the new advances in image uploading, tagging, mapping, and sharing applications from camera phone UGC is the mobile social network GyPSii. This "market-leading mobile digital lifestyle application and geo-mobility social media platform" added one million new users in the last quarter of 2009 (GyPSii, 2010). Not stopping there, GyPSii, as part of a 2010 deal with mobile operator Telefonica, extended its reach to include 130 million subscribers in Latin America (mocoNews.net, 2010). GyPSii, via its GyPSii CONNECT app, integrates with both Facebook and Twitter, making it a true social meta-aggregator.

The camera phone plays a critical part in many of the above noted projects. This is due, in part, to a social norm, as people usually do not leave the house without their phones, while the DSC only comes out when the main purpose is to take pictures (though the compact nature of the DSC maybe be changing that perception). It is this ubiquitous nature of the camera phone that is causing this change in the way we perceive and use images. With more than 50% of all U.S. households now using camera phones, these image-driven social posts will only grow in scope (PMA, 2010). The quality of the camera phone's image resolution has also increased, as the average resolution is expected to be 5.7 megapixels by 2013 (iSuppli, 2010). It should be noted that the number of megapixels is not the only determining factor in image quality. Factors such as dynamic range, low light capabilities, and noise level reduction must be improved for camera phones to truly replace DSCs, but it is believed that these technologies, including the addition of optical zoom, auto focus, and improved flash will migrate from the compact DSC to the camera phone in the next few years, if not sooner (iSuppli, 2010). With camera phones such as the 12.1 megapixel Satio from Sony Ericsson already on the market, complete with touch focus and xenon flash, the ability to take quality images with a cell phone is a reality (Sony Ericsson, 2010). With this increased image quality available on the camera phone (other companies are sure to follow Sony's lead if sales are brisk), is the end of the "phone-less" DSC near?

Effect on Older Technologies

Obviously, it is too soon to actually make that prediction, as older technologies that were thought to be dead have actually evolved. Polaroid is a great example of this mediamorphosis theory. Current Polaroid executive Jon Pollock states, "We joke that Polaroids really were the first social medium before YouTube, Facebook, and Twitter" (Lagesse, 2010). As with Kodachrome, Polaroid discontinued production of instant film for their analog cameras in 2008, but not their original focus on instant imaging. Stepping into the instant film void is ZINK (Zero Ink), whose second generation films work with Polaroid cameras and printers. One such device is the PoGo printer, the first new, ZINK-enabled Polaroid product (Zink Imaging, 2010). Perhaps hoping for the same market bump they received in 2003 after Outkast's hit single *Hey Ya* went number one (with the lyric, "Shake it like a Polaroid picture!"), Polaroid hired musical artist Lady Gaga as the creative director and inventor of specialty products (Polaroid, 2010). And the original Polaroid film isn't gone yet. A group of engineers, many who worked for Polaroid, formed The Impossible Project and purchased the old Polaroid factory in Enschede, Netherlands. Their mission is to produce "a new product with new characteristics, consisting of new optimised components", resulting in "innovative and fresh analog material" that can be used in traditional Polaroid cameras, like the SX-70 (The Impossible Project, 2010).

CURRENT STATUS

DSLR vs. DSC

A distinction must be made between the types of DSCs used in order to better understand how we capture the majority of our images. Sales of point-and-shoot compact DSCs made up the majority of the total number of DSC units sold, but sales figures show a 4% drop in revenue in the past year (Bogaty, 2010a). However, revenue from DSLR cameras increased 44% over the same time span (Bogaty, 2010a). One reason for the growth is that the average price of DSLR cameras dropped 16% (Bogaty, 2010b). The growth of DSLR cameras in Australia is even greater, as DSLRs accounted for 27% of total DSC sales in 2009, an 11% increase from 2007 (Canon, 2010). And DSLR unit sales grew a record 13% in western European markets (Bryant, 2010). Because market sales of DSCs are now driven by repeat buyers, it seems they are upgrading to the more option laden DSLR. However, this option "gap" is closing, as features like the Micro Four Thirds interchangeable lens for point and shoot cameras are added to the compact cameras (PMA, 2010).

Despite the increase in DSLR sales, combined DSC sales are projected to decrease in the 2010 U.S. market for the third straight year, and it is projected that the DSC market value will show a decrease of more than 11% since 2008 (PMA, 2010). One area of the market that is holding steady is the aftermarket camera accessory area, as the same figure (17%) is spent on accessories during the initial purchase and up to six months after, as was the case in 2007 (Bogaty, 2010c). Another area responsible for the declining market value is the printing sector. Though the number of digital images printed is projected to be stable for the fourth straight year (approx. 14 billion), the total number of images printed will fall for the ninth straight year (PMA, 2010). The real culprit is the steep decline of prints made from traditional sources (film). When DSC sales surpassed film camera sales in 2004, DSC usage followed suit, surpassing the number of images printed from film cameras in 2007. Prints made from film cameras have declined 72% since then. That year also represented the high water mark for the number of prints made from DSCs, even though DSC adoption continues to grow, as household penetration has increased by over 13% since 2007 (PMA, 2010). The economy is blamed in part for this decline, as economists state that 2007 was the start of the economic downturn, but other factors probably play a more significant role. One is the aforementioned jump to screen phenomenon, as images are more often shared via the screen than by prints. The second factor is that when traditional film was developed, it was standard operating procedure to get prints (often double prints) from an entire roll of film. That package driven procedure no longer is in play with digital images, as users pick and chose only their favorite images to print.

Photo Publishing

One bright spot in the digital imaging industry is photo publishing. Initially starting in the analog era with photo calendars and custom holiday gift cards, photo publishing represents 35% of the total digital photo printing revenue, up 11% from 2005, with projected growth of 9% in 2010. Card products are responsible for almost half of this market, with customizable photo books, of which numbers were first measured in 2008, making up 30% of the market (PMA, 2010). The growth of photobooks in western Europe was even more pronounced, growing 36% in 2009 with a projection that 23 million photobooks will be shipped in 2012 (Watson, 2010a). Online printing of these goods remains the number one method of obtaining the product, with home printing second. The most popular online sources were Apple iPhoto (21% of the market), Blurb (19%) and Shutterfly (10%) (frankb, 2010a). This points to an observation that, despite the fact that we mainly record our lives via the digital image with the majority of photo sharing done electronically (via DSC, camera phone and email), we still want to preserve our fondest memories for safekeeping in an analog format.

One electronic product that actually treats digital images somewhat traditionally (though the "jump to the screen" principle still applies) is the digital photo frame. Growth in this market continues, as it is not forecasted to peak until 2011. Increased frame size is one reason for the continued success of this product, as 8" screens (up from the original 3.5" screens) have hit the market. Other growth factors include the "emergence of crossover products, such as portable/docking photo frames, leather-bound electronic 'photobooks', fridge-mounted messaging centres and products with integrated cameras, microphones and speakers which allow for communication over the Internet" (Watson, 2010b). According to 2009 statistics, 20% of U.S. households own a digital photo frame, and that number increases to 26% of DSC households. The percentage further increases based on income, as a digital photo frame will be found in 29% of households with an annual income of $75,000 or more (frankb, 2010b).

Camera Phones

Perhaps the biggest continuing trend is the number of households owning camera phones. From only 2.5% of all households owning one camera phone in 2003 (Wong, 2007), this number has jumped to 62% in 2009, with an average of two phones per household (PMA, 2010). This growth is not expected to slow, as the installed base of approximately 850 million units in 2006 is projected to reach 1.5 billion units in 2010 (CEA, 2010a). Camera phone owners took an estimated 62% of all digital images (Newton, 2010), with the total number of images taken projected to be 228 billion in 2010 (CEA, 2010b). However, of all the digital images uploaded to the most popular image sharing site Flickr in 2009, only 11% came from camera phones. "The shortage of camera phone photos posted to the web presents a unique challenge for image hosting services," said Dan Shapiro, CEO of Ontela. "Obviously, people are finding the process of getting the photos posted to be too cumbersome" (Newton, 2010). Perhaps the process will be less cumbersome in the future, as many apps that allow for streamlined image uploads exist. Three such apps for the iPhone are Reflections 1.2 from Orange Petal, Darkslide Premium 1.6.2 from Connected Flow, and Mobile Fotos 2.5.1 from Karl Von Randow. Photostream, Upload2Flickr, and PicUp are other apps available for the Android model camera phones. Additionally, the number of apps recently introduced on the market that allow for all kinds of digital manipulation to images captured by a camera phone is staggering. These apps can apply filters, control dynamic range, and create mattes, as well as reduce blurry images (anti-shake technology and image stabilizer technology), produce postcard-perfect PhotoCards, perform automatic continuous shooting, and walk the dog (Evans, 2010). OK, they don't have a camera phone app for that…yet!

🌎 Sustainability 🌎

Consumer spending in the digital imaging industry decreased in three of the four major categories in 2008 and 2009, with that trend projected to continue through 2010. Sales of DSCs peaked in 2007 and have declined every year since, as household saturation of DSCs has slowed growth, with camera replacement being the main driving force in new camera sales. Because DSC replacement is expected to occur every three to four years, a slight increase is expected in the market in 2011. Home printing consumables has followed the same path as DSC sales, peaking in 2007 and declining every year since. Retail/online printing peaked a year later, in 2008, but is expected to show the same decline. Only the photo publishing category has shown growth, as revenues increased every year since 2006. One new area for growth could be the personal and business stationery market, as a U.S. Census Bureau estimate states that these products generate more than $20 billion in revenue every year (PMA, 2010).

The good news is that image taking and sharing practices have not slowed, as the number of images saved continues to increase every year. This explains the phenomenal growth in companies such as Sandisk (flash memory/storage), and Shutterfly (social media/image sharing), whose last quarter 2009 earnings showed a 43.7% and 21.7% revenue growth rate, respectively (PMA, 2010). As long as people are still capturing images at the current growth rate, business opportunities in the $10 billion U.S. photo industry will be available.

Economic sustainability is not the only way to look at the industry, as environmental sustainability is also important. The current "green" movement affects the digital imaging industry in two distinct ways. One is the public policy stance of many of the leaders of DSC manufacturing, led by the Consumer Electronics Association (CEA). The CEA promotes their site, myGreenElectronics.org, to consumers, legislators and the press. The goal is to teach responsible purchasing and disposal practices for all electronics (CEA, 2010c). Similar efforts by Canon (Environmental Activities), Kodak (Global Sustainability Report) and Nikon (Corporate Social Responsibility), to name a few of the leading industry icons, are underway. In fact, many of these companies have been involved in this type of activity before the recent green push made it fashionable. One reason for this is that digital images, (and the previous images captured on film), have always been used to record, document and archive the state of the world, including nature photography and climate change.

This is the second way that digital imaging is involved in sustainability. For example, a recent survey, one that was accomplished only because of the advances in digital imaging, documents the earth's disappearing glaciers. This ongoing study by the Extreme Ice Survey (EIS) uses thirty three DSCs on location, recording time-lapse sequences of glaciers in the northern hemisphere. James Balog, trained geologist and photographer, leads the EIS in documenting the glaciers retreat over the period of several years. The Columbia Glacier, for example, was recorded by remotely taking snapshots during daylight hours, with a minimum of 8,000 digital images captured per year. Placed in a timeline, these images animate the life of the glacier. "People think that glaciers are these big, dead, static objects where nothing happens," says Balog. "But they're alive, and they're reacting to the climate all the time" (Ritchin, 2010b). This survey and other similar projects demonstrate digital imaging's importance in defining global sustainability issues. (Note: The digital images taken by Balog show that the Columbia Glacier retreated more than two miles in a 13 month period.)

FACTORS TO WATCH

❖ *More standard options will appear on compact, point and shoot DSCs.* Samsung's Perfect Portrait System is one example of this. Features like Face Detection, Beauty Shot, and Red Eye Fix mode, along with Samsung's Smile Shot and Blink Detection technologies will add professional capabilities to lower end DSCs (dpreview.com, 2010). Additionally, GEO-tagging capabilities will be a standard feature on many new models released in 2010, adding to the contextual information about a digital image, leading to more smart aggregation applications.

❖ *Moore's Law remains in play,* as seen with the release of the SanDisk Ultra 64 GB SDXC (secure digital extreme capacity) memory cards, as well as a 64 GB Extreme Pro card with a read and write performance of up to 90 Mb/s. Newer cards will continue to offer more storage in years to come, as they increased in capacity from 32 GB to 64 GB between 2008 and 2010, with further increases to come.

❖ *DSCs Vanishing Point (the option gap closure) becomes a reality.* This convergence is happening in two directions, as features once found only on high end expensive DSLRs are now standard on compact, point and shoot DSCs, and image quality not available on camera phones until now will soon match DSCs, as a 14.6 megapixel CMOS sensor for camera phones from Toshiba is scheduled to ship in July, 2010 (3G.co.uk).

❖ *New, powerful hardware and software will take the digital image away from its role of recording the past.* Advances to screen technology (Seadragon Ajax) will change the way we view and use the screen, and thus the images displayed on it. Meta "beehive" algorithms will alter the single image into a collective virtual footprint of our world. Manipulation software will continue to alter captured digital images; often times before they even leave the camera. How will this manipulation change the way we record our past, and how will it change the role of the digital image in society? As Frances Richard states in an article on the state of photography, "Media deliver data, and the opportunity to rewrite data, with instantaneous rapidity" (Richard, 2010).

❖ *Other sociological implications triggered by ubiquitous digital photography and the malleability of the digital image.* Sociologist Pierre Bourdieu, studying French families in the 1950s, called the camera a "festive technology," referring to the posed snapshots of extended family members (Lagessse, 2003). It has been suggested that, by capturing more images, the posed, perfect family portraits will give way to more candid snapshots, thus altering our perception of family life. Will hyper-photography, Ritchin's name for interactive digital images that provide feedback about the subject matter from the subject themselves, give us an even better understanding of the image, and thus our lives? "Whereas analog documentary photography shows what has already happened when it is often too late to help," writes Ritchin, "a proactive photography might show the future, according to expert predictions, as a way of trying to prevent it from happening" (Ritchin, 2010a).

❖ *Privacy issues will remain, as the dissemination of digital photos over the Internet increases.* Computational photography algorithms aggregate digital images from image data banks such as Flickr without regard to Flickr's Creative Commons licensing, or general copyright laws. Recently, a family portrait that was used on a Missouri family's Christmas card that was posted on a few social networking sites was later used as a storefront advertisement for a super market chain in the Czech Republic town of Prague. In a recent UK poll, two-thirds of the respondents thought that images used on Google Maps Street View were "intrusive," while 24% believed that it was a "service for burglars" (Barnett, 2010). And the Electronic Privacy Information Center (EPIC) has received complaints about the Department of Homeland Security's whole body imaging technology. EPIC president Marc Rotenberg and Ralph Nader have asked for "a comprehensive evaluation of the devices' effectiveness, health impacts, and privacy safeguards" (EPIC, 2010).

◈ *Growth in watermarking technology to communicate ownership and other information about digital images.* Digimarc for Images adds "a persistent, yet imperceptible digital watermark to your images to communicate your copyright ownership" (Digimarc, 2010). Additionally, their LicenseStream technology lets potential buyers find and pay for content with the click of a mouse.

BiblioGraphy

3G.co.uk. (2010). 15 Megapixel Camera Phone Image Sensor. *Press Release.* Retrieved March 14, 2010 from http://www.3g.co.uk/PR/Nov2009/15-Megapixel-Camera-Phone-Image-Sensor-3G.html.

Aaland, M. (1992). *Digital photography.* Avalon Books, CA: Random House.

Adobe. (2010a). Digital camera raw file support. *Adobe Photoshop CS4.* Retrieved March 8, 2010 from http://www.adobe.com/products/dng/.

Adobe. (2010b). The public, archival format for digital camera raw data. *Digital Negative (DNG).* Retrieved March 8, 2010 from http://www.adobe.com/products/dng/.

Arcas, B. A. (2010a). Talks. *Blaise Aguera y Arcas: Jaw-dropping Photosynth demo.* Retrieved March 07, 2010 from http://www.ted.com/index.php/talks/view/id/129.

Arcas, B. A. (2010b). Talks. *Blaise Aguera y Arcas demos augmented reality maps.* Retrieved March 08, 2010 from http://www.ted.com/talks/blaise_aguera.html.

Barnett, E. (2010). Google Street View: survey raises privacy concerns. *Technology.* Retrieved March 14, 2010 from http://www.telegraph.co.uk/technology/google/7430245/Google-Street-View-survey-raises-privacy-concerns.html.

Bogaty, S. (2010a). November Consumer Technology U.S. Retail Sales Revenue Positive for First Time in 2009, According to NPD. *NPD Market Research.* Retrieved March 11, 2010 from http://www.npd.com/press/releases/press_091217.html.

Bogaty, S. (2010b). NPD Retail Sales Data Shows Consumer Technology Sales down Less Than 1 Percent for the Holiday Season. *NPD Market Research.* Retrieved March 11, 2010 from http://www.npd.com/press/releases/press_100108.html.

Bogaty, S. (2010c). DSLR Aftermarket Attach Rates Decline, But Accessory Sales Still Driving Dollars, According to NPD. *NPD Market Research.* Retrieved March 11, 2010 from http://www.npd.com/press/releases/press_091111b.html.

Bryant, S. (2010). The Portable Consumer Electronics Market in Europe. *FutureSource Consulting.* Retrieved March 11, 2010 from http://www.futuresource-consulting.com/press/2009-09_ConvergingPortableDevices_release.pdf.

Business Wire. (2010a). Topaz Labs Unveils Topaz Adjust 4. *News.* Retrieved March 8, 2010 from http://www.businesswire.com/portal/site/home/permalink/?ndmViewId=news_view&newsId=20100228005111&newsLang=en.

Business Wire. (2010b). Smith Micro Software to Publish STOIK Imagic Media Management Software for Enhancing and Managing Photos and Video. *News.* Retrieved March 8, 2010 from http://www.businesswire.com/portal/site/home/permalink/?ndmViewId=news_view&newsId=20100303006643&newsLang=en.

Canon, (2010). Canon Digital Lifestyle Index. *Graph.* Retrieved March 12, 2010 from http://www.photoreview.com.au/news/education/australians-hanker-for-dslrs.aspx.

Carter, R. L. (2010a). *DigiCam History Dot Com.* Retrieved March 6, 2010 from http://www.digicamhistory.com/1980_1983.html.

Carter, R. L. (2010b). *DigiCam History Dot Com.* Retrieved March 6, 2010 from http://www.digicamhistory.com/1995%20D-Z.html.

Carter, R. L. (2010c). *DigiCam History Dot Com.* Retrieved March 6, 2010 from http://www.digicamhistory.com/1996%20S-Z.html.

Clairmont, S. (2010). Data watch: Digital camera household penetration slowing down, but sales continue. *Trends. PMA Newline International.* Retrieved March 6, 2010 from http://www.photomarketing.com/newsletter/ni_Newsline.asp?dt=07/28/2008.

Clark, R. N. (2010). Film versus digital information. *Clark Vision.* Retrieved March 6, 2010 from http://clarkvision.com/articles/how_many_megapixels/index.html.

Consumer Electronics Association. (2010a). *Digital America 2007: U.S. consumer electronic industry today.* Retrieved March 8, 2010 from http://www.nxtbook.com/nxtbooks/cea/digitalamerica07/.

Consumer Electronics Association. (2010b). *Digital America 2006: Camera phone mania.* Retrieved March 12, 2010 from http://www.ce.org/Press/CEA_Pubs/2088.asp.

Consumer Electronics Associaton. (2010c). Electronics Recycling. CEA Initiatives. Retrieved March 14, 2010 from http://www.ce.org/AboutCEA/CEAInitiatives/3645.asp.

Curtin, D. (2010). *How a digital camera works.* Retrieved March 6, 2010 from http://www.shortcourses.com/guide/guide1-3.html.

Digimarc. (2010). Digimarc for Images. *Solutions.* Retrieved March 14, 2010 from https://www.digimarc.com/solutions/

dpreview.com (2010). Capture every moment with the compact Samsung PL80. *Press Release.* Retrieved March 14, 2010 from http://www.dpreview.com/news/1001/10011901samsungsl630.asp#press

EPIC. (2010). EPIC and Ralph Nader Host Event on Body Scanners. *Top News.* Retrieved March 14, 2010 from http://epic.org/privacy/airtravel/backscatter/.

Evans, G. (2010). Archive. *Iphoneography.* Retrieved March 12, 2010 from http://www.iphoneography.com/archive.

Eye-Fi. (2010). Google + Eye-Fi. *Make your camera wireless.* Retrieved March 8, 2010 from http://www.eye.fi/.

Farace, J. (2010). Melancholytron. Digital Innovations: Joe Farace. *Shutterbug. March 2010.* p. 46.

Fidler, R. (1997). *Mediamorphosis: Understanding new media.* Pine Forge Press, p. 9

Flake, G. (2010) Talks. *Gary Flake: Is Pivot a turning point in web exploration?* Retrieved March 10, 2010 from http://www.ted.com/talks/gary_flake_is_pivot_a_turning_point_for_web _exploration.html.

Four Thirds. (2010). *About Four Thirds.* Retrieved March 6, 2010 from http://www.four-thirds.org/en/fourthirds/index.html.

Four Thirds Photo. (2010). *Micro Four Thirds Press Release.* Retrieved March 6, 2010 from http://fourthirdsphoto.com/micro43/02.php.

frankb. (2010a). PMA Data Watch: Photo Book activity of advanced amateurs. *PMA Foresight.* Retrieved March 12, 2010 from http://pmaforesight.com/?author=3.

frankb. (2010b). PMA Data Watch: A look at digital photo frame ownership and purchasing. *PMA Foresight.* Retrieved March 12, 2010 from http://pmaforesight.com/?author=3.

Goldman, J. (2010). Tap, point, and shoot: Touch-screen digital cameras. *Cnet reviews.* Retrieved March 8, 2010 from http://reviews.cnet.com/touch-screen-cameras/.

GyPSii. (2010). GyPSii Leads the Way with Mobile Social Media Content and Contextual Targeted Mobile Advertising Adds 1M New Users in Last Quarter. *News Release.* Retrieved March 10, 2010 from http://corporate.gypsii.com/docs/02122010_GyPSii_1M.pdf.

Harry Ransom Center - The University of Texas at Austin. (2010). The First Photograph. *Exhibitions.* Retrieved March 6, 2010 from http://www.hrc.utexas.edu/exhibitions/permanent/wfp/.

Hasselblad. (2010). H4D Launch. *Promotions.* Retrieved March 7, 2010 from http://www.hasselbladusa.com/media/2081132/uk_h4d_datasheet_v3.pdf

Hopkinson, M. (2010). Head to Head: A conversation with Marc Riboud and Elliot Erwitt. *Aperture. 198,* 24-28.

iSuppli. (2010). Cell phones pressure low-end digital still camera market. *News.* Retrieved March 10, 2010 from http://www.isuppli.com/News/Pages/Cell-Phones-Pressure-Low-end-Digital-Still-Camera-Market.aspx.

Kodak. (2010). *Kodachrome film. Kodachrome Discontinued.* Retrieved March 6, 2010 from http://www.kodak.com/global/en/professional/products/films/catalog/kodachrome64ProfessionalFilmPKR.jhtml?pq-path=13364.

Lagesse, D. (2003). Are photos finished? Digital makes memories easier to capture and share—But harder to hold on to. *U.S. News & World Report,* 66-69.

Lagesse, D. (2010). Suddenly, instant photos are everywhere. *U.S. News & World Report.* Retrieved March 6, 2010 from http://www.usnews.com/money/personal-finance/articles/2010/02/19/suddenly-instant-photos-are-everywhere.html.

Lester, P. (2006). *Visual communication: Images with messages.* Belmont, CA: Wadsworth.

Mandle, N. (2010). Beware shutter lag in digital cameras. *Consumer Electronics.* Retrieved March 6, 2010 from http://blogs.consumerreports.org/electronics/2010/02/buzzword-shutter-lag-first-shot-delay-lindsey-vonn-point-and-shoot-digital-photography-slr-camera-ratings-reviews.html.

many eyes. (2010). A bit of history. *About many eyes.* Retrieved March 10, 2010 from http://manyeyes.alphaworks.ibm.com/manyeyes/page/About.html.

Microsoft (2010). Innovation and research. Media and entertainment. Retrieved March 8, 2010 from http://www.microsoft.com/media/en/us/media-entertainment-solutions/innovation-research-microsoft-media-entertainment-industry.aspx.

Mobile Acuity. (2010). *Mobile Acuity.* Retrieved March 10, 2010 from http://www.mobileacuity.com/.

mocoNews.net. (2010). Mobile content bits: Gypsii/Telefonica, Red Cross, American Greetings, Handmark's Olympics App. *Topics.* Retrieved March 10, 2010 from http://moconews.net/article/419-mobile-content-bits-gypsiitelefonica-red-cross-american-greetings-handm/.

Naone, E. (2010). Making sense of mountains of data. *Technology Review.* Retrieved March 10, 2010 from http://www.technologyreview.com/web/24645/page1/.

National Press Photographers Association. (2010). Digital manipulation code of ethics. *NPPA statement of principle.* Retrieved March 6, 2010 from http://www.nppa.org/professional_development/business_practices/digitalethics.html

Newton, R. (2010). Camera Phone Pictures Still Stuck. *PR Web.* Retrieved March 12, 2010 from http://www.prweb.com/releases/2009/06/prweb2584154.htm.

Pavlik, J. & McIntosh, S. (2004). Converging media: An introduction to mass communications. Pearson Education, MA: Allyn & Bacon.

PCMAG.com. (2010). 21 Great Technologies That Failed. Features. Retrieved March 6, 2010 from
    http://www.pcmag.com/article2/0,2817,2325943,00.asp

Phase One. (2010). *Capture One 5PRO*. Retrieved March 8, 2010 from http://www.phaseone.com/Software/Capture-One-5-Pro/Pro-
    Features.aspx.

Photo Marketing Association Research Department. (2010). *Photo Industry 2010: Review and Forecast*. Jackson, MI: Photo Marketing
    Association.

Photoshop.com. (2010). *Test drive*. Retrieved March 8, 2010 from https://www.photoshop.com/?wf=testdrive

Pictures that lie. (2010). *C/NET News*. Retrieved March 14, 2010 from http://news.cnet.com/2300-1026_3-6033210-20.html?tag=mncol.

Polaroid. (2010). Lady Gaga Named Creative Director for Specialty Line of Polaroid Imaging Products. *News*. Retrieved March 6, 2010
    from http://www.polaroid.com/About/News/Press+Release:+Lady+Gaga+Named+Creative+
    Director+for+Specialty+Line+of+Polaroid+Imaging+Products/4339.

Richard, F. (2010). Photography's Ghosts: The Image and Its Artifice. *The Nation*. Retrieved March 14, 2010 from
    http://www.thenation.com/doc/20090316/richard.

Ritchin, F. (2008). Of other times and places. *Aperture, 190*, 74-77.

Ritchin, F. (2010a). Exposure Time. *Essay – Change Observer*. Retrieved March 14, 2010 from
    http://changeobserver.designobserver.com/entry.html?entry=11447#last.

Ritchin, F. (2010b). Of Art and Ice: James Balog. *Aperture, 196*, 80-81.

Saffo, P. (2010). *Technological ages*. Retrieved March 8, 2008 from http://www.saffo.com/idea3.php.

Sci_Fun. (2010). Mobile Acuity – Spellbinder. *Research Projects*. Retrieved March 10, 2010 from http://www.scifun.ed.ac.uk/main.html.

Seadragon. (2010). *Seadragon Developer*. Retrieved March 8, 2010 from http://www.seadragon.com/developer/.

Sheerin, M. (2008). Digital imaging and photography. In Grant, A. and Meadows, J. (Eds.) *Communication Technology Update and
    Fundamentals*, Eleventh Edition. Boston: Focal Press.

Smart, E.J., Cascio, J., and Paffendorf, J. (2007). *Metaverse Roadmap. Pathways to the 3D Web (pdf)*. San Pedro, CA: Accelerated
    Studies Foundation

Sketch2Photo. (2010). *Sketch2Photo: Internet Image Montage*. Retrieved March 10, 2010 from
    http://www.ece.nus.edu.sg/stfpage/eletp/Projects/Sketch2Photo/index.htm.

Sony Ericsson. (2010). Satio specifications. *Phones and accessories*. Retrieved March 10, 2010 from
    http://www.sonyericsson.com/cws/corporate/products/phoneportfolio/specification/satio.

The Impossible Project. (2010). Will there ever be new film for Polaroid cameras? *Press Release*. Retrieved March 6, 2010 from
    http://www.the-impossible-project.com/resources/press_releases/2010-02-08.pdf.

Tuckman, B. (2010, March 8). *Personal communication*.

Watson, A. C. (2010a). Digital photo frame market worth 750m Euros in Western Europe. *Press release*. Retrieved March 12, 2010 from
    http://www.futuresource-consulting.com/press/2009-10_PhotoBooks-Europe_release.pdf.

Watson, A. C. (2010b). Photobook market to grow 36% in Western Europe this year. *Press release*. Retrieved March 12, 2010 from
    http://www.futuresource-consulting.com/press/2009-04_DPF-follow-up_release.pdf.

Wauters, R. (2010). Kooaba debuts image recognition API. *TechCrunch*. Retrieved March 10, 2010 from
    http://techcrunch.com/2010/03/04/kooaba-debuts-image-recognition-api/.

Wong, M. (2007). Camera phone pioneer mulls gadget impact. Technology. Wi-Fi center. *USA Today*. Retrieved March 11, 2008 from
    http://www.usatoday.com/tech/wireless/ phones/2007-05-19-camera-phone_N.htm.

YouTube. (2010). *Kooaba screencast*. Retrieved March 10, 2010 from http://techcrunch.com/2010/03/04/kooaba-debuts-image-
    recognition-api/.

Zink Imaging. (2010). Developing with Zink. *Meet Zink Imaging*. Retrieved March 6, 2010 from
    http://www.inkless.com/files/ZINK_Imaging_Corp_brochure_9_04_08.pdf.

IV

Networking Technologies

18

Telephony

Jack Karlis, M.A.M.C. & Matthew Telleen, J.D.*

When AT&T launched its slogan "Reach out and touch someone" in 1979, it surely had in mind only the wired telephones that have existed for most of the 20th Century.

If AT&T was to relaunch its slogan in 2010, it might say, "Reach out and text, call, ping, IM, Facebook, and while you're at it, surf the Web, do your shopping, banking, and learn something new." The new slogan may have grown larger than the original, but so have the capabilities of phones that have become one of the most important, if not *the* most important, technology in the 21st Century—telephony.

Mobile phones have become an extension of our lives, containing vital information, data, social networking tools, and customized to our personal tastes. Our phones can give us step-by-step geographic directions, inform us what our friends and family are doing, provide instantaneous communication with others, tell us how our stocks are doing, and let us know what the weather is like half a world away. That is only the tip of what we are going to be able to do with phones in the very near future.

The complex history of telephony reads like a roadmap with twists and turns through the forest of legislation and deregulation and ultimately to where we stand now—looking at a wide open plain with endless possibilities we couldn't have imagined or intended when voice communication technology began.

Background

Traditional Wired Telephony in the United States

The telephone was invented by Alexander Graham Bell in 1876, but like most technological advances, it didn't appear from out of the blue (AT&T, 2010a). There had been several other inventions and discoveries that led to the technology used in the telephone. The telephone operates by converting sound waves into electrical impulses, transferring them across a wire, and then converting them back into a tone similar to the original. One invention that preceded the telephone and played a role in the development of telephony was the telegraph, invented by Samuel Morse in 1838 (Bellis, 2010d). Once the telegraph demonstrated the ability to transfer signals via a wire, the next step was to find a way to transfer voice. In fact, there were at least two other inventors working on the technology at the same time as Bell. One of them, Elisha Gray, arrived at the patent office only hours after Bell (Bellis, 2010b). Another, Antonio Meucci, had filed paperwork called a patent

---

*Doctoral Candidates, School of Journalism and Mass Communications, University of South Carolina (Columbia, South Carolina).

caveat with the U.S. Patent Office in December 1871, five years before Bell (Bellis, 2010c). A patent caveat is basically a placeholder for an invention one intends to patent, but is not yet ready to present (Gray was also intending to file a caveat). Meucci renewed his caveat in 1872, 1873 and 1874, but then let it lapse, so Bell was able to receive his patent in 1876 and ultimately credit for the telephone (Bellis, 2010a).

The question of who actually came up with the idea was incredibly controversial, and led to more than 600 lawsuits (Ament, 2006). However, none of them successfully proved that Bell did not invent the technology himself and file the first legal patent for the technology (Bellis, 2010a). The controversy lives on, however, and as recently as 2001, a resolution was brought before U.S. Congress to formally recognize the role Meucci played in inventing the telephone (Fossella, 2001).

Bell moved forward with his invention by forming the Bell Telephone Company, which would later become AT&T (AT&T, 2010a). Under the leadership of Theodore Vail, AT&T began pushing for universal service in the early 1900s, and began fighting with the government over its monopoly status. However, after the *Communications Act of 1934*, AT&T was authorized as an American telephone monopoly, providing local telephone service to about 90% of the country and providing the interconnections (long distance service) among the 5000+ smaller companies that served the other 10% (AT&T, 2010b).

AT&T continued to operate as a monopoly for much of the next 40 years. During that time, telephones nearly reached complete universal adoption as the number of households with telephones rose from 50% in 1945 to 90% in 1969. Two factors worked to assist AT&T with their monopoly status; the first was government acquiescence and the second was technological dominance. The government did decide to allow AT&T to function as a monopoly, but the technological advancements produced by Bell Labs, AT&T's research and development arm, helped the government justify its decision. From 1940 to 1970, Bell Labs played a role in the development of the laser, the transistor, the solar cell, data networking, communications satellites, the Unix operating system, and the C programming language.

But others were creating telephone innovations as well, and these innovations played a role in the eventual downfall of the AT&T monopoly. Lawsuits by inventors of complimentary or competing technologies chipped away at AT&T's monopoly. At the same time, Department of Justice attorneys were realizing that, in many ways, AT&T's monopoly was limiting some innovations and price competition.

In 1982, AT&T agreed to a final agreement that it would divest itself of its local telephone operations (AT&T, 2010b). This dramatic change in corporate structure was happening at the same time that another, more significant change was being developed that would change the telephone landscape forever.

The Evolution of Wireless Telephony Technologies

Wireless telephones are portable telephones with a built-in antenna that communicate over radio waves. AT&T first developed the concept of a cellular telephone in 1947. A mobile telephone transmits a call to a tower, which then routes the call to a switching office, which then transmits the call to the appropriate switching office for the receiving phone and finally through another tower to the receiving phone or through the wired network if the call is to a landline phone. The towers are spaced throughout a geographic area, dividing the area into "cells." Therefore, mobile phones that use this process came to be known as cellular phones (Brain et. al, 2010).

Just as with the traditional phone, the cellular phone was not invented out of the blue. Even though AT&T developed the concept in the 1940s, it was decades before anyone successfully utilized the technology to make phone calls from remote locations (AT&T, 2010b) The first cellular phone call was made in April 1973.

Dr. Martin Cooper had developed the technology while working for Motorola's Communications Systems Division. His first call was to a rival at AT&T's Bell Labs, which was trying to create a similar device. Ten years later, Motorola developed the first commercial cellular phone, the DynaTAC. It became known as "The Brick," because it weighed 16-ounces and cost $3500 (Marples, 2008).

The first cellular phone network used the 800 MHz and 900 MHz frequency bands and was referred to as IG. It was an analog network that only allowed for voice communications. In the early 1990s, the FCC allocated spectrum for PCS (personal communications services). This technology along with digital cellular became known as 2G, and it used smaller cells than the IG technology. That innovation allowed for more cells to inhabit one area while providing for better and faster coverage. The technology was also digital, which used a more advanced system of binary decoding to break down messages faster. 2G was capable of delivering wireless voice and data with 14.4 Kb/s data bandwidth (Phifer, 2009).

2G was the first available on a system called GSM (global system for mobile communications). GSM was the standard technology in Europe, but in the United States, there is no regulated standard, and different providers use different systems. AT&T and T-Mobile both used GSM, but Sprint and Verizon used an alternative technology called CDMA (code division multiple access) (Chavis, 2010).

While 2G was a significant improvement over IG, it was soon overwhelmed by the demand to connect to the Internet and send text messages in addition to phone conversations. An improved set of systems dubbed 2.5G increased speeds further, introducing General Packet Radio Service (GPRS) which enabled packet switching and increasing speeds to 80 Kbps. GPRS was superseded by Enhanced Data rates for Global Evolution (EDGE) which provided download speeds of up to 200 Kbps.

The next generation of wireless technology was called 3G. Like 2G, there is no single system for 3G, rather 3G is a term coined by the International Telecommunications Union (ITU) which describes systems that can handle voice and data simultaneously and provide higher data rates than 2G networks, ranging from 300 Kbps to 1 Mbps. Providing faster service required technological upgrades, and competing wireless companies in the United States have attempted to use the scope of their 3G network coverage as a competitive marketing tool (Phifer, 2009).

Figure 18.1

The Evolution from 2G to 3G Mobile Technologies

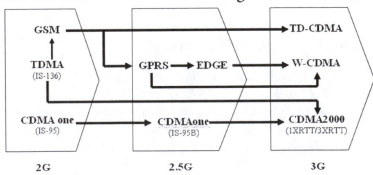

Source: ITU (2000)

Internet Telephony: VoIP

There is not a real difference between the underlying science involved in traditional telephones and mobile phones. In both cases, a device is created that can transform information into a form that can be transferred and then reversing the process so the information appears at the other end the same way it started. Whether the information is a voice, text, or Web site, the process is the same. The big difference between the two telephone technologies is the methods for transporting the information. Once we understand this, it seems natural that other modes of communicating information could be used for telephony. One such development is VoIP or Voice over Internet Protocol.

VoIP can use hardware identical to traditional telephone lines. You can still plug your phone into the wall and send your voice into the phone and into the wires in your wall. The only difference is the technology that is then used to transform and then transport your voice. Traditional telephone lines use the public switched telephone network (PSTN), which transports the data on the two wire cords we associate with home phones and the phone lines we see in our neighborhoods and along our highways. VoIP uses the wiring that is used to deliver high speed Internet into the home (Valdes, 2010).

VoIP can describe two very different services. The first, as mentioned above, uses the same phones as traditional telephone lines. Examples of this type of service include phone service provided by cable companies and devices such as MagicJack. The second can use personal computers and devices that can access the Internet using services such as Skype. Both require broadband Internet access to work and are addressed later in this chapter in the Current Status section (Valdes, 2010).

VoIP has several advantages over using the PSTN. The first is that using the PSTN is inherently limited because each connection becomes a closed loop, meaning only two people can use that line at a time. This means that circuits can become jammed, and it is expensive to connect two people who are far away from each other, which is why companies have traditionally charged for long distance calls. VoIP calls only use bandwidth when sound is being communicated, which means that many calls can use the same line. This means that VoIP is both more efficient and less expensive (RADDataCommunications, 2001). Another advantage is mobility. When using the VoIP services that utilize Internet-capable devices such as laptops, a person can make a phone call anywhere an Internet connection is available.

One problem for VoIP is the need to have enough bandwidth to deliver quality. If some packets of information are lost or dropped because of a lack of bandwidth, the audio quality suffers, and the call becomes unclear. Cable companies using VoIP can account for this by prioritizing voice data on their own networks, but external services such as Skype and Vonage cannot control for this, and call quality can suffer because of it. VoIP quality can improve as compression technology improves.

VoIP faces other challenges as well. Landlines are more reliable than VoIP and use an independent power source. VoIP is dependent upon Internet service, which use modems with traditional power sources that may be lost during a power outage. In addition, landlines have worked with emergency services to provide additional details when someone dials 911. The FCC has started requiring VoIP providers to meet Enhanced 911 (E911) obligations, but as of mid-2010 there is still not complete compliance.

Recent Developments

In 2009, the United States Government passed a $787 billion Stimulus Bill to help the slumping economy. Included in the bill was $7.2 billion for the expansion of broadband Internet coverage (IBISWorld, 2010a). This legislation is significant because increased broadband will provide a competitive advantage to VoIP, allowing more people to choose this alternative form of telephony. One of the challenges facing VoIP's adoption is the need discussed above to ensure packet delivery. While increased broadband access should help, bandwidth issues could be exacerbated by the increase in Internet capable technologies. Mobile devices designed to utilize Wi-Fi instead of cellular access to the Internet could increase competition for bandwidth and challenge the ability of providers to handle increased traffic, a problem discussed in the Factor to Watch section.

A similar problem is facing cellular companies as smart phone growth is prompting a huge increase in demand for data traffic on wireless networks. This problem continues to loom as smart phones continue to grow in popularity. Smart phones are making up an increasing percentage of cell phone sales. In 2009, mobile phone sales as a whole actually decreased worldwide by 0.9%, possibly because of the global economic downturn. At the same time, global sales of smart phones rose by 23.8%. Smart phones only made up roughly 14% of total, global phone sales for 2009, but they made up almost 16% in the fourth quarter so their share of the market should continue to grow (Whitney, 2010).

As more users purchase smart phones and use their phones for data as well as voice, they will continue to demand fast and uninterrupted access. In the same way that carriers have been using the size of their 3G networks as a marketing device, at least one major U.S. wireless company is relying on the expansion of its 4G network to woo customers. At the end of 2009, Sprint began promoting itself as having the only 4G network (Sprint, 2010). Just like 3G, 4G is a standard that has been defined by the ITU. However, there is debate as to what can be labeled 4G and whether 4G coverage is markedly superior to 3G coverage and worth the cost of upgrading technology (Chavis, 2010).

The percentage of Americans who rely exclusively on their cell phone is growing. In the first six months of 2009, 22.5% of households had no landline but at least one cell phone. In 2008, that number was 17.5% and in 2005, it was only 7.8%. Even some of those adults with landlines are receiving all or almost all of their phone calls via cell phones. During the first six months of 2009, 16.2% of adults lived in "wireless-mostly" homes, an increase of 2.2% over the same period in 2008 (Blumberg, 2009).

Over the past several years, various sectors of the telephony industry have seen substantial mergers resulting in changes in the power structure and the major players involved. Chapter 4 explained the mergers of various service providers. In addition, the hardware side saw substantial mergers when Alcatel and Lucent merged in 2006, (Gubbins, 2006) followed by Nokia and Siemens in 2007 (Fitchard, 2007). In 2009, Nortel Networks declared bankruptcy, with, several companies buying portions of the fallen giant. Ericsson purchased Nortel's wireless assets for $1.13 billion, outbidding Nokia Siemens. (Austen, 2009a). Avaya paid $900 million for a unit that makes communications equipment for corporations and governments. (Austen, 2009b). Ciena purchased Nortel's Metro Ethernet Network (MEN) for $773.8 million and Genband paid $282 million for Nortel's VoIP assets. (Fitchard, 2010).

One aspect it seems that the U.S. media is not picking up on, but is being speculated in other areas of the world, are the long-term effects of mobile phone use. Medical scientists have looked at the lack of adolescents' recall of mobile phone use in Australia and found that the recall of their actual use was not accurate with recording software estimates, which makes it difficult to truly measure phone use (Inyang et al., 2009). Others have looked at the microwave exposure and nonionizing radiation emitted by mobile phones and have predicted "consequential biological effects" (Rothman, 2009).

CURRENT STATUS

It's a Wireless World

The most important aspect of telephony to examine from the financial, technological and societal views is the wireless sector. By the end of 2009, there were almost 4.7 billion mobile subscribers worldwide, a figure more than 2.5 times the count five years prior (IBISWorld, 2009).

While mobile telephony is prevalent in U.S. society, consider the magnitude it has globally. In the global market, wireless telecommunications providers yielded a crop of $927.8 billion in total revenue with more than 4,676.6 million subscribers and employed 1,767,860 people in 2009 (IBISWorld, 2009). Global Systems for Mobile communications or GSMs (2G and 2.5G technologies) devoured 78.8% of the global market share. Earning 8.5% and 8.3% respectively, W-CDMA (3G and 3.5 G technologies, Wireless Code Division Multiple Access) and CDMA trailed GSMs considerably during the same time frame (IBISWorld, 2009).

Geographic location had a significant influence on revenue streams. Europe was the leader with $304 billion in revenue, followed by North America ($226 billion), North Asia ($186 billion), Africa and the Middle East ($85 billion), South America ($56 billion), India and Central Asia ($43 billion), Oceania ($14.5 billion), and South East Asia ($13 billion) (IBISWorld, 2009). Revenues are projected to arrive at the level of $1.4 trillion by 2015 (IBISWorld, 2009).

As of mid 2010, the global wireless market is dominated by five major wireless telecommunication providers: Vodafone Group Pic (7.1% market share), China Mobile Limited (7.1%), AT&T, Inc. (5.7%), Deutsche Telekom AG (5.4%), and NTT DoCoMo (4.5%) with the other 70.2% remaining comprised of a potpourri of carriers (IBISWorld, 2009). Other notable carriers include U.S. Cellular, Bharti Airtel, Singapore Telecommunications, America Movil, Sprint Nextel, France Telecom, Alltel, Telenor, Telstra, Hutchinson, KPN, Mobile Telesystems and Singapore Telecommunications.

In 2010, the number of mobile subscribers is expected to grow by 15.4% with new growth in the India, Central Asia, Africa, Middle East, and South East Asia markets (IBISWorld, 2009). The ascension to 3G, 3.5G and ultimately 4G technologies may generate more revenues and subscribers.

Europe, North America and North Asia alone were predicted to account for 77.2% of the global market share in 2009 with the United States expected to account for 20.8% of global wireless revenues, but just 6.2% of subscribers, compared with China's 16.2% of the total global number of subscribers (IBISWorld, 2009).

The United States of America, by comparison, produced revenue of $205 billion from more than 296 million wireless subscribers (IBISWorld, 2010a). General consumers and residential customers comprised the majority (55%) of the wireless market segment, and is expected to grow even more in the coming years, while small/medium businesses (30%) and corporate segments (15%) trailed (IBISWorld, 2010a).

Geographically, the Southeast (25.2%) made up the largest percentage of wireless subscribers, while the West (18.1), Mid-Atlantic (16.3), Great Lakes (14.4), Southwest (11.6), Plains (6.3), New England (4.7) and Rocky Mountains (3.2) trailed behind (IBISWorld, 2010a).

Just as in the global market, a few major carriers dominate the market. Verizon Wireless, AT&T Mobility, Sprint Nextel and T-Mobile. Verizon Wireless, jointly owned by Verizon Communications and British wireless giant Vodafone, had 32.2% of the U.S. wireless market share in 2009 (IBISWorld, 2010a). AT&T laid claim to second with 27.4% of the market share (IBISWorld, 2010a). Sprint Nextel owned 14.4%, T-Mobile (part of German company Deustche Telekom) owned 11%, and a mixture of other smaller wireless providers accounted for the last 15% (IBISWorld, 2010a). Other smaller wireless providers include U.S. Cellular, Metro PCS, and Cox Communications.

T-Mobile might be a company to watch, given that it is selling the Google phone, a handset that doesn't require a wireless carrier to subsidize it. T-Mobile introduced contract-free EMP (Even More Plus) plans in 2009 that did not require subscribers to agree to subsidized cell phone price as a term of purchase (IBIS-World, 2010a). The EMP plans and the Google phone are a natural fit. The two companies also have a history of collaborating as four of T-Mobile's phones already use the Google Android platform. The Google phone is addressed in greater detail later in this chapter.

Don't look for the wireless market to recede in the coming years. Some projections find that 91.3% of the U.S. population currently has a cell phone as the wireless penetration rate has jumped 30% in the past five years with nearly 20% of the U.S. population living in a wireless-only household (IBISWorld, 2010a). The future has a decidedly wireless flavor in its forecast. Nearly 66% of Americans between the ages of 16 and 29 would opt for a cell phone over a landline and 34% of Americans between the ages of 25 and 29 live in a wireless-only household (IBISWorld, 2010a).

The motivations behind the use of wireless handsets may be another indicator used to predict where the wireless technology may be headed. While sociability, instrumentality, and reassurance were found to be the main gratifications of the conventional household telephone (Dimmick et al., 1994), mobile phones opened new uses and gratifications of telephony. Even before Leung and Wei (2000) found that the strongest motives for using cellular phones were mobility, immediacy and instrumentality, they found information seeking and instrumentality were significant predictors for mobile pager use for news (Leung & Wei, 1999). When looking at the motivations for using mobile phones for mass communications and entertainment, Wei (2008) found that the mobile phone was a hybrid medium that combined both interpersonal and mass communication. He also found that the instrumental use motives were for seeking news and surfing the Web (Wei, 2008). With Internet ready phones in today's market, consumers can access news anytime they want.

According to a Pew Research Center study, 33% of cell phone users (26% of all Americans) access news on their phones (Purcell et al., 2010). Users look the most closely for weather (26% of mobile phone users), news and current events (25%), a news application (18%), sports scores and stories (16%), traffic information (13%), financial information (12%), and news via e-mails or texts (11%) (Purcell, et, al., 2010).

M-Commerce

Besides providing social interaction and information seeking, mobile phones are becoming electronic retail outlets. Naturally, retailers and big businesses will look to take advantage of this growing revenue channel.

M-Commerce or Mobile Commerce can be defined as any transaction with monetary value that is made from an online mobile device. In 2009, ABI Research projected m-commerce sales of physical items to reach $544 million in North America alone with some estimates as high as $800 million, a number up from $346 million in 2008 (Kharif, 2009). In 2006, it was predicted that 25% of all cell phones users would use m-commerce to buy physical items and content, but recent figures show only 7% of U.S. Consumers used their phones to make purchases according to a Nielsen Mobile survey (Kharif, 2009). During the 2009 holiday season, 19% of Americans planned to use their mobile device for shopping (finding store locations, obtaining coupons and sales information, and researching products and prices) while 39% of the 18-19 age demographic said they would use their devices for shopping (USA Today, 2009). In a survey of 407 mobile users in Singapore, Wei, Hao and Pan (2009) found that when users respond positively to SMS ads, the ads themselves can affect purchasing. The financial impact of m-commerce may currently be small, but there is potential for dynamic growth in the near future.

While just two online retailers (e-Bay and Amazon.com) sold 70% of all physical goods through m-Commerce in 2008, less than 20% of established retailers had a mobile Web site (Kharif, 2009). Consumers can expect that market share to change as half of established retailers were expected to have a mobile outlet by the end of 2009 (Kharif, 2009). Papa John's took a dip into the m-commerce pool in the middle of 2008 by offering its product for order through its mobile Web sites. By December of that year, sales had reached $1 million through the mobile site, and growth is expected to continue "ten-fold" through m-commerce for the company (Kharif, 2009). Content such as apps, music, and electronic media content are also making their mark. Mobile content stores report sales increasing by double and triple digits, and Apple alone reported two billion app downloads for its iPhones and iPod Touch (Kharif, 2009) as of September 2009. Companies such as Starbucks are launching their own apps (Kharif, 2009).

In order to access and use mobile sites for m-commerce, users must have a Web-capable phone such as a BlackBerry, iPhone, or other Internet ready device. During the second fiscal quarter of 2008, only 19% of all handset purchases were smart phones (Kharif, 2009). By comparison, during the same time period in 2009, 28% of all phones sold were smart phones and in a statistic that is even more telling of future growth, 33% of mobile phone service subscribers without data or Web plans were looking to purchase a smart phone within the next year (Kharif, 2009). Globally, markets in Asia have led the way in m-commerce and there is dynamic growth expected in South American markets (Burger, 2007).

There are, however, deterrents to the growth of m-commerce, namely limited bandwidth coverage and security concerns. A few select devices and services are devouring the majority of the bandwidth as it currently stands. AT&T's iPhone has received the majority of blame and has even been labeled by Sanford C. Bernstein analyst Craig Moffett as "a kind of predator parasite on the wireless network, sucking out the value and leaving networks gasping for air" (Kharif, 2009) for its bandwidth troubles during its first three years of existence (Gruman, 2010). Consumers can expect the problem to exacerbate by 2014 as mobile data traffic is expected to increase by a factor of 12 since 2008 with the spread of 3G smart books, laptops, and net books (Gruman, 2010). The projected figures add up to 9.7 exabytes (9.7 million terabytes) of data, but only 10% of that total will come from smart phones according to ABI Research (Gruman, 2010). Slow access speeds are currently a problem as a Keynote study recently found the download times for homepages of major retailers to be a fair 8.3 seconds to a paltry 34.4 seconds (Hornick, 2010). The study also found the product search results to range from 4.5 seconds to 37.9 seconds and product information with a best time of 5.7 seconds to 26.8 seconds (Hornick, 2010).

With 4G technologies not expected to arrive in full force until 2015 (Gruman, 2010), m-commerce is facing a major problem with the limited bandwidth resources and unlimited data plans. However, Sprint has jumped ahead of the curve by introducing 4G service in 27 U.S. markets and plans to offer service in Cleveland, Cincinnati, Los Angeles, Miami, Pittsburgh, Salt Lake City, St. Louis, Boston, Denver, Kansas City, Houston, Minneapolis, New York City, San Francisco, and Washington, D.C (Sprint, 2010).

Security is another major concern for proposed m-commerce users. From 2002 to 2006, a time of large mobile expansion, the Federal Trade Commission reported identity theft cases at their highest numbers in states and geographic regions with the largest populations (Koong et al., 2008). When the population was factored in, however, the trends of concentration were not as bad as initially reported and 2006 was the first year that displayed a decline in the number of reported cases (Koong et al., 2008). According to 41st Parameter, a fraud detection and prevention firm, there will be more mobile channel cybercrime and decreased effectiveness of traditional anti-fraud tactics due to the rapid adoption of new mobile handsets and multiple operating systems (Hartz, 2009).

Transactions trust significantly affects consumers' intentions adopt to m-commerce (Kao, 2009). In a study of Korean m-commerce in digital music transactions, Choi found that content reliability and transaction process were significant factors to customer satisfaction and loyalty in m-commerce transactions (Choi, et. al., 2008). There are also technical limitations in the hardware, specifically processing power, battery life, communication bandwidth, and device memory that limit the available cryptography standards for mobile security (Hamad et al., 2009).

Despite these constraints, m-banking and m-commerce are expected to blossom. More than 60% of Americans have expressed an interest in accessing credit card details, balances, and transactions through their mobile phones, while 64% would use their device for price comparisons, according to research by m-banking firm Firethorn (Over half, 2009). In a surveillance capacity, 85% say they like to access their finances daily through a mobile phone, and nearly 66% of all respondents are likely to download and use a free account management application (Over half, 2009).

Measures are being put into place to improve financial transactions through mobile devices. Zarifopoulos and Economides (2009) proposed a 164-criteria based Mobile Banking Evaluation Framework that focuses on interface, navigation, content, offered services, reliability, and technical aspects. In October 2009, Amazon introduced its "Mobile Payments Service," which lets customers pay using shipping and financial information stored on Amazon (Kharif, 2009). Visa is releasing an app that stores a user's credit-card information on a mobile phone and, when a consumer goes to a retailer's mobile Web site to purchase something, it prequalifies the purchaser in the payment field (Kharif, 2009).

The Status of VoIP

VoIP (Voice over Internet Protocol) is another option in voice communication that is surpassing the traditional hard-wired phones lines that have been around for most of the 20th Century. The VoIP industry accounted for $12.3 billion in revenue with 29.8 million subscribers (IBISWorld, 2010b) in the United States. Cable VoIP providers, which account for 71% of the total VoIP subscribers, have a decidedly important advantage over pure VoIP providers. In addition to VoIP services that they sometimes refer to as "digital telephone" services, cable VoIP providers offer television programming packages, Internet services, and standard wireless services. U.S. households (76% of the market) consume the vast majority of VoIP, distantly followed by businesses (22%) (IBISWorld, 2010b). Government accounted for only 2% (IBISWorld, 2010b), but as VoIP technology begins to replace existing traditional communication technologies, new opportunities will inevitably arise (Subramaya et al., 2009).

Mirroring the geographic concentration of wireless services in the United States, VoIP has greater penetration in the Southeast, followed by the West, Mid-Atlantic, Great Lakes, Southwest, Plains, New England, and the Rocky Mountains (IBISWorld, 2010b).

There are four major VoIP providers in the United States: Comcast, Time Warner Cable, Cox and Vonage. Comcast is the leader in market share (31.5%) nearly doubling its closest competitor, Time Warner Cable (16.2%). Cox (9.6%), and Vonage (8.3%) significantly trail Time Warner in market share, but a subplot drawing considerable interest is the 34.4% of the market share filled by other companies. Skype may be one of the more highly publicized free VoIP services (1.5% of market share), but there are a variety of other enterprises trying to make a name for them in the VoIP market (IBISWorld, 2010b). MagicJack, another VoIP service that boasts free long distance service over the first year for less than $50, has received ample attention from the media (Mossberg, 2010; Magicjack, 2010)

VoIP may also be provided through Wi-Fi and Wi-Max technologies as VoIP providers, specifically cable companies, look to maximize their services and profits. Some are investing capital in Clearwire, most notably with its major shareholder Sprint (Sprint, 2010), a Wi-Max company that offers 4G technology (as discussed in Chapter 21), while others are developing their own networks with 3G capability but with aspirations of becoming 4G networks.

Although price and perceived quality of services are key determinants of VoIP adoption, it cannot be overlooked that an Internet connection is required in order to make it work correctly, adding another complication to the spread of VoIP services. When looking at VoIP from a theoretical perspective, the perceived ease of use of VoIP technology has an impact on its perceived usefulness, while perceived usefulness had a positive effect on actual use of the technology (Park, 2010).

Wired Telephone Service

Household telephones with hard-wired lines, the traditional units that have been a part of American society for most of the 20th Century, first started out with a low percentage of housing units with service before becoming ubiquitous. As of November 2009, 95.7% of all U.S. households (119 million) had telephone service, an increase of 0.7% from the year before and the highest number ever reported by the Census Population Survey (FCC, 2010).

The telephone penetration rate for households in income brackets below $15,000 was 94.0%, and the rate for households with $50,000 or more was at least 98.2% (FCC, 2010). The rate for unemployed subscribers was 94.7% compared with 96.8% for employed adults (FCC, 2010). Penetration rates varied by state, with rates bottoming out at 90.9% (New Mexico) and topping out at 99% (Oregon) (FCC, 2010). Age is related to penetration rate, with households under the control of a person under the age of 25 having the lowest reported penetration rate of 93.1% as opposed to the 96.6% rate reported by households headed by a person over 55 (FCC, 2010).

There are some advances coming in wired phone technology. Comcast Corp.'s digital enhanced cordless telecommunications (DETC) is interface free and can handle Internet applications while Cox Communications is adding new applications to its voice model such as unified messaging and voicemail on the desktop (Hardesty, 2009).

With the looming threat of wireless only households and VoIP, telephone providers will likely concentrate most of their efforts on offering "bundles" or improving Internet service. As "bundles" become more prevalent, it is interesting to compare the major players that offer cable, Internet, and telephone services for the United States with traditional phone companies. In 2009, Comcast was the leader in market share among bundle providers (37.4%), followed by Liberty Media (20.5%), DISH Network (13.4%), Time Warner (6.5%), and Charter Communications (4%) (IBISWorld, 2010c). Conversely, the major wired telecommunication providers in the United States are AT&T (30.5% market share), Verizon (23.4%), Qwest Communications International (4.8%) and a mixture of smaller companies (Sprint Nextel, Century Link, Frontier Communications, Windstream and Level 3) comprising the remaining 41.3% of the market (IBISWorld, 2010d).

At the beginning of 2010, Verizon laid claim to 9.22 million total wireline broadband connections (Verizon, 2010). The company's FiOS (fiber optic) Internet division served more than 3.43 million households in 16 states (Verizon, 2010).

While the technology and coverage areas are expanding, so, too, are the problems associated with them. At the forefront of controversy is the use of mobile devices to talk or text while driving an automobile. According to a report by the National Center for Injury Prevention and Control and the Division of Unintentional Injury Prevention, transportation is the largest cause (72.3%) of unintentional injury deaths among 15-19 year olds (Sleet et, al., 2010). The study specifically cites the use of mobile phones, texting, and Internet use as major contributors to unplanned deaths in automobile accidents. The National Highway and Safety Administration reported 5,870 deaths and 500,000 injuries due to distracted or inattentive drivers in 2008 (Copeland, 2010a). As of mid 2010, 19 states and the District of Columbia prohibit texting while driving, and 23 more are deliberating a ban on texting while driving to avoid losing 25% of their federal highway funds (Copeland, 2010b). The Department of Transportation recently passed legislation prohibiting drivers of commercial vehicles from sending text messages or they will face civil or criminal penalties up to $2,750 (Industry Notes, 2010). The Federal Motor Carrier Safety Administration states that drivers who send texts while driving are 20 times more likely to get in an accident than non distracted drivers (Industry Notes, 2010).

🌍 Sustainability 🌍

As consumers, we get excited when we imagine what the changes in technology will allow our cell phones to do in the coming years. As an industry, the projected advances provide opportunities for companies to offer exciting new products. Having smarter phones will make our worlds more connected, more convenient and more accessible. But with all these new phones changing the way we live, one question emerges: What happens to all the old phones?

That is a question that is concerning the United Nations. In February 2010, the UN's Environmental Programme (UNEP) released a report addressing the environmental hazards posed by the rapid increase in the production of cell phones and other electronics (UN, 2010).

The problem is twofold. On the one hand, there is simply a large increase in the quantity of e-waste, and cell phones are a major contributor. After all, there were more than a billion cell phones sold in 2007. The United States produces an estimated 3 million tons of e-waste, and China produces 2.3 million tons (UN, 2010).

In addition to the raw quantity, e-waste like cell phones contain dangerous chemicals and is frequently mishandled. Cell phones contain precious metals like gold and silver. Although there isn't enough value in these metals to justify breaking open your phone, there are operations where large quantities of e-waste is destroyed for the purpose of extracting these metals (UN, 2010). The problem is that the phones also may contain metals like mercury and cadmium as well as brominated flame retardants. These substances have been linked to cancer and other health problems (Kinver, 2006).

The "backyard recyclers", as they are dubbed by the UN report, are not very efficient at getting out the precious metals relative to the "release of steady plumes of far-reaching toxic pollution" (UN, 2010). There are facilities that can do a more efficient job, but the UN report suggests that government intervention is needed to ensure that proper procedures are followed (Lasar, 2010).

The report encourages the development of state of the art e-waste recycling technologies in developing countries like Brazil, Colombia and Morocco. "One person's waste can be another's raw material," according to Konrad Osterwalder, UN Under-Secretary General (UN, 2010). "The challenge of dealing with e-waste represents an important step in the transition to a green economy (UN, 2010)." One thing seems clear: telephony technology will continue to grow and that will mean new products replace old ones that need to be disposed of.

AT&T and Verizon are two wireless companies attempting to curb texting while driving with their respective campaigns, "Txting & Drivng ... It Can Wait" and "Don't Text and Drive" (Copeland, 2010a). AT&T's campaign will use advertising in 72 malls promoting a site (att.com/txtngcanwait) where parents and teens can sign pledges prohibiting texting while driving.

FACTORS TO WATCH

Telephony, specifically wireless telephony, seems to be growing faster than society or even the U.S. Government can handle as the thirst for bytes, especially for mobile data access, has become insatiable.

The Limited Resource of Broadband

Broadband connectivity is necessary to move data, and, as mentioned earlier in this chapter, its demand is only expected to increase. Although some users log onto the Internet through the use of a wireless card, which uses the same network as mobile phones, others opt for the allocated network available in their physical proximity.

Ovum, a research company, estimate revenues generated from mobile broadband will grow 450% from the period of 2008 to 2014 with the security, retail and transport sectors driving the adoption (Jones, 2010). Wireless providers, realizing that communication is only one use of personal wireless communication, have begun to make a push for their 3G net books, which eat up a lot of the bandwidth along with the conventional laptops and PCs that are 3G capable.

In order to limit the amount of bandwidth used by individual devices, some providers have begun charging by the amount of data usage (Gruman, 2010). AT&T has been scrambling since the iPhone's launch in 2007, with its unlimited data plans, to stop heavy congestion on its networks (IBISWorld, 2010a) and as a result, has nearly doubled its 3G access speeds. Apple plans to limit data use by iPad owners by charging by the amount of data used (Gruman, 2010). Sprint and T-Mobile are also increasing network capacity. Verizon Wireless and AT&T have dropped ominous hints that the days of unlimited data usage are ending and "variable pricing" is coming (Milian, 2010).

4G technologies may be the answer due to its data capacity. It can transmit data up to 100 Mb/s for a traveler at high speeds and 1 Gb/s for travel at low speeds. The speeds will allow any network to deliver service over any device (IBISWorld, 2010a) and ultimately cement the transition of the wireless industry to a data-dominated service. While some critics think the idea of 4G coming to the aid of the broadband crisis won't happen until 2015 (Gruman, 2010), companies have already made moves to a 4G-laden future. International telecom giant NTT DoCoMo has become a major proponent of 4G technology, while Verizon plans to roll out 4G services in 2010, with a full service rollout by the conclusion of 2013 (IBISWorld, 2010a). Sprint Nextel has begun its 4G rollout with Wi-Max standardized technology that allows mobile broadband coverage and provides greater geographic coverage (IBISWorld, 2010a).

Mobile Television

What was once an idea relegated to spy and science fiction movies, mobile television delivered via mobile phones might be coming to life at long last. While many providers have made a concentrated effort towards marketing mobile television, it is the technological and service limitations, mainly network speeds, which have stalled the migration towards mobile television adoption (IBISWorld, 2010a). In 2007, less than 1% of mobile subscribers watched broadcast television programming on their devices one or more times per month (Frommer, 2007), but according to a report by ABI Research, mobile television subscribers are expected to grow from their 2006 numbers (11 million) to a much larger contingent of 462 million in 2012 (ABI Research, 2007). With improving network speeds, providers may finally be able to comprehensively offer this service based on a flat pricing service and an on-demand format. More content providers will gear their products for mobile consumption (IBISWorld, 2010a).

There are other factors to consider for mobile television adoption besides Rogers' *Diffusion of Innovations* (2003). From a business perspective, factors including video quality, type of content, transmission format, and pricing need to be decided before mobile television can be marketed (Kalba, 2009). Video quality, screen size, channel capacity, channel-switching latency, handset design, and digital interface are variables that users may or may not decide to adopt (Kalba, 2009). Perhaps it will be the interactions between the technology, the users' environment, content options, and development of service that will shape mobile television in ways originally unintended, much like we have seen with mobile phones and television, themselves (Kalba, 2009). And, as discussed in Chapter 6, there are multiple forms of mobile television, some of which are compatible with and offered by wireless telephone carriers, with others offered by companies seeking to compete with these wireless carriers.

Screen size and mobile browsing will also have an impact on mobile television's adoption. While two of the earliest mobile browsers, Opera Mobile and Blazer, struggled with minimizing content from desktop to mobile viewing size, it was not until the debut of 2007's iPhone and its mobile Safari browser that users were able to zoom in and digest all the mobile information available to conventional computer users (Lewis and Moscovitz, 2010). Although Opera Mobile and Opera Mini are the most commonly installed browsers on mobile hardware, other browsers currently available are Internet Explorer Mobile, Blazer, Openwave Mobile Browser, Fennec, Mobile Safari and Android (Lewis and Moscovitz, 2010). Each offers its own resolution and varies by size and picture quality. Mobile television may have to wait for a standard to be adopted. One key difference among these browsers is whether they are capable of displaying video distributed in the Flash format. Many browsers, including those distributed by Apple, don't have Flash plug-ins, preventing these mobile browsers from displaying mobile video distributed in this format.

The VoIP battlefield

While VoIP may ultimately be the most cost effective solution for long distance calls (Leung, 2010), not every communications provider was a fan at first. AT&T, in an effort to herd customers to use its international calling options, attempted to bar Skype and restrict applications such as SlingPlayer Mobile (Moren, 2010), but in January 2010, the company relented on allowing long distance VoIP capability when it launched iCall, the first app to offer free VoIP on its mobile network (Furchgott, 2010).

In December 2009, AT&T found itself again in the crux of talk of the future of VoIP when its FCC proposal suggested that voice service be delivered through VoIP service over broadband in the future (Engebretson, 2010b). The catch is that while 22% of AT&T customers have already shut off traditional phone service, those who want only voice service would be issued a Notice of Inquiry by the FCC to address "how to ensure that the phase-out of the PSTN does not leave individuals who do not use computers without service" through the use of inexpensive devices that allow VOIP customers to plug traditional telephones directly into broadband connections (Engebretson, 2010a). This effort could allow voice-only customers to take the wireless route for communications, leaving smaller telecommunications companies without wireless interests behind and requiring a complete overhaul of the emergency 911 system.

New Operating Systems

As the wireless market becomes more lucrative, more and more companies, including some big business-es, will try and get into the wireless market. Software giant Microsoft plans to launch Windows Mobile 7, an operating systems that borrows design elements from its Zune portable music player and is compatible with Microsoft's Xbox Live, by the end of 2010 (Baig, 2010). More than 18.3 million mobile phones with Microsoft software were shipped in 2009, following 19.8 million units in 2008 (Baig, 2010). Research in Motion's Black-Berrys, popular among the corporate crowd, and Apple's iPhones, popular among the general consumer, are more prevalent in public opinion (Baig, 2010) and have put a mountain in front of Microsoft's path to gain a larger share of the wireless market.

Google's Android software, the fastest growing operating system in the wireless market (Baig, 2010) seems to be the answer to iPhone's meteoric three-year rise. Google's Android software isn't its only effort to take over the wireless market as it launched its Google's Nexus One Web phone, a handset that is a break from the usual contract and carrier-bound handsets. The Web-enabled device does not require the user to choose a specific carrier and uses a ported phone number (Google, 2010). Google's achievement is offering the first carrier-independent smart phone store: where you first pick which phone you want, then a network on that plat-form and a plan on that network. Users can now shop among networks and choose wireless plans based on price and network quality without the constraints of having limited handset options (Stokes, 2010). The Nexus One phone may force wireless carriers to reinvent their marketing approach and service quality.

Risks of Mobile Telephony

The growing need for wireless security will continue to flourish, as handsets serve as a bridging medium and move closer and closer to the power of a home computer. As cell phones have grown in power, mobile security systems are well behind the technology required to access a remote desktop (Sabzevar & Sousa, 2009). Wireless networks may allow prepared attackers to listen in on any conversation and can jam even sen-sitive and life-dependent applications despite encryption (Pelzl & Wollinger, 2006). Since handsets are in ef-fect mini-computers, they are not immune to viruses that could pose a serious threat to mobile communications (Wang et al., 2009). but, as of early 2010, a major virus has yet to affect mobile telephony in the United States.

The Future Looks Bright

As mobile telephony become more and more personalized, their initial use, voice communications seems antiquated. There are a number of burgeoning applications for mobile phones on the horizon.

◆ MediNet, a mobile healthcare system that uses monitoring devices on a user's mobile phone, can help keep watch on and offer self care for those with diabetes and cardiovascular disease (Mohan et al., 2009). General medical diagnostic information, such as blood pressure, oxygen saturation, internal pressures, orthopedic device loading, and gastrointestinal endoscopy, can now be moni-tored by individuals, patients, and caregivers through wireless communications (Budinger, 2004).

◆ MMS images delivered over mobile phones that have the same quality as common optical micro-scopes, are being used in connecting isolated laboratories without Internet access (Bellina & Mis-soni, 2009). SMS texting has been proven to be effective in outreach communication for underprivileged communities (Gomez, et. al., 2008). Security of medical records is being im-proved to maintain confidentiality (Weerasinghe et al., 2010).

◈ Wireless handsets can also be used to locate people through RFID (Radio Frequency Identification) middleware in times of emergency or surveillance needs (Schwieren & Vossen, 2009). Mobile social computing applications (MSCAs) are middleware that a "common platform for capturing, managing, and sharing the social state of physical communities" and consequently improved response time between the participants (Gupta et al., 2008, p. 35).

◈ The future may see more user feedback in the design process for handsets and services (van de Kar & den Hengst, 2009). Maybe there will be an impetus for mobile educational games, much like the European Union is addressing (Maxl & Tarkus, 2009). Maybe even voting or "convenience voting" (Gronke et al., 2008) is in the not too distant future.

Bibliography

Ament, P. (2006). Fascinating facts about the invention of the telephone by Alexander Graham Bell in 1876. *The Great Idea Finder.* Retrieved from http://www.ideafinder.com/history/inventions/telephone.htm

ABI Research (2007). Mobile marketing and advertising: Marketing brands and products on mobile web. Retrieved 2008, Jan 15, from http://www.abiresearch.com/products/market_research/Mobile_Marketing_and_Advertising

AT&T (2010a). Inventing the Telephone. *AT&T Corporate History.* Retrieved from http://www.corp.att.com/history/inventing.html

AT&T (2010b). Milestones in AT&T History. *AT&T Corporate History.* Retrieved from http://www.corp.att.com/history/milestones.html

Austen, I.(2009a, July 27). Ericsson Wins Auction for Nortel Assets. *New York Times,* Retrieved from http://www.nytimes.com/2009/07/27/technology/companies/27iht-nortel.html.

Austen, I. (2009b, September 15). Avaya Wins the Auction for Key Nortel Unit. *New York Times,* from http://www.nytimes.com/2009/09/15/technology/companies/15nortel.html

Baig, E. (2010, February 15). Windows Mobile 7 could be on phones by year's end. *USA Today,* p. 1.

Bell. (2010). "Historical Timeline." Retrieved 3/12/2010, 2010, from http://www.alcatel-lucent.com/wps/portal/!ut/p/kcxml/04_Sj9SPykssy0xPLMnMz0vM0Y_QjzKLd4w3MXMBSYGYRq6m-pEoYgbxjggRX4_83FT9IHlv_QD9gtzQiHJHR0UAaOmbyQ!!/delta/base64xml/L3dJdyEvd0ZNQUFzQUMvNElVRS82XzIfSVA!

Bellina, L., & Missoni, E. (2009). Mobile cell-phones (M-phones) in telemicroscopy: Increasing connectivity of isolated laboratories. *Diagnostic Pathology.* 4(19), 4.

Bellis, M. (2010a). The History of the Telephone, Alexander Graham Bell. *About.com : Inventors.* Retrieved from http://inventors.about.com/od/bstartinventors/a/telephone.htm

Bellis, M. (2010b). Elisha Gray - The Race to Patent the Telephone. *About.com : Inventors.* Retrieved from http://inventors.about.com/od/gstartinventors/a/Elisha_Gray.htm

Bellis, M. (2010c). The History of the Telephone - Antonio Meucci. *About.com : Inventors.* Retrieved from http://inventors.about.com/library/inventors/bl_Antonio_Meucci.htm

Bellis, M. (2010d) "The History of the Electric Telegraph and Telegraphy." About.com : Inventors.

Blumberg, S. J. P. (2009) "Wireless Substitution: Early Release of Estimates from the National Health Interview Survey, January - June 2009." Center for Disease Control.

Brain, M., Tyson, Jeff, Layton, Julia (2010) "How Cell Phones Work." How Stuff Works.

Budinger, T. (2004). Biomonitoring with Wireless Communications. *Annual Review of Biomedical Engineering,* 5, 19.

Burger, A. (2007). M-commerce hot spots, Part I: Beyond ringtones and wallpaper. *E-Commerce Times.* Retrieved from http://www.ecommercetimes.com/story/57109.html

Chavis, J. (2010). What is a 4G network? *Wise Geek.* Retrieved from http://www.wisegeek.com/what-is-a-4g-network.htm

Choi, J., Seol, H., Lee, S., Cho, H., & Park, Y. (2008). Customer Satisfaction Factors of Mobile Commerce in Korea. *Internet Research,* 18(3), 23.

Copeland, L. (2010a, March 8). Word to youth: Texting, driving don't mix. *USA Today.*

Copeland, L. (2010b, January 25). States go after texting drivers. *USA Today.*

Dimmick, J. W., Sikand, J., & Patterson, S. J. (1994). The gratifications of the household telephone: sociability, instrumentality, and reassurance. *Communication Research 21(5),* 643-663.

Engebretson, J. (2010a). How will telcos convert voice-only customers to VOIP? *Connected Planet.* Retrieved from http://connectedplanetonline.com/IP-NGN/news/converting-voice-customers-to-voip-0222/

Engebretson, J. (2010b). FCC provides additional broadband plan details. *Connected Planet.* Retrieved from http://connectedplanetonline.com/residential_services/news/broadband-plan-details-0222/

FCC. (2010). *Telephone Subscribership in the United States.* Washington, D.C.: Federal Communications Commission.

Fitchard, K. (2007). 3GSM: Nokia, Siemens kick off joint venture ahead of closing. *Connected Planet.* Retrieved from http://connectedplanetonline.com/wireless/finance/nokia_siemens_merger_021206/index.html

Fitchard, K. (2010). Tiny Genband swallows Nortel's giant VoIP business. *Connected Planet.* Retrieved from http://connectedplanetonline.com/IP-NGN/news/Genband-swallows-nortel-voip-0224/index.html

Fossella, V. (2001). H.Res.269. C. Resolution.

Frommer, D. (2007, October 9). As AT&T Bulks Up on Spectrum, Another Mobile TV Plan Fizzles. *Silicon Alley Insider.*

Furchgott, R. (2010, February 4). App of the week: The phone call is free, but keep it short. *New York Times,* B9..

Gomez, E. A. (2008). *Connecting communities of need with public health: Can SMS text-messaging improve outreach communication?* Paper presented at the 41st Annual Hawaii International Conference on System Sciences, Hawaii.

Google. (2010). google.com/phone. Retrieved 3/12, 2010, from www.google.com/phone

Gronke, P., Galanes-Rosenbaum, E., Miller, P., & Toffey, D. (2008). Convenience Voting. *Annual Review of Political Science, 11,* 437-455.

Gruman, G. (2010). Mobile data explosion: Not the iPhone's fault. *InfoWorld.* Retrieved from http://www.infoworld.com/d/mobilize/mobile-data-explosion-not-iphones-fault-308?source=IFWNLE_nlt_networking_2010-03-09

Gubbins, E. (2006). Alcatel Lucent merger closes. *Connected Planet.* Retrieved from http://connectedplanetonline.com/access/finance/alcatel_lucent_merger_113006/index.html.

Gupta, A., Kalra, A., Boston, D., & Borcea, C. (2009). MobiSoC: A middleware for mobile social computing applications. *Mobile Networks and Applications, 14,* 35-52.

Hamad, F., Smalov, L., & James, A. (2009). Energy-aware Security in M-Commerce and the Internet of Things. *IETE Technical Review, 26*(5), 6.

Hardesty, L. (2009). Telephony Calls Opportunities. *Communications Technology, 26*(11), 20.

Hartz, D. (2009). M-Commerce fraud to increase to rapid adoption of mobile. *The America's Intelligence Wire.* Retrieved from http://infotrac.galegroup.com.wf2dnvr14.webfeat.org/itw/infomark/369/433/10227467lwl6/purl=rcl_GBFM_0_A212532989&dyn=4!xrn_1_0_A212532989

Hornick, B. (2010). M-commerce websites show poor performance. *The America's Intelligence Wire.* Retrieved from http://infotrac.galegroup.com.wf2dnvr14.webfeat.org/itw/infomark/26/932/9847111 9wl6/purl=rcl_GBFM_0_A218025375&dyn=4!xrn_1_0_A218025375

IBISWorld. (2009). *Global Wireless Telecommunications Carriers* (No. 15111GL): IBISWorld.

IBISWorld. (2010a). *Wireless Telecommunications Carriers in the U.S.:* IBISWorld.

IBISWorld. (2010b). *Voice Over Internet Protocol Providers (VoIP) in the US* (No. 51331a).

IBISWorld. (2010c). *Cable, Internet & Telephone Providers in the U.S.* (No. 51322): IBISWorld.

IBISWorld. (2010d). *Wired Telecommunications Carriers in the U.S.* (No. 51331b): IBIS World.

Industry Notes. (2010). *Professional Safety, 55*(3), 4.

Inyang, I., Benke, G., Morrissey, J., McKenzie, R., & Abramson, M. (2009). How Well Do Adolescents Recall Use of Mobile Telephones? Results of a Validation Study. *BMC Medical Research Methodology, 9,* 36.

Jones, J. (2010). Keeping Pace with Mobile Broadband. *Electronics Weekly*(2412), 13.

Kalba, K. (2009). Adopting Mobile TV: Technologies Seeking Content and Cool. In D. Gerbag (Ed.), *Television Goes Digital* (pp. 63-77). New York: Springer.

Kao, D. T. (2009). The Impact of Transaction on Consumers' Intentions to Adopt M-Commerce: A Cross-Cultural Investigation. *CyberPsychology & Behavior, 12*(2), 5.

Kharif, O. (2009). M-Commerce's Big Moment. *BusinessWeek Online,* 1. Retrieved from http://www.businessweek.com/technology/content/oct2009/tc20091011_278825.htm

Kinver, M. (2006). Do mobile phones cost the Earth? *BBC News.* Retrieved from http://news.bbc.co.uk/2/hi/sci/tech/6174422.stm

Koong, K. S., Liu, L. C., Bai, S., & Lin, B. (2008). Identity Theft in the USA: Evidence from 2002 to 2006. *International Journal of Mobile Communications, 6*(2), 18.

Lasar, M. (2010). Add billions of mobile phones to the world's e-waste problem. *Ars Technica.* Retrieved from http://arstechnica.com/tech-policy/news/2010/02/united-nations-add-mobile-phones-to-the-world-e-waste-crisis.ars

Leung, L., & Wei, R. (1999). Seeking News via the Pager: An Expectancy-Value Study. *Journal of Broadcasting & Electronic Media, 43*(3), 299-315.

Leung, L., & Wei, R. (2000). More than just talk on the move: Uses and gratifications of the cellular phone. *Journalism & Mass Communication Quarterly, 77*(2), 308-320.

Leung, Y. (2010). Sparse Telephone Gateway for Internet Telephony. *Computer Networks, 54*(1), 150.

Lewis, J., & Moscovitz, M. (2009). Developing for Small Screens and the Mobile Web *AdvancED CSS* (pp. 149-186). New York: Springer-Verlag.

Li, S., Glass, R., & Records, H. (2008). The Influence of Gender on New Technology Adoption and Use-Mobile Commerce. *Journal of Internet Commerce, 7*(2), 20.

magicjack.com. (2010). magicjack.com. Retrieved 3/12, 2010, from www.magicjack.com

Marples, G. (2008) "The History of Cell Phones - A Vision Realized." The History Of.net. Retrieved May 11, 2010 from http://www.thehistoryof.net/history-of-cell-phones.html.

Maxl, E., & Tarkus, A. (2009). Definition of User Requirements concerning Mobile Learning Games within the mGBL Project. In O. Petrovic & A. Brand (Eds.), *Serious Games on the Move* (pp. 91-104): Springer Vienna.

Milian, M. (2010). Verizon Wireless' teach chief says unlimited Internet access 'has to change,' echoing AT&T. *Los Angeles Times*. Retrieved from http://latimesblogs.latimes.com/technology/2010/03/verizon-metered-internet.html

Mohan, M., Marin, D. D., Sutan, S. S., & Deen, A. A. (2008). *MediNet: Personalizing the Self-Care Process for Patients with Diabetes and Cardiovascular Disease Using Mobile Telephony.* Paper presented at the Annual International Conference of the IEEE Engineering in Medicine and Biology Society.

Moren, D. (2010). AT&T Changes Stance on VoIP Apps. *Macworld, 27.*

Mossberg, W. (2010, February 18). MagicJack: Way Overhyped, But Really Works. *Wall Street Journal-Eastern Edition.*

Over half of US citizens interested in m-commerce. (2009). *The America's Intelligence Wire,*

Park, N. (2010). Adoption and Use of Computer-Based Voice Over Internet Protocol Phone Service: Toward an Integrated Model. *Journal of Communication, 60*(1), 33.

Pelzl, J., & Wollinger, T. (2006). Security Aspects of Mobile Communications. In K. Lemke, C. Paar & M. Wolf (Eds.), *Embedded security in cars.* Berlin: Springer.

Phifer, L. (2009) "3G." *Search Telecom.*

Purcell, K., Rainie, L., Mitchell, A., Rosenstiel, T., & Olmstead, K. (2010). *Understanding the participatory news consumer: How internet and cell phone users have turned news into a social experience:* Pew Research Center.

RADDataCommunications. (2001). "Voice over IP: History of voice over IP." Retrieved 3/12/2010, 2010, from http://www3.rad.com/networks/2001/voip/.

Rogers, E. (2003). *Diffusion of Innovation* (Fifth ed.). New York: Free Press.

Rothman, K. J. (2009). Health Effects of Mobile Telephones. *Epidemiology, 20*(5), 2.

Sabzevar, A., & Sousa, J. P. (2009). Secure Mobile Phone Access to Remote Personal Computers: A Case Study. In J. Cordeiro, B. Shishkov, A. Ranchordas & M. Helfert (Eds.), *Software and Data Technologies* (Vol. 47, pp. 76-90): Springer Berlin Heidelberg.

Schwieren, J., & Vossen, G. (2008, June12-June 16). *ID-services: An RFID middleware architecture for mobile applications.* Paper presented at the 2nd International Workshop on RFID Technology-Concepts, Applications, Challenges, Barcelona, Spain.

Sleet, D., Ballesteros, M., & Borse, N. (2010). A review of unintentional injuries in adolescents. *Annual Review of Public Health, 31,* 195-212.

Sprint. (2010). Sprint 4G expansion plans to stretch coast-to-coast from Los Angeles to Miami. *News Release* Retrieved 4/12, 2010, from http://newsreleases.sprint.com/phoenix.zhtml?c=127149&p=irol-newsArticle_newsroom&ID=1404958&highlight=.

Stokes, J. (2010). Google's biggest announcement was not a phone, but a URL. *Ars technica.* Retrieved from http://arstechnica.com/gadgets/news/2010/01/googles-big-news-today-was-not-a-phone-but-a-url.ars

Subramanya, S., Wu, X., Schulzrinne, H., & Buriak, S. (2009). VoIP-Based Air Traffic Controller Training. *IEEE Communications Magazine, 47*(11), 8.

UN (2010) Urgent need to prepare developing countries for surge in e-waste. United Nations Press Releases. Retrieved from http://www.unep.org/Documents.Multilingual/Default.asp?DocumentID=612&ArticleID=6471&l=en&t=long

USA Today. (2009, November 27). When shopping, they'll phone it in. *USA Today.*

Valdes, R. (2010) "How VoIP works." How Stuff Works.

van de Kar, E., & den Hengst, M. (2009). Involving Users Early on in the Design Process: Closing the Gap Between Mobile Information Services and Their Users. *Electronic Markets, 19*(1).

Verizon. (2010). Verizon FiOs-Fact Sheet. Retrieved 3/14/2010, 2010, from http://newscenter.verizon.com/kit/fios-symmetrical-internet-service/all-about-fios.html

Wang, P., Gonzalez, M., Hidalgo, C., & Barbasi, A. (2009). Understanding the Spreading Patterns of Mobile Phone Viruses. *Science, 324*(5930).

Weerasinghe, D., Rajarajan, M., & Rakocevic, V. (2009). *Security Protection on Trust Delegated Data in Public Mobile Networks.* Paper presented at the Second International ICST Conference.

Wei, R. (2008). Motivations for using the mobile phone for mass communications and entertainment. *Telematics & Informatics, 25*(1), 10.

Wei, R., Eiamong, H., & Pan, J. (2010). Examining User Behavioral Response to SMS Ads: Implications for the Evolution of the Mobile Phone as a Bona-fide Medium. *Telematics & Informatics, 27*(1), 32.

Wei, R., Hao, X., & Pan, J. (2009). Examining user behavioral response to SMS ads: Implications for the evolution of the mobile phone as a bona-fide medium. *Telematics & Informatics, 27*, 32-41

Whitney, L. (2010). Apple, RIM spark quarterly mobile-phone sales. *CNET.* Retrieved from http://news.cnet.com/8301-17938_105-10458135-1.html

Zarifopoulos, M., & Economides, A. A. (2009). Evaluation Mobile Banking Portals. *International Journal of Mobile Communications, 7*(1), 25.

19

THE INTERNET

Tim Brown, Ph.D. & Heather Halter, B.A.[*]

I t is arguable that as a technology, the Internet has single-handedly changed the way we do nearly everything. It is so pervasive in our lives that our use of the Internet and the World Wide Web prompted *Time* magazine to name "You"—the Internet using public—its "Person of the Year" in 2006, because of how much the public contributes to the world through this medium. It has come a long way from its beginnings as a military project 40 years ago. The Internet has gone beyond being just a useful tool in the workplace and the business world to becoming an integral interpersonal and mass communication medium.

Millions of people access the Internet; nearly 75% of Americans use the Internet (Rainie, 2010), and, as of mid-2010, China boasted the largest Internet-using population at 384 million people (Miniwatts Marketing Group, 2010). Our online activities both force and are enhanced by other technologies that keep growing and updating themselves to accommodate that use, such as Apple's iPad, the netbook, and smartphones. Many public places now offer free Wi-Fi as a selling point.

What exactly is this technology that has taken over our lives? Martin Irvine of Georgetown University said that there are three components to the Internet. It is "a worldwide computing system using a common means of linking hardware and transmitting digital information, a community of people using a common communication technology, and a globally distributed system of information" (DeFleur & Dennis, 2002, p. 219). It is important to note, however, that the Internet does not act alone in providing us with seemingly endless information-seeking and communication opportunities. An integral part of this technology is the World Wide Web. While the Internet is a network of computers, the World Wide Web allows users to access that network in a user-friendly way. It provides an audio visual format and a graphical interface that is easier to use than remembering lines of computer code.

This chapter examines the quickly changing medium that is the Internet (and the World Wide Web) by reviewing its origins, the current state of Web 2.0, Internet mobility, security, and economics, and will introduce several topics that will be important areas of research in the future.

---

[*] Tim Brown, Ph.D. is Assistant Professor, and Heather Halter, B.A., is a Master's Degree candidate, Nicholson School of Communication, University of Central Florida (Orlando, Florida).

Background

Though it is now accessible to virtually anyone who has a compatible device, the Internet began as a military project. During the Cold War, the United States government wanted to maintain a communication system that would still function if the country was attacked by missiles and existing radio transmitters and telephone poles were disabled. The solution was to transmit information in small bits so that it could travel faster and be sent again more easily if its path were disrupted. This concept is known as packet-switching.

Many sources consider the birth of the Internet to have occurred in 1968 when the Advanced Research Projects Agency Network (ARPANET) was founded. Several universities, including UCLA and Stanford, were collaborating on military projects and needed a fast, easy way to send and receive information for those projects. Thus ARPANET became the first collection of networked computers to transfer information to and from remote locations using packet switching.

ARPANET users discovered that, in addition to sending information to each other for collaboration and research, they were also using the computer network for personal communication, so individual electronic mail, or e-mail, accounts were established. E-mail accounts allow users to have a personally identifiable user name, followed by the @ sign, followed by the name of the host computer system.

USENET was developed in 1976 to serve as a way for students at The University of North Carolina and Duke University to communicate through computer networks. It served as an electronic bulletin board that allowed users on the network to post thoughts on different topics through email. USENET then expanded to include other computers that were not allowed to use ARPANET.

In 1986, ARPANET was replaced by NSFNET (sponsored by the National Science Foundation) which featured upgraded high-speed, fiber-optic technology. This upgrade allowed for more bandwidth and faster network connections because the network was connected to supercomputers throughout the country. This technology is what we now refer to as the modern day Internet. The general public could now access the Internet through Internet service providers (ISPs), such as America Online, CompuServe, and Prodigy. Every computer and server on the Internet was assigned a unique IP (Internet Protocol) address that consisted of a series of numbers (for example, 209.152.74.113).

The theory of Diffusion of Innovations (discussed in Chapter 3) points out that people look for low levels of complexity in an innovation to determine whether or not they want to adopt it; in other words, they want to know how easy the innovation is to use. That qualification presented a problem for the early versions of the Internet—much of it was still being run on "text-based" commands. Even though the public could now access the Internet, they needed a more user-friendly way to receive the information it contained and send information to others that didn't involve learning text based commands. In 1989, Tim Berners-Lee created a graphical interface for accessing the Internet and named his innovation the "World Wide Web." One of the key features of the World Wide Web was the concept of hyperlinks and common-language Web addresses known as "URLs" (uniform resource locators). This innovation allows a user to simply click on a certain word or picture and automatically retrieve the information that is tied to that link. The hyperlink sends a request to a special server known as a "domain name server," the server locates the IP address of the information, and sends that back to the original computer, which then sends a request for information to that IP address. The user's computer is then able to display text, video, images, and audio that has been requested. Today we know this as simple "point-and-click" access to information, but in 1989 it was revolutionary. Users were no longer forced to memorize codes or commands to get from one place to the next on the Internet—they could simply point to the content they wanted and access it.

It is worthwhile at this point to explain the IP address and domain name system in more detail. The domain name (e.g. google.com) is how we navigate the World Wide Web, but on the back end (which we don't see), the IP addresses—numbers—are the actual addresses. The Internet Corporation for Assigned Names and Numbers, or ICANN, is responsible for assigning domain names and numbers to specific websites and servers. With 1.6 billion users on the Internet, that can be quite a task (ICANN, 2010b). To try and keep things simple, ICANN maintains two different sets of "top level domain" names: generic TLD names (gTLD) such as .edu, .com, and .org; and country codes (ccTLD) such as .br for Brazil, .ca for Canada, and .ru for Russia. Table 19.1 lists the 21 gTLD names (there are 250 ccTLD names). This information will be discussed later in this chapter.

Table 19.1
Top Level Domain Names

Top Level Domain	Definition
.aero	Air-transport industry sites
.arpa	Internet Infrastructure sites
.asia	Pan-Asia communication
.biz	Business sites
.cat	Catalan language and culture sites
.com	Commercial sites
.coop	Cooperative organization sites
.edu	Educational institution sites
.gov	Government sites
.info	General usage sites
.int	International sites
.jobs	Companies advertising jobs
.mil	Military sites
.mobi	Mobile devices
.museum	Museum sites
.name	Individuals' sites
.net	Networking and Internet-related sites
.org	Sites for organizations
.pro	Sites for professions
.travel	Travel related sites
.tel	Business and individuals to publish contact data

Source: Internet Corporation for Assigned Names and Numbers, 2010

The impact of the Internet upon business and commerce has been significant, creating new categories of each, e-business and e-commerce. Mesenbourg (1999) defines e-business as any procedure that a business organization conducts over a computer mediated network. E-business thus includes processes such as ordering new materials to aid in the production of goods, marketing to customers, or processing their orders, as well as automated employee services, such as training information housed on a company Intranet. E-commerce, on the other hand, is defined as any transaction over a computer mediated network that involves the transfer of owner-ship or rights to use goods or services. For example, when you purchase a song from iTunes or any other electronic music store on the Internet, you are engaging in e-commerce.

These definitions also point out the similarities between e-business and e-commerce. Certainly some of the processes involved in e-business could be classified as commerce—that is, the exchange of ownership rights. If a pharmacy electronically orders its drugs from pharmaceutical companies, that is an exchange of ownership rights of a good. Using the definitions above, such a transaction would be considered e-commerce, not e-business. However, the above scenario also involves the order of new materials to aid in the production of goods (e.g., filling prescriptions), which would fall under the definition of e-business. So, is there any real difference between the two?

Perhaps an easier way to define the difference might be to examine the recipient of the transaction. In the above example, one business is ordering goods from another business; that is, business to business or B2B. The pharmacy needs to purchase the raw materials (large quantities of medicine) in order to provide a finished product (filled prescriptions, packages of cold medicine) to the consumer. Therefore, the transaction between the two businesses (from one to the other) seems best to fall under the e-business category. However, the purchase of a song from iTunes is the transaction between the business (record company) and you (consumer), or business to consumer (B2C). Because so many transactions between businesses and consumers are retail based (a business selling a finished product to a consumer), it is perhaps best to view transactions to consumers as e-commerce.

Even with the clarification above, one can see that e-commerce can very easily be classified as a subset of e-business. The U.S. Federal Government defines both that way, and its figures offer support for those definitions. Revised figures from 2007 show that e-commerce accounted for 3.4% of all commerce that year; up from 2.9% in 2006 (Scheleur et al., 2008). E-commerce transactions in 2007 grew by 19% over the previous year, while total retail in the United States (both e-commerce and face-to-face) grew by only 4%. Basically, that means that electronic commerce growth is outpacing traditional commerce, although it is still a minor part of the economic equation.

Recent Developments

Web 2.0

The World Wide Web has come a long way since its invention. It is currently in a phase that has become known as "Web 2.0," which, according to The Pew Internet and American Life Project "is an umbrella term that is used to refer to a new era of Web-enabled applications that are built around user-generated or user-manipulated content, such as wikis, blogs, podcasts, and social networking sites" (*Web 2.0*, 2010). In other words, Web 2.0 is powered by the people who control the content.

Wikis are informational Web sites that are open for editing. Virtually anyone can edit a subject posting to include any sort of fact or opinion. This function can be troublesome, because not all information posted is factual. To test the credibility of one of the most popular wiki sites, Wikipedia, an instructor at the University of Central Florida modified the school's entry. The instructor claimed that he designed the school's Pegasus logo, when in fact, he did not. This entry remained on the Web site until he removed it several months later.

A blog is very similar to a wiki, except it is not generally open for anyone to edit. Typically it is run by one host, who can post anything from news, information, or simply his or her own opinion (De Zúñiga, Puig-I-Abril & Rojas , 2009). On demand video is another part of Web 2.0. Web sites such as YouTube allow users to watch, share, and publish videos, making the users active participants in media distribution (Hanson &

Haridakis, 2008). Other video sites such as Hulu allow users to watch network television shows online at their convenience. Instant messaging was once one of the most popular uses of the Web, but its use has stagnated over the last few years.

Some of the most popular Web 2.0 applications are social networking sites. Social networking sites are generally defined as "a social utility that connects people, to keep up with friends, upload photos, share links and videos" (Top Sites, 2010). These sites are some of the most commonly visited Web sites in the country, and indeed the world. The number two most visited Web site in the world is Facebook. Also, in the top 20 most visited Web sites are Twitter and MySpace (Top Sites, 2010).

Facebook, in particular, is quickly becoming a one-stop shop for practically any type of information. It is a portal to the rest of the Internet in one convenient location, much like AOL portals were in the early days of the World Wide Web. It is an interpersonal communication medium, in that you can send direct messages to friends, family members, and acquaintances. It has also become a mass communication medium. Businesses and corporations can now have "fan pages," where Facebook users can "become a fan" of that company. This feature allows the companies to communicate or market to a large number of people with one simple wall posting or message. Facebook status updates, along with other social networking sites, have also become a popular way to spread late breaking news, by posting links to or videos from news corporation Web sites. For example, in 2009, celebrity news Web site TMZ.com broke the story of pop singer Michael Jackson's death. Within minutes, a link to this story had popped up on Facebook and Twitter, and hundreds of people were updating statuses and tweets about the death (Ostrow, 2009a). (Social Networking is discussed in more detail in Chapter 20.)

Mobility

For a good portion of the Internet's history, desktop computing stations or stand-alone PC's were the only way to "get online." That was primarily because of the need for cables to connect the computer's modem to either a phone line or a broadband modem/connection. But the growth of wireless technologies (Wi-Fi, Wi-Max, and cellular wireless broadband) has expanded both the types of devices that can access the Internet and the type of content that is being generated and posted "online." In 2009, the Pew Internet and American Life Project noted that more than half of online Americans had accessed the Internet wirelessly, and that "one-third of Americans (32%) have used a cell phone or Smart phone to access the Internet for emailing, instant-messaging, or information-seeking" (Horrigan, 2009). Both of those percentages were increases from the previous two years, and they point to the growing trend of users wanting their information "on the go." That is also borne out by statistics from JiWire, a consumer Wi-Fi hotspot finder. The company points to a projected 21% growth in free Wi-Fi hotspots around the U.S. during 2009 and notes that 56% of the people in the survey they connect to these Wi-Fi spots through a mobile, handheld device (*JiWire*, 2009).

Security

A constant concern for users of the Internet is security. One area of security that needs to be closely watched is cyberterrorism. Director of National Intelligence Dennis Blair said that cyberterrorism, defined as when a secure computer system is compromised and protected information is stolen, is our country's biggest threat (Gjtelen, 2010). An act of cyberterrorism occurred in December 2009, when a computer located in China managed to hack into several Internet, finance, technology, media, and chemical sector companies to steal account information (Drummond, 2010a). America is so dependent upon computers that a major breach could shut down our power grid, communication systems, and transportation systems. We have "cyber-offense" but no "cyber-defense" (Gjtelen, 2010). America can launch a cyber attack on another country, but if another country launches a cyber attack on America, these experts say we are powerless to stop it.

Domain Names

Earlier in this chapter we talked about IP addresses and domain names. Did you notice how all of the 21 gTLD names were in "Latin" letters or text? One of the controversies surrounding ICANN is that critics believe that it is controlled too much by western business influences. In April 2010, ICANN approved the use of "non-Latin" letters for domain names (ICANN, 2010a). Essentially, that means that Internet users in Egypt, Saudi Arabia, Russia, the United Arab Emirates, and other countries can now use characters from their own languages for Internet addresses. They will no longer be forced to use a traditional Latin alphabet (.ru for Russia, for example). ICANN also announced that it would likely speed up the process for four other countries, including China and Thailand, to do the same.

Cyber-Squatting

"Cyber-Squatting" has also become a bit of a problem. Just as real-life "squatters" will occupy a home or piece of land that may or may not be theirs, cyber-squatters register and control a domain name that may or may not be directly related to their business, in an effort to sell that domain name to someone who will use it for business or personal purposes (Cybersquatting.com, 2010). For example, if you want to find out what's happening in the White House, you might type in www.whitehouse.com. However, as of late April, 2010, that would take you to a site that has nothing to do with the home of the President of the United States. (NOTE: you would want to type in www.whitehouse.gov to reach the real White House Web site). The owners of whitehouse.com may be hoping for the government to offer to buy that domain name, and they are also probably asking for quite a bit of money for it as well—that in itself is not necessarily a problem. What does become a problem is when the cyber-squatters decide to use their registered domain name "in bad faith"—or to lower the value of the legitimate trademark holder. At least one estimate shows there are more than 10,000 domain names that have variations on the name "Coke/Coca Cola." Many celebrities have seen their own names taken by cyber-squatters (Celine Dion, for example), preventing them from using their most important "brand," their name, as their Web address.

Legislation has been passed to help legitimate trademark holders who want to take control of "squatted" domain names. ICANN has developed its Uniform Domain Name Dispute Resolution Policy, and the U.S. Congress has enacted the *Anti-Cyber-squatting Consumer Protection Act*. Both are aimed at allowing those companies and individuals who have legitimate claims to domain names within their trademark to keep (or in some cases obtain) those domain names.

CURRENT STATUS

According to the Pew Internet and American Life Project, as of December 2009, 74% of American adults are online, with no significant gender difference. 93% of young people from ages 18-29 are online, 81% of people from ages 30-49 are online, 70% of people from ages 50-64 are online, and 38% of people over the age of 65 are online. Internet usage also varies by ethnicity; whites are online the most, while English- and Spanish-speaking Hispanics have shown the most growth of any ethnic group. Pew also reports that the more education one has, the more likely one will be online, and the more income one makes, the more likely one will be online. 60% of Americans have home broadband access, which means that the Internet is not simply a novelty to be taken advantage of at work. 55% of Americans have accessed the Internet via a wireless connection, either using a laptop or mobile device (Rainie, 2010).

poverty, and drought in the developing world (Cohen, 2009; Dvorak, 2007). One note should be made about the digital divide statistics: the ITU reports that *mobile* Internet access is growing in developing countries; perhaps a sign that people in those countries are finding their own ways of accessing online content without programs such as those listed above (ITU, 2010).

Table 19.2

Internet Users by Level of Development

Year	Level	% (per 100 inhabitants)
2006	Overall	16
	Developing	9
	Developed	52
2007	Overall	19
	Developing	10
	Developed	55
2008	Overall	22
	Developing	14
	Developed	60
2009	Overall	26
	Developing	17.5
	Developed	64

Source: International Telecommunications Union, 2010

Table 19.3

Mobile Cellular Subscriptions by Level of Development

Year	Level	% (per 100 inhabitants)
2006	Overall	37
	Developing	24
	Developed	95
2007	Overall	43
	Developing	30
	Developed	99
2008	Overall	58
	Developing	50
	Developed	103
2009	Overall	67
	Developing	56.8
	Developed	113.6

Note: percentages over 100 reflect more than one cell phone per person

Source: International Telecommunications Union, 2010

Teens and the Future of the Internet:

American teenagers have become a driving force in the growth of Web 2.0, primarily through their use of social networking sites and information sharing. However, that sharing can sometimes come at a price. Much like the young driver who speeds through intersections and takes chances on the roads, the young Internet user sometimes takes chances that create tragic consequences. News accounts of teenagers "sexting" one another (sending sexually suggestive emails, text messages, and photos to one another) have increased over the past few years. Many teens don't realize the legal implications of sending such information over the Internet, either hard wired or mobile. Some states see that type of material as pornographic in nature (Keys, 2009), which is even worse if the senders/receivers/subjects of the content are under 18. This is another example of the "cognitive" digital divide—teenagers may know how to use the basics of digital technology and the Internet, but their experience level is below that of technology users who are older and/or more experienced.

Economics

Another concern is the viability of the Internet, more specifically, the applications and products that many people use on the Internet. While Google may be among the more valuable media companies in world, with a market capitalization of $169.12 billion as of April 30th, 2010, other companies (Facebook, MySpace) have been popular and have brought in revenue, but have not found a way to generate profits the way that Google has (Ostrow, 2009b). On April 14, 2010, Twitter announced that it was going to start offering "promoted Tweets" (advertisements) when users search its Web site. Even though the company reports having 150 million users (Ostrow, 2010), none of them pay for access, and the company needed a way to pay for the services. While research has shown that users are willing to accept a limited amount of advertising to keep information free (Epps, 2009) the question remains as to how much they will accept and when they will have to start paying for content. This dilemma has already hit the news industry, which once saw the Internet as an experiment and gave away its content for free, but now sees online readership as a way to improve economic viability and is now trying to monetize online content.

What seems clear from this chapter is that the Internet is, in many ways, an evolving entity. While packet switching and IP assignments don't change too much, the use of the Internet and the potential for it seem to grow and change with each person who logs on. What remains to be seen is how much things will continue to change. The growth of mobile access and the desire of many to have ubiquitous access to the Internet may lead us to realize that we really *do* need to be "on the grid" all the time. However, there are just as many critics who would argue the opposite—that too much of a good thing is, well, too much. Whatever the direction may be, it's clear that the uses of the Internet are as varied as the needs of the users who use it.

Bibliography:
50X15.org (2010). Retrieved April 29, 2010 from http://50x15.org/connected-global-population
Block, R. (2007). Net neutrality and the FCC: what's being done to preserve it. Retrieved April 5, 2010 from: http://www.engadget.com/2007/03/29/net-neutrality-and-the-fcc-whats-being-done-to-preserve-it/.
Cohen, B. (2009) *The problems with One Laptop per Child.* (Blog) Retrieved April 28, 2010, from http://scienceblogs.com/worldsfair/2009/01/the_problems_with_one_laptop_p.php
Cybersquatting.com – Lawsuits and Domain Law Resource (2010). Website; Published by Kronenberger-Burgoyne, LLP, San Francisco, CA. Retrieved April 29, 2010 from http://cybersquatting.com/
Davis, W. (2010). Fed court rules FCC has no authority in net-neutrality case. Retrieved April 7, 2010 from: http://www.mediapost.com/publications/?fa=Articles.showArticle&art_aid=125618&nid=113010.
DeFleur, M. L. & Dennis, E. E. (2002). *Understanding mass communication: A liberal arts perspective.* Boston: Houghton-Mifflin
De Zúñiga, H. G., Puig-I-Abril, E. and Rojas, H. (2009). Weblogs, traditional sources online and political participation: an assessment of how the internet is changing the political environment. *New Media and Society, 11*(4), 553-574.
Dominick, J. R., Messere, F., & Sherman, B.L. (2008). *Broadcasting, cable, the Internet, and beyond: An introduction to modern electronic media.* New York: McGraw-Hill.
Drummond, D. (2010a). A new approach to China. Retrieved March 22, 2010 from: http://googleblog.blogspot.com/2010/01/new-approach-to-china.html
Drummond, D. (2010b). A new approach to China: An update. Retrieved April 1, 2010 from: http://googleblog.blogspot.com/2010/03/new-approach-to-china-update.html

Dvorak, J.C. (2007) One laptop per child doesn't change the world. *PC Magazine* (2007, Dec. 4). Retrieved April 29, 2010 from http://www.pcmag.com/article2/0,2817,2227850,00.asp

Epps, S.R. (2009) Publishers need multichannel subscription models. (Nov. 10) Forrester Research, Inc. (Report). Cambridge, MA. Retrieved on April 28, 2010 from http://www.forrester.com/rb/Research/publishers_need_multichannel_subscription_models/q/id/53822/t/2

Gelsi, S. (2010) Green computing catches Silicon Valley's eye. *Marketwatch* (April 30, 2010). Retrieved April 30, 2010 from http://www.marketwatch.com/story/venture-capitalist-steve-jurvetson-eyes-green-it-2010-04-29?reflink=MW_news_stmp

Gibs, J. (2010) Do we watch the web the same way we watch TV? *Nielsen Wire.com* (Report) The Nielsen Company, New York, N.Y. Retrieved April 29, 2010, from http://blog.nielsen.com/nielsenwire/consumer/ do-we-watch-the-web-the-same-way-we-watch-tv-not-really/

Gjelten, J. (2010). Cyber insecurity: U.S. struggles to confront threat. Retrieved April 5, 2010 from: http://www.npr.org/templates/story/story.php?storyId=125578576.

Green Information Technology Strategic Plan (2009). United States Department of Agriculture (Report). Washington, D.C. Retrieved April 29, 2010 from http://www.educause.edu/Resources/TheGreenInformationTechnologyI/163740

Green PC made from recyclable materials (2010) *Ubergizmo.com.* Retrieved April 30, 2010 from http://www.ubergizmo.com/15/archives/2010/01/green_pc_made_from_recyclable_materials.html

Hanson, G. & Haridakis, P. (2008). YouTube users watching and sharing the news: A uses and gratifications approach. *The Journal of Electronic Publishing, 11*(3). Horrigan, J. (2009). *Wireless Internet Use.* Pew Internet and American Life Project. Pew Research Center, Washington D.C, Retrieved April 10, 2010 from http://www.pewinternet.org/Reports/2009/12-Wireless-Internet-Use.aspx

Horrigan, J. (2009). Wireless Internet Use. Pew Internet and American Live Project. Retrieved May 12, 2010 from http://www.pewinternet.org/reports/2009/12-wireless-internet-use.aspx

ICANN (2010a) ICANN gives final approval for four countries to use non-Latin languages in Internet address names (News Release). Retrieved April 30, 2010 from www.icann.org/en/news/releases/release-22apr10-en.pdf

ICANN Internet Corporation for Assignment Names and Numbers (2010b). Accessed April 30, 2010 from http://www.icann.org/

International Telecommunications Union (2010). *Measuring the Information Society* (Report). ITU, Geneva, Switzerland. Retrieved April 29 2010, from http://www.itu.int/ITU-D/ict/publications/idi/2010/index.html

JiWire Mobile Audience Insights Report (2010) JiWire Mobile Audience Media. Retrieved April 28th, 2010, from http://www.jiwire.com/downloads/pdf/JiWire_MobileAudienceInsights_Q409.pdf

Keys, M. (2009). Sexting shatters lives, turns children into sex offenders Retrieved April 14, 2010 from: http://www.orlandosentinel.com/news/education/back-to-school/ktxl-news-sexting0814,0,4842001.story

Lamonica, Martin (2010). Greenpeace lauds Cisco, chides Google. *Cnet News Greentech* (April 29, 2010). Retrieved April 30, 2010 from http://news.cnet.com/8301-11128_3-20003584-54.html

Mesenbourg, T. L. (1999). *Measuring electronic business: Definitions, underlying concepts, and measurement plans.* Retrieved March 1, 2006 from http://www.census.gov/epcd/www/ebusiness.htm.

Miniwatts Marketing Group (2010). China Internet usage stats and population report. Retrieved March 30, 2010 from: http://www.internetworldstats.com/asia/cn.htm

One Laptop per Child (2010) Accessed April 29, 2010 from http://www.laptop.org/en/vision/index.shtml

Ostrow, A. (2009a). Michael Jackson's massive impact (On Google, Facebook, and Yahoo). Retrieved April 1, 2010, from: http://mashable.com/2009/06/26/michael-jackson-web-impact/

Ostrow, A. (2009b) Facebook's 2010 revenue estimated at $710 million. Retrieved April 28, 2010, from http://mashable.com/2009/12/07/facebook-2010-revenue/

Ostrow, A. (2010). Twitter has 105 million registered users. Retrieved April 1, 2010, from: http://mashable.com/2010/04/14/twitter-registered-users/

Rainie, L. (2010). Internet, broadband, and cell phone statistics. Retrieved April 10, 2010 from: http://www.pewinternet.org/Reports/2010/Internet-broadband-and-cell-phone-statistics.aspx

Scheleur, S., King, C., & Kinyon, D. (2008). *Quarterly retail e-commerce sales: 4th quarter 2007.* Retrieved March 4, 2008 from http://www.census.gov/mrts/www/data/html/07Q4.html.

Top Sites. (2010). Alexa: A web information company. Retrieved April 2, 2010 from: http://www.alexa.com/topsites

Trend Data-Online activities, 2000-2009 (2009). Pew Internet and American Life Project (Report). Pew Research Center, Washington, D.C. Retrieved April 10, 2010 from: http://www.pewinternet.org/Static-Pages/Trend-Data/Online-Activities-20002009.aspx

U.S. Census Bureau (2010). Quarterly retail e-commerce sales 4th quarter 2009. Retrieved May 7, 2010 from http://www.census.gov/retail/mrts/www/data/html/09Q4.html

Web 2.0 (2010). Pew Internet and American Life Project (Report). Pew Research Center, Washington, D.C. Retrieved April 10, 2010 from http://www.pewinternet.org/topics/Web-20.aspx

20

Social Networking

Rachel A. Sauerbier[*]

Social networking has become a global phenomenon. From its humble beginnings with SixDegrees.com, to Friendster, to MySpace, Facebook, Twitter and everything in between, the role of social networking Web sites has come to permeate almost every aspect of online experience. Even with so much exposure, there is still some confusion on what constitutes a social network site (SNS), and which of the literally hundreds of Web pages on the Internet can be considered SNSs.

What is an SNS? According to boyd and Ellison (2008), there are three criterion that a Web site must meet to be considered an SNS. A Web site must allow users to "(1) construct a public or semi-public profile within a bounded system, (2) articulate a list of other users with whom they share a connection, and (3) view and traverse their list of connections and those made by others within the system" (boyd & Ellison, 2008, p. 211). These guidelines may seem to restrict what can be considered an SNS, as there are still literally hundreds of vastly diverse Web sites that are functioning as such.

One of the most exciting SNSs that has exploded in the past few years is Twitter. Twitter can be seen as the perfect storm of social networking. Twitter is a microblogging SNS that allows users to update their messages—or "feeds"—in 140 characters or less. It is fast, easy, advertising free (as of mid-2010), and accessible with either a computer or any wireless device. It is social networking on the go, where users anywhere can update millions of people of their comings and goings. With so many different types of SNSs branching out in different directions, the question that faces many users looking to adopt a new online social network is "how do I want to connect to people?" Or, "who am I looking to connect to?" Whether their goals are personal, professional, romantic, or nostalgic, sites like Facebook.com, LinkedIn.com, Match.com or Classmates.com can get a person hooked into the social network he or she is looking for.

Background

SNSs have taken on many forms during their evolution. Social networking on the Internet can trace its roots back to listservs such as CompuServe, BBS, and AOL where people would converge to share computer files and ideas (Nickson, 2009). CompuServe was started in 1969 by Jeff Wilkins who wanted to help streamline his father-in-law's insurance business (Banks, 2007). During the 1960s, computers were still prohibitively expensive, so many small, private businesses could not afford a computer of their own. During that time, it was common practice to "timeshare" computers with other companies (Banks, 2007). Timesharing, in this sense,

---

[*] Graduate Student, Communication Studies Department, California State University, Chico (Chico, California).

meant that there was one central computer that allowed several different companies to share access in order to remotely use them for general computing purposes. Wilkins saw the potential in this market, and with the help of two college friends, talked the board of directors at his father-in-law's insurance company into buying a computer for timesharing purposes. With this first computer, Wilkins and his two partners, Alexander Trevor and John Goltz, started up CompuServe Networks, Inc. By taking the basic concept of timesharing already in place, and improving upon it, Wilkins, Trevor, and Goltz created the first centralized site for computer networking and sharing. In 1977, as home computers started to become popular, Wilkins started designing an application that would connect those home computers to the centralized CompuServe computer. The home computer owner could use the central computer for access, for storage or—most importantly—for "person-to-person communications—both public and private" (Banks, 2007).

Another two decades would go by before the first identifiable SNS would appear on the Internet. Throughout the 1980s and early 1990s, there were several different bulletin board systems (BBSs) and sites including America Online (AOL) that provided convergence points for people to meet and share online. In 1996, the first "identifiable" SNS was created—SixDegrees.com (boyd & Ellison, 2008). SixDegrees was originally based upon the concept that no two people are separated by more than six degrees of separation. The concept of the Web site was fairly simple—sign up, provide some personal background and supply the e-mail addresses of 10 friends, family, or colleagues. Each person had his or her own profile, could search for their friends, and for the friends of friends (Caslon Analytics, 2006). It was completely free and relatively easy to use. SixDegrees shut down in 2001 after the dot com bubble popped. What was left in its wake, however, was the beginnings of SNSs as they are known today. There have been literally hundreds of different SNSs that have sprung from the footprints of SixDegrees. In the decade following the demise of SixDegrees, SNSs such as Friendster, MySpace, LinkedIn, Facebook and Twitter have become Internet zeitgeists.

Friendster was created in 2002 by a former Netscape engineer, Jonathan Abrams (Milian, 2009). The Web site was designed for people to create profiles that included personal information—everything from gender to birth date to favorite foods—and the ability to connect with friends that they might not otherwise be able to connect to easily. The original design of Friendster was fresh and innovative, and personal privacy was an important consideration. In order to add someone as a Friendster contact, the friend requester needed to know either the last name or the e-mail address of the requested. It was Abrams' original intention to have a Web site that hosted pages for close friends and family to be able to connect, not as a virtual popularity contest to see who could get the most "Friendsters" (Milian, 2009).

Shortly after the debut of Friendster, a new SNS hit the Internet, MySpace. From its inception by Tom Anderson and Chris DeWolfe in 2003, MySpace was markedly different from Friendster. While Friendster focused on making and maintaining connections with people who already knew each other, MySpace was busy turning the online social networking phenomenon into a multimedia experience. It was the first SNS to allow members to customize their profiles using HTML. So, instead of having "cookie-cutter" profiles like Friendster offered, a MySpace user could completely adapt their profile to their own tastes, right down to the font of the page and music playing in the background. As Nickson (2009) puts it "It looked and felt hipper than the major competitor Friendster right from the start, and it conducted a campaign of sorts in the early days to show alienated Friendster users just what they were missing." This signaled trouble for Friendster, which was slow to adapt to this new form of social networking. A stroke of good fortune for MySpace also came in the form of rumors being spread that Friendster was going to start charging fees for its services. In 2005, with 22 million users, MySpace was sold to News Corp. for $580 million (*BusinessWeek*, 2005). MySpace, now with approximately 130 million users, has since been toppled as the number one SNS by Facebook, which has over 400 million users worldwide (MySpace, n.d. & Facebook, n.d.a).

From its humble roots as a way for Harvard students to stay connected to one another, Facebook has come a long way. Facebook was created in 2004 by Mark Zuckerberg with the help of Dustin Moskovitz, Chris Hughes and Eduardo Saverin (Facebook, n.d.b). Originally, Facebook was only open to Harvard students, however, by the end of the year, it had expanded to Yale University, Columbia University, and Stanford University—the latter's hometown providing the new headquarters for the company in Palo Alto, CA. In 2005, the company started providing social networking services to anyone who had a valid e-mail address ending in .edu. By 2006, Facebook was offering its Web site to anyone over the age of 13 who had a valid e-mail address (Facebook, n.d.a). What made Facebook unique, at the time, was that it was the first SNS to offer the "news feed" on a user's home page. With all other SNSs before Facebook, in order to see what friends were doing, the user would have to click to that friend's page. Facebook, instead, put a live feed of all changes users were posting—everything from relationship changes, to job changes, to updates of their status. In essence, Facebook made microblogging popular. This was a huge shift from MySpace, which had placed a tremendous amount of emphasis on traditional blogging, where people could type as much as they wanted to. With Facebook people were limited to 420 character status updates. Facebook changed the way people were using Web sites for social networking and paved the way for sites like Twitter, with its limitation of 140 character "tweets" (Dsouza, 2010).

Figure 20.1:
Top 10 Social Networking Sites Ranked by Unique Monthly Visitors, May 1, 2010

Rank	Site	Unique Monthly Visitors
1	Facebook	250,000,000
2	MySpace	122,000,000
3	Twitter	80,500,000
4	LinkedIn	50,000,000
5	Ning	42,000,000
6	Tagged	30,000,000
7	Classmates	29,000,000
8	Hi5	27,000,000
9	MyYearbook	12,000,000
10	Meetup	8,000,000

Source: ebizmba.com (2010)

Twitter was formed in 2006 by Jack Dorsey, Evan Williams, and Biz Stone (Beaumont, 2008). It was created out of a desire to be able to stay in touch with friends easier than allowed by Facebook, MySpace, and LinkedIn. Taking the concept of the 160 character limit text messaging imposed on users, Twitter shortened the message length down to 140 (to allow the extra 20 characters to be used for a user name) (Twitter, n.d.a). Twitter attributes a huge amount of its initial success to its usage at festivals like Austin, Texas' South by Southwest (SXSW). Twitter had already gone live a year before, but it was at the 2007 SXSW that the SNS exploded (Mayfield, 2007). Another helpful, if not totally unexpected, promotion of Twitter came from the unusually large number of celebrities who adopted the use of Twitter fairly early—so much so that Web sites like followfamous.com emerged to track which celebrities are using Twitter, even going so far as to have the tagline of their Web site as "find-follow-spy" (followfamous, n.d.).

Not all SNSs have been used for social, personal, dating, or celebrity-stalking purposes. LinkedIn was created in 2003 by Reid Hoffman, Allen Blue, Jean-Luc Vaillant, Eric Ly, and Konstantin Guericke (LinkedIn, 2010). LinkedIn returns the concept of SNSs to its old CompuServe roots. According to the LinkedIn.com history

Web page, the purpose of LinkedIn is to "help you make better use of your professional network and help the people you trust in return. Our mission is to connect the world's professionals to make them more productive and successful" (LinkedIn, n.d.). So instead of helping the user find the long, lost friend from high school, LinkedIn helps build professional connections, that in turn could lead to better job opportunities and more productivity. With over 60 million members worldwide, LinkedIn leads the way in the unique section of SNSs that deal strictly with business relationships.

RECENT DEVELOPMENTS

SNSs have been gaining in popularity over the past five years. With each new technological advancement, the capabilities of SNSs have increased. These changes, though, are not always positive, and many people and companies have realized that they come with a price. This section, will explore how SNSs are using multiple platforms of technology to keep users connected to one another; how entrepreneurs are creating new, niche SNSs; how well-established sites like Facebook, Twitter, and MySpace are adapting to compete with rapid change and not become obsolete; how social networking online has created a whole new issue with privacy and safety; and how social networking is affecting other aspects of life-like employment and relationships.

Until very recently, SNSs could only be as comprehensive as the technology they were using. A case-in-point is the original CompuServe where the most daunting challenge was the necessity for more storage. Today, with all of the advancements in technology, the sky is the limit to what SNSs can do. "Multiple platform" technology has been one of the biggest areas of growth for SNSs. Multiple platforms refers to how a user can access an SNS. Users can now access Facebook, MySpace, Bebo, and Twitter—to name a few—on both their computers and mobile phones. Apple's iPod Touch, for example, allows users to connect to the Internet and update profiles via a wireless connection. With the technology barrier down, SNSs are able to flourish and grow in ways that were not deemed possible five years ago. From March 2009 to March 2010, the number of mobile users accessing their Facebook and Twitter accounts rose 112% and 347% respectively (Walsh, 2010).

Figure 20.2
Online Three Month Average ending January 2010

	Total Audience (000)		
	Jan-09	Jan-10	% Change
Facebook	11,874	25,137	112
MySpace	12,338	11,439	-7
Twitter	1,051	4,700	347

Source: comScore

Much of the social networking growth is attributed to the proliferation of smartphone users (Walsh, 2010). According to Walsh (2010), almost 30% of smartphone users accessed an SNS with their smartphone. Twitter users almost exclusively access Twitter via mobile phones. The ability to update and post to Twitter through both a mobile Web browser and via text message is the reason Twitter has found such success. (Walsh, 2010). The idea of Twitter's microblogging was born from the format of text messaging, so this development is not entirely surprising. Facebook and MySpace have also adopted the ability to update status via text message, but because the interface of both these SNSs are much more comprehensive than Twitter—Web sites are more than just status updates—mobile phone users must have access to the mobile Web.

Twitter's relevance as an SNS goes beyond finding friends and updating the comings and goings of its users. Twitter has recently become a unique, and initially unexpected, source of up-to-date news. The first photo of the crash of US Airways Flight 1549 was posted on Twitter by Janis Krums (Ovide, 2009). The photograph is now one of the most famous photographs of the amazing crash-landing of the flight into the Hudson River. Several months later, when the Iranian presidential elections ended in mass protests and riots, Twitter was used to globally spread images and updates from Tehran and across Iran. When the Iranian government tried to stifle coverage of the protests by not allowing any news coverage to leave the country, and completely deleting stories from newspapers—literally leaving large blocks of white space in the newspapers—Twitter users in Iran were spreading the word across the world. The "promiscuous" nature of Twitter is what made it such an invaluable tool for the election crisis in Iran. A tweet from Twitter goes out over two networks, both a text messaging network and the SNS network, so it can be "received and read on practically anything with a screen and a network connection" (Grossman, 2009, par. 3). After receiving a tweet, users have the option to "retweet" it, in essence, forwarding it on to their followers.

Twitter has also become a significant rival to traditional news sources. Savvy Twitter users use their feeds to judge what the breaking news of the day is. This, however, has not been without some difficulties. Some breaking news stories have been misreported or even wrong when published on Twitter (Gilbertson, 2009). Major news sources understand the potential for this new dissemination of the major stories of the day. Yahoo engineer, Vik Singh, created *TweetNews*, which takes the actual news stories that are being reported on *Yahoo! News* and cross-references them against the most prevalent Twitter feeds (Gilbertson, 2009). While not completely foolproof, it does help control the accuracy of the news coming from Twitter feeds. In November 2009, MSNBC acquired the rights to supply the content sent out over the wildly-popular Twitter newsfeed, @BreakingNews (paidContent, 2009). This is a strategic move for MSNBC because they will be gaining the over 1.4 million followers of @BreakingNews to add to the 40,000 users who already follow their newsfeed, @msnbc_breaking (paidContent, 2009).

The activity of Twitter, both as a zeitgeist for microblogging and as a cutting-edge news source, has not been lost on other SNSs. In February 2010, Facebook patented their "news feed" (*Fox News*, 2010). While the overall implications for this are still unfolding, it could mean that Facebook would "own" the rights to the way people use their sites to make status updates. If the patent covers all aspects of the Facebook "news feed," the results could be troubling for other SNSs that use status updates as part of their user-platform. It should not however, change the way that sites like Twitter provide feeds to their users (O'Neill, 2010).

The popularity of SNSs has not been without significant troubles. Employers are facing the unique issue of their employees using company time to update and maintain their social networking profiles. A study conducted in 2009 found that 54% of companies ban the use of SNSs on company time (Gaudin, 2009). The same study also found that of the companies that do allow full access to SNSs, overall employee productivity drops 1.5%. Of those surveyed who used company time to use an SNS, many spent up to two hours a day on them (Gaudin, 2009).

Many employers are also using SNSs to vet their employees. The inappropriate comment or less-than-flattering picture that gets posted on a user's profile page has begun to have serious professional repercussions. In 2008, 13 Virgin Atlantic flight crew members were fired after using the company's Facebook fan page to insult passengers (O'Neill, 2008). The case of the Virgin Atlantic employees is blatant, but employers are using SNSs to keep an eye on their employees and also as a sort of "informal" background check to look at potential employees. Social Sentry is a company that offers a Web-based subscription service to companies that essentially spies on the usage of SNSs by employees. The company can track who, where, and for how long an employee uses a site. Social Sentry can even track the usage of an employee who is signed into an SNS with an alias (Dash, 2010). Many companies are monitoring their employees' usage of SNSs the old-fashioned way: Logging in and searching for employees manually. Employees should seriously consider whether to accept their boss' friend request.

The SNSs users' ability to share their lives with friends and family via online social profiles has also created the grave, unintended issue of privacy violations. As many people have found out the hard way, they are not only sharing their information with their friends and family, but also with millions of strangers. The privacy violations can, at times, be nothing more than a mere annoyance, however there have been numerous reports of SNSs becoming havens for pedophiles and scammers (Poulsen, 2006; Goodin, 2007; Krebs, 2008). The situation becomes even more tenuous because of the nature of SNSs. Legislators and the SNSs themselves have tried to curb the problem with everything from a proposed e-mail registry (Lemos, 2006a) to creating databases within the site to try to filter out registered sex offenders (Lemos, 2006b). The issue with this—and similar methods to try and catch scammers—is as technology makes SNSs more user-friendly and dynamic, the same technology makes it easier for criminals to prey on their cyber-victims relatively unnoticed.

The other issue is, while there is an obvious problem with dangerous sex offenders, stalkers, and scammers, the more pressing and growing problem on SNSs is cyberbullying (Zetter, 2009). Children, for the most part, do not have to worry about the dangers of an adult preying on them as much as they have to worry about other children harassing them. One of the more bizarre cases of cyber-bullying occurred in April, 2010 where a 16-year-old is suing his mother for harassment stemming from her interference with his life via Facebook. The unnamed teenager claims that his mother hacked into his account and posted "slanderous" things about him (Matyszczyk, 2010). Denise New, the boy's mother, claims that it was well within her rights to monitor his account and "have a conversation with him, whether it's his account, or your account, or whoever's account" (Matyszczyk, 2010).

Because of the clear and present danger facing the younger users of SNSs today, the government has stepped in. In 2008, the Internet Safety Technical Task Force was created to make sure that the online experience for minors is a safe as possible (Berkman Center for Internet & Society, n.d). Even with findings from studies the task force has conducted (like the one about cyberbullying mentioned above), there are still issues regarding a minor's safety and privacy online. Another area that is drawing concern is SNSs privacy policies. As more and more people find the details of their private life being shared with unintended people, each SNS is trying to give users the sense of security without sacrificing the "openness" of social networking.

In December 2009, Facebook founder Mark Zuckerberg sent out a message to all Facebook users detailing the new privacy settings that were being enacted. The message stated that it gives the user more control over who sees what on each profile. It also gives the user different privacy settings within each section. Now, a user can either let his or her friends, networks, friends of friends, or everybody see each specific part of their profile (Zuckerberg, 2009). However, the new privacy settings have not proven to be very user-friendly, and unless users do some digging through the layers of privacy settings, many people wind up making more of their personal profile public than intended (Needleman, 2009). MySpace was created with black and white privacy settings in place—either a profile was public or private. Private profiles can only be viewed by approved friends (MySpace, n.d.). This method of "public/private" has not proved foolproof, however, as many sites give instructions on how to view and download pictures and information from private MySpace profiles (Articlesbase, 2007). Twitter has all but circumvented the privacy issue by making all content on their site available to the public. They have given users the ownership of what should be put on display for the general public to see, a sort of *caveat emptor*. Setting a Twitter account to private is possible, but the theory is, privacy defeats the purpose of Twitter—which is to engender a true sense of openness and sharing on its site (Twitter, n.d. a).

The necessity for user awareness about privacy has been prompted for several reasons. There are, of course, the reasons that have already been mentioned—like children's safety, scammers, and employers using it to vet employees—but SNSs are also being used by the Government to obtain information about people. In February 2010, documents acquired by the *Freedom of Information Act* found that the Federal Bureau of Investigation (FBI) was creating fake profiles on popular SNSs to communicate with suspected criminals and gather personal information about them (Lardner, 2010). Now, while training new agents, the FBI and other government agencies extol the benefits of using SNSs to facilitate investigations (Lardner, 2010). The Internal Revenue Service (IRS) also trains its employees to use SNSs and other Internet applications, like Google Maps, to gather information about taxpayers (Prince, 2010). An interesting site that has gained attention recently is pleaserobme.com. Please Rob Me urges users of Twitter, Foursquare, and Gowalla, to name a few, to be mindful of posting updates that state where they are—especially if where they are is not home (McCarthy, 2010). Most people do not realize that a savvy criminal can find out where just about anyone lives. If users are using a very public SNS to brag about being on vacation, it is an open invitation for burglars to rob their house while they are not home. The fundamental issue is clear: there is no guarantee of privacy if the information is on an SNS.

A trend that is gaining steam is that of niche SNSs. Sites like Bebo, DeviantArt, Ning, BlackPlanet, and Chatroulette are catering to users who want something more specific than a broad-based SNSs like Facebook or MySpace. Bebo (blog early, blog often), for example, is catering to those who want to use an SNS as a platform for their blogs. Ning is unique in that it builds networks of relative strangers that share similar interests (Ning, n.d.). Another SNS that has gained a lot of attention is ChatRoulette, a hybrid of video chat and social networking where the user logs-in to the Web site and is randomly paired up with other ChatRoulette users. The two people can talk as long as they want, but either party can terminate the conversation at any time. The Web site is causing concern because it is rapidly turning into a video version of the "causal encounters" page on Craigslist (Hackman, 2010). The creators of Chatroulette are working furiously to reduce the number of "nude encounters" by working on the "report members" feature (Hackman, 2010).

One interesting site that has taken the concept of a niche SNS to a whole new level is A Small World. A Small World is an SNS that "is by invitation only, which is part of what makes this network unique, and the connections, authentic. Trusted, and loyal ASW members, who meet certain criteria, have the privilege of inviting a limited number of their friends to the network" (A Small World, n.d., par. 2). A Small World is, in other words, an SNS devoted to affluent, traveled, cultured people. It is the American Express Centurion Card of SNSs. Each day, more and more niche SNSs pop up, attracting Internet users who are looking for something more than re-friending the 500 people they haven't thought about since the third grade.

CURRENT STATUS

SNSs are here to stay. The Internet has become an essential part to the everyday workings of the postmodern world. As more and more developing countries obtain reliable Internet access, the need to stay connected will become stronger. What is the status of SNSs today? How are they changing the way people interact with one another? How have they changed the online culture?

One area that has seen a major impact from SNSs is online advertising. About 20% of online advertising hits come from SNSs (comScore, 2009). MySpace and Facebook account for almost 80% of SNSs advertising hits (comScore, 2009). Among companies using SNSs to advertise their products, AT&T led the way in 2009 (comScore, 2009). The attraction for many companies is the huge potential for market saturation by advertising on SNSs. Companies like AT&T and the others on the top list of social networking advertisers realize that people spend a tremendous amount of time on social networking sites, which gives these companies a better chance their advertisements will be seen.

Figure 20.3

Top Online Display Ad Publishers in Social Networking Category (June 2009)

	Total Display Ad Impressions (MM)	Share of Display Ads	Ad Exposed Unique Visitors (000)
Total Internet : Total Audience	326,899	100.0	188,589
Social Networking	68,927	21.1	129,620
MySpace	30,004	9.2	64,472
Facebook	26,813	8.2	67,389
Tagged	1,940	0.6	7,422
MocoSpace	496	0.2	1,067
Hi5	461	0.1	3,459
Bebo	435	0.1	6,350
Classmates	400	0.1	9,181
BlackPlanet	345	0.1	2,084
GaiaOnline	258	0.1	1,859
DeviantArt	204	0.1	3,681

Source: comScore

Figure 20.4

Top Online Display Advertisers in Social Networking Category (June 2009)

	Total Display Ad Impressions (MM)	Share of Advertiser Ad Impressions	Ad Exposed Unique Visitors (000)
Social Networking Category	68,927	21.1	129,620
AT&T, Inc.	2,067	29.5	87,080
Experian Interactive	1,250	23.9	58,991
Ask Network	950	44.6	41,379
Sprint Nextel Corporation	790	26.3	68,581
Pangea Media	572	89.6	33,079
Microsoft Sites	564	16.8	60,148
Apollo Group, Inc.	510	41.4	51,981
Zynga.com	484	96.8	40,009
GameVance.com	450	33.9	34,762
Verizon Communications Corporation	435	10.5	54,010

Source : comScore

Figure 20.5

Top 10 Social Networking and Blog Sites Ranked by Total Minutes for April 2009 and Their Year-over-Year Percent Growth

Rank	Site	April 2008 Total Minutes (000)	April 2009 Total Minutes (000)	Year-over-Year % Growth
1	Facebook	1,735,698	13,872,640	699
2	MySpace	7,254,645	4,973,919	-31
3	Blogger	448,710	582,683	30
4	Tagged	29,858	327,871	998
5	Twitter	7,865	299,836	3712
6	MyYearbook	131,105	268,565	105
7	LiveJournal	54,671	204,121	273
8	LinkedIn	119,636	202,407	69
9	SlashKey	N/A	187,687	N/A
10	GaiaOnline	173,115	143,909	-17

Source: Nielsen

How much time is being spent on SNSs? In 2009, time spent on SNSs accounted for 11% of all time spent on the Internet (Curve, 2010). Twitter saw the largest growth in user time, with a 3712% growth from April 2008 to April 2009. Facebook overtook MySpace as the overall leader in user time spent on its site per year, skyrocketing to almost 14 million minutes spent there, accounting for an almost 700% growth (Nielsen, 2009a).

Different age demographics have begun to adopt the social networking trend. The fastest growing age demographic to start updating their profiles are the people between 35 and 54 years old (comScore, 2010). Baby Boomers are also starting to find their friends online, but are slowest, second only to the toddlers to tweens age demographic (comScore, 2010).

Figure 20.6

Social Network Users by Age

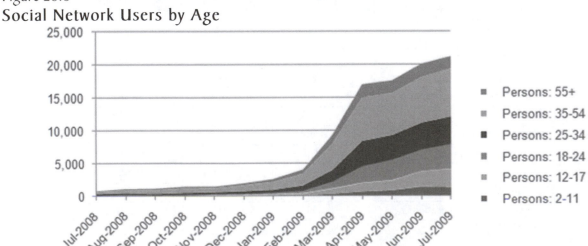

Legend:
- Persons: 55+
- Persons: 35-54
- Persons: 25-34
- Persons: 18-24
- Persons: 12-17
- Persons: 2-11

Source: comScore

Another interesting trend is that not only are more people spending more time on SNSs, but they are spending more time on SNSs than any other Internet application (Nielsen, 2009b). February 2009 marked the first month that SNSs usage outpaced the use of e-mail (Nielsen, 2009b). SNSs eclipsed search engines in mid-2005 and video well before that (Nielsen, 2009b).

The growth of SNSs has been steady and shows no signs of slowing. The question that begs to be asked next is: Where does social networking go from here?

⊕ Sustainability ⊕

SNSs are heeding the call to save the planet. Here's what some of the most popular SNSs are doing to keep the planet green:

Facebook: In 2009, Facebook expanded into four new data centers to keep up with their growth. All four of the new data centers Facebook moved into are Leadership in Energy & Environmental Design (LEED) gold certified (Miller, 2009). This is not only good for the environment, but also a wise business move; the new LEED centers run more efficiently so Facebook can get more productivity from the new, sustainable data centers than from a traditional data center (Miller, 2009).

Twitter: Twitter actively works at giving back to the world that has made it such a success. Twitter is committed to improving the world's water supply (Twitter, n.d. a). Twitter has also supported World AIDS day and promotes global literacy (Twitter, n.d. a).

Here are a few new SNSs that have been created with global sustainability in mind:

Makemesustainable: This SNS is dedicated to helping people reduce their carbon footprint (Fehrenbacher, 2008). There are different sections on this Web site that allow the user to see what their carbon footprint is based upon different actions the user has taken (Fehrenbacher, 2008).

Zerofootprint: One of the few non-profit, green SNSs on the Web right now, this SNS creates carbon footprint calculators for large companies and communities (Fehrenbacher, 2008).

Carbonrally: Carbonrally was created by Jason Karas with the idea that members of a social network could be joined together to form teams that help individual members strive for sustainable practices like reducing carbon emissions (Fehrenbacher, 2008). This site is gaining attention from businesses that need an extra hand in team building.

FACTORS TO WATCH

What is in store for SNSs? What can we expect to see from these Internet giants in the coming years?

On April 6, 2010, AOL announced they are looking to off-load Bebo (Ingram, 2010). AOL admitted that Bebo business is declining and the company is no longer able to invest resources into the SNS. AOL would like to sell the SNS, but if there are no interested parties, they will be forced to shut the SNS down (Ingram, 2010). AOL will make a decision about Bebo by late-May 2010.

Expect to see more integration. It is already starting to happen with many Web pages offering links to post their articles, updates, etc. on favorite SNSs like Facebook, Twitter, Blogger, Flickr, and so on. There are already applications—both for mobile phones and the computer—that allow users to publish status updates to Facebook, Twitter, and MySpace simultaneously. The trend to watch is whether the individual SNSs will allow users to import and export their unique profiles from one site to another using an application programming interface (API) (Farber, 2007). With the use of an API, users will be able to not only update their statuses simultaneously, but also transfer all information back and forth—including friends. If the SNSs themselves do not come up with an API, third party programmers will come up with software to allow it—much like Adobe did with their new product, AIR. AIR allows seamless interfacing between multiple platforms using the same code (Hollister, 2010).

Expect mobile phones to play an increasing role in SNSs. Mobile technology is no longer an issue for SNSs, so there should be more growth and adaptation to serve the needs of mobile SNSs users (Lichtenberg, 2009).

Employers will not only use SNSs to spy on their employees, but also to recruit them. It will be a tool that can be used in the best interest of both parties involved (Pennock, 2009). The employer can learn how the prospective employee presents themself to the world, who they associate with, etc., and the prospective employee can check out the employer's profile page to see if the company is "cool enough" to work for.

Most importantly, expect to see more Web sites like Failbook.com. Failbook.com is a Web site dedicated to celebrating the questionable content and ridiculous messages people post on their Facebook profiles. There are numerous sites on the Web that are highlighting the often amusing posts from various Internet sites, but Failbook is one of the first and most entertaining. The posts included on Failbook range from unfortunate spelling errors, all the way to awkward cyber encounters between kids and their parents—with everything else in between. Failbook is run by Pet Holdings, Inc., the same company that runs FAIL Blog and I Can Has Cheezburger (Cheezburger, n.d.). With the amount of questionable material people put on their SNSs profiles, it is a wonder that, as of mid-2010, there is only one site completely dedicated to finding it.

Bibliography

A Small World. (n.d.). About ASMALLWORLD. *A Small World.* Retrieved April 5, 2010 from http://www.asmallworld.net/about

Articlesbase (2007, July 24). Tips how to view private MySpace profiles. *Articlesbase.* Retrieved April 5, 2010 from http://www.articlesbase Fx/computers-articles/tips-how-to-view-private-myspace-profiles-186819.html

Banks, M.A. (2007, January 1). The Internet, ARPANet, and consumer online. *All Business.* Retrieved March 31, 2010 from http://www.allbusiness.com/media-telecommunications/Internet-www/10555321-1.html

Beaumont, C. (2008, November 25). The team behind Twitter: Jack Dorsey, Biz Stone and Evan Williams. *Telegraph.* Retrieved March 31, 2010 from http://www.telegraph.co.uk/technology/3520024/The-team-behind-Twitter-Jack-Dorsey-Biz-Stone-and-Evan-Williams.html

Berkman Center for Internet & Society. (n.d.). Internet safety technical task force. *Berkman Center for Internet & Society at Harvard University.* Retrieved April 5, 2010 from http://cyber.law.harvard.edu/research/isttf

boyd, d.m., & Ellison, N.B. (2008). Social networking sites: Definition, history, and scholarship. *Journal of Computer-Mediated Communication,* 13, 210-230

BusinessWeek. (2005, July 29). MySpace: WhoseSpace?. *BusinessWeek.* Retrieved March 31, 2010 from http://www.businessweek.com/technology/content/jul2005/tc20050729_0719_tc057.htm

Caslon Analytics. (2006). Caslon Analytics social networking services. *Caslon Analytics.* Retrieved March 31, 2010 from http://www.caslon.com.au/socialspacesprofile2.htm

Cheezburger. (n.d.). Failbook- Funny Facebook status messages. Failbook. Retrieved April 26 from http://failbook.com/

comScore. (2009, September 1). Social networking sites account for more than 20 percent of all U.S. online display ad impressions, according to comScore ad metrix. comScore. Retrieved March 28th, 2010 from http://www.comscore.com/Press_Events/Press_Releases/2009/9/Social_Networking_Sites_Account_for_More_than_20_Percent_of_All_U.S._Online_Display_Ad_Impressions_According_to_comScore_Ad_Metrix/(language)/eng-US

comScore. (2010). The 2009 U.S. digital year in review: A recap of the year in digital marketing. *comScore.*

Curve, H. (2010, February 10). Comscore: 2009 social networking stats. *Computerworld.* Retrieved from http://news.idg.no/cw/art.cfm?id=B8790C25-1A64-6A71-CEDC88EAA45BCE6F

Dash, R. (2010, March 30). How to monitor your employees' Facebook use. *All Facebook.* Retrieved April 5, 2010 from http://www.allfacebook.com/2010/03/monitor-employees-facebook/

Dsouza, K. (2010, March 14). Facebook status update has 420 character limit too. *Techie Buzz*. Retrieved March 31, 2010 from http://techie-buzz.com/social-networking/facebook-has-a-420-character-status-update-limit-too.html

eBizMBA. (2010, March). Top 20 most popular social networking Web sites. *eBizMBA*. Retrieved March 28, 2010 from http://www.ebizmba.com/articles/social-networking-Web sites

Facebook (n.d. a). Timeline. Retrieved March 31, 2010 from http://www.facebook.com/press/info.php?timeline

Facebook (n.d. b). Factsheet. Retrieved March 31, 2010 from http://www.facebook.com/press/info.php?factsheet

Farber, D. (2007, August 2). The future of social networks. *ZDNet*. Retrieved on March 28, 2010 from http://blogs.zdnet.com/BTL/?p=5848

Fehrenbacher, K. (2008, April 11). 10 green social networks you should know. *Earth2tech*. Retrieved April 5, 2010 from http://earth2tech.com/2008/04/11/10-green-social-networks-you-should-know/

FollowFamous. (n.d.). Find famous celebrities on Twitter. *Follow Famous*. Retrieved April 1, 2010 from http://www.followfamous.com/

Fox News. (2010, February 26). Watch out, Twitter: Facebook patents 'news feed.' *Fox News*. Retrieved March 29, 2010 from http://www.foxnews.com/scitech/2010/02/26/facebook-patents-news-feed/

Gaudin, S. (2009, October 6). Study: 54% of companies ban Facebook, Twitter at work. *Computerworld*. Retrieved April 5, 2010 from http://www.computerworld.com/s/article/9139020/Study_54_of_companies_ban_Facebook_Twitter_at_work

Gilbertson, S. (2009, January 16). Twitter-Yahoo mashup yields better breaking news search. *Wired*. Retrieved March 28, 2010 from http://www.wired.com/epicenter/2009/01/twitter-yahoo-b/

Goodin, D. (2007, September 25). NY probes Facebook over pedophile controls. *The Register*. Retrieved from http://www.theregister.co.uk/2007/09/25/facebook_subpoena/

Grossman, L. (2009, June 17). Iran protests: Twitter, the medium of the movement. *Time*. Retrieved April 3, 2010 from http://www.time.com/time/world/article/0,8599,1905125,00.html

Hackman, M. (2010, April 5). Chatroulette tries to fix its penis problem. *PCMag*. Retrieved April 5, 2010 from http://www.pcmag.com/article2/0,2817,2362256,00.asp

Hollister, S. (2010, April 5). Adobe AIR developer demonstration: One game, five platforms, all the same code. *Endagaget*. Retrieved April 5, 2010 from http://www.engadget.com/2010/04/05/adobe-air-developer-demonstration-one-game-five-platforms-all/

Ingram, M. (2010, April 6). Facebook wins: AOL throws in the towel on Bebo. *GigaOm*. Retrieved April 6, 2010 from http://gigaom.com/2010/04/06/facebook-wins-aol-throws-in-the-towel-on-bebo/?utm_source=feedburner&utm_medium=feed&utm_campaign=Feed:+OmMalik+(GigaOM)

Krebs, B. (2008, October 8). Spear phishing scam targets LinkedIn users. *The Washington Post*. Retrieved from http://voices.washingtonpost.com/securityfix/2008/10/spear_phishing_attacks_against.html

Lardner, R. (2010, March 16). Break the law and your new 'friend' may be the FBI. *USA Today*. Retrieved May 12, 2010 from http://www.usatoday.com/tech/news/2010-03-16-fbi-facebook_N.thm

Lemos, R. (2006a, December 7). E-mail, IM registry for sex offenders proposed. *Security Focus*. Retrieved April 5, 2010 from http://www.securityfocus.com/brief/378

Lemos, R. (2006b, December 5). MySpace teams to create sex-offender database. *Security Focus*. Retrieved April 5, 2010 from http://www.securityfocus.com/news/11428

Lichtenberg, R. (2009, December 11). 10 ways social media will change in 2010. *ReadWriteWeb*. Retrieved March 31, 2010 from http://www.readwriteweb.com/archives/10_ways_social_media_will_change_in_2010.php

LinkedIn. (2010, March 29). Company history. *LinkedIn*. Retrieved March 29, 2010 from http://press.linkedin.com/history

Matyszczyk, C. (2010, April 7). Son plans to sue mother over Facebook interference. *Cnet*. Retrieved April 9, 2010 from http://news.cnet.com/8301-17852_3-20001917-71.html

Mayfield, R. (2007, March 10). Twitter tips the tuna. *Ross Mayfield's Weblog*. Retrieved March 31, 2010 from http://ross.typepad.com/blog/2007/03/twitter_tips_th.html

McCarthy, C. (2010, February 17). The dark side of geo: PleaseRobMe.com. *Cnet*. Retrieved April 9, 2010 from http://news.cnet.com/8301-13577_3-10454981-36.html

Milian, M. (2009, July 22) Friendster founder on social networking: I invented this stuff (updated). *The Los Angeles Times*. Retrieved from http://latimesblogs.latimes.com/technology/2009/07/friendster-jonathan-abrams.html

Miller, R. (2009, November 5). Facebook goes green with new data centers. *Data Center Knowledge*. Retrieved April 5, 2010 from http://www.datacenterknowledge.com/archives/2009/11/05/facebook-goes-green-with-new-data-centers/

MySpace. (n.d.). MySpace safety tips & settings. MySpace. Retrieved April 5, 2010 from http://www.myspace.com/index.cfm?fuseaction=cms.viewpage&placement=safety_pagetips&sspage=4

Needleman, R. (2009, December 10). How to fix Facebook's new privacy settings. Cnet. Retrieved April 5, 2010 from http://news.cnet.com/8301-19882_3-10413317-250.html

Nickson, C. (2009, January 21). The history of social networking. *Digital Trends*. Retrieved March 28, 2010 from http://www.digitaltrends.com/features/the-history-of-social-networking/

Nielsen. (2009a, June 2). Time spent on Facebook up 700%, but MySpace still tops for video. *Nielsenwire*. Retrieved April 5, 2010 from http://blog.nielsen.com/nielsenwire/online_mobile/time-spent-on-facebook-up-700-but-myspace-still-tops-for-video/

Nielsen. (2009b). The global online media landscape: Identifying opportunities in a challenging market. *Nielsen.* Retrieved April 5, 2010 from http://blog.nielsen.com/nielsenwire/wp-content/uploads/2009/04/nielsen-online-global-lanscapefinal1.pdf

Ning. (n.d). Why you'll (heart) Ning. *Ning.* Retrieved April 5, 2010 from http://about.ning.com/

O'Neill, N. (2008, October 31). Virgin crew fired after insulting passengers on Facebook. *All Facebook.* Retrieved April 5, 2010 from http://www.allfacebook.com/2008/10/virgin-crew-fired-after-insulting-passengers-on-facebook/

O'Neill, N. (2010, February 25). Facebook patents the news feed. *All Facebook.* Retrieved April 5, 2010 from http://www.allfacebook.com/2010/02/facebook-feed-patent/

Ovide, S. (2009, January 15). Twittering the USAirways plane crash. *The Wall Street Journal.* Retrieved April 3, 2010 from http://blogs.wsj.com/digits/2009/01/15/twittering-the-usairways-plane-crash/tab/article/

paidContent.org. (2009, November 23). MSNBC.com taking over @BreakingNews Twitter feed; signs on as BNO news' first client. *paidContent.org.* Retrieved March 28th, 2010 from http://paidcontent.org/article/419-msnbc.com-taking-over-breakingnews-twitter-feed-signs-on-as-bno-news-fi/

Pennock, R. (2009, April 7). Social networking sites: A new recruiting tool. *Lab Manager Magazine.* Retrieved April 5, 2010 from http://www.labmanager.com/articles.asp?ID=243

Poulsen, K. (2006, October 16). MySpace predator caught by code. *Wired.* Retrieved April 5, 2010 from http://www.wired.com/science/discoveries/news/2006/10/71948

Prince, B. (2010, March 16). Social network privacy concerns raised by undercover police tactics. *eWeek.* Retrieved April 5, 2010 from http://www.eweek.com/c/a/Security/Social-Network-Privacy-Concerns-Raised-by-Undercover-Police-Tactics-409306/

Technology Review. (2008, July). The social networking story. *Technology Review,* 111(4), 40-41

Twitter. (n.d. a). Twitter 101: A special guide. *Twitter.* Retrieved March 31, 2010 from http://business.twitter.com/twitter101

Twitter. (n.d. b). Twitter privacy policy. *Twitter.* Retrieved April 5, 2010 from http://twitter.com/privacy

Walsh, M. (2010, March 3). Facebook, Twitter soar on mobile web, MySpace slides. *MediaPost.* Retrieved April 3, 2010 from http://www.mediapost.com/publications/?fa=Articles.showArticle&art_aid=123650&nid=111810

Zetter, K. (2009, January 16). Bullies worse than predators on social networks. *Wired.* Retrieved April 5, 2010 from http://www.wired.com/threatlevel/2009/01/bullies-worse-t/

Zuckerberg, M. (2009, December 1). An open letter from Facebook founder Mark Zuckerberg. *Facebook.* Retrieved April 5, 2010 from http://blog.facebook.com/blog.php?post=190423927130

21

Broadband & Home Networks

John J. Lombardi, Ph.D. with Jennifer H. Meadows, Ph.D.[*]

Tim Berners-Lee, the man credited with developing the World Wide Web has said "Anyone who has lost track of time when using a computer knows the propensity to dream, the urge to make dreams come true and the tendency to miss lunch" (FAQ, n.d.). The World Wide Web is just a bit more than two decades old. However, it is deeply engrained in the daily lives of millions of people worldwide. But the World Wide Web is just part of the growing Internet experience. The Internet is used in virtually all aspects of our lives. In addition to surfing the Web, the Internet allows users to share information with one another. The Internet can be used to send and receive photos, music, videos, phone calls or any other type of data.

High speed Internet connections are typically referred to as "broadband" connections. What constitutes "high speed," though, is subject to debate, but the FCC considers Tier I high speed Internet to be greater than or equal to 768 Kb/s, but less than 1.5 mbls (FCC, 2008). The Organisation for Economic Co-Operation and Development (OECD), an organization based in France that collects and distributes international economic and social data, considers broadband any connection with speeds of at least 256 Kb/s. Meanwhile the International Telecommunication Union considers broadband to be connection speeds of between 1.5 and 2.0 Mb/s (ITU, 2003).

While the FCC defines broadband as connections equal to or greater than 768 Kb/s, actual speeds in the U.S. are generally much faster. Although the U.S. may lag behind other countries, the average speed in the U.S. is 5.1 Mb/s (Whitney, 2009). South Korea, the current world leader, boasts an average speed of over 20 Mb/s.

The increased connection speeds afforded by broadband technology allow for users to engage in increasingly complex activities such as VoIP, IPTV, and interactive gaming. Additionally, the "always on" approach to broadband allows for consumers to easily create wireless home networks. Such configurations can allow for wireless data sharing between numerous devices. For instance, a wireless home network can allow for multiple computers to connect to the Internet at one time. Such networks can also allow for audio and video content to be moved around your home wirelessly. For instance, with a wireless broadband connection you could view videos on your television that are stored on your computer. Movie rental firms such as Netflix allow subscribers to access certain content instantly. In this case subscribers could add movies to their "instant queue" and then access them directly through their television.

---

[*] Dr. Lombardi is Associate Professor, Department of Mass Communication, Frostburg State University (Frostburg, Maryland). Dr. Meadows is Professor, Department of Communication Design, California State University, Chico (Chico, California).

The key device in most home networks is a residential gateway, or router. Routers are devices that link all IP (Internet protocol) devices to one another and to the home broadband connection. The capability of routing any type of data stream to set-top boxes, telephones, and other devices will eventually allow audio, video, and telephone signals to be distributed throughout the home in the same manner as computer data streams are routed.

This chapter briefly reviews the development of broadband and home networks and residential gateways, discusses the types and uses of these technologies, and examines the current status and future developments of these exciting technologies.

Background

Broadband networks can use a number of different technologies to deliver service. These technologies include digital subscriber line (DSL), cable modem, satellite, fiber, wireless, and broadband over power line (BPL). Thanks in part to the *Telecommunication Act of 1996* broadband providers include telephone companies, cable operators, public utilities, and private corporations.

DSL

DSL stands for digital subscriber line. This technology supplies broadband Internet access over regular telephone lines with service being provided by local carriers such as Verizon, Qwest, and AT&T. There are several types of DSL available, but asymmetrical DSL (ADSL) is the most widely used for broadband Internet access. "Asymmetrical" refers to the fact that download speeds are faster than upload speeds. This is a common feature in most broadband Internet network technologies because the assumption is that people download more frequently than upload, and they download larger amounts of data. With DSL, the customer has a modem that connects to a phone jack. Data moves over the telephone network to the central office. At the central office, the telephone line is connected to a DSL access multiplexer (DSLAM). The DSLAM aggregates all of the data coming in from multiple lines and connects them to a high-bandwidth Internet connection.

A DSL connection from the home (or office) to the central office is not shared. As such, the connection speed is not affected by other users. However, ADSL is a distance sensitive technology. This means that the distance from your home to the central office affects the connection speed, because the farther your home is from the central office, the slower your connection speed will be. Also, this technology only works within 18,000 feet (about 3 ½ miles) of the central office (though "bridge taps" may be used to extend this range a bit). ASDL typically offers download speeds up to 1.5 Mb/s and upload speeds from 64 Kb/s to 640 Kb/s. Some areas have more advanced DSL services called ADSL2 and ADSL2+. These services offer higher bandwidth, up to 12 Mb/s with ADSL2 and 24 Mb/s with ADSL2+. Prices vary from a low of $19.95 per month for 768 Kb/s download to $40 per month for up to 6 Mb/s with AT&T's DSL service (AT&T, n.d.).

FTTN

Fiber-to-the-node is a hybrid form of DSL often times referred to as VDSL (very high bit-rate DSL). This service, used for services such as Verizon's FiOS, offers speeds up to 50 Mb/s downstream and 20 Mb/s upstream. This system employs a fiber optic cable that runs from the central office to a node in individual neighborhoods. A traditional copper wire then runs from the node (or VDSL gateway) to the home. The neighborhood node is a junction box in the neighborhood that contains a VDSL gateway that converts the digital signal on the fiber optic network to a signal that is carried on ordinary copper wires to the residence.

Verizon's FiOS service offers speeds from 15 Mb/s downstream and 5 Mb/s upstream for $49.99 a month to 50 Mb/s downstream and 20 Mb/s upstream for $139.95 per month (Verizon, 2010).

FTTH

Fiber-to-the-home employs fiber optic networks all the way to the home. Fiber optic cables have the advantage of being extremely fast (speeds up to 1 Gb/s) and are the backbone of both cable and telecommunications networks. Extending these networks to the home is rare, as costs are incredibly high—connection costs per home run about $700. As of October 2009, FTTH/FTTN connections were deployed in approximately 18 million U.S. homes (up from just under three million homes in early 2008) (Corning, 2009).

Cable Modem

Cable television providers offer Internet service. In this system a customer's Internet service can come into the home on the same cable that provides cable television service and for some, telephone service. With the upgrade to hybrid fiber/coaxial cable networks, cable television operators began offering broadband Internet access. But how can the same cable that supplies your cable television signals also have enough bandwidth to also supply high speed Internet access? They can do this because it is possible to fit the download data (the data going from the Internet to the home) into the 6 MHz bandwidth space of a single television channel. The upload speed (the data going from the computer back to the Internet) requires only about 2 MHz of bandwidth space.

In the case of Internet through a cable service, the signal travels to the cable headend via the cable modem termination system (CMTS). The CMST acts like the DSLAM of a DSL service. From the cable headend, the signal travels to a cable node in a given neighborhood. A coaxial cable then runs from the neighborhood node to the home.

Cable modems use a standard called data over cable service interface specifications (DOCSIS). First generation DOCSIS 1.0 , which were used with first-generation hybrid fiber/coax networks, was capable of providing bandwidth between 320 Kb/s and 10 Mb/s. DOCSIS 2.0 raised that bandwidth to up to 30 Mb/s (DOCSIS, n.d.). DOCSIS 3.0 provides bandwidth well in excess of 100 Mb/s. In fact, some modem chipsets can bond up to eight downstream channels thus creating the possibility of delivering up to 320 Mb/s (Docsis 3.0, 2009). Comcast is the number one U.S. cable broadband provider with 15.9 million customers as of the December 31, 2009 (Corporate overview, n.d.).

Cable Internet service costs range from about $40 per month for a service with 15 Mb/s download speeds to up to $150 per month for 50 Mb/s service. Prices for cable broadband service are usually lower when bundled with other services.

Although cable Internet provides fast speeds and, arguably, reasonable rates, this service is not without problems. Unlike DSL, cable Internet users share bandwidth. This means that the useable speed of individual subscribers varies depending upon the number of simultaneous users.

Satellite

For those people who live out of DSL's reach and in rural areas without cable, satellite broadband Internet access is an option. With this service, a modem is connected to a small satellite dish which then communicates with the service providers' satellite. That satellite, in turn, directs the data to a provider center that has a high-capacity connection to the Internet. Satellite Internet service cannot deliver the bandwidth of cable or DSL, but speeds are a great improvement over dial-up. For example, HughesNet offers home service with 1 Mb/s download and 128 Kb/s upload for $59.99 a month. Its highest speed service for the residential market, ProPlus, offers 1.6 Mb/s download and 250 Kb/s upload for $79.99 a month. Higher speeds are available for home or small office networks, but the price goes up considerably. The fastest speed available is 3 Mb/s download and 300 Kb/s upload for $189.99 a month. These prices do not include the cost of installation or the purchase or leasing of equipment (HughesNet, 2010).

The two most popular satellite services in the U.S. are HughesNet and Wild Blue. HughesNet uses three DBS satellites on the high-power Ku band, while Wild Blue uses the Ka-band and 11 gateways located throughout the U.S. (Wild Blue, n.d).

Wireless

There are two different types of wireless broadband networks: mobile and fixed. Mobile broadband networks are offered by wireless telephony companies and employ 3G (and increasingly 4G) networks (discussed in more detail in Chapter 18). Second generation (2G) mobile broadband networks generally use the Enhanced Data GSM Environment (EDGE) protocol (some refer to this as 2.75G because it is better than traditional 2G, but not quite at the level of true 3G networks). Third generation (3G) networks generally use Evolution, Data Optimized (EVDO), or High-Speed Uplink Packet Access (HSUPA). In mid-2009, Verizon and AT&T began rolling out 4G networks. These fourth generation networks will provide 50–100 Mb/s bandwidth to individual cells. This capacity should translate to 5 Mb/s to 10 Mb/s download speeds to individual users (Bangeman, 2009). Users can access these networks using a laptop card.

Fixed broadband wireless networks use either Wi-Fi or WiMAX. Wi-Fi uses a group of standards in the IEEE 802.11 group to provide short-range, wireless Internet access to a range of devices such as laptops, cell phones, and PDAs (personal data assistants). Wi-Fi "hotspots" can be found in many public and private locations. Come businesses and municipalities provide Wi-Fi access for free. Other places charge a fee.

WiMAX, which stands for worldwide interoperability for wireless access, is also known as IEEE 802.16. There are two versions: a fixed point-to-multipoint version and a mobile version. Unlike Wi-Fi which has a range of 100 to 300 feet, WiMAX can provide wireless access up to 30 miles for fixed stations and three to ten miles for mobile stations (What is wimax, n.d.). As of mid-2010, Clearwire provides WiMAX service in selected locations throughout the United States, but service availability is still modest. A regularly updated coverage map can be found at http://www.wimaxmaps.org/.

BPL

Broadband over power line (BPL) uses existing power lines to deliver broadband services directly into the home. The modem is actually plugged into an electrical outlet in the subscriber's home as a means of obtaining the service. Several factors, however, are causing this technology to lose its appeal. BPL is quite susceptible to interference from radio frequencies, and other broadband services (listed above) provide a faster and more reliable connection.

Manassas, Virginia was one of the first cities in the U.S. to deploy a BPL network in October 2005. By late 2008 the City had assumed control of the service formally offered by ComTek. As of late 2009 the City was losing money and on the verge of abandoning attempt to provide BPL service to residents (Bode, 2009).

Home Networks

Computer networking was, at one time, only found in large organizations such as businesses, government offices, and schools. The complexity and cost of such networking facilities was beyond the scope of most home computer owners. At one time a computer network required the use of an Ethernet network and expensive wiring called Category 5 (or Cat 5). Additionally, a server, hub, and router were needed. And all of this required someone in the household to have computer networking expertise as network maintenance was regularly needed.

Several factors changed the environment to allow home networks to take off: broadband Internet access, multiple computer households, and new networked consumer devices and services. Because of these advances, a router (costing as little as $30) can be quickly installed. This router essentially splits the incoming Internet signal and sends it (either through a wired or wireless connection) to other equipment in the house. Computers, cell phones, televisions, DVD players, stereo receivers, and other devices can be included within the home network. This setup allows for quick and easy file sharing. With a home network users can, among other things, send video files from their computer to their television; they can send audio files from their computer to their stereo receiver; they can send a print job from their cell phone to their printer; or with some additional equipment they could use their cell phone to control home lighting and other electrical devices within the home.

There are four basic types of home networks:

◆ Traditional

◆ Phone line

◆ Power line

◆ Wireless

When discussing each type of home network, it is important to consider the transmission rate, or speed, of the network. Regular file sharing and low-bandwidth applications such as home control may require a speed of 1 Mb/s or less. The MPEG-2 digital video and audio from DBS services requires a speed of 3 Mb/s, DVD-quality video requires between 3 Mb/s and 8 Mb/s, and compressed high-definition television (HDTV) requires around 20 Mb/s.

Traditional networks use Ethernet, which has a data transmission rate of 10 Mb/s to 100 Mb/s. There is also Gigabit Ethernet, used mostly in business, that has transmission speeds up to 1 Gb/s. Ethernet is the kind of networking commonly found in offices and universities. As discussed earlier, traditional Ethernet has not been popular for home networking because it is expensive to install and maintain and difficult to use. To direct the data, the network must have a server, hub, and router. Each device on the network must be connected, and many computers and devices require add-on devices to enable them to work with Ethernet. Thus, despite the speed of this kind of network, its expense and complicated nature make it somewhat unpopular in the home networking market, except among those who build and maintain these networks at the office.

Many new housing developments come with "structured wiring" that includes wiring for home networks, home theatre systems, and other digital data networking services such as utility management and security. One of the popular features of structured wiring is home automation including the ability to unlock doors or adjust the temperature or lights. New homes represent a small fraction of the potential market for home networking services and equipment, so manufacturers have turned their attention to solutions for existing homes. These solutions almost always are based upon "no new wires" networking solutions that use existing phone lines or power lines, or they are wireless.

Phone lines are ideal for home networking. This technology uses the existing random tree wiring typically found in homes and runs over regular telephone wire—there is no need for Cat 5 wiring. The technology uses frequency division multiplexing (FDM) to allow data to travel through the phone line without interfering with regular telephone calls or DSL service. There is no interference because each service is assigned a different frequency. The Home Phone Line Networking Alliance (HomePNA) has presented several standards for phone line networking. HomePNA 1.0 boasted data transmission rates up to 1 Mb/s. It was replaced by HomePNA (HPNA) 2.0, which boasts data transmission rates up to 10 Mb/s and is backward-compatible with HPNA 1.0. HomePNA 3.1 provides data rates up to 320 Mb/s and operates over phone wires and coaxial cables, which makes it a solution to deliver video and data services (320 Mbps, n.d.). HomePNA 4.0 is expected sometime in 2010 (Lawson, 2008).

The most popular type of home network is wireless. Currently, there are several types of wireless home networking technologies: Wi-Fi (otherwise known as IEEE 802.11a, 802.11b 802.11g, and 802.11n), Bluetooth, and wireless mesh technologies such as ZigBee and Z-wave. Wi-Fi, Bluetooth, and ZigBee are based on the same premise: low-frequency radio signals from the instrumentation, science, and medical (ISM) bands of spectrum are used to transmit and receive data. The ISM bands, around 2.4 GHz, not licensed by the FCC, are used mostly for microwave ovens and cordless telephones (except for 802.11a, which operates at 5 GHz).

Wireless networks utilize a transceiver (combination transmitter and receiver) that is connected to a wired network or gateway (generally a router) at a fixed location. Much like cellular telephones, wireless networks use microcells to extend the connectivity range by overlapping to allow the user to roam without losing the connection (Wi-Fi Alliance, n.d.).

Wi-Fi is the most common type of wireless networking. It uses a series of similarly labeled transmission protocols (802.11a, 802.11b, 802.11g, and 802.11n). Most of these protocols operate in the 2.4 GHz frequency band (except for 802.11a which utilizes the 5.4 GHz frequency band). Wi-Fi was originally the consumer-friendly label attached to IEEE 802.11b, the specification for wireless Ethernet. 802.11b was created in July 1999. It can transfer data up to 11 Mb/s and is supported by the Wi-Fi Alliance. A couple years later 802.11a was introduced, providing bandwidth up to 54 Mb/s. This was soon followed by the release of 802.11g, which combines the best of 802.11a and 802.11b, providing bandwidth up to 54 Mb/s. The 802.11n standard was released in 2007 and amended in 2009 and provides bandwidth over 100 Mb/s (Mitchell, n.d.).

Because wireless networks use so much of their available bandwidth for coordination among the devices on the network, it is difficult to compare the rated speeds of these networks with the rated speeds of wired networks. For example, 802.11b is rated at 11 Mb/s, but the actual throughput (the amount of data that can be effectively transmitted) is only about 6 Mb/s. Similarly, 802.11g's rated speed of 54 Mb/s yields a data throughput of only about 25 Mb/s (802.11 wireless, 2004). Tests of 802.11n have confirmed speeds from 100 Mb/s to 140 Mb/s (Haskin, 2007).

Security is an issue with any network. Wi-Fi uses two types of encryption: WEP (Wired Equivalent Privacy) and WPA (Wi-Fi Protected Access). WEP has security flaws and is easily hacked. WPA fixes those flaws in WEP and uses a 128-bit encryption. There are two versions: WPA-Personal that uses a password and WPA-Enterprise that uses a server to verify network users (Wi-Fi Alliance, n.d.). WPA2 is an upgrade to WPA and is now required of all Wi-Fi Alliance certified products (WPA2, n.d.).

While Wi-Fi can transmit data up to 140 Mb/s for up to 150 feet, Bluetooth was developed for short-range communication at a data rate of up to 3 Mb/s and is geared primarily toward voice and data applications. Bluetooth technologies are good for transmitting data up to 100 meters. Bluetooth technology is built into devices such as laptop computers, music players (including car stereo systems), and cell phones. Bluetooth-enhanced devices can communicate with each other and create an ad hoc network. The technology works with and enhances other networking technologies.

Zigbee is also known as IEEE 802.15.4 and is classified, along with Bluetooth, as a technology for wireless personal area networks (WPANs). ZigBee is low power, but it also has a low data rate making it good for ad hoc mesh networks for home security, home automation, and smart lighting (ZigBee, n.d.). Z-Wave is very similar to Zigbee in that it is a low-power, low-bandwidth technology for wireless mesh networks. Z-Wave is RF based and operates in the 900 MHz range. It is useful for lighting, security, health-care monitoring, and utility control (Z-Wave, n.d.; Castle, 2008).

Usually, a home network will involve not just one of the technologies discussed above, but several. It is not unusual for a home network to be configured for HPNA, Wi-Fi, and even traditional Ethernet. Table 21.1 compares each of the home networking technologies discussed in this section.

Residential Gateways

The residential gateway, also known as the broadband router, is what makes the home network infinitely more useful. This is the device that allows users on a home network to share access to their broadband connection. As broadband connections become more common, the one "pipe" coming into the home will most likely carry numerous services such as the Internet, phone, and entertainment. A residential gateway seamlessly connects the home network to a broadband network so all network devices in the home can be used at the same time.

The current definition of a residential gateway has its beginnings in a white paper developed by the RG Group, a consortium of companies and research groups interested in the residential gateway concept. The RG Group determined that the residential gateway is "a single, intelligent, standardized, and flexible network interface unit that receives communication signals from various external networks and delivers the signals to specific consumer devices through in-home networks" (Li, 1998). Residential gateways can be categorized as complete, home network only, and simple.

A **complete residential gateway** operates independent of a personal computer and contains a modem and networking software. This gateway can intelligently route incoming signals from the broadband connections to specific devices on the home network. Set-top box and broadband-centric are two categories of complete residential gateways. A broadband-centric residential gateway incorporates an independent digital modem such as a DSL modem with IP management and integrated HomePNA ports. Set-top box residential gateways use integrated IP management and routing with the processing power of the box. Complete residential gateways also include software to protect the home network, including a firewall, diagnostics, and security log.

Home network only residential gateways interface with existing DSL or cable modems in the home. These route incoming signals to specific devices on the home network, and typically contain the same types of software to protect the home network found in complete residential gateways.

Simple residential gateways are limited to routing and connectivity between properly configured devices. Also known as "dumb" residential gateways, these have limited processing power and applications, and only limited security for the home network.

Table 21.1

Comparison of Home Networking Technologies

	How it Works	Standards	Specifications	Transmission and Rate	Cost Reliability	Security
Conventional Ethernet	Uses Cat 5 wiring with a server and hub to direct traffic	IEEE 802.3xx IEEE 802.5	10 Mb/s to 1 Gb/s	High	High	Secure
HomePNA	Uses existing phone lines and OFDM	HPNA 1.0 HPNA 2.0 HPNA 3.0 HPNA 3.1	1.0, up to 1 Mb/s 2.0, 10 Mb/s 3.0, 128 Mb/s 3.1, 320 Mb/s	High	Low	High
IEEE 802.11a Wi-Fi	Wireless. Uses electromagnetic radio signals to transmit between access point and users.	IEEE 802.11a 5 GHz	Up to 54 Mb/s	High	Moderate	High to Moderate
IEEE 802.11b Wi-Fi	Wireless. Uses electromagnetic radio signals to transmit between access point and users.	IEEE 802.11b 2.4 GHz	Up to 11 Mb/s	High	Low	High to Low
IEEE 802.11g Wi-Fi	*Wireless. Same as 802.11b*	*IEEE 802.11g 2.4 GHz*	*Up to 54 Mb/s*	*High*	*Low*	*High to Low*
IEEE 802.11n Wi-Fi	*Wireless. Same as 802.11g*	*IEEE 802.11n*	*Up to 140 Mb/s*	?	?	*High to Low*
WiMAX	Wireless. Uses electromagnetic radio signals to transmit between access point and users.	IEEE 802.16 Fixed IEEE 802.20 Mobile	Up to 75 Mb/s	High	High	Not yet determined
Bluetooth	Wireless.	Bluetooth V 1.0 2.4 GHz V 2.0 + EDR	1 Mb/s 3 Mb/s	High to Moderate	Low	High to Moderate
Powerline	Uses existing power lines in home.	HomePlug v1.0 HomePlug AV HPCC	Up to 14 Mb/s Up to 200 Mb/s low	Moderate	Moderate	High
ZigBee	Wireless. Uses Electromagnet radio signals to transmit between access point and users	IEEE 802.15.4	250 Kb/s	High	Low	High to
Z-Wave	Uses 908 MHz "2-Way RF	Proprietary	9.6Kbps	High	Low	Moderate

Source: J. Meadows

Working Together—The Home Network and Residential Gateway

A home network controlled by a residential gateway or central router allows multiple users to access a broadband connection at the same time. Household members do not have to compete for access to the Internet, printer, television content, music files, or movies. The home network allows for shared access of all controllable devices. Technological innovations have made it possible to access computer devices through a home network in the same way as you would access the Internet. Televisions and Blu-Ray DVD players regularly come configured with hardware that allows for accessing streamed audio and video content without having to funnel it through a computer. Cell phone technology is more regularly being used to access home networks remotely. With this technology it is now possible to set your DVR to record a show or to turn lights on and off without being in the home. The residential gateway or router also allows multiple computers to access the Internet at the same time. This is accomplished by creating a "virtual" IP address for each computer. The residential gateway routes different signals to appropriate devices in the home.

Home networks and residential gateways are key to what industry pundits are calling the "smart home." Although having our washing machine tell us when our clothes are done may not be a top priority for many of us, utility management, security, and enhanced telephone services including VoIP are just a few of the potential applications for this technology. Before these applications can be implemented, however, two developments are necessary. First, appropriate devices for each application (appliance controls, security cameras, telephones, etc.) have to be configured to connect to one or more of the different home networking topologies (wireless, HPNA, or power line). Next, software, including user interfaces, control modules, etc., needs to be created and installed. It is easy to conceive of being able to go to a Web page for your home to adjust the air conditioner, turn on the lights, or monitor the security system, but these types of services will not be widely available until consumers have proven that they are willing to pay for them.

Recent Developments

On March 16, 2010, the Federal Communications Commission unveiled its National Broadband Plan. The primary purpose of the nearly 376 page plan is to "create a high-performance America—a more productive, creative, efficient America in which affordable broadband is available everywhere, and everyone has the means and skills to use valuable broadband applications" (FCC, 2010a, p. 9). The plan was drafted after the U.S. Congress, in early 2009, directed the FCC to develop a plan to ensure every American has access to broadband capabilities (FCC, 2010a)

In a 2010 press release discussing the release of the National Broadband Plan, Blair Levin, Executive Director of the Omnibus Broadband Initiative, explains how significant this plan is. He stated, "In every era, America must confront the challenge of connecting the nation anew. Above all else, the plan is a call to action to meet that challenge for our era. If we meet it, we will have networks, devices, and applications that create new solutions to seemingly intractable problems" (FCC, 2010b, p. 1). FCC Chairman Julius Genachowski calls the Plan "a 21st century roadmap to spur economic growth and investment, create jobs, educate our children, protect our citizens, and engage in our democracy. It's an action plan, and action is necessary to meet the challenges of global competitiveness, and harness the power of broadband to help address so many vital national issues" (FCC, 2010b, p. 1).

The assumption, according to the report, is that the U.S. government can influence the broadband landscape in four general ways. First, the government can create policies that ensure robust competition among broadband players. The thought is that this competition will maximize consumer welfare, innovation, and investment. Second, the government can ensure efficient allocation and management of broadband assets. Third, the government can reform current service procedures that will support the launching of broadband in more affluent areas, and ensure that low-income Americans have physical and financial access to broadband technology. Fourth, the government can reform laws and policies to maximize broadband usage in areas traditionally overseen by the government such as public education, health care, and other government operations (FCC, 2010a).

In the National Broadband Plan, the FCC outlined six primary goals. They are:

◈ **Goal 1:** At least 100 million U.S. homes should have affordable access to actual download speeds of at least 100 megabits per second and actual upload speeds of at least 50 megabits per second.

◈ **Goal 2:** The United States should lead the world in mobile innovation, with the fastest and most extensive wireless networks of any nation.

◈ **Goal 3:** Every American should have affordable access to robust broadband service, and the means and skills to subscribe if they so choose.

◈ **Goal 4:** Every community should have affordable access to at least 1 Gb/s broadband service to anchor institutions such as schools, hospitals and government buildings.

◈ **Goal 5:** To ensure the safety of Americans, every first responder should have access to a nation-wide public safety wireless network.

◈ **Goal 6:** To ensure that America leads in the clean energy economy, every American should be able to use broadband to track and manage their real-time energy consumption (FCC 2010a).

There are approximately 200 specific recommendations within the plan, directed toward President Obama's administration, the U.S. Congress, or the commission itself. Nonetheless, each of these recommendations must be dealt with separately. In the coming months the FCC plans to issue dozens of notices of proposed rulemaking (NPRMs) (Gross, 2010a).

One of the main points of contention is likely to revolve around funding for the plan. As part of the proposal, the FCC is planning to redirect $15.5 billion of the Universal Service Fund over 10 years to broadband deployment (Gross 2010a). This may not be easy, however, since the USF is primarily used to subsidize phone service in rural areas (Gross, 2010b).

In order to increase broadband access it will be necessary for the FCC to secure additional spectrum space. The FCC is likely to ask Congress to give it new authority to sell unused spectrum space. One potential source of this unused spectrum space is current television licensees. A potential method of acquiring spectrum space from current television licensees is to ask television stations to voluntarily give up their unused spectrum space in exchange for sharing the revenue that would come from auctioning off this space (Gross 2010b).

While the cable and telephone companies have been successful with their broadband services, municipal Wi-Fi networks and BPL have not shown the success once touted. In some cases the general concept of city-wide Wi-Fi is being created by combinations of commercial Wi-Fi services. For example in New York City, Comcast, Cablevision, and Time Warner Cable cover the city, and the service is free for their customers (Gardner, 2010) BPL might be faring a little better as it is being proposed as an option for rural broadband access (Hansell, 2009).

HomePNA is a non-profit association that brings together various companies in an effort to create multimedia home networking technology. Collectively these companies create appropriate infrastructure to deliver Internet Protocol services such as IPTV and VoIP. HomePNA's current standard, which was adapted by the ITU, is HPNA 3.1 (HomePNA, nd). At present HomePNA technology provides data rates up to 320 Mb/s. Recently, the HomePNA Alliance has added several more telcos to its group. HomePNA now has more telco members than any wired home networking alliance. With the addition of Bell Canada, the HomePNA alliance now has four of the top five largest carriers in North America. Collectively, the alliance has generated IPTV revenue of more than $1 billion (HomePNA, 2010).

With home networking speeds increasing and costs decreasing more and more, home networks are likely to be deployed. Advances in technology are making it increasingly possible to use home networks to do much more than simply access the Internet. With newer technology it is now possible to control household appliances remotely. Through a home networking system, washers and dryers, for instance, can send messages to a phone or television alerting you when your clothes are clean or dry. Combined with smart phone technology, users can also set their home DVR, control the lights in their home, access their business's security cameras, or access their home computer remotely through their smart phone..

Home networking can also be used to manage photos, audio content, and video content. With corresponding hardware, a home network can allow such files to be accessed from multiple devices (both computer and non-computer) wirelessly. Apple has an iPhone "app" that will allow for the manipulation of one's iTunes jukebox (housed on the user's computer) through an iPhone.

Increasingly, Blu-ray DVDs are including special "BD Live" access. BD Live content is Internet-based content that can be played through an appropriately equipped Blu-ray player while playing certain Blu-ray DVDs. BD Live content generally includes special features that go beyond what may be included on the actual DVD. The beauty of BD Live content is that, if configured properly, it can be played back seamlessly, even though it is coming from the Internet. As an example, assume a recent movie production company has "deleted scenes" housed on a Web site as BD Live content. Using an appropriately equipped and configured Blu-ray player, this content can be played through the Blu-ray player at the appropriate point in the movie you're watching on the Blu-ray player. Also, if the movie production company creates new content that corresponds to the movie after releasing the DVD, the BD Live feature can be used to access this new content.

CURRENT STATUS

The statistics on broadband penetration vary widely. The OECD keeps track of worldwide broadband penetration. According to the OECD, broadband subscribers in the U.S. have gradually increased over the last few years. As Table 21.2 illustrates, an estimated 26.65% of Americans had access to broadband service by mid-2009. This is nearly a 400% increase since 2002. Despite this increase, the U.S.'s world standing for broadband access is considered low. The OECD has the U.S. ranked 15th in the world in broadband penetration (see Table 21.3). Another source reports the U.S. has dropped from 22nd place in 2008 to 25th place in 2009. On the plus side, nearly 95% of Internet users in the U.S. have access to broadband service (US broadband, n.d.).

Table 21.2
U.S. Broadband Penetration History

2002	2003	2004	2005	2006	2007	2008	2009
6.71	9.57	12.76	16.32	20.27	23.44	25.43	26.65

Source: OECD (2009)

The United States currently ranks 15th in the world for broadband penetration with 26.7 subscribers per 100 inhabitants (up from 22.1 in 2007). The rankings are presented in Table 21.3. The United States has the largest number of broadband subscribers with 81.17 million. Fiber connections were most numerous in Korea (15.1) and Japan (12.4). The U.S. is above the OECD average penetration rates for overall broadband usage and for the usage of cable modems. However, the U.S. is below the OECD average for DSL and fiber penetration.

Approximately 271 million people worldwide subscribe to some type of broadband service. Nearly 163 million of those people subscribe to DSL service. More than 78 million people have cable Internet and nearly 25 million have fiber (see Table 21.4). As mentioned above, Japan and Korea lead the way in terms of fiber usage. Figure 21.1 shows in Japan, 51% of all broadband subscribers utilize fiber networks. In Korea that number is just below 46%. In the U.S., however, the number is 6%. The OECD global average is 9%.

Table 21.3

Broadband Subscribers per 100 Inhabitants, by Technology, June 2009

	Rank	DSL	Cable	Fiber/LAN	Other	Total	Total Subs
Netherlands	1	22.5	13.7	1.1	0.8	38.1	6,262,500
Denmark	2	22.4	9.9	3.9	0.9	37.0	2,031,000
Norway	3	22.7	7.7	3.5	0.7	34.5	1,645,619
Switzerland	4	23.3	10.0	0.2	0.3	33.8	2,603,400
Korea	5	7.2	10.5	15.1	0.0	32.8	15,938,529
Iceland	6	30.7	0.0	1.3	0.7	32.8	104,604
Sweden	7	18.5	6.3	6.7	0.1	31.6	2,915,000
Luxembourg	8	26.0	5.3	0.0	0.0	31.3	153,172
Finland	9	24.9	4.1	0.0	0.8	29.7	1,579,600
Canada	10	13.2	15.2	0.0	1.3	29.7	9,916,217
Germany	11	26.7	2.4	0.1	0.1	29.3	24,043,000
France	12	27.5	1.6	0.1	0.0	29.1	18,675,000
U.K.	13	22.8	6.1	0.0	0.1	28.9	17,742,676
Belgium	14	16.3	11.8	0.0	0.2	28.4	3,041,311
United States	15	10.3	13.8	1.6	0.9	26.7	81,170,428
Australia	16	19.4	4.3	0.0	1.2	24.9	5,356,000
Japan	17	8.5	3.3	12.4	0.0	24.2	30,927,003
New Zealand	18	20.4	1.4	0.0	1.0	22.8	980,649
Austria	19	14.5	6.8	0.1	0.5	21.8	1,821,000
Ireland	20	15.5	2.8	0.1	3.0	21.4	950,082
OECD	Average	13.7	6.6	2.1	0.5	22.8	

Source: OECD (2009)

Table 21.4

Worldwide Broadband Use by Technology, June 2009

	Totals
DSL	162,798,177
Cable Modem	78,255,562
Fibre + LAN	24,566,216
Other	5,514,437
TOTAL	271,134,392

Source: OECD (2009)

Figure 21.1
Percentage of Broadband Subscribers Using Fiber, June 2009

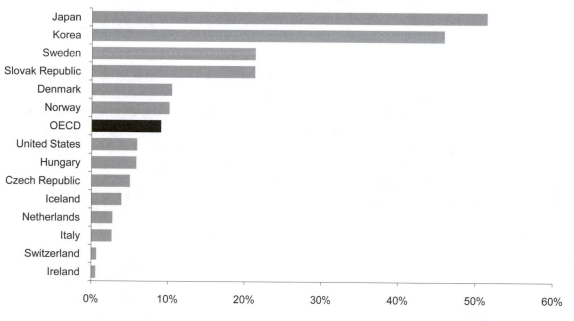

Source: OECD (2009)

AT&T and Comcast continue to be two of the largest Internet service providers (ISP) in the country. As of early 2008, AT&T had 18.3 million subscribers while Comcast had 13.2 million subscribers. However, as of early 2010, Comcast subscribers increased to 15.9 million (Comcast, n.d.) and AT&T subscribers dipped to 16.3 million (AT&T, n.d.).

Parks Associates reported that approximately 35 million homes had data networks as of the end of 2008, nearly 38% had such networks by the end of 2009, and an estimated 42% would have home networks by the end of 2010 and more than 50% of homes would have data networks by 2013 (Scherf, 2009).

FACTORS TO WATCH

Home networking offers countless global opportunities. In Korea, for instance, it is expected that the majority of homes will be connected to advanced home networking systems by 2015. This advanced system goes beyond what has been described above. The idea here is to network all home appliances as well as traditional electronic devices. Additionally, the advanced home networking system should support telemedicine and teletherapy processes. The development of home networking applications will continue to escalate if the overall market share continues to expand. As of 2008 the market for home networking was just over $80 billion. It is expected to nearly double, to over $150 billion, by 2012 (Tae-gyu, 2010).

Access and Speed

The FCC has proposed sweeping changes in the broadband landscape, but implementation is to be slow and will come in stages. By 2015, for instance, the plan calls for 100 million U.S. homes to have affordable broadband service with actual download speeds of 50 Mb/s and actual upload speeds of 20 Mb/s. By 2020, the plan calls for 100 million U.S. homes to have access to upload speeds of 100 Mb/s and download speeds of 50 Mb/s.

While the FCC, Congress, and the White House make plans to increase Internet speeds up to 100 Mb/s, Internet giant Google is planning to install fiber optic networks in a select community or communities in the U.S. These networks are supposed to generate speeds of up to 1 Gb/s (or 1,000 Mb/s). As of early 2010, Google was soliciting interest from communities across the country. By April 2010, it is expected that Google will select the community or communities in which to install fiber networks. It is believed that between 50,000 and 500,000 homes will be involved in the trial (Letzing, 2010). In attempt to become one of the selected communities for Google's fiber network trial, the city of Topeka, Kansas has temporarily changed its name to Google, Kansas (Raphael, 2010).

Home Networks

The FCC believes that increased broadband capacities in the home can help save energy. The National Broadband Plan suggests that people who receive consistent feedback regarding their energy consumption are more likely to make simple changes to reduce consumption. The plan calls for the ability of Americans to be able to use broadband technologies to quickly and accurately track their own real-time energy consumption.

Additionally, the market for home networking and networked devices in the home will continue to grow. More and more electronics manufactures will develop devices that can be linked to home networks. Currently it is possible to link televisions, Blu-ray DVD players, DVRs, and home stereo equipment to your home network. It's also possible to purchase add-ons that will allow for the control of home appliances, lights, and heating and cooling equipment.

Mobile Broadband

Mobile technology continues to evolve. Mobile devices are used to do much more than make phone calls. More and more mobile technology is used to surf the Internet, shop for goods, track shipping, read books, and even monitor patients. Because of the ever-evolving use of mobile devices, the FCC believes mobile broadband speeds must increase. The National Broadband Plan calls for making an additional 300 MHz of spectrum space available for mobile broadband by 2015 and 500 MHz available by 2020.

Health and Education

Most Americans believe that health care and education in the U.S. could be improved. The FCC has recommended that every community in the U.S. have at least one 1 Gb/s broadband service anchored to a community institution such as a hospital, library, or school. Providing high speed broadband connectivity to hospitals can allow for quicker access to medical records, faster test results, and more efficient treatments. High speed Internet connections in libraries and schools can allow for expanded Internet access to students, teachers, and community members.

🌍 Sustainability 🌍

One may not immediately link issues of sustainability with improved broadband technologies. However, there are several ways in which broadband technologies can help with environmental sustainability. One way in which broadband technologies can help the environment is by making it easier for employees to telecommute, thereby saving fuel costs and reducing CO_2 emissions. But the possibilities go well beyond this one.

With increased access to broadband technologies, lower cost and easier access to education and business services would be possible. According to Fehrenbacher (2009) improved broadband services could lead to replacing physical goods with virtual goods. Books, CDs, and DVDs could be sent electronically thereby eliminating the need to make physical copies of these products greatly reducing energy consumption and CO_2 output. Products could also be made to order thus reducing the need to store large quantities of goods in warehouses requiring heating and cooling (Environmental sustainability, n.d.). According to Broadband for America, ecommerce can reduce air pollution by 36% and requires 16% less energy than conventional shopping (Environmental sustainability, n.d.).

Broadband technology can be used to improve home networks to allow for the control of home appliances, heating/cooling systems, sprinkler systems, and more. This allows for homeowners to continually and expeditiously monitor resource consumption. According to the FCC's National Broadband Plan, consumers who can easily monitor their own consumption are more likely to modify their usage thus eliminating or at least reducing waste.

Smart grid technology, which relies on high-speed data transmissions, can significantly reduce energy usage. Most of the current electrical grids in the U.S. send power across many miles of power lines to various locations just in case a need for that electricity exists. A tremendous amount of electricity is wasted simply from its dissipating as it travels along power lines. Smart grid technology allows for electricity to travel only when needed and in the shortest distance possible, thus greatly reducing waste. Computer networks, with high-speed broadband, would be at the center of this technology. Additionally, smart grids can incorporate energy from a variety of sources (wind, solar, hydro-electric, etc.). Standard grids can only work with energy from one source at a time.

Public Safety

Since the tragic events of September 11, 2001 there has been a call to have more effective and efficient communication between and among first responders. The 9/11 Commission's report, released in June 2004 concluded that a significant communication breakdown occurred at each crash site because a compatible communication system was not in place. The National Broadband Plan believes it is necessary for every first responder to have access to a wireless public safety network.

Net Neutrality

The issue of "net neutrality" continues to circulate. Currently it is possible for Internet Service Providers to block or prioritize access to Web content. The Obama administration and the FCC, however, want to prevent this from happening. The proponents of net neutrality believe this is a free speech issue. They suggest that ISPs who block or prioritize access to certain Web content can easily direct users to certain sites and away from others. Supporters of the current system believe that new regulations would serve only to minimize investment (Bradley, 2009). FCC Chairman Julius Genachowski, in a 2009 statement said that "it is vital that we safeguard the free and open Internet" (FCC, 2009).

The U.S. Court of Appeals for the District of Columbia disagrees. On April 6, 2010 the court ruled that the FCC has only limited power over Web traffic under current law. As such, the FCC cannot tell ISPs to provide equal access to all Web content. This ruling could, however, prompt Congress to enact legislation that would increase the authority of the FCC, giving it the authority to regulate Internet service. It is, nonetheless, uncertain whether Congress will be successful. It is also uncertain how, if at all, this ruling will impact the FCC's National Broadband Plan (Wyatt, 2010).

Regardless of the ruling, though, the FCC is still committed to promoting an open Internet. The FCC, in a statement released shortly after the court ruling said: "Today's court decision invalidated the prior Commission's approach to preserving an open Internet. But the Court in no way disagreed with the importance of preserving a free and open Internet; nor did it close the door to other methods for achieving this important end" (FCC, 2010c, p. 1).

Bibliography

320 Mbps home networking specification released (n.d.). Retrieved March 1, 2010, from HomePna website: http://www.homepna.org/products/specifications/.

AT&T. (n.d.). Retrieved March 1, 2010 from http://www.att.com/gen/general?pid=6431&GUID=767c62da-f369-41ba-a372-962815120fc1&gclid=CPbrjL_7j5MCFSH_iAodel6JUw.

AT&T U-verse Residential Gateway. (n.d.). *AT&T U-verse.* Retrieved May 5, 2008 from https://uma.att.com/assets/files/installation_equipment.html.

Bangeman, E. (2007, June 7). Ham radio group says FCC turns deaf ear to BPL interference complaints. *Ars Technica.* Retrieved March 5, 2010 from http://arstechnica.com/news.ars/post/20070607-ham-radio-group-says-fcc-turns-deaf-ear-to-bpl-interference-complaints.html.

Bangeman, E. (2008, April 28). Judge tells FCC to rework power line broadband regulations. *Ars Technica.* Retrieved March 5, 2010 from http://arstechnica.com/news.ars/post/20080428-judge-tells-fcc-to-rework-powerline-broadband-regulations.html.

Bangeman, E. (2009, April 2). 4G wireless broadband coming to rural areas, says Verizon. *Ars Technica.* Retrieved March 1, 2010 from http://arstechnica.com/telecom/news/2009/04/4g-wireless-broadband-coming-to-rural-areas-says-verizon.ars.

Bode, K. (2009, November 19). Broadband over powerline's poster child pulling the plug. *DSLReports.com.* Retrieved March 1, 2010 from http://www.dslreports.com/shownews/Broadband-Over-Powerlines-Poster-Child-Pulling-The-Plug-105576.

Bradley, T. (2009, September 22). Battle lines drawn in FCC net neutrality fight. *PC World.* Retrieved March 16, 2010 from http://www.pcworld.com/businesscenter/article/172391/battle_lines_drawn_in_fcc_net_neutrality_fight.html.

Castle, S. (2008). Saving energy with wireless mesh networks. *Electronic House.* Retrieved March 5, 2010 from http://www.electronichouse.com/article/energy_saving_with_mesh/C94.

Comcast reports fourth quarter and year end 2009 results (n.d.). Retrieved March 5, 2010 from Comcast website: http://www.cmcsk.com/releasedetail.cfm?ReleaseID=442388.

Consumer services (n.d.) Retrieved March 5, 2010 from AT&T website: http://www.att.com/gen/general?pid=7506.

Corning. (2009). FTTH deployment assessment. Boston, MA. Retrieved from http://www.ftthcouncil.org/sites/default/files/FTTH Deployment Assessment - Corning 10 12 09 FINAL.pdf

Corporate overview (n.d.). Retrieved March 1, 2010, from Comcast website: http://www.comcast.com/corporate/about/pressroom/corporateoverview/corporateoverview.html.

D-Link showcases advanced, easy-to-use home networking and digital home solutions at CES 2008. (2008). Retrieved March 5, 2010 from http://www.dlink.com/press/pr/?prid=374.

DOCSIS: Data over cable service interface specifications. (n.d.). Retrieved March 1, 2010, from Javvin website: http://www.javvin.com/protocolDOCSIS.html.

Docsis 3.0. (2009, March 13). Retrieved March 1, 2010, from Light Reading website: http://www.lightreading.com/document.asp?doc_id=173525.

Environmental sustainability (n.d.). *Broadband for America.* Retrieved March 16, 2010 from http://www.broadbandforamerica.com/benefits/environmental.

FAQ (n.d.) w3.org. Retrieved April 30, 2010 from http://www.w3.org/People/Berners-Lee/FAQ.html

Federal Communications Commission. (2008, June 12). Report and order and further notice of proposed rulemaking (WC Docket No. 07-38). Washington, DC: Federal Register.

Federal Communications Commission (2009, September 21). FCC chairman Julius Genachowski outlines actions to preserve the free and open internet [Press release]. Retrieved from http://hraunfoss.fcc.gov/edocs_public/attachmatch/DOC-293567A1.pdf.

Federal Communications Commission. (2010a). The national broadband plan. Retrieved from http://download.broadband.gov/plan/national-broadband-plan.pdf.

Federal Communications Commission (2010b, March 16). FCC Sends National Broadband Plan to Congress: Plan Details Actions for Connecting Consumers, Economy with 21ˢᵗ Century Networks. [Press release]. Retrieved from http://hraunfoss.fcc.gov/edocs_public/attachmatch/DOC-296880A1.pdf.

Federal Communications Commission (2010c, April 6). FCC Statement of Comcast v. FCC Decision. [Press release]. Retrieved from http://hraunfoss.fcc.gov/edocs_public/attachmatch/DOC-297355A1.pdf

Fehrenbacher, K. (2009, August 26). How high-speed broadband can fight climate change. *Benton Foundation*. Retrieved March 9, 2010 from http://www.benton.org/node/27386.

Gardner, W. D. (2010, April 16). Cable companies partner on Wi-Fi network. Information Week. Retrieved April 30, 2010 from http://www.informationweek.com/news/storage/fabrics/showArticle.jhtml?articleID=224400567

Gross, G. (2010a, March 16). FCC officially releases national broadband plan. *PC World*. Retrieved March 16, 2010 from http://www.pcworld.com/businesscenter/article/191666/fcc_officially_releases_national_broadband_plan.html.

Gross, G. (2010b, March 16). FCC's national broadband plan released. *Computerworld*. Retrieved March 16, 2010 from http://www.computerworld.com/s/article/9171298/FCC_s_national_broadband_plan_released?taxonomyId=15&pageNumber=2.

Hansell, S. (2009, February 19). I.B.M. delivers rural broadband over powerlines. Bits Blogs/New York Times. Retrieved April 30, 2010 from http://bits.blogs.nytimes.com/2009/02/19/ibm-delivers-rural-broadband-over-power-lines/

Haskin, D. (2007). FAQ: 802.11n wireless networking. *MacWorld*. Retrieved March 5, 2010 from http://www.macworld.com/article/57940/2007/05/8021infaq.html.

HomePNA. (nd). *FAQ*. Retrieved April 30, 2010 from http://www.homepna.org/en/about/faq.asp#about1.

HomePNA. (2008). *FAQ*. Retrieved March 5, 2010 from http://www.homepna.org/en/about/faq.asp#about1.

HomePNA (2010). *Bell Canada*. Retrieved May 1, 2010 from http://www.homepna.org/press/releases/?release=30.

HomePlug Powerline Alliance. (n.d.). *FAQs*. Retrieved March 5, 2010 from http://www.homeplug.org/about/faqs/.

HughesNet. (2010). Retrieved March 5, 2010 from http://www.nationwidesatellite.com/HughesNet/service_plans/HughesNet_plans.asp.

International Telecommunications Union. (2003). *Birth of broadband*. Retrieved March 1, 2010 from http://www.itu.int/osg/spu/publications/birthofbroadband/faq.html.

Lawson, S. (2008, December 16). ITU aims to defragment home networks with G.hn. *PC World*. Retrieved March 1, 2010 from http://pcworld.about.com/od/networkinI/ITU-Aims-to-Defragment-Home-Ne.htm.

Letzing, J. (2010, March 16). Google's fiber "experiment" details still scant. *Wall Street Journal*. Retrieved March 16, 2010 from http://online.wsj.com/article/BT-CO-20100316-707590.html?mod=WSJ_latestheadlines.

Li, H. (1998). Evolution of the residential-gateway concept and standards. *Parks Associates*. Retrieved April 22, 2000 from http://www.parksassociates.com/media/jhcable.htm.

Mitchell, B. (n.d.). Wireless standards- 802.11b 802.11a 802.11g and 802.11n: The 802.11 family explained. About.com. Retrieved March 5, 2010 from http://compnetworking.about.com/cs/wireless80211/a/aa80211standard.htm.

Raphael, J. (2010, March 2). Topeka: That's Google, Kansas to you. *PC World*. Retrieved March 16, 2010 from http://www.pcworld.com/article/190601/topeka_thats_google_kansas_to_you.html.

Reardon, M. (2007, January 9). Cisco touts the networked home of the future. *C/NET News*. Retrieved March 5, 2010 from http://www.news.com/2100-1033_3-6148728.html.

Scherf, K. (2009). Connected home: Global outlook. *Parks Associates*. Retrieved March 5, 2010 from http://www.parksassociates.com/research/reports/tocs/2009/connectedhome.htm.

Smith, A. (2008, May 2). Broadband over power lines plan is dead in Dallas. *Dallas Morning News*. Retrieved May 3, 2008 from http://www.dallasnews.com/sharedcontent/dws/bus/stories/DN-current_02bus.ART.State. Edition1.460d413.html.

Tae-gyu, K. (2010, February 7). Seamless home networking to debut in 2011. *Korea Times*. Retrieved March 16, 2010 from http://www.koreatimes.co.kr/www/news/biz/2010/02/123_60437.html.

Urbina, I. (2008, March 22). Hopes for wireless cities fade as internet providers pull out. *New York Times*. Retrieved March 5, 2010 from http://www.nytimes.com/2008/03/22/us/22wireless.html.

US broadband penetration drops to 25ᵗʰ worldwide (n.d.). *WebSiteOptimization*. Retrieved March 5, 2010 from http://www.websiteoptimization.com/bw/1001/.

Verizon. (2010). *FiOS Internet*. Retrieved March 1, 2010 from http://www22.verizon.com/Residential/FiOSInternet/Plans/Plans.htm

What is wimax (n.d.). Retrieved March 5, 2010 from http://www.wimax.com/education.

Whitney, L. (2009, August 25). U.S. lags other nations in internet speed. *C/Net News*. Retrieved March 1, 2010 from http://news.cnet.com/8301-13578_3-10317118-38.html.

Wi-Fi Alliance. (n.d.). *Wi-Fi overview*. Retrieved March 26, 2004 from http://www.wi-fi.org/OpenSection/ why_Wi-Fi.asp?TID=2.

Wild Blue. (n.d.). *About Wild Blue*. Retrieved May 5, 2008 from http://www.wildblue.com/aboutwildblue/index.jsp.

WPA2. (n.d.). Retrieved March 5, 2010 from http://www.wi-fi.org/knowledge_center/wpa2/.

Wyatt, E. (2010, April 6). U.S. court of curbs F.C.C. authority on web traffic. *The New York Times*. Retrieved April 11, 2010 from http://www.nytimes.com/2010/04/07/technology/07net.html

ZigBee. (n.d.). *ZigBee Alliance*. Retrieved May 5, 2008 from http://www.zigbee.org/en/index.asp.

Z-Wave. (n.d.). Retrieved May 5, 2008 from http://www.z-wave.com/modules/Z-Wave-Start/.

22

TElEPRESENCE

Michael R. Ogden, Ph.D. & Steve Jackson, M.A.[*]

Telepresence is a series of technologies that allow for "face-to-face" meetings between people who are separated geographically. Sometimes described as being a generation or more beyond videoconferencing, telepresence aims to create an environment where "real-to-life" participants interact in a shared boardroom—even though they may be separated by thousands of miles (Nortel Networks, 2010). The enabling technologies that comprise what is referred to as "telepresence" include videoconferencing (use of video to facilitate meetings), videotelephony (use of video for person-to-person communication), telerobotics (use of video to manipulate objects at a distance), and avatar-based virtual presence. The goal of telepresence is to provide immediate, deep feedback to meetings, group communication settings, and to remote operation settings such as telerobotics. John Chambers, the CEO of Cisco Systems, calls telepresence "advanced teleconferencing that will allow cameras to follow subjects and users to detect subtle nuances of communication" (Neel, 2006).

In settings such as education, telepresence is credited with increasing social presence and thus, improving the communication of information (Tu, 2002). There is little doubt that communication systems are changing the face of higher education. Universities are augmenting traditional physical settings with virtual learning tools and building virtual learning communities enabling students to connect with educators and other students in an unprecedented manner. Illustrative of this trend, in February 2010, Duke University and Cisco Systems unveiled a "first-of-its-kind" virtual lecture hall for students enrolled in Duke's Fuqua School of Business. Custom-built using Cisco's TelePresence technology, the new lecture facility provides business school students with access to professors, business leaders, and guest lecturers located around the globe, extending the classroom environment across campuses and into the business world

In the business environment, telepresence—and by extension, other modes of teleconferencing—always held out the promise of increased productivity and efficiency, improved communications, enhanced business opportunities, and reduced travel expenses. But "we humans are a 'touchy-feely' species, who, in general, prefer travel and face-to-face encounters over the more impersonal [teleconference] experience" (Kuehn, 2002). This "human touch" versus mediated interaction served as the backdrop to the Academy Awards nominated film *Up In The Air* (2009) starring George Clooney and Anna Kendrick. Clooney's character responds to his boss that firing people by Internet-teleconference ignores the importance of the in-person social interaction. This point was driven home when Kendrick's character fires the first person using the teleconferencing system; the audience sees the man crying to himself inconsolably, alone, in an empty room (IMDB, 2010).

---

[*]Michael R. Ogden is Professor & Director, Film & Video Studies Program, and Steve Jackson is Assistant Professor of Convergent Media, Department of Communication, Central Washington University (Ellensburg, Washington).

Popular culture references aside, BT Conferencing's Chief Executive, Aaron McCormack, tells customers that if the nature of their business requires a lot of travel and collaboration among different locations and across multiple time zones, then telepresence can offer a more cost effective alternative to the traditional face-to-face business meeting (Knights, 2010). However, McCormack points out that telepresence is only a viable solution if the company has a large travel budget, a sizable distributed workforce, or mobile workers who need to communicate with each other and/or corporate headquarters on a regular basis (Knights, 2010). Beyond the obvious elimination of direct travel expenses, the key benefit of telepresence is that it eliminates the hours of downtime and days away from the office. Even with the proliferation of handheld communication devices (smart phones, personal digital assistants, etc.), people in transit are not able to conduct business as efficiently as they can from their offices. Even so, McCormack recognizes the importance of the "human touch" and emphasizes that telepresence still "shouldn't replace those regular get-togethers" (Knights, 2010). However, Cisco's CEO John Chambers believes that his experience will become more typical in the future, "I've had 261 direct meetings with customers around the world this year [2009], and 200 of them were done using telepresence" (BBC News, 2009). According to Chambers, "Business travel is dead" (BBC News, 2009).

Perhaps presaging such sentiments as Mr. Chambers', a 2006 consulting report indicated that 55% of Americans saw audio-, video-, and Web-conferencing as good alternatives to face-to-face meetings; while 56% of their European and 55% of their Asia-Pacific counterparts felt the same (Frost & Sullivan, 2006a). Although U.S. business professionals agree with their international counterparts that travel is still an essential part of business (Frost & Sullivan, 2006a), travel appears to no longer be the first choice, nor even the preferred choice, for conducting business globally. With newer telepresence technologies and more teleconferencing services to choose from, people are better able to communicate interactively. As we enter a new era of communication and collaboration, business professionals are no longer bound by the limitations of time, location, or the traditional office. Telepresence provides the power of choice for interactive communication and offers a positive alternative for many business professionals to have the ability to remain productive while maintaining business relationships without the need for extensive travel.

Definitions of what exactly constitutes "telepresence"—or even the older, arguably more inclusive term, "teleconferencing"—tend to differ across the industry. As for the more contemporary term, "telepresence," it could be argued that this is merely whatever the best videoconferencing technology happens to be at the moment with the inclusion of immersive environmental factors (Grigonis, 2010). Wainhouse Research defined telepresence as conferencing "solutions [that] use video- and audioconferencing components as well as other 'arts and sciences' to create a two-way immersive communications experience that simulates an in-person, interactive encounter" (Wainhouse Research, 2008). However, even as it may be difficult to conceptually distinguish high-end videoconferencing from genuine telepresence, it is also becoming difficult to separate either one from the broader convergent business communications model of "unified communications"—a framework for integrated collaboration which strives to unify all forms of messaging, conferencing, video and the Internet (Grigonis, 2010). Attempts to find a consensus in defining such terms is not entirely an academic exercise. It has been the experience of many industry professionals that disputes over the feasibility of teleconferencing are often perpetuated by the fact that few of the negotiating parties know exactly what the other party believes a teleconference to be (Hausman, 1991).

Nevertheless, in the broadest sense, teleconferencing can be defined as "small group communication through an electronic medium" (Johansen, et al., 1979, p. 1). *Electronic Telespan* defines teleconferencing as "an electronic meeting that allows three or more people to meet, be it across time zones or across office cubicles" (Gold, 2004). However, these very broad definitions have not proven very useful in defining the widely varying means of conducting "electronic meetings." Jan Sellards, then president of the International Teleconferencing Association, defined the term in 1987 as, "the meeting between two or more locations and two or more people in those remote locations, where they have a need to share information. This does not necessarily mean a big multimedia event. The simplest form of teleconferencing is an audioconference" (Hausman, 1991, p. 246). Some practitioners prefer to call conferences using video "videoconferences," those employing mainly audio "audioconferences," and those using a range of computer-based technologies either "computer-conferences" or "Web-conferences"—oftentimes arranged on a continuum to distinguish those technologies that facilitate the "most natural" type of meetings from those that are "least natural" (see Figure 22.1). More typically, the term "teleconferencing" is used as a shorthand term to represent an array of technologies and services ranging from a three-way telephone conversation to full-motion color television to highly interactive, multipoint Web-based electronic meeting "spaces" to even the experience of "being there without being there" via telepresence technologies—each varying in complexity, expense, and sense of immediacy.

"Integrated collaboration" has also emerged as a preferred term emphasizing the functionality of teleconferencing without dwelling excessively on the technology. Whereas most definitions of teleconferencing focus on the use of audio/video/computer communications to facilitate meetings without the burden of travel, "integrated collaboration is a *process* that allows two or more users to interact with audio, video, and/or data streams in both real-time and non-real-time communications modes across packet and circuit switched networks" (Davis, 1999, p. 5, emphasis added). According to Andrew Davis, Managing Partner at Wainhouse Consulting Group, teleconferencing is primarily about meetings, but "integrated collaboration is about meetings, corporate communications, sales, training, and enhanced customer services" (Davis, 1999, p. 5).

Figure 22.1
Teleconferencing Continuum

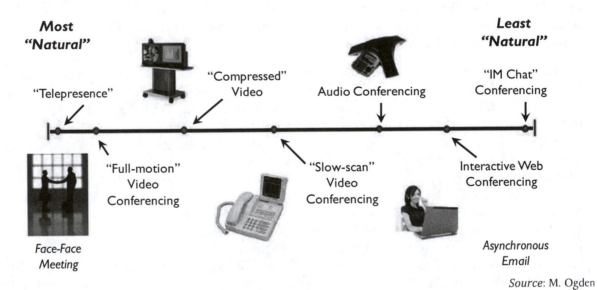

Source: M. Ogden

As what constitutes telepresence &/or teleconferencing continues to evolve, users look for easy-to-use, standards-based solutions that can integrate across all their communication needs. Whether referred to as "integrated collaboration," "collaboration solutions" (Glenwright, 2003), "conferencing and collaboration" (Polycom, 2003), unified communications or any of the other process-oriented, use-based terms, trends in convergent media are fueling a paradigm shift as geographically-dispersed work teams become the rule rather than the exception, and as price reductions and connectivity improvements make the various technologies of teleconferencing more dynamic and available to a wider constituency.

While seeking a meaningful definition for "teleconferencing," it is also important to distinguish between the two different "modes" of teleconferencing: *broadcast* and *conversational*. In broadcast teleconferences, the intention is to reach a large and dispersed audience with the same message at the same time, while providing a limited opportunity to interact with the originator. Typically, this takes the form of a "one-to-many" video broadcast with interaction facilitated via audience telephone "call-ins." These events (e.g., "state of the organization" addresses, employee relations conferences, new product kickoffs, etc.) require expensive transmission equipment, careful planning, sophisticated production techniques, and smooth coordination among the sites to be successful (Stowe, 1992). Increasingly, though, corporate "Webinars" and Internet video streaming technologies are replacing such events.

On the other hand, conversational teleconferences usually link only a few sites together in an "each-to-all" configuration with a limited number of individuals per site. Although prior arrangement is usually necessary, such meetings are often more spontaneous, relatively inexpensive, and simple to conduct. They seldom require anything more complicated than exchanging e-mail messages, synchronizing meeting times (especially if across time zones), and/or making a phone call to a colleague. Conversational teleconferencing supports numerous kinds of business activities from management and administrative meetings (*e.g.*, project, budget, staff, etc.), to marketing, sales, finance, and human resources (Stowe, 1992).

Another way to categorize teleconferencing applications is according to whether the facilities are used *in-house* as part of the normal routine, or *ad hoc*, only occasionally as the need arises. Once the exclusive domain of Fortune 500 firms, in-house or institutional teleconferencing—dedicated, room-based, and/or roll-about audio- and/or videoconferencing systems—are becoming more commonplace across a wide spectrum of organizations (*e.g.*, schools, churches, hospitals, etc.). For example, Tribal Data Resources (TDR), a company that provides American Indian tribes and tribal service organizations with the tools and training necessary to increase self-sufficiency and administrative resources, began using Web-conferencing for customer support and training in 2002. The company found Web-conferencing to be cost-effective and so valuable and intuitive to use that they integrated the Web-conferencing functionality directly into the latest version of their membership and enrollment data management software (iLinc, 2007).

Ad hoc teleconferencing, more commonly referred to as "conferencing on demand," accounts for the majority of corporate meetings and can run the gamut from large-scale, one-off regional sales meetings via video-conferences, occasional audioconferences between work-teams, or to much smaller-scale, client review desktop Web-conferences. Catering mostly to the needs of larger corporations, many of the major hotel chains (*e.g.*, Holiday Inn, Hilton, Marriott, Sheraton, Hyatt, etc.) first began offering sophisticated teleconferencing services in the 1980s to attract corporations and professional associations (Singleton, 1983), and several business copy centers such as FedEx Kinko's developed their own teleconferencing networks tailored for occasional use by small businesses and/or individuals. As teleconferencing choices expanded and prices dropped, such "third-party options" for ad hoc teleconferencing services waned, as teleconferencing became an extension of doing business and moved in-house. With the growth and maturation of telepresence since 2005, up-market hotel chains that cultivate a brand identity of catering to the business traveler are once again embracing technology. Both Marriott International and Starwood Hotels and Casinos have opened public telepresence rooms in a couple of pilot locations across the US, Europe, Australia, China, and Brazil using Cisco's TelePresence technology (McGillicuddy, 2010). Mary Casey, Vice President of Corporate Global Sales at Starwood, stated that their large corporate clients, especially those who have already invested in telepresence, are the main targets of her hotels' telepresence rooms, filling the niche of a regional hub service in locations where company owned facilities would not be cost effective (McGillicuddy, 2010). Although smaller companies have yet to express much interest in telepresence services, Casey believes it might just be a matter of educating the market on the experience such technologies can offer (McGillicuddy, 2010).

After years of false starts and unfulfilled promises, telepresence and integrated collaboration solutions have reached reliability, ease-of-use, and utility levels such that the technologies are finally being integrated into everyday business processes. Although there are no "true" substitutes for in-person meetings, those who subscribe to the "integrated collaboration" model of teleconferencing believe that the long-term growth of the industry will contribute real human value only to the extent that it improves the productivity of its users beyond the conservation of time and material resources expended in travel. Given the ease and flexibility of today's teleconferencing options, the most difficult challenge will be to hold more meaningful and productive meetings instead of just more meetings.

Background

The basic technology for telepresence has existed for years. In its simplest form, telepresence has been around since the invention of the telephone—allowing people for the first time to converse in "real time," even though they were separated physically (Singleton, 1983). Today, we understand telepresence to be more involved than a simple telephone conversation. Some contend that telepresence has its roots in comic strips and science fiction. Certainly, comic strips such as *Buck Rogers*, popular in the early 1900s, made it easy to imagine people of the future communicating with projected images, or *Dick Tracy* calling instant meetings through a communication device on his wrist. The videophone in Stanley Kubrick's *2001: A Space Odyssey* (1968) furthered the notion of interactive video communications as a common feature of our near future. Likewise, *Star Trek's* holodeck popularized the notion of fully-immersive virtual environments for diversion or business as accepted conventions of our far future. Robert A. Heinlein's story Waldo, found in *Waldo & Magic Inc.*, first published in 1950, provided perhaps the ultimate model for telepresence, including the use of remote controlled robotics (Heinlein, 1986). In this story the titular character, Waldo, used remote video and grasping devices named after himself to interact with people he did business with. This allowed him to conduct affairs around the planet without being present in person.

AT&T pioneered the teleconferencing gear that was, until the 1950s and 1960s, merely speculative science fiction. These early efforts were impressive for their time, but were also considered little more than novelties and failed to catch on with consumers (Noll, 1992). Today, these visions have been brought to life in three alternatives to face-to-face meetings easily classified by their broad medium of application: audio, video (including telepresence), and computer-mediated teleconferencing.

Audio

In 2005, audioconferencing was credited with over 20 billion minutes of use per year, had an annual unit volume growth rate of over 20%, and was the most commonly-used form of teleconferencing (Davis & Weinstein, 2005). As businesses gravitated toward audioconferencing to trim travel costs during the most recent economic downturn, the market saw a sharp upswing in demand as well as an increase in competition. Core markets have now become mostly saturated, and entry barriers are rapidly dropping. Competition now stems mainly from the availability of free audio conferencing services offered on the Web (*e.g.*, Skype, iChat, etc.). Ironically, the Web has also emerged as a key tool for providing integrated, value-added services and applications that are being bundled with traditional audioconferencing services. Thus, the industry is in a state of flux, the increased adoption of converged collaboration services has slowed down the growth of stand-alone audioconferencing services (Frost & Sullivan, 2009). Instead, audio conferencing minutes are now more likely to be bundled with collaboration solutions offered via the Web (Frost & Sullivan, 2009).

For a basic telephone conference involving a limited number of participants between two sites, a telephone set with either a three-way calling feature or a conferencing feature supported by the PBX (private branch exchange) or key system is all that is required. If participants are expected to be in the same room at each location, a speakerphone can be used. Adding additional sites to an audioconference requires an electronic device called a bridge to provide the connection (Singleton, 1983)—simply plugging several telephone lines together will not yield satisfactory results. Audio bridges can accommodate a number of different types of local and wide area network (LAN and WAN) interfaces and are capable of linking several hundred participants in a single call, while simultaneously balancing the volume levels (allowing everyone to hear each other as though they were talking one-on-one) and reducing noise (echo, feedback, clipping, dropout, attenuation, and artifacts) (Muller, 1998).

A bridged audioconference can be either attended (operator-assisted) or unattended (reservationless) and implemented in one of several ways: dial-out, prearranged, or meet-me. In the dial-out mode, the operator (or conference originator) places a call to each participant at a prearranged number and then connects each one into the conference. Prearranged audioconferences are dialed automatically, or users dial a predefined code from a touch-tone telephone. In either case, the information needed to set up the conference is stored in a scheduler controlling the bridge. In the meet-me mode, participants are required to call into a bridge at a prearranged time to begin the conference. Regardless of the mode of implementation, the more participants brought into an audioconference through the bridge, the more free extensions are required (Muller, 1998).

Video & Telepresence

Humans are inherently visual beings—we want to see as much as we want to hear. Since AT&T demonstrated the Picturephone at the 1964 World's Fair, corporate America has had an on-again/off-again fascination with video communications (Borthick, 2002). The assumption behind videoconferencing, usually unquestioned, has been that the closer the medium can come to simulating face-to-face communications, the better (Johansen, et al., 1979). Unfortunately, high-end videoconferencing has had a bumpy past, seldom living up to its hype. Plagued by jerky gestures, out-of-sync audio and cumbersome equipment, few executives liked what they saw (Finney, 2007). "As a result, many enterprises ended up installing these solutions 20 years ago, only to find that this equipment ended up sitting unused, fully depreciated, and trivialized as a toy that failed the crucial enterprise test of providing ROI [Return On Investment] and utility at the end of the day" (Park, 2008, p. 5). Engineers have since struggled to make video images more lifelike in size and quality. Now, thanks to new technologies, videoconferencing is delivering on its promise; high-definition TV images are sharp, broadband fiber-optic cable has replaced telephone lines, and the equipment is often installed in studios that are handsome and appropriately corporate (Finney, 2007).

Today, the videoconferencing industry is undergoing an important transformation. Social adoption of new collaborative and communicative technologies, improvements to digital compression, and an increased focus on remote communications and collaboration driven by globalization have allowed videoconferencing and telepresence to allay decades-old concerns and provide real tangible benefits in the workplace (Park, 2008). Thus, in 2007, Andrew Davis, of the research and consulting firm Wainhouse Research, noted "spectacular" growth in the videoconferencing industry with revenues up 38% based upon 27% growth in units shipped industry-wide (Davis, 2008a). Although a far more costly visual communications tool when compared with conventional videoconferencing systems, revenues for ready-built telepresence suites in Asia–Pacific (representing approximately 15% of the world telepresence market) grew at an estimated 71.1% in 2009—

up from 46.6% in 2008 (Frost & Sullivan, 2010). Frost & Sullivan expects a growth of 64.4% in the Asia–Pacific telepresence market, with revenues of over $73 million by the end of 2010 and an expected market size of $110 million by the end of 2015 (Frost & Sullivan, 2010). Globally, ABI Research Vice President Stan Schatt is forecasting the telepresence market to grow from almost $126 million in 2007 to almost $2.5 billion in 2013 (Weinschenk, 2009). However, most vendors' top-of-the-line virtual conference room environments typically cost between $200,000 and $500,000 for each office location, along with thousands of dollars a month in broadband connection charges—not a casual commitment by any means (Grigonis, 2010).

The mainstream videoconferencing market, on the other hand, is dominated by simpler systems that use less advanced equipment and cost from about $10,000 to $50,000, depending on location, room size and other features (Finney, 2007). As a result, the industry is already witnessing a blurring of boundaries between the immersive telepresence suites and conventional high-definition (HD) videoconferencing systems, and this trend should accelerate in the coming years (Frost & Sullivan, 2010). Telepresence is therefore expected to face stiff competition in the next few years from more affordable mid-range, HD videoconferencing systems as well as customized immersive solutions, which many system integrators are now starting to offer at lower price points. Although telepresence is currently a small—but very visible—segment of the videoconferencing market (estimated at 3% in 2009), it is expected to have a significant impact on the visual collaboration market (Frost & Sullivan, 2010).

There are only a few large dominant players in the videoconferencing and telepresence hardware market; namely, Cisco Systems (which acquired former market leader Tandberg in December 2009), Hewlett-Packard (HP) and Polycom, with a few other companies (such as Avaya, BT Conferencing, and Teliris) maintaining smaller, more tenuous market shares. Of these companies, Cisco and Hewlett-Pakard (with their HP Halo system) have a strong focus on the telepresence market. In 2007, Polycom had a market share of 31% but was looking to increase its market share with a broader product line that also addressed small and medium sized businesses and branch offices of larger entities. To this end, the company introduced the QDX6000, a high-quality video product priced at $4,000 in 2008 (Davis, 2008c). In early 2010, HP and Polycom announced that HP will start selling Polycom's portfolio of voice and video technologies as part of its UC&C (Unified Communications and Collaboration) Services offerings, and that Polycom's line of telepresence and video conferencing products will interoperate with HP's Halo telepresence solution (Burt, 2010). HP officials reportedly also have cut ties with Tandberg, which was bought by Cisco for $3.4 billion (Burt, 2010). Polycom's deal with HP includes Polycom's video and voice solutions for Avaya and the CX5000 Unified Conference Station—known earlier as Microsoft Roundtable—which integrates with Microsoft's Office Communications Server Wave 14, the software maker's version of its UC (Unified Communications) platform (Burt, 2010).

As an important side note illustrating the introduction of consumer videoconferencing, in 2003, with the slogan "videoconferencing for the rest of us," Apple Computers introduced the iChat AV videoconferencing software application along with the iSight digital video camera as a low-cost, two-way desktop videoconferencing solution for the Macintosh. Starting with the Tiger operating system (Mac OS 10.4) and continuing with Leopard (10.5) and Snow Leopard (10.6), iChat AV takes advantage of the H.264 video codec and launches a multi-way video- and audioconference directly on the desktop with a sharper picture and improved color accuracy. Also, iChat allows for high-quality audioconferences with up to 10 participants, integrated instant text messaging, and drag-and-drop file sharing (Apple, 2006). Other features in iChat include the ability to share Keynote slide presentations, control a single desktop for collaboration with colleagues, and the ability to record the iChat session (audio or video) playable in either iTunes or QuickTime (Apple 2008). With today's options, videoconferencing becomes just another application running on the user's computer desktop.

Only a small fraction of the 230,000 videoconferencing systems sold worldwide in 2009 were telepresence systems (Engebretson, 2010). Globally, around 225 companies are active users of telepresence. Technology and service providers argue that telepresence allows users to develop a closer rapport with each other, because everyone can see who is talking, see their facial expression and have eye-contact—things traditional videoconferencing systems cannot provide. However, videoconferencing and telepresence systems come in three basic formats, each having benefits and drawbacks in terms of suitability for different purposes and sizes of business (Knights, 2010):

◆ *Desktop models*: best suited to smaller offices, ad-hoc use, and one-to-many communication. The illusion of "being there" can be strained when trying to replicate a formal meeting scenario because such systems are not located in a purpose-built meeting room. Likewise, desktop telepresence systems have difficulty creating the conditions of a live meeting—most notably, the illusion of eye-to-eye contact.

◆ *Meeting-room systems*: better suited to companies with a large, distributed network of sites that need to hold regular, formal meetings that involve a number of people. On the downside, users may find the numbers of people these systems can accommodate at each location somewhat limiting.

◆ *Boardroom suites*: with the biggest high definition screens with hidden cameras and microphones situated in purpose-built suites that are designed to replicate the look, feel, and even sound of a live meeting (on both sides of the technology interface), these telepresence facilities are the most immersive. Specialized surround audio and life-sized screen technology makes this the most expensive option.

Videoconferencing and telepresence between more than two locations requires a multipoint control unit (MCU). An MCU is a switch that acts as a video "bridge" connecting the signals among all locations and enabling participants to see one another, converse, and/or view the same graphics (Muller, 1998). The MCU also provides the means to control the videoconference in terms of who is seeing what at any given time. Most MCUs include voice-activated switching, presentation or lecture mode, and moderator control (Muller, 1998). Likewise, because of the large amount of information contained in an uncompressed full-motion video signal (about 90 million bits per second), two-way videoconferencing that even remotely approaches broadcast television quality would require incredible bandwidth at equally great cost. Therefore, all but the most expensive full-motion videoconferencing options utilize video compression/decompression technology to take advantage of the fact that not all of the 90 million bits of a video signal are really necessary to reconstruct a "watchable" image. In fact, the majority of the information in a typical videoconferencing image is redundant: most of the image remains exactly the same except for the speaker's head movements and occasional gestures.

Computer-Mediated

Whereas videoconferencing and telepresence are about "see me," computer or Web conferencing is about "see what I see" (Davis & Weinstein, 2005). Murray Turoff developed one of the first computer conferencing systems in 1971 for the Office of Emergency Preparedness (EMISARI, a management information system) to deal with the wage-price freeze (Lucky, 1991). Since then, the capacity of two or more personal computers to interconnect, send, receive, store, and display digitized imagery has expanded rapidly—thanks, in large part, to rapid developments in computer hardware and the spread of the Internet. At the most basic level, computer conferencing is the written form of a conference call. Participants in a computer conference could communicate via a simple conferencing application such as Internet Relay Chat (IRC) or AOL's Instant Messenger, both of which provide a simple text-based chat function.

Another form of computer conferencing takes advantage of the ability to "time-shift" a presentation via Webcasting. Many "meetings" are actually one-way presentations with limited questions and answers. In such situations, a Webcast or Webinar may actually be a better choice. For such Web-based information sharing, the originator tries to anticipate the viewer's questions and concerns during the recording of a presentation, then makes the finished product available to anyone who wants to stream or download it at a time more convenient to the viewer—sort of an asynchronous broadcast on the Web.

To make a computer-based meeting more interactive, however, most users want to do either real-time audio or video (or both), while sharing documents or a common workspace. Enter Web conferencing—also known as online meetings—perhaps one of the fastest-growing sectors in teleconferencing. Frost & Sullivan define Web conferencing as, "a set of technologies and services that allow people to hold real-time and synchronous conferences over the Internet. In order to hold a Web conference, each participant needs to use a PC and a Web browser to share information. The most basic feature of a Web conference is screen sharing, whereby conference participants see whatever is on the presenter's screen. Additionally, audio communication in a Web conference can either be done through traditional PSTN [public switched telephone network] networks or through VoIP" (Frost & Sullivan, 2006b). Online meeting services have now been around for more than a decade and the basic concept has not changed much—using Webcam-enabled computers and phones, dozens of users can see and chat with one another, share documents in real time, type messages to the whole group or a few individuals, and write on a shared virtual whiteboard (Alsever, 2009). Web conferencing market revenue is forecast to increase from $136.3 million in 2006 to $538.0 million by 2011 (Frost & Sullivan, 2007a). In 2008, the Web conferencing industry grew by 19%, topping $1.1 billion in sales (Alsever, 2009). Some of the key factors driving the Web conferencing market include the increasing globalization of large companies, recognition of the downside of business travel, and the need for businesses to become more competitive (Frost & Sullivan, 2007a).

The Web conferencing industry quickly differentiated itself into three deployment options for users to choose from. In the hosted model, the most popular online meeting services include GoToMeeting (owned by Citrix Online), WebEx (acquired in 2007 by Cisco), Premiere Global Services' Netspoke, and Microsoft. Although most offer product lines tailored to small businesses, comparing their functionality can be a daunting task. Pricing options make it more complicated; providers charge per-minute, by the month, or through licensing agreements (Foley, 2006), but most comprehensive packages range from $40 to $60 per month (Alsever, 2009). Some service providers, such as Yugma.com, Dimdim.com and Skype, offer basic computer-to-computer connections virtually for free. On Dimdim you can text chat, share slides, whiteboard, documents, and Web pages and record your call. To share your desktop, however, you must download software. For $99 a year, you can have two-way video chats and get custom branded meeting rooms (Alsever, 2009). However, for most Web conferencing systems, a service provider's Web conferencing software is "hosted" on the vendor's (or a partner's) system—known as the SaaS (Software as a Service) model—and the user accesses the capabilities over the Internet, paying a "one-time" or monthly subscription fee based on the number of users. The on-premises model, such as Polycom's WebOffice, Oracle's Collaboration Suite, Skype, or even Apple's iChat, installs software on systems owned-and-operated by the business and uses the business's existing Internet connectivity. The blended model, from companies such as Interwise, combines both of these, typically recommending the use of a telephone to augment the poor sound quality of some computers. Typically, everyday meetings are run using on-premises facilities, while large, multi-nodal meetings use software running on external servers. Obviously, the most affordable is on-premise Web conferencing, running on a typical office computer with little or no added equipment beside a Webcam. On-premise software has a strong following in Japan, China and South Korea, while SaaS solutions are favored in Australia, India and Southeast Asian nations—in the US and Europe, the blended model is prevalent (PR Newswire, 2009).

There is no denying that Web conferencing is an area of high interest to conferencing users. Effective organizations are using Web conferencing as more than just a substitute for face-to-face meetings. Web conferencing can help people work together with colleagues and business partners, share information, make better decisions, work on more projects simultaneously, and increase the impact of their work provided they are afforded a minimum of functional tools. Users expect all participants to be able to see presentations, share desktops and/or applications, have the ability to exchange real-time text messages with other participants, and have a shared whiteboard (Mann & Latham, 2005).

Obviously, the key to a successful and effective collaboration experience is achieving a level of "connectedness" between the participants. Social psychologists have pointed out that "in terms of the immediacy [i.e., 'connectedness'] that they can afford, media can be ordered from the most immediate to the least: face-to-face, [videoconferencing], picturephone, telephone, [below this, synchronous and asynchronous computerized conferencing]…the choice of media in regard to intimacy should be related to the nature of the task, with the least immediate or intimate mode preferable for unpleasant tasks" (Hiltz & Turoff, 1993, p. 118). This suggests that, for the less intimate task, the most immediate medium (face-to-face) would lead to favorable outcomes. In this same vein, a slightly more intimate task would require a medium of intermediate immediacy (telepresence or videoconferencing), while those tasks that are highly intimate, perhaps embarrassing, personal, or charged with potential conflict would benefit from using a medium of low immediacy (audio or even computer conferening).

Interestingly, though, Hiltz and Turoff (1993)—reporting the results of a 1977 study—indicated that "numerous carefully conducted experiments…found all vocal media to be very similar in effectiveness [including face-to-face, audio, and video]. However, …people *perceived* audio to be less satisfactory than video" and both to be less satisfactory than face-to-face (emphasis added, p. 121). Although much anecdotal information attesting to the highly satisfactory and "life-like" attributes of telepresence have been reported, little recent work has been done in this area and it appears that there is still a great deal of room for further research.

Recent Developments

Opinions vary, but past circumstances have led many corporate IT managers to take a long, hard look at telepresence and other collaboration tools in light of rapidly-expanding corporate communication needs and converging technologies. With multiple devices and interfaces to access content, learning curves and complexity become major challenges. One of the most important recent developments is the linkage of telepresence with convergence media in redefining the unified communications model (see Figure 22.2). Thus, unified communications (UC) has emerged as the catch-phrase *du jour* to describe the planned, coordinated use of key technologies for integrated collaboration. "UC is a direct result of the convergence of communications and applications. Differing forms of communications historically have been developed, marketed, and sold as individual applications. In some cases, they even had separate networks and devices. The convergence of all communications on IP networks and open software platforms enables a new UC paradigm and is changing how individuals, groups, and organizations communicate" (Elliot, 2007). UC applications are, therefore, expected to including such facilities as VoIP, PC-based presence, e-mail, audio and Web conferencing, videoconferencing, voice mail, find-me/follow-me capabilities (for call routing), unified messaging, Wikis/blogs, mobile clients, and IM and social networking capabilities—all used to serve a wide array of communication needs and goals in a "click to communicate" interface (Elliot, 2007).

Figure 22.2
Evolution of Telepresence

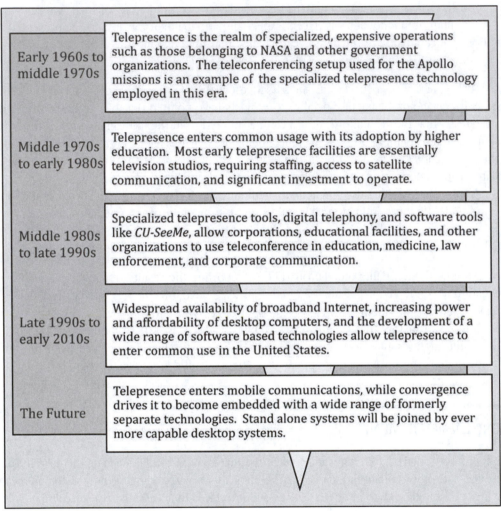

Early 1960s to middle 1970s	Telepresence is the realm of specialized, expensive operations such as those belonging to NASA and other government organizations. The teleconferencing setup used for the Apollo missions is an example of the specialized telepresence technology employed in this era.
Middle 1970s to early 1980s	Telepresence enters common usage with its adoption by higher education. Most early telepresence facilities are essentially television studios, requiring staffing, access to satellite communication, and significant investment to operate.
Middle 1980s to late 1990s	Specialized telepresence tools, digital telephony, and software tools like *CU-SeeMe*, allow corporations, educational facilities, and other organizations to use teleconference in education, medicine, law enforcement, and corporate communication.
Late 1990s to early 2010s	Widespread availability of broadband Internet, increasing power and affordability of desktop computers, and the development of a wide range of software based technologies allow telepresence to enter common use in the United States.
The Future	Telepresence enters mobile communications, while convergence drives it to become embedded with a wide range of formerly separate technologies. Stand alone systems will be joined by ever more capable desktop systems.

Source: S. Jackson

Several business and IT-related trends are contributing to the trend toward unified communication, but the largest is the growth of the virtual workplace, in which an increasing number of employees work in a location that is different from that of their coworkers or managers. These employees must continue to communicate and collaborate, but they have the challenge of having to do so over the telephone and the Internet, rather than in person—and they require technology to help them do so. Also impacting the need for UC tools is the need to support global business, the desire to cut back on travel for budgetary and productivity reasons, the spread of IP (specifically, voice over IP) in the enterprise, and the need to cut cycle times around production and decision-making (Frost & Sullivan, 2007b). Still, skeptics of UC exist. Elliot Gold of *Electronic Telespan* sees a rush toward the UC enterprise, but remains convinced that "...while the sales pitches and even the RFPs out there will talk loudly about UC, the majority of the usage will be plain old voice, as it is today, and will be for many years to come. Yes, we will see Web; yes, we will see video in UC on desktops, available from the new media servers, but in the beginning, and frankly for some time to come, the applications will come out of people's mouths and into their ears" (I can see..., 2007).

Unified communications efforts notwithstanding, many business people still maintain that face-to-face meetings will always offer the best level of interactivity. They are also beefing up their Web sites for actual end users "...using animation for demonstrations of products as well as using streaming video for testimonials" (Vinas, 2002, p. 32). The key point in the use of teleconferencing is ease-of-use and ease-of-access.

The other obstacles to ubiquitous adoption are cultural—many people are uncomfortable speaking to a camera and very uncomfortable knowing they are being recorded. Paul Saffo, a director of the Institute for the Future in Menlo Park (California), believes this is normal. "It takes about 30 years for new technolog[ies] to be absorbed into the mainstream. Products for videoconferencing [and by extension, Web conferencing]... invented 15 to 20 years ago are just now beginning to come into their own" (Weiland, 1996, p. 63). By Saffo's standard, U.S. society is probably entering its second stage of acceptance of teleconferencing technology— perhaps accelerated by the events of September 11, 2001 and the most recent economic downturn. While this transformation is underway, the industry may seem in a constant state of flux and somewhat confusing. The most confusing and yet promising of the newest teleconferencing developments are not in hardware or software, but in the international standards that make it all work.

Standards

International standards for teleconferencing promulgated by the International Telecommunications Union (ITU) have set the foundation for network transmission technologies and vendor interoperability in the teleconferencing industry, especially videoconferencing. Prior to the establishment of these standards, vendors employed a range of proprietary algorithms and packaged hardware and software so that systems from different vendors could not communicate with each other. By establishing worldwide teleconferencing standards, the ITU helps ensure that teleconferencing technologies can "talk" to each other regardless of brand. Likewise, as new innovations are developed, the new systems remain "backward-compatible" with existing systems. The most important standards are under the umbrella standard of H.320 that defines the operating modes and transmission speeds for videoconferencing system codecs, (Muller, 1998). All videoconferencing codecs and MCUs that comply with H.320 are interoperable with those of different manufacturers. Other important standards for the implementation and adoption of teleconferencing are:

◆ *H.322*—LAN-based videoconferencing with guaranteed bandwidth (ITU, 1996).

◆ *H.323*—LAN-based videoconferencing with non-guaranteed bandwidth such as LAN and WAN networks using packet switched Internet protocol (ITU, 2000). This standard supports the move by many desktop teleconferencing systems to sophisticated bridging systems and IP multicasting software that reduces desktop clutter and frees up valuable bandwidth on the network.

◆ *H.324*—Originally developed to facilitate low bit-rate video telephony by specifying a common method for video, voice, and data to be shared simultaneously over modem connections via standard analog telephone lines (ITU, 1998). In 2002, this protocol was modified for 3G wireless networks (H.324M or 3G-324M) enabling real-time conversational multimedia communication services and applications on 2.5G and 3G mobile devices (Radvision, 2002).

◆ *H.263*—This video coding protocol for low bit rate communication supports 30 frames per second video at the narrow bandwidths used in videoconferencing.

◆ *H.264*—A more advanced video codec for audio/visual services, H.264 is a relatively new ITU protocol that improves the video resolution quality in the H.323 protocol suite by encoding and transmitting two interlaced fields for each frame. This process allows the decoded video to be more fluid and lifelike, approaching or matching MPEG-2 quality at a 64% lower bandwidth.

Video conferencing applications designed for desktop and cell phone use have a range of standards and a great deal of interconnectivity. Applications such as Apple Computer's iChat use Session Initiation Protocol (SIP) to allow connections between desktop computers and services such as America Online (Petersen, 2008). SIP, according to the standardization document, is "...an application-layer control protocol that can establish, modify, and terminate multimedia sessions (conferences) such as Internet telephony calls" (Rosenburg et al., 2002). These technologies have created seamless and easy to use video conferencing that allow telepresence to be available to a wide audience. Industry leaders such as Google Chat are compatible with a wide range of video conferencing technologies, such as Pidgin, Psi, iChat, or Trillian Pro (Google Talk, 2010). In a similar manner, Skype, a video and telephone software application has developed cell phone tools for Nokia and Android phones (Ricknäs, 2010).

Cisco Systems has likewise launched efforts to create more open interoperation between equipment and software from different vendors. The Telepresence Interoperability Protocol (TIP) is being offered royalty-free to industry competition in an effort to create systems that can communicate with each other (Modine, 2010).

CURRENT STATUS

As technologies have expanded, morphed, and matured, teleconferencing options have transformed and expanded as well. As discussed earlier, teleconferencing is no longer a simple conference call, nor is it exclusively the domain of complex two-way high-definition video hook-ups. Furthermore, the cost of video codecs and other end-user equipment continues to fall. Fifteen years ago, a standard videoconferencing system could cost $75,000 or more, and for that, you could buy only enough gear to outfit a couple of conference rooms. Currently, such room-based systems can be found for as little as $10,000, and desktop PC-based Webcams and software are available for a few hundred dollars, making videoconferencing much more attractive than ever before. Also, early videoconferencing systems depended on ISDN (Integrated Services Digital Network) lines to transmit data because they were the only connections that provided the bandwidth and stability that videoconferencing applications needed. Early in the 21st Century, however, videoconferencing vendors shifted from ISDN lines, which were expensive and required special skills to manage, to IP networks. IP has become the de facto networking standard for most conferencing networks and a wide variety of applications, such as electronic messaging, telephone services, and data sharing (Videoconferencing..., 2007).

Not to be counted out, audioconferencing has also jumped on the IP bandwagon. Paul Berberian, co-founder, president, and CEO of audio and data conferencing provider Raindance Communications, notes that, "for every boardroom-type videoconference, there are thousands of audioconferences" (Borthick, 2002). Audioconferencing over IP networks (VoIP) has garnered much attention lately as Internet telephony software makes it possible for users to engage in long-distance conversations between virtually any location in the world without regard for per-minute usage charges. In most cases, all that the user needs is an Internet-connected computer equipped with telephony software, a sound card, microphone, and speakers or a headset (Muller, 1998). As was mentioned earlier, one of the most popular business features of Skype is their free conference calling, now capable of handling up to 10 individuals per conference session and point-to-point video calls are also easy to set-up—all you need is a Webcam (Skype, 2008). However, because the voice of each party is compressed and packetized, there can be significant delays that result in noticeable gaps in a person's speech.

Web-based conferencing systems are rapidly gaining in popularity. According to Wainhouse Research, 75% of small business respondents see the ability to use Web conferencing to reach more people and save time and travel costs as its major benefits (Foley, 2006). Also, 59% said it made meetings more productive. According to a Time.com article, Web videoconferencing is seeing an upturn as employers seek to save time and cut travel costs during the latest economic downturn by interviewing job candidates using Skype (Kiviat, 2009).

As mentioned earlier, in 2009, Microsoft and Polycom announced that the two companies were deepening their strategic relationship to deliver the broadest and most powerful sets of voice and video solutions for unified communications and collaboration. As a result, Polycom added the CX5000 Unified Conference Station (formerly Microsoft RoundTable) into its suite of devices optimized for Microsoft Office Communicator. Originally launched by Microsoft in October 2007, the CX5000 is a plug-and-play device that connects to a PC through a USB connection, so no extra provisioning or configuration is needed—any user can walk into a conference room, plug in a laptop, and start a meeting. Listing for approximately $4,300, the CX5000 is actually an unusual Webcam that gives remote participants a 360° view of the conference room. (Yes, it is a room-based group videoconferencing system.) When used with Office Live Meeting service, or as part of Office Communications Server, the CX5000 combines content, a panoramic 360-degree view of the entire meeting room, and a separate view of the active speaker for a unique voice and video experience (Polycom, 2009).

🌍 Sustainability 🌍

Telepresence and its related technologies (telecommuting, videoconferencing, and audio conferencing) may have the greatest potential of all technologies discussed in this book to reduce environmental impact. Of the three, telecommuting may have the greatest potential as a "green" solution because of the fact that it offers systematic bypass of energy use. Estimates of the extent of telecommuting in the U.S. vary, but all of the estimates indicate that telecommuting has become a major factor in corporate America. According to a custom analysis of a national study of telecommunications use, 21.5 million workers in the U.S. spend more than 20% of their work week telecommuting (Grant, 2010). Presuming that each telecommuter saves one gallon of fuel per day just one day a week, the total impact is a reduction in fuel consumption of more than a billion gallons per year!

The potential for reduction in travel from teleconferencing is more limited. In a classic study of the potential of teleconferencing to reduce travel, Noll (1986) indicated that teleconferencing is appropriate for meetings in which 1) participants already know each other, 2) the meeting is scheduled far enough in advance to allow reservation of conference rooms and other resources, and 3) the business transacted was routine business, not involving complex negotiation. Noll concluded that only about three to five percent of all business meetings meet these criteria, reducing the potential of teleconferencing to reduce travel.

But "telepresence," as defined in this chapter, may offer significantly richer communication experience. In exploring "media richness," Daft, Lengel, & Trevino (1987) indicate that the "richer" a medium is in its ability to transmit non-verbal cues, allow the use of natural language, and allow instant feedback, the more complex messages can be communicated through that medium. High-bandwidth telepresence technologies may thus have the potential to expand the replacement of traditional meetings with virtual meetings.

The reduction in energy use is the most significant factor from a sustainability perspective, but the primary incentive for adoption of these technologies is that they offer a combination of a reduction in travel expenses and an increase in productivity. As with most technological adoption by businesses, the primary motivator will probably be the bottom line.

—August E. Grant, Ph.D.

FACTORS TO WATCH

Convergence has created a wide range of telepresence products and services, many of which are capable of interacting with each other. Telepresence is coming to portable communication devices such as the iPhone (Dupree, 2010), delayed mostly by the limited bandwidth of cell phone networks. Current cell phones such as the iPhone have all of the technology needed to participate in video conferencing, while video conferencing technology firms are producing tools needed for developers to create video conferencing tools inside of their own phone applications (Brandenburg, 2010).

Telepresence will continue to make inroads in high-end corporate and military applications. Military organizations are using telepresence, in the form of telerobotic operations of bomb disposal, reconnaissance vehicles, and combat aircraft, many of which allow user-friendly operation without putting operators at risk. In some cases, skilled aircraft pilots can be replaced by specialized telerobotics operators (Page, 2009). NASA, when discussing technology requirements for astronauts in future manned lunar missions, identified remote telepresence when performing extra-vehicular activities such as moon walks as being an important capability (Connors et al., 1994).

Telepresence will become a linchpin of unified communication. Future systems will allow transmission of images and presentation files, linking between asynchronous and synchronous communication forms, allow integration of video, audio, text, and graphics, and teleoperation. As this technology converges with other technologies, information will move more efficiently and transparently through communication systems.

Another trend to watch is the integration of telepresence into consumer electronics. Consumers have many options to connect their television sets to the Internet. An extreme example is Skype's partnership with television manufacturers Panasonic and LG, allowing higher end television sets by these manufacturers to connect to Skype with the addition of a Web camera. This development may help bring telepresence to the masses, as ubiquitous and easy to use home televisions can now become telepresence units without a separate computer or expensive hardware or software additions (Ray, 2010).

Convergence is a factor in virtual presence as well. IBM uses an internal version of Second Life to create avatar based virtual meetings that exceed the normal scope and size of Web-based meetings or conference calls. The potential advantages for these meetings are numerous. IBM Chief Technology Officer for Sales, Francoise LeGoues, claims that traditional telepresence meetings became ineffective after 45 minutes when too many people join a meeting. However, avatar based meetings proved excellent for building teams. IBM currently has 10,000 employees able to participate in virtual meeting spaces using a secure Second Life Engine (Digital Nation, 2010).

The potential advantages of a virtual environment meeting are immense. The first is that the modern technical workforce already has experience with virtual environments. Most people in the next generation will have played video games that allow them to move avatars through a virtual space and interact with others in that space. The second advantage is that virtual environments represent a culturally level playing field. In face-to-face communications people draw on social convention to avoid embarrassment and to keep from embarrassing their peers. Goffman likens this process to a theatrical presentation, with the "actor" only able to be themselves behind the curtains when they are not on physical display (Goffman, 1956). This obviously creates a situation where the better actor controls the debate, and where handicaps in voice, physical presence, and the like can inhibit effective collaborations. In addition, actors may spend more time trying to decode the cultural requirements of different members of the group than actually communicating with them. Avatars represent a way of allowing the actors in a telepresence setting to forget about one aspect of the theatrical presentation, and concentrate on other aspects that are more important to productivity.

William Gibson's book, *Virtual Light* (1993), outlines another possible direction for telepresence through the interaction between real and virtual world constructs. In Gibson's work, glasses are equipped with a database that allows the user to see information overlaid on images from a user's actual visual spectrum. A user looks at a building, and can see architectural plans for that building overlaid on the actual real world-view. Two doctors, separated by thousands of miles, will be able to look in on the same patient. The doctor present in person can receive images overlaid on an image of her own patient, while carrying on a consult with the second doctor who is thousands of miles away. With the significant shortage of medical practitioners in rural areas of the United States and the complete absence of medical personnel in some areas of the world, telemedicine represents an exciting way to bridge the gap caused by the lack of trained doctors. It also allows specialists, often concentrated in large urban areas, to treat patients from around the globe.

Telepresence systems such as those promoted by Cisco may become increasingly important. With high end compression engines, high-quality cameras, large flat panel displays, and carefully designed and integrated furniture and room elements, telepresence systems such as the one illustrated in Figure 22.3 cost much more than standard "vanilla" videoconferencing solutions. Most telepresence systems currently cost $200,000 to $400,000 each, with a $300,000 list price perhaps representing the average for a six-seat room. In contrast, traditional videoconferencing systems range from $10,000 to $65,000, with perhaps $25,000 representing a good industry average (Wainhouse Research, 2008). In addition, because they strive for the highest-quality images, telepresence systems require more bandwidth. Many vendors are recommending 10 Mb/s to 15 Mb/s connections for each telepresence room, while high-end standard definition conference room videoconferencing systems typically operate between 384 Kb/s and 1.5 Mb/s and high-definition videoconferencing systems typically operate at 2 Mb/s (Wainhouse Research, 2008).

Figure 22.3
Cisco System, Inc.'s TelePresence Screen Shot

Source: Cisco Systems, Inc.

Cisco counters that TelePresence rooms are used an average of five hours per day, compared with an average of only 30 minutes for other teleconferencing offerings. Based on this data, Cisco estimates that its customers have saved "more than $60 million in productivity improvement" (Cisco Notches Telepresence Milestone, 2008). Just how Cisco came up with their numbers is not very clear; nevertheless, a clear pattern of usage has emerged—"system usage increases over time and as the number of systems increases" (Wainhouse Research, 2008). In a company with two telepresence rooms, usage typically starts at a few hours per day and increases regularly until it stabilizes. To some extent, usage also increases as the number of systems increase—a classic illustration of Metcalfe's law: the value of a network is proportional to the square of the number of endpoints; or the value of an endpoint is proportional to the square of the number of endpoints to which it can connect (Wainhouse Research, 2008). According to a Sage Research report on future benefits of telepresence, employee collaboration benefits are among the top improvements companies expect (Sage Research, 2006). Other anticipated benefits include improved productivity and cost savings from cut-backs in business travel and other conference services (video-, Web- and audioconferencing).

Though most existing videoconferencing and telepresence systems attempt to humanize the mediated communication experience, they are still unable to provide the immersive components that define actual face-to-face communication. As discussed earlier, attempts have been made to create a more immersive experience using large HD displays, gaze preservation through multi-camera capturing, and matching the physical environments between the remote locations—creating the illusion of a continuity of the physical space through the screen. However, some researchers believe the experience of telepresence can be further enhanced using virtual reality where the remote users are rendered inside a shared virtual environment (Kurillo, et al., 2008).

UCBerkeley's Tele-immersion Lab defines tele-immersion as enabling "users in geographically distributed sites to collaborate in real time in a shared simulated environment as if they were in the same physical room" (Tele-Immersion @ UC Berkeley, 2010). Having participated in and learned from earlier experiments, UC Berkeley's Tele-immersion lab's system has 360-degree stereo capturing capability that allows full-body 3D reconstruction of people and objects. The data is captured in real time and projected into a virtual environment as a point cloud that can be combined with virtual objects and scenes. The current apparatus includes 48 cameras arranged in 12 stereo clusters. A stereo reconstruction program running in parallel on 12 computers processes the images from each cluster. The acquired data can be sent via Gigabit Internet two connections to another computer to be rendered into a three-dimensional scene. The data is then displayed using passive stereo projection to increase the perception of depth. UC Berkeley's Tele-Immersion Lab also has hardware capable of capturing and playing sound from four microphones and four speakers, and eight infrared lights that project patterns that facilitate depth detection (Tele-Immersion @ UC Berkeley, 2010).

As broadband access continues to increase, fully-immersive three-dimensional virtual conferencing may one day become a reality, but today, it is still awkward and "kludgy" at best. Still, if we go back just a couple of years, who would have imagined that virtual events—real-time integrated collaboration via audio-, video-, and Web-conferencing—would be a business reality today?

Bibliography

Alsever, J. (2009, March 11). Skip the trip: Web conferencing booms. *CNNmoney.com*. Retrieve April 3, 2010 from http://money.cnn.com/2009/02/24/smallbusiness/online_conferencing.fsb/index.htm.

Apple Computers. (2006). *iChat AV: Videoconferencing for the rest of us*. Retrieved April 7, 2006 from http://www.apple.com/macosx/features/ichat/.

Apple Computers. (2008). *iChat. Not Being There is Half the Fun.* Retrieved April 27, 2008 from http://www.apple.com/ma-cosx/features/ichat.html.

BBC News (2009, April 13*). Can Cisco turn the downturn into opportunity?* Retrieved March 30, 2010 from http://news.bbc.co.uk/2/hi/business/7992417.stm.

Borthick, S. (2002, March). Video: Nice but not necessary? *Business Communications Review.* Retrieved March 24, 2002 from http://www.bcr.com/bcrmag/2002/03/p10.asp.

Brandenburg, M. (2010). GIPS Brings Video Conferencing Tech To iPhone Developers, Retrieved March 29, 2010. http://www.networkcomputing.com/wireless/gips-brings-video-conferencing-tech-to-iphone-developers.php

Burt, J. (2010, March 22). HP Partners with Polycom as Cisco Split Grows. *Enterprise Networking.* Retrieved April 2, 2010 from http://www.eweek.com/c/a/Enterprise-Networking/HP-Partners-with-Polycom-as-Cisco-Split-Grows-384994/.

Cisco notches telepresence ,ilestone. (2008, April 22). TelecomWeb News Break. Retrieved April 27, 2008 from http://www.telecomweb.com/tnd/260415.html.

Connors, M., Eppler M., and Morrow, G. (1994). Interviews with the Apollo Lunar Surface Astronauts in Support of Planning for EVA Systems Design. NASA Technical Memorandum 108846.

Daft, R.L., Lengel, R.H., & Trevino, L.K. (1987). Message equivocality, media selection, and manager performance: Implications for information systems. *MIS Quarterly,* 355-366.

Davis, A. (1999, June). *Integrated collaboration: Driving business efficiency into the next millennium.* Tempe, AZ: Forward Concepts.

Davis, A. (2008a, February 22). Videoconferencing industry statistics—Q4-2007. *The Wainhouse Research Bulletin, 9,* 7. Retrieved April 25, 2008, from http://www.wainhouse.com/files/wrb-09/wrb-0907.pdf.

Davis, A. (2008c, March 3). Radvision to support Microsoft OCS 2007 and Thinking about RoundTables and square rooms. *The Wainhouse Research Bulletin, 9,* 8. Retrieved April 26, 2008, from http://www.wainhouse.com/files/wrb-09/wrb-0908.pdf.

Davis, A., & Weinstein, I. (2005, March). *The business case for videoconferencing: Achieving a competitive edge.* Wainhouse Research.

Digital Nation. (2010). Interview Francoise LeGoues. *Frontline, PBS.* Retrieved April 2nd, 2010, from http://www.pbs.org/wgbh/pages/frontline/digitalnation/interviews/legoues.html.

Dupree, C. (2010). Video Chat coming in future iPhones/iPads? Retrieved March 29, 2010 http://9to5mac.com/iphone-video-chat-340968306

Elliot, B. (2007, August 20). Magic quadrant for unified communications, 2007. Retrieved April 27, 2008 from http://mediaproducts.gartner.com/reprints/microsoft/article3/article3.html.

Engebretson, J. (2010, March 10). Telepresence: Not just for meetings any more. *Connected Planet.* Retrieved March 12, 2010 from http://connectedplanetonline.com/business_services/news/telepresence-not-just-for-meetings-anymore-0310/.

Festa, P. (2003, December 26). Microsoft settles in whiteboard patent dustup. *C/NET News.com.* Retrieved April 1, 2004 from http://zdnet.com.com/2100-1104-5133588.html.

Finger, R. (1998, June). Measuring quality in videoconferencing systems. Business Communications Review. Retrieved March 24, 2002 from http://www.bcr.com/bcrmag/1998/06/p51.asp.

Finney, P (2007, May 29). Telepresence TV. *The New York Times.* Retrieved March 30, 2010 from http://www.nytimes.com/2007/05/29/technology/29video.html?_r=1.

Foley, M. (2006, December). The basics: Web conferencing. Inc. Retrieved April 27, 2008 from http://technology.inc.com/managing/articles/200612/webconference.html.

Frost & Sullivan. (2006a). Meetings around the world: The impact of collaboration on business performance. Retrieved April 26, 2008 from http://newscenter.verizon.com/kit/collaboration/MAW_WP.pdf.

Frost & Sullivan. (2006b, September 29). World Web conferencing market. Retrieved April 27, 2008 from http://www.frost.com/prod/servlet/report-homepage.pag?repid=F764-01-00-00-00&ctxst=FcmCtx1&ctxht= FcmCtx2&ctxhl= FcmCtx3&ctxixpLink=FcmCtx4&ctxixpLabel=FcmCtx5.

Frost & Sullivan. (2007a, September 5). European Web conferencing software and srvices markets. Retrieved April 27, 2008 from http://www.frost.com/prod/servlet/report-homepage.pag?repid=BA0F-01-00-00-00&ctxst= FcmCtx11&ctxht=FcmCtx12&ctxhl=FcmCtx13&ctxixpLink=FcmCtx14&ctxixpLabel=FcmCtx15.

Frost & Sullivan. (2007b, December 21). World unified communications market. Retrieved April 27, 2008 from http://www.frost.com/prod/servlet/report-homepage.pag?repid=N180-01-00-00-00&ctxst=FcmCtx16&ctxht= FcmCtx17&ctxhl=FcmCtx18&ctxixpLink=FcmCtx19&ctxixpLabel=FcmCtx20.

Frost & Sullivan (2009, June 19). North American Audio Conferencing Service Markets. Retrieved April 3, 2010 from http://www.marketresearch.com/map/prod/2286717.html.

Frost & Sullivan (2010, March 15). Telepresence growth peaks in 2009-10, Frost & Sullivan predicts (Press Release). Retrieved April 3, 2010 from http://www.frost.com/prod/servlet/press-release-print.pag?docid=195819181.

Gibson, W. (1993). *Virtual light.* New York, NY: Bantam Books.

Glenwright, T. (2003, January). Digital dialogue. *PM Network, 17* (I), 47, 49.

Goffman, E. (1956). *The Presentation of self in everyday life.* New York: Anchor.

Gold, E. (Ed.). (2004). *Telespan's definitive buyer's guide to teleconferencing.* Retrieved April 12, 2004 from http://www.telespan.com/buyersguide/index.html.

Google talk (2010). Other IM Clients. Retrieved March 29, 2010 from http://www.google.com/talk/otherclients.html.

Grant, A. E. (2010). Enhanced telecommuting: The mobile telepresence opportunity. Columbia, SC; Focus 25 Research & Consulting.

Grigonis, R. (2010). Telepresence: Business travel goes virtual. *Forbescustom.com.* Retrieved March 30, 2010 from http://www.forbescustom.com/TelecomPgs/TelepresPl.html.

Hausman, C. (1991). *Institutional video: Planning, budgeting, production, and evaluation.* Belmont, CA: Wadsworth Publishing Company.

Heinlein, R. A. (1986). *Waldo & Magic, Inc.* New York: Del Rey.

Hiltz, S., & Turoff, M. (1993). *The network nation: Human communication via computer.* Cambridge, MA: The MIT Press.

I can see for miles, and miles: Telespan's 2007 predictions. (2007, January 22). Electronic Telespan, 27 (4), Retrieved April 27, 2008 from http://www.telespan.com/editorial.html.

iLinc. (2007). Tribal Data Resources integrates iLinc software into its flagship application to give customers direct access to online support. Retrieved April 26, 2008 from http://www.ilinc.com/pdf/case-studies/ilinc-tribal-data-resources-case-study.pdf.

International Telecommunications Union. (1996, March). *Visual telephone systems and terminal equipment for local area networks which provide a guaranteed quality of service (H.322).* Retrieved April 14, 2002 from http://www.itu.int/rec/recommendation.asp? type=folders&lang=e&parent=T-REC-h.322.

International Telecommunications Union. (1998, February). *Terminal for low bit-rate multimedia communications (H.324).* Retrieved April 14, 2002 from http://www.itu.int/rec/recommendation.asp? type=folders&lang=e &parent=T-REC-h.324.

International Telecommunications Union. (2000, November). *Packet-based multimedia communications systems (H.323).* Retrieved April 14, 2002 from http://www.itu.int/rec/recommendation.asp? type=folders&lang=e &parent=T-REC-h.323.

Internet Movie Database (IMDB). (2010). Synopsis for *Up In The Air.* Retrieved april 2, 2010 from http://www.imdb.com/title/tt1193138/synopsis.

Johansen, R., Vallee, J., & Spangler, K. (1979). *Electronic meetings: Technical alternatives and social choices.* Reading, MA: Addison-Wesley.

Kiviat, B. (Oct. 20, 2009). How Skype Is Changing the Job Interview. *Time.com.* Retrieved April 2, 2010 from http://www.time.com/time/business/article/0,8599,1930838,00.html.

Knights, M. (2010). Telepresence: A better way to spend your travel budget? *BNET.* Retrieved March 30, 2010 from http://www.bnet.com/2403-13240_23-330128.html.

Kowalke, M. (2006, November 13). Radicati Group: Unified communications market driven by adoption of 3G, VoIP. TMCnet, Retrieved April 27, 2008 from http://www.tmcnet.com/ channels/unified-communications/articles/3549-radicati-group-unified-communications-market-driven-adoption-3g.htm.

Kretkowski, P. (2007, January 24). Can Skype Cut It for Business? VOIP News. Retrieved April 3, 2010 from http://www.voip-news.com/feature/can-skype-work-for-business-012507.

Kuehn, R. (2002, January). 2002: Year of the conundrum. *Business Communications Review.* Retrieved March 24, 2002 from http://www.bcr.com/ bcrmag/2002/01/p66.asp.

Kurillo, G., Vasudevan, R., Lobaton, E. & Bajcsy, R. (2008). A framework for collaborative real-time 3D teleimmersion in a geographically distributed environment. *Proceedings of IEEE International Symposium on Multimedia.* Retrieved April 3, 2010 from http://tele-immersion.citris-uc.org/sites/ti6.citris-uc.org/files/ism2008.pdf.

Lucky, R. (1991). In a very short time. In D. Leebaert, Ed. *Technology 2001: The future of computing and communications.* Cambridge, MA: The MIT Press.

Macromedia. (2004). **Corporate Web site**. Retrieved April 1, 2004 from http://www.macromedia.com/software/ breeze/.

Mann, J., & Latham, L. (2005, September 29). *Magic quadrant for Web conferencing, 2005.* Retrieved April 25, 2006 from http://mediaproducts.gartner.com/reprints/macromedia/131153.html.

McGillicuddy, S. (2010, March 5) Telepresence and the travel industry: If you can't beat them, join them. *Unified Communications Nation.* Retrieved March 30, 2010 from http://itknowledgeexchange.techtarget.com/unified-communications/telepresence-and-the-travel-industry-if-you-cant-beat-them-join-them/.

Microsoft. (2004). Corporate Web site. Retrieved April 1, 2004 from http://www.microsoft.com/office/ livemeeting/.

Microsoft NetMeeting 3.0 Preview. (1999, May). Internet telephony. *TMCNet.* Retrieved April 1, 2004 from http://www.tmcnet.com/articles/itmag/0599/0599labs1.htm.

Microsoft unveils office communicator mobile. (2006, February 17). *Corporate Media News.* Retrieved February 21, 2006 from http://www.corporatemedianews.com/articles/viewarticle.jsp?id=37613.

Modine, A. (2010). Cisco sets free video con protocol: Big enough to share. Retrieved March 29, 2010 from http://www.theregister.co.uk/2010/01/27/cisco_networkers_live_protocol/

Muller, N. (1998). *Desktop encyclopedia of telecommunications.* New York: McGraw-Hill.

Neel, K. (2006). Cisco's Chambers Predicts Dawn Of 'Telepresence'. Retrieved March 29, 2010 from http://www.networkcomputing.com/other/ciscos-chambers-predicts-dawn-of-telepresence.php?keyword=teleconferencing.

Noll, A. M. (1986). Teleconferencing target market. *Information Management Review,* Fall, 1986, pp. 65-73.

Noll, A. (1992). Anatomy of a failure: Picturephone revisited. *Telecommunications Policy,* 307-317.

Nortel Networks (2010). Telepresence: Reducing the impact of business travel (White Paper). Retrieved March 30, 2010 from http://www.nortel.com/services/collateral/nn123551.pdf.

Page, L. (2009). US killer robo-plane makes strike without remote pilot: Automated killware now handled by sergeants. Retrieved March 29, 2010 from http://www.theregister.co.uk/2009/03/06/warrior_no_pilot_required/.

Park, H. (2008, December). Being in two places at once: Telepresence versus videoconferencing in the enterprise. Aberdeen Group. Retrieved March 30, 2010 from http://www.tandberg.com/collateral/Telepresence%20vs%20Videoconferencing%20-%20Aberdeen%20Group.pdf.

Parkes, P. (2009, December 7). Maxim: It's just about getting stuff done. Better. Faster. Cheaper. Retrieved April 3, 2010 from http://share.skype.com/sites/business/2009/12/maxim.html.

Paul, G. (2000, February). An overview of the ITU videoconferencing and collaboration standards. *The Edge Perspectives, 1* (1). Retrieved April 1, 2004 from http://www.mitre.org/news/edge_perspectives /february_00/paul.html.

Petersen, R. (2008). iChat AV versus my home router (SIP, NAT and firewalls oh my). Retrieved March 29, 2010 from http://emperor.tidbits.com/TidBITS/Talk/1805/

Polycom (2009, March 30). Microsoft and Polycom Expand Their Relationship to Enhance Unified Communications and Collaboration Solutions. Retrieved April 3, 2010 from http://www.polycom.com/company/news_room/press_releases/2009/20090330_1.html.

Polycom. (2003). *Polycom guide to conferencing and collaboration.* Pleasanton, CA: Polycom.

PR Newswire (2009, December 14). Frost & Sullivan: Web Conferencing Market Defies Economic Decline. Retrieved April 3, 2010 from http://www.prnewswire.com/news-releases/frost--sullivan-web-conferencing-market-defies-economic-decline-79216042.html.

Radvision (2002). 3G powered 3-G-324M protocol. Retrieved April 27, 2008 from http://www.radvision.com/ NR/rdonlyres/6066D65E-9E2E-4786-822A-B1FDBF59A86A/0/3GPowered3GH324MProtocol.pdf

Ray, B. (2010). Skype offers living room TV action. Retrieved April 2nd, 2010, http://www.theregister.co.uk/2010/01/06/skype_tv/.

Rendleman, J. (2001, June 25). Sprint offers IP-based videoconferencing. *Information Week, 843*, 91.

Ricknäs, M. (2010). Nokia smartphones get Skype client: Skype is also working on a client for Google Android-based smartphones. Retrieved March 29, 2010 from http://www.infoworld.com/d/mobilize/nokia-smartphones-get-skype-client-514?source=rss_infoworld_news.

Rosenberg, J., Schulzrinne H., Camarillo, G., Johnston, A., Peterson, J., Sparks, R., Handley, M., and Schooler, E. (2002). SIP: Session Initiation Protocol. Retrieved March 29, 2010 from http://tools.ietf.org/html/rfc3261.

Sage Research (2006). Cisco TelePresence trends: Future benefits outlook. Retrieved April 26, 2008 from http://www.cisco.com/en/US/prod/collateral/ps7060/ps8329/ps8330/ps7073/prod_white_paper0900aecd8054f897.pdf

Singleton, L. (1983). *Telecommunications in the information age.* Cambridge, MA: Ballinger.

Skype. (2008). *Corporate Web site.* Retrieved April 27, 2008 from http://www.skype.com/business/.

Stowe, R. (1992). Teleconferencing. In A. Richardson, Ed. *Corporate and organizational video.* New York: McGraw-Hill.

Tele-Immersion @ UCBerkeley (2010). *Official Website.* Retrived April 3, 2010 from http://tele-immersion.citris-uc.org/.

Tu, C. H. (2002). The Measurement of Social Presence in an Online Learning Environment. Retrieved March 29, 2010 http://goliath.ecnext.com/coms2/gi_0199-1822824/The-measurement-of-social-presence.html.

Videoconferencing is a comeback hit. (2007, April 30). *Federal Computer Week.* Retrieved April 27, 2008 from http://www.fcw.com/print/13_13/news/102549-1.html.

Vinas, T. (2002, February). Meetings makeover. *Industry Week, 251* (2), 29-35.

Wainhouse Research. (2008, January 28). *Telepresence vs. videoconferencing: Resolving the cost-benefit conundrum.* Retrieved April 27, 2008 from http://www.wrplatinum.com/Downloads/8349.aspx

Weiland, R. (1996). 2001: A meetings odyssey. In, R. Kling, Ed. *Computerization and controversy: Value conflicts and social choices,* 2nd edition. San Diego, CA: Academic Press.

Weinschenk, C. (2009, January). Telepresence Market Set for Growth. IT Business Edge. Retrieved March 30, 2010 from http://www.itbusinessedge.com/cm/community/features/interviews/blog/telepresence-market-set-for-growth/?cs=23219.

23

Conclusions
...and the Future

August E. Grant, Ph.D.*

T his book has introduced you to a range of ideas on how to study communication technologies, given you the history of communication technologies, and detailed the latest developments in about two dozen technologies. Along the way, the authors have told stories about successes and failures, legal battles and regulatory limitations, and changes in lifestyle for the end user.

So what can you do with this information? If you're entrepreneurial, you can use it to figure out how to get rich. If you're academically inclined, you can use it to inform research and analysis of the next generation of communication technology. If you're planning a career in the media industries, you can use it to help choose the organizations where you will work, or to find new opportunities for your employer or for yourself.

More importantly, whether you are in any of those groups or not, you are going to be surrounded by new media for the rest of your life. The cycle of innovation, introduction, and maturity of media almost always includes a cycle of decline as well. As new communication technologies are introduced and older ones disappear, your media use habits will change. What you've learned from this book should help you make decisions on when to adopt a new technology or drop an old one. Of course, those decisions depend upon your personal goals—which might be to be an innovator, to make the most efficient use of your personal resources (time and money), or to have the most relaxing life style.

This chapter explores a few of these issues, starting with a list of media that were not covered in this book, but which should be considered as the next generation of "new" communication technologies.

Other New Technologies

It is virtually impossible to discuss all of the technologies that may impact your life and career in a book such as this one. Some are so new that there is little written about them. Others have been in the "introduction" stage for so long that there is little "new" to discuss. And others we simply did not have the space to include. Here are a few to keep your eyes on:

---

* Professor, College of Mass Communications and Information Studies, University of South Carolina (Columbia, South Carolina).

◆ **E-books** have been mentioned in many chapters. They are almost important enough to have their own chapter. E-books have the potential to revolutionize the publishing industry. Indeed, this book (and the previous edition of the book) is available in e-book format. (You might ask why a compilation of information on new technology uses old technology like a paper book. The answer is simple: Paper books are still one of the most efficient ways of distributing information in a format that can be stored and accessed over time. E-publishing does not yet offer the reach, the financial return, or the reputation for the authors that are offered by old-fashioned books, and the authors in this book are concerned about all three of these.)

◆ **The "cloud"** is a nebulous term that refers to computing power and storage that take place remotely from a computer or other device, somewhere on the Internet. Cloud computing promises to bring virtually unlimited computing power and storage capacity to any user by using capabilities of servers and other computers distributed across the Internet. Issues of privacy, security, and control of content remain, but any discussion of this term bears watching during the coming decade.

◆ **Mobile Internet access** has the potential to revolutionize many aspects of our society, including advertising, education, law enforcement, and medicine. This book has touched on a few of the emerging applications related to ubiquitous mobile Internet access, but these applications will likely pale in comparison with new applications that will apply the potential of anytime, anywhere connectivity. Among all of these applications, education may be affected the most, as students, teachers, workers, managers—virtually everyone—will have answers to almost any question available instantly from any location.

◆ **Virtual reality** was promised as a cutting-edge entertainment technology, but has emerged as a key technology in a number of industries including architecture and education. In some ways, it is the antithesis of the Internet, conceived for entertainment but finding its role as a key technology in industry.

◆ **Health and medical applications** represent a huge set of opportunities to leverage the power of communication technologies. Spending on health care will increase globally over the next 20 years, and communication technologies have great potential to revolutionize health care delivery and preventive care.

These are just a few of the technologies that are just over the horizon as this book is being finalized in May 2010. By the time you read this, you will certainly know of others to add to the list. The key for you is to be able to apply the "umbrella perspective," the lessons from the history of other technologies, and the theories discussed in Chapter 3 to help you analyze those technologies and predict their place in your future.

Making Money from New Technologies

You have the potential to get rich from the next generation of technologies. Just conduct an analysis of a few emerging technologies using the tools in the "Fundamentals" section of the book; choose the one that has the best potential to meet an unmet demand (one that people will pay for); then create a business plan that demonstrates how your revenues will exceed your expenses from creating, producing, or distributing the technology. Sounds easy, right?

Conceptually, the process is deceptively easy. The difficult part is putting in the hours needed to plan for every contingency, solve problems as they crop up (or before they do), make the contacts you need in order to bring in all of the pieces to make your plan work, and then distribute the product or service to the end users. If the lessons in this book are any indication, two factors will be more important than all the others: the interpersonal relationships that lead to organizational connections—and a lot of luck!

Here are a few guidelines distilled from 20-plus years of working, studying, and consulting in the communication technology industries that might help you become an entrepreneur:

◆ **Ideas are not as important as execution**. If you have a good idea, chances are others will have the same idea. The ones who succeed are the ones who have the tools and vision to put the ideas into action.

◆ **Protect your ideas**. The time and effort needed to get a patent, copyright, or even a simple non-disclosure agreement will pay off handsomely if your ideas succeed.

◆ **There is no substitute for hard work**. Entrepreneurs don't work 40-hour weeks, and they always have a tool nearby to record ideas or keep track of contacts.

◆ **There is no substitute for time away from work**. Taking one day a week away from the job gives you perspective, letting you step back and see the big picture. Plus, some of the best ideas come from bringing in completely unrelated content, so make sure you are always scanning the world around you for developments in the arts, technology, business, regulation, and culture.

◆ **Who you know is more important than what you know**. You can't succeed as a solo act in the communication technology field. You have to a) find and partner with or hire people who are better than you in the skill sets you don't have, and b) make contacts with people in organizations that can help your business succeed.

◆ **Keep learning**. Study your field, but also study the world. The technologies that you will be working with have the potential to provide you access to more information than any entrepreneur in the past has had. Use the tools to continue growing.

◆ **Create a set of realistic goals**. Don't limit yourself to just one goal, but don't have too many. As you achieve your goals, take time to celebrate your success.

◆ **Give back**. You can't be a success without relying upon the efforts of those who came before you and those who helped you out along the way. The best way to pay it back is to pay it forward.

This list was created to help entrepreneurs, but they may be equally relevant to any type of career. Just as the communication technologies explored in this book have applications that permeate industries and institutions throughout society, the tools and techniques explored in this book can be equally useful regardless of where you are or where you are going.